"let the little children
come to me"

Cornelia B. Horn & John W. Martens

"let the little children come to me"

*Childhood and Children in
Early Christianity*

The Catholic University of America Press
Washington, D.C.

The paper used in this publication meets the minimum requirements
of American National Standards for Information Science—Perma-
nence of Paper for Printed Library Materials, ANSI z39.48-1984.

∞

Library of Congress Cataloging-in-Publication Data

Horn, Cornelia B.

Let the little children come to me : childhood and children in early

Christianity / Cornelia B. Horn and John W. Martens.

p. cm.

Includes bibliographical references and index.

ISBN 978-0-8132-1674-4 (pbk. : alk. paper)

1. Children—Religious aspects—Christianity.   2. Children—

History.   I. Martens, John W., 1960–   II. Title.

BT705.H67 2009

270.1083—dc22

This book is dedicated to the

children in our families:

John's sons, Jacob Peter and

John Samuel Luke,

and Cornelia's children,

Katharina Jane

and Lucas Origène

Contents

Preface

This book is a collaborative effort in several ways. First, it is designed to join together insights to be gained from the disciplines of biblical studies, patristics, and early Church history. The goal of this work is to set out on the path of telling the story of children through the first six centuries of the Christian era, with a particular focus on the life, experience, and perception of children within the Christian community. During this time, Christianity went through its formative and expansive stages in the Mediterranean world. The Church was in the making, and so were Christian perspectives on children.

We do not see as our primary goal to write the ultimate and comprehensive study on children in the early Christian world. Instead we aim to contribute a seminal and foundational work on the topic, which clarifies many of the important themes that emerged with regard to early Christians' concern for children and which locates the sources that will serve others, and ourselves, for continued study in the future. As such, this project also is collaborative insofar as it aims to be even more broadly interdisciplinary than we described above, relying on previous research conducted on children in Greco-Roman and in Jewish contexts. This study utilizes methods and data derived from a number of disciplines, such as philological and text-critical approaches, historical reconstruction, social and cultural historical inquiry, theological and philosophical approaches to early Christian literature, insights gained from the examination of archaeological data, approaches to ancient medical and child-rearing texts, pedagogical considerations, and much other data which can illuminate the history of childhood.

The structure employed in approaching and organizing the material is grounded in our primary interest in this book, namely, to define many of the most important themes that reflect the concerns and the realities of life related to "children" in the early Christian world. We examine family life, issues of marriage and celibacy, asceticism, discipline and education, play and work, and the place of the child within the Christian community. There are further concerns and areas of life, or death, that affected children's lives and that shaped the ways in which ancient Christians thought of children. As childhood studies continue to grow and develop, some areas that we have treated in a single chapter might gain in clarity, and the availability of further data that we have not seen or that have not even been discovered yet might call for separate, monograph-length studies. Since this book is intended not as the ultimate study but as a foundational one on children and childhood in the early Christian community, paving the way, we hope, for many more studies to come, such limitations to the scope of this work are not so much a deficiency as a sign of an actively growing, excitingly new, and promising area of scholarship.

Because of the large quantity and variety of sources that we have utilized in this study, it is necessary to address briefly the question of how one might approach such manifold data. One of the distinctions to be kept in mind when examining sources for insights they may have to offer on children in particular, but in fact on any other subject matter or topic more generally, is the difference between historical and historiographical sources on the one hand, those that tell of how history was and how people thought and conceived of how events in history happened or were to be understood, and theological sources, such as the New Testament and various hagiographical martyrdom accounts, on the other. While theological sources clearly have historical value insofar as they offer information on the intellectual history of people in a given era, the precise place of theological sources in the reconstruction of the history of children is a difficult issue. New Testament texts are valuable for the historical reconstruction of some aspects of life in the Mediterranean world in the first and second centuries. There is no doubt that they are part of the early Christian period. Still, they are not historical sources in a straightforward manner. While we do not engage in extensive discussions of the "historical Jesus," or questions of authorship of individual texts of the New Testament, or of other early Christian sources for that matter, on occasion we do argue that certain texts give us historical data. On other occasions, this study employs the New Testament texts and other sources in order to reconstruct concepts and beliefs that guided the Christian understanding of the place of children and the role of the family. Such a use of sources is to be distinguished from considering data contained in these texts for reconstructing the history of the society in which the Christian believers interacted. In effect, historical criticism consists of a two-pronged approach to the material it examines: at times, the message that texts convey and the historical reality that underlies them and that can be glimpsed, at least, in some instances, have a varyingly close or more distant relationship. Yet still, both are valid: the message communicates the conceptual and spiritual assumptions of the religious communities in question. Extracting and presenting data that allow one to identify the statement of the message of a given text provides the author and the audience of a given study with insights into the history of the intellectual development of the community or communities studied. With regard to the New Testament in particular, an added dimension of the value of these texts for the history of early Christianity is to be considered as well. Since Christian writers subsequent to the first and second centuries assumed that the New Testament Gospels, Acts, letters, and apocalypse were historically accurate, these texts are essential to unlocking the assumptions of Christian authors and Christian practices also during the post-apostolic centuries of the early Church. For the scope of this study, this then means that New Testament material has a bearing on perceptions of historical realities of the lives of children also for the time between the second and the sixth centuries. Exegesis and the writing of early Christian history often went hand in hand during that time. A modern study would miss out if it did not take account of this interrelationship as well. Clearly to expound the perceptions of and statements made concerning children in the Gospels and in Paul's letters is an important task also for the historian of early Christianity who studies that subject matter, since these texts were at the heart of much of early Christian self-definition, interpretation, and development. The theology of the early Church influenced the practice of the early Christians and vice versa. The New Testament is important because the construction of the life of Jesus and the first-century Christians that it offered (and *not* the "historical Jesus" or our reconstruction of the historical reality in Palestine) was a core element of what was received by later Christian writers.

This study is not limited to the canonical New Testament or to the traditions of those strands of Christianity that eventually and through the support of the Roman emperor were recognized and further developed as the Great Church. In addition to patristic and biblical sources, we consider some aspects of apocryphal Christian literature and other documents considered marginal by the Great Church tradition. We do not pursue as a separate goal to evaluate distinct understandings of childhood in circles such as those of the Gnostics, Marcionites, or Manicheans. For the moment, this area of study has to remain a desideratum for further research. We also utilize Greco-Roman and Jewish texts and ideas, as these are important for providing context for understanding the reality and development of early Christianity. Most of these sources are charged with their own reflections or understanding, theological or philosophical, about the nature of human life and development. The same care that has to be applied when examining Christian sources and their ideological framework and context also has to be carefully utilized when employing Greco-Roman and Jewish sources for historical reconstruction of the world of early and late ancient Christianity.

This book addresses both scholars and students of the ancient world. It is our hope that it may be of aid to those first encountering the study of early Christianity. Yet we also hope that it may encourage the one who is already well-seasoned in this field to embark on the exploration of a topic to which she or he has not given much attention thus far. Wherever this book inspires further reflection, research, and writing on questions of childhood, children, and family life it has achieved its goal.

This book was in the making for a long time. Work on it began in the fall of 2001, when we became colleagues in the Department of Theology at the University of Saint Thomas. The manuscript was completed in the summer of 2005. For reasons beyond our control, publication was delayed for more than three years, a period of time during which research on children in early Christianity has made good progress. To the extent possible, we have taken account of the new research that was published up to December 2007. Yet there is no doubt in our mind that we have missed valuable contributions in that process. The responsibility for such shortcomings rests with the present authors.

Along the way, several individuals have assisted us in the process of researching and writing this book. We wish to acknowledge here with special gratitude the many thoughts contributed and hours of revising that Robert R. Phenix Jr. invested in this project, helping all along the way to let the two different voices of the authors better meld into one. Through his labor this has become a better book.

Various audiences at regional, national, and international meetings of the American Academy of Religion, the Society of Biblical Literature, the North American Patristics Society, the Symposium Syriacum, and ARAM have listened to our ideas and offered feedback. Two anonymous reviewers of the manuscript for the Catholic University of America Press have given precious advice and directions for improvement. We are grateful to both of those audiences.

Finally, we also thank two outstanding librarians, Jan Malcheski and Ron Crown, as well as our former and current research assistants at the University of Saint Thomas, in Saint Paul, Minn., and Saint Louis University, in Saint Louis, Mo., especially Inta Ivanovska, Fr. Oliver Herbel, and Aaron Overby, for their support in gathering data, checking references, discussing ideas, proofreading, and indexing. We are very pleased that our book has found a formidable home in the repertoire of publications offered by the Catholic University of America Press. To its director, David McGonagle, the editors Theresa Walker and James G. Kruggel, and especially our copyeditor, Ellen Coughlin, whose attention to detail and scrutinizing eye have been so well invested in this project, we wish to extend our thanks. It goes without saying that any remaining omissions, mistakes, or other shortcomings fall back on the authors.

Cornelia Horn and John Martens
December 2007

Abbreviations

ANF	Ante-Nicene Fathers
CBQ	*Catholic Biblical Quarterly*
CCL	Corpus Christianorum Latinorum
CCSA	Corpus Christianorum Series Apocrypha
CCSL	Corpus Christianorum Series Latina
CSEL	Corpus Scriptorum Ecclesiasticorum Latinorum
GCS	Die griechischen christlichen Schriftsteller der ersten Jahrhunderte
JECS	*Journal of Early Christian Studies*
JSNT	*Journal for the Study of the New Testament*
JSOT	*Journal for the Study of the Old Testament*
JThS	*Journal of Theological Studies*
LCL	Loeb Classical Library
NPNF	Nicene and Post-Nicene Fathers
PG	Patrologia Graeca
PL	Patrologia Latina
RAC	*Reallexikon für Antike und Christentum*
SCh	Sources Chrétiennes
WUNT	Wissenschaftliche Untersuchungen zum Neuen Testament

"let the little children
come to me"

one

What Is a Child?

*He called a child, whom he put among them, and said, "Truly I
tell you, unless you change and become like children, you will never
enter the kingdom of heaven."*

Matthew 18:2–3

Some Methodological Considerations at the Outset

When the Gospel of Matthew has Jesus call upon his disciples to "become
like children," what was in the minds of the earliest hearers or readers
of this text? What did they consider a child to be? Would a Jewish audience understand what it meant to be a child in ways that differed from the
perception of a Roman or Greek audience? Did Christians have specific
views of children that shaped their thinking when they pondered these
words from the Gospel? Did they see children and their roles in family and
society through different eyes from those of Jews and adherents of Greek
and Roman religions? Christians were part of the Greco-Roman world.
Their parent religion, Judaism, offered a range of responses to Greco-
Roman learning, along a spectrum from direct assimilation of its institutions
and ideas, through adaptation to express Judaism in a language amenable
to a Hellenized audience, to outright hostility. This spectrum of responses also influenced Christian attitudes to Greco-Roman ideas, including
assumptions concerning children and childhood. The approach to a picture of the development of the Christian concept of a child followed in this

study is through the experiences of children from various classes and within this broader distinction between the ideal Jewish and Greco-Roman families.[1]

The goal of the present study is to determine significant differences Christianity made in the lives of children, historically, sociologically, and culturally. The evidence, partial and limited as it often is, must be allowed to speak for itself. Peter Garnsey once stated that "the influence of Christianity on attitudes toward childhood" was "too large a subject" to be treated by him, but that "continuities with and divergences from the Jewish and pagan traditions merit explanation." He saw as "the main theme . . . the comprehensive reorientation of attitudes about childhood that was achieved by the Church fathers."[2] This reorientation began with the teachings of Jesus and expressed itself throughout the Christian writings of antiquity.

As a designation for human beings, the word "child" functions in multiple ways. It may designate a person's age, or origin—for example, when someone is spoken of as being the "child of" another. At times it may emphasize a person's character or behavior, for example, when someone is described as "childish." The term may also indicate a person's status within society, especially in reference to situations of social dependency.[3] Given the diversity of connotations for "child," writers reflecting on childhood in antiquity, perhaps in any age, arrived at different conclusions. Among Greco-Roman and Jewish sources, some aspects are clear: persons of a certain age—for example, five years old—are to be considered children. Yet the ancient world shared with the modern one the same liminal concern about the question of when a child ceased being a child. In the first century A.D., a ten-to-twelve-year-old person was on the cusp of becoming an adult. The lengthy, drawn-out, and well-defined period of youth that is part of the modern experience of transitioning from childhood to adult life, and is characterized by certain boundaries defined legally, emotionally, and by increasing responsibilities, did not exist in the same way in the ancient

1. Among other studies, the articles collected in Shaye J. D. Cohen, ed., *The Jewish Family in Antiquity* (Atlanta: Scholars Press, 1993), and the work by Thomas Wiedemann, *Adults and Children in the Roman Empire* (London: Routledge, 1989), can function as important guides to some of the dimensions of Jewish and Greco-Roman childhood.

2. Peter Garnsey, "Child Rearing in Ancient Italy," in *The Family in Italy from Antiquity to the Present*, eds. D. I. Kertzer and R. P. Saller (New Haven, Conn.: Yale University Press, 1991), 48–65, here 49, n. 2.

3. See Lothar Coenen and Klaus Haacker, eds., *Theologisches Begriffslexikon zum Neuen Testament* (Wuppertal: R. Brockhaus Verlag and Neukirchener Verlag, 1997), "Kind," vol. 2, 1121–35, here 1121.

world.[4] Ancient *adolescentia* was more a part of the realm of adult life than is the experience of one's teenage years in modern Western cultures. As we explore the basic boundary between childhood and adulthood at the beginning of Christianity, we must allow for the fact that such boundaries were fluid and shifting, both for boys and girls. Drawing these borderlines more closely permits us to delve into the world of children, even if it will not determine definitively the nature of childhood.

In examining these boundaries we must note that much of this study focuses on children who were free citizens, mainly because of the availability of data for reconstructing the lives of such children. It is important to emphasize this limitation at the outset. Children of slaves followed a different path to adulthood than their freeborn peers. Slaves were not able to marry legally, and therefore their children were not their own.[5] A child of a slave belonged to the owner of the child's mother. We know little about child slaves beyond their work and their submission to their masters. We can assume that childhood for a slave might have included a relatively short period of carefree life before work began. Some slave children might have had favored positions in their masters' homes, or may even have been treated as a *delicium,* a sort of "pet,"[6] but the condition in which they lived should not be forgotten. At various points we will discuss the childhood of slaves. In addition, it might be suggested that the childhood of the slave and of the freeborn child of the impoverished classes that formed the vast majority of Roman society were not so different; child labor would have been essen-

4. Whereas Emiel Eyben, *Restless Youth in Ancient Rome* (London: Routledge, 1993), argued for a distinct period of "youth" or "adolescence" in the ancient world, Marc Kleijwegt, *Ancient Youth: The Ambiguity of Youth and the Absence of Adolescence in Greco-Roman Society* (Amsterdam: J. C. Gieben, 1991), disagreed. See also Emiel Eyben, "Jugend," in *RAC* 19 (2001), 388–442.

5. For a discussion of slaves in the family in the ancient world, see also Dale B. Martin, "Slave Families and Slaves in Families," in *Early Christian Families in Context: An Interdisciplinary Dialogue,* ed. David L. Balch and Carolyn Osiek (Grand Rapids, Mich.: Eerdmans, 2003), 207–30. More specifically on young female slaves and the conflicts between their situation and Christian teachings, see the studies by Beate Wehn, "'Geschunden die einen, und die anderen leben . . .' Über Herrschaft, Gewalt und Tod in einem christlichen Schreckenstext (Andreas-Akten 17–22)" (465–87), and Bernadette J. Brooten, "Der lange Schatten der Sklaverei im Leben von Frauen und Mädchen" (488–503), both in *Dem Tod nicht glauben. Sozialgeschichte der Bibel. Festschrift für Luise Schottroff zum 70. Geburtstag* (Gütersloh: Gütersloher Verlagshaus, 2004). See also Carolyn Osiek, "Female Slaves, *Porneia,* and the Limits of Obedience," in *Early Christian Families in Context,* 255–74.

6. On *delicia* children, see Christian Laes, "Desperately Different? *Delicia* Children in the Roman Household," in *Early Christian Families in Context,* 298–324, with much prior literature cited there. See also Cornelia Horn, "Children's Play as Social Ritual," in *Late Ancient Christianity. A People's History of Christianity,* ed. Virginia Burrus, vol. 2 (Minneapolis: Fortress Press, 2005), 95–116.

tial to keeping the members of the family alive. Such families did not possess the skills or means to record their stories, and the writers of the Roman world—including even Christian authors—mostly ignored these day-to-day aspects of the masses. Hence our data on childhood in the Greco-Roman world are heavily biased toward the children of the upper classes, the privileged few whose parents were able to buy the toys that became archaeological artifacts, and whose problems with child-rearing were deemed worthy of discussion, such as in the letters of Jerome or the treatises and homilies of John Chrysostom. Thus most of our study reconstructs what might be the ideal picture of a free child, with parents who had the means to raise, educate, and form that child for life as a free man or woman.

In the Greco-Roman literature on anthropology and childhood, a person's life was often divided into stages, which we will present in the following pages. Yet childhood development did not then, nor does it now, fall into idealized stages of seven to ten years. The perceptions of childhood in ancient society were not completely defined by these theoretical stages. Furthermore, the stages presented in ancient sources most often take boys rather than girls as their measure; discussions of education, for instance, often omit girls' education. Consequently, we do not have a clear sense of much of the education girls received, even if it was in the home.

Determining the parameters of childhood is only the beginning point of a study on ancient children.[7] One also has to ask what it meant to be a child in the ancient world. At the advent of Christianity, how parents and families thought about children, how they perceived and treated them, was informed and shaped by the culture in which they lived.[8] These cultural settings, whether Jewish or Greco-Roman, did not cease to influence Christians' understanding of children until late in the historical development of Christianity. We depend, then, on relevant information about children and childhood as found in Jewish, Greco-Roman, and Christian sources.[9]

---

7. For guides to the history of scholarship on children and family matters see, for example, Reidar Aasgaard, "Children in Antiquity and Early Christianity: Research History and Central Issues," *Familia* 33 (2006), 23–46; Joseph M. Hawes and N. Ray Hiner, eds., *Children in Historical and Comparative Perspective: An International Handbook and Research Guide* (Westport, Conn.: Greenwood Press, 1991); N. Ray Hiner and Joseph M. Hawes, "Standing on Common Ground: Reflections on the History of Children and Childhood," in *Children in Historical and Comparative Perspective*, 1–9; Valerie French, "Children in Antiquity," in *Children in Historical and Comparative Perspective*, 13–29; and Gerald L. Soliday, ed., *History of the Family and Kinship: A Select International Bibliography* (Millwood, N.Y.: Kraus International Publications, 1980).

8. See Marc Kleijwegt, "Kind," in *RAC* 11 (2004), 865–947.

9. For studies on family and childhood questions in the ancient world in a variety of set-

Accordingly, to sketch the life of an average child in the ancient Mediterranean world is probably not possible.[10] Apart from differences among classes—whether a child was a slave, freeborn, or an aristocrat—one also has to account for gender differences.[11] In addition one needs to consider what separated Jews, Greeks, Romans, and other cultures and peoples of the region from one another. Since here is not the place to lay out in detail the areas of such differences between various ancient cultures that contributed to the milieu in which early Christianity arose, it might suffice to refer to the Carthaginian practice of child sacrifice, which still seems to have been current in the Roman period.[12] Such a locally defined and delimited

---

tings, see for example Peter Hatlie, "The Religious Lives of Children and Adolescents," in *Byzantine Christianity. A People's History of Christianity,* ed. Derek Krueger, vol. 3 (Minneapolis: Fortress Press, 2006), 182–200; Anne Behnke Kinney, *Representations of Childhood and Youth in Early China* (Stanford, Calif.: Stanford University Press, 2004); Beryl Rawson, *Children and Childhood in Roman Italy* (Oxford: Oxford University Press, 2003); Suzanne Dixon, ed., *Childhood, Class, and Kin in the Roman World* (London: Routledge, 2001); A. R. Colón, with P. A. Colón, *A History of Children: A Socio-Cultural Survey across Millennia* (Westport, Conn.: Greenwood Press, 2001); Brian C. Daleas, "Children in the Roman World: Status and the Growth of Identity" (Ph.D. thesis, Indiana University, 1998); Jane F. Gardner, *Family and "Familia" in Roman Law and Life* (Oxford: Clarendon Press, 1998); Sarah B. Pomeroy, *Families in Classical and Hellenistic Greece* (Oxford: Clarendon Press, 1997); Beryl Rawson and Paul Weaver, eds., *The Roman Family in Italy: Status, Sentiment, Space* (Oxford: Clarendon Press, 1997); Richard P. Saller, *Patriarchy, Property, and Death in the Roman Family* (Cambridge: Cambridge University Press, 1994); Suzanne Dixon, *The Roman Family* (Baltimore: Johns Hopkins University Press, 1992); Keith R. Bradley, *Discovering the Roman Family: Studies in Roman Social History* (New York: Oxford University Press, 1991); Jane F. Gardener and Thomas Wiedemann, *The Roman Household: A Sourcebook* (London: Routledge, 1991); Beryl Rawson, ed., *Marriage, Divorce, and Children in Ancient Rome* (New York: Oxford University Press, 1991); Mark Golden, *Children and Childhood in Classical Athens* (Baltimore: Johns Hopkins University Press, 1990); Thomas Wiedemann, *Adults and Children in the Roman Empire* (London: Routledge, 1989); James Casey, *The History of the Family,* New Perspectives on the Past (Oxford: Basil Blackwell, 1989); Suzanne Dixon, *The Roman Mother* (Norman: University of Oklahoma Press, c1988); Beryl Rawson, ed., *The Family in Ancient Rome: New Perspectives* (Ithaca, N.Y.: Cornell University Press, 1986); and Walter Kirkpatrick Lacey, *The Family in Classical Greece* (Ithaca, N.Y.: Cornell University Press, 1984).

10. See Jill Korbin, "Prologue: A Perspective from Contemporary Childhood Studies," in *Coming of Age in Ancient Greece: Images of Childhood from the Classical Past,* ed. Jenifer Neils and John H. Oakley (New Haven, Conn.: Yale University Press, c2003, 2004), 7–11, here 9–10.

11. Ibid., 10.

12. Naomi J. Norman, "Death and Burial of Roman Children: The Case of the Yasmina Cemetery at Carthage—Part II, The Archaeological Evidence," *Mortality* 8.1 (2003), 36–47; on this issue in particular see 37–38. Children up to age five were sacrificed at Punic Carthage. Norman disputes Tertullian's evidence that the practice continued until Tiberius (Tertullian, *Apologia* 9.2–3 [ed. and trans. T. R. Glover, *Tertullian. Apology. De Spectaculis* (Cambridge, Mass.: Harvard University Press, 1966), 2–227, here 46–47]), suggesting rather that the practice came to an end in the second century B.C.

particularity offers at least a brief indicator, albeit a rather gruesome one, of the extremes to which attitudes toward children might go in some areas and cultures.

Different Stages in the Life of a Child

Methodological and factual limitations on any plausible sketch of children and childhood have moved scholarship to a new orientation. As more data from the ancient world become available, the picture of children will no doubt continue to change.[13] What is clear is that childhood was both a conceptual and a social reality in the ancient Jewish and Greco-Roman worlds. There were clear divisions to childhood, as numerous texts from the ancient world state. In the first century A.D., Philo of Alexandria, a Jewish author strongly influenced by Hellenistic culture, provided a perspective on the stages of life, one which he acknowledged was dependent upon Greek conceptions of human development.[14]

Physiognomic Developments

In *De opificio mundi* 103–4, Philo spoke of ten stages of a person's life from *brephos* (infant) to *gerōn* (old person).[15] He divided these stages into segments of seven years, following the scheme attributed to Solon, the Athenian lawgiver. It is to be kept in mind that Philo favored males in his categorization of life stages, offering observations at most stages mainly with respect to the development of the male body. The development of the female body was not seen as significant.[16] In the first stage, the *pais* (child) was a *nēpios* (young boy, or even an infant). At the second stage, which ended at about age fourteen, the individual was called a *hēbē* (youth). This stage was

13. Philip Ariès, *L'Enfant et la Vie familiale sous l'Ancien Régime* (Paris: Plon, 1960), trans. Robert Baldick, *Centuries of Childhood: A Social History of Family Life* (New York: Vintage Books, 1962).

14. Golden, *Children and Childhood*, discusses the notion of Greek childhood in full; see also the shorter discussions on the nature of the Greek terminology in Mark Golden, "*Pais*, 'Child' and 'Slave,'" *L'Antiquité Classique* 54 (1985), 91–104, here 93; Mark Golden, "Childhood in Ancient Greece," in *Coming of Age in Ancient Greece*, 12–29, here 14; and Kleijwegt, "Kind," 866.

15. All translations of Philo's work, unless otherwise noted, are from *Philo*, 12 vols., Loeb Classical Library (vols. 1–5, trans. Francis Henry Colson and Rev. George Herbert Whitaker; vols. 6–10, trans. F. H. Colson; vols. 11–12, trans. Ralph Marcus) (Cambridge, Mass.: Harvard University Press, 1929–62, reprinted 1981).

16. See Dorothy Sly, *Philo's Perception of Women* (Atlanta: Scholars Press, 1990).

marked by the first production of sperm. At the third and fourth stages the person also was called a "youth," but these stages were marked by the growing of the beard and, at the fourth stage, by the increase of strength. At the fifth stage Philo suggested that the young man take a bride and have children. Immediately following this division, he cited the seven stages of Hippocrates (fifth–fourth centuries B.C.), in which each stage received its own separate title: a person moved from *paidion* (infant, young child), to *pais* (child), *meirakion* ("a lad," perhaps a teenager),[17] *neaniskos* (young man), *anēr* (man), *presbytēs* (old[er?] man), and, finally, *gerōn* (old man) (*Opif.* 105). Hippocrates's description of a child as recounted in Philo stated that the individual ceased to be a *pais* (child) when he reached puberty at the ideal age of fourteen, being now able to produce offspring and found a family. The person remained a *meirakion* until age twenty-one, when he could grow a beard. In each of these cases, Hippocrates depended upon physiological characteristics of the male body; each physiological stage determined a properly ordered aspect of the child's or man's stage of life. Hippocrates, like Solon, wrote for males and was concerned only with male development.

Development of the Soul

Philo also proposed a development of the soul corresponding to his physiological scheme. In *Quis rerum divinarum heres sit,* he wrote that in "childhood" *(paidikē),* the first seven years of life, a child's soul was in a "simple" state and the child was a *brephos* (*Her.* 294–96). In the second stage, *neotēs* (youth), when the body was "in bloom" *(hēba),* opportunities and desires for sin ran rampant. Philo characterized the four subsequent stages in reference to progress made in the process of the "healing" of the soul which is stricken by the increase of desire, which Philo understood to be sinful, in the second stage.[18] He did not label these four stages with specific titles. The first two correlated to physical stages of the body, and the second two stages divided the balance of one's life, as one's soul grew in virtue (*Her.* 297–99).[19]

17. Next to *pais,* a dominant term for child in Philo, Greek availed itself of other terms to define a child as well, for instance *teknon.* Henry George Liddell and Robert Scott, *A Greek-English Lexicon: Abridged* (Oxford: Clarendon Press, 1958), 431, suggest the translation "lad" for *meirakion.*

18. See David Winston, "Philo and the Rabbis on Sex and the Body," in *The Ancestral Philosophy: Hellenistic Philosophy in Second Temple Judaism,* ed. Gregory E. Sterling (Providence, R.I.: Brown Judaic Studies, 2001), 199–219, on the question of the body's relation to the healthy functioning of the whole person.

19. For a standard discussion of virtue in Philo, see Harry A. Wolfson, *Philo: Foundations of*

In other works, Philo described human development in terms of slightly different stages, each being seven to ten years in duration. In *De congressu,* he spoke of childhood *(paidikos)* as a stage of ten years after which one passed through puberty *(meirakiouomai)* for the next ten years *(Congr.* 82). Here Philo talked about the journey of the soul, but he did so in a manner that partially corresponded to the stages of life a child had to pass through to achieve maturity. Philo said that he had been a *neos* (a youth) when he first started to study philosophy *(Congr.* 74). This enterprise began when one left childhood *(paidikos)* and entered puberty *(meirakiouomai) (Congr.* 82). For Philo, one reached maturity through engaging in a journey that began with preliminary studies, moved on to the study of wisdom, and then to the study of God, in Philo's context understood as the study of revealed religion in the Jewish Scriptures. Philo's description of the soul's progress is defined in response to the challenges of the physical body. As the body gains strength, the soul must also become strong so as to master the body, and not be damaged through acquiescence to Philo's understanding of physical temptation. The activity of the individual must then be to gradually train the soul for its struggle with the corporeal passions, beginning with philosophy and culminating in the study of the divine law. In so describing the reality of the soul's journey, Philo linked spiritual maturity to physical growth.

Philo also interpreted the individual stages of life allegorically, based on important episodes in the history of Israel presented in the Pentateuch and Deuteronomistic history.[20] He explained that childhood, which was associated with passion *(pathos),* was Egypt, while puberty, which was associated with vice *(kakia),* was Canaan *(Congr.* 83–85). Only after spending ten years in Canaan could one wed Hagar *(Congr.* 88); after this, of course, the next step was to move beyond Hagar, who allegorically represented the preliminary studies, and join the true bride, Sarah, the embodiment of phi-

---

Religious Philosophy in Judaism, Christianity, and Islam (Cambridge, Mass.: Harvard University Press, 1947), vol. 2, 268–79.

20. On allegorical interpretation in Philo, see Harry A. Wolfson, *The Philosophy of the Church Fathers: Faith, Trinity, Incarnation* (Cambridge, Mass.: Harvard University Press, 1956), 24–72; and David Runia, *Philo in Early Christian Literature. Compendia Rerum Iudaicarum ad Novum Testamentum,* section III, vol. 3 (Assen: Van Gorcum, 1993), who discusses allegorical method in Philo at various instances throughout the entire study, especially as it relates to the patristic use of his methods. For a discussion of how Philo employed allegory with regard to childbirth, see the enlightening treatment in Verna E. F. Harrison, "The allegorization of gender: Plato and Philo on spiritual childbearing," in *Asceticism,* eds. Vincent L. Wimbush and Richard Valantasis (New York: Oxford University Press, 1995), 520–34.

losophy (*Congr.* 121). Philo envisioned two ten-year stages for both childhood and puberty, almost equaling the scheme of Solon and Hippocrates, which described youth as a twenty-one-year period divided into three stages of seven years each.

Since Philo, and the Greek authors he cited, seemed to be concerned with males only, one has to look elsewhere in Jewish literature of this period for Jewish conceptions of female development. Rabbinical views on children are found scattered throughout many places. For this study we have relied on the earliest rabbinic Jewish source, the Mishnah. Although compiled probably in the late second or early third century A.D., the Mishnah reflects the views of earlier historical periods.[21]

Mishnah

The rabbis structured their approach to childhood quite differently from Philo. What they thought about children can be drawn from remarks made in their halakha, that is, the interpretation of legal passages of Torah.[22] Many of the relevant passages deal specifically with marriage, particularly the earliest legal age of marriage for girls, and thus with the age at which a girl grew from childhood into adulthood. Among the rabbis, marriage played a larger role in the understanding of girls' development than that of their male cohorts.[23] Discussing sexual matters with women was taboo for pious men, and human female sexual reproduction was poorly un-

21. For the Hebrew text of the Mishnah and an English translation, see the seven-volume edition of Philip Blackman, *Mishnayoth. Pointed Hebrew Text, English Translation, Introductions, Notes, Supplement, Appendix, Indexes, Addenda, Corrigenda* (New York: The Judaica Press, 1990). Admittedly, this is not a critical edition of the Hebrew text, but such editions of the Mishnah are difficult to come by. Unless otherwise noted, we cite the Mishnah from Blackman's edition.

22. Little work has been accomplished on matters of childhood in rabbinic literature. See David Kraemer, "Images of Childhood and Adolescence in Talmudic Literature," in *Exploring Judaism: The Collected Essays of David Kraemer*, ed. David Kraemer (Atlanta: Scholars Press, c1999), 37–50; the short anonymous article "Children," in *Encyclopaedia Judaica* 5 (Jerusalem: Keter Publishing, 1971), 426–28; Ephraim Kanarfogel, "Attitudes toward Childhood and Children in Medieval Jewish Society," in *Approaches to Judaism in Medieval Times*, vol. 2, ed. David R. Blumenthal (Chico, Calif.: Scholars Press, 1985), 1–34; and I. Lebendiger, "The Minor in Jewish Law," *Jewish Quarterly Review* 6 (1915–16), 459–93 and 7 (1916–17), 89–111 and 145–74. See also some discussion in Cornelia B. Horn, "Challenges to Childhood in the Eastern Mediterranean World in Ancient Christianity," (unpublished manuscript), ch. 2.

23. Helen Foley, "Mothers and Daughters," in *Coming of Age in Ancient Greece*, 113–37, here 113, calls marriage "the" coming of age ritual for girls. See also Ben Zion (Benno) Schereschewsky, "Child Marriage," in *Encyclopaedia Judaica* 5, 423–26, who discusses rabbinic texts regarding child marriage and even some current, North African practices.

derstood in many of its fundamentals. It may be inferred that the biology of female reproduction was a source of consternation to these otherwise learned men, and therefore shameful to those who had to make decisions about all aspects of creation and human society. Presumably, the men who were the sole arbiters of Jewish legal interpretation were not entirely certain about the sexual maturity of any given young female. It seems that for the ancient world in general, girls undertook the passage into adulthood at the point of marriage. Rabbinic texts also shed some light on male childhood, although on this topic they are a less abundant source and the categories that define an adult male are more complex.[24]

M. Yebamoth 4:10 offers insight into the rabbinic view of girls. The text distinguishes between two types of widow: the *betulah*, that is, a widow who has biological children, and the *be'ulah*, who is a widow without issue. Some scholars render the second term for widows (pl. *be'ulot*) as "virgins."[25] Yet one has to wonder as to the plausibility of this translation, since the woman thus designated was married. Perhaps the term indicated simply that the female person had entered the betrothal period but had not yet married when her fiancé died, in which case she could have been a virgin but would still have been considered a "widow."[26] Nevertheless, we probably ought to move away from the translation "virgin" altogether and instead take the root of the word— *'ullah*,[27] "girl"—as the basis for translation, thus indicating that the widow was young and that at this point she was considered physically unable to bear children. The latter suggestion could indicate girls who were married but unable to bear children since they were still too young and not mature physically; that is, they were of an age and condition prior to puberty.

The dividing line for the marriage of girls becomes clearer in *m. Yebamoth* 6:10. That passage states that a High Priest was not to marry a *bogeret* (a girl who had reached the age of maturity),[28] but only one younger than

---

24. In general on rabbinic anthropological views, see Ephraim Elimelech Urbach, *The Sages: Their Concepts and Beliefs*, trans. Israel Abrahams (Jerusalem: Magnes Press and Hebrew University, 1975), vol. 1, 214–54, and vol. 2, 784–800. Yet that study offers little discussion of the transition from child (read: boy) to man.

25. See Blackman, *Mishnayoth: Nashim (3)*, 49.

26. For a helpful study of Jewish marriage and betrothal, see Michael L. Satlow, *Jewish Marriage in Antiquity* (Princeton, N.J.: Princeton University Press, 2001).

27. See Marcus Jastrow, *Dictionary of the Targumim, Talmud Babli, Yerushalmi, and Midrashic Literature* (New York: The Judaica Press, 1982), 1051.

28. Both Blackman, *Mishnayoth: Nashim (3)*, 140, and Jastrow, *Dictionary of the Targumim*, 137, declare this age to be twelve and a half years. The root from which the word is derived,

that. The *bogeret*, defined by commentators as a girl of twelve and a half years of age, was set apart in *m. Ketuboth* 3:8 from the *katanah* (less than twelve years and a day) and the *na'arah* (a girl twelve years and a day). *M. Niddah* 5:7 schematizes the stages of a girl's life in much the same manner. The stages of childhood are compared to three stages of the ripening process of a fig. The Mishnah distinguishes between an undeveloped fig, corresponding to the *yaldut*, the period from three to twelve years; a ripening fig, which indicates the *na'arah*, who is no older than twelve years and a day; and the ripe fig, representing the *bogeret*, who is no older than twelve and a half years. These ages are clearly associated with physical sexual maturity, and the concern over what constitutes a "pure" marriage for different groups in Judaism, principally along the line of division between priest or Levite and layman.

As much as Philo's description of the stages of life revealed a gender-biased perspective, so do the rabbinical classifications. Philo's concern with the male body rests partly on his sources and partly on his ideas about the development of the soul, which for Philo define following the laws of Torah. Underlying Philo's perspective is perhaps that only men are required to follow all the laws of Torah, with some exceptions outlined below. Rabbinic interests shared this assumption to a certain extent (*m. Sotah* 4:3; cf. however *m. Niddah* 6:3), and therefore addressed female sexual maturity as a problem for males observing Torah, a minefield filled with traps for sin that must be clearly demarcated, particularly as it applies to consummation of the marriage.

Although the rabbis also focused on the early stages of life of a female child, and so supply us with significant information regarding the development of a girl in a Jewish context, their male perspective saw women both as a source of (preferably male) offspring and a source of sexual pleasure.[29] In the ancient world, the fig was a symbol of fecundity and ripeness.[30]

---

boger, means "to be wrinkled," "to be rough." See also Schereschewsky, "Child Marriage," 423, for a description of these terms.

29. Peter Garnsey, *Food and Society in Classical Antiquity* (Cambridge: Cambridge University Press, 1999), 9–10, draws the connection between sex and food in the ancient world; one of these images is that of "woman as food to be consumed" (9).

30. On "figs," see *The Oxford Classical Dictionary,* eds. Simon Hornblower and Antony Spawforth (Oxford: Oxford University Press, 1996), 595. As the entry makes clear, because of the relative lack of sources of sugar in the ancient world, figs were renowned for their sweetness and delicacy. They were sweet by nature. See also V. Reichmann, "Feige I (Ficus Carica)," in *RAC* 7 (1969), 640–82, who notes that the fig was a sign of luxury (646), and was seen as being in clear reference to the sexual organs (650–57).

Thus the rabbis focused on determining the point at which the fruit, and ultimately the female body, was best matured, that is, when a girl reached puberty. The physical component is made even more explicit in *m. Niddah* 5:8, where the rabbis argued that a number of physical signs give evidence of the transition to womanhood: each of these signs was related to the change in the girl's breasts. The physical signs of female pubescence are not the only determining factors for the consummation of a marriage. *M. Niddah* 4:4 discusses whether a girl three years and one day old may be betrothed by sexual intercourse. In this instance, the girl is not seen as an adult, clearly not biologically. The discussion here seems to revolve around whether she can be betrothed to a priest. The Mishnah makes clear that a girl of that age does not possess reason, and so cannot willingly engage in sexual intercourse. This is suggested by the subsequent ruling that, if this was an act of incest (and it most probably was), the male partner (father) was liable to death but she was not. One hopes, however, that such instances of marriage were only theoretical.[31]

For the rabbis, the transition from boyhood to manhood also could be defined with respect to the age at which boys could marry, but the issue for boys was more complex. For some rabbis a boy was ready for marriage at the age of eighteen (*m. Aboth* 5:21).[32] Others, especially when they had levirate marriage in mind, ruled that a boy nine years old and a day might marry his childless sister-in-law (*m. Niddah* 5). These fault lines appear elsewhere in *m. Niddah,* for both boys and girls. According to *m. Niddah* 5:6, a girl who was eleven years and a day had to be questioned to see if she comprehended her marriage vows; a girl of twelve years and a day had to be questioned throughout her twelfth year to make certain that she indeed understood what she entered into when she took the vow of marriage, although the vow remained valid in both instances. The same held for boys, but the ages at which they were to be questioned were twelve years and one day and thirteen years and one day, respectively. Before those ages, regardless of what the children said, the vows were not valid; after those

31. Continuing the treatment of questions pertaining to levirate marriage, *m. Niddah* 4:4 discusses a girl three years and one day who may be betrothed by sexual intercourse. The girl is not seen as an adult, although she may be rendered invalid for the priest's due; if the relationship was incestuous, the male partner was liable to death but she was not. See, in *m. Niddah* 5:5, the following discussion for the parallel situation with a boy nine years and one day.

32. There is little historical information on this rabbi. H. L. Strack and G. Stemberger, *Introduction to the Talmud and Midrash* (Minneapolis: Fortress Press, 1992), 89, place him in the fourth generation of Tannaim, concurrent with R. Judah ha-Nasi, but no dates are offered. This would locate him in the late second or early third century.

ages, however, even if the children were to eschew their vows, saying they did not comprehend them, the vows remained valid.

This passage then allows us to draw some conclusions concerning the setting of boundary lines for the transition from childhood to adulthood in early rabbinic Judaism. For girls, the point after twelve years was a key liminal age; for boys, the age of thirteen indicated one crucial transition point to adulthood, unlike, for instance, the age of nine years and a day, at which the boy, regardless of the implications of his behavior, was considered to be a child.[33] It becomes clearer that puberty was one of the defining marks of adulthood. With girls it appears to have been *the* defining moment. While puberty may not have been the only category by which to judge the transition to adulthood, it played the most important role. That emerges even more clearly from *m. Niddah* 5:9, which states that both a boy who had attained twenty years and a girl who had reached eighteen years without showing signs of sexual maturity were deemed incapable of contracting a levirate marriage.[34]

In addition to questions of sexual maturity, a person's transition to adulthood also involved his or her education, particularly the study of the Torah. Here, again, childhood found its end and adulthood its beginning. Girls probably did not receive the same kind of formal education as boys did.[35] Most rabbis seem to have rejected in principle that a girl would be educated in the Torah (*m. Sotah* 3:4), although there is evidence that some women received training in the Torah; Rabbi Beruria, whose father trained her, is a famous case in point.[36] In fact the education of girls in the Torah appears to have been the exception, not the rule. As numerous passag-

33. For further discussion of the boy nine years and a day, see *m. Yebamoth* 10:6–9.

34. Indeed *m. Yebamoth* 10:9 indicates that the regulations which applied to the boy nine years and a day likewise were valid for the twenty-year-old one who had not yet shown signs of sexual maturity.

35. Lee I. Levine, *The Ancient Synagogue: The First Thousand Years* (New Haven, Conn.: Yale University Press, 2000), 376, speaks of "daily study" for children in the synagogues, but nowhere mentions girls actually studying.

36. On Beruria, the daughter of Rabbi Chanina ben Teradion and the wife of Rabbi Meir, see Leonard Swidler, *Women in Judaism: The Status of Women in Formative Judaism* (Metuchen, N.J.: Scarecrow Press, 1976), 93–111. Swidler thinks Beruria was an exception to the practice of not educating girls. Daniel Boyarin, *Carnal Israel: Reading Sex in Talmudic Culture* (Berkeley: University of California Press, 1993), 168–80 and 180–96, however, has a more nuanced discussion. While he acknowledges that in Talmudic Judaism women—and thus girls—did not study, he distinguishes between the trends in ancient Palestinian Judaism, which did allow for some study by women (cf. *t. Berakoth* 2:12), and Babylonian Judaism, which did not. Yet it is rather clear that girls did not study at the same level as boys did. David Goodblatt, "The Beruriah

es in the Mishnah make plain, boys were to be educated in the Torah.[37] Yet the fact that boys were instructed in the Torah while girls for the most part were not did not mean that, when girls reached the proper age, they were not required to follow the dictates of the Torah in the same manner as boys. For example, a girl was to fast at age twelve and a boy at age thirteen. In fact, we can be certain that the age at which other obligations began to take place were twelve for girls and thirteen for boys (*m. Aboth* 5:21, *m. Yoma* 8:4, and *m. Berakoth* 3:3).[38]

As for the stages of life, Jewish sources describe divisions much like those found in Greek and other Hellenistic works. The Mishnaic distribution of stages of a person's development did not follow Philo's stages exactly, but it was quite similar. A boy of age five, but not a child in general, began to study Scripture. At ten, he studied the Mishnah. At thirteen, he fulfilled the commandments, and at fifteen, he began his study of the Talmud.[39] At eighteen he was ready for marriage and at twenty he began to pursue a vocation.[40] From this point on, we reach ages that determine the stages of adulthood, rising in multiples of ten until one hundred years. For boys, the transition to adulthood was more complex than for girls. For girls it began and ended at the age of twelve. For boys, it began at thirteen, but if we see eighteen as the age for marriage and twenty for "pursuing" a career, we might say that there were gradations in the achievement of one's role as an adult male.

The discussion of childhood and adulthood in the Mishnah seems to have been rooted in the life of Judaism, especially with the pursuit of life in accord with the rules of the Torah, prayer, and participation in Temple

---

Traditions," *Journal of Jewish Studies* 26 (1975), 68–85, argues that the traditions concerning Beruriah's family background and rabbinical training were late additions.

37. The relevance of this will be considered in greater depth in chapter 4, on education. But see Levine, *The Ancient Synagogue*, 98, 133, and 374–80, who acknowledges that the evidence for schools in the pre-70 period is negligible, but also maintains—rightly, we think—that the boys must have been studying somewhere, and that the rabbinic explosion is hardly explicable in the second century A.D. without some formal mode of education. For a helpful recent discussion of the training of children in Torah, see Günter Stemberger, "Kinder lernen Tora. Rabbinische Perspektiven," *Jahrbuch für Biblische Theologie* 17 (2002), 121–37.

38. See *m. Hagigah* 1:1 and *m. Arachin* 2:6 for the general prohibition on children participating in Temple services, except when the Levites were singing.

39. While this is not the place to make the argument, the references to the study of Mishnah and Talmud within the Mishnah suggest a late redaction for this tractate and passage. See Strack and Stemberger, *Introduction to the Talmud and Midrash*, 137.

40. So according to Blackman, *Mishnayoth: Nezikin (4)*, 537; the verb itself, *radaf*, is more general: "to seek after," "to pursue something," "to run," as in Jastrow, *Dictionary of the Targumim*, 1453. Blackman's reading is explicable, however, and seems probable.

service functioning as the lines dividing adulthood from childhood. Yet in common with the Greco-Roman world, puberty was the obvious transitional stage. Philo had adopted the language of the Greeks to express the stages of life, using them to understand the child's development in his own Jewish community and, it must be said, universally.

Roman and Greek Childhood

According to Roman medical texts, a girl reached puberty at the age of fourteen, but according to Roman legal and literary texts, girls could marry at age twelve and boys at fourteen.[41] These dates align with the second stage of human development recognized in Roman law and thought, that of the *impuberes*, whose limit was reached at twelve for girls and fourteen for boys.[42] Prior to this came the age of the *infans*, literally "the one who does not speak," a child until the age of seven. Reflected in this terminology we find the view that the first period of a person's life was one of basic growth and development, particularly with regard to the child's teeth and thus its ability to use language. Once a child had acquired a basic command of language, the second phase of childhood, or *impuberitia*, was characterized as *pueritia*, from age seven to fourteen. It marked the onset of puberty and the accompanying ability to procreate.[43] This second longer stage of life might be compared to the modern concept of "youth." During this period the young people first were called *adolescentes* and subsequently *adulti*, with both phases combined lasting until the age of twenty-five. The age at which

41. For a fine discussion, with ancient sources listed throughout, see also Marcel Durry, "Le Marriage des Filles Impubères à Rome," *Comptes Rendus de l'Académie des Inscriptions* (1955), 84–91. See also Gillian Clark, *Women in Late Antiquity: Pagan and Christian Lifestyles* (Oxford: Clarendon Press, 1993), 80–81; Brent D. Shaw, "The Age of Roman Girls at Marriage: Some Reconsiderations," *Journal of Roman Studies* 77 (1987), 30–46; and Richard P. Saller, "Men's Age at Marriage and its Consequences in the Roman Family," *Classical Philology* 82 (1987), 21–34.

42. Technically children in this class were defined as *qui fari possunt*, whose range of age is from seven to twelve/fourteen. Both they and the *infantes* are termed *impuberes*, but the term came to be applied to this second stage as a matter of common usage. See Durry, "Le Marriage des Filles Impubères," 87. On Roman legal views of children see Kleijwegt, "Kind," 880–81 and 891–93. For the development of an awareness of subcategories of childhood, see also M. Manson, "The emergence of the small child in Rome (third century BC—first century AD)," *History of Education* 12 (1983), 149–59.

43. See also Isidore of Seville, *Etymologiae* 11.2.3 (ed. W. M. Lindsay, *Isidori Hispalensis Episcopi Etymologiarum sive originum libri XX* [New York: Oxford University Press, first ed. 1911, reprinted 1985]): *Secunda aetas, pueritia, id est, pura, et necdum ad generandum apta, tendens usque ad decimum quartum annum.* See also K. Arnold, "Kind," in *Lexikon des Mittelalters* vol. 5, fasc. 6 (Munich: Artemis Verlag, 1991), cols. 1142–45, here 1142.

children entered into "youth" depended on a range of factors, including a person's legal status, gender, social status, and economic position. For the wealthy and privileged, the transition from childhood to youth often coincided with one's entrance into public office in the Roman administration, especially for upper-class youth; otherwise this period marked the child's definitive entry into the world of physical labor. Many children of the lower classes and certainly those of slave families would have begun hard labor during their earlier childhood years.[44] Finally, following this period of "youth" came the age of *maioritas*. Here Roman usage of the term seems clearer in many respects than Greek or Jewish equivalents. Even after having contracted a marriage, having begotten children, and having achieved standing in the realm of public and military life, the son, *filius familias*, remained under the power of his father, that is, in his father's *patria potestas*, until his father died. Grandchildren also fell under the *patria potestas*.[45] So, although the attainment of adulthood could take place through marriage, for which the father's commendation was necessary for both a son and a daughter, the son continued under his father's authority even as an adult.

The status of a daughter after marriage depended on the type of marriage she entered into. If she married *in manum*, she would find herself after the wedding under either her husband's or her husband's father's *patria potestas*. If she married *sine manu*, she remained under that of her own father.[46] Thus, in Roman law and custom adulthood did not coincide with independence

44. See Arnold, "Kind," 1142.

45. *Patria potestas* is a well-studied concept of Roman familial organization. See for example Antti Arjava, "Paternal Power in Late Antiquity," *Journal of Roman Studies* 88 (1988), 147–65; William V. Harris, "The Roman Father's Power of Life and Death," in *Studies in Roman Law in Memory of A. Arthur Schiller,* ed. Roger S. Bagnall and William V. Harris (Leiden: E. J. Brill, 1986), 81–95; Beryl Rawson, "The Roman Family," in *The Family in Ancient Rome,* 1–57, especially 15–31; Walter Kirkpatrick Lacey, *"Patria Potestas,"* in *The Family in Ancient Rome,* 121–44; G. Matringe, "La puissance paternelle et le mariage des fils et filles de famille en droit romain (sous l'Empire et en Occident)," in *Studi in onore di Edoardo Volterra,* 6 vols., Pubblicazioni della Facoltà di giurisprudenza dell'Università di Roma 40–45 (Milan: A. Giuffrè, 1971), vol. 5, 191–237; Naphtali Lewis, "On Paternal Authority in Roman Egypt," *Revue internationale des droits de l'antiquité* 17 (1970), 251–58; D. Daube, *Roman Law: Linguistic, Social and Philosophical Aspects,* Gray Lectures 1966 (Chicago: Aldine, 1969); John A. Crook, *"Patria Potestas,"* *Classical Quarterly* 17 (1967), 113–22; and D. Volterra, "Quelques observations sur le mariage des *filiifamilias,*" *Revue internationale des droits de l'antiquité* 1 (1948), 213–42. More recently, Mathew Kuefler, *The Manly Eunuch: Masculinity, Gender Ambiguity, and Christian Ideology in Late Antiquity* (Chicago: University of Chicago Press, 2001), 70–76, discussed how the effectiveness of *patria potestas* declined over time.

46. For helpful discussions of the history of Roman marriage, including marriage in the Roman world in early Christian times, see, for example, Susan Treggiari, *Roman Marriage: iusti coniuges from the Time of Cicero to the Time of Ulpian* (Oxford: Oxford University Press, 1991);

from parental authority. Nevertheless, it is clear that adulthood was reached, if not in law, then through various achievements of age and activity.

A Roman daughter could be married off between twelve and fourteen. In fact, Romans considered marriage the natural state for adult women. Both boys and girls wore the *toga praetexta* while they were *impuberes*, but the boy graduated to the *toga virilis* while the daughter graduated to marriage. Education was often available for girls until ten years of age, while boys might continue their studies into *adolescentia*.[47] The boy, too, would receive his formal induction into Roman society at the festival of *Liberalia*, when he gained the *toga virilis* and his full incorporation as a citizen into Roman society, usually at the age of fifteen to seventeen.[48] After this he could continue to study or could join the army and take part in military life. He could also give himself over to a period of youthful indulgence prior to marriage.[49]

Greek society in the Hellenistic period had much the same demarcation as Roman society, particularly in areas under strong Roman cultural influence. The transitional phase for girls was from twelve to fourteen. Boys had much the same education as in Roman society. The power of the father, however, was not as absolute among the Greeks as it was among the Romans, and so a Greek boy following his education might find himself engaged in political and military life, just like a Roman youth, but with a greater sense of autonomy. The Greek boy would not wed at the same time as a girl, but would be at least in his late teens if not older when he finally entered marriage. More often than their Roman peers, Greek boys may have experienced sexual intimacy with members of the same sex prior to entering married life.[50]

---

and Judith Evans Grubbs, *Law and Family in Late Antiquity: The Emperor Constantine's Marriage Legislation* (Oxford: Oxford University Press, 1995).

47. For a still useful overview of education in the ancient world and how Christians accommodated it, see P. Blomenkamp, "Erziehung," in *RAC* 6 (1966), 502–59.

48. On the Roman feast of the *Liberalia*, see H. Dessau, "Liberalia," in *Paulys Real-encyclopädie*, vol. 13, cols. 81–82. For recent work on Roman festivals related to life in the household, see Fanny Dolansky, "Ritual, Gender, and Status in the Roman Family" (Ph.D. thesis, University of Chicago, 2006). For a detailed study of the *toga virilis* ceremony in context, see Fanny L. Dolansky, "Coming of Age in Rome: The History and Social Significance of Assuming the *toga virilis*" (M.A. thesis, University of Victoria, Canada, 1999). Walter Hatto Gross, "Toga," in *Der Kleine Pauly: Lexikon der Antike* (Munich: Druckenmüller, 1964–75), vol. 5, cols. 879–80; and Fritz Heichelheim, "Toga," in *Paulys Real-encyclopädie der classischen Altertumswissenschaft* (Stuttgart: J. B. Metzler, 1937), vol. 6, cols. 1651–60.

49. For a study of the structures of life for youths in the ancient world in the West, see Pierre Ginestet, *Les organizations de la jeunesse dans l'Occident Romain* (Brussels: Revue d'Études Latines, 1991).

50. On the connection between homosexual relationships and the education and training

The Age of Childhood

In order to determine the end of a boy's childhood, one ought to look at the stages of incorporation into the institutions of society rather than simply calendrical age. For males in Rome, most commentators point to the accession of a youth to the *toga virilis* at about the age of seventeen. In Greek areas youth seems to have come to an end and adulthood begun with a boy's ability to enter into the body politic proper as well as his entrance into the army. This would put the end of childhood at seventeen or eighteen. In a Jewish setting, a boy's transition to adulthood seems to have been completed between the ages of eighteen and twenty. It is possible to go higher or lower, but these ages offer reasonable points of reference. In all of the cultures we have examined, the basic point of transition to adulthood for girls was puberty, which was generally defined as occurring between twelve and fourteen, although sometimes girls were married at an earlier age. Thus in the larger context of the early and late ancient Christian world with which this study is concerned, childhood ended for girls at about twelve to fifteen, and for boys at about seventeen to eighteen.[51] With the basic chronological parameters in place for determining the overall age limits of childhood, the remainder of the discussion of the present chapter considers in a more detailed outline how individual stages of a child's life were filled and related to one another.

Conception and Birth of a Child

Abortion, Exposure, and Infanticide

Customs and practices accompanying the initial entrance of the child into the world significantly differed between Jews and their Greco-Roman neighbors.[52] To various degrees Greeks and Romans practiced abortion,

---

of young men in Greek culture, see Jeffrey Henderson, "Greek Attitudes Toward Sex" (1249–63), and Judith P. Hallett, "Roman Attitudes Toward Sex" (1265–78), in *Civilization of the Ancient Mediterranean: Greece and Rome,* eds. Michael Grant and Rachel Kitzinger (New York: Charles Scribner's Sons, 1988). See especially Henderson, 1258–63.

51. For a consideration of the representation in Christian sources of twelve as the ideal age of transition from childhood to adulthood, see two contributions by Elena Giannarelli, "Nota sui dodici anni—l'età della scelta—nella tradizione letteraria antica," *Maia* 29–30 (1977–78), 127–33; and "Infanzia e santità: un problema della biografia cristiana antica," in *Bambini santi: rappresentazioni dell'infanzia e modelli agiografici,* eds. Anna Benvenuti Papi and Elena Giannarelli (Turin: Rosenberg & Sellier, 1991), 25–58.

52. For a wealth of information concerning ancient perspectives on birth-giving and earli-

exposure, and infanticide. These practices were linked not only to basic beliefs concerning childhood, but about the human person in general.[53] Everywhere in the Hellenistic world, Jews rejected these practices[54] because they believed that each child was created in the image of God (Gn 1:26–27) and so deserving of life.[55]

The reasons Greeks and Romans practiced abortion, exposure, and infanticide are varied. In a series of works,[56] Eleanor Scott warns scholars not

---

est childhood, see the numerous articles collected in Véronique Dasen, ed., *Naissance et petite enfance dans l'Antiquité. Actes du colloque de Fribourg, 28 novembre–1er décembre 2001* (Fribourg: Academic Press Fribourg, 2004); and Véronique Dasen, ed., *Regards croisés sur la naissance et la petite enfance: actes du cycle de conferences "Naitre en 2001" / Geburt und frühe Kindheit: interdisziplinäre Aspekte: Beiträge der Vortragsreihe "Geboren im Jahr 2001"* (Fribourg: Éditions Universitaires, 2002).

53. Golden, "Childhood in Ancient Greece," 15, speaks of the entry of the child into the family not by virtue of birth, but by virtue of rituals. For a brief overview of views on the pre-born child in the ancient classical, Jewish, and early Christian world, see, for example, E. Lesky and J. H. Waszink, "Embryologie," in *RAC* 4 (1959), 1228–44. For some consideration of Christian views of abortion, see also Odd M. Bakke, *When Children Became People: The Birth of Childhood in Early Christianity*, trans. Brian McNeil (Minneapolis: Fortress Press, 2005), ch. 4; Anastasia D. Vakaloudi, *Contraception and Abortion from Antiquity to Byzantium* [in Greek] (n.p.: Ant. Stamoulis Editions, 2003); Andreas Lindemann, "'Do Not Let a Woman Destroy the Unborn Baby in Her Belly': Abortion in Ancient Judaism and Christianity," *Studia Theologica* 49 (1995), 253–71; Michael J. Gorman, *Abortion and the Early Church: Christian, Jewish and Pagan Attitudes in the Greco-Roman World* (Downers Grove, Ill.: InterVarsity Press, 1982); and Enzo Nardi, *Procurato aborto nel mondo Greco Romano* (Milan: Dott. A. Giuffrè Editore, 1971), chs. 5–7. Our discussion here forgoes a consideration of the pre-born child. A study that examines in fuller detail early Christian views of the individual stages of a child's life would have to address this question at length.

54. See Philo, *Spec. Laws*, 3.110–19; Josephus, *Against Apion*, 2.202 (ed. and trans. H. St. J. Thackeray, *Josephus*, LCL 9 vols., vol. 1: *The Life. Against Apion* [Cambridge, Mass.: Harvard University Press, 1926], 161–411, here 372–75); Pseudo-Phocylides, *Sentences* 184–85 (ed. P. W. Van der Horst, *The Sentences of Pseudo-Phocylides. With Introduction and Commentary* [Leiden: E. J. Brill, 1978], 100–101); *The Sibylline Oracles* 2.280–82 and 3.765–66 (ed. Johannes Geffcken, *Die Oracula Sibyllina* [Leipzig: J. C. Hinrichs'sche Buchhandlung, 1902, repr. 1979], 41–42 and 87); etc. Daniel Schwartz, "Did the Jews Practice Infant Exposure and Infanticide in Antiquity?" *Studia Philonica Annual* 16 (2004), 61–95, has challenged scholars who argue that the Jews were no better than their neighbors in these regards. Schwartz is convincing in restoring the consensus position to prominence. See also chapter 6 of this volume.

55. The often-cited words of the Roman historian Tacitus, who remarked on the peculiar practice of the Jews of raising all children born to them, gives substance to the assumption that this belief also manifested itself in practice; see Tacitus, *Histories* 5.5 (ed. Karl and Wilhelm Heraeus, *Historiarum libri qui supersunt*, 2 vols. [Leipzig: B. G. Teubner, 1927–29; repr. Amsterdam: A. M. Hakkert, 1966], vol. 2, 183); cf. Strabo, *Geography* 17.2.5 (ed. and trans. Horace Leonard Jones, *The Geography of Strabo*, LCL, 8 vols. [Cambridge, Mass: Harvard University Press, 1982], vol. 8, 152).

56. Eleanor Scott, "Unpicking a Myth: The Infanticide of Female and Disabled Infants in Antiquity," in *TRAC 2000*, Proceedings of the tenth annual Theoretical Roman Archaeology

to be hasty in accepting previous judgments regarding the preponderance of infanticide among girls or deformed and disabled children.[57] Infanticide could be linked to economics, superstition,[58] the health of the child, the belief that one had too many children, the suspect parentage of a child, or, indeed, to gender or deformation.[59] More significant than the reasons per se was the acceptance of exposure or infanticide as methods of birth control or household management. Abortion was chosen for similar reasons, most often as a form of birth control or because the origin of a woman's pregnancy was suspect.[60]

In the Greco-Roman world, particularly in the Roman Empire, exposure and infanticide were also conditioned by *patria potestas,* the seemingly overwhelming legal authority of the male head of a household, usually the father. The *potestas* of the father extended over the life and death of his children. Although numerous sources point out that it was exercised in the realm of a child's life only at the time of infancy, if at all, it extended theoretically even into adulthood.[61]

The mere birth of a child did not yet signify its entrance into the family. On the eighth day, the father would "raise up" (*tollere,* Latin) the child and so accept it into the household. Or he would not, thus rejecting it from the family. The origin of this practice might be related to the high infant mortality rate, about which more shall be said shortly. People shaped by Greco-Roman perspectives on life and death would have no reason to ac-

---

Conference held at the Institute of Archaeology, University College London, April 6–7, 2000 (Oxford: Oxbow Books, 2001), 143–51; Eleanor Scott, *The Archaeology of Infancy and Infant Death* (Oxford: Archaeopress, 1999); and Eleanor Scott, "Killing the Female? Archaeological Narratives of Infanticide," in *Gender and the Archaeology of Death* (New York: Alta Mira Press, 2001), 3–21. For other studies witnessing to archaeological inquiry into the life of children, see Mary E. Lewis, *The Bioarchaeology of Children: Perspectives from Biological and Forensic Anthropology* (Cambridge: Cambridge University Press, 2007); see also several of the contributions collected in Jenny Moore and Eleanor Scott, eds., *Invisible People and Processes: Writing Gender and Childhood into European Archaeology* (London: Leicester University Press, 1997); and M. J. Becker, "Roman period amphora burials of young children dating to the third century C.E. at Metaponto (Basilicata), Italy," *Archaeological News* 21–22 (1996–97), 20–26.

57. Such, for instance, is Peter Garnsey's conclusion in "Child Rearing in Ancient Italy," 56: "only those suffering from physical weakness or deformity are likely to have met with direct infanticide more or less invariably." This is precisely the kind of conclusion for the support of which, according to Scott, there is little evidence.

58. The birth of twins, for instance, was considered a bad omen, and one of the children often was killed. See Scott, "Unpicking a Myth," 148–49.

59. Mark Golden, "Demography and the Exposure of Girls at Athens," *Phoenix* 35.4 (1981), 316–31.

60. Scott, "Unpicking a Myth," 148.   61. Lacey, *"Patria Potestas,"* 133–35.

cept into the household a child who was soon to die. Such a reality of life also may have provided the ground for the Jewish practice of circumcision on the eighth day.[62] Although Jews accepted all children into the family, male or female, it may have been considered best to circumcise and welcome the infant boy into the covenant only when one was certain that the child would survive the procedure.

Child Mortality

One of the starkest realities of the ancient world, regardless of people or culture, was child mortality. The rate of death of children, specifically infants, was extremely high, as was maternal mortality in childbirth. Some conservative estimates place the rate at about twenty-eight infant deaths per hundred births.[63] This phenomenon crossed all class, ethnic, and gender boundaries. It shaped the view of childhood itself as liminal, vulnerable, dependent, and in some ways skirting the boundaries of human existence.[64] The Christian view of death, not any reduction in the child mortality rate, would later help to alter and shape a new view of childhood. Without such a shift in the understanding of the nature and meaning of death, the reality of infant mortality might have continued to make it easier to turn infants out of the family, given that from the very outset their status was marginal. We should not assume, however, that infant mortality or even the practice of infanticide and exposure indicated that ancient Greco-Roman parents did not love the progeny they chose to raise.[65]

62. For evidence from the first century A.D., see also Philippians 3:5, where Paul informs his audience about his circumcision on the eighth day.

63. Garnsey, "Child Rearing in Ancient Italy," 51–52, states that "28 percent of those born alive, or 280 out of 1,000 children, died in the course of the first year, and around 50 percent died before the age of ten." Mark Golden, "Did the Ancients Care When Their Children Died?" *Greece & Rome* 35.2 (1988), 152–63, here 155, suggests that the number might be closer to 30 to 40 percent. Closely related to the matter of child mortality is that of children's health, or rather, their lack thereof. A systematic examination of children's sickness and their medical treatment, to the extent that it occurred in whatever form, is a desideratum. On that matter, see also Keith Bradley, "The Roman child in sickness and health," in *The Roman Family in the Empire: Rome, Italy, and Beyond,* ed. Michele George (Oxford: Oxford University Press, 2005), 67–92.

64. For some discussions of the representation of children in funerary art, see for example J. Huskinson, "Disappearing Children? Children in Roman Funerary Art of the First to the Fourth Century A.D.," in *Hoping for Continuity: Childhood, Education and Death in Antiquity and the Middle Ages,* ed. K. Mustakallio, J. Hanska, H.-L. Sainio, and Ville Vuolanto (Rome: Institutum Romanum Finlandiae, 2005), 91–103; and J. Huskinson, *Roman Children's Sarcophagi: Their Decoration and Its Social Significance* (Oxford: Clarendon Press, 1996).

65. Golden, "Did the Ancients Care?" 152–60; see especially Golden's closing comments.

Child mortality might explain the ease with which wealthy parents gave their children into the care of nurses for the first years of their lives. The nurse could be a slave on a country estate or a free woman, often in the country also, contracted for the task. Nurses could play major roles in the development of the children in their care,[66] which extended beyond breast-feeding to nurture and play.[67] Poorer families could not afford to contract nurses for their children. Today we know that being nursed by one's own mother gives a child the advantages of receiving first *colostrum* and then human milk, which aids in fighting off and preventing disease and generally improves the baby's health. It is quite likely that the infants of poorer families who were breastfed also had a greater opportunity to benefit from the affection of their own mothers.[68] Interestingly, it was possible in the ancient world that slave children were sent to nurses, both because in infancy they could perform no work and so were not needed in the home and, more significantly, so that their mothers could return to work immediately.[69]

The Role of the Mother

No clear legal definition described the role of the mother as the key female figure in the structure of the Roman household. Although, parallel to *pater familias,* the term *mater familias* was in use,[70] this designation of a central female figure in the household did not have the same legal underpinnings as *pater familias. Mater familias* functioned initially as a title of honor. It described a wife who through entering into marriage with her husband had left the *patria potestas* of her father and had submitted her-

66. See, for example, S. Joshel, "Nurturing the Master's Child: Slavery and the Roman Child Nurse," *Signs* 12 (1986), 3–22.

67. This is also documented in early Christian sources. See, for example, *Acts of Thomas* X.120 (ed. Maximilian Bonnet, "Acta Philippi et Acta Thomae accedunt Acta Barnabae," *Acta Apostolorum Apocrypha,* vol. 2.2, eds. Richard A. Lipsius and Maximilian Bonnet [Hildesheim: Georg Olms, 1959], 229–30), on Mygdonia and her nurse Marcia.

68. Foley, "Mothers and Daughters," discusses the close, at times affectionate, relationship between daughters and mothers in ancient Greece.

69. The extent to which Jewish families employed nurses is not clear. According to *m. Ketubot* 5:5, nursing an infant was a mother's obligation, unless she had two servants or slaves (bondwomen). *M. Avodah Zarah* 2:1, however, states that while a Jewish woman may not nurse a Gentile child, a Gentile woman can nurse a Jewish child. The text is not clear as to when this might take place. It presents two possible readings: a Gentile woman might nurse a Jewish child if the Jewish woman is not able to produce enough breast milk ("in her poverty"), or if the Jewish woman is present ("in her domain/home").

70. Gottfried Schiemann, *"Mater familias,"* in *Der Neue Pauly. Enzyklopädie der Antike* 7 (Stuttgart: J. B. Metzler, 1996), col. 998.

self together with her (future) children to the *manus* of her husband.[71] The *mater familias* occupied the second place of honor in her household, coming right after her husband and before her male children.[72]

Giving birth to children was one of the ways by which a Roman wife could gain independence from her husband. Emperor Augustus's legislation had decreed that a legally married wife who had left the *patria potestas* of her father and borne three children no longer needed a guardian, and thus was no longer under *tutela*.[73] If the wife had been a slave earlier in her life and had been set free, she gained the same right after giving birth to four children.[74] Whereas children in the Greco-Roman household were subjected legally to the will of the *pater familias*, it is to be noted that early Christian texts witness to the relatively greater role that mothers played in the process of the formation of their children's faith.[75] The relatively distinguished social role a *mater familias* was able to play in her family and the accompanying recognition accorded her in the Christian community may have been a factor that helped to facilitate the Christianization of the young in the Greco-Roman household.

71. The best source text on a *manus* marriage relationship is Gaius's *Institutiones* from the second century A.D. By the time of Justinian's *Digest*, regulations regarding *manus* marriage were no longer to be found in the law codes, since this form of marriage had gone out of usage. See also Gottfried Schiemann, "*Manus*," in *Der Neue Pauly* 7, cols. 839–41.

72. During the first few centuries of early Christian history, at a time when marriage *in manu* had almost disappeared, the title *mater familias* changed in meaning. Law texts from the beginning of the third century A.D., for example, identify *mater familias* as a term that applied to any chaste woman, independent of whether she was married or a widow, freeborn or freed (Ulpian, *Digest* 50.16.46.1 [ed. Theodor Mommsen with the aid of Paul Krueger, English trans. Alan Watson, *The Digest of Justinian* (Philadelphia: University of Pennsylvania Press, 1985), vol. 4, 937]; see also Schiemann, "*Mater familias*," 998).

73. On *tutela*, see Judith Evans Grubbs, *Women and the Law in the Roman Empire: A Sourcebook on Marriage, Divorce and Widowhood* (London: Routledge, 2002), ch. 1, sec. 3. On Augustus's legislation concerning marriage regulations, see, for example, Grubbs, *Law and Family in Late Antiquity*, 103–12, with the rest of chapter 3 being a discussion of Constantine's repeal of the Augustean laws. For further discussions of Augustus's marriage laws, see Angelika Mette-Dittmann, *Die Ehegesetze des Augustus. Eine Untersuchung im Rahmen der Gesellschaftspolitik des Princeps* (Stuttgart: F. Steiner, 1991); Karl Galinsky, "Augustus' legislation on morals and marriage," *Philologus* 125 (1981), 126–44; and L. F. Raditsa, "Augustus' Legislation Concerning Marriage, Procreation, Love Affairs and Adultery," in *Aufstieg und Niedergang der römischen Welt* 2.13 (1980), 278–339.

74. See Schiemann, "*Manus*," 840.

75. See, for example, Gregory Nazianzen's dedication to the Christian life at the hands of his mother, Nonna, and Theodoret of Cyrrhus's comments on the role of women in creating a pious education for their children. See Gregory Nazianzen's panegyric at the occasion of the funeral of his father, Gregory the Elder (see Gregory Nazianzen, *Orations* 18.7–11 [*Funebris in*

The Child up to the Age of Seven

Care of the Child, Play, and Work

Up until the age of seven, the usual age at which school began for Jewish and Greco-Roman children, the young child tended to be in the care of his or her mother or other female caregivers.[76] The father had little concern for the raising of the child at this age.[77] Greco-Roman sources provide only limited information about these aspects of youth. From the limited sources available we know that children played, and we are informed about some of the types of games with which they entertained themselves.

Toys like rattles were given to children even in infancy.[78] Other toys might be pull-toys and dolls. The known games of children in ancient Greece and Rome are quite extensive, in fact, even if the ancient names are no longer known.[79] At an early age, boys and girls might play games together, although gender separation was common in play after the age of seven. Play, with toys or without, often mimicked the behavior and realities of adult life in the given culture or was engaged in simply for its own

---

Patrem] [ed. PG 35.985–1044, here 992–997; trans. Leo P. McCauley, and others, *Funeral Orations by Saint Gregory Nazianzen and Saint Ambrose* (New York: Fathers of the Church, 1953), 119–56, here 124–28]) and remarks Theodoret of Cyrrhus made regarding 1 Timothy 5:10 (see Theodoret of Cyrrhus, *Commentary on the Letters of Paul* [ed. PG 82.35–878, here 817; trans. Robert Hill, *Theodoret of Cyrus. Commentary on the Letters of St. Paul* (Brookline, Mass.: Holy Cross Orthodox Press, 2001), vol. 2, 224]).

76. Henri Irénée Marrou, *Histoire de l'éducation dans l'antiquité* (Paris: Editions du Seuil, 1948); English translation, *A History of Education in Antiquity,* trans. George Lamb, Wisconsin Studies in Classics (Madison: University of Wisconsin Press, c1956, repr. 1982), 142.

77. This is not to imply that fathers did not love or care for their children. Psalm 127 speaks of the joy of children, and Ben Sirach 25:7 speaks of a man rejoicing in his children. According to the rabbinic tradition, to provide for children also was a moral duty (*m. Baba Kamma* 10:1). See also Philo, *Spec. Laws,* 2.240. The Greco-Roman tradition also refers to children as sources of joy: see Cicero, *Letters to Atticus,* 5.9.3, 6.4.3, 6.8.5, 13.33.2 (ed. David Roy Shackleton Bailey, *M. Tullius Cicero. Epistulae ad Atticum,* 2 vols. [Stuttgart: B. G. Teubner, 1987], vol. 1, 177, 229–30, and 236, and vol. 2, 549); Pliny the Younger, *Epistulae* 4.21.3 (ed. and trans. Betty Radice, *Pliny, Letters and Panegyricus,* LCL, 2 vols. [Cambridge, Mass.: Harvard University Press, 1972], vol. 1, 300). On Greek fathers and sons, see H. A. Shapiro, "Fathers and Sons, Men and Boys," in *Coming of Age in Ancient Greece,* 85–111. On aspects of the relationship between Roman fathers and their daughters, see Judith P. Hallett, *Fathers and Daughters in Roman Society: Women and the Elite Family* (Princeton, N.J.: Princeton University Press, 1984).

78. Aristotle, *Politics,* 1340b, 25–35 (ed. W. D. Ross, *Aristotelis Politeia* [Oxford: Oxford University Press, 1973], 262–63), speaks of the invention of the rattle. See Marina Plati, *Playing in Ancient Greece . . . with Lysis and Timarete* (Athens: N. P. Goulandris Foundation—Museum of Cycladic Art, 1999), 24.

79. Marrou, *History of Education,* 142–43.

sake.[80] Whether slave children continued to have opportunities for play as they grew older is unclear; one may suspect that this was the case, although the type of tasks set for these children would also determine the type of leisure activities open to them.[81] We may say the same for poorer freeborn children. The evidence, however, does not permit a clear picture of how much playtime such children may have had.[82]

Here the ancient model of childhood can seem quite different from what we might expect. Apart from aristocratic and upper-class boys and girls who lived a life of ease, comfort, and education,[83] most children had to go to work, some even before the age of seven. The contractual documentation indicates that children, freeborn boys and slave boys and girls, were apprenticed in their early teens and sometimes much earlier in life.[84] Most of these apprenticeships were for the purposes of mastering a skilled trade, such as weaving or coppersmith work. As apprentices, freeborn boys and slaves of either gender learned skilled trades for a profession. Those who were free were enabled to gain a living for themselves and their family, both at the time of their apprenticeship and later. The training slaves received either prepared them for work on the master's estate or enabled their master to sell them for a higher price.

The date of apprenticeship suggests that for freeborn males some form of schooling preceded entry into the workforce. While it is reasonable to assume that this was the case, it was not necessarily so in each instance.[85] Slaves were put to work at the earliest date possible, in tasks involving unskilled labor: grave markers indicate dates of death for slave actors and dancers at five, nine, ten, eleven, and twelve.[86] Emperor Justinian's *Digest*

---

80. Jenifer Neils, "Children and Greek Religion," in *Coming of Age in Ancient Greece*, 139–61, here 146–50, discusses the wide variety of children's play in ancient Greece.

81. Golden, "Childhood in Ancient Greece," 18–19, discusses how early slave children, and free children, would have started their work lives. For many it would have been before the age of ten.

82. Keith R. Bradley, "Child Labor in the Roman World," in *Discovering the Roman Family*, 103–24, here 103, states that the upper-class boy and girl in an aristocratic family in Rome had a life of ease and comfort, but "by contrast, the vast majority of children in Roman society were denied the benefits of upper-class life." This often meant that freeborn males and male and female slaves were apprenticed to learn a trade. Yet, according to Bradley (107–9) this seems to have taken place in their early teens.

83. Ibid., 103–6.

84. Ibid., 108.

85. Golden, "Childhood in Ancient Greece," 18–19, also speaks of the cost of school and the inability of most Greeks to afford it.

86. Bradley, "Child Labor," 115.

states that "if a slave is under five years of age or is infirm or is one who was unable to do any work for his owner, no estimation of the value of his services will be made."[87] This also implied that a slave of five years or older might be assumed to be working, even if such a child slave was performing only light tasks. Indeed, young slave children often served at the master's table, pouring wine or serving food. Several contracts regarding apprenticeships indicate that the child was expected to work from sunrise to sunset.[88]

Whether freeborn or slave, children who worked were expected to be productive: masters demanded productive labor of their slave, and the families of freeborn children relied on their income.[89] We do not see freeborn girls in apprenticeships, perhaps because they received training in the home, learning weaving and cooking, to prepare them for marriage.[90] As a result, girls were usually sheltered from the world outside the home.[91] Evidence indicates that girls learned to weave at a young age.[92] Freeborn girls were not trained to support a family financially, but instead to grow into their primary role in life as wives and mothers. Playing with dolls was probably seen to aid in this task. In addition, they were being educated, perhaps at home or in schools. For most lower-class girls such education ceased at the primary school level. There is evidence that upper-class girls continued to the grammatical, or secondary, level of education, as pedagogues and teachers attended them, but they, too, were prepared first of all for marriage.

Depending upon class, the life of the young child might focus more on play and education or on work and apprenticeship. The data presented in this study, however, primarily concern urban children. It may very well

87. Justinian, *Digest* 7.7.6.1 (Mommsen, Krueger, and Watson, vol. 1, 242). Justinian, *Codex* 6.43.3.1 (ed. P. Krueger, *Corpus Iuris Civilis*, 3 vols., vol. 2: *Codex Iustinianus* [Berlin: Apud Weidmannos, repr. 1929], 274), indicates that slaves were working at the age of ten.

88. Bradley, "Child Labor," 110. See also Orsamus Pearl, "Apprentice Contract," *Bulletin of the American Society of Papyrologists* 22 (1985), 255–59, here 255, in which the child apprentice is not allowed any sick days.

89. This was the situation for freeborn children in poorer families; slave children worked because, from the perspective of their masters, that was what they were born for.

90. Foley, "Mothers and Daughters," 118, discusses the high prominence placed on weaving in the mother-daughter relationship; see also Marrou, *History of Education*, 232–33.

91. According to data collected in Bradley, "Child Labor," 107, however, female slaves were sent out of the home for apprenticeship in weaving skills.

92. Jerome, *Letters*, 107.10 and 128.1 (ed. Isidorus Hilberg, *Sancti Eusebii Hieronymi Epistulae*, 3 vols., CSEL 54–56 [Vindobonae: F. Tempsky, 1910–18; 2nd ed., Vindobonae: Verlag der Österreichischen Akademie der Wissenschaften, 1996], vol. 2, 300–302, and vol. 3, 162–64).

have been the case that rural children spent even more of their childhood engaged in simple chores such as gathering wood or tending sheep.[93] The reality of a child's work ought not lead us to think that Greeks and Romans considered children merely useful entities. Children's work prepared them for life in their society, in the manner best suited to the means and abilities of the individual families. The parents and slave owners had obligations to their charges and in a reciprocal manner children had duties to fulfill for their parents and masters. No more or less than formal education, work also was intended to prepare the child for life. We ought not think of the children as missing out on a childhood as such, but rather as having a normal childhood for their time, given a family's social and economic situation and a child's gender. Admittedly, this cannot be argued for slave children: their lot clearly was not dependent on a parent's desire or choice, but on what suited the needs of the master and his or her household.

Jewish Children

Jewish children started their education at home at a young age. It was an education focused on the teachings of the Bible and in particular the study of Torah. Whether all children were actually taught to read and write is not as obvious as the rabbinic texts claim. As far as the sources are concerned, most also focus on the education of boys, not girls.[94] One text considers a five-year-old ready to study the Scriptures (*m. Aboth* 5:21)[95] and assumes that the father will be involved in this education, but not all Jewish fathers were capable of educating their children. A Jewish education in the

93. See Golden, "Childhood in Ancient Greece," 19, on agricultural work, which small children could perform.

94. See, for instance, the discussion in *m. Sotah* 3:4 in which Ben Azzai sees limited teaching in the Torah as necessary for a daughter so that she would know the laws of adultery. Rabbi Eliezer, on the other hand, strongly rejected any such education. Twice in Proverbs the suggestion is made to the ideal young man to adhere to the laws of his father and the teachings of his mother. In the Septuagint (LXX), "law" is translated as *nomos* and teaching/instruction as *thesmos*. Both words could be translated as "law." It is not clear what implications can be drawn from this, except to say that the family was the locus of teaching and the child, male or female, was to pay due deference to the parent, whether mother or father. Perhaps one might conclude that mothers had responsibility for a particular type of teaching based in the home. See also John W. Martens, *One God, One Law: Philo of Alexandria on the Mosaic and Greco-Roman Law* (Leiden: E. J. Brill, 2003), 147–49. Tobit 1:7–8 presents the young Tobit being instructed in religious law by his paternal grandmother, but the explanation for this seems clear: "for my father had died and left me an orphan" (Tob 1:8).

95. See further Deuteronomy 4:4, 6:7, 31:12–13; Proverbs 4:1–4, 22:6; Tobit 4; and 4 Maccabees 18:10–19.

Bible, for young boys, probably did cross class lines, at least if this meant hearing the Bible read or memorizing passages of the text. Still, it is difficult to imagine that slave children had the same opportunity to learn as was available to the son of a wealthy landowner.

The paucity of sources on Jewish children at work should not be taken to mean that work was not a part of the life of most Jewish children as well, especially those of the majority whose families were engaged in agricultural pursuits.[96] Similarly, Jewish sources say little about play, but this does not need to imply that play was not a part of Jewish children's lives.[97] Sources tend to note religious obligations more often than day-to-day activities. Children were exempt from fulfilling some commandments, e.g., to assemble to hear the law (Dt 3:12), or to appear at the Temple (*m. Hagigah* 1:1). A young child was not to recite the *shema'*, but a child could read from the Torah or the prophets at the synagogue service (*m. Megillah* 4:5–6). Finally, a child was able to appear at the Temple for only one purpose, namely, to sing with the Levites (*m. Arachin* 2:6).[98]

The Child until Puberty

In this stage, education and apprenticeship remained the key elements in a child's life. Yet as this study considers this phase of the young person's life, it also addresses questions of pederasty, discipline, religious obligations of the child, and the movement toward puberty with the physical and sociological changes it brought, especially for girls.

Education

The formal education of children in the Greco-Roman world started at the age of seven for children in those families who were able to afford an education for their offspring. Girls and boys could be educated together; in the Hellenistic period girls were educated beyond the elementary level, together with boys.[99] Jewish girls, however, had fewer opportu-

---

96. Ecclesiastes 9:9 and *b. Kiddushin* 30b note the obligation of the father to find work for his son. *M. Aboth* 5:21 notes that the age for choosing or entering a vocation is twenty.

97. For a study of toys in Israel/Palestine in antiquity, see Ulrich Hübner, *Spiele und Spielzeug im antiken Palästina* (Freiburg: Vandenhoek & Ruprecht, 1992).

98. Such young children were known as "tormentors" of the Levites because their voices were so sweet. O. Larry Yarbrough, "Parents and Children in the Jewish Family of Antiquity," in *The Jewish Family in Antiquity*, 39–59, here 47.

99. Marrou, *History of Education*, 232, indicates that the pattern of education in Rome was more home-based than that of Greece. In Greece there was no question that the child at seven

nities for formal education than their Greek and Roman counterparts.[100]

The curriculum for elementary education was fixed. Both Greco-Roman and Jewish children learned how to read and write, beginning with the alphabet, then the writing of letters, and progressing on to reading. Basic arithmetic also was a part of many children's curriculum. While elementary education began at seven, children started secondary schooling whenever they were able to read and write fluently.[101]

Many class sessions were held in open areas, where only sheets protected the students from the elements and from prying eyes, and blocked some of the distractions from their own wandering eyes.[102] Some schools, of course, gathered their pupils inside buildings or more specifically in a room inside a building.[103] These rooms were sparsely decorated, with stools for the children and a chair for the teacher. The children wrote, taking notes on tablets placed on their knees, not on desks.

Greek children were brought to school by a *paedagogus,* a practice soon adopted by the Romans.[104] This was typically a slave who served not only as a caregiver for the child, but at times even more as a guardian from harmful outside influences. The *paedagogus* stayed with the child for the

---

should attend school; in Rome the merits of home schooling were still debated by Quintilian. The Roman mother had authority for raising the child until seven, as in Greece, but the difference was that the Roman child came under his father's tutelage to a greater degree than in Greece, where his education was placed more formally in his teachers' hands. We shall maintain this distinction between Greek and Roman models of education while acknowledging the formal similarity of curricula and method. Marrou, *History of Education,* 274, acknowledges that co-education was "not the usual thing."

100. See the discussion in William A. Smith, *Ancient Education* (New York: Philosophical Library, 1955), 240–48. For Jews, most elementary education took place in the home, but this began to change in the Hellenistic period. Girls do not seem to have been a part of this formal education.

101. Marrou, *History of Education,* 161. For accompanying circumstances, see also K. Hopkins, "Everyday Life for the Roman Schoolboy," *History Today* 43.10 (1993), 25–30.

102. Mary Ann Beavis, "'Pluck the Rose but Shun the Thorns': The Ancient School and Christian Origins," *Studies in Religion/Sciences Religieuses* 29.4 (2000), 411–23, here 413. Marrou, *History of Education,* 267, states that this was more common in Roman schools, which were often in a *pergola* that opened "on to the porticos of the forum."

103. Marrou, *History of Education,* 145.

104. Ibid., 144, suggests that the etymology for this word is "slave companion," yet it seems more likely that the term referred to the child who was being "guided" or "led," thus designating a "companion" or "guide" of the child. This reflects the meaning of the word *pais* in Greek, which may refer to a boy, or, more broadly, a child, and also a slave. See also the treatment in Golden, "*Pais,* 'Child' and 'Slave.'" See further Marrou, *History of Education,* 267–68, who discusses the adoption of the *paedagogus* by the Romans.

duration of the lessons and made sure that the child arrived at home safely. If a slave, the *paedagogus* might remain a part of the child's life throughout his or her entire schooling. Indeed, a *paedagogus* could even be at a child's side until adulthood. Both *paedagogus* and teacher could administer punishment to the child—the teacher could also use the rod[105]—but given the long hours with the child, the *paedagogus* most likely was the one to carry out discipline.

Discipline and Punishment

Discipline was a part of a child's life, although sources speak more frequently of its application to boys than to girls. The father wielded authority primarily within the household, which included the right to inflict corporal punishment.[106] In both Greek and Roman settings physical punishment was taken for granted; the same can be said for the Jewish family, in which attitudes favorable to corporal punishment and discipline could be justified by appeal to biblical passages. Discipline could be meted out for poor work at school, insolence, bad behavior, or disobedience of any sort.[107]

105. Augustine, *Confessions* I.ix (14–15), xvii (27) (ed. Lucas Verheijen, *Sancti Augustini Confessionum Libri XIII*, CCL 27 [Turnhout: Brepols, 1981], 8–9 and 15; trans. Henry Chadwick, *Saint Augustine: Confessions*, Oxford World Classics [Oxford: Oxford University Press, c1991], 11–12, 19), seems to indicate that corporal punishment came from his teacher, but he himself does not suggest punishment exercised at the hands of his *paedagogus*.

106. Richard Saller, "Corporal Punishment, Authority, Obedience in the Roman Household," in *Marriage, Divorce and Children in Ancient Rome*, 144–65, here 157. Nevertheless, among the child's relations, punishment did not rest only with the father: Seneca, *Controversiae* 9.5.7 (ed. Lennart Håkanson, *L. Annaeus Seneca. Oratorum et Rhetorum Sententiae, Divisiones, Colores* [Leipzig: B. G. Teubner, 1989], 266), describes a grandfather hitting his grandson for naughty behavior; Cicero, *Tusculan Disputations* 3.64 (ed. Otto Heine, *Cicero. Tusculanarum Disputationum*, 2 vols. [Leipzig: B. G. Teubner, 1957; repr., Amsterdam: Verlag Adolf M. Hakkert, 1965], vol. 2, 38–39), describes mothers and grandmothers disciplining boys with corporal punishment. For a discussion of the image of the *pater flagellans,* also as it pertains to the approximation of the concepts of "child" and "slave" with regard to identifying individual members of the church, see Theodore S. DeBruyn, "Flogging a Son: The Emergence of the *pater flagellans* in Latin Christian Discourse," *Journal of Early Christian Studies* 7.2 (1999), 249–90. Considerations of the beatings which children received need to be set against the larger background of domestic violence. For that issue, see for example John T. Fitzgerald, "Early Christian Missionary Practice and Pagan Reaction: 1 Peter and Domestic Violence against Slaves and Wives," in *Renewing Tradition: Studies in Texts and Contexts in Honor of James W. Thompson,* ed. M. W. Hamilton, T. H. Olbricht, and J. Peterson (Eugene, Ore.: Pickwick Publications, 2007), 24–44; and John T. Fitzgerald, "Proverbs 3:11–12, Hebrews 12:5–6, and the Tradition of Corporal Punishment," in *Scripture and Traditions: Essays on Early Judaism and Christianity,* ed. G. O'Day and P. Gray (Leiden: E. J. Brill, 2008), 291–317.

107. Justinian, *Digest* 48.19.16.2 (Mommsen, Krueger, and Watson, vol. 4, 849), discusses

For slaves, the range of disciplinary measures to be considered encompasses the exercise of discipline, which may have been intended to correct a child's behavior; corporal punishment, with perhaps the same goal; and finally savagery. We cannot always be certain that the slaves discussed in certain texts, both literary and historical, were children. Such distinctions are not always made. A given slave might be called *pais*, "child," in Greek, but it is not clear when this refers to status and when to age, even in cases where we can determine that a slave is clearly implied. Mark Golden notes, however, that diminutives of *pais*, such as *paidion*, do indicate a young child or a child slave, and when the word *paidiskē* is used, it always seems to indicate a slave girl.[108]

While the corporal punishment of freeborn girls is not described in many sources, that of slave girls is.[109] From instances where it is clear that slave children receive corporal punishment, it is often the case that female slaves of childhood age were being beaten. Indeed, age did not enter into the consideration of the flogging and beating of slaves and neither did gender. In fact, because of the "intimacy" in which female slaves lived with their female masters, they were often targets for abuse.[110]

Child slaves can be distinguished from freeborn children by the kinds of punishment they received. Boys of all classes were subject to corporal punishment, but it rarely seems to have been the case that upper-class boys were subjected to the flogging and whipping that slaves regularly endured. Too much corporal punishment, it was said, encouraged a child to become servile like a slave, and it is obvious that beatings and the fear of the whip defined the slave's existence even from childhood.

While this held true for Greco-Roman child slaves, less evidence is forthcoming from Jewish sources. Slaves who were born and reared within the Jewish family are noted.[111] Jewish child slaves are also mentioned in

---

both the father's right to punish his children and the master's right to punish his slaves; on the *patria potestas* see Kleijwegt, "Kind," 891–93.

108. Golden, "*Pais*, 'Child' and 'Slave,'" 91. It does not seem that Latin has a common word for child in the same manner as Greek does to refer to slaves. On relatively rare occasions *puer* might have been employed to refer to a slave. See, for example, Cicero, *Rosc. Am.* 28, 77 (ed. Karl Halm, *Ciceros Ausgewählte Reden, Vol. 1: Die Reden für Sex. Roscius aus Ameria and über das Imperium des Cn. Pompeius* [Berlin: Weidmannsche Buchhandlung, 12th ed., 1910], 52–53).

109. Saller, "Corporal Punishment," 158.

110. Ibid., 159. Saller also points out that torturers (*tortures*) were available for hire to beat slaves.

111. Dale B. Martin, "Slavery and the Ancient Jewish Family," in *The Jewish Family in Antiquity*, 113–29, here 124–25, for a discussion of the Greek terms *threptos*, *thremma*, and the Latin

sales, with one sale involving a girl of seven and another, the sale of four slave boys, whose ages are not mentioned.[112] Discipline and punishment of child slaves in Jewish families are not addressed in these sources, but we ought to assume they occurred, since slavery in Jewish families was little different from that found in the Greco-Roman world.[113] Given that Jewish sources speak highly of corporal punishment for one's children, slaves presumably received the same sorts of beatings, and most likely worse ones. Given also the parables of Jesus in which slaves are beaten both lightly and severely (e.g., Lk 12:47–48), we might assume that the nature of slave life for Jewish child slaves was similar to that found in Greco-Roman settings.

Physical Training and Games

In contrast to the bodies of slaves, which they tended to view as property to be used and abused according to the master's whim, Greeks and Romans idealized the physical form of the human body, especially that of boys and young men. Physical education was a major part of the life of the Greco-Roman freeborn child, and opportunities for physical education were available for girls in some cities as well. Physical education began for children at the age of seven or eight.[114] It served not simply for relaxation or exercise but to form children both in body and mind. Many Jews who had adapted to Hellenistic culture would also have embraced the physical arts of the *gymnasium*, engaging in sports that are part of modern athletic culture: track and field games, boxing, and wrestling.[115] In contrast, Jewish writers had a much more ambivalent view of the body, at least with regard to the body as cultivated in the *gymnasium*. This is reflected particularly in Palestinian Jewish texts where the rebellion against Hellenistic rule was most acutely expressed.[116]

---

verna, which generally, but not always, referred to slaves; one inscription speaks of a little girl, named Eirene, who died at "three years, seven months, and one day" and who was identified as *threptē*. For further consideration of epigraphical evidence for children in ancient sources, see for example Mary T. Boatwright, "Children and Parents on the Tombstones of Pannonia," in *The Roman Family in the Empire*, 287–318; and Christian Laes, "High Hopes, Bitter Grief. Children and Their Virtues in Latin Literary Inscriptions," in *Virtutis imago. Studies on the Conceptualisation and Transformation of an Ancient Ideal*, ed. Gert Partoens, Geert Roskam, and Toon Van Houdt (Louvain: Peeters, 2004), 43–75.

112. Martin, "Slavery," 123.   113. Ibid., 126.

114. Marrou, *History of Education*, 117. This evidence is literary, historical, epigraphical, inscriptional, and monumental.

115. Mark Golden, *Sport in the Ancient World from A to Z* (London: Routledge, 2004), 114–19, on the sports of the Olympic Games, but consult the various entries for each sport.

116. See 2 Maccabbees 4:9–17.

Children did engage in such athletic exercises, but other games were also considered suitable for them. These activities often used a ball, and one game looked very much like hockey, while another one was similar to rugby. There were also ancient playgrounds, in part used for ball games. Some of these games were played by boys almost exclusively; but girls also played ball games, including one known as *aporraxis*.[117] Children amused themselves with hoops, knucklebones, and various other toys, including dolls for girls. Carts, balls, and sticks, and pets such as mice, birds, ducks, geese, rabbits, dogs, and goats also functioned as children's playthings in ancient Greece. We hear little about the games of Jewish children, but we know that their parents' ambivalence toward the *gymnasium* was fraught with concerns related to religion. Religious qualms suffused Jewish concerns regarding physical education. Primary among them was the association of physical education with the gods, and the practice and performance of games while naked.

Religious Duties

Among Greeks, Romans, and Jews, children's religious duties were considerable, and it was expected that they would be raised in the manner of life of their parents. In the Greco-Roman context, children did take part in many religious activities, some of which were especially reserved for them.

Religious rites in Athens were a core aspect of family life. Some elements of such rites centered on children, who had specific responsibilities in performing religious rituals. Children not only participated in the rites of the household gods, the gods of the hearth, i.e., the *lares,* but were also seen as mediators between adults and the divine world.[118] The identity fostered by such activities cemented children's attachment to their parents' culture, household, and community.[119] These religious rituals drew mothers and daughters together, in particular as the domain of the woman was

117. See Plati, *Playing in Ancient Greece,* 27, for a photograph of a scene resembling a hockey game on a marble relief, which resides in the Archaeological Museum of Athens. Marrou, *History of Education,* 142–43, claims that although these games "were generally played by younger children, the figures depicted on the relief seem to be teenagers." It depends, of course, on what exactly is meant by "younger" or "older" in the definition of terms. On rugby, see Plati, *Playing in Ancient Greece,* 26; on playgrounds, Neils, "Children and Greek Religion," 146 and 150; on *aporraxis,* Plati, *Playing in Ancient Greece,* 26.

118. Golden, *Children and Childhood,* 30–32; and Wiedemann, *Adults and Children,* 177.

119. Neils, "Children and Greek Religion," discusses children as objects of worship (140–43), as mediums in augury (158), rituals for children (143–46), and children as assistants in rituals (157–59).

the home and their responsibilities included the propitiation of deities associated with domestic well-being.[120] Religious activities offered fathers and young sons the unusual opportunity to spend time together, because until reaching the age when they would be turned over to their fathers for instruction and begin assisting them with work in the case of most households, young boys were at the hems of their mothers, and so would not be a part of the daily activities of their fathers.[121] A similar function of religious festivals as a time for father-son relationships obtained in Roman households.[122]

Jewish children also played a role in the religious life of the family. Although participation in cultic activities at the Temple was proscribed for Jewish children until they reached the appropriate age, and certainly daily libations and offerings of Greco-Roman families could not be a part of the Jewish home, Jewish children did participate in household ritual activities, including celebrations on the Sabbath and other festivals. Primary among these activities was the reading and studying of Scripture, which was reserved for boys. A Jewish boy from seven to fourteen also might receive a religious education at the local synagogue, whether this was a daily activity or, more likely, one reserved for the Sabbath.

Pederasty

One aspect of childhood which separated Jews from the Greco-Roman world was the less frequent practice of pederasty. The sources have much to say about its occurrence as a regular part of Greco-Roman culture.[123] Greek sources from the classical period present pederasty as a means by which the adult male guided the young male through friendship to knowledge.[124] It was a part of Greco-Roman culture that Jewish commentators, and later, Christian commentators most frequently condemned.

120. Foley, "Mothers and Daughters," 118 and 126.

121. Shapiro, "Fathers and Sons, Men and Boys," 96; see his discussion of religion and fathers on 96–98 and 102–3.

122. Karl Olav Sandnes, "Equality within Patriarchal Structures," in *Constructing Early Christian Families: Family as Social Reality and Metaphor*, ed. Halvor Moxnes (London: Routledge, 1997), 150–65, here 154.

123. Marrou, *History of Education*, 143–44; and Mark Golden, "Slavery and Homosexuality at Athens," *Phoenix* 38 (1984), 308–24, here 309. Golden states that male homosexuality at Athens defined both slavery and childhood for boys, indicating the "quasi-servile" status of boys.

124. The ideal of classical Greece seems to have been a relationship between an adult male and an adolescent. In the Hellenistic, or Greco-Roman, period this more limited age range of the younger partner was not always maintained. See Marrou, *History of Education*, 26–35.

A part of the role of the *paedagogus* was to protect a boy from men, while the nurse played the equivalent role for a girl. Indeed, Greco-Roman men pursued girls too, yet girls seem to have been abused with less frequency than boys, since they were less often to be found in the public square, and were under the watchful eyes of the women of the house. Adult males in Greece and Rome looking for child sexual partners had other choices as well. A master could take sexual advantage of his own slave children, male or female, or engage child prostitutes, many of whom would have been slaves or poorer freeborn children.[125] In Greco-Roman culture these sexual liaisons were acceptable and thus the lives of many children, slave and free, would have been marked by involuntary sexual activity.

The Young Adolescent

Marriage of Girls

Adolescence was the time of transition for children in the ancient world, especially for girls. Jewish girls' transition to adulthood was defined by marriage. The time for marriage seems to have been set both by age—twelve or older—and the physical signs of puberty. Sources posit the age of marriage for girls in ancient Greece around puberty, which is often set at age fourteen, but could be younger. For them, marriage marked the transition to womanhood.[126] While some studies have argued that we need to revise our assumptions concerning the marriage age for boys and girls,[127] the best evidence suggests that most girls and even some boys married at puberty or in their late teens.[128] A part of the preparation for the marriage ceremony was the ritual offering of a girl's dolls and toys to the appropriate

125. Florence Dupont, *Daily Life in Ancient Rome* (Oxford: Basil Blackwell, 1993), 228.

126. John H. Oakley and Rebecca H. Sinos, *The Wedding in Ancient Athens* (Madison: University of Wisconsin Press, 1993), 10; and Golden, *Children and Childhood*, 48. Foley, "Mothers and Daughters," 122–25, commenting on the Hellenistic period, indicated the mother's role in helping to choose a husband for her daughter and even in aiding to draw up marriage contracts.

127. Brent D. Shaw, "The Age of Roman Girls at Marriage: Some Reconsiderations," *Journal of Roman Studies* 77 (1987), 30–46; and Richard P. Saller, "Men's Age at Marriage," 21–34. See also Arnold A. Lelis, William A. Percy, and Beert C. Verstraete, *The Age of Marriage in Ancient Rome* (Lewiston, N.Y.: Edwin Mellen Press, 2003); W. Ingalls, "*Paida Nean Malista:* When Did Athenian Girls Really Marry?" *Mouseion* 1 (2001), 17–29; M. M. Aubin, "More apparent than real? Questioning the difference in marital age between Christian and non-Christian women of Rome during the third and fourth century," *Ancient History Bulletin* 14 (2000), 1–13; and M. K. Hopkins, "The Age of Roman Girls at Marriage," *Population Studies* 18 (1965), 309–27.

128. Shaw, "The Age of Roman Girls at Marriage," 43.

goddess.[129] Once the girl was married, the transition to womanhood was complete, except for the arrival of motherhood. In the Greek world, the married girl was under the authority of her husband, having passed from the authority of her father. In the Roman context, authority for the new bride was not specifically passed to her husband, but to her father-in-law, if he was alive, and his *potestas*. At the death of the father-in-law, authority over her would pass into the hands of her husband. The Roman girl married at much the same age as Greek girls did, with the laws of Rome indicating twelve as the earliest age for marriage.[130] In both Greek and Roman law and custom, the decision concerning the betrothal rested with the father, and the girl could reject it only under limited circumstances.[131]

"Marriage" of Slave Girls

According to Greco-Roman law, slaves could not marry. Still, there is some evidence that slaves formed families, despite not having the legal right to establish families or the ability to keep them intact, since parents or children could be sold. It was not always clear who the father of a slave child was, or whether this mattered to the masters. Also, a slave child's family often could not trace its own lineage. In such a situation it is not clear how one might mark a slave girl's transition from childhood to womanhood. Given that her body was not her own, neither she nor her parents could preserve it inviolate for her and her husband. Lacking any formal ceremony to signal such a transition, a plausible assumption is that slave girls defined their entrance to womanhood by the birth of a child.

129. On the rituals preceding the wedding ceremony, see Oakley and Sinos, *The Wedding in Ancient Athens*, 9–21.

130. Justinian, *Digest* 23.1.9; 23.2.4 (Mommsen, Krueger, and Watson, vol. 2, 656 and 657). The same is true of concubines: Justinian, *Digest* 25.7.1.4 (Mommsen, Krueger, and Watson, vol. 2, 744), states that a concubine can be "any age," "unless she is less than twelve years of age." See also Durry, "Le Mariage des Filles Impubères a Rome," 85–88, who remarks that the general age given for a girl's marriage was around fourteen, that is, more or less the age of puberty, but that the law's setting of the age at twelve would mean that some girls were married prior to puberty. This must indeed have been the case, since Justinian, *Digest* 23.1.14 (Mommsen, Krueger, and Watson, vol. 2, 657), suggests that a girl could be betrothed at seven years. Justinian, *Digest* 23.1.17 (ibid.), stipulated that a betrothal could be delayed for four years or more for a number of reasons; none of these reasons specify the age of the betrothed.

131. Justinian, *Digest* 23.1.11–12 (Mommsen, Krueger, and Watson, vol. 2, 657): the daughter had to give consent to the betrothal, but could reject her future spouse only for bad behavior and character. The consent of the son, in the Roman context, seems to have been primarily his prerogative (Justinian, *Digest* 23.1.13 [ibid.]), but the authority of the father must be kept in mind here. In the Greek context, the son, who passed out of his father's authority at the age of eighteen, possessed greater freedom to make his own match.

Marriage of Boys

Marriage as the transition to adulthood did not have the same force for boys or young men. We hear of Jewish, Greek, and Roman boys marrying in their late teens and older.[132] Boys were expected to enter political life, engage in military service, continue their education, and enter into their careers, or all of the above, prior to marriage. This is not to say that marriage was not a decisive factor in determining a young man's passage into adulthood. Yet it was not the only factor. The Jewish boy, who had taken on the responsibility of the commandments at age thirteen, was expected to enter into marriage at eighteen, or younger, and into a vocation at the age of twenty. Jewish boys who married as teenagers continued their studies and training for their professions after marriage. The age gap between wife and husband in Rome was often quite large and most Roman husbands married in their twenties, not late teens.[133] In contrast, Greek youths tended to enter political and military life at about sixteen or seventeen and had more of the responsibilities of adulthood bestowed upon them.

Education could retard marriage and other responsibilities as the young man was preparing for his life in the political forum. Yet this delay manifested itself only for those who were members of the upper classes. The tertiary stage of education, attendance at the rhetorical school, which was the equivalent of going to a college or university or of training for a profession in modern times, was not available for most. The rabbinical school was initially limited to those of certain wealth, but this changed after the third century A.D., when the school of Hillel, which believed that the best way to produce disciples of Torah was to admit students of all abilities and all economic classes, came to dominate rabbinic Judaism. Most young Jewish men were at work and married by the age of eighteen or twenty. Yet the coming of adulthood seems to have been devised purposefully—whether consciously is harder to say—to make the transition for boys a gradual one.[134]

"Marriage" of Slave Boys

Slave boys would not marry, though many had children, of whose existence they may not have been aware. Slave boys were not given any of the rites of passage, such as marriage, upper-level education,[135] citizenship, mil-

132. Oakley and Sinos, *The Wedding in Ancient Athens*, 10.

133. Saller, "Men's Age at Marriage," 31–34.

134. Golden, "Slavery and Homosexuality," 311.

135. Wiedemann, *Adults and Children*, 162–63, argued that in the later Empire tertiary education, more than citizenship, came to set off the adult from the child.

itary service, or political service, nor were they permitted to hold authority over their own bodies. Their transition to adulthood is more difficult to determine, since slave boys did not pass through any of the acknowledged gateways to manhood. Slavery was intended to keep them as children by a fiction of law and practice. Some boys, who became eunuchs, were made child slaves permanently by castration, but others were rendered into such a state simply by permanent humiliation and degradation. In the ancient Mediterranean world, the stage of becoming an adult male was marked off by assuming or achieving power—freedom, authority, and right—a status which a slave could never fully attain, even high-placed slaves who were responsible for the wealth of some members of the landed aristocracy. The slave's servile status is seen in the fact that he had no choice in homosexual relationships, and that he was forced to be the servile partner, the catamite who could never initiate sexual contact.[136] Viewed in this way, a slave remained a child forever.

The Question under Investigation

Christianity arose and developed in a world that was shaped to a large extent by factors derived from Greco-Roman and Jewish life and culture. It was this world that gave Christianity its form; and it was this world that Christianity partially assimilated and partially transformed in the course of late antiquity. In what way, then, can we speak about "Christian" childhood or children in Christianity? Is it, ultimately, simply a matter of describing the sources, stating where children are mentioned and how these sources differ in their portrayal of children from the Greco-Roman or Jewish sources? The heart of the matter is to ascertain the difference that Christianity made in the lives of Christian children and the transformation of childhood—theoretical and practical—that Christianity inaugurated in this period.[137] This investigation attempts to make sense of the sources in the context of the transformed lives of what could now be called "Christian children." In approaching this question it is necessary to consider the real-

136. See also the discussion in Golden, "Slavery and Homosexuality," 312–20.

137. Gillian Clark, "The Fathers and the Children," in *The Church and Childhood: Papers Read at the 1993 Summer Meeting and the 1994 Winter Meeting of the Ecclesiastical History Society*, ed. Diana Wood (Oxford: Basil Blackwell, 1994), 1–27, here 4. See also John W. Martens, "What Difference Did Christianity Make?" paper presented at the annual meeting of the American Academy of Religion/Society of Biblical Literature, Toronto, Canada, November 2002. See also Aasgaard, "Children in Antiquity and Early Christianity," 35–36.

ity that Christian children were a heterogeneous group. Some were slaves; others were peasant children; some came from the privileged classes and from the aristocracy, while others were of humble origins. Just as with Jewish sources and in Greco-Roman society, gender was a substantial factor in determining the expectations of parents and society and the kind of childhood a boy or girl would experience. To speak of Christian children requires of us to be aware that we cannot describe only one type of child.

We also need to be aware of the particular family structure from which a child came, even though in individual cases this might be impossible to determine. The impact of Christianity on society was felt primarily at the level of the individual and the implications for social relationships, perhaps more so than as a phenomenon of intellectual or religious culture.[138] With respect to changing family structures and relationships in Rome at the time Christianity emerged, scholars have posed the question of what difference Christian popular and normative beliefs made in real life.[139] The sociology of early Christianity inspires many important questions with regard to children that this study will attempt to address. Did Christianity lead to social dislocation in the family?[140] Did the earliest Christians come from "extended kinship groups"?[141] Did the respective families have slaves? How did the free children and slave children in a Christian household interact? Did a house church lead to tension and difficulty for family members who were not Christians?[142] Did children participate in worship? Did the type of home play a role in how children interacted with each other and with other family members?[143] How did Christianity impact families divided by faith, both in terms of worship at household hearths, but also as related to

138. Ramsey MacMullen, *Changes in the Roman Empire* (Princeton, N.J.: Princeton University Press, 1990), 142–43.

139. Peter Garnsey, "Sons, Slaves—and Christians," in *The Roman Family in Italy*, 101–21, here 102.

140. See for example, Peter Balla, *The Child-Parent Relationship in the New Testament and Its Environments* (Tübingen: Mohr-Siebeck, 2003), 138–42.

141. Santiago Guijarro Oporto, "Domestic Space, Family Relationships, and the Social Location of the Q People," *JSNT* 27.1 (2004), 69–81, here 70–72 and 75–76.

142. David Balch, "Rich Pompeiian Houses, Shops for Rent, and the Huge Apartment Building in Herculaneum as Typical Spaces for Pauline House Churches," *JSNT* 27.1 (2004), 27–46, here 37–40. The connection between family life and the formation of house churches also has been examined in Carolyn Osiek, Margaret Y. MacDonald, and Janet H. Tulloch, *A Woman's Place: House Churches in Earliest Christianity* (Minneapolis: Fortress Press, 2006).

143. Peter Richardson, "Towards a Typology of Levantine/Palestinian Houses," *JSNT* 27.1 (2004), 47–68, here 53–61, for discussion and analysis of the types of homes that can be documented.

extended kinship networks? Some scholars have suggested that Christiani-ty did not substantially change the conditions of the significant slave popu-lation of the Roman Empire,[144] indeed, that the life of an adult slave was all the worse. The present study will attempt to address the implications for slave children, as well as other issues relevant to the complex changes that Christianity introduced in the Greco-Roman world.

As we approach this task, we turn from the concrete evidence of birth, work, school, and play to the seemingly ephemeral theological teaching of the Jews and early Christians. From an understanding of the religious thought of Jesus and the early Christians the impact of changes, real and potential, on children in the first Christian centuries can be assessed. Far from being ephemeral or removed from the daily lives of children, the theological aspect of childhood imagery is an important feature of early Christians' depictions of the individual's relationship to God and the larger realm of the divine. To address the function of the child in the religious thought of early Christians' descriptions of their religion is to peer into the primary evidence for understanding the basic assumptions about children and childhood among their audiences. Whatever the historical value of the events they purport to describe, the New Testament and other early Chris-tian texts are the best data for ascertaining the idealizations and actual sta-tus of early Christian children.[145]

144. Geoffrey Ernest Maurice de Ste. Croix, *The Class Struggle in the Ancient Greek World: From the Archaic Age to the Arab Conquests* (Ithaca, N.Y.: Cornell University Press, 1981), 419.

145. Aasgaard, "Children in Antiquity and Early Christianity," 32, also notes the attention which the metaphorical dimensions of language related to childhood in early Christianity have received in research in the past two and a half decades. Related studies would be welcome for late ancient Christianity as well.

two

𝒦

The Christian Framework

From "Child of God" to "Son/Daughter of the Church"

While the social history of children in the early Church is the central concern of this study, one must account for the fact that one of the key ways in which early Christians understood their relationships to God and to each other was through the metaphor of the child of God.[1] The theological understanding of the human being as a child of God orients the Christian by giving him or her a core identity. Although not unique to Christianity,[2] such an understanding derives from the nature of the relationship of God to the people of Israel, a relationship principally manifested and un-

---

1. For work on "child of God" as metaphor, see for example Peter Müller, "Gottes Kinder. Zur Metaphorik der Gotteskindschaft im Neuen Testament," *Jahrbuch für Biblische Theologie* 17 (2002), 141–61; P. Müller, "Die Metapher vom 'Kind Gottes' und die neutestamentliche Theologie," in *"... was ihr auf dem Weg verhandelt habt": Beiträge zur Exegese und Theologie des Neuen Testaments. Festschrift für Ferdinand Hahn zum 75. Geburtstag,* eds. Peter Müller, Christine Gerber, and Thomas Knöppler (Neukirchen-Vluyn: Neukirchener Verlag, 2001), 192–203; and D. Rusam, *Die Gemeinschaft der Kinder Gottes: Das Motiv der Gotteskindschaft und die Gemeinden der johanneischen Briefe* (Stuttgart: Kohlhammer, 1993).

2. Shapiro, "Fathers and Sons, Men and Boys," 85–88, discusses Zeus as father in Greek theological thought as well as the son as hero in Greek myth (88–95). Yet Christianity certainly accepted the idea of God's fatherhood, and implied by it the notion of the believer being God's child. For a study of the notion of God's fatherhood in Greek patristic thought, see, for example, Peter Widdicombe, *The Fatherhood of God from Origen to Athanasius* (Oxford: Clarendon Press, 2000).

derstood corporately. One also finds the portrayal of the Messiah as the Son of God, particularly in some of the royal or messianic Psalms, many of which became part of the Christian understanding of Jesus' messiahship.[3] This special relationship between God and the individual as God's child has implications in Judaism and in Christianity, which use the language of "children" to express the understanding of Israel, or the Church respectively, as the community of the children of God. The precise extent to which this image affects the discussion of children and their place in the community varies, and it is not always clear. Yet a more conscious awareness of the image is valuable as we explore the lives of children. Theological language about childhood can be resolved and properly received only in light of the historical realities of children's lives. At the same time, any differences Christianity made in the concrete lives of children grew out of religious or theological motivations and the realization that the child, from all eternity, was with God. Throughout the discussion we have to ask what it was about children and childhood that made that particular image so powerful for the early portraits of Jesus and for Christianity.

Old Testament

The Old Testament presents passages that speak of Yahweh's heavenly attendants as "gods, children of 'elyon," who still will die like mortals (Ps 82:7), and passages that speak of the destruction of children, including the ritual sacrifice of children to Yahweh or other deities. In other texts, children, particularly orphans, are among the marginalized groups of Israelite society that are under Yahweh's special care. There is no argument from historical development that can explain the discrepancy between the use of child terminology to describe fallen deities on the one hand and the divine mandate to sacrifice firstborn male children on the other. In the polemic against Israel in Ezekiel 20:24–26, Yahweh gave Israel bad laws, including the law of child sacrifice (cf. Ex 22:29b–30). By even conservative dating, the setting of Ezekiel is situated in the last years of the kingdom of Judah (beginning of the sixth century B.C.). Ezekiel 16 presents the allegory of

---

3. Gerhard Delling, "Gotteskindschaft," in *RAC* 11 (1981), 1159–85, discusses these in his study, speaking of the people as God's child (col. 1162) and Jesus as God's child (cols. 1164–65). See also the magisterial study of Walther Zimmerli and Joachim Jeremias, "παῖς θεοῦ," in *Theological Dictionary of the New Testament*, ed. G. Kittel and G. Friedrich (Grand Rapids, Mich.: Eerdmans, 1967), vol. 5, 654–717; as well as James Limburg, "The Book of Psalms," in *The Anchor Bible Dictionary*, vol. 5 (New York: Doubleday, 1992), 522–36, esp. 533 and 536.

the covenant relationship between Yahweh and Israel as (an incestuous) one between a father and an adopted daughter. These passages are roughly contemporary to Isaiah 49:15, written perhaps as early as the exilic period (ca. 587–529 B.C.), which describes Yahweh as a mother who nurses Israel. The law in Exodus 22:29b–30 that requires the offering of firstborn males of humans and animals to Yahweh certainly was reinterpreted in Judaism, and may have been reinterpreted even before the Second Temple (fifth century B.C.–A.D. 70). However, its inclusion in the final form of the Pentateuch suggests that the redactors did not wish to amend the traditional law due to respect for its antiquity, as Ezekiel 20:24–26 suggests. This may have been reinforced by the story of the sacrifice of the firstborn male Egyptians (Ex 12:29). Even the passage at Ezekiel 20:25–26 does not attempt to reform this statute or declare it no longer binding, but merely provides an etiology: "Moreover, I [Yahweh] gave them statutes which were not good and ordinances by which they could not live. I defiled them through their very gifts, in their offering up all their firstborn, in order that I might horrify them, so that they might know that I am Yahweh." The examples of child sacrifice could be multiplied, such as the near-sacrifice of Isaac in Genesis 22, or Mesha''s sacrifice of his firstborn son and heir to Chemosh in order to (successfully!) repel the Israelite siege of his city (2 Kg 3:26–27).[4]

The role of children in the Hebrew Bible in some instances refers to historical religious practices or, if the practice was abandoned, to past religious rites, in other passages recalls stories regarding the origins of humans as fallen deities, and in other cases (perhaps the majority of instances) is a literary device to indicate the complete dependency of Israel in its binding treaty with Yahweh. Far from a systematic view of children, the Old Testament witnesses to the view of children as essentially a benefit to adults. Like all benefits, such as livestock or crops, children were understood as proof of divine favor. This notion of children as a blessing may be found in passages such as the narrative of Sarah's miraculous conception (Gn 18). Since children were seen as important to the continuation of society, depriving one's enemies of their children was an act of extermination, such as in Psalm 137:8–9: "O daughter of Babylon, you devastator! Blessed shall they be who pay you back what you have done to us, blessed shall they be who take your little ones and dash them against the rock!" Like all benefits, when humans felt that they had lost divine favor, children, particularly first-

---

4. See John D. Levenson, *The Death and Resurrection of the Beloved Son: The Transformation of Child Sacrifice in Judaism and Christianity* (New Haven, Conn.: Yale University Press, 1993).

born males, could be sacrificed to appease the deity (Abraham, Mesha'), and were possibly sacrificed as a prophylactic, an insurance policy to assure the survival of society (Ex 22). Christianity understood the death of Jesus of Nazareth as God's giving his only son over to death as a father sacrificing a beloved child for the sake of his creation: "For God so loved the world that he gave his only Son" (Jn 3:16). This sacrifice of the only son probably reflects an interpretation of the Old Testament inheritance of Christianity, rather than an adoption of contemporary Greco-Roman or Jewish practice. The silence of the sages of the Mishnah on passages in Torah requiring the sacrifice of the firstborn at a minimum reflects the interpretation of the 'Aqedah of Isaac (Gn 22), which is an etiology for the substitution of an animal for the firstborn male offspring. Similarly, the New Testament, and the Gospel of John in particular, associates the sacrifice of Jesus with the sacrifice of the paschal lamb, which reflects the substitution of an animal to redeem a firstborn child that became part of the Jewish reinterpretation, in Exodus 20, of offering male children to Yahweh.

Torah regulates the obligations that bind children and parents, creating the parent-child relationship within the foundational concept of the treaty between Yahweh and Israel. In the background to early Christianity, the Mishnah is selectively interested in these many regulations. The frequent allusions to children bearing the punishment of the parents (Ex 20:5, etc.) is not at all of interest for the sages of the Mishnah, though it seems to have been a matter of debate even in the first century A.D., as John 9:2 places the question of the status of the inherited sin of the man born blind into the mouths of his disciples.

Neither the New Testament writers nor the compilers of the Mishnah were concerned with the many laws in Torah governing the fate of child slaves, or the sacrifice of children (to Yahweh or to Molech). The Mishnah treats the rights of the firstborn male humans (*m. Bekhoroth* 8–9), as well as regulations for the marriage of priests and high priests. Where the New Testament is silent on these and other matters one can only speculate that the apocalyptic outlook of Paul, or the post-Second Temple composition of the Gospels (with the possible exception of Mark), or the silent assumption that the matters of Jewish law would apply to Christians as well in matters that did not pertain specifically to their new messianic orientation are the causes.

In other areas, the Old Testament obligations enjoined on children are adopted as part of Christian morality and good order in the family. Perhaps the most important example of this is Exodus 20:12 (Dt 5:16; see also the curse of Dt 27:16), in which children must honor their fathers and mothers. As Ephesians 6:2–3 points out, this is the first commandment with a promise, "so that it may be well with you in the land [or: on the earth]." This is also one of the few passages concerning children in Torah on which the Gospels attribute to Jesus a legal ruling. Matthew 15:4–9 (Mk 7:10–12) states that if a child dedicated his or her possessions to God, then there was no obligation to assist the parents in old age, a practice which Jesus condemns. Mark 7:10–12 interprets this to mean that the children were not required to do anything for the parents at all if they declared their possessions *qurbān*. In the Mishnah there is no evidence for the interpretation that Jesus condemns. *M. Kerithoth* 6:9 argues that the children and the mother must respect the father, as the father is always mentioned first; this order within the family was typical for the Greco-Roman world, and so the similar arrangement found in Ephesians 6 may be due more to a broad Greco-Roman institution than to a particularly Jewish one.

Children as a blessing and a promise that Yahweh remains with his people abounds in the literary imaginations of the writers of the Old Testament, and nowhere is this clearer than in the language of the covenant community of Israel, as the child of God.[5] Many of these images come in the prophetic books, but Exodus 4:22 demonstrates the fact that God acts for the people of his covenant. Here Israel is designated as the "firstborn son." In Isaiah 49:15 and 66:13, Israel is cast as the nursing child and God as its caring mother.[6] This imagery may also be approbative, at least as it depicts Israel as the wayward child.[7] Hosea presents the child Israel called

5. For context on the metaphor of Israel as the "child" of God, see Janet L. R. Melnyk, "When Israel was a child: ancient Near Eastern adoption formulas and the relationship between God and Israel," in *History and Interpretation: Essays in Honour of John H. Hayes*, eds. M. Patrick Graham, William P. Brown, and Jeffrey K. Kuan (Sheffield: JSOT Press, 1993), 245–59; and John Rogerson, "The Family and Structures of Grace in the Old Testament," in *The Family in Theological Perspective*, ed. Stephen C. Barton (Edinburgh: T&T Clark, 1996), 25–42, an article which provides a discussion of the family in the Old Testament from the combined perspectives of social history and theology.

6. See Andreas Reichert, "Israel, the firstborn of God: a topic of early Deuteronomic theology," in *Proceedings of the Sixth World Congress of Jewish Studies*, vol. 1, Hebrew University of Jerusalem, 1973, ed. Avigador Shinan (Jerusalem: World Union of Jewish Studies, 1977), 341–49. On the motherhood and fatherhood of God, see Hans-Winfried Jüngling, "'Was anders ist Gott für den Menschen, wenn nicht sein Vater und seine Mutter?' Zu einer Doppelmetapher der religiösen Sprache," in *Ein Gott allein? JHWH-Verehrung und biblischer Monotheismus im Kontext der israelitischen und altorientalischen Religionsgeschichte*, eds. Walter Dietrich and Martin A. Klopfenstein (Göttingen: Vandenhoeck & Ruprecht, 1994), 365–86, which considers the cultural background to "mother" and "father" language for God in the Old Testament. See also John J. Schmitt, "The Motherhood of God and Zion as Mother," *Revue biblique* 92 (1985), 557–69.

7. For the sake of ease and consistency we speak of Israel, but the prophetic texts some-

from Egypt, a son nurtured by the love and care of God (Hos 11:1–4).⁸
When the child turns from God, abandoning God, God decides not to ex-
ecute his anger, but to roar until "his children shall come trembling from
the west" (Hos 11:10). Jeremiah 31:20 speaks of "Ephraim my dear son," but
later of "virgin Israel," the "faithless daughter" (Jer 31:21–22). Here gender-
qualifications that modify offspring terminology carry the weight of illustrating parental pleasure and displeasure. Indeed, these passages point to a
constant theme in the relationship of child and parent: the faithlessness of
the child who constantly wanders away from the parent.

In some passages, the image of the child is developed in a rather star-
tling way. Israel is indeed the child of God, but Israel is also portrayed as
the faithless spouse. These twin themes are developed in Jeremiah 3 and
Ezekiel 16.⁹ The woman who "played the whore with many lovers" (Jer 3:1)
calls out to God "[her] father ... the friend of [her] youth" (Jer 3:4). Later, God calls out to his "faithless children" (Jer 3:14), Israel and Judah. The
scenario is fully developed in Ezekiel 16, in which the foundling girl Jerusalem has been abandoned by her parents and raised by God, only to abuse
and sacrifice the children she was to have with God later on (Ez 16:20–
21).¹⁰ The covenant, which God established with Jerusalem, was a marriage covenant, enacted when Jerusalem came of age (Ez 16:8) and from
which Jerusalem then turned away. Nevertheless, the strong sense that permeates all of these passages is that God wishes to turn away from his anger and care for his child(ren), if only they would return to him (cf. Mal
1:2–9). A remnant theology also begins to emerge from these images: even
if the nation, or the people, of Israel will not serve God, God will care for
those within the nation who do serve and honor God as father. Malachi
3:17 speaks of the children who turn to God: "They shall be mine, says the
Lord of hosts, my special possession on the day when I act, and I will spare
them as parents spare their children who serve them." The focus on those

---

times speak of Ephraim, Judah, and Israel. All of these are presented as God's child and all, of
course, formed a part of the same covenant.

8. See also Duane Andre Smith, "Kinship and Covenant in Hosea 11:1–4," *Horizons in Biblical Theology* 16 (1994), 41–53.

9. See also Hosea 2 for the imagery of Israel as faithless spouse.

10. See also Meir Malul, "Adoption of Foundlings in the Bible and Mesopotamian Documents: A Study of Some Legal Metaphors in Ezekiel 16.1–7," *Journal for the Study of the Old Testament* 46 (1990), 97–126. Linda Day, "Rhetoric and Domestic Violence in Ezekiel 16," *Biblical
Interpretation* 8 (2000), 205–30, here 210, n. 10, comments on how children who are abused during their youth become abusers themselves later in life.

who turn and cling to God as his true children is one that reemerges in the New Testament.[11]

Another theme found in the Old Testament is that of the chosen child of God. Like the prophet or some other person whom God chose for a special purpose, such as Abraham, Jacob, Samuel, or Jeremiah, the Old Testament also speaks of the one who alone is seen as God's child.[12] This is the king, or the king to come *(melkiah)*. The earliest mention could be in 2 Samuel 7, in which God promises to David a house "forever." With respect to the son of David, God is made to state, "I will be a father to him, and he shall be a son to me" (2 Sm 7:14). Likewise, Psalm 2:7 has the king state, "He [i.e., God] said to me, 'You are my son, today I have begotten you.'" This verse especially grounds divine enthronement of the son in early Christian literature. Psalm 69 speaks of the king calling out to God, his father (v. 26), and God making him his "firstborn" (v. 27).[13]

The image of the child that emerges in the Old Testament and its reception in early Christianity and in the roughly contemporary legislation of the sages of the Mishnah are difficult to harmonize. Clearly, passages such as Matthew 15:6–10 and Mark 7:10–12 are familiar with matters of inheritance in Jewish law. The silence of the New Testament on most of the passages of Torah with regard to children may reflect an entirely new orientation, or may be an acquiescence to Jewish or Greco-Roman family law. The New Testament authors did embrace the language of childhood that characterizes the relationship between the Father and his disciples, in large measure to adopt and adapt the covenant terminology of the prophetic books to reflect the opening of the promise of Abraham to the Gentiles through the sacrifice of God's son.

---

11. See, for example, Matthew 11:25, and 1 John 2:1.

12. Zimmerli and Jeremias, "παῖς θεοῦ," 663. For extensive discussion of the term *pais theou* (Hebrew: *ˈebed Yahweh*) ranging from the OT to later Judaism and the NT, see Zimmerli and Jeremias, "παῖς θεοῦ."

13. See K. Koch, "Der König als Sohn Gottes in Ägypten und Israel," in *"Mein Sohn bist du" (Ps 2,7): Studien zu den Königspsalmen,* ed. Eckart Otto and Erich Zenger (Stuttgart: Verlag Katholisches Bibelwerk, 2002), 1–32. See, e.g., the discussion in Agustin del Agua Pérez, "Procedimientos derásicos del Sal 2:7b en el Nuevo Testamento: Tu eres mi hijo, yo te he engendrado hoy," *Estudios bíblicos* 42 (1984), 391–414. Psalm 69 also speaks of the children of the king who may wander from God and so be punished. Such behavior, however, will not affect the king, whose kingship will not end through the children's erring behavior. Rather, "his line shall continue forever" (v. 36).

New Testament: Gospels and Acts of the Apostles

The passages from the Old Testament discussed above orient the New Testament understanding of the people of God as children of God and the Christian reflection upon Jesus the Messiah as Son of God, but they do not explain the ways in which the New Testament writers interpreted this image. They also do not reveal what this understanding means for the identity of both the Church and its individual members. Thus one has to ask in what way this material helps to understand the nature of Christianity and its orientation to children in its midst. Jesus was the obedient son, called at his baptism (Mk 1:11 and par.) and again at his Transfiguration (Mk 9:7 and par.). Not only is he called the Son of God here, but God is shown as announcing his love and good pleasure in the son. Two passages from Isaiah help to understand Jesus' call in the Gospels as God's son: Isaiah 52:13–53:12 and 42:1–4.

One of the most significant biblical passages for early Christianity's self-definition is one of the Servant Songs of Isaiah, 52:13–53:12, and, to greater or lesser degrees, the four other Servant Songs in Isaiah.[14] That this passage was essential to the developing formulation of who Jesus was in the early Church is incontrovertible. Part of situating the meaning of the passage rests in the task of clarifying the relationship of the servant to God: the Hebrew word 'ebed can indeed refer to "slave" or "servant"; thus context is the determining factor. It is important to note, as Walther Zimmerli argued, that the "true essence of this figure is to be found in its belonging to another, in this instance Yahweh."[15] In this "belonging," the servant works on behalf of God, serves to make God known, and although the servant suffers on behalf of God, ultimately he (or she) is vindicated by God. While we cannot review the possible answers as to the identity of the Servant historically, we note that for Christians, this was Jesus.[16]

14. For explorations of the influence of these Servant Songs in the New Testament and later early Christian literature, see Robert F. O'Toole, "How Does Luke Portray Jesus as Servant of YHWH," *Biblica* 81 (2000), 328–46; J. Duncan M. Derrett, "Midrash in the New Testament: The Origin of Luke 22:67–68," *Studia Theologica* 29 (1975), 147–56; and Herbert Haage, "Der Gottesknecht bei Deuterojesaja im Verständnis der alten Kirche," *Freiburger Zeitschrift für Philosophie und Theologie* 31 (1984), 343–77.

15. Zimmerli and Jeremias, "παῖς θεοῦ," 668.

16. For different models of identification see, for example, Peter Fiedler, "'The Servant of the Lord': Israel (Isaiah 42:1–4) and Jesus (Matthew 12:18)," *Covenant Quarterly* 56 (1997), 119–29; and D. W. Van Winkle, "The Relationship of the Nations to Yahweh and to Israel in Isaiah 40:55," *Vetus Testamentum* 35 (1985), 446–58.

In understanding Jesus as the "Servant," his role is identified in close correlation with his relationship to God. This relationship might also have been seen as that of a "child." It is difficult to determine whether this view is located in the earliest understanding of the Christian use of this image, or in Jesus' self-understanding. We do know, however, that when 'ebed was translated from Hebrew to Greek in the Septuagint (LXX), it was translated with roughly equal frequency as *pais* and as *doulos*.[17] It is true that *pais* can have the sense of either "child" or "slave," as noted in the previous chapter,[18] and that 'ebed has the sense of "slave" or "servant." For both words, context determines the translation one must choose. It might be that the LXX translators opted for *pais* when it was recognized that *doulos* was too strong a word in context—this seems entirely probable.[19] For instance, in the case of Isaiah 42:1, where the Hebrew has "here is my servant ['ebed]," the LXX has "Jacob is my child/servant [*pais*]" and complements this with "Israel is my chosen one." The sense of Israel as the (corporate) child seems very clear in this instance. Likewise, when we come to Isaiah 52:13–53:12, we are met with two occurrences of *pais*, one being the diminutive *paidion*. In Isaiah 52:13, the former translates 'ebed; the other translates *yonek*, "young shoot," with *paidion*, "young child" (Is 53:2). Christians understood this passage to refer to an individual rather than a nation. The interpreting translator may have moved from a reading of "servant" to "child," especially in light of the second reference to "young child" in Isaiah 53:2. This translation then could have made it easier for Christians to connect the understanding of the Messiah as Son of God, as seen in Psalm 2 and 2 Samuel 7, to that of the servant as God's child. In this case, the portrait of the servant might indicate "childlike nearness to God."[20]

What we have observed may point to the melding of categories which would become complete in the New Testament portrait of Jesus. Such a joining of ideas occurs again in Matthew 12:18, where the translation of Isaiah 42:1 includes for Matthew a designation of Jesus as "my child" (*pais*),

17. Zimmerli and Jeremias, "παῖς θεοῦ," 673–77. This section, written by Walther Zimmerli, discusses where the LXX renders the Hebrew 'ebed with *pais* or *doulos*. Other terms were also supplied to translate the word 'ebed, but these two dominate.

18. See also Golden, "*Pais*, 'Child,' and 'Slave,'" 91–97, especially the notes on 91.

19. At times, however, the context of the translators themselves may have been decisive. See, for example, Arie van der Kooij, "'The Servant of the Lord': A Particular Group of Jews in Egypt according to the Old Greek of Isaiah—Some Comments on LXX Isa 49,1–6 and Related Passages," in *Studies in the Book of Isaiah: Festschrift Willem A. M. Beuken*, eds. Jacques van Ruiten and Marc Vervenne (Louvain: Louvain University Press, 1997), 383–96.

20. Zimmerli and Jeremias, "παῖς θεοῦ," 673–77.

even though this is a translation from the Hebrew and is not taken from the LXX, in which the *pais* is clearly identified as the people of Israel. In Matthew it manifestly refers to Jesus.[21] In the canonical Acts of the Apostles, Jesus is identified as *pais* on three occasions, each time from the mouth of Peter, who describes Jesus as God's "child" in Acts 3:13, 3:26, and 4:30. On one occasion, Peter speaks of David as God's "child" (Acts 4:27). It is possible, of course, that these instances ought to have the sense of "servant," but such a meaning becomes increasingly difficult to determine for the audience, especially for those in the Gentile world, who brought no particular knowledge of Hebrew to their hearing or reading of the story of Jesus. Such hearers or readers had to choose whether to see Jesus as the servant of God, one who served the master obediently, or as the child of God, the one who attained the position of the master. Joachim Jeremias suggested another connection. He argued that what lay behind the "lamb" *(amnos)* of God who takes away the sin of the world in John 1:29 was a translation of the Aramaic *ṭalya,* which might be read as "boy," "child," or "servant," but also as "lamb."[22] In fact, it can mean both, because the root *ṭly* means "young." Further support for Jeremias's conjecture and for this double meaning can be derived from data provided by Syriac hagiography.[23] In the light of this explanation, the origin of the term *pais* of God to describe Jesus "must have its origin in the Aramaic-speaking primitive Church"[24] and in the transformation of the servant language, already accomplished to some degree in the LXX. There are certainly echoes of this language in later Christian documents, to which we will return, but the earliest of our texts, Paul's letters, do not share this language. In his letters, the Apostle Paul does not refer to Jesus as the child of God, but consistently uses the term "son" *(huios)* of God, because Paul primarily is concerned to explain the adoption of the nations together with Israel.[25]

---

21. For other discussions of Matthew's relation to Isaiah 42 at this instance, see also Martinus J. J. Menken, "The Quotation from Isaiah 42:1–4 in Matthew 12:18–21," *Bijdragen* 59 (1998), 251–66; Fiedler, "'The Servant of the Lord'"; Claude Tassin, "Matthieu 'targumiste?': L'exemple de Mt 12,18 (–Is 42,1)," *Estudios bíblicos* 48 (1990), 199–214; and John A. Grindel, "Matthew 12:18–21," *Catholic Biblical Quarterly* 29 (1967), 110–15.

22. Zimmerli and Jeremias, "παῖς θεοῦ," 702–3.

23. See the discussion in chapter 6.

24. Zimmerli and Jeremias, "παῖς θεοῦ," 702.

25. One passage where it might have been expected is in the Christ Hymn of Phil 2:6–11. Instead Paul uses *doulos* not *pais* in a passage that seems clearly based on Is 52:13–53:12. For a study of this influence, see Leo Krinetzki, *Der Einfluß von Is 52:13–53:12 Par auf Phil 2:6–11* (Rome: Pontificium Athenaeum Anselmianum, 1959). See also Ben F. Meyer, *Reality and*

While the servant language might have become subsumed under the language of the "child" of God, or have given it impetus, there are other clear examples which locate the origin of Jesus as God's son. These are the passages which speak of the king, the son of David, as the special son of God. In each of the Gospels, Jesus is seen as the unique Son of God.[26] All three of the synoptic Gospels designate Jesus as such in the Baptism and Transfiguration accounts, but this is only one aspect of what we find in the Gospels as a whole. The Gospel of John does not contain the identification of Jesus as "son"—unless Jeremias's conjecture regarding "lamb" (ṭalya) in John 1:29 and 36 is correct—but nevertheless has the most extensive portrait of the close relationship between the son and his father in all the Gospels.

Jesus' identification as the Son of God takes place by various means. All three synoptic Gospels designate him as God's son near the beginning of the text. Mark 1:1 proclaims Jesus as the Son of God. Matthew 2:15 hearkens back to Hosea 11:1 in designating Jesus as the son called out of Egypt, rather than referring to the people of Israel. In the angel's proclamation Luke twice places the announcement that Jesus is the Son of the Most High (Luke 1:32, 35). In Matthew and Luke, it is the devil that plays on Jesus' sonship to tempt and torment him (Mt 4:3, 6; Lk 4:3, 9). While this is missing in Mark's account, demons do identify him there as God's son (Mk 3:11; 5:7; cf. Mt 8:29; Lk 4:41; 8:28). Peter also sees in Jesus the "son of the living God" (Mt 16:16), a perspective lacking in Mark ("you are the Christ": Mk 8:29) and Luke ("the Christ of God": Lk 9:20). Jesus further bolsters the relationship when he responds to Peter by saying that "[Jesus'] father in heaven" had revealed this to him (Mt 16:17). The disciples as a whole are credited with acknowledging Jesus as Son of God in a sea miracle in Matthew 14:33. Neither the parallel in Mark 6:45–52 nor that in John 6:15–21 has the disciples identify Jesus in this manner. At the scene of his trial, either Jesus' own claims about being the Son of God, or common knowledge and acceptance that the one who is the Messiah is also the Son of God, leads to questions as to whether Jesus is indeed the Son of God

---

Illusion in New Testament Scholarship (Collegeville, Minn.: Liturgical Press, 1994), 15–19, on the "Servant" motif of Is 52:13–53:12 underlying Phil 2:6–11.

26. Some of this language appears in the canonical Acts of the Apostles. Paul, following his conversion, immediately proclaims Jesus the son of God in the synagogues (Acts 9:20); in Acts 13:33 Paul links this image of Jesus the son by citing Ps 2:7. The only other proclamation of Jesus as son of God occurs in Acts 8:37, in which the Ethiopian eunuch declares Jesus the son of God upon having Is 53:7–8 expounded to him by Phillip.

(Mk 14:61; Mt 26:63; 27:40, 43; Lk 22:70), something he either explicitly (Mk 14:62) or implicitly (Mt 26:64; Lk 22:67, 70) accepts. Finally, two of the synoptic Gospels place on the lips of a centurion the claim that Jesus was God's son (Mk 15:39; Mt 27:54).

Jesus' own claims of sonship often take place in narrative contexts, which reflect his manner of teaching. Especially powerful is the association of his special knowledge of the father precisely because of his relationship as "son" in Matthew 11:25–27 (par. Lk 10:21–22). Preceding the passage in verse 27 is the claim that God reveals the truth to "infants" (*nēpioi*) not to the wise, but the crux of Jesus' revelation is his close relationship to the father as the son and the intimacy of knowledge given to him because of this relationship. This passage expresses the common ancient belief that a son should know the father, be like the father, and express in will and action the desires of the father: his task was to represent and model the father.[27] The son knows only what the father reveals to the son (Mk 13:32; Mt 24:36; Acts 1:7). This dependency, however, is a part of the nexus of the father-son relationship in the ancient world.[28]

Another passage in which Jesus explains his relationship as son to the father is expressed through exegesis of Psalm 110:1. All three synoptic Gospels contain this passage (Mk 12:35–37; Mt 22:41–45; Lk 20:41–44).[29] In his explanation of the psalm verse, Jesus is presented as stating that the Messiah is not the son of David, or at least that the human lineage is not the dominant or foundational identity. Rather, divine origin from and relationship to God identify the Messiah: as such his divine sonship is defined by his relationship to God. This focus on divinity does not remove the need for obedience to the father. In the depiction of Jesus in the garden of Gethsemane (Mk 14:32–36; Mt 26:36–46; Lk 22:39–46), Jesus is portrayed as

27. See, for example, the discussion by Joachim Kügler, "Der Sohn als Abbild des Vaters: kulturgeschichtliche Notizen zu Sir 30,4–6," *Biblische Notizen* 107–8 (2001), 78–92. For other qualities of the father-son relationship in the ancient Near Eastern world, see for example F. C. Fensham, "Father and Son as Terminology for Treaty and Covenant," in *Near Eastern Studies in Honor of William Foxwell Albright*, ed. Hans Goedicke (Baltimore: Johns Hopkins University Press, 1971), 121–35.

28. For studies of the father-son relationship in the Greco-Roman world, see for example Emiel Eyben, "Fathers and Sons," in *Marriage, Divorce, and Children in Ancient Rome*, 114–43; and Lacey, "*Patria Potestas.*" For the Jewish setting, see Samuel Krauss, *Talmudische Archäologie II* (Hildesheim: Georg Olms, 1966), 254–55, on the father as the teacher and trainer of the son.

29. Commentators are more often concerned with the exegesis of the psalm verse in Paul or Acts. See William R. G. Loader, "Christ at the Right Hand: Ps 110:1 in the New Testament," *New Testament Studies* 24 (1978), 199–217; and Michel Gourgues, "Lecture christologique du Psaume CX et fête de la Pentecôte," *Revue biblique* 83 (1976), 5–24.

the son struggling to do the will of the father, but asking that the task be removed. The key to Jesus' sonship is found in the desire to do only what is the will of the father: he is the obedient son.[30] These images are part of the stock portrayal and the common reality of the good son in relationship to his father in the ancient Mediterranean world.

The Gospel of John's portrayal of Jesus as the Son of God is the most extensive and also the most spiritualized. On the other hand, the images of Jesus as son are drawn from the same well as many of the synoptic passages: the son is obedient to the will of his father and the will of the father is made manifest in the son because he knows the father and his ways best. According to John, Jesus is the only begotten (son) of the father (1:14) and thus the only one able to reveal the father (1:18). The entire section in John 3:1–21 is, in some part, related to ideas of sonship or more broadly to the idea of the child of God. Jesus is seen as the executor of God's will: through one's response to the only son one gains salvation or condemnation (3:16–18). The broader imagery, however, indicates that the response to the son allows one to become a child of God as well (3:3–9). Indeed, later, in John 3:35–36, the text states that "the father loves the son and has placed all things in his hands. Whoever believes in the son has eternal life; whoever disobeys the son will not see life, but must endure God's wrath." The spiritualizing language of being born from above, or anew, ought not hide the concreteness of the image. One becomes a child to the extent that one manifests the will of the parent and it is the only son, Jesus, who makes the will of the father known to humanity.

The idea of the son's dependence upon the father for what he knows, his obedience to the father's will, and the response given to the son as being the equivalent of the response given to the father all come together again in John 5:19–46 (cf. also Jn 6:35–51). The will of Jesus is equivalent to that of his father because the father's authority is in the son. What Jesus knows, he has learned from his father. Charles H. Dodd has an interesting interpretation of this passage:

There is a parable about a son learning his trade by watching his father at work: "A son can do nothing on his own account, but only what he sees his father doing. What the father does, the son does in the same manner. For the father

---

30. In support of this reading, which assumes as basis the experience of obedience of son to father, or more generally of child to parent, on the human level, see also Joseph A. Grassi, "Abba, Father (Mark 14:36): Another Approach," *Journal of the American Academy of Religion* 50 (1982), 449–58, who argues also for a parallel to the ʿAqedah in Genesis 22.

loves his son and shows him everything that he does himself" (all the secrets of the craft). It is perhaps not too bold to find here a reminiscence of the family workshop at Nazareth. There Jesus learned to be a "carpenter."[31]

Dodd saw the image as one taken from daily life, one in which the son learned his craft or trade from the father: "Basically, this is a picture from daily life, but John, after his manner, has made use of it to enforce a theological point."[32] Yet we might argue that the force of the theological point rises from its indebtedness to daily life, that Jesus' sonship is explicable precisely because it makes sense of spiritual sonship by means of the images of daily life.

Indeed, in all of the passages from the Gospels certain themes emerge: God's son must be obedient to the will of the father, he cannot be a wayward son and be a true child of God at the same time; he must make known the father and so model himself on the father; his task, his work, is that of the father, and so he is the student of the father; he acts only on the authority of the father. In all this, images of daily life emerge. Jesus is God's son because he does the work of the father, just like the child of any father in the ancient world was expected to do.

In some passages in the Gospel of John, the discussion of Jesus' sonship is connected with descriptions of those who believe and follow him and so become children of God (Jn 3:16–18, 35–36; 8:34–38). Here are echoes of the Old Testament notion of the people of Israel as God's children. The idea that Jesus has come only for the "lost sheep of the house of Israel" (Mt 10:6, 15:24), the children of God, is found especially in Matthew. In Mark 7:27 (par. Mt 15:26), however, Jesus pronounced Israel as "children" in contrast to the Gentiles whom he called "dogs." The Syro-Phoenician woman, who is identified as a Canaanite in Matthew, did not turn away from Jesus, but stood her ground in seeking aid for her daughter; Jesus relented and healed the daughter, thus acknowledging that the woman and her child were children of God as well. The transition to seeing all people, or certainly those who responded to and followed Jesus, as children of God was the major development in the Gospel material and was quickly supplanting an exclusivist notion, based strictly on ethnicity, of who could call God father.

Jesus is presented as having referred to his followers or those who

---

31. Charles H. Dodd, *The Founder of Christianity* (New York: Macmillan, 1970), 120. The Scripture quotation is from John 5:19–20.

32. Dodd, *The Founder of Christianity*, 179, n. 4.

heard him as "little" children. Clearly, if those who responded to the Son of God became children of God then Jesus' own disciples were such. Yet the language was used in a special way of his followers when it was phrased as coming from the lips of Jesus himself. In John 13:33, Jesus referred to his apostles and disciples as "little children" *(teknia)* and later in the Gospel again as "little children" *(paidia)* (21:5). This language is mimicked throughout the synoptics, sometimes using different terms, but always seemingly having the same sense.[33] Those who respond to Jesus are not only children, but somehow and in some way they are the "little" children.

All of the synoptic Gospels show Jesus as sending out his disciples to minister, and he warns them of persecution to come (Mk 13:11; Mt 10:21; Lk 21:15), but only Matthew has him tell them that the "Spirit of [their] Father" will speak through them when they are required to testify, supporting his children in their time of need. This same sense of the father's care and concern for those who follow Jesus, the son, is made manifest in Matthew 11:25–30 (par. Lk 10:21–22). Not only are the followers of Jesus privy to the revelation of the father through the son, but they are contrasted with those who consider themselves wise and understanding. The followers of Jesus are infants *(nēpioi)* (Mt 11:25). This status is part of their identity, it seems, and may describe something of their earthly status, but without question it indicates their orientation to the father, upon whom their dependence is absolute.

Another term, which according to the Gospel writers Jesus used in order to describe at least some of his followers, is "little ones" *(mikroi)*. This term might go back to the Hebrew *qāṭān*, a word which both the Old Testament and rabbinic literature use for children in numerous places.[34] It is not always clear whether children are on the mind of the respective authors, or whether Jesus was understood to have included in this grouping all of his disciples. The diminutives used, for instance, in the Gospel of John make one wonder whether the terms are inclusive of all of Jesus' followers. While the use of "little ones" in Mark 9:42 (par. Mt 10:42) seems to designate any follower of Jesus, at least as the pericope now stands, the use of the term in Matthew 18:6 (par. Lk 17:2), 10, and 14 specifically seems to single out children.[35] It is possible that Jesus employed the word to refer both

33. For example, Mark 10:24; Matthew 5:45, 7:11; Luke 6:35.

34. See J. Conrad, "קָטֹן *qāṭōn*; קָטָן *qāṭān*; קֹטֶן *qōṭen*." in *Theological Dictionary of the Old Testament* (Grand Rapids, Mich.: Eerdmans, 2004), vol. 13, 3–9, here 6–9.

35. For a broader discussion of the "little ones," see David E. Orton, "We felt like grasshoppers: The little ones in biblical interpretation," *Biblical Interpretation* 11 (2003), 488–502; and

to children and to his disciples. In this case, there was something about his disciples, in their dependence upon the father, their vulnerability, or their lack of prestige, which caused them to be included among the "little ones." Nevertheless, it seems fair to say that the disciples, too, were among the children: "Children [*tekna*], how hard it is to enter the kingdom of God!" (Mk 10:24). For this to take place, reliance on the father seems to have been the essential and necessary step, especially as revealed through the son. Therefore Jesus is presented as calling upon his disciples to pray, "Our Father . . . your kingdom come, your will be done" (Mt 6:9–10; par. Lk 11:2).

Apart from Jesus' teachings on the specific role and function of actual children as spiritual models, to the fuller discussion of which we will turn later, the specification of all people as children of God reveals aspects of the character not only of humanity and the followers of Jesus, but of the nature of the biblical God. Jesus' teaching is fully and unmistakably rooted in the message of the Old Testament. Much of that text shows that the biblical God stands aside with the minors, the forgotten, the weak, the foreigners, the youngest, and the oppressed. The biblical God is father and mother, is parent to all.

A true child of God represents that parent as only the son of God can do in fullness. Yet all disciples of the son of God must strive to emulate this model (Mt 5:48). As a special possession of their father, children are the ones who in will and action imitate the father, who are obedient, not wayward, whose close relationship with the father aims at living in accord with the model he sets, and who complete the task given to them by the father. The ideal child is the image of the ideal disciple.

New Testament: Pauline Literature and Beyond

As the Son of God, by definition Jesus is the child of God. In Paul's formulation one continues to see the extension of this status to all who follow Jesus' welcome into God's family. Paul and the Pauline tradition describe Jesus as "son" on numerous occasions (1 Thes 1:10; 1 Cor 1:9; 2 Cor 1:19; Gal 2:20; 4:4; Rom 1:3, 4, 9; 5:10; 8:3, 32; Col 1:13; and Eph 4:14) in order to speak of Jesus' relationship with the father. Quite explicitly in Romans 8:29 and Galatians 4:6, 7 Paul links Jesus' sonship to Christian participation in the family of God. In both of those passages, Christians who are under-

---

also Savvas Agouridēs, "'Little Ones' in Matthew," *Bible Translator* 35 (1984), 329–34, who sees in the "little ones" a group of young disciples in the community, for whom Matthew wished to establish their function in the Church.

stood as participating in Jesus' life and death become a part of God's family and are able to cry out to God as Father (Gal 4:7). As a result, Christians become "members of the household" *(oikeioi)* or family of those who believe (Gal 6:10). The language of belonging to the family as so stated is unique to this passage,[36] but it derives from the implication of being a son or daughter of God. In the Pauline tradition, a passage in Ephesians 2:19 duplicates the language of Christians, specifically Gentiles, being brought into God's family, by designating them as "fellow citizens" of "God's household."[37] Ephesians 3:15 uses similar language to illustrate the bringing together of Jew and Gentile through Jesus Christ: it describes those who are a part of the *patria* of God. This could mean the "fatherhood" of God or it may imply the "family" (or even "homeland") of God, but in either case it indicates the new relationship of the individual to God as Father gained through his Son, Jesus Christ.

Paul himself had no hesitation to call Christians "children" of God. In most cases he described them not as *pais/paides*, but as *teknon/tekna*. Christians share in Christ's suffering and will also share in his glory as children of God (Rom 8:16, 17, and 21). Utilizing the remnant theology of the Old Testament, Paul did not extend this family membership to all of Israel, however, but only to those who believe in Christ (Rom 9:7–10; cf. Gal 3:7). In Galatians 4:21–5:1 Paul developed an analogy of complexity and depth; our purpose in referring to it is simply to note that through it Paul designated his children, the Church, as the children of God, those who were "heirs" of the inheritance of God, an image which utilized clear examples from both Jewish and Greco-Roman inheritance law.[38] Paul argued that under the Torah the person was "restrained" until the revealing of Christ, as under a *paedagogus*, the image of the slave guardian whose purpose it was to see the child disciplined and educated (Gal 3:23–24).[39] Now that Christ

36. For developments in the usage of this language in eastern Christian society in the Byzantine period, see Jean Verpeaux, "Les *oikeioi*: notes d'histoire institutionnelle et sociale," *Revue des études byzantines* 23 (1965), 89–99.

37. See also the discussion in Carmen Bernabé Ubieta, "'Neither *xenoi* nor *paroikoi*, *sympolitai* and *oikeioi tou theou*' (Eph 2:19): Pauline Christian Communities: Defining a New Territoriality," in *Social Scientific Models for Interpreting the Bible: Essays by the Context Group in Honor of Bruce J. Malina*, ed. John J. Pilch (Leiden: E. J. Brill, 2001), 260–80.

38. For discussion of some legal background to these passages, see Nigel M. Watson, "'And if children, then heirs' (Rom 8:17)—why not sons?" *Australian Biblical Review* 49 (2001), 53–56; and Francis Lyall, "Legal Metaphors in the Epistles," *Tyndale Bulletin* 32 (1981), 79–95. See also Alfio Marcello Buscemi, "Libertà e *huiothesia*: studio esegetico di Gal 4,1–7," *Liber Annuus* 30 (1980), 93–136.

39. For the role of the *paedagogus* in the ancient world, see Marrou, *History of Education*,

was revealed, Christians were "sons" (*huioi*) of God and so had come into their inheritance (Gal 3:25–29).

Paul regularly referred to the members of his churches as his children. On occasion he would speak as their father, urging and encouraging them (1 Thes 2:11) or threatening discipline and punishment if need be (1 Cor 4:14–21). He used images of tenderness to describe his role as parent to the members of his churches, his children. Two passages in 2 Corinthians (6:14 and 12:14) speak of how in his tumultuous relationship with his Corinthian children Paul desired to talk to them openly and not to be a burden to them. Paul also could present himself as the mother of his churches, designating himself as the nurse who tenderly fed her own children in Thessalonica (1 Thes 2:7), or as the mother who was bringing to birth once again her children in Galatia (Gal 4:19). In later apocryphal literature, other apostles also are depicted as caring for the faithful like nurses, feeding the little ones with their milk. The portrait of the apostle John in the *Acts of John* is a case in point.[40] This particular image of believers as children being cared for by a given apostle as their parent has some currency in early Christianity at least into the third century.[41]

One of the tasks Paul saw for himself as a parent was to bring his children to maturity. In 1 Corinthians 14:20 he associated childhood with immaturity and asked the Corinthians to stop being "children" (*paidia*) in their thinking, but to "be childlike" (*nēpiazete*) in evil. The same image had already appeared earlier in the letter when Paul addressed the Corinthians as "infants" (*nēpioi*) (1 Cor 3:1). For Paul, maturity was equal to growing in

---

144. See also Gregory of Nyssa, *De beneficentia* (ed. Adrianus van Heck, in *Gregorii Nysseni Opera*, ed. Werner Jaeger [Leiden: E. J. Brill, 1952–], vol. 9, 91–108, here 93), who describes how the *paedagogus* receives the children from their father, yet before teaching them higher sciences, first makes them memorize the alphabet and then guides them in writing the shapes of the letters in wax. Eventually, he teaches them the names of the letters, then the syllables, and also practices with them how to pronounce difficult words properly. See also chapter 1 of this volume.

40. *Acts of John* 45 (ed. and trans. Eric Junod and Jean-Daniel Kaestli, *Acta Iohannis. Praefatio—Textus* [Turnhout: Brepols, 1983], 227, §45, ll. 7–10 [Greek], 226 [French]). For fuller discussion, see Cornelia B. Horn, "The Depiction of Children and Young People as Literary Device in Canonical and Apocryphal Acts," in *Bringing the Underground to the Foreground: New Perspectives on Jewish and Christian Apocryphal Texts and Traditions*, Proceedings of the Apocrypha and Pseudepigrapha Section of the Society for Biblical Literature, Groningen, the Netherlands, July 25–28, 2004, ed. Pierluigi Piovanelli, forthcoming.

41. For the relative dating of the *Acts of John* in comparison to other apocryphal Acts of Apostles, see Jan N. Bremmer, "The Apocryphal Acts: Authors, Place, Time and Readership," in *The Apocryphal Acts of Thomas*, ed. Jan N. Bremmer (Louvain: Peeters, 2001), 149–70, here 152–53.

Christ continuously.[42] In Philippians 2:15, he designated the congregation as children of God, but spoke of his need to present them as "blameless and pure children of God" on the day of the Lord and so referred back to his role as their spiritual father. He referenced the time before the Christians in Galatia knew Christ as a time when they were "infants" *(nēpioi)* (Gal 4:3). The Pauline tradition, for example Ephesians 4:14, also described Christians as "infants" *(nēpioi)*, who are growing to maturity in Christ. Finally, Paul saw himself in 1 Corinthians 13:11 as a *nēpios* or infant who on becoming an adult "put away" childish things *(ta tou nēpiou)*.

These images reveal to us that part of what it meant to be a child of God was to have a relationship with God that paradoxically was unencumbered by the restraints of childhood. As an infant or a child, one's relationship necessarily was limited; once one reached the age of majority and gained maturity, childhood technically was put aside, and a deeper relationship, without intermediary forces, could be established between the parent and the child. The child, it would seem, was free to enter into a relationship in which his or her life was modeled after that of the father or parent, and in which he or she was free to choose to live a life in obedience to and in the likeness of the father or parent. This idea lies behind much of Paul's image of the *nēpios*.

On occasion Paul spoke of his co-workers as his children, particularly Timothy. He referred to Timothy as his "son" (1 Cor 4:17; Phil 2:22). In 1 Corinthians 4:17 he called him "my beloved child" *(mou teknon agapēton)*, paralleling the language that is applied to Jesus when he is called "son" of God at the baptism in the Jordan.[43] Furthermore, Timothy was called "faithful in the Lord" precisely because he would remind the Corinthians of all that Paul taught in all of his churches. Therefore, as Jesus was the faithful Son of God because of his obedience to the will of God, Timothy was the child of Paul due to his obedience to Paul and his ministry. The same sense of obedience is present in Philippians: Timothy was the child to Paul as father because he had "served" Paul in the Gospel. In fact,

---

42. In a generalized statement Paul speaks of Jewish teachers as teachers "of infants" *(nēpioi)* (Rom 2:20). Here, it seems, his use of infants has a pejorative sense, with none of the concomitant understanding that those who are infants will grow in spiritual insight. It is possible that Paul is actually speaking of infants here.

43. On the central importance of this scene for early Christian theology, see the studies by Kilian McDonnell, *The Baptism of Jesus in the Jordan: The Trinitarian and Cosmic Order of Salvation* (Collegeville, Minn.: Liturgical Press, 1996); and Daniel Vigne, *Christ au Jourdain: Le Baptême de Jésus dans la tradition judéo-chrétienne* (Paris: Librairie Lecoffre, 1992).

one can discern the case of Timothy's obedience even more clearly. The verb Paul used, *edouleusen,* a form related to *doulos,* can be translated more properly as "he performed the duties of a slave" or, stemming from its integral meaning, "he obeyed." In the ancient world, fathers, and mothers as well, demanded obedience and this was a key element of the child's relationship with parents.[44] Independent of the authenticity of some of the letters included in the Pauline corpus, the same images appear in the Pastoral Epistles.[45] First Timothy 1:2 called Timothy Paul's "true child in the faith." First Timothy 1:18 referred to him as "child" and gave him a religious charge again connected to his faith. He also was called "beloved child" in 2 Timothy 1:2 and later in the letter was given his task in his ministry due to his knowledge of Paul's teaching (2 Tm 3:10). Elsewhere in Paul's own letters, Timothy was called "brother" (2 Cor 1:1; 1 Thes 3:2; Phlm 1; cf. also Col 1:1 in the Pauline tradition), indicating, it appears, the relationship of Timothy with the whole Church, not just Paul. This seems especially to have been the case in 1 Thessalonians 3:2, where the author called Timothy "our" brother, specifically in the work of the Gospel, thus reflecting the familial nature of the Church as a whole.[46]

Already from this relatively early point in the study we can formulate

44. Philip F. Esler, "Family Imagery and Christian Identity in Gal. 5:13 to 6:10," in *Constructing Early Christian Families,* 121–49, here 124–25; Yarbrough, "Parents and Children in the Jewish Family of Antiquity"; and Grassi, "Abba, Father (Mark 14:36)." For a discussion of psychological aspects of children's obedience, see also Giovanni Cattanei, "Significato formativo dell'obbedienza," in *L'educazione morale,* eds. Enzo Giammancheri and Marcello Peretti (Brescia, Italy: Editrice la Scuola, 1977), 247–77.

45. For questions related to the authorship of the Pastoral Epistles, see Anthony E. Bird, "The Authorship of the Pastoral Epistles—Quantifying Literary Style," *Reformed Theological Review* 56 (1997), 118–37; I. Howard Marshall, "Recent Study of the Pastoral Epistles," *Themelios* 23 (1997), 3–29; Jean-Daniel Kaestli, "Luke-Acts and the Pastoral Epistles: The Thesis of a Common Authorship," in *Luke's Literary Achievement: Collected Essays,* ed. Christopher M. Tuckett (Sheffield: Sheffield Academic Press, 1995), 110–26; Gerhard Lohfink, "Die Vermittlung des Paulinismus zu den Pastoralbriefen," *Biblische Zeitschrift* 32.2 (1988), 169–88; Anthony T. Hanson, "The Domestication of Paul: A Study in the Development of Early Christian Theology," *Bulletin of the John Rylands University Library of Manchester* 63.2 (1981), 402–18; Edgar Hennecke, "Apostolische Pseudepigraphen," in *Pseudepigraphie in der heidnischen und jüdisch-christlichen Antike,* ed. Norbert Brox (Darmstadt: Wissenschaftliche Buchgesellschaft, 1977), 82–89; and Bela Bates Edwards, "The Genuineness of the Pastoral Epistles," *Bibliotheca Sacra* 150 (1993), 131–39 (reprinted from 1851 edition).

46. For a study of the function of family and kinship language in some early Christian churches, see Philip E. Esler, "'Keeping it in the family': Culture, Kinship and Identity in 1 Thessalonians and Galatians," in *Families and Family Relations as Represented in Early Judaisms and Early Christianities: Texts and Fictions,* eds. Jan W. van Henten and Athalya Brenner (Leiden: DEO Publishing, 2000), 145–84.

two general comments. Christians were understood to be children of God, and Paul always utilized *teknon* to describe them as such. This world of ideas and this language are connected to the vision of the relationship to God, which Christ had gained for his disciples. When Paul talked about the members of his churches as spiritual children, however, he designated them exclusively as "infants" who had to grow up both to maturity and in their relationship with the father. At some level they became children upon entry into the Church, but as far as their spiritual maturity was concerned, they remained infants until they grew in the faith. When Paul described Timothy, he also used the word *teknon*. This term seems to bespeak a part of the new identity of the follower of Christ. Yet it also reflects an ideal father-son relationship between Timothy and Paul. It was based on Timothy's fidelity and loyalty, not just to the Gospel, but also to the Apostle himself: Timothy was the obedient child.

Highlights from the Post-Apostolic Early Christian Period

Whereas Paul never referred to Jesus as the "child" of God, the phrase did continue to be utilized as a regular designation in later texts. Jesus as the Son of God, as one might expect, had a provenance which was extremely wide. The phrase itself was foundational and at the bedrock of the Christian understanding of Jesus' identity, not just as the son who was obedient to the father, but in Christological definitions which shape Christian belief to this day. The declaration of Jesus as "the only-begotten Son of God . . . begotten not made"[47] in the creed that was promulgated at the Council of Nicaea (A.D. 325) continues to have formative impact *par excellence* throughout the Christian churches. In the course of time, Christian theology has become accustomed to refer to Christ as the "Son of God" *(huios theou)*. Yet in official definitions the son is not necessarily ever the child, even if, after the manner in which all ancients hoped for it, he was always obedient to the father. "Child of God" as a designation for Christ, however, was used in a number of biblical and extra-biblical texts in early Christianity.

The evidence of Christian literature from the first through the fifth cen-

---

47. The Greek formulates: "καὶ εἰς ἕνα κύριον Ἰησοῦν Χριστὸν τὸν υἱὸν τοῦ θεοῦ γεννηθέντα ἐκ τοῦ πατρὸς μονογενῆ . . . γεννηθέντα οὐ ποιηθέντα." On the basis of the edition by G. Alberigo et al., *Conciliorum Oecumenicorum Decreta* (Bologna: Istituto per le Scienze Religiose, 1973), the text is reprinted and translated into English in Norman P. Tanner S.J., *Decrees of the Ecumenical Councils*, vol. 1: *Nicaea I to Lateran V* (Washington, D.C.: Georgetown University Press, 1990), 5.

turies attests that the epithet *pais theou* was used as a Christological title. The LXX, significantly, appears to have reserved the designation *ho pais tou theou* to Moses (Jo 14:7; 1 Chr 6:34; 2 Chr 24:9), who also could be called *pais kyriou* (2 Chr 1:3). This title is customarily rendered as "servant of God," since the LXX translates the Hebrew *'ebed*. In the New Testament, designations of Christ as "child" *(pais)* appear in Acts 3:13, Acts 3:26, and Acts 4:30,[48] yet in none of these instances are they presented in the formula "child of God" *(pais theou)*.

Modern translators of Acts usually prefer to render *pais* in the relevant passages as "servant." Ludger Bernhard, however, has demonstrated that from the Syriac Peshitta, as well as from the Armenian, Georgian, Ge'ez, and Sahidic (Coptic) versions down to the Old Latin version, almost all early Christian versions of the Scriptures understood and translated the word with their respective word for "son"[49] or "(male) child."[50] For instance, the Bohairic (Coptic) word employed the term ⲁⲗⲟⲩ, which is as broad in meaning as the Greek *pais,* thus rendering the designation for anyone from small child, boy, youth, to girl, and servant or slave.[51]

The first reference to Christ as "child" *(pais)* of God in non-canonical texts seems to be the occurrence in *First Clement* 59:4. On four occasions, all in the context of the Eucharistic blessing, the *Didache* speaks of Jesus as "child of God" (9.2, 3; 10.2, 3). The same language is also used in the *Martyrdom of Polycarp* 14:1. Especially significant in these passages is the designation of Jesus the child as "beloved" (and "blessed" in the *Martyrdom of Polycarp*), the same word that is used to describe him in the baptism scene in the synoptic Gospels.[52]

---

48. Jacques E. Ménard, "*Pais Theou* as Messianic Title in the Book of Acts," *Catholic Biblical Quarterly* 19 (1957), 83–92, considers the occurences in Acts strictly in reference to the image of the Suffering Servant and does not explore the connotations of "child" of God that the title may bear. Yet it is to be noted that Is 53:2 (LXX) renders the Hebrew *yonek* with *paidion*.

49. Ludger Bernhard, "Das frühchristliche Verständnis der Formel ΙΗΣΟΥΣ ΠΑΙΣ ΘΕΟΥ aufgrund der alten Bibelübersetzungen," in *Lingua Restituta Orientalis: Festgabe für Julius Aßfalg*, eds. Regine Schulz, Julius Aßfalg, and Manfred Görg (Wiesbaden: Otto Harrassowitz, 1990), 21–29, here 23 (Syriac, Georgian, and Armenian evidence), 24 (Ge'ez, Sahidic-Coptic, and Old Latin evidence).

50. So Jerome in the *Vulgate*. See Bernhard, "Das frühchristliche Verständnis," 26.

51. Bernhard, "Das frühchristliche Verständnis," 25.

52. *First Letter of Clement to the Corinthians* 59:4 (ed. and trans. Bart Ehrman, *The Apostolic Fathers* [Cambridge, Mass.: Harvard University Press, 2003], vol. 1, 34–151, here 142): ὅτι σὺ εἶ ὁ θεὸς μόνος καὶ Ἰησοῦς Χριστὸς ὁ παῖς σου. For an edition of the Greek text of the *Didache*, accompanied by a French translation, see Willy Rordorf and André Tuilier, eds. and trans., *La Doctrine des Douze Apôtres* (Paris: Les Éditions du Cerf, 1998). The Greek text of *The Martyr-*

Adolf Harnack, Joachim Jeremias, David Ison, J. T. Brothers,[53] and in supplementary fashion also Ludger Bernhard have analyzed and discussed much of the available textual material for how the title *pais theou* was understood in early and late ancient Christian times. Already in 1926 Harnack concluded that initially *pais theou* functioned as a messianic title, yet soon the designation became limited in its usage to liturgical texts. Harnack, and Jeremias following him, identified the fifth century as the period of time after which the epithet had disappeared completely as a title for Christ.[54] In 1987, Ison was able to demonstrate on the basis of Constantine's *Oratio ad sanctorum coetum*[55] that, against Harnack's assumption of an early restriction of the use of *pais theou* to texts employed in sacred discourse, *pais* in reference to Christ in fact functioned also in the fourth century in early Christian rhetoric in at least a twofold manner. First, the title could serve "as a bridge in the discussion between Christianity and paganism."[56] The title's presence in Constantine's *Oratio ad sanctorum coetum* in particular gains weight by virtue of this work's role in initiating the Christian interpretation of Virgil's famous *Fourth Eclogue*.[57] Virgil had spoken of a time

---

dom of Polycarp is accessible in Herbert Musurillo, ed. and trans., *The Acts of the Christian Martyrs* (Oxford: Clarendon Press, 1972), 2–21.

53. Adolf Harnack, "Die Bezeichnung Jesus als 'Knecht Gottes' und ihre Geschichte in der alten Kirche," *Sitzungsberichte der preussischen Akademie der Wissenschaften* 28 (1926), 212–38; Zimmerli and Jeremias, "παῖς θεοῦ"; David Ison, "ΠΑΙΣ ΘΕΟΥ in the Age of Constantine," *Journal of Theological Studies* 38 (1987), 412–19; and J. T. Brothers, "The Interpretation of παῖς θεοῦ in Justin Martyr's *Dialogue with Trypho*," *Studia Patristica* 9 (1966), 127–38.

54. Harnack, "Die Bezeichnung Jesus als 'Knecht Gottes,'" 238; and Zimmerli and Jeremias, "παῖς θεοῦ," 703.

55. For the critical edition of Emperor Constantine's *Oratio ad sanctorum coetum* ("Oration for the Saints"), see Ivar August Heikel, ed., *Über das Leben Constantins; Constantins Rede an die heilige Versammlung; Tricennatsrede an Constantin* (Leipzig: J. C. Hinrichs, 1902), 149–92. While previous scholarship doubted the authenticity of Constantine's speeches, the opinion of scholars regarding the *Oratio ad sanctorum coetum* has turned more toward the positive since the middle of the twentieth century. See I. C. Skeat, "Appendix to A. H. M. Jones, Notes on the Genuineness of the Constantinian Documents in Eusebius's *Life of Constantine*," *Journal of Ecclesiastical History* 5 (1954), 196–200; and David J. Ison, "The Constantinian Oration to the Saints—Authorship and Background" (Ph.D. thesis, University of London, 1985). See also H. R. Seeliger, "Constantine I (the Great), Emperor," in *Dictionary of Early Christian Literature*, eds. Siegmar Döpp and Wilhelm Geerlings (New York: Crossroad, 2000), 141–42.

56. Ison, "ΠΑΙΣ ΘΕΟΥ in the Age of Constantine," 418.

57. Virgil, *Eclogae* 4.1–63 (ed. Robert Coleman, *Vergil: Eclogues* [Cambridge: Cambridge University Press, 1977], 52–54). For the classic discussion of the myth of the heavenly, divine child, see Eduard Norden, *Die Geburt des Kindes: Geschichte einer religiösen Idee* (Leipzig: B. G. Teubner, 1924, repr. 1958). See also Coleman, *Vergil: Eclogues*, 150–54.

of peace the beginning of which was marked by the birth of a child.[58] Ison showed that the *pais theou* title also was employed in the fourth century "as an analogy for the divine Father/Son relationship drawn from imperial terminology for the emperor and his sons."[59] In the end, however, its usage did not survive. If it could be reintroduced into the discourse of Christian churches, it might not only have a positive effect on developing a more deeply grounded theology of childhood, but also would take seriously and respond constructively to requests for the re-conceptualization of Christological discourse in the interest of emancipatory practices.[60]

Early Christian texts from across the Mediterranean world, both from the west and from the east, availed themselves in theological discourse of the image of the believer as a child of God, at times in disciplinary contexts and at times with clear signs of a personal identification of the faithful individual with the image. The *Shepherd of Hermas,* a second-century work situated in the Roman Church, compared and identified the believers "from the twelfth mountain" with "infant children, in whose hearts no evil originates; nor did they know what wickedness [was]."[61] These believers "always remained as children." Such believers, like children, "dwell in the kingdom of God, because they defiled in nothing the commandments of God." The text further specified that these types of believers "remained like children all the days of their life in the same mind." The author worked on the basis of conceptions of young children as being free of and immune to evil inclinations. At the same time, the ideal believer also is presented as the one who managed to remain a child for the whole course of his or her life.

The *Shepherd of Hermas* further commented on God's appreciation of children as well as God's respect for those who were able to remain "like children all the days of their life." "All infants are honorable before God," and accordingly "are the first persons with Him." The figure of the angel of repentance, one of the main characters in the text, specified that those who were "innocent like children" would have a part that was "good and honor-

---

58. Whether acquaintance with this tradition may form part of the background to Luke 10:6 has not been decided definitively. For some discussion of this verse, see William Klassen, "'A Child of Peace' (Luke 10:6) in First Century Context," *New Testament Studies* 27 (1981), 488–506.

59. Ison, "ΠΑΙΣ ΘΕΟΥ in the Age of Constantine," 418–19.

60. See for example Elisabeth Schüssler Fiorenza, *Jesus: Miriam's Child, Sophia's Prophet. Critical Issues in Feminist Christology* (New York: Continuum, 1994), 61–63.

61. *Shepherd of Hermas,* bk. 3, par. 106, *simil.* 9, ch. 29 (ed. Bart Ehrman, *The Apostolic Fathers* [Cambridge, Mass.: Harvard University Press, 2003], vol. 2, 174–473, here 456 [modified]). The remainder of the citations in this paragraph are taken from the same passage.

able before God." Thus those who steadfastly were "as children, without doing evil," were promised to receive great honor. With a *makarism*, the *Shepherd of Hermas* announced to them, "Blessed, then, are you who put away wickedness from yourselves, and put on innocence. As the first of all will you live unto God."[62] The imitation and acquisition of a child's innocence is what in the end guaranteed the believer his or her elevated rank in God's eyes.

The *Odes of Solomon* captured the personal voice of the prayerful believer who identified with the image of the "child of God." This text consists of a collection of hymns that probably dates to the early second century and provides the modern reader with a taste of some of the most beautiful creations of the early Christian poetic spirit.[63] These odes are especially sensitive to describing the Godhead in gender-inclusive terms while making use of a plethora of parental images. In such settings, the believer emerges as a child in relationship to God. The poet cast this connection to God in language that bespeaks the relationship of a child to his mother. In Ode 35, for example, the poet described his rest in the Lord as the experience of being "carried like a child by its mother" and of being nourished by the "milk, the dew of the Lord," which God gave him. Two verses later the poet continued his verbal representation of his experience, and exclaimed: "[I] spread out my hands in the ascent of myself, and . . . directed myself towards the Most High" in his prayer, search, and enjoyment of redemption. This gesture of worship and longing for God has all the qualities of the image of a child lifting up its arms and stretching itself out toward its mother or father for help, comfort, and protection. The voice of the poet, who may have been male, nevertheless is sensitively expressive of female experience when, for instance in Ode 28, he could say, "My heart continually refreshes itself and leaps for joy, like the babe who leaps for joy in his mother's womb." Such language may be grounded in Scriptural examples, particularly that of the Visitation of Mary and Elizabeth in Luke 1:41. Yet such a restriction in possible sources of inspiration aims at too narrow a

---

62. Ibid., chs. 29 and 31 (Ehrmann, vol. 2, 456 and 460).

63. We take as the basis for our discussion the Syriac text as edited and translated into English in James H. Charlesworth, ed. and trans., *The Odes of Solomon. The Syriac Text*, Society of Biblical Literature Texts and Translations 13, Pseudepigrapha Series 7 (Missoula, Mont.: Scholars Press, c1977, 1978). See now also Michael Lattke, *Oden Salomos: Text, Übersetzung, Kommentar*, Novum Testamentum et orbis antiquus 41.1–3 (Freiburg: Universitätsverlag, 1999–2005), vol. 1 (odes 1 and 3–14), vol. 2 (odes 15–28), and vol. 3 (odes 29–42; with transcription of the Syriac by Klaus Beyer).

goal, given that in the immediately preceding verse, the odist had compared "the wings of doves over their nestlings, and the mouths of their nestlings towards their mouths" directly to "the wings of the Spirit over [the odist's] heart."[64] Here such comparison might have originated from the direct observation of the feeding which young birds demand of their parents. The comparison of the believer to a child in the womb is not to be missed. With regard to this particular image, moreover, the student of literature from the early Christian east will also draw a line from the *Odes of Solomon* to later Syriac traditions. For instance, in his *Homily* 9 ("On Poverty"), the native Syriac theologian Philoxenus of Mabbugh, who lived from the middle of the fifth century to the beginning of the sixth, availed himself of the image of the child in the mother's womb as a fitting simile for the faith development and growth of the believer, but also for progress to be made in the spiritual life of the ascetic.[65]

The religious, poetic imagination of the author of the *Odes of Solomon* is intriguing, especially when it comes to applying gendered language to God. In that realm the odist not only comfortably spoke of the Spirit in female imagery, but also envisioned, for instance, breasts of the Father.[66] The odist's imagination also was versatile and flexible when it employed metaphors of the child. The relationship between the believer and God allowed for depictions of God in the role of the child while the believer fulfilled the role of the caring mother, overflowing with sweet streams of tenderness. In Ode 40 the odist sang, "As honey drips from the honeycomb of bees, and milk flows from the woman who loves her children, so also is my hope upon You, O my God."[67]

In the end, the more dominant emphasis discernible in the *Odes of Sol-*

64. *Odes of Solomon* 28.1 and 35.5 and 7 (ed. and trans. Charlesworth, *Odes of Solomon*, 107–8 and 124–25).

65. See Philoxenus of Mabbugh, *Discourses. Homily 9: On Poverty* (ed. and trans. E. A. Wallis Budge, *The Discourses of Philoxenus Bishop of Mabbôgh, A.D. 485–519* [London: Asher, 1893–94], vol. 1, 257–352 [Syriac], and vol. 2, 247–336 [English], here vol. 1, 339–40 [Syriac], and vol. 2, 324–25 [English]). For some discussion, see Cornelia Horn, *Asceticism and Christological Controversy in Fifth-Century Palestine: The Career of Peter the Iberian* (Oxford: Oxford University Press, 2006), 348–50.

66. See, for example, *Odes of Solomon* 19. For a discussion of gendered imagery for God in these odes, see, for example, Susan Ashbrook Harvey, "Feminine Imagery for the Divine: The Holy Spirit, the Odes of Solomon, and Early Syriac Tradition," *St. Vladimir's Theological Quarterly* 37.2 (1993), 111–39. For a discussion of the merging of maternal images used for the Spirit and Mary in *Odes of Solomon* 19, see Cornelia B. Horn, "The Virgin and the Perfect Virgin. Traces of Early Eastern Christian Mariology in the *Odes of Solomon*," *Studia Patristica* 40 (2006), 413–28.

67. *Odes of Solomon* 40.1 (Charlesworth, 137–38).

omon saw the believers, old and young, as children in their relationship to God. This relationship of child to parent marked the interaction between the faithful person and God. The odist explained that "as the eyes of a son upon his father, so are my eyes, O Lord, at all times towards You." When in Ode 41 the poet exhorted his audience, "Let all the Lord's babes praise Him, . . . and His children shall be acknowledged by Him," he likely had in mind all ranks and ages of Christians, spiritual and otherwise, who "live in the Lord by His grace."[68]

As structures within the early Christian community took on an ever more clearly defined shape, the use of the image of the believer as a "child of God" was also transformed. Already Ignatius of Antioch had spoken of the bishop as father of the faithful.[69] Composed in a genre of writing commonly called "church orders," the fourth-century *Didascalia Apostolorum*, preserved in complete form only in Syriac in a translation from the late fifth or possibly early sixth century, urged the layman to love, honor, and fear "the bishop . . . as father and lord and god after God Almighty."[70] This relationship between the faithful and their bishop was described not only as that of a child to its father.[71] The Syriac *Didascalia Apostolorum*, which conceived of the hierarchical relationship of the members of the Christian community to one another as a patriarchal system of love,[72] was at ease

---

68. Ibid., 14.1 and 41.1–3 (Charlesworth, 65 and 139–40).

69. Ignatius of Antioch, *Letter to the Trallians* 3.1 (ed. and trans. Ehrmann, *The Apostolic Fathers*, vol. 1, 256–69, here 258–59).

70. Syriac *Didascalia Apostolorum* 7 (ed. and trans. Arthur Vööbus, *The Didascalia apostolorum in Syriac*, CSCO 401–2 and 407–8, Script. Syr. tt. 175–76 and 179–80 [Louvain: Secrétariat du CorpusSCO, 1979], vol. 401, 81 [Syriac], and vol. 402, 75 [English]). For recent studies on the *Didascalia apostolorum*, see Charlotte Fonrobert, "The *Didascalia apostolorum*: A mishnah for the disciples of Jesus," *Journal of Early Christian Studies* 9.4 (2001), 483–509; Michael L. Penn, "'Bold and Having No Shame': Ambiguous Widows, Controlling Clergy, and Early Syrian Communities," *Hugoye: Journal of Syriac Studies* 4.2 (2001), http://syrcom.cua.edu/Hugoye/Vol4No2/HV4N2Penn.html; Karen Jo Torjesen, "The episcopacy—sacerdotal or monarchical? The appeal to Old Testament Institutions by Cyprian and the *Didascalia*," *Studia Patristica* 36 (Louvain: Peeters, 2001), 387–406; and Charlotte Methuen, "Widows, Bishops and the Struggle for Authority in the *Didascalia Apostolorum*," *Journal of Ecclesiastical History* 46 (1995), 197–213. For the revised dating of this translation, see also Sebastian Brock, "Diachronic Aspects of Syriac Word Formation: An Aid for Dating Anonymous Texts," in *V Symposium Syriacum 1988*, Katholieke Universiteit, Leuven, August 29–31, 1988, ed. René Lavenant, S.J., Orientalia Christiana Analecta 236 (Rome: Pont. Institutum Studiorum Orientalium, 1990), 321–30, here 328–30.

71. On the father-metaphor for the bishop, see also Georg Schöllgen, *Die Anfänge der Professionalisierung des Klerus und das kirchliche Amt in der Syrischen Didaskalie* (Münster: Aschendorffsche Verlagsbuchhandlung, c1998), 135–39.

72. J. Colson, "L'évêque dans la Didascalie des Apôtres," *La Vie Spirituelle. Supplément* 5 (1951), 271–90, here 281; and Schöllgen, *Die Anfänge*, 135.

to compare the love of a bishop for the faithful of his church, who were identified as children, to the love of a mother-bird for her chicks when she "breeds and keeps them warm through zest of love as eggs from which young birds are to come, or broods over them and breeds them as young birds, for their rearing up as winged fowl."[73]

The Syriac *Didascalia Apostolorum* featured this relationship between the faithful as sons (and daughters) and the bishop as father and mother "after God." Of frequent occurrence are images related to the process of procreating, raising up, and educating children. Among them one finds the following formulations:

"O man [*bar nāshā*], know your bishops, those through whom you were made a son of God [*bar lalāhā*], and the right hand, your mother. And love him who, after God, has become your father and your mother—for 'whosoever shall revile his father or his mother, shall suffer death [Ex 21:16; see also Mt 15:4].' But honor the bishops, those who have loosed you from sins, those who by the water have begotten you anew, those who filled you with the Holy Spirit, those who brought you up with the word as with milk, those who established you with doctrine, those who confirmed you with admonition, and made you to partake of the holy eucharist of God, and made you partakers and joint heirs of the promise of God."[74]

It was in this setting of the faithful regarding themselves as children or little chicks, who saw their bishop as their mother, caring, warming, and breeding them, that education and instruction in the community was to take place. The bishop was to teach, admonish, rebuke, chasten, and correct the faithful, "as for restitution and not as for destruction," "as for repentance," intending to "amend and clarify the . . . ways [of the faithful], and restore the conduct of their life in the world."[75] In the course of the more detailed formulation of hierarchical structures in the early Church, the language describing the individual believer as the child of God developed to give expression to and foster these growing structures. Increasingly also the emphasis shifted. From being a "child of God" the Christian came to be a "child of Mother Church" and was to understand himself or herself as being under the direction of the bishop as father. The use of family language as such continued throughout both of these realms of discourse without interruption.

73. Syriac *Didascalia Apostolorum* 7 (Vööbus, vol. 401, 81 [Syriac], and vol. 402, 76 [English]). For the image of the bishop as mother, see Schöllgen, *Die Anfänge*, 139–40.

74. Syriac *Didascalia Apostolorum* 9 (Vööbus, vol. 401, 109–10 [Syriac], and vol. 402, 104 [English; modified]).

75. Syriac *Didascalia Apostolorum* 7 (Vööbus, vol. 401, 81 [Syriac], and vol. 402, 76 [English]).

three

🖋

Children and Family Life in the Christian Household

This chapter moves on to consider aspects of the lives of children, both real and implied, in the texts of early Christianity. While theological concerns continue to play a major role in these texts, the examination concentrates on the implications and possibilities these ideas bring to our understanding of the day-to-day lives of children and their families.

All of the first followers of Jesus were Jewish and as such had been raised in Jewish homes.[1] Those among them who were married were raising their children in Jewish homes and according to Jewish customs.[2] It is worth considering how their children's lives were affected by Jesus' teach-

1. More comprehensively on questions of architecture, space, and family life in ancient Jewish and non-Jewish settings, see Guijarro Oporto, "Domestic Space, Family Relationships"; Balch, "Rich Pompeiian Houses"; Richardson, "Towards a Typology of Levantine/Palestinian Houses"; Michele George, "Domestic Architecture and Household Relations: Pompeii and Roman Ephesos," *JSNT* 27.1 (2004), 7–25; Beryl Rawson, "'The Roman Family' in Recent Research: State of the Question," *Biblical Interpretation* 11.2 (2003), 119–38; and Carolyn Osiek and David L. Balch, *Families in the New Testament World: Households and House Churches* (Louisville, Ky.: Westminster John Knox, 1997).

2. According to information provided in canonical and apocryphal Gospels and Acts, at least the apostles Peter and Philip had children. For Philip's daughters, see e.g., Acts 21:8–9. See also references below in note 94. For some discussion of Peter's daughter, see Cornelia Horn, "Suffering Children, Parental Authority and the Quest for Liberation? A Tale of Three Girls in the *Acts of Paul (and Thecla)*, the *Act(s) of Peter*, the *Acts of Nerseus and Achilleus*, and the *Epistle of Pseudo-Titus*," in *A Feminist Companion to the New Testament Apocrypha*, ed. Amy-Jill Levine with Maria Mayo Robbins (New York: Continuum, 2006), 118–45, here 130–43.

ings and by the formation of the Church. Following considerations of these initial stages of historical development, this chapter attempts to answer the same questions in the context of Greco-Roman society and asks how Christianity altered the lives of those who first experienced a Christian upbringing in the Greco-Roman world.

The "Status" of the Child

Some scholars describe children in the biblical world as occupying "the lowest status in society" and as having a "social status . . . little better than that of a slave."[3] It seems now de rigueur to speak of children as the lowliest of creatures in the ancient world, and some evidence we have examined may point in that direction. Yet one should not accept such an assumption blithely. Certainly the ancient world was rigidly hierarchical in how it defined social roles, including those at the bottom. However, this sort of rigidity was enforced on all members of society, given their relative positions, and so the hierarchical structure impacted all members of a given society. Yet the fact that children were at the lower end of the hierarchy did not imply that their place was not secure or not valued. "Social status" in this context meant that children did not have the same duties, abilities, responsibilities, and possibilities as adults had in their societies. Nevertheless, they were valuable and necessary members of their families and cultures.[4] The cultural predisposition and a certain amount of cruelty that allowed

3. See, for example, Richard A. Horsley, providing the introduction and notes to the "Gospel of Mark" (NT 56–92, here NT 76), and J. Andrew Overman to "Gospel of Matthew" (NT 7–55, here NT 34) in Michael D. Coogan, ed., Mark Z. Brettler, Carol A. Newsom, and Pheme Perkins, associate editors, *The New Oxford Annotated Bible, Third Edition, with the Apocryphal/ Deuterocanonical Books, New Revised Standard Version* (Oxford and New York: Oxford University Press, 2001). Paul, in fact, engages in a discussion of this very issue of status versus no status in Galatians 4:1–3 when he says, "My point is this: heirs, as long as they are minors, are no better than slaves, though they are the owners of all the property; but they remain under guardians and trustees until the date set by the father. So with us; while we were minors, we were enslaved to the elemental spirits of the world." The child has a well-defined and proscribed role, but the reality is, and it is not a fiction *per se*, that the child will own the property, including the slave, at some point in the future. The child was valued as heir, as the one who would continue the family name, and as the one who would perpetuate the family lineage. This is much better than the lot of the slave, even if at times childhood could also be miserable. Some children would argue in much the same way about childhood today: it can be miserable.

4. See Garnsey, "Sons, Slaves—and Christians"; Golden, "*Pais*, 'Child' and 'Slave'"; and Golden, "Slavery and Homosexuality." In different ways and dealing with different elements of life, each of these articles makes clear the similarities, but also the profound differences, between children and slaves.

Greco-Roman families to expose children do not indicate that children as such had no value. Some contexts illustrate how decisions for the exposure of children were made, for example when a father, acting upon *patria potestas,* simply refused to accept a newborn child into his household. Yet why these decisions were made is often not clear. The fact that children were exposed or abandoned does not in itself reveal that they were not essential to the family and to society. One may also emphasize that, according to literary and archaeological evidence, such practices appear to have been less widespread in the Jewish community.[5] If they occurred, they were qualified as practices appropriate to Canaanites, Amorites, Hittites, and Egyptians, not as something Jews did, except when they themselves were subject to foreign pressures.[6]

To say therefore that a given child was "little better than a slave" both does injustice to ancient notions of childhood and dismisses the harsh differences between slavery and belonging to a family as a child.[7] No doubt there were slave children, but this is another matter;[8] to be a child in a Jewish family in the first century A.D. did not mean that the life one lived approximated slavery. It was a life in which one was expected to be obedient and in which one could be punished severely. Yet it also was a life in which one was a part of a household and a family, a life that a slave did not have.

The Child in the Jewish Family

As in the ancient world in general, in Judaism the family was the key building block of society. While we have no sense that in Judaism the *oikos* consisted of patrons and clients in the formal manner one finds in Roman society,[9] we do know that the members of the extended family were often

5. See the discussion on this issue in the introductory chapter above as well as in chapter 6 below, and in Schwartz, "Did the Jews Practice Infant Exposure and Infanticide in Antiquity?"

6. See the discussion in Malul, "Adoption of Foundlings in the Bible and Mesopotamian Documents."

7. On this score, see John 8:35 for an ancient example of the difference between a child and a slave as defined via belonging to the household (*oikos*). See Garnsey, "Sons, Slaves—and Christians," 101–21, for an index to the differences between sons and slaves. See also Jennifer Glancy, *Slavery in Early Christianity* (New York: Oxford University Press, 2002), 4 and 10–28.

8. On slave children, see especially our discussion below in chapter 6.

9. On the family in first-century Galilee and the stresses to which it was exposed, see Jonathan Reed, *Archaeology and the Galilean Jesus: A Re-examination of the Evidence* (Harrisburg, Pa.: Trinity Press International, 2001), 77–99; on the Jewish family in a broader sense, see John J. Collins, "Marriage, Divorce, and Family in Second Temple Judaism," in *Families in Ancient Israel,* eds. Leo J. Perdue, Joseph Blenkinsopp, John J. Collins, and Carol Meyers (Louisville, Ky.:

living in close proximity to one another.[10] We know, too, that in Judaism the family was further defined by tribe, admittedly limited in number in Jesus' day, and by class, at least as far as the priestly class and high priestly houses were concerned.[11] Priests were also placed under other limitations, for example that of being able to marry only within other priestly families.[12] That one's family lineage mattered in Jewish society is suggested by the fact that both Luke and Matthew provide genealogies for Jesus (Mt 1:1–17; Lk 3:23–28). As literary elements within the context of the Gospels, these have clear theological purposes, connecting Jesus to the lineage of Adam (Lk 3:38) or David (Mt 1:1).[13] While we do not contend that they represent true genealogical records, these examples point to a common concern in Judaism: that one ought to know one's family and its background. Genealogies certainly served a variety of other purposes,[14] yet the frequent use the Old Testament makes of them is evidence of a concern with family lineage (Gn 10 and 1 Chr 1–9).

In significant strands of Judaism, the family is based upon the child (Ps 128:3–4). There are other ways of conceiving of the family, especially with respect to more hierarchical societies or in light of modern discussions,[15] but without children the family ceases to exist. It is for this reason that the promises to Abraham include that of children (cf. Gn 13:14–16, 15:2–5) as a

---

Westminster John Knox, 1997), 104–62. See also Bruce Malina, "Patron and Client: The Analogy behind Synoptic Theology," in *The Social World of Jesus and the Gospels* (London: Routledge, 1996), 143–75.

10. See also Richardson, "Towards a Typology of Levantine/Palestinian Houses"; and Reed, *Archaeology and the Galilean Jesus*, 76 and 86.

11. Carol Meyers, "The Family in Early Israel," in *Families in Ancient Israel*, ed. Leo Perdue and others (Louisville, Ky.: Westminster John Knox, 1997), 1–47, here 36–38, on "blood ties" whether real or not that bound the ancient Israelites; and Joseph Blenkinsopp, "The Family in First Temple Judaism," in *Families in Ancient Israel*, 48–103, here 49–51, on "clan" relationships. According to Collins, "Marriage, Divorce, and Family in Second Temple Judaism," 105, "priests who could not establish their genealogies were excluded from the priesthood as unclean." See Exodus 6:14–27 and Numbers 3 for the genealogical descent of the priests. See also Merlin D. Rehm, "Levites and Priests," in *ABD* 4 (1992), 297–310.

12. See Roland J. Faley, "Leviticus," in *The New Jerome Biblical Commentary*, eds. Raymond E. Brown, Joseph A. Fitzmyer, and Roland E. Murphy (Englewood Cliffs, N.J.: Prentice Hall, 1990), 61–79, here 74–75. See Leviticus 21:1–24.

13. See also Raymond E. Brown, *The Birth of the Messiah* (New York: Random House, 1993), 64–69.

14. Marshall D. Johnson, *The Purpose of the Biblical Genealogies*, 2nd ed. (Cambridge: Cambridge University Press, 1988).

15. See the website of the Family Diversity Project, based in Amherst, Mass. (http://www.lovemakesfamily.org), for current examples of changing models of the family.

promise of the first order. Indeed Abraham's name itself is understood to *mean* "father of many,"[16] for among the Israelites and subsequently among the Jews nothing spoke of the blessings of God like children. The concern with the barrenness of the mother, which is at the heart of so many of the accounts of patriarchs, prophets, and heroes in the Old Testament,[17] witnesses to a society that was receptive to this motif as an expression of fear of the loss of the continuation of the family.[18] Indeed, the practice of a woman's giving her servant to her husband in order that a child might be born through her (Gn 16:2; 30:3, 9) appears to be a means for the wife to have a child in her name. As barrenness was perceived as a great loss, the loss of God's blessing (Gn 30:23; 1 Sm 1:18), of family, of the future, so God's granting of children in unlikely circumstances was the greatest of blessings. While the accounts of Sarah, Rebekah, Rachel, Hannah, and Samson's mother seem to focus on the miraculous, in fact they focus on the mundane, the common occurrence of conception and birth.

The desire for children is also seen in the practice of levirate marriage. According to this custom, a brother or kinsman of a man who had died childless was to marry the widow in order to raise up the first child that was born in the deceased one's name (Dt 25:5–10).[19] One reason, if not perhaps the only one, for this practice was that Israelite society regarded it as a curse for a man to die childless, a status equivalent to the end of his name, in the same way that barrenness brought shame, "reproach," upon a woman for ending a lineage.[20] This reality of childlessness was so serious

---

16. See Genesis 17:5. See also A. R. Millard, "Abraham," in *ABD* 1 (1992), 35–41, here 39.

17. For example, the accounts of Sarah-Abraham, Rebekah-Isaac, Rachel-Jacob, Samson's mother, and Hannah, mother of Samuel. For a discussion of "barrenness" in the Old Testament, see Irmtraud Fischer, "'. . . und sie war unfruchtbar.' Zur Stellung kinderloser Frauen in der Literatur Alt-Israels," in *Kinder machen. Strategien der Kontrolle weiblicher Fruchtbarkeit*, eds. Gertrude Pauritsch, Beate Frakele, and Elisabeth List (Vienna: Wiener Frauenverlag, 1988), 116–26; Irmtraud Fischer, "Über Lust und Last, Kinder zu haben. Soziale, genealogische und theologische Aspekte in der Literatur Alt-Israels," *Jahrbuch für Biblische Theologie* 17 (2002), 55–82, here 69–71; for a discussion of the topic in the ancient and early Christian world, see also P. Thrams and W. Drews, "Kinderlosigkeit," in *RAC* 20 (2004), 947–64.

18. For a study concerning conventions of the use of the motif of "barrenness" in Scripture, see for example James G. Williams, "The Beautiful and the Barren: Conventions in Biblical Type-Scenes," *JSOT* 17 (1980), 107–19.

19. Richard Kalmin, "Levirate Law," in *ABD* 4 (1992), 296–97.

20. Samuel H. Dresner, "Barren Rachel," *Judaism* 40 (Fall 1991), 442–51; and Judith R. Baskin, "Rabbinic Reflections on the Barren Wife," *Harvard Theological Review* 82 (January 1989), 101–14. See also Brant James Pitre, "Blessing the barren and warning the fecund: Jesus' message for women concerning pregnancy and childbirth," *JSNT* 81 (2001), 59–80, who argues

that the fiction of a child's being born in one's name, through the divine-
ly ordained requirement of levirate marriage, was created to overcome it.
Therefore, whether levirate marriage was a common practice or whether
barrenness was a common concern, the reality of both pointed to the centrality and necessity of having children in the family. The story of Ruth,
which probably deals with a form of levirate marriage, emphasized the
need to continue the family line and ended with a short genealogy (Ru
4:18–22) precisely to show how God was seen as acting in these situations
to maintain the family name for God's own purposes.[21]

These same concerns, the joy of children and the good of the family,
including the reality of the extended family, appear at the beginning of
the Gospels of Matthew and Luke and later in the text of the Gospels of
John and Mark.[22] Theological concerns are paramount in the New Testament consideration of children. One could even argue that reference to
the child in the New Testament functions primarily as a cipher for theo-

---

that barrenness had become a blessing, since it fit well with Jesus' apocalyptic asceticism. For
a more conventional take on barrenness, see the *Protoevangelium of James* 3.3 (ed. and trans.
Ronald F. Hock, *The Infancy Gospels of James and Thomas* [Santa Rosa, Calif.: Polebridge Press,
1995], 32–77, here 36–37), where Anna, Mary's mother, states that she was born under a curse
because of her barrenness.

21. Phyllis Trible, "Ruth," in *ABD* 5 (1992), 842–47.

22. For studies of children in the New Testament, see for example Peter Balla, *The Child-
Parent Relationship in the New Testament and Its Environments* (Tübingen: Mohr Siebeck, 2003);
Martin Ebner, "'Kinderevangelium' oder markinische Sozialkritik? Mk 10,13–16 im Kontext,"
Jahrbuch für Biblische Theologie 17 (2002), 315–36; Bettina Eltrop, "Kinder im Neuen Testament.
Eine sozialgeschichtliche Nachfrage," *Jahrbuch für Biblische Theologie* 17 (2002), 83–96; John T.
Carroll, "Children in the Bible," *Interpretation* 55 (2001), 121–34; Judith M. Gundry-Volf, "The
Least and the Greatest: Children in the New Testament," in *The Child in Christian Thought*, ed.
Marcia J. Bunge (Grand Rapids, Mich.: Eerdmans, 2001), 29–60; William A. Strange, *Children
in the Early Church: Children in the Ancient World, the New Testament and the Early Church* (Car-
lisle, England: Paternoster, 1996; repr. on demand: Eugene, Ore.: Wipf & Stock, 2004); Bettina
Eltrop, *Denn solchen gehört das Himmelreich. Kinder im Matthäusevangelium. Eine feministisch-
sozialgeschichtliche Untersuchung* (Stuttgart: Ulrich E. Grauer, 1996); James Francis, "Children
and Childhood in the New Testament," in *The Family in Theological Perspective*, ed. Stephen C.
Barton (Edinburgh: T&T Clark, 1996), 65–85; O. L. Yarbrough, "Parents and Children in the
Letters of Paul," in *The Social World of the First Christians: Essays in Honor of Wayne A. Meeks*,
ed. L. M. White and O. L. Yarbrough (Minneapolis: Fortress, 1995), 126–41; Peter Müller, *In
der Mitte der Gemeinde. Kinder im Neuen Testament* (Neukirchen-Vluyn: Neukirchener Verlag,
1992); Hans-Ruedi Weber, *Jesus and the Children: Biblical Resources for Study and Preaching* (Atlanta: John Knox, 1979); Hans-Hartmut Schroeder, *Eltern und Kinder in der Verkündigung Jesu:
Eine hermeneutische und exegetische Untersuchung* (Hamburg-Bergstedt: Herbert Reich, Evangelischer Verlag GmbH, 1972); Simon Légasse, *Jésus et l'enfant: "enfant," "petits" et "simples" dans la
tradition synoptique* (Paris: Lecoffre, 1969); and George R. Beasley-Murray, "Church and Child
in the New Testament," *Baptist Quarterly* 21 (1965–66), 206–18.

logical concerns. This is not to say that we do not gain real information about the actual lives of children. In fact, theological concerns have real-life implications.

In Focus: The Gospels

Birth of Children in the Gospels

Given the significance of Jesus' words and actions for the self-definition and self-understanding of early Christians, we shall first consider the presentation of Jesus as a child and his life in the setting of his family in the Gospels. The story of his infancy fits within the context of ancient Judaism, but his unique status and character potentially distort the picture and perception of the experience of the average child. Jesus the child is not, in most respects, a model for understanding the infancy of other children; nor does the limited portrayal of his childhood in the canonical Gospels give the reader serious data to enhance his or her understanding of the life of children in general at the time. The same statement can be formulated concerning the portrait of Jesus' childhood in the *Infancy Gospel of Thomas*.[23] Nevertheless, one can derive some insights from this material about Jesus as infant and boy and about his family life that are valuable for attempts to understand children in the family in early Christianity. The kinds of portraits of Jesus and his family that one finds may be those of a chosen family and of a child unique in stature, yet common cultural understandings of childhood and family life often underlie such stereotypical portrayals. This child and his family are special precisely because we can see the way in which they transcend the common norms.

That Jesus' conception is presented as not having taken place by normal means becomes a consideration when we think about the status of marriage, procreation, and celibacy in later Christian documents. It does not diminish the reality of his family life and of his parents. Yet his special nature as "Son of God" and "Son of Man" grounds the New Testament portrait of his childhood and his family life in theological realities, such as

23. Relatively convenient access to the Greek text of the *Infancy Gospel of Thomas*, accompanied by an English translation, is available in Ronald F. Hock, *The Infancy Gospels of James and Thomas* (Santa Rosa, Calif.: Polebridge Press, 1995), 104–43. For recent work toward establishing a critical text, see Tony Chartrand-Burke, "The Infancy Gospel of Thomas: The Text, Its Origins, and Its Transmission," Ph.D. thesis, University of Toronto, 2001 (Ottawa: National Library of Canada, 2002). A new critical edition of the *Infancy Gospel of Thomas* by S. Voicu and T. Chartrand-Burke is in preparation for CCSA.

the wondrous conception, the unusual birth, and the twelve-year-old boy's discussion with the priests and sages in the Temple (Mt 1–2; Lk 1–2). Still, we can learn something about the day-to-day life of the child in the family based on the wondrous child's portrait in the canonical Gospels. Also, the *Infancy Gospel of Thomas* takes seriously this family life, showing Jesus learning a trade from his father and at times frustrating at least one of his parents' wishes and desires for him.[24]

The infancy narrative in Luke presents us with two motifs, which appear regularly in the Old Testament: that of the barren woman and that of the joy of children. These two themes are inextricably linked. In addition, we find as a minor theme that of Mary's journey to Elizabeth, the visit of two pregnant women with one another. Theologically the inclusion of this scene is intended to tie Jesus to John the Baptist. Yet through the motif of Mary's joy at the news of Elizabeth's pregnancy, the scene takes as its base the reality of the extended family in first-century Judaism. Elizabeth's miraculous pregnancy in her old age, mimicking that of the matriarchs of old, removes her "reproach" or "disgrace" (*oneidos*: Lk 1:25), for now she, too, will have a child.[25] The annunciation to Mary of her own miraculous conception includes the news of Elizabeth's pregnancy (Lk 1:37). The miraculous nature of these pregnancies is not our concern here, for at its heart Judaism considered pregnancy an act of God (Gn 4:1). In some cases God's activity was especially apparent for Jews and Christians (Lk 1:37).[26] Two details in this story provide us with clues as to the value of children and the joy their birth brought for the family. First, Luke tells us that Mary stayed with Elizabeth for three months before she returned home (Lk 1:56). Independent of whether or not one considers this a historical event,[27] it indicates the reality that pregnancy was a shared experience, at least by women in a fam-

24. See, for example, *Infancy Gospel of Thomas* 2, 5, 11, 13–14, and 18 (ed. and trans. Hock, *The Infancy Gospels of James and Thomas*, 104–7, 110–11, 126–29, 130–33, and 138–39).

25. Arie Troost, "Elizabeth and Mary—Naomi and Ruth: Gender-Response Criticism in Luke 1–2," in *A Feminist Companion to the Hebrew Bible in the New Testament*, ed. Athalya Brenner (Sheffield: Sheffield Academic Press, 1996), 159–96.

26. See also Philo, *De Abrahamo* 107–18 and 167–68, commenting on the conception and birth of Isaac in Genesis 18 and 21:1–2.

27. Victor H. Matthews and Don C. Benjamin, *The Social World of Ancient Israel, 1250–587 B.C.E.* (Peabody, Mass.: Hendrickson Publishers, 1993), 67–81, discusses midwifery in ancient Israel. The *Protoevangelium of James* deals with midwifery with respect to Mary's birth (5.5) and especially at chapters 18–20, when Mary gives birth to Jesus (see Hock, *The Infancy Gospels of James and Thomas*, 19, 41, and 65–69). The text assumes the necessity and presence of a midwife. See also Gillian Clark, *Women in Late Antiquity: Pagan and Christian Lifestyles* (Oxford: Clarendon Press, 1993), 67, 69–70, and 74.

ily. Luke might include it precisely because such a practice would resonate with his readers. It precedes the notice in Luke 1:57–58 of the birth and the subsequent celebration (*synchairon autē,* "rejoicing with her") of her neighbors (*perioikoi,* "those who lived near her") and her relatives (*syngeneis*). Such joy was at the heart of any birth, for the parents and the family as a whole. We cannot overlook some of the basic reasons for this joy: both the child and the mother survived the birthing process.[28] The family does not disappear from the scene. It is involved with the continuing reception of the child into the family through the process of circumcision and the naming of the newborn baby (Lk 1:59–66).[29] The notice that John, a *paidion,* grew up and came to maturity in the wilderness is a standard and formulaic summation, similar to that in 1 Samuel 2:26. Later, the portrait of John as a little boy in the desert provided a model for the ascetic life.[30]

Both Luke and Matthew narrated the birth of Jesus. Both focused even more on the miraculous nature of his conception, birth, and attendant events. Due to the remarkable nature of the circumstances, joy did not seem to be on the participants' minds when they first heard the news. Mary responded with proper surprise, asking how it could at all be if she was a virgin (Lk 1:34). Luke did not record Joseph's response, but one suspects that joy may not have been the first emotion Joseph experienced. In Matthew, he in fact is presented as having desired to end the betrothal to Mary and as having relented only after an angelic visitation (Mt 1:19–21). In this case, disgrace came from the appearance of a child born outside of a proper marriage, whereas Elizabeth's pregnancy removed the disgrace of being married for a long period without a child.

According to both Luke and Matthew, Jesus' conception took place during the time of his parents' betrothal. As in Greco-Roman society, be-

28. The saying in John 16:21 reflects positively on the process of childbirth and the process of bringing a child into the world: "When a woman is in labor, she has pain, because her hour has come. But when her child (*paidion*) is born she no longer remembers the anguish because of the joy (*dia tēn charan*) of having brought a human being into the world." Without question, the main import of the teaching is to wait with anticipation for the return of the Lord, but in this context Jesus speaks positively of a woman having brought a child (*paidion*) into the world—she has "joy." This is especially interesting since Jesus' teaching regarding childbirth and barrenness also comes in the synoptic Gospels (Mk 13:17; Mt 24:19; and Lk 21:23) in the context of teaching about the Last Days. These passages also affirm the goodness of birth, albeit by stressing how even this most joyous of events will be transformed by the eschaton.

29. See Leviticus 12:2–8 on the circumcision of the newborn boy and the purification of the mother; see also Leonard V. Snowman, "Circumcision," in *Encyclopaedia Judaica* 5 (Jerusalem: Keter Publishing, 1978), 567–76.

30. See below, chapter 8.

trothal or engagement was a formal, contractual procedure most often initiated by the bride's father and the potential husband (Dt 22:13–21, 29; Ex
22:16–17).[31] The bride-to-be did not live with her husband until the bride
price had been paid, a detail that also emerges from Deuteronomy 22:23–30.
Throughout the discussion of marriage and betrothal in Deuteronomy 22,
the father's role is clear: he was, in a sense, the owner of his daughter. In Hebrew, the daughter was known as the *na'arah,* the girl, a term translated in
the LXX as *pais.* This alerts one, again, to the common age of a bride in Judaism, somewhere around the time of puberty, at the point of moving from
childhood to adulthood. This also seems to have been the age of Mary, a girl
preparing for marriage, a virgin on the cusp of the transition to adulthood,
when she and Joseph learned of her pregnancy. Far from leading to celebration, such a pregnancy would have been proof of her loss of virginity and
was punishable by death (Dt 22:20–21, 23–24).[32]

Reactions to the news of the birth of Jesus would have been different
from that at the birth of John the Baptist. Given the unusual circumstances, it is hard to imagine the larger family's celebration at Jesus' birth. Indeed, we are led to believe that neither family nor neighbors were present for the birth of the child, the circumcision, or the naming (Lk 2:16, 21;
Mt 1:25). Admittedly, both accounts present a wondrous birth and odd
circumstances—either traveling to Bethlehem (Luke) or fleeing to Egypt
(Matthew)—but the absence of family and friends from the description
of the birth of Jesus set this event apart from births more commonly experienced in his day. The infant Jesus was cared for by his parents, Mary and
Joseph, and like every child, he was vulnerable and dependent upon the
adults around him. In Matthew's infancy narrative, Joseph and Mary saved
Jesus from death by taking him to Egypt, something Joseph is said to have
done at divine urging. In Luke's narrative, Jesus' vulnerability is exempli-
fied by the location of his birth: in a manger or crib (Lk 2:12: *phatnē;* in Mt
2:11, Jesus is in a house).

On the other hand, the kinship network that is lacking in the birth narrative is assumed in the discussion of Jesus' travel to and from Jerusalem

31. The term used in Luke and Matthew for betrothal, *mnēsteuo,* is derived from the same
verb as the one used in Deuteronomy (LXX); in Luke and Matthew the verb is used exclusively
in its passive form, indicating that the bride *was* engaged, likely by her father. For discussions
of betrothal and engagement in the Greco-Roman and Jewish worlds, see also Clark, *Women in
Late Antiquity,* 13–15; and Paul Gaechter, "The Chronology from Mary's Betrothal to the Birth
of Christ," *Theological Studies* 2.2 and 3 (1941), 145–70 and 347–68, here 147–56.

32. See also Jane Schaberg, *The Illegitimacy of Jesus: A Feminist Theological Interpretation of
the Infancy Narratives* (New York: Crossroad, 1990), 91–101.

when he was a twelve-year-old boy (Lk 2:44–45). When Jesus was found missing from the midst of the family, his parents returned to Jerusalem to find him. They did not know he was missing when they left the city because their assumption was that he would be among the relatives and neighbors. His parents did not think much of it at all—the extended family was a real part of Jesus' family.[33]

The Boy Jesus and Children's Obedience

The canonical Gospels preserve one account of events during Jesus' boyhood in Luke 2:41–52, when the boy *(pais)* was twelve years old.[34] The narrative plays to a tension one can spot over and over in the Gospels: the priority of God the Father over human parents and family. Jesus is shown as being preeminently the child of God and he is found in his Father's house following the Passover. In contrast, Mary and Joseph as his earthly parents are full of anxiety when they find him and ask their child *(teknon)*, "Why have you done this to us?" (Lk 2:48). With his reply, Jesus points them to the precedence of God the Father in his life, but his parents do not understand. Nevertheless, the story ends with Jesus acknowledging his earthly parents' authority, and Luke states that Jesus was obedient, or "subject" to them *(hypotassō)* (Lk 2:51), following this escapade. The significance of Jesus' obedience to his parents became an important element of the ideals of Christian obedience to God and of the obedience of children to their parents. Jesus became the model, obedient both to his earthly parents and to his father in heaven. Through the emphasis on his obedience, one can detect a sense of the behavior expected, at least ideally, of all other children. One can also see points of connection to other parents in the concern Jesus' parents showed for the vulnerability and well-being of their child, the abject fear perhaps at the loss of their only son, given that here we are not told of other children.

The theme of children's obedience runs strong in early Christian literature. Throughout the texts two words come to the fore regarding children in the Christian family: discipline and obedience. These characteristics

33. See notes 9–11. Apart from this incident, the only further information about Jesus' childhood in the NT is found in the two summary statements in Luke 2:40 and 2:52, which bracket the account of the boy Jesus in the Temple. These are formulaic, similar to 1 Samuel 2:26, and they point to the desirable development of any child, but especially of the chosen son of God: he grew and matured; he was filled with wisdom; and he was loved by God and man.

34. For a discussion of the literary quality of this passage as ancient biography see Nils Krückemeier, "Der Zwölfjährige Jesus im Tempel (Lk 2:40–52) und die biografische Literatur der hellenistischen Antike," *New Testament Studies* 50.3 (2004), 307–19.

are common in Greco-Roman and Jewish thought regarding parents and children.[35] Children *(tekna)* were to obey their parents, and fathers—not parents—were not to provoke their children, but were to bring them up in the discipline *(paideia* and *nouthesia)* of the Lord (Eph 6:1–4). These two terms, *paideia* and *nouthesia,* imply both education and discipline and can be understood as referring to Christian instruction.[36] Some support is gained from 1 John. When providing directions to the community, the First Letter of John mentions *teknia* (children) whose sins are forgiven in God, *neaniskoi* (teenagers) who have conquered the Evil one and in whom the word of God abides, and *paidia* (children) who know the father (1 Jn 2:12–14). The various terms for children in this letter are rightly understood also as metaphorical. Yet these stages also connect the life of children to steps of development in the training and instruction in the teaching of the Church. Colossians, which probably was the source of the teachings in Ephesians, has the same admonitions to children *(tekna)* to obey parents and to fathers not to provoke children (Col 3:20–21).[37] The caution expressed to fathers not to provoke their children points to the power of the father within the family, Christian or otherwise, and the common conception, and reality, that fathers often were harsh disciplinarians. Paul's First Letter to the Thessalonians shows that this was not the only frame of reference, since he tells the church there that he acted "like a father with his children" when he was with them, "urging, pleading, and encouraging" them (1 Thes 2:11–12). Yet the later tradition recorded in the Letter to the Hebrews stressed that God disciplines human beings as children just as earthly parents discipline their children; although as children we may have chafed at this "painful" discipline, it yields great fruit (Heb 12:7–11). In the first-century world of the New Testament, such discipline was simply a part of childhood.

35. See, for example, Reinhold Bohlen, *Die Ehrung der Eltern bei Ben Sira. Studien zur Motivation und Interpretation eines familienethischen Grundwertes in frühhellenistischer Zeit* (Trier: Paulinus-Verlag, 1991), who considers questions related to this topic from the perspective of the requirement for children to honor their parents. For a broader study of the theme of respect that is to be shown to one's parents throughout the biblical tradition, see also H. Jungbauer, *"Ehre Vater und Mutter": Der Weg des Elterngebots in der biblischen Tradition* (Tübingen: Mohr-Siebeck, 2002).

36. For a fuller examination of this topic, see chapter 4.

37. For a helpful commentary on Colossians and Ephesians that is sensitive to social-scientific questions and that sees Ephesians as having been written in A.D. 90 and as being dependent on Colossians, see Margaret Y. MacDonald, *Colossians and Ephesians* (Collegeville, Minn.: Liturgical Press, 2000).

Discipline clearly was the role of the father, or the task of a servant *(paedagogus)* to whom the father had delegated that role. The Pastoral Epistles point to this primary responsibility of the father as the head of the family. One's office in the Church was connected to one's patriarchal duties. A bishop should manage his own household well, which included having children *(tekna)* "in submission" *(en hypotagēi)* (1 Tm 3:4). The qualifications for a deacon or deaconess likewise included that he or she should be able to manage his or her own children and household well. This *oikonomia,* "management" of the children and household included both discipline and instruction, as is made more explicit in the Letter to Titus. There elders are chosen on the basis of "having believing children" *(tekna echōn pista),* who are not debauched or "unsubmissive" *(anypotakta)* (Ti 1:6). That someone properly manages his or her children shows forth in the children's adherence to the faith. Concern about this connection may also be in the background of Titus 1:1, which speaks of "whole households" being upset by improper teaching; some of those responsible for the troubling teaching are described in Titus 1:10 as *anypotaktoi.* They could be the "unsubmissive" children of these very households, or their teachers. Second Timothy 3:4 sees disobedience to parents as a sign of the last days. Titus 2:4 encourages "young women" *(neas—* the feminine equivalent of *neos),* who according to our earlier discussion should be regarded as belonging to the age group of teenagers, to love their husbands and their children, and be good household managers in order that God's name may not be "blasphemed." This instruction may have had its source in actual behavior within the community (cf. Ti 2:4). As in Greco-Roman communities, in Judaism the undisciplined, wild child was a sign of poor parenting; in the Christian community, lack of discipline in children appears to have been seen as going hand in hand with a lack of adherence to the faith.[38]

In the second century, Theophilus of Antioch witnessed to the same parallel that ancient Christian authors saw between authority and enforcement of the law on the one hand, and the authority of the father and the means to enforce his authority on the other hand. As much as the law may, for instance, "command . . . abstinence from anything" so also it may be the case that "a father sometimes orders his own child to abstain from cer-

---

38. Examples of ill-behaving children have not received much study yet. Among the few exceptions is Eric Ziolkowski, *Evil Children in Religion, Literature, and Art* (New York: Palgrave, 2001), who discusses interpretations of 2 Kings 2:22–23 throughout the centuries, including ancient, patristic, and medieval explanations in his chapters 1 and 2.

tain things." In both instances it happens that "someone does not obey [the law]" or that "the child does not obey the paternal command." Punishment is the consequence. Yet, as Theophilus emphasized, the cause of that punishment "is not the law" or the father, but "disobedience" and "transgression."[39]

Children's obedience as a necessary element of family life continued to be repeated and emphasized in early Christian sources. *Didache* 4.9 and *Barnabas* 19.5 warned parents not to withhold corporal punishment from son or daughter but to "teach [*didaxeis*] them the fear of God" from their "youth" (*neotētos*).[40] Like *First Clement,* Polycarp encouraged parents "to teach the children the instruction [*ta tekna paideuein tēn paideian*] of the fear of God."[41] Clement of Alexandria devoted a large section of his *Paedogogus* to the discipline and instruction of children as well.[42] This instruction is for all "children" of God, but Clement took examples from the correction and reproof of actual children, stressing their need to be instructed and corrected as the model for God's reproof and instruction through his Son. These examples demonstrate the fusion of actual and spiritual childhood in the development of early Christian delineation of the obligations of family members.

Early Christian authors insisted that there had to be a right ordering of relationships between parents and children. Attention and respect that a father might show to his sons, or a parent to his or her children, had to be subordinate to the honor the Christian parent owed to God. Thus in the longer recension of Pseudo-Ignatius of Antioch's *Letter to the Magnesians*,[43] the author employed the example of the young Samuel reproving the priest Eli, a man who at the time had taken on the role of substitute father and priestly authority for him (1 Sm 2–3; esp. 3:10–18), "for giving honor to his sons rath-

39. Theophilus of Antioch, *To Autolycus* 2.25 (ed. and trans. Robert Grant, *Theophilus of Antioch. Ad Autolycum* [Oxford: Clarendon Press, 1970], 66–69).

40. *Didache* 4.9 (ed. and trans. Ehrman, *Apostolic Fathers,* vol. 1, 405–43, here 424–25); and *Letter of Barnabas* 19.5 (Ehrman, *Apostolic Fathers,* vol. 2, 3–83, here 76–77).

41. Polycarp, *Letter to the Philippians* 4.2 (Ehrman, *Apostolic Fathers,* vol. 1, 332–53, here 338); see also *First Clement* 21:6, 8 (Ehrman, *Apostolic Fathers,* vol. 1, 74 and 76).

42. Clement of Alexandria, *Paedagogus* 1.8, 9 (ed. M. Marcovich and C. M. van Winden, *Clementis Alexandrini. Paedagogus* [Leiden: E. J. Brill, 2002], 39–54).

43. The letters of Ignatius of Antioch are preserved in three recensions: a shorter recension in Greek, a longer recension in Greek, and a relatively short Syriac recension. The longer recension in Greek dates to the fourth century. See Johannes Quasten, *Patrology,* vol. 1: *The Beginnings of Patristic Literature* (Allen, Tex.: Christian Classics, 1950, repr. 1995), 74. See also F. R. Prostmeier, "Ignatius of Antioch," in *Dictionary of Early Christian Literature,* eds. Siegmar Döpp and Wilhelm Geerlings, trans. Matthew O'Connell (New York: Crossroad, 2000), 296–98.

er than to God."[44] Here was an example found in the Scriptures of a father who had placed the interests of his sons above those of God. A father had to exercise his authority, but right authority derived from knowing and acting according to an acknowledgment of God's primacy. In the perspective of Pseudo-Ignatius, if a parent did not place God first, and his or her children second, anyone else devoted to God, certainly including a bishop, had authority to correct such a parent, even if that admonisher was younger in age.

The second-century *Shepherd of Hermas* contains a passage that helpfully illustrates how the *patria potestas* of the Roman father received an interpretation of spiritual authority of the Christian father over his family. Hermas was instructed on how to correct the evil ways of both his children and his wife. In response to fifteen days of fasting and prayer before God, Hermas received the following revelation:

> Your seed, O Hermas, has sinned against God, and they have blasphemed against the Lord, and in their great wickedness they have betrayed their parents. And they passed as traitors of their parents, and by their treachery they did not reap benefit. And even now they have added to their sins lusts and iniquitous pollutions, and thus their iniquities have been filled up. But make known these words to all your children, and to your wife, who is to be your sister. For she does not restrain her tongue, with which she commits iniquity; but, on hearing these words, she will control herself, and will obtain mercy. For after you have made known to them these words which my Lord has commanded me to reveal to you, then shall they be forgiven all the sins which in former times they committed, and forgiveness will be granted to all the saints who have sinned even to the present day, if they repent.[45]

Thus, the father was to function as a messenger and minister of repentance for his family. In contrast to the seemingly unchecked authority of the *pater familias*, however, who had the right to exercise the *ius vitae necisque*, the Christian father who felt wronged still was encouraged not to act and administer punishment against his children out of revenge and hurt feelings. Rather, Hermas was advised not to remember the wrongs done to him.[46] The principle at work here was that "the remembrance of wrongs

---

44. Ignatius of Antioch, *Letter to the Magnesians* 3 (ed. and trans. Ehrman, *Apostolic Fathers*, vol. 1, 240–55, here 242–44). For a rewriting of the same theme see also the spurious *Epistle of Mary the Proselyte (Mary of Cassobola) to Ignatius* ch. 2.2 (ed. and trans. F. X. Funk, *Patres Apostolici*, vol. 2 [Tübingen: Libraria Henrici Laupp, 1901], 46–53, here 48–49). This letter is part of the longer recension.

45. *Shepherd of Hermas*, bk. 1, *visio* 2, ch. 2 (ed. Ehrman, *Apostolic Fathers*, vol. 2, 186).

46. Ibid., ch. 3 (Ehrman, *Apostolic Fathers*, vol. 2, 188).

works death." Moreover, as father Hermas was reminded that in cases of misbehavior and wrongs against the father of the family, he carried a certain responsibility for the wrongdoings of its members. Thus, Hermas was told that he "did not attend to them, but [was] careless and engaged in [his own] wicked transactions."[47]

Of particular interest is the way the *Shepherd of Hermas* phrased its words of consolation and hope for Hermas. Although Hermas was scolded and held partially responsible for the misdeeds of his children and his wife, and although he was blamed for his own "wicked transactions," the promise of salvation from condemnation was given to him "because [he] did not depart from the living God, and on account of [his] simplicity and great self-control." Moreover, "all who act in the same manner, and walk in guilelessness and simplicity," were promised to be saved. Early Christian perceptions of the characteristic features of a child and its typical behavior saw the qualities of "simplicity" and "guilelessness" as those most characteristic of a child. Thus, Hermas was promised salvation if, when, and for as long as he became and remained a child. "Unless you become like little children" (Mt 18:3) was lurking in the background.

Theophilus of Antioch also reflected the notion current in early Christian communities that an infant was simple and sincere. According to him, the qualities of simplicity and guilelessness characterized the submission that children owed to their parents.[48] Obedience to one's parents, moreover, was distinguished as something "holy" and "right." Thus, the child owed this obedience not only to its parents, but also to "the God and Father of the universe."[49] Obedience in the family and religious obedience went hand in hand. Disobedience brought along punishment, which most often the father administered.

In cases where a father was not present, children or grandchildren were to fulfill their religious duty to their mother or grandmother by caring for them financially (1 Tm 5:3–8). As in Jewish literature, this was a part of the child's obligations and the child who did not provide for his or her family "denied the faith and [was] worse than an unbeliever" (1 Tm 5:8). Roman law preferred that parents continue to support children, even if they were emancipated (*Digest*, 25.3.5), but a child, particularly a son, could be compelled by law to support even his father if need be, and even if the son was emancipated (*Digest*, 25.3.5, 13).

47. Ibid. (Ehrman, *Apostolic Fathers*, vol. 2, 190).
48. Theophilus of Antioch, *To Autolycus* 2.25 (ed. Grant, *Theophilus. Ad Autolycum*, 66–67).
49. Ibid.

Obedience was to be embedded in a personal relationship with the parent. When writing to the Philadelphians, Ignatius of Antioch had already instructed the children of the community to "obey [their] parents" and to "have an affection for them." The affection that was to be shown to the parents was understood as being grounded in the parents' being "workers together with God for [their children's] birth [in this world]."[50] The child Jesus' model of the obedient son clearly helped to emphasize that children's obedience was a necessary link in the web of family relationships.

The Child in the Family

While no other incidents of Jesus' childhood beyond the episode of the twelve-year-old in the Temple are described in the canonical Gospels, the incident in the Nazareth synagogue offers information about the kind of childhood Jesus was thought to have had (Mt 13:53–58; Mk 6:1–16; Lk 4:16–30; cf. Jn 6:42, 7:15). From these passages one may derive that Jesus was a known member of the community, whose wisdom shocked the assembly that was gathered together, perhaps, as the Gospel of John states, because he had no formal education (Jn 7:15). The manner in which the crowd understood Jesus, however, put him in his place, one might say, or connected him to his family. In John, Luke, and Matthew, Jesus is identified as the son of Joseph (Lk 4:22; Jn 6:42) or the carpenter's son (Mt 13:55), a comment that contextualized and identified him as the son of his father. This seems more likely than Jesus' self-identification as a carpenter *(tektōn)* in Mark 6:3, unless the implication was that identifying Jesus by his trade identified his father and his father's trade.[51] In the passages just discussed, Jesus' mother is identified only in Luke's Gospel. Further, in Mark and Mat-

---

50. Ignatius of Antioch, *Letter to the Philadelphians* 4 (ed. Ehrman, *Apostolic Fathers*, vol. 1, 282–94, here 286).

51. W. F. Albright and C. S. Mann, *Matthew* (New York: Doubleday, 1971), 172–73, see Joseph's identification as *tekton*, placing him as a skilled master builder, who may have been an itinerant craftsperson working in one town or another depending upon demand. See Benedict T. Viviano, "The Gospel According to Matthew," in *The New Jerome Biblical Commentary*, 630–74, here 657, who says that "in the Talmud carpenters or joiners *(naggâr)* are praised for their knowledge of the Torah (y. *Yebamot* 8.9b; y. *Kiddushin* 4.66b)." For one of the very few texts on Joseph preserved in ancient Christian literature see the apocryphal *History of Joseph the Carpenter*, a text whose style is related to that of Coptic homilies from the time between the sixth to eighth centuries. The earliest Sahidic fragments are found in manuscripts from the tenth to eleventh centuries. For a brief introduction and recent French translation of the Bohairic witness, see Anne Boud'hors, "Histoire de Joseph le Charpentier," in *Ecrits apocryphes chrétiens II*, eds. Pierre Geoltrain and Jean-Daniel Kaestli (Paris: Éditions Gallimard, 2005), 27–74. For a critical edition of the Arabic text, accompanied by an Italian translation, see A. Battista and

thew, brothers (*adelphoi*) are noted by name (James, Joses/Joseph, Judas, and Simon) and sisters (*adelphai*) as a group. The initial purpose of specifying all of these family members on the part of the synagogue assembly was to locate Jesus as someone whom they knew in the context of a family setting, and by virtue of his humble origins Jesus was not perceived to be deserving of honor, at least as a scholar of Scripture or as someone with claims to be the Messiah or a prophet. To a large extent, in the ancient world one was defined by virtue of one's family. Society did not identify individuals independently of their larger family. It was for this reason that the rebellious son or the wayward daughter, transgressing the boundaries of family and family identity, brought shame on the entire family.

The identification of the brothers and sisters of Jesus has been at the heart of a controversy that this study cannot attempt to solve. However, some aspects of this problem shed light on the dimension of family in the Gospel portraits of Jesus.[52] In the ancient world, it would not be unusual to identify someone not only by father, which would be the primary referent, or mother, but by the family as a whole. Nothing inherently speaks against the brothers and sisters of Jesus being related to him.[53] Kinship patterns were extensive, and extended family was and still is a part of one's real family.[54] In the canonical New Testament documents apart from the Gospels, there is little concern with the question of Jesus' family (cf. Gal 1:19). While each reader will weigh the evidence in determining the meaning of references to brothers and sisters in these passages, one might take into account that Mark 6:4 does include the notification that a prophet's honor did not extend to his hometown (*patridi autou*) (Nazareth),[55] to his relatives (*syngeneusin autou*), or to his house (*oikia autou*), suggesting some difference between the circle of relatives and the tighter circle of the household. Whether Jesus had full brothers and sisters, half-brothers and

---

B. Bagatti, eds. and trans., *Edizione critica del testo arabo della "Historia Iosephi Fabri Lignarii" e ricerche sulla sua origine* (Jerusalem: Franciscan Printing Press, 1978).

52. Joseph A. Fitzmyer, *Luke*, Anchor Bible, vol. 28 (New York: Doubleday, 1981–85), 723–24; and Raymond E. Brown et al., eds., *Mary in the New Testament* (Philadelphia: Fortress Press, 1978), 65–72 and 167–80. For a helpful discussion, see also Richard Bauckham, *Jude and the Relatives of Jesus in the Early Church* (Edinburgh: T&T Clark, c1990).

53. Albright and Mann, *Matthew*, 161.

54. When traveling in the Middle East and throughout the Mediterranean world, as well as through contacts with immigrant families from these regions, we both had ample opportunities to witness this phenomenon.

55. Greek *patris*, fatherland, homeland, or hometown, which is telling in this context as an identification of Nazareth: the land of one's father or family.

half-sisters, or merely cousins, he was known, understood, and identified by his family, including those of his household.

The exact role of the priority of the family, however, was not so clear-cut, either in Jesus' own life or in that of his disciples. One needs to consider further some statements that diminish the role of family and obligations to family in Jesus' teachings regarding discipleship, some of which directly concern children. A significant passage is found in Mark 3:31–35 (Mt 12:46–50; Lk 8:19–21).[56] The story concerning Jesus and his ministry in those passages[57] pertains to the definition of Jesus' true family. It also gives the reader insight into the nature of the extended family and the intimate connection, which everyone who was understood to belong to the family shared. Indeed the phrase used to identify Jesus' family is especially significant when one is considering the nature of the extended family; the Greek literally speaks of "his own people" or "those people who belong to him."[58] Jesus' family intervened when they began to hear negative reports about him, especially concerning potential madness or about his relationship to demonic forces (Mk 3:21–22). This intervention was part of their role as the family, particularly with respect to a child, in order to preserve the family name. Yet when the crowd announced the presence of his mother and brothers, Jesus did not go to inquire of his family, a behavior that would be expected of the good and obedient son. Instead, Jesus challenged the crowd: those who listened to the word of God and did the will of God were Jesus' true family—"my brother, and sister, and mother" (Mk 3:34–35; Mt 12:49–50; Lk 8:21; cf. Jn 15:14).

56. One may take this account to reflect a historical event in the life of Jesus, due to the indices of discontinuity (the priority of family was paramount in Judaism and enjoined by honor of father and mother in the Ten Commandments) and of offensiveness (Mark has people say about Jesus, just prior to the pericope, that he is "beside himself" or "out of his mind" [v. 21] and "had" or was "possessed" by Beelzebul [v. 22]; it is omitted in Matthew and Luke). For a survey of methods and criteria for the study of the historical Jesus see, for example, Christopher Tuckett, "Sources and Methods," in *The Cambridge Companion to Jesus,* ed. Markus Bockmuehl (Cambridge: Cambridge University Press, 2001), 121–37.

57. The pericope in Mark truly extends from 3:20–35. The Beelzebul passage of Mark appears in Matthew 9:32–34 and 12:22–30 and Luke 11:14–15, 17–23 (cf. Jn 7:20, 8:48, 8:52, and 10:20). That Mark locates the passage in the proper historical context of the family seems likely, as the potential offense of the family is more likely to have been excised by Matthew and Luke than to have been added by Mark. John 8:48 does add a claim that Jesus is a Samaritan, a slur it would seem that is designed to deny his family or tribal kinship.

58. On the Greek of this phrase, see F. Blass and A. Debrunner, *A Greek Grammar of the New Testament and Other Early Christian Literature,* trans. and ed. Robert W. Funk (Chicago: University of Chicago Press, 1961), 124, #237; *para* is used with the genitive only with respect to persons.

The Priority of the Family of God

As we saw in the previous chapter, and even in the one account of Jesus' boyhood contained in Luke, God the Father (only in Mt 12:50) was shown to be the true father of the Son of God and of those who followed him. Thus, Jesus diminished the role and significance of one's biological family for the priority of the family of disciples. That this had an impact on children among Jesus' disciples, also in a practical way, can only be surmised. Nevertheless, other statements in the Jesus tradition, and in later Christian tradition, make such a conclusion seem likely. In Mark 10:23–31 (Mt 19:23–30; Lk 18:24–30, 22:28–30) Jesus explained the demands of discipleship, referring to his disciples as "children" (*tekna*) in Mark 10:24. Astonished at Jesus' claim that entering the kingdom of heaven is a task that is more difficult than it is for a camel to walk through the eye of a needle, Peter pleaded with Jesus and said, "We have left everything [Mark and Matthew = *panta*; Luke = *ta idia*[59]] and followed you" (Mk 10:28). In his response, Jesus confirmed that there was no one who had left houses, brothers, sisters, mothers, and fathers for the sake of the Gospel who would not receive a hundredfold in this life and eternal life (Mk 10:29–30; Mt 19:29; Lk 18:29–30). Whether or not Jesus intended for his followers to leave their parents or their children for the sake of the Gospel cannot be known with certainty. The authors of the Gospels thought he did. It is telling that the plea initiating Jesus' comment came from the lips of Peter. He was the one apostle about whom the canonical record stated that he was married (Mk 1:30; Mt 8:14; Lk 4:38; 1 Cor 9:5).[60] In the canonical texts, we never hear of Peter's children and it is possible that he had none. Yet Christians in the second and third centuries thought Peter was the father of one daughter, at least.[61] Given that the apostle Philip had daughters, it is likely that he was married. Paul also referred to other married apostles (1 Cor 9:5), without providing names. It is unlikely that none of the couples mentioned or alluded to in the New Testament had any children. Therefore, the call to leave behind everything to follow Jesus was understood to imply leaving behind children or parents as well. Peter's heartfelt cry that he had left "all" may have included children, and therefore his outburst may take on more resonance

59. A common locution in Luke for "all that belongs to someone."

60. See also the discussion by Martin Hengel, "Apostolische Ehen und Familien," in *The Interpretation of the Bible. The International Symposium in Slovenia* (Sheffield: Sheffield Academic Press, c1998), 257–74.

61. For further discussion of Peter's daughter, see Horn, "Suffering Children, Parental Authority, and the Quest for Liberation?" 130–43.

for the modern reader. It also suggests that the absence of one parent or both tempered the meaning of "following Jesus" for children. Jesus' radical revision of the accustomed priority of the family is also seen in Luke 11:27–28, and Jesus did not reserve the challenge for his disciples alone. In a passage that rings with the authentic voice of a spontaneous call from a crowd ("blessed be the womb that bore you and the breasts that you sucked": Lk 11:27) and the likewise spontaneous response Jesus offered, he rejected the claim that blessings rested upon his mother for raising him. In Jesus' reply, "Blessed are those who hear the word of God and keep it" (Lk 11:28),[62] the author of Luke indicates the priority of the family that was gathered around God. Discipleship to Jesus, and not familial ties, was to define the new Christian society.

This conjecture puts in a new light the warning in Mark 13:9–13 (Mt 10:17–22; 24:19; Lk 21:12–17) about the unraveling of social order that precedes the *eschaton*. If Jesus' call for children to leave their parents and parents their children was heeded, the Gospels' claims that a father will betray his child *(teknon)* and children *(tekna)* their parents may have had a basis in the social realities of the early Christian Church. The social dislocation caused by the new Christian movement allows one to presume a breakdown in familial ties,[63] at least in some instances. Without question the idea that a family member would betray another family member ranked as an apostasy of the worst sort in the ancient context, functioning as a negative marker for the importance of family. Even if this was not an indication of social reality directly but instead a sign of how horrible the end was expected to be, the supposition that it reflects real situations should not be rejected out of hand.

Social dislocation is also at the heart of Matthew's description of the arrival of the heavenly kingdom (Mt 10:34–39; Lk 12:51–53, 14:26–27), in which the disciples of Jesus, and the priority of the kingdom among Jesus' followers, were seen to bring violence to the household: father was poised against son, mother against daughter, and mother-in-law against daughter-in-law. Such hostility in the family supposedly was of little consequence to Jesus' followers, whose priority of focus was not to be on the love of father and mother or wife (in Luke) or children, but solely on Jesus. The conse-

---

62. See also Luke Timothy Johnson, *The Gospel of Luke*, Sacra Pagina Series, vol. 3 (Collegeville, Minn.: Liturgical Press, 1991), 184–87.

63. John M. G. Barclay, "The Family as the Bearer of Religion in Judaism and Early Christianity," in *Constructing Early Christian Families*, 66–80, here 74; see also S. C. Barton, *Discipleship and Family Ties in Mark and Matthew* (Cambridge: Cambridge University Press, 1994), 222.

quences of this for children in these early Christian families who took this message as a model for discipleship are not considered in the texts. Jesus demanded the subordination or abandonment of the life of the family in order to pursue a higher call. Luke 9:61 preserves Jesus' refusal of an anonymous disciple's request to first bid farewell to those in his "household" (*oikos*) before committing himself to the kingdom. The same overturning of the present familial order is noticed in Jesus' ignoring the call of one brother to ask his older brother to divide the family inheritance with him (Lk 12:13–15).[64] Jesus met the younger brother's call for justice with a warning to avoid avarice and greed. Luke 20:34 offers an interesting addition to Jesus' teaching in Matthew and Mark regarding resurrection and marriage. All three Synoptic parallels contain a saying of Jesus about the resurrection and the new condition in the age to come, specifically that there will be no marriage in heaven (Mk 12:25; Mt 22:30; Lk 20:35).[65] Only Luke added that "the sons [*huioi*; or 'children'] of this age marry and are given in marriage" (Lk 20:34), but those that "are worthy to attain to that age" do not marry and are not given in marriage (Lk 20:35). This passage makes the implied contrast between ages in Mark 12:25 and Matthew 22:30 explicit, but it also connects the diminution of marriage to this age and to those "worthy to attain" the resurrection in this age. That is, marriage, the heart and foundation of family life, is minimized in significance. It is only relevant in this age, but has no lasting value and may keep one from attaining that prize which is of eternal value. One further passage from Luke, found in the road-to-Golgotha pericope in Luke 23:28–29, has Jesus turning to the lamenting people and connecting his suffering to the greater suffering to come. He told the women to weep for their own children (*tekna*), for the time was coming when people would say, "Happy are the barren ones, and the wombs that never bore, and the breasts that never nursed," turning upside down the message regarding Elizabeth and her son, John the Baptist, that the end of barrenness is the beginning of joy. Jesus' orientation to the Father and to the kingdom also redirected him away from the ties of this world to those of the world to come. In all of these passages from the Gos-

---

64. Luke Timothy Johnson, *Sharing Possessions: Mandate and Symbol of Faith* (Philadelphia: Fortress Press, 1981), 1–78; Abraham J. Malherbe, "The Christianization of a *Topos* (Luke 12:13–34)," *Novum Testamentum* 38 (1996), 123–35. For a helpful discussion of Luke 15:11–32, a subsequent story that also features the relationship of two brothers with one another, see Wolfgang Pöhlmann, *Der Verlorene Sohn und das Haus. Studien zu Lukas 15,11–32 im Horizont der antiken Lehre von Haus, Erziehung und Ackerbau* (Tübingen: Mohr-Siebeck, 1993).

65. Fitzmyer, *Luke*, Anchor Bible, vol. 28a, 1298–1308.

pel of Luke, the priority of following Jesus is stressed and familial life is discouraged in light of the *eschaton*.

Spiritual and Earthly Families

The rejection of family ties in individual instances did not mean that family ties as such were without value; rather they were relativized only in light of God's fatherhood and the new familial ties. At times, the spiritual and earthly families were compatible: for example, in the pairs of brothers among Jesus' disciples: Simon Peter and Andrew (Mk 1:16 and parallels) and James and John (Mk 1:19). One can also see aspects of this occasional correspondence in the life of Jesus' disciples, when a number of them traveled together with their mothers. While the presence of mothers traveling with their sons may simply point to the mothers' own discipleship, it may also indicate the youthfulness of certain disciples and apostles of Jesus. Some of them may not yet have been of an age to marry. In Mark 15:40, we are told of Mary the mother of James the Younger and Joses (cf. Mt 27:56 and Lk 24:10). Matthew also mentions the mother of the sons of Zebedee in 27:56 and in 20:20–23; in Matthew 20, she pleaded before Jesus for her sons' place in glory. These disciples (James the Younger and Joses) and apostles (James and John) may have been of a relatively young age, given that they were unmarried. Instead of traveling with wives, they were still accompanied by their mothers, who cared for their needs. Given that in Judaism young men tended to marry at about the age of eighteen, the age of these unmarried brothers may have been somewhat below this age.

Evidence that some of those who followed a Christian teacher on his journeys were of a relatively young age is available from documents of the second and third centuries. Apocryphal acts of apostles provide several examples of children and youth leaving their parents and becoming followers of a given apostle, or being recruited by the apostle even against their parents' wishes. The *Acts of Thomas* tells of a flute-girl who joined the king's young daughter and her newlywed bridegroom in following the apostle Thomas.[66] In Gregory of Tours's Latin translation of the *Acts of Andrew*, the apostle made Exoos follow him, although the young boy's parents were opposed to it.[67] Earlier, the same apostle had restored another boy to life,

---

66. *Acts of Thomas* I.16 (ed. Maximilian Bonnet, *Acta Philippi et Acta Thomae accedunt Acta Barnabae*, in *Acta Apostolorum Apocrypha* 2.2 [Leipzig: Hermann Mendelssohn, 1903; repr. Hildesheim: Georg Olms, 1959], 99–291, here 122–24).

67. *Acts of Andrew* 12 (ed. and trans. Jean-Marc Prieur, *Acta Andreae. Textus* [Turnhout: Brepols, 1989], 592–97).

but instead of accepting the parents' gifts, which they had offered to him in gratitude, Andrew preferred to take the youth with him on his journey.[68] In these cases, the separation of family ties is more pronounced than in the canonical material.[69] These passages, however, also lend support to the likelihood that in some cases people of a young age joined a wandering preacher and followed him on his journeys, both as a kind of apprentice and as a disciple.

Children in Jesus' Ministry

Children appear in a number of Gospel pericopes, sometimes among Jesus' disciples, sometimes in the crowds, and sometimes they are said to have been brought to him by grieving parents. In Mark 9:33–37, 42–48 (Mt 18:1–14; Lk 9:46–48; 17:1–2) and Mark 10:13–16 (Mt 18:3; 19:13–15; Lk 18:15–16), Jesus is shown receiving children and presenting them as models for the kingdom of God. In the scenes of miraculous feedings found in all four Gospels, Matthew mentions that women and children *(paidia)* were also present (14:21), and John 6:9 specifies that it was a "little boy" who supplied the food.

According to the Gospel accounts, children and their parents were among those who experienced Jesus' ministry. Whether the presence of only one parent reflected the reality of higher mortality rates in the ancient world or simply offered a stylized dramatic element of the miracle accounts is difficult to determine in a given instance, but Jesus often is portrayed as having healed children in the presence of only one parent. The Gospel of Mark offers four such healings: the paralytic child (2:1–10; Mt 9:1–8; Lk 5:17–26; cf. Jn 5:1–9); Jairus's daughter (5:21–43; Mt 9:18–26; Lk 8:40–56); the Syro-Phoenician woman's daughter (7:24–30; Mt 15:21–28); and the epileptic child (9:14–29; Mt 17:14–21; Lk 9:37–43). Three of these accounts clearly deal with children; translators of the account of the paralytic often assume that he was a man. In the accounts of Mark and Matthew, the person in question, who is brought in by four friends, is designated by the term *paralytikos,* which does not necessarily mean a "paralytic man" as the NRSV translates. In healing the paralytic, Jesus refers to him as *teknon* in both Mark 2:5 and Matthew 9:2, which could indicate a spiri-

68. Ibid. 7 (Prieur, *Acta Andreae. Textus,* 586–87).

69. For the relevance of the theme of the separation of family ties, see also Cornelia Horn, "Children at the Intersection of Classical and Early Christian Popular Literature," paper delivered at the annual meeting of the American Academy of Religion/Society of Biblical Literature, San Diego, Calif., November 2007.

tual child, but which can also refer to an actual child. Luke employed the term *anthropos* (5:18, 20), both in his description of the person and in Jesus' address to him, which seems to refer to an adult. John's possible parallel clearly described a man who had been ill for thirty-eight years (Jn 5:5). While we consider the person being healed in the account a child, one can argue that the age of the person is indeterminate. Yet we also note here the methodological problem that in translations of ancient texts children may at times be concealed by inattentive renditions of a given phrase or expression into the target language.[70]

In each of the four cases of healing in Mark referred to above, people sought out Jesus on behalf of their sick or dying children. In three cases parents did so, and in the case of the paralytic four of his friends approached Jesus. In two of the accounts, only one parent was present—the Syro-Phoenician woman and the father of the epileptic boy—while the other parent is not mentioned. In the case of Jairus's daughter, the father sought out Jesus, but the mother was present at home with the child when Jesus arrived.

All of these accounts show great concern on the part of caregivers for their children, independent of whether the child was a girl or a boy. This concern emerges as having been the impetus for seeking Jesus. In not one of the cases did the children speak to Jesus on their own behalf: the parent or the friends pleaded the child's case. A key characteristic of all of these healings is the persistence of the parents and friends. The friends of the paralytic refused to be stymied by a crowded house or even a roof. Jairus begged Jesus to heal his dying daughter. The Syro-Phoenician woman refused to be put off by Jesus' challenge to her, and the father of the epileptic boy sought out Jesus by himself after Jesus' disciples were unable to heal his son. In all instances, Jesus responded to the pleas presented to him. These children were loved, and their parents' or friends' concern transcended any roadblocks, physical or verbal, that were put in their path.[71] It is also fair to say that the authors of the Gospels portrayed Jesus as taking the pain and suffering of the children and their caregivers as worthy of his intervention, not simply for the sake of the parents, but for the children's own well-being. While one may suspect that the children were happy to be healed, their actual responses are not recorded. In all of these cases, Jesus

---

70. See also below, chapter 8, for the discussion of the extent of meaning of the noun *parthenos*.

71. Alan Richardson, *The Miracle-Stories of the Gospels* (London: SCM Press, 1969), 63.

acted for a child on behalf of family or friends; the value of the child for the grieving parents was clear: these were not lesser beings, but loved and integral members of the family. In their sickness, the vulnerability of the children was not only increased, but also extended to their parents; it was to the combined vulnerability of the parent and child that Jesus was shown to have responded.

Slave Children and Slave Families

The vulnerability of children and parents is seen most profoundly in the slave family.[72] In the parable of the debtors in Matthew 18:23–35, the master ordered a slave with his wife and children (*tekna*) to be sold in order to repay the slave's debt. Although this is a parable, it portrays the worst conditions of the social reality of slaves and their children in this period: slaves could be sold and separated from their families.[73] One should not assume that the slave, his wife, and his children were sold to the same buyer.

The parable raises the question of slave children in the early Christian world and community, again in light of the philological question addressed at the beginning of this study.[74] Slaves were sometimes referred to as *pais* in the case of males (as in the story of the centurion's servant, called *pais* in Mt 8:5, 7, and 13, and only referred to as *doulos* in v. 9; in Lk 7:1–10, *pais* is used only in v. 7) or as *paidiskē* in the case of females (as in Mk 14:66–69; Mt 26:69–75; and Lk 22:55–62). The question arises whether or not these are references to actual children. One must also consider whether the repeated reference to *pais* with respect to a slave indicates a child slave. At least three observations can be made: the intimate connection a slave could have with his family or master, the separation that could rend a child from parents, and the reality of slavery throughout the Roman Empire. Independent of whether a given specific slave in a story was a child, there is no question that child slaves were a part of real life throughout the New Testament world.

One may consider the relation of *pais* to *doulos* in light of a possible parallel in John 4:46–54 to the accounts in Matthew 8:5–13 and Luke 7:1–10. In all three accounts, a healing is said to have occurred in Capernaum

---

72. See also Martin, "Slavery."

73. Glancy, *Slavery in Early Christianity,* 112–29. Dupont, *Daily Life in Ancient Rome,* 56–62, brings evidence of a different sort which nevertheless bears on the slaves' family status: the slave was there for the master; his or her task was not to care for a family or be a part of a family, but to be available for the service of the master's needs and to serve the master's whims.

74. See chapter 1.

involving a centurion in the synoptic accounts and a "royal official" (*basilikos*) in John. In John, however, the one who was lying ill was the official's little son, his *paidion* (Jn 4:47; 4:51 speaks of *pais*). In all three accounts the person who was ill was healed due to the faith of the master/father. While there are clear connections and parallels among all the accounts, it is more difficult to determine what was at the heart of the original account: the exegete is confronted with the need to judge whether it is more likely that the healing account originally concerned a child or a slave. If it concerned a slave, one also has to weigh whether or not it was likely that the slave *was* a child, a detail that would have been lost in the synoptic accounts, except for the use of *pais*. In the end, perhaps no decision on these questions can be reached, but the presence of the Johannine account leads one to consider at least the age of the slave in the synoptic versions.

By way of summary one may say that the Gospels provide evidence, at least in contours, for Jesus' own extended family and that of John the Baptist. Children are present in the midst of Jesus and his followers; perhaps even some of his closest followers had children or may have been children. Several healing miracles portray Jesus' own concern for children when he responded to the determination and faith of loving and caring parents or caregivers. Finally, one notices that the life of slave families was part of the reality presented in the New Testament, and so also the lives of slave children, even if the family life of slaves, unlike that of free persons, was an ephemeral concern.

In Focus: The Pauline Letters, the Post-Pauline Letters, and the Acts of the Apostles

The Baptism of Children and the Ancient Household

Children appear in Paul's letters only in relief. Almost half a century ago, Joachim Jeremias argued that infants were baptized as a part of the *oikos*. First Corinthians 1:16 supplied his primary piece of data, when Paul mentioned in an aside that he baptized the household of Stephanus. Jeremias argued that little children were baptized as a part of the household.[75] Setting aside a review of all the evidence Jeremias marshaled for his argument, the basis for his analysis and conclusion seems to be correct. Insofar as children were baptized, the setting for these baptisms was the gather-

---

75. For further comment on the debate that ensued between Joachim Jeremias and Kurt Aland, see below, chapter 7.

ing of the community in the household or house church. To illustrate this, Jeremias utilized three passages from Acts in his discussion: Acts 16:15, in which Lydia and her *oikos* are baptized; Acts 16:32–34, the baptism of the Philippian jailer and "all his house"; and Acts 18:8, which tells of the baptism of Crispus, a leader of the synagogue, and his "whole house."[76] This evidence makes plausible the conclusion that children and a spouse as a part of a household also were baptized. Nevertheless, it is not clear whether the evidence necessarily implies that slaves and slave children were baptized as well.

There is further evidence from John 4:46–54 of a "whole household" believing in Jesus. Following the healing of his *pais,* the royal official in John's account "believed" in Jesus "along with his whole household." Some would argue regarding the exegesis of the passage that it is not possible to move from "belief" to "baptism." Yet "belief" is the Johannine key to following Jesus, which is evident in the passage concerning the Samaritan woman and her kin who believe (Jn 4:39–42), just prior to this account. From John 4:1–2 we learn also that the disciples of Jesus were baptizing new disciples. It seems possible that this account points to the slaves of the official "believing" with the "whole household," since the slaves figure prominently in the account (v. 51).

Following Ethelbert Stauffer, Jeremias pointed out that an "*oikos*-formula" of the form "he and his (whole) house" existed in the Hebrew Bible, and he adduced numerous references to it as proof that children were included among those baptized.[77] One may also consider that welcoming a child, at least a boy, into the covenant through circumcision was and is standard practice in Jewish families. As for the dedication of the infant, the same was true of Greco-Roman religious practice.[78] While the child's individuality was not as significant in the ancient world, the child was more a part of the fabric of family and community life, including religious life.

---

76. Joachim Jeremias, *Infant Baptism in the First Four Centuries,* trans. David Cairns (London: SCM Press, 1962), 20–21.

77. See Ethelbert Stauffer, "Zur Kindertaufe in der Urkirche," *Deutsches Pfarrblatt* 49 (1949), 152–54; and Jeremias, *Infant Baptism,* 20–21. See also the discussion by Peter Weigandt, "Zur sogenannten 'Oikosformel,'" *Novum Testamentum* 6 (1963), 49–74.

78. See Golden, *Children and Childhood in Classical Athens,* 23–25, on the bringing of the child into the home by means of ritual; on Roman families see Dupont, *Daily Life in Ancient Rome,* 220–22, and the discussion by Brent D. Shaw, "Raising and Killing Children: Two Roman Myths," *Mnemosyne* 54.1 (2001), 31–77, who in the first part of his article shows that phrases like *tollere liberos* or *suscipere liberos* did not refer to a specific ritual. Instead they were used simply to speak of having or raising children.

Infant baptism fits in well with this evidence. In light of Jewish and Greco-Roman religious practices of the inclusion of children, the practice of the baptism of children in Christian settings was not an innovation, but simply functioned as a shifting of allegiances.

Social Dislocation for the Earliest Christian Children

One should not pass over the aspect of the "shifting of allegiances" too quickly.[79] The formal initiation of both boys and girls into the Church via the rite of baptism constituted a shift when compared to Jewish religious initiatory practice, partly through the inclusion of girls in one and the same rite with boys.[80] Apart from that, however, one needs to consider the social impact on people who shifted their allegiance to the early Christian movement.[81] Full incorporation into the Christian Church had repercussions for children with respect to their larger kinship network. Their participation in the rites and festivals of their extended family, whether Jewish or pagan, was affected. This was the case quite clearly if one was Jewish (e.g., Acts 2:46; 3:1; 5:42). If one's relatives came from a Gentile context (1 Cor 8–10), Paul did not want children to maintain their participation in the rites and festivities of the pagan environment. Yet later evidence from early Christian sources suggests that in practice Christian children continued to be exposed to and participate in non-Christian religious celebrations. In mixed households such cases would have been more frequent. Christian practices also may have led to ostracism from grandparents, aunts, uncles, and cousins.[82] While Paul "advanced in Judaism beyond many among [his] people of the same age" (Gal 1:14), the concrete education that awaited those children baptized in the new faith was a matter of new developments in the Christian community.[83] A synagogue that was not too welcoming to Christian adults may not have received such parents' offspring with any greater dedication, enthusiasm, or openness. These are some of the practicalities of the Christian decision to bring the "whole household" into the faith; while the adults of the family may have been somewhat prepared for the consequences of the decision, it is not clear that the children would have been.

---

79. We take up the question again in chapter 7.

80. In Judaism, women also went to the *mikvah* for ritual cleansing. Yet these rites of cleansing, while inclusive of both genders, did not function as the main part of the initiation into the religion.

81. Barclay, "The Family as the Bearer of Religion," 73.

82. Ibid.; cf. also 1 Peter 1:18.

83. Barclay, "The Family as the Bearer of Religion," 76.

Considerations along these lines may form part of the background to the Galatians' decision to circumcise, generally understood in light of adult converts returning to, or beginning, Jewish practice.[84] Yet we can also discern concern for children in this letter. If the members of the Galatian church started to implement circumcision, they also had their sons in view. The difficulty for those who were encouraging them to be circumcised may not have been simply theological, but also practical: people wanted their children to be seen as being a part of this "new" covenant. Paul's arguments with the Galatians concerning the Law as the *paedagogus* (Gal 3:23–26) and the question of who was the heir of the covenant (Gal 4:21–31) take on a social dimension. Likewise, Paul's theological arguments assume a new resonance in this light. He stated that, far from bringing one into the covenant, circumcision simply was the maintenance of the status of a *nēpios*, or minor (Gal 4:3). The step to maturity had to be realized with a step of faith in order to become a true heir, a *huios theou* or "son of God." If the social dimension of circumcision with respect to both adults and children came into play in the Galatian community, then Paul's argument in Galatians 4 was an attempt to resist seeing circumcision as necessary for the children of Galatian Christians. Paul's telling the Jews living among the Gentiles "not to circumcise their children" seems to have been at the heart of the accusation of James in Acts 21:21. The perceived threat was that such a decision could cut one off from family and kin, and therefore was a decision against one's own family of birth, a family that was genealogically rooted in the descendants of Abraham, and therefore in God's chosen nation, Israel.

Part of what replaced the family in Christianity's initial Judean setting was the Church itself. The language of brothers (and sisters),[85] of the Son

---

84. J. Louis Martyn, *Galatians* (New York: Doubleday, 1997), 470, sees Paul as addressing "the male heads of the Galatian households," though understanding that sons would be included. Yet Hans Dieter Betz, *Galatians* (Philadelphia: Fortress Press, 1979), 258–63; Richard N. Longenecker, *Galatians* (Dallas, Tex.: Word Books, 1990), 225–26; J. B. Lightfoot, *St. Paul's Epistle to the Galatians* (repr. Lynn, Mass.: Hendrickson Publishers, 1982), 203–7; and Ernest De Witt Burton, *The Epistle to the Galatians* (Edinburgh: T&T Clark, 1975), 272–81, as examples of studies on Galatians as a whole, do not seem to consider the circumcision of children as a possible issue for Paul.

85. For studies of the use of *adelphoi* in biblical, early Christian, and intertestamental literature see, e.g., Troy W. Martin, "The Brother Body: Addressing and Describing the Galatians and the Agitators as Ἀδελφοί," *Biblical Research* 47 (2002), 5–18 ; David Horrell, "From ἀδελφοί to οἶκος θεοῦ: Social Transformation in Pauline Christianity," *Journal of Biblical Literature* 120.2 (2001), 293–311; Vincent Skemp, "ΑΔΕΛΦΟΣ and the Theme of Kinship in Tobit," *Ephemerides theologicae Lovanienses* 75.1 (1999), 92–103; and Reidar Aasgaard, "Brotherhood in Plutarch and Paul: Its Role and Character," in *Constructing Early Christian Families*, 166–82.

and of the Father, functioned as more than theological language; it grounded the life of at least one community. One learns from Acts 2:43–47, 4:32–37 that in Jerusalem all things were held in common and given to the community.[86] Even if this represents an ideal portrait in Luke-Acts, what this meant for children in the community and family life is difficult to determine in all its complexity, since we neither know if children continued to live in family homes at this stage nor whether people lived communally, or whether great breaches took place within families in their extended or nuclear form. Despite the lack of direct evidence for the shape of children's lives at this stage of Christian development, however, children were present.[87] We hear of them occasionally in Acts, and there is no reason to assume that their presence in the life of the community was not constant.

Children at Worship

In light of the social and familial dislocation caused by a family's adherence to the new way, life in the first generations of Christians offered opportunities for children to experience Christian identity through liturgy. Given that household churches were the norm in Christian worship life during the Church's early existence,[88] the attendance of children at these services as part of family life is certain. When early Christians were sharing everything, including meals (Acts 2:44–46), children were present among them.[89] Children were in the midst of the community, whether at home or in the Tem-

---

86. Andreas Lindemann, "The beginnings of Christian life in Jerusalem according to the summaries in the Acts of the Apostles (Acts 2:42–47; 4:32–37; 5:12–16)," in *Common Life in the Early Church: Essays Honoring Graydon F. Snyder,* ed. Julian V. Hills (Harrisburg, Pa.: Trinity Press International, 1998), 202–18; Luke Timothy Johnson, *The Acts of the Apostles,* Sacra Pagina Series, vol. 5, (Collegeville, Minn.: Liturgical Press, 1991), 58–63 and 82–93; and J. Dupont, "Community of Goods in the Early Church," in *Salvation of the Gentiles,* ed. J. Keating (New York: Paulist Press, 1979), 85–102.

87. For a consideration of some of the evidence on children in Acts, see Horn, "The Depiction of Children and Young People as Literary Device."

88. As much research of the last two decades or so has made clear, the locus of the early Christian Church was the household: Hans-Josef Klauck, *Hausgemeinde und Hauskirche im frühen Christentum* (Stuttgart: Verlag Katholisches Bibelwerk, 1981); W. A. Meeks, *The First Urban Christians* (New Haven, Conn.: Yale University Press, 1983); Margaret Y. McDonald, *The Pauline Churches: A Socio-historical Study of Institutionalization in the Pauline and Deutero-Pauline Churches* (Cambridge: Cambridge University Press, 1988); Harry O. Maier, *The Social Setting of the Ministry as Reflected in the Writings of Hermas, Clement, and Ignatius* (Waterloo: Wilfrid Laurier University Press, 2002); Barclay, "The Family as the Bearer of Religion," 76; and Carsten Claussen, *Versammlung, Gemeinde, Synagoge: das hellenistisch-jüdische Umfeld der frühchristlichen Gemeinden* (Göttingen: Vandenhoeck & Ruprecht, 2002).

89. See the work by Hanne Sigismund Nielsen, "Roman Children at Mealtimes," in *Meals*

ple. Children were simply a part of daily Christian life, and it was their life as much as it was their parents' life. There is no positive evidence to show how children participated in the formal services at this stage, to the extent that services were formal. On the other hand, there is no reason to consider silence regarding children as suggesting their exclusion.

Following the discussion in Acts 4:32–37 regarding the Church's holding all things in common, the reader is confronted with the account of Ananias and Sapphira, a married couple who withheld part of their promised wealth from the Church and paid for this with their lives (Acts 5:1–11). While no arguments for or against the historicity of this account need to be considered here, two details deserve attention.[90] Both the body of Ananias and the body of Sapphira were said to have been carried out from the apostles' midst by "young men" (so the NRSV translation; Greek *neōteros* in Acts 5:6; *neaniskos* in 5:10). It cannot easily be determined whether these are the children of Church members or believers themselves apart from their families, or whether these "young men" are still to be regarded as children in age. Depending on the breakdown of ages he utilized, Philo could locate the *neotēs* (in *Heres* 294–296) as a fourteen-year-old and the *neos* from ten to twenty years of age (*Congr.* 74–82). The word used in Acts 5:6, *neōteros*, is the comparative of *neos* and is related to *neotēs*; these "young men" or boys could be anywhere from ten to twenty. The word *neaniskos* found in Acts 5:10, however, is used by Philo in *De opificio mundi* 103–104 to designate the fourth stage of Hippocrates's generations of man and so gives us an age range from twenty-one to twenty-eight. Which solution is the better one is hard to say. Against the background of Philo's usage the one term clearly identifies a younger person than the other. Yet we also cannot know that Luke's use of these terms is the same as that of Philo.[91] A

---

in a Social Context: Aspects of the Communal Meal in the Hellenistic and Roman World*, eds. Inge Nielsen and Hanne Sigismund Nielsen (Aarhus, Denmark: Aarhus University Press, 1998), 56–66, for a discussion of the place of children in meal settings in the ancient world.

90. J. M. D. Derrett, "Ananias, Sapphira, and the Right of Property," *Downside Review* 89 (1971), 225–32; and Ph.-H. Menoud, "La mort d'Ananias et de Sapphira (Actes 5.1–11)," in *Aux Sources de la Tradition Chrétienne: Mélanges offerts à M. Maurice Goguel à l'occasion de son soixante-dixième anniversaire* (Neuchatel: Delachaux et Nièstle, 1950), 146–54.

91. A few studies on connections between Philo and Luke have appeared. Among them are Joachim Kügler, "Die Windeln Jesu als Zeichen: Religionsgeschichtliche Anmerkungen zu ΣΠΑΡΓΑΝΟΩ in Lk 2," *Biblische Notizen* 77 (1995), 20–28; Joachim Kügler, "Die Windeln Jesu (Lk 2)—Nachtrag. Zum Gebrauch von ΣΠΑΡΓΑΝΟΝ bei Philo von Alexandrien," *Biblische Notizen* 81 (1996), 8–14; Hans-Josef Klauck, "Die heilige Stadt: Jerusalem bei Philo und Lukas," *Kairos* 28.3–4 (1986), 129–51; and James R. Royse, "A Philonic use of ΠΑΝΔΟΧΕΙΟΝ (Luke X 34)," *Novum Testamentum* 23 (1981), 193–94.

twenty-eight-year-old would still have been considered a relatively young person in antiquity, but nevertheless an adult. Yet if only the expression of physical strength to carry away the dead bodies was to be emphasized, it is not clear why the author needed to distinguish the "young men" apart from other adult men and women. It seems most likely that the youths in question were older teenagers, selected because the task they were given required strong, youthful hands.

A related question arises concerning Saul, when we find him in Acts 7:58. Like Eutychos in Acts 20:9, he is called a *neanias*. In *De cherubim* 114, Philo placed the *neanias* just prior to being a "mature man," the seventh of his eight stages. Yet, if we were to employ a ten-year breakdown of ages, we would find the *neanias* as a sixty- to seventy-year-old; a seven-year breakdown in stages would give us an age of forty-two to forty-nine. This is clearly too old to be a "young man," even in the ancient world. The gradations used by Philo in *De Cherubim* do not seem to be formal, but rather function in an almost romantic manner as Philo recounted his past youth in light of the coming separation of body and soul. The *neanias* of Acts 7:58 and 20:9 must be seen in the same light as the *neaniskos* of Acts 5:6, namely as an older teenager. We can insist on this at least insofar as, after his fall from a window, Eutychos is called not a *neanias*, but a *pais* (Acts 20:12). This last piece of data tells us quite clearly that young people were present at Church meetings, but we do not know if other members of Eutychos's family were present as well. When the fellow believers found that he was alive, there was comfort and relief among those gathered, but parents or family are not mentioned explicitly.

Children in Families with One Believing Parent

That many children in earliest Christianity were raised in a household with only one believing parent is highly probable.[92] As in the Gospels, where we hear of mothers of some of the disciples as followers of Jesus, we also encounter in Paul's epistles and the pseudo-Pauline literature, as well as in Acts, some women who followed Jesus apart from their husbands. Best known perhaps are the mother and grandmother of Timothy. The author of 2 Timothy spoke of the faith that lived in Timothy's grandmother Lois and in his mother, Eunice, and that lived on in him (2 Tm 1:5). From Acts 16:1 one learns that Timothy's father, a Greek, did not believe, yet

92. For a helpful study of some aspects of mixed marriages, see Margaret Y. MacDonald, "Early Christian Women Married to Unbelievers," *Studies in Religion/Sciences religieuses* 19 (1990), 221–34.

that his Jewish mother, Eunice, was a believer in Christ. That Timothy was raised in the Christian faith emerges from 2 Timothy 3:14–15, where the author encouraged him to continue in what he had learned and believed, since "from infancy" he had known the sacred writings which were able to "instruct" one to salvation.[93] Accepting that Timothy was not literally reading the Scriptures "from infancy," we may suppose that he was present with his mother and grandmother in church from infancy and was exposed to the Scriptures there. Whether this indicated a more formal training in the Scriptures from childhood is not possible to determine. Yet we can be certain that Timothy was not raised as a Jew, since he was circumcised only as a young man or child (Acts 16:3). This evidence suggests that his religious identity was "from infancy" a Christian identity, perhaps mentioned in order to suggest baptism in his infancy. It also leads one to wonder about Timothy's age as a disciple of Jesus and co-worker with Paul. If Timothy was truly a Christian "from infancy," and still young when he began to travel with Paul, his mother and grandmother may have become Christians in the thirties or early forties of the first century. Timothy could have been a young teenager when Paul first met him.

Although we do know that Timothy was young when he traveled with Paul, how young exactly he was is beyond precise determination. An intriguing piece of data concerning his age is the use of the verb *kataphroneō* ("to look down on," "despise") in Matthew 18:10 ("do not look down on the children"), which finds a parallel usage in 1 Timothy 4:12 *(kataphroneitō)*. There the author tells Timothy not to let anyone "look down on [his] youthfulness." While some may argue that this detail is of little relevance for establishing Timothy's actual age, since Paul's authorship has been dismissed so often for this letter, it is helpful to turn to the authentically Pauline letter of 1 Corinthians for further clues. In 1 Corinthians 16:10–11, Paul urged a welcome acceptance in Corinth, free from fear. He stressed that no one "despise," "scorn," or "look down with contempt on *(exoutheneō)*" Timothy. One wonders what reason Paul might have had to fear such contempt. It could be related to ongoing strife between Paul and the church in Corinth. Yet one should not overlook the data regarding Timothy's youth. His youth would have been a major issue in accepting the Christian teachings in a culture that valued the adult male, educated and discerning, as the typical age for a person of disciplined mind. It is possible that references to

---

93. See Philo, *Legatio* 115; and Philo, *Spec. Leg.* 4.149–50, for the claim that Judaism was learned "from the cradle"; cf. Barclay, "The Family as the Bearer of Religion," 72.

Timothy as *teknon* (1 Tm 1:2; 1:18; 2 Tm 1:2; 2:1) reflect not only his spiritual relationship to Paul, but also his physical age.

Other families in which one parent may have been a convert included that of Lydia and her household (Acts 16:14–15). We cannot be certain how she became head of the household, perhaps through widowhood. Such a situation would not necessarily imply that her husband was not a Christian. It also does not provide information on how many children she had or what their ages had been. Other families may have been those of Mary, the mother of John Mark (Acts 12:12), and of Philip and his four unmarried *(parthenos)* daughters (Acts 21:8–9).[94] Some of the family groupings Paul listed in Romans may indicate a parent with children. Paul mentioned "those from [the family of] Aristobulus" (Rom 16:10) and "those from [the family of] Narcissus who are in the Lord" (Rom 16:11). This possibly refers to a parent and the children who believed, although it could also refer to the entire family of each man. The same was the case with the previously mentioned "household of Stephanus" (1 Cor 1:16), Crispus and his entire household (Acts 18:8), Cornelius and his entire household (Acts 10:24, 48; 11:14), and the Philippian jailer and his entire family (Acts 16:33). The author of Acts also had Paul refer to Rufus and his mother (Acts 16:13) and a possible family grouping including Nereus and his sister in Acts 16:15. One cannot say what age Rufus was in this context, or determine at what age each of those mentioned entered the Christian community. Other families may have been intended by the reference to Nympha and the church in her house (Col 4:15), Philemon and the church in his house (Phlm 1), and the household of Onesiphorus (2 Tm 4:19). One can observe a similar phenomenon when at the beginning of the second century Ignatius of Antioch wrote to the Christians in Smryna and sent greetings, for example, "to the families of my brothers, along with their wives and children" and "to Tavia's family," encouraging her especially "to be firmly and thoroughly grounded in faith and love."[95] These were Christian households, where children were a natural part of the web of faith relationships as well.

Without direct mention of children, such as the four daughters of Phil-

---

94. For comments on this passage on Philip and his daughters *(thygatēr)*, see also Eusebius of Caesarea, *Church History* 3.30.1, 3.31.5–6, 3.39.9, and 5.17.3 (ed. Eduard Schwartz, Theodor Mommsen, and Friedhelm Winkelmann, *Eusebius Werke, Zweiter Band, Erster Teil, Die Kirchengeschichte*, GCS, n.s. vol. 6.1 [Berlin: Akademie Verlag, repr. 1999], 262, 266, 288, and 470). See also below, chapter 8, for a discussion of the relative age of *parthenoi*.

95. Ignatius of Antioch, *Letter to the Smyrneans* 13 (ed. and trans. Ehrman, *Apostolic Fathers*, vol. 1, 294–309, here 308; also trans. Cyril C. Richardson, *Early Christian Fathers* [New York: Simon & Schuster, 1996], 116).

ip or the children of whom Ignatius spoke when writing to the Smyrneans, it is impossible to determine how many children these families had or what their ages might have been. Yet the preponderance of families listed with a single parent, the fact that only mothers are listed among the parents of Jesus' disciples, and the complementary evidence that often women alone responded to the message (Acts 17:4) lead one to the conclusion that belonging to the Church in the first and early second centuries often led to disruptions of the family structure. It meant that children were in families that were separated by the Gospel.

This reality is alluded to in Paul's epistles. In 1 Corinthians 7:12–16, Paul engaged in a discussion of the case of a Christian believer married to an unbelieving spouse,[96] either male or female. Paul asked believers to remain with their unbelieving partners, unless the unbeliever wished to separate. The reasons for suggesting persistence in the marriage commitment were twofold: the unbelieving partner was "made holy" through the believing partner; and the children *(tekna)* were holy and did not become "unclean." Theologically, Paul's claim raises ambiguities about the precise meaning intended. Holiness may have been seen as having a contagious effect by which those who lived "close" to the believer were "infected," as it were, by the faith of the believer. That the children would be "unclean" if the partners separated suggests that the faith of one, like a little bit of leaven, was seen as imparting something to the whole household. Socially, it suggests certain realities about early Christian families. It was not necessarily "whole households" which believed, and since believing husbands at times would have unbelieving wives (1 Cor 7:12–16), it also seems that the belief of a "whole household" was not simply a matter of the father imposing his faith on the family.[97] Paul's statement also suggests that since the children were "made holy" by the believing parent, these particular children did not choose the faith by themselves or were brought into it through baptism. Certain early Christian families were divided in faith, if not in household. The unbelieving parent might object to his or her children being brought

96. For further discussion of the phenomenon particularly of women being married to unbelieving husbands, see MacDonald, "Early Christian Women Married to Unbelievers."

97. What we know of women's religious life in the ancient world supports the assumption of a significant level of independence regarding the choice the individual had when selecting what cult to follow. For a wealth of evidence pointing to women's manifold religious practices see, for example, Ross Shepard Kraemer, *Her Share of the Blessings: Women's Religions among Pagans, Jews, and Christians in the Greco-Roman World* (New York: Oxford University Press, 1992); and Deborah F. Sawyer, *Women and Religion in the First Christian Centuries* (London: Routledge, 1996, repr. 1998).

to the Church. Perhaps the believing spouse did not have the right to take the children away from the familial and local belief system. In this case Paul states that it is permissible for the non-Christian spouse to leave the household, and that in such instances "the brother or sister is not bound" (1 Cor 7:15). Paul's concluding statement in 1 Corinthians 7:16, that the wife may be the salvation of the husband and vice versa, is ambiguous: does Paul refer here to instances in which the spouses of mixed religious backgrounds remain together, or to instances where the non-Christian leaves the marriage, thereby granting "peace" to the household (cf. 7:15)? No matter which interpretation one accepts, Paul seems to blithely ignore his earlier statement in 7:14, that the children of a mixed marriage in which the parents separate are "unclean." In 7:16, Paul is no longer concerned for the fate of the children in such marriages. This discrepancy may suggest that 1 Corinthians 7:12–16 contains two different solutions to the problem of mixed marriages, in which one or both of the statements on children of such marriages may reflect the post-Pauline Church.

A further observation is in order: if according to Paul the children of a mixed marriage were holy within the marriage, but became unclean if the marriage ended, this may simply have indicated a theological reality for Paul about the nature of divorce, with divorce rendering the children unclean. It could also point to a social reality that in the case of the end of a mixed marriage the children might end up living with the unbelieving spouse, whether male or female, and so become unclean by virtue of no longer being in the presence of the believing parent. That these issues were not limited to Paul's churches is clear from 1 Peter 3:1–6, in which the wife was encouraged to be a model that could lead her husband to salvation. While the husband's salvation obviously was a concern, the children's salvation may also have been in view. Hand in hand with the growth in the number of early Christians, particularly women, mixed marriages increasingly were perceived as creating troublesome situations for family life. Tertullian, for example, warned women not to marry an unbeliever, who would only object to his wife's attendance at church functions and rather involve her in public events and social receptions at home that required her active participation in worldly, pagan affairs.[98] The same interest in leading his children to participate in socially acceptable, secular affairs, and the same resistance to their attendance at church services may be assumed.

---

98. Tertullian, *To His Wife*, bk. 2, ch. 4 (ed. and trans. Charles Munier, *Tertullien. A Son Épouse* [Paris: Les Éditions du Cerf, 1980], 134–37).

Marriage without Children?

It is instructive to note that when we do read about married Christian couples in the New Testament, we do not hear about their children. This is the case with Peter and his wife (1 Cor 9:5), Prisca and Aquila (Rom 16:3; 1 Cor 16:19; 2 Tm 4:19; Acts 18:2, 18), Ananias and Sapphira (Acts 5:1–11), and (possibly) Andronicus and Junia (Rom 16:7).[99] Perhaps these couples did not have children; perhaps it was not deemed significant to mention any children they may have had. All of the family groupings listed further above, those of Philemon, Aristobulus, Narcissus, Onesiphorus, and perhaps others, may have included wives and children, but, if present, the wives and children were subsumed in the family structure. As Carolyn Osiek and David Balch have formulated, "Paul never refers to procreation, even when discussing Christian heterosexual couples' relationships."[100] Neither did he refer to their offspring. In New Testament accounts of Paul's life, a small number of children were present. On one occasion, we learn from Acts that while Paul was stopping in Tyre, he sought out the Christians in the city, who escorted him from the city with their "wives and children" (Acts 21:5). The children were there, but they did not form the main focus. They came, or did not come, together with the whole household.

Marriage, Celibacy, and Children

As Christians began to create a religious identity apart from their Jewish lineage and attempted to convert non-Jews in the Greco-Roman world, morality played a significant role, in part because markers that were available to others—such as circumcision and the Sabbath or the participation in local cults from childhood on—were discouraged. Peter Brown argued that Christian self-definition was created especially through sexual morality,[101] a marker of identity that Christians inherited from Judaism. This is particularly evident in Paul's own conflict in setting aside Torah as a re-

---

99. On the identification of Junia as a female person, see most significantly the work by Bernadette Brooten, "'Junia—outstanding among the apostles' (Romans 16:7)," in *Women Priests: A Catholic Commentary on the Vatican Declaration,* eds. Leonard and Arlene Swidler (New York: Paulist Press, 1977), 141–44. See also Eldon Jay Epp, *Junia: the First Woman Apostle* (Minneapolis: Fortress Press, 2005).

100. Osiek and Balch, *Families in the New Testament World,* 118.

101. Peter Brown, "Late Antiquity," in *A History of Private Life: I. From Pagan Rome to Byzantium* (Cambridge, Mass.: Harvard University Press, 1987), 237–311, discusses the easy-going pagan sexual morality (243–46) in contrast to Christians who increasingly used sexuality to define morality (257, 259, 263–67, and 297–304).

quirement for being a "child of the promise" of Abraham on the one hand, and his insistence that the moral code of Torah be the basis for Christian conduct on the other. Brown's conclusion overlooks other important elements of Christian identity and the fact that morality certainly did not separate Christians, especially Jewish Christians, from Jews who did not accept Jesus of Nazareth as the Messiah. Yet it is with respect to sexual morality and practice, in this case the tension between marriage and celibacy, that freeborn children may have been profoundly affected by being and becoming Christians. We hasten to add that we do not know much about how children of slaves were affected by teachings on Christian sexual morality. Where they were owned by pagan slave masters their bodies were not their own, as many Roman authors stressed, and they were not able to contract legal Roman marriages. The acceptance of the Roman institution of slavery on the part of Paul and the Pauline tradition gave little incentive to Christian slave owners to distinguish their treatment of slaves from the way their non-Christian neighbors treated them.[102] Hence the present discussion focuses on the children of freeborn converts to Christianity.

A sense of the shift in children's lives, as related to early Christian teaching on marriage and sexuality, emerges in 1 Corinthians 7:36–38. Now often translated and interpreted as relating to the practice of "spiritual" marriage in Corinth, it is equally plausible that Paul advocated an ideal of celibacy for girls reaching the age of marriage. The matter at hand which can be inferred from this passage is whether a Christian father had the right or perhaps the obligation to allow his daughter not to marry.[103] If one reads these verses as an instance of Paul telling fathers that they could decide to keep their daughters from marriage, the consequences for such girls were potentially profound. Paul's apocalypticism, which insisted on an imminent arrival of a new age in which the social conventions of society, including the bedrock of the Roman family, would be swept away, placed on such girls the burden of self-sufficiency. A woman was expected to marry as part of the social contract that protected her when her father died. If she would or could not be married, it was no longer clear who was to take care of her on the death of her guardian. In the Roman world it is clear that some women were skilled and thus could support themselves, but the extent to which single women established Roman households is uncertain. Thus Christian

102. Brooten, "Der lange Schatten der Sklaverei im Leben von Frauen und Mädchen," has discussed evidence from apocryphal acts of apostles and other texts that suggests that Christian slave masters did not necessarily treat young slaves any better than non-Christian slave masters.

103. For fuller discussion of this passage, see below, chapter 8.

celibacy emerged as a two-edged sword: it could be embraced as a new and fresh opportunity, but it could also spell the end of the dream of a secure married life in Greco-Roman or Jewish society.

Conversion and Social Change

Conversion to Christianity before Constantine was disruptive of family life, as Barclay noted when he commented that "certain trends in the new movement constituted a challenge to the common assumptions of family solidarity and loyalty, a challenge which endured beyond the first convulsive generation in the form of a powerfully persistent ascetic ideal."[104] Certainly, a conversion to Christianity upset the style of life, worship, and even attitudes expected of children in a Greco-Roman setting. Even accounting for the polemic of Celsus, there likely was at least a grain of truth in the disruption, which so riled him:

In private houses one can see wool workers, cobblers, laundry workers, and the most illiterate country bumpkins, who would not venture to voice their opinions in front of their intellectual betters. But let them get hold of children in private houses—let them find some gullible wives—and you will hear some preposterous statements: You will hear them say, for instance, that they should not pay any attention to their fathers or teachers, but must obey them. They say that their elders and teachers are fools, and are in reality very bad men who like to voice their silly opinions. These Christians claim that they alone know the right way to live, and that, if only the children will believe them, they will be happy and their homes will be happy as well. Now if, as they are speaking thus to the children, they happen to see a schoolteacher coming along, some intelligent person, or even the father of one of the children, these Christians flee in all directions, or at least the more cautious of them. The more reckless encourage the children to rebel. They tell the children that they remain silent in the presence of the parents and the schoolteachers only because they do not want to have anything to do with men as corrupt as these pagans, who, did they know what the children had been hearing, would likely punish them for hearing it. These Christians also tell the children that they should leave their fathers and teachers and follow the women and their little chums to the wooldresser's shop, or to the cobbler's or to the washerwoman's shop, so that they might learn how to be perfect. And by this logic they have persuaded many to join them.[105]

104. Barclay, "The Family as the Bearer of Religion," 72.

105. Origen, *Contra Celsum* 3.55 (ed. Marcel Borret, *Origène. Contre Celse*, vol. 2, books 3 and 4 [Paris: Les Éditions du Cerf, 1968], 128–31; trans. R. Joseph Hoffmann, *Celsus. On The True Doctrine. A Discourse Against the Christians* [New York: Oxford University Press, 1987], 73–74).

Celsus's objection to what he saw as the Christians' preying upon children, women, and other people he regarded as of low standing reveals a fear of losing children to Christianity and of disrupting the orderly familial, educational, and social structures. As the Christian families featured in the Pastoral Epistles feared the disruption of their families, so did the Greco-Roman families, which were cast in disarray by the new framework of social loyalties that came with acceptance of the Christian message.

The family continued to take its place as the locus of much of Christian life. The evidence for children being raised as Christians from their youth is well known.[106] It includes the biographical information concerning Ignatius, bishop of Antioch, as well as some distinguished early Christian figures who were part of the network of Christians in the city. Writing to Polycarp in Smyrna, Ignatius asked him to greet the wife of Epitropus with "all her house and children" (*Poly.* 7).[107] Irenaeus met Polycarp, then the Bishop of Smyrna, in his "early youth."[108] A fragment from his *Letter to Florinus* tells in greater depth of Irenaeus's memories of Polycarp, and he recalled them more vividly than recent events. He remembered where he sat, where Polycarp sat, how he looked, his remembrances of John and others who had seen the Lord, and his discourses to the Church, to all of which Irenaeus had "listened eagerly at the time, . . . not committing them to writing, but learning them by heart."[109] In the *Martyrdom of Polycarp,* Polycarp attested that he had "served" Jesus for eighty-six years.[110] Papias, himself from nearby Hierapolis, as a child had "listened to John" and later had been "a companion of Polycarp."[111] All of these details and remem-

106. For example, in the *Martyrdom of Saints Justin and Companions,* Paeon and Euelpistus both claimed to have been raised as Christians by their parents, one in Cappadocia and the other in Iconium. The account of their martyrdom is found in Herbert Musurillo, ed. and trans., *The Acts of the Christian Martyrs* (Oxford: Clarendon Press, 1972). These accounts are from Recension A, 6, 23; 7, 24–25; Recension B, 4.3, 9–10; 4.6, 15–17; and Recension C, 3.4, 24–26, on pages 41–61.

107. That he wrote in a similar vein to the Smyrneans, greeting also the children in the family, has been mentioned above already.

108. Irenaeus of Lyons, *Adversus haereses* 3.3.4 (ed. Adelin Rousseau and Louis Doutreleau, *Irénée de Lyon; Contre les Hérésies,* book 3 [Paris: Les Éditions du Cerf, 1974], 38).

109. Eusebius of Caesarea, *Church History* 5.20.5–6 (ed. Schwartz, Mommsen, and Winkelmann, *Eusebius Werke, Zweiter Band, Erster Teil, Die Kirchengeschichte,* GCS N. F. vol. 6.1, 482–84; trans. Williamson, *Eusebius: The History of the Church from Christ to Constantine,* 168–69).

110. *Martyrdom of Polycarp* 9.3 (ed. and trans. Musurillo, *The Acts of the Christian Martyrs,* 8–9).

111. Eusebius of Caesarea, *Church History* 3.39 (ed. Schwartz, Mommsen, and Winkelmann, *Eusebius Werke, Zweiter Band, Erster Teil, Die Kirchengeschichte,* GCS N. F. vol. 6.1, 286; trans.

brances speak to the reality of growing numbers of Christians in the second century who had been raised in the faith from childhood on. Much of their initial exposure to the Christian religion occurred in contexts related to their family.

Children in the Christian household were expected to be obedient and to submit to discipline,[112] but the newly emphasized reality of celibacy also continued to define the life of Christian children and families. Although we discuss this aspect of Christian children's life more fully in chapter eight, it is to be noted here that celibacy applies almost exclusively to Christian daughters. Sons who eschewed marriage were also in violation of the social order. Some early Christian writers vaunted the sexual abstinence of their coreligionists as evidence of the superiority of their religion. Indeed, Christian condemnation of pagan sexual practice often focused on the Greco-Roman gods' participation in incest and pederasty.[113] Christians, however, as Justin Martyr claimed, were chaste from childhood into old age.[114] In a treatise long erroneously ascribed to Cyprian, the more rigorous Novatian saw virginity as the continuation of infancy *(perseverans infantia)*, and since virginity did not have children *(virginitas filios non habet)*, but instead had "contempt for offspring [*filiorum contemptum habet*]," it was free "from the calamity of the death of children [*extra funerum filiorum calamitatem*]."[115] This was a mixed message to be sure. Children were called to chastity, yet chastity had contempt for children. Cyprian himself expressed that all were called to this path, men and women, boys and girls, and girls who heeded this call no longer had to worry about bearing children or having a hus-

---

Williamson, *Eusebius: The History of the Church from Christ to Constantine*, 101), citing and then modifying Irenaeus, *Against Heresies* 5.33.4.

112. See above, chapter 3.

113. See, for example, Clement of Alexandria, *Protreptikos* II (ed. Miroslav Marcovich, *Clementis Alexandrini "Protrepticus"* [Leiden: E. J. Brill, 1995], 19–64). See also Cornelia B. Horn, "The *Pseudo-Clementines* and the Challenges of the Conversion of Families," *lectio difficilior. European Electronic Journal for Feminist Exegesis* 2 (2007), http://www.lectio.unibe.ch/07_2/horn.html.

114. Justin Martyr, *First Apology* 15 (ed. Miroslav Marcovich, *Iustini Marytris. Apologiae Pro Christianis* [Berlin: de Gruyter, 1994], 31–133, here 54).

115. Novatian, *De bono pudicitiae* 7 (ed. G. Hartel, *S. Thasci Caecilli Cypriani Opera Omnia*, CSEL 3.3 [Vienna: Apud C. Geroldi Filium, 1871], 13–25, here 18; trans. Ernest Wallis, "Treatises Attributed to Cyprian: 'Of the Discipline and Advantage of Chastity,'" in *Hippolytus, Cyprian, Caius, Novatian, Appendix*, ANF 5 [republished: Peabody, Mass.: Hendrickson Publishers, 2004], 587–92, here 589). For the identification of Novatian as author of the treatise, see Johannes Quasten, *Patrology*, vol. 2: *The Ante-Nicene Literature After Irenaeus* (Allen, Tex.: Christian Classics, 1950, repr. 1995), 225–26 and 367.

band rule over them. Besides, Cyprian said, the earth was full enough already: stop begetting![116] Polycarp also exhorted the younger men or boys *(neōteroi)* in Philippi to remain chaste *(hagneias)* and the virgins to remain "in blameless and pure conscience."[117] If one did marry, Athenagoras commented, it was only for procreation; otherwise one should remain in a state of virginity.[118] In his *Exhortation to Chastity,* Tertullian could hardly approve of sex even within marriage, and certainly not of a second marriage. His view of children bears recitation:

> The fact that children are a troublesome burden, especially in our times, should be a significant argument for widows and widowers to remain unmarried. *Men have to be forced by law to father a family, because no man in his right sense would ever care to have children.* But suppose that, in spite of this reluctance of yours, you do cause your wife to conceive. What will you do? Will you interrupt her pregnancy by the use of drugs? I rather imagine that we have no more right to murder a baby before birth than after it.[119]

Like Cyprian, who later was to encourage girls to remain chaste partly to free them from the pain at the death of a child, but also due to "contempt of offspring," Tertullian simply had found the prospect of having children unbearable. His contempt for children was thinly veiled here. It is tempting to understand Tertullian's position as an extreme or idiosyncratic distaste for sex or children, but the widespread encratite movement that was a feature of parts of early Christianity, particularly in Syria, also reveals that some Christians, perhaps a good number of them, saw the new religion as an escape from the drudgery of childrearing imposed on them by Roman society

116. Cyprian, *On the Dress of Virgins* 2, 22, and 23 (ed. G. Hartel, *S. Thasci Caecilli Cypriani Opera Omnia,* CSEL 3.1 [Vienna: Apud C. Geroldi Filium, 1868], 185–205, here 188–89 and 202–4; trans. Roy J. Deferrari, *St. Cyprian. Treatises* [New York: Fathers of the Church, 1958], 33 and 50–51).

117. Polycarp, *Letter to the Philippians* 5.3 (ed. Ehrman, *Apostolic Fathers,* vol. 1, 340).

118. Athenagoras, *A Plea for the Christians* 33 (ed. Miroslav Marcovich, *Athenagoras. Legatio Pro Christianis* [Berlin: de Gruyter, 1990], 104–5).

119. Tertullian, *Exhortation to Chastity* 12.5 (ed. Aem. Kroymann, "Q. S. Fl. Tertulliani *De Exhortatione Castitatis,*" in *Quinti Septimi Florentis Tertulliani Opera,* vol. 2: *Opera Montanistica* [Turnhout: Brepols, 1954], 1013–35, here 1032–33; trans. William P. Le Saint, *Tertullian. Treatises on Marriage and Remarriage* [Westminster, Md.: Newman Press, 1951], 42–64, here 61 [italics added]). Later on, Augustine would take a similar view, but more nuanced. In *De bono conjugale* 9.9 and 10.10 (trans. Charles T. Wilcox and others, *St. Augustine, Treatises on Marriage and Other Subjects* [New York: Fathers of the Church, 1955], 9–51, here 21–23) he argued that the world already had enough children and so even those drawn to marriage should choose celibacy instead. See also the discussion by David G. Hunter, "Marriage," in *Augustine through the Ages: An Encyclopedia* (Grand Rapids, Mich.: Eerdmans, 1999), 535–37.

and state. There also is a potential danger to any such teaching. Once one sees chastity as the norm, for the good of the chaste subject, the fruits of marriage can come to be seen as contemptible.

In *Paedagogus* 2.10, addressing the questions of Christian marriage and children in a more balanced way than Tertullian,[120] Clement of Alexandria saw children as the necessary fruit of marriage,[121] but condemned "wantonness" within and outside of marriage. Having sex while one's wife was pregnant was strongly discouraged. In *Stromateis* 3.6, he condemned those who saw sexual intercourse as inherently "polluted," and asked whether they did not know that they themselves were also the result of intercourse.[122] Marriage and childbearing did not simply add "more wretches" to the world, but fulfilled an essential duty to procreate. Even the apostles Peter and Philip had children, he claimed, a reflection of his knowledge of extracanonical traditions that featured Peter's daughter.[123] Clement argued that the distress of many couples in being unable to procreate was evidence that bringing children into the world was a fundamental good.[124] Despite this understanding of children, Clement had a strong sense that chastity was still best and within marriage self-control should be practiced. He even intimated a negative sense of children that is present in canonical and apocryphal New Testament texts: marriage in Christ was a positive experience, if one did not "find it bitter" to raise children because it took "him" (not her) away from the things of God.[125] This, of course, found its basis in 1 Corinthians 7, particularly verses 32–34, but the idea was supported and accepted in all subsequent Christian centuries.

120. For a fuller treatment of Clement of Alexandria's view of marriage, family life, and women, see J. P. Broudéhoux, *Marriage et Famille chez Clément d'Alexandrie* (Paris: Beauchesne et ses fils, c1970); and Donald Kinder, "Clement of Alexandria: Conflicting Views on Women," *Second Century: A Journal of Early Christian Studies* 7.4 (1989–90), 213–20.

121. Clement of Alexandria, *Paedagogus* 2.10.83 (ed. Marcovich, *Clementis Alexandrini. Paedagogus,* 119).

122. Clement of Alexandria, *Stromateis* 3.6.45–56 (ed. Otto Stählin and Ludwig Früchtel, *Clemens Alexandrinus. Zweiter Band. Stromata. Buch I–VI* [Berlin: Akademie Verlag, 1960], 216–22).

123. For such extra-canonical witnesses, particularly in the form of the Coptic fragment featuring Peter's daughter, a text that quite likely derives from the apocryphal *Acts of Peter,* see James Brashler and Douglas M. Parrott, eds. and trans., "The Act of Peter, BG, 4: 128,1–141,7," in *Nag Hammadi Codices V,2–5 and VI with Papyrus Berolinensis 8502,1 and 4,* ed. Douglas M. Parrott, Nag Hammadi Studies 11 (Leiden: E. J. Brill, 1979), 473–93.

124. Clement of Alexandria, *Stromateis* 3.9.67 (ed. Stählin and Früchtel, *Clemens Alexandrinus. Zweiter Band. Stromata. Buch I–VI,* 226, l. 21).

125. Clement of Alexandria, *Stromateis* 3.9.67, 1 (ed. Stählin and Früchtel, *Clemens Alexandrinus. Zweiter Band. Stromata. Buch I–VI,* 226, ll. 20–24).

These criticisms of married life, and of the place of children within it, reflect common early Christian views. We do not hear overly much about the love between parents and children or about relationships with parents, or siblings, or the extended family in Christian sources. Yet, children were present and children did participate in family life and in the life of the early Christian community. Thus it is fair to ask how children experienced Christianity and how this experience shaped their relationship with their families and the world around them. It is a safe assumption that children in the first centuries of the Christian movement perceived the new religion as socially dislocating. While Jesus welcomed them into the kingdom, and held children up as models of discipleship, their exposure to Christian discipleship appears to have been confusing and disorienting for them as it disturbed familial and kinship structures. It is possible that disciples left families behind and that often only one parent joined and followed the movement. The fact that we often hear of only one parent becoming one of Jesus' disciples could mean that only one parent remained fully involved in a child's life. The scraps of the biography of Timothy that may be patched together from the New Testament suggest that although his father was alive only his mother and grandmother became part of the Christian movement, and it was they who decisively influenced and shaped the young boy's Christian formation.

One seems to be justified in assuming the presence of children in most if not all congregations. Yet the relative silence in early Christian sources on the roles of children in Christian communities is all the more profound when one compares in the Torah and in rabbinic sources the concern with the education of children and the care in delimiting the age of consent to marriage and of maturity in religious practice. Regardless of Jesus' teaching about children, it is difficult to hold that children were indeed considered and accepted as the models of discipleship at this time. Instead, they blended silently into the background. Indeed, it is likely that adults were generally the targets of most preaching within the Church. When the adults converted, the children were sure to follow. Children do not seem to have been considered as entities separate from their families and often were not considered capable of making decisions regarding religious adherence. When children are mentioned it is with respect to a parent and a parent's duties to her or his children. Celsus does refer to Christian preaching directed at non-Christian children, but for the early centuries it is not clear how many children responded to the call alone. Celsus himself responded with outrage, and most Roman parents would have reacted similarly.

Conclusions

What Christianity may have meant to children in the household in the Pauline, post-Pauline, apostolic, and later Christian communities is not always easy to ascertain. Like their Greco-Roman neighbors, Christian parents were expected to impose discipline on their children, and obedience was demanded of all children in the ancient world. Greco-Roman and Jewish fathers were called on to exercise their absolute authority with restraint,[126] a belief which lies beneath the counsel in Ephesians "not to provoke" one's children, but to provide for them. Yet the obedience of the children was expected and their lack of submission was viewed as a stain on the parents as well as the children, and on the Christian community as a whole.

The social implications of Christian belief within the family and wider kinship network were far-ranging. Christianity seems to have divided families. Parents could be on opposite ends of religious adherence and larger familial units likewise were divided at times on the same grounds. These implications are hard to define specifically. It would also have led to a different kind of kinship network for children, that of the Church, in which all members were said to be children, either of God or of an apostle, such as Paul, and brothers and sisters of each other. How children's lives were affected by these changes in the home and in the family is also difficult to determine. Apart from these divisions in family life, the major change seems to have resided in questions pertaining to children and marriage. Whether for a lack of Christian suitors that would have been accepted as appropriate spouses for Christian girls or due to the choice of celibacy, some girls would not have been married because of the new Christian movement. Whether Christian girls themselves perceived this as a choice or as an imposition upon them cannot be determined.

The explicit focus on celibacy was a Christian innovation in family life. It seems impossible to determine for the earliest centuries how children responded to the option of celibacy. With Osiek and Balch we suspect that most Christians continued to marry and be given in marriage, but we are led to wonder about the impact this teaching had on children. As to the time of marriage, it seems likely that Christian girls continued to marry at the same age as other girls of the day. This is probably the case for young Christian men as well. Yet celibacy and the hope of the return of Jesus may

126. See Eyben, "Fathers and Sons," for a balanced portrait of the father; the author stresses that neither excessively strict nor excessively indulgent fathers were praised.

have cut into the number of men available to Christian girls for marriage.

Christian teaching on the superiority of chastity would have been a constant clarion call in the ears of children. Marriage, even when practiced with continence, was second best. Children may have experienced their own sexuality as a burden or as a welcome renunciation in the battle with this world, from which they were constantly being asked to distinguish themselves, for instance in the realms of behavior, clothing, footwear, and make-up. By the second century, this formed a substantial part of the definition of Christian identity, which could be increasingly distinguished from that of the surrounding world. Families were more settled in the faith and we begin to hear of numerous children being raised in the faith. Children experienced Christianity as a part of their life from a young age and it shaped their life. While for initial generations it often meant the social dislocation of separating from family and household life, or the experience of gaining a whole new sense of community, in the course of the second century it became the determining form of life Christian children knew.

four

Children and Daily Life

Christian Children's Education

This chapter reconstructs the larger context of the child's education in the early Christian world, considering factors not only of class and social location, but also of religious affiliation.[1] Our discussion highlights the fact that the process of educating and raising up a Christian child, of leading

---

1. Several texts and studies have shaped this inquiry. Among them are the impact of ascetico-practical ideas as expressed in John Chrysostom's treatise *Against the Opponents of the Monastic Life* (ed. PG 47.319–386; trans. David G. Hunter, *A Comparison between a King and a Monk / Against the Opponents of the Monastic Life. Two Treatises by John Chrysostom* [Lewiston, N.Y.: Edwin Mellen Press, c1988], 77–176), and the differences in the education available for the wealthiest of children as opposed to slaves, demonstrated, for example, in Basil of Caesarea's *Ad adolescentes* (ed. N. G. Wilson, *Saint Basil on the Value of Greek Literature* [London: Duckworth, c1975], 19–36; convenient access to an English translation and a Greek text based on earlier editions by Roy Joseph Deferrari and Martin R. P. McGuire, "Address to Young Men on Reading Greek Literature," is also available in Roy J. Deferrari, *Saint Basil. The Letters* [London: William Heinemann, 1926–34], vol. 4, 378–435). Wilson's text is valuable in part because he took into account the witness of two translations into Syriac, one preserved in two manuscripts from the sixth century and thus constituting the earliest textual witness to the work. The earliest manuscript that contains the Greek text is dated to A.D. 899. See Wilson, *Saint Basil on the Value of Greek Literature*, 72–73. Other key texts that guided our inquiry include John Chrysostom's *On Vainglory, and the Right Way for Parents to Raise Their Children* (ed. and trans. Anne-Marie Malingrey, *Jean Chrysostome. Sur la vaine gloire et l'éducation des enfants* [Paris: Les Éditions du Cerf, 1972]; English trans. by M. L. W. Laistner, *Christianity and Pagan Culture in the Later Roman Empire together with An English Translation of John Chrysostom's Address on Vainglory and the Right Way for Parents to Bring up Their Children* [Ithaca, N.Y.: Cornell University Press, c1951, paperback 1967], 85–122; see also the editions by Basileios K. Exarchos, *Johannes Chrysostomos.*

and guiding him or her into adulthood, was at the same time a process of socializing the child into the community of the Church and ideally into the "City of God," to borrow a title from Augustine of Hippo.[2] As an exercise in socialization, the education of the Christian child was intrinsically a political act.

Definitions and Perspectives

To some it may seem that education was at the heart of a child's life in the ancient world. Yet evaluation of this claim depends on how one defines "education." If one considers only the standard, three-stage Greco-Roman education, moving through a primary training in writing, reading, and arithmetic; to a secondary, often called "grammatical," education; and then to the third stage of rhetorical and philosophical education, one easily omits the majority of children in antiquity.[3] Such an education at its

Über Hoffart und Kindererziehung [Munich: Max Hueber Verlag, 1952]; and by Franciscus Schulte, *S. Joannis Chrysostomi De inani gloria et de educandis liberis* [Monasterii Guestfalorum: Ex Officina Societatis Typographiae, 1914]); and Jerome's *Letters* to Laeta (*Ep.* 107) and Pacatula (and her father Gaudentius) (*Ep.* 128) (ed. Hilberg, *Sancti Eusebii Hieronymi Epistulae*, CSEL 55, 290–305 [*Ep.* 107] and CSEL 56, 156–162 [*Ep.* 128]). The discussion in the present chapter will highlight John Chrysostom's and Jerome's contributions only. Basil's may be left for future study.

2. See Augustine's *De civitate Dei* (ed. and trans. R. W. Dyson, *Augustine, The City of God against the Pagans* [Cambridge: Cambridge University Press, 1998]). For other areas of Christian socialization in a child's life, see also the discussion in Horn, "Children's Play as Social Ritual."

3. On the stages of education see Marrou, *History of Education*, 142–59 (primary schools), 160–75 (secondary schools), 186–216 (tertiary education)—all in Greek settings; for Rome, see 265–73 (primary schools), 274–83 (secondary schools), and 284–91 (tertiary schools). Marrou refers to a tertiary level of education as "higher education." See also Stanley F. Bonner, *Education in Ancient Rome* (Berkeley: University of California Press, 1977), parts 1 and 3, and especially 34–35, 41–42, 84–85, 136–37, and 250–76. See Smith, *Ancient Education*, chs. 6 (Greece) and 8 (Rome); and Aubrey Gwynn, *Roman Education from Cicero to Quintilian* (New York: Teachers College Press, 1926), 79–122, 153–79, and 180–241. For a more localized discussion of education during the relevant period, see also Raffaella Cribiore, *Gymnastics of the Mind: Greek Education in Hellenistic and Roman Egypt* (Princeton, N.J.: Princeton University Press, c2001). Other helpful studies of ancient education include Johannes Christes, Richard Klein, and Christoph Lüth, eds., *Handbuch der Erziehung und Bildung in der Antike* (Darmstadt: Wissenschaftliche Buchgesellschaft, 2006); Teresa Morgan, *Literate Education in the Hellenistic and Roman Worlds*, Cambridge Classical Studies (Cambridge: Cambridge University Press, 1998); Robin Barrow, *Greek and Roman Education* (London: Bristol Classical Press, c1976, reprinted 1996), a study that is very accessible to undergraduate students; James Bowen, *A History of Western Education*, vol. 1: *The Ancient World: Orient and Mediterranean 2000 B.C.–A.D. 1054* (New York: St. Martin's Press, 1972); and Horst-Theodor Johann, ed., *Erziehung und Bildung in der heidnischen und christlichen Antike* (Darmstadt: Wissenschaftliche Buchgesellschaft, 1976).

secondary and tertiary levels was reserved almost exclusively for wealthy, freeborn, and aristocratic boys. If we consider education as the process of being "raised" into a particular culture, craft, and family, then all children were educated. Education at this level is so broad as to have few parameters to limit the discussion. Some aspects of this broader kind of "education," particularly into a craft or profession, shall be considered in the following chapter. In the present one, the investigation concentrates on what one can say about a formal Christian education and its relationship to its Jewish and Greco-Roman models. Also of interest are the means by which children were educated in the Christian faith by family and Church.

Basic Questions Regarding Ancient Education

Whether Jewish, Greek, or Roman, the kind of education a child received varied according to ethnicity, religion, gender, and class. There were similarities in basic education that crossed cultural boundaries and these are seen at the most elementary level of learning letters, reading, writing, and arithmetic. According to most studies of education, elementary education seems to have been available to both boys and girls, and not only those of the highest socioeconomic status. Yet these studies often consider only free and urban children.[4] One cannot be certain to what extent the majority of children, free, slave, or poor, who lived in the countryside, gained an education, even at the elementary level.[5] For instance, most early education in Judaism, at least from the period reflected in the Mishnah, is assumed to have taken place in the home and to have consisted of instilling the core elements of Jewish religious identity and morality. Yet this presupposes that Jewish peasant fathers had the time to educate their sons, were capable of exercising or even possessed the skills necessary to offer sufficient education, such as reading and writing, and knew the Torah well

4. Marrou, *History of Education,* 144, distinguishes between those who were free and those who were slaves when he discusses children's education, but the schools children attended primarily seem to have been based in urban areas; on the other hand, he points to the origin of Roman education as a rural, peasant innovation that had come to be in the hands of the aristocracy (230–31).

5. Marrou, 103, states that sometimes slaves were admitted to primary education, above and beyond the slaves who functioned as *paidagogoi* after they had become educated by taking their young charges to school (142). He also mentions masters who owned hundreds or even thousands of slaves, some of whom were educated in a literary manner to serve as secretaries or readers (266). According to him, in Greece (103) and Rome (266) girls did attend school, perhaps more readily in Rome than in Greece at public schools. Of course there the available data pertains to girls whose parents could afford the luxury of school or a tutor.

enough to teach it to their sons (and perhaps daughters), since they could not have afforded Torah scrolls. The existence of the kind of parental literacy that this required is unlikely. Rather, the education of men in Torah (the Mishnah speaks with ambivalence on the education of women in this area) was conducted at the rabbinical court, where the students would gather in front of the master or his more advanced students to learn the Torah and its commentary in the Mishnah through aural reception and mnemonic characteristics of oral reception. For this reason *m. Kerithoth* 6:9 states that just as child and mother are bound to honor the father (based on Lv 19:3), so too are the son and the father bound to honor the son's teacher.

Moving to a consideration of higher levels of education, one does find profound differences, mostly between Jews on the one hand and Greeks or Romans on the other, but also between Greeks and Romans themselves. In whatever manner it took shape, Jewish education focused on the Scriptures and later, when we observe the rise of rabbinical academies, on the learning transmitted in the Talmud.[6] This focus on the Scriptures set Jewish levels of secondary or tertiary education apart from those found elsewhere in the Greco-Roman world. Greco-Roman education, which focused on grammar, rhetoric, philosophy, and the training of the body in the *gymnasium,* was also found among Jews, but it was available only to a limited number of upper-class young men,[7] and the attitude toward it reflected in Jewish sources is mixed at best. One needs to keep in mind that the majority of Jews, Greeks, and Romans did not participate in such higher education. This, in fact, is one of the major issues in studying education in the ancient world. Too often factors such as the limited number of children who had the opportunity to be formally educated, or the limited knowledge we have of how education actually took place, are not made explicit. We have much theoretical information, but often we lack answers to basic questions, such as whether girls were educated formally or what school buildings were like, or even if education in a formal sense existed in Palestine in Jesus' day.[8]

---

6. Levine, *The Ancient Synagogue,* 377, for Leviticus as the book of first study for boys.

7. Alan Mendelson, *Secular Education in Philo of Alexandria* (Cincinnati: Hebrew Union College Press, 1982), 1–16.

8. Levine, *The Ancient Synagogue,* 133, for instance, states that "evidence for schools in synagogues is negligible for the pre-70 period," but suspects that they must have been there somewhere. Likewise, we do not know if girls learned Torah in official capacities; see also above, chapter 1. Swidler, *Women in Judaism,* 93–111, believes girls were not regularly educated, whereas Boyarin, *Carnal Israel,* 168–80 and 180–96, thinks that at least in Palestine they were.

Physical Discipline as Education

Discipline and its immediate relevance for education is an important dimension of any discussion of this period. Much of the tradition regarding Jewish education that is evidenced in the Hebrew Bible points to a great emphasis on moral formation closely linked to physical discipline. Characteristically, Old Testament texts connect the concepts of education and correction, primarily by use of physical violence. The Hebrew verb *yasar* can range in its meaning from "discipline," "chasten," and "chastise" to "correct" and "admonish," and more directly also "instruct."[9] Likewise, the noun *mûsār* conveys the meanings "discipline," "chastening," "chastisement," and "correction."[10] Especially relevant for early Christian contexts of discourse on the education of children is that, in general, these Hebrew terms derived from *yasar* and *mûsār* are translated by the respective forms of the Greek *paideuein* and *paideia* (see, for example, Dt 8:5b–c and Prv 3:11a). Greek education, like Roman education, often relied on physical punishment to help "educate" the child, as Augustine painfully recalled in his *Confessions*.[11] Physical punishment as a means of education or formation of the young person toward betterment was known and advised in both the Jewish and the Greco-Roman world, although Quintilian called for its cessation in the Roman educational system.[12] The roots of this form of education, however, ran deep and were impossible to extract.

Jewish Education up to the First Century A.D.

Jesus and his first apostles have to be situated in a Jewish context. Thus initial questions about a "Christian" education have to account for the type of education they may have received as Jewish children, given their social, economic, and geographic location, and the clues we receive to how the authors of the New Testament presented their education. Such a setting also is the location of the earliest Christians and a suitable beginning point of

9. See, for example, Deuteronomy 8:5b–c; "as a parent disciplines a child, so the Lord your God disciplines you."

10. Proverbs 3:11a: "My child, do not despise the Lord's discipline." F. Brown, S. Driver, and C. Briggs, *The Brown-Driver-Briggs Hebrew and English Lexicon* (Boston, 1906; repr. Peabody, Mass.: Hendrickson Publishers, fourth printing 1999), 415–16.

11. See Augustine of Hippo, *Confessions* I ix (14–15), xvii (27) (ed. Verheijen, *Sancti Augustini. Confessionum Libri XIII*, 8–9, 15; trans. Chadwick, *Saint Augustine: Confessions*, 11–12, 19).

12. Quintilian, *De institutione oratoria*, 1.3.13–17 (ed. and trans. H. E. Butler, *The Institutio oratoria of Quintilian /with an English translation*, LCL 124 [Cambridge, Mass.: Harvard University Press, 1961], 58–61).

a study of education in the early Church. Certainly no exaggerated claims for Jesus or any of his followers with respect to their formal education are in place. Indeed, what is remarkable is how unimportant formal education is in the New Testament, with the possible exception of Paul's brief statement in Philippians 3:4–6 concerning his own training. Nevertheless, it is possible for this study to show what a basic education may have been in Judea in the first century and, more broadly, in the Hellenistic and Greco-Roman eras.

The basic understanding of education in the ancient Near East was that it was restricted to those of the scribal and priestly classes, in order to produce the *ḥakam*, or wise man, in Hebrew parlance. Elias Bickerman and others have noted a shift in the Hellenistic period, when the understanding of education, which was heavily influenced by the school systems of the Greeks, began to include ideas of democratization, both in Jewish consciousness and practice. Part of this development was due to the rise of the Pharisees, who adopted the Greek notion that "piety was teachable" and who attempted to transform Judaism through education; for this reason study was based on the Torah, but not limited to it. According to Bickerman, even in Jewish villages there were persons who were able to draw up contracts in Greek.[13]

Another element of Greek education was that of physical culture, which began to make inroads into Judea, into Jerusalem in particular, and into neighboring regions in the Hellenistic period. One has to keep in mind that this kind of education was directed in particular at wealthy young men; often overlooked in the Jewish opposition to the *gymnasium* in Jerusalem is the fact that it was dedicated to inculcating Greek culture and education in young men of the upper and priestly classes in Jerusalem, the heart of Judaism for the next generation.[14] Without question, commentators agree that this was education for the upper classes, the priests, and the aristocracy (cf. 2 Mc 4:10–13).

Forty years ago, Saul Lieberman noted how disturbing this trend in education was to the later rabbis, given the nudity it involved and the gods whose statues were present at the *gymnasium* and as patrons of the games.[15] One of the problems the rabbis faced in their rejection of such trends was that no biblical prohibition existed against such education. They demanded

13. Elias Bickerman, *From Ezra to the Last of the Maccabees* (New York: Schocken Books, 1970), 59 and 161–70.

14. Ibid., 104–7.

15. Saul Lieberman, *Greek in Jewish Palestine* (New York: Philip Feldheim, 1965), 92.

limitations, but could not ban activities at the *gymnasium* on the Sabbath. *Mishnah Shabbat* 22:6, for example, states that "they may oil and massage their stomach, but not exercise (the body) and not scrape. They may not go down to the [wrestling ground] and may not use artificial emetics."[16] All of these restrictions, or allowances, concern wrestling at the *gymnasium* on the Sabbath;[17] what is surprising is that the text does not simply formulate a blanket prohibition, but rather that the rabbis, in principle, accepted wrestling and, hence, the *gymnasium*.

Martin Hengel located *gymnasia* not only in cities, but also in larger villages, and noted that they were sponsored by associations or private foundations. The focus was on the education of *ephebes*, or "teenagers," about fourteen to seventeen years in age. This education was not only physical, but also literary and philosophical. Hengel also stressed that guardian deities were seen as being present at the *gymnasium* and at the festivals and competitions, at which the *ephebes* often played an important role. He further noted that the establishment of the *gymnasium*, which first opened in Jerusalem in 175 B.C., was not possible without a long period of preparation and a group of men willing to send their sons to partake in such an education.[18] To prepare for such an education also implied that previously one had received an education at an elementary level. From this portrait questions arise as to how this was carried out in the Greco-Roman period in Palestine. It must be asked whether such education focused on the Torah or on Greek learning, and whether all or many boys would have received a basic education in the Torah.

The traditional teaching was based on the Torah and the responsibility for such an education was placed on the father (cf. Dt 11:19). Yet for most fathers, the ability to fulfill such a responsibility was probably lacking, with regard to the availability of both time and skill. We cannot romanticize this tradition, knowing that the vast majority of fathers were peasant farmers or craftsmen. Strack and Stemberger commented that "most fathers were not in a position either to meet this obligation personally or to hire private tutors; and hence came about the early establishment of boys' schools." If

---

16. Ibid., 93–96. This translation is taken from Lieberman, except for "wrestling ground," which he would translate as "exercise the body." We emend it as "exercise [the body]." For Lieberman's detailed discussion of this passage see the listed pages.

17. The prohibition on emetics seems to be a prohibition on purging, apparently a common practice among wrestlers in ancient times. See Lieberman, *Greek in Jewish Palestine*, 96–97.

18. Martin Hengel, *Judaism and Hellenism* (Minneapolis: Fortress Press, 1991), 66–67 and 70–75.

Strack and Stemberger are clear-eyed about the ability of fathers, it is not as obvious that they are equally so about boys' schools in Jewish Palestine. They seem to accept the Talmudic traditions about Simeon ben Shetah and Yehoshua ben Gamala as historical, that is, that they started schools for boys all over the land.[19] Shaye Cohen doubted the basic historicity of these accounts and, as it seems, with good reasons. First, education was not possible for many boys for economic reasons: even if schools had been available, the time necessary to leave the farm or workshop and study at them would not have been readily available. Secondly, there is no evidence for the establishment of such schools in the first century B.C. or the first century A.D.[20] Finally, the rabbis of the second century hardly would have been as critical as they were of the education of the "people of the land" if such schools had existed to train their sons and if they had taken advantage of such education.[21]

It is true that sometime in the second century A.D. we begin to find schools of a rabbinic type and, as Hengel argued, something must have preceded this:

Without a considerable number of Jewish elementary schools, the rise of the Rabbinate, the extension of the popular Pharisaic movement and even the establishment of the institution of the synagogue, which presupposes a basic stock of people knowledgeable in the law in particular places, would be inconceivable: "The beginnings of a popular school had to arise as a preliminary to the liturgy of reading and preaching."[22]

It is likely that formal education preceded the rise of the rabbinate. It is not so obvious why this education had to have been popular, that is, available to all. Scholars of this period generally point to education in Jewish Palestine as part of the life of the elite classes, scribal and aristocratic, as it had been since time immemorial. Ben Sirach, who is the earliest witness to the term *bet ha-midrash,* still desired the exclusion of the common worker from education (Sir 38:24–34). Apart from traditional education in the To-

19. Strack and Stemberger, *Introduction to the Talmud and Midrash,* 10–11. See also Hengel, *Judaism and Hellenism,* 81, who sees the origin of the elementary school *(bêt sefer)* in Simeon ben Shetah's Talmudic decree.

20. Shaye J. D. Cohen, *From the Maccabees to the Mishnah* (Philadelphia: Westminster Press, 1987), 120.

21. Ibid., 225; Lieberman, *Greek in Jewish Palestine,* 2; and Bickerman, *From Ezra to the Last of the Maccabees,* 114.

22. Hengel, *Judaism and Hellenism,* 82, citing from Adolf Schlatter, *Geschichte Israels von Alexander dem Großen bis Hadrian* (Stuttgart: Calwer, 1925), 59.

rah, the members of the upper classes in the third and second century B.C. would have enjoyed Greek education through tutors and perhaps private schools.[23] This seems to have continued into the rabbinic period, as Rabbi Gamaliel was given permission to teach those in his "house" Greek wisdom as well as the Torah.[24]

Yet between the early Hellenistic period, when the upper classes and priestly castes enjoyed Greek wisdom through private tutors and schools and established *gymnasia* in Palestine, and the rise of rabbinic schools and learning, some change took place, for the school did become a part of the life of Judaism, even if not available to all. The change is grounded in historical events, primarily the destruction of the Temple.[25] This led to a focus on piety expressed through learning and the establishment of rabbinic learning as the key means of understanding what it meant to be a loyal Jew. The development of the synagogue and the learning associated with it was a further result of this change. Learning as an act of piety and the development of the synagogue as a center of learning were for the most part independent phenomena. Cohen has made clear that synagogues, though they were places of learning, were not initially bulwarks of rabbinic learning alone and that we cannot speak of rabbis running synagogues between the second and sixth centuries A.D.[26]

If the centrality of education itself was a Hellenistic innovation among Jews, it seems to have taken root precisely within another innovation of the Hellenistic period, that of the synagogue. It was in the synagogues of this period that education in the Torah spread to all of the populace, while schools dedicated to children also started in the synagogues.[27] Education took place on the Sabbath primarily and, secondarily, it grounded schools of rabbinic learning for those wealthy enough to partake of it. Synagogues

23. Hengel, *Judaism and Hellenism,* 76.

24. Lieberman, *Greek in Jewish Palestine,* 20.

25. Shaye J. D. Cohen, "The Significance of Yavneh," *Hebrew Union College Annual* 55 (1984), 27–53.

26. Cohen, *From the Maccabees to the Mishnah,* 223.

27. Much scholarly literature occupies itself with the origin of the synagogue and whether it began in the Hellenistic or Exilic period. Yet here is not the place to revisit this discussion in detail. We are also certain that other institutions preceded the synagogues as gathering places for Jews in the Diaspora. For a short, substantive discussion, see Cohen, *From the Maccabees to the Mishnah,* 111–15; Levine, *The Ancient Synagogue,* 374–80; see also Anders Runesson, "The Origins of the Synagogue in Past and Present Research—Some Comments on Definitions, Theories, and Sources," *Studia Theologica* 57 (2003), 60–76, for a review of the basic data regarding the origins of synagogues. Runesson, however, does not consider the issue of synagogues functioning as schoolhouses for children.

are attested in the Gospels (for Palestine), and in Acts and the Pauline epistles (accounting for Asia Minor, Macedonia, Achaia, and Rome). Synagogues may have existed in the Diaspora perhaps since the third century B.C. Yet we also begin to hear about synagogues in the land of Judea and in Galilee in the first century A.D., both in the Gospels and Acts and in Josephus. A major focus of the synagogues in Judea and its environs was reading the Torah and studying the commandments.[28] The question arises whether this referred to the teaching of children as well. Cohen rejected the historicity of the tradition found in the Palestinian Talmud (*Ketuboth* 8:11, 32c, attributed to Simeon ben Shetah, first century B.C.) and in the Babylonian Talmud (*Baba Bathra* 21a, attributed to Yehoshua ben Gamala) that there was "compulsory education for all children."[29] There is no evidence of Jewish public schools in Judea or in the Diaspora, which has suggested to scholars that public education amounted to the reading, or probably more often the hearing, of Torah in synagogues.[30] For Cohen, "in all likelihood elementary education was the responsibility of the family. Wealthy (or ignorant!) people might hire a tutor for their children, but generally in the ancient world elementary education did not go beyond paternal education in a craft."[31] Thus the vast majority of people would have received whatever education they had in reading and writing or in the Torah in the synagogue. For most people this may have required some literacy, but it could also have been education transmitted primarily via oral means: listening, memorizing, and reciting.[32] Communal prayer and Scriptural study took place in synagogues; the Torah was not only read, but also explained and interpreted.[33] Children may have learned in this setting, yet the extent to which education in the synagogues was a formal one for children is not clear. Cohen cautioned that "advanced study, beyond the public reading and explication of the Torah every Sabbath in the synagogue was almost exclusively the prerogative of the wealthy and the privileged, since only they had the means and leisure . . . to pursue higher education instead

---

28. Cohen, *From the Maccabees to the Mishnah,* 112–13.

29. Ibid., 120.

30. Levine, *The Ancient Synagogue,* 376 and 378, argues that daily study was available in the synagogue and that wealthy and poor studied together.

31. Cohen, *From the Maccabees to the Mishnah,* 120.

32. See Birger Gerhardsson, *Memory and Manuscript: Oral Tradition and Written Transmission in Rabbinic Judaism and Early Christianity* (Lund: C. W. K. Gleerup, 1961; English edition, Grand Rapids, Mich.: Eerdmans, 1998), 59–66, on the essential and central role of memorization in Jewish education.

33. Cohen, *From the Maccabees to the Mishnah,* 72–73.

of trying to make a living."[34] We cannot assume that every child, even if he or she attended the synagogue regularly, would have become literate. Rabbinic schools were located in some synagogues, but very many schools were located in a rabbi's home or at some other site, especially as the rabbinic movement grew. While this education influenced the community greatly, it was never available to everyone, due to the inability to send a son or daughter to school. The rise of the rabbinic school system in the first or second century A.D. did not mean that the majority of peasant farmers or craftsmen could afford an education for their children at that time. On the basis of "the evidence of the Mishnah and other tannaitic corpora," Cohen observed that "most of the rabbis of the second century . . . were well-to-do landowners who lived in villages and small towns."[35] On the other hand, as the school system of the rabbis spread, it came to include the urban population and the poor,[36] but long after the rise of Christianity. Any formal education that Jesus or his apostles might have experienced as children would have taken place in villages and would have been available to those of a wealthy or landed class. The impact of the rabbinic school system on Christian education resided in inspiring the development of Christian schools in later years.

We do not know much about the rabbis of the first century,[37] but we do know that they had more in common with lay people than with priests, and belonged more to the artisan class than to the aristocracy. Although they were influenced by Greek learning, they would not necessarily have acknowledged it.[38] The rabbis' focus was on the Torah and education in the emerging oral traditions which would become known as the oral law, recorded in the discussions of the Mishnah, Tosefta, and Talmud.[39] Those who became rabbis certainly received an education, either from Greek tutors and schools or from the traditional scribal teaching of the priests or through a combination of both, and then they began to form schools. Bickerman argued that the formation of schools by a "Jewish intelligentsia," as

34. Ibid., 120.

35. Ibid., 222.

36. Ibid.; and Levine, *The Ancient Synagogue,* 378.

37. The relationship between the Pharisees and the rabbis is a difficult one to solve historically, but we follow Cohen, *From the Maccabees to the Mishnah,* 157, on this matter. For a fuller discussion, see Cohen, "The Significance of Yavneh."

38. Cohen, *From the Maccabees to the Mishnah,* 43; and Bickerman, *From Ezra to the Last of the Maccabees,* 162.

39. Bickerman, *From Ezra to the Last of the Maccabees,* 163, argues that education in the Torah led to interpretation, which necessarily led to the "oral law."

opposed to clergy who were dependent on the sanctuary, was the most significant Greek impact on education at this time.[40]

These schools can be characterized as having functioned according to the "master-disciple" type, a system in which a group of disciples followed a master, lived and ate with him, and learned from him at every step of the way.[41] The school may have ended with the master's death, and so perpetual institutions were not yet envisaged. We also do not know at what age students began to live with a master and follow him, but if this was to be the life of the disciple, it may be assumed that some of them at least came as boys and, certainly, as teenagers.[42] Indeed, the Mishnah sees boys as beginning their study of Scripture at the age of five and of Mishnah at ten (*m. Aboth* 5:21). Yet when exactly this was introduced is difficult to determine. In the first century, these private institutions did not have an authorizing or supervising body, but it is also clear that "schools" of thought began to emerge and certain teachers would have been sought out for their great learning and perhaps also for their connections. This may also have been the case with a rabbi like Gamaliel and the school in his "house." Noted for great learning, both Jewish and Greek, the school also came to be passed down in his family. Like any other profession, the skills were transmitted within the family, and the business, as such, was passed on to the children. While Cohen noted that as time marched forward "the rabbis triumphed over the indifference of the masses by gradually gaining control of the schools and the synagogues," he dated this no earlier than the seventh century.[43] In the interim, the rabbis competed for students with other teachers, increasingly determining the kind of education a Jew received not only in Palestine but also throughout the Jewish world.[44] One other aspect of education in Judaism, which was similar to what occurred in the Greco-Roman world, merely is to be mentioned without further discussion here.

40. Ibid., 67.

41. Cohen, *From the Maccabees to the Mishnah*, 121; and Gerhardsson, *Memory and Manuscript*, 57–59.

42. Lieberman, *Greek in Jewish Palestine*, 16, writes that R. Eliezer "was the son of a rich landowner. He joined the school of R. Johanan ben Zaccai when he was more than twenty years old. Prior to that he had been entirely ignorant of Jewish learning. It is possible he acquired his secular learning in his youth, while still at home." This tells us three things: that education was not usually started at this late date, but in one's childhood; that R. Eliezer was wealthy enough to pursue an education as a young man, a necessity for such a life; and that he nevertheless had received an education in secular learning before joining a rabbinic circle.

43. Cohen, *From the Maccabees to the Mishnah*, 221.

44. Hengel, *Judaism and Hellenism*, 59.

As with Greco-Roman schools, Jewish sources relay information regarding the beating of children by their teachers (*y. Mo'ed Qatan* 3.1, 81d).[45]

Education in the Gospel Record

This study has already examined the possible conclusions concerning the circumstances of Jesus' life as a child that derive from the data of the accounts of Jesus' birth and childhood. Information that impinges on any speculation on his education is limited to one statement, Luke 2:46–47. Yet Luke's account is a typical idealized story of a child prodigy,[46] not so different from accounts, for example of Cyrus in Xenophon's *Cyropaideia* or Apollonius in Philostratus' *Life of Apollonius of Tyana*.[47] Jesus' ability to sit with the teachers (*didaskaloi*), listen, and ask questions is miraculous exactly because one would not expect this from a boy (Lk 2:46). He amazed his adult audience because his wisdom surpassed his years (Lk 2:47) and was beyond whatever kind of education children would have received by then. As a result, it is not possible to use Luke's account to reconstruct Jesus' education, since any education he received ran counter to the point of the story. Nevertheless, there are some significant details which are to be brought to bear on the question of education in the course of this discussion. Luke, the learned Gentile, speaks of "teachers" at the Temple, without knowing well the actual situation in Palestine. More likely, these "teachers" were clergy, representing the locus of education in Judea: scholars of the Torah or members of the Sanhedrin, interpreting matters of the Torah. They may have been of the scribal or priestly caste and as such they may have been representatives of the Near Eastern model of the educated man as a wise man, a *ḥakam*.

As to other evidence of how the Gospel authors portrayed Jesus' education, we note that a couple of passages in the canonical Gospels suggest his ability to read and to write, even if his ability to do so was not the focus of any of these pericopes. In Luke 4:16, Jesus is said to have read in the synagogue; the parallels in Mark 6:1–6 and Matthew 13:53–58 do not mention that Jesus reads, but that he "teaches" (*didaskō*) in the synagogue (Mk 6:2; Mt 13:54; Lk 4:21), which may imply his ability to read. The numerous times

---

45. Levine, *The Ancient Synagogue*, 378–79.

46. Krückemeier, "Der Zwölfjährige Jesus."

47. For a translation of the *Cyropaideia*, see Wayne Ambler, trans., *Xenophon. The Education of Cyrus* (Ithaca, N.Y.: Cornell University Press, 2001). For a critical edition and translation of the text of Apollonius's story, see Christopher P. Jones, ed. and trans., *Philostratus. The Life of Apollonius of Tyana* (Cambridge, Mass.: Harvard University Press, 2005).

that Jesus rhetorically asks of the learned men of Judea "have you not read in . . ." suggests his own ability to read the texts he is citing or to which he is referring (Mk 2:25, 12:10, 12:26; Mt 12:3, 5, 19:4, 21:16, 42, 22:31; and Lk 6:3, 10:26). As far as Jesus' writing ability is concerned, one can find only one passage, in the Gospel of John. Jesus writes with his finger on the ground, twice, for a purpose that remains unclear (Jn 8:6, 8).[48] All in all, this evidence does not further much the efforts at reconstructing education in first-century Palestine, even though it does allow us to approach the presentation of Jesus in the Gospels through the lens of ancient literacy.

Apocryphal early Christian traditions from post-apostolic times believed in the existence of a letter that Jesus wrote to King Abgar of Edessa. In his *Church History,* Eusebius of Caesarea reported that, when he was writing in the early fourth century, the letter was still being kept in the city's archives.[49] While this evidence is central to determining the belief of early fourth-century Christians regarding Jesus' literacy, it has little value for establishing Jesus' actual literacy in first-century Palestine.[50]

Jesus' Education according to the *Infancy Gospel of Thomas*

One text does consider Jesus' education in the context of the type of "village teacher" mentioned above. The *Infancy Gospel of Thomas* speaks of Jesus' education while a boy in Nazareth.[51] While we make no claims

48. This account is not found in the earliest manuscripts, but it represents an early stream of tradition, which in an offhand way assumes Jesus' literacy. Pheme Perkins, "The Gospel according to John," in *The New Jerome Biblical Commentary,* 942–85, here 949, states that "this story is more in the style of the Synoptics than of the Fourth Gospel"; she also notes its similarity to Lukan traditions about Jesus (965).

49. Eusebius of Caesarea, *Church History* 1.13.5–11 (ed. Schwartz, Mommsen, and Winkelmann, *Eusebius Werke, Zweiter Band, Erster Teil, Die Kirchengeschichte,* GCS N. F. vol. 6.1, 84–88; also ed. Kirsopp Lake, *Eusebius. The Ecclesiastical History,* LCL 153 [Cambridge, Mass.: Harvard University Press, 1926], vol. 1, 86, ll. 5–11; trans. Williamson, *Eusebius: The History of the Church from Christ to Constantine,* 31).

50. For some consideration of the status of literacy at the time, see, for example, Alan Millard, "Literacy in the time of Jesus: Could his words have been recorded in his lifetime?" *Biblical Archaeology Review* 29.4 (2003), 36–45.

51. Unless otherwise noted, all translations from the *Infancy Gospel of Thomas* in the following discussion are taken from David R. Cartlidge and David L. Dungan, *Documents for the Study of the Gospels* (London: Collins, 1980). For an important study of the textual history of the *Infancy Gospel of Thomas,* see Stephen Gerö, "Infancy Gospel of Thomas: A Study of the Textual and Literary Problems," *Novum Testamentum* 13.1 (1971), 46–80. More recently, see the work by Tony Chartrand-Burke: "The Infancy Gospel of Thomas"; "The Greek Manuscript Tradition of the Infancy Gospel of Thomas," *Apocrypha* 14 (2004), 129–51; and "Authorship and Identity in the Infancy Gospel of Thomas," *Toronto Journal of Theology* 14.1 (1998), 27–43.

regarding the historicity of this text and clearly acknowledge the rhetorical function of this typical encomiastic element of ancient biography, the comments in the text allow us to examine what second- and third-century Christians deemed reasonable to expect for a boy growing up in a Galilean village.[52] It offers a window into education from the second century on, yet less so into the life of Jesus of Nazareth.

According to the *Infancy Gospel of Thomas,* Jesus first had contact with a teacher as a boy around the age of five. The entire account is cast as having taken place when he was between the ages of five and twelve. A teacher by the name of Zacchaeus overheard Jesus make a wise remark and so asked his father, Joseph, if the boy might be allowed to receive an education under his auspices, since he was "a smart child, and . . . has a mind" (6:2). Zacchaeus offered to teach him his Greek letters, and also respect for his elders, both of which he began to do (6:2–3). Jesus, however, discerned that his teacher had no "inner" knowledge of the letters and challenged his understanding (6:3–4). Eventually the teacher was unable to answer Jesus and begged that the boy be taken away from him, as he was not "earthborn. . . . Perhaps he was begotten before the world's creation" (7:2). Zacchaeus was confused: he had sought a pupil and disciple, but had become a student; he had sought to teach, but learned the limit of his knowledge; he was an old man, but had been "conquered" by a child (7:2–3).[53] The same impression one carries away from the story of Jesus' foray into the Temple as a twelve-year-old, one also gains here: Jesus knows more than the teachers. Indeed, the material covered in the Lukan account ends this infancy Gospel and the whole text may be seen as having been written to fill in the blanks left by the infancy narratives of Luke and Matthew and the Temple story told by Luke.[54]

52. See Hock, *The Infancy Gospels of James and Thomas,* 84–85, for a general introduction and the dating of the text. The text is clearly written in Greek and the author does not show great knowledge of Judaism (91); even the lessons, in Greek, seem to be based on a Greco-Roman model (102, 113, and 119), but village teaching was a possibility (113, note on 6:2) and there is no reason to doubt the basic possibility of such teaching in a Jewish setting, as we discussed above. In the second century, Irenaeus of Lyons reflects some acquaintance with traditions contained in the text, yet the form of the text as we have it is the product of subsequent centuries, at times dated to the sixth century. Manuscript evidence is even later than that. See also Oscar Cullmann, "Kindheitsevangelien," in *Neutestamentliche Apokryphen in deutscher Übersetzung,* vol. 1: *Evangelien,* eds. Edgar Hennecke and Wilhelm Schneemelcher (Tübingen: Mohr-Siebeck, 1987), 330–72, here 349–53.

53. Brian McNeil, "Jesus and the Alphabet," *JThS* 27 (1976), 126–28, here 128, stated that the "schoolmaster is baffled, not simply because of the superior learning of his pupil, but rather because his 'pupil' is of a quite different order of being."

54. It does more than filling in the blanks, but it does do that as well. Oscar Cullmann,

The second attempt at educating the young boy took place some time later and on this occasion Joseph wished to find a teacher for Jesus since he did not want his growing boy to be ignorant of his letters (14:1). Jesus is presented as having been past six years of age (11:1), and thus as reaching the proper age for education, at least according to Greco-Roman standards. This time the teacher decided to give him instruction in Greek first and then in Hebrew. Yet as he taught, Jesus never answered (14:1). Instead, Jesus challenged his new teacher with the request that he should explain to him "Alpha," the first letter of the Greek alphabet—"if you really are a teacher"—and in his anger the teacher hit Jesus on the head (14:2). In response, Jesus cursed him and the teacher fainted (14:3). A third teacher who was trying his luck on the boy was a friend of Joseph's and Joseph was reluctant to have his friend take Jesus on as a student (15:1). Yet Jesus entered the school, picked up a book, and began not to read—"he did not read the letters in it"—but to teach by the Holy Spirit (15:2). In this "foreshadowing" of Luke 4:16–30 and Jesus' teaching in the synagogue, Jesus astounded and amazed the crowd that gathered to hear him (15:2). Joseph, however, became frightened when he heard about it and ran to find out what the cause of the commotion was, "wondering whether this teacher was also without skill" (15:3). Finally this third teacher recognized Jesus' ability and said to Joseph, "Know, brother, that I took this child as a disciple, but he is full of much grace and wisdom, and I beg you brother, take him into your house" (15:3).

How does one educate the Son of God? The answer provided in the *Infancy Gospel of Thomas* is clear: one does not. Yet, the village picture of the old teacher ("I am an old man": 7:3), of the age of learning (14:1), of learning the alphabet first (6:2; 14:1), of physical punishment in response to an unruly student (the teacher "hit Jesus on the head": 14:2), and even of the reality of village teachers who take a "disciple" into their home (15:3) all resonate with what we know of education during this period. Questions that arise from a review of the data are whether the portraits also conform to what we know about first century A.D. Jewish education or that of the second century, whether the focus on teaching Greek may indicate a Greco-Roman educational context, and whether the model of the age of education as well as the presence of the disciple in the home of the master

---

"Infancy Gospels," in *New Testament Apocrypha*, vol. 1, *Gospels and Related Writings*, ed. Wilhelm Schneemelcher, trans. R. McL. Wilson (Tübingen: Mohr-Siebeck, 1959; English translation: Philadelphia: Westminster Press, 1963), 363–69, here 363–64, also detects Gnostic themes of the revealer who does not need to learn or grow in wisdom as Luke states in 2:40.

indicate a Jewish or Greco-Roman education. It is difficult if not impossible to come to a definitive description of these aspects of Jewish education in this period. One suspects that the nature of education at the basic elementary level in a Jewish village did not change much from the first to the second or even subsequent centuries. Although a shift may have come with the development of rabbinic schools, such a form of education is not in view here. The focus on Greek does not necessarily rule out a Jewish education, as Hengel, Bickerman, Lieberman, and Cohen have made clear. Nevertheless, one may assume that a village education began with Hebrew and the Torah. In the *Infancy Gospel of Thomas* Joseph takes his son to the local teacher. This may indicate the reality for most men of this time: although the responsibility of education was placed upon the father, most would have allowed others to fulfill this duty for them. Finally, one can say that teachers and small village schools were available to those of a certain economic class. Jesus may have fit into such a class,[55] and probably the picture of the village teacher would not have changed much if at all from the first to the second century.

Jesus' Apostles and Disciples

Some of those who gathered around Jesus in the first century also may have had a village education and been able to read and write. Peter and John are described as "uneducated and common" *(agrammatoi* and *idiōtai)* (Acts 4:13), although they did not necessarily come from a class without any learning. Raymond Brown argued that the author of Acts intended to portray the apostles only as "unlettered," not as "illiterate."[56] Santiago Gui-

---

55. Jesus' social class has been a focal point for some recent research and reevaluation. The longstanding portrayal of Jesus as a poor peasant has been subject to revision. Albright and Mann, *Matthew*, 172–73, noted that the word *tektōn* used to describe Joseph in Matthew 13:55 "generally indicates a craftsman of considerable skill" (172). They concluded that Joseph was not "the simple—and poor—village carpenter," but "a builder of some consequence" (173). Reed, *Archaeology and the Galilean Jesus*, 136–37, however, still places Jesus among "the lower classes" and surmises that he does not visit Sepphoris or Tiberias due to comfort among the lower classes and not the wealthy of the city. Richard L. Rohrbaugh, "Ethnocentrism and Historical Questions about Jesus," in *The Social Setting of Jesus and the Gospels* (Minneapolis: Fortress Press, 2002), 27–43, here 36–37, placed Jesus among the "lowest-status persons" in his social and historical context. On the other hand, Tor Vegge, "The Literacy of Jesus the Carpenter's Son," *Studia Theologica* 59 (2005), 19–37, here 31, concluded that the "literary style of the teaching in the gospels" presupposes an elite education. Yet Rainer Riesner, *Jesus als Lehrer* (Tübingen: Mohr-Siebeck, 1988), 206–45, claimed that Jesus probably had only an elementary education.

56. Raymond Brown, *An Introduction to the New Testament* (New York: Doubleday, 1997), 291.

jarro stressed that Simon, Andrew, James, and John came from families with backgrounds that were not among the aristocratic or wealthy classes, but that were not among the peasant classes either. Like Jesus, they came from the artisan class.[57] Members of this social stratum were able to afford a basic education with a village scribe. The tax collector Levi, who became one of Jesus' apostles (Mk 2:14–17; Lk 5:27–33; in Mt 9:9–13 the tax collector is "Matthew"), probably had a more than basic level of education.

The teacher-disciple relationship between Jesus and his apostles offers reason to consider the age of Jesus' disciples. Students—Greek, Roman, or Jewish—tended to follow a teacher in their teenage years. Jesus is portrayed as having called them from their families and their vocations to follow him and he became their "father," as was common in rabbinic circles.[58] It seems likely that many of these disciples were of a young age and that Pharisaic opposition to Jesus partly came from his influence as a teacher of the young.[59] That Jesus did not have an education as a rabbi is of little concern. As Cohen has demonstrated, rabbinic, or Pharisaic, learning had not become dominant in the first century. A teacher who could attract students could teach them, although not all would be pleased with what he had to teach.

Jesus' proclamation is presented as having been accompanied by constant teaching, especially in the form of parables, for those who gathered around him. These were young men and women whose desire for a deeper education was preceded by at least some form of education and a quest for further study. The age of disciples who were following a thirty-year-old

---

57. Santiago Guijarro, "The Family in First-Century Galilee," in *Constructing Early Christian Families*, 42–65, here 60.

58. Cohen, *From the Maccabees to the Mishnah*, 122.

59. In support of this one may note that apart from information about Peter, we have no clear indication that any of the apostles were married, a step in life that generally took place at a young age. One also notes that it was young people who were able to follow a teacher, and that it was at a young age when students gathered around a master. That it was "Pharisaic" opposition may be a statement open to modification, yet much of the Pharisees' questioning of Jesus has to do with how he taught his disciples. They were less interested in questioning him directly. See, e.g., Matthew 9:11 ("Why does your teacher eat with tax collectors and sinners?"), 12:2 ("Your disciples are doing what is not lawful on the Sabbath"), 15:2 ("Why do your disciples break the tradition of the elders?"), 15:12; Mark 2:18–28, 7:2–5 (eating with defiled hands); Luke 5:30, 6:1–11; and John 4:1–2. Adrian Destro and Mauro Pesce, "Fathers and Householders in the Jesus Movement: The Perspective of the Gospel of Luke," *Biblical Interpretation* 11.2 (2003), 211–38, here 211, 216–19, and 222, noted the absence of fathers from Jesus' following, but claimed that the disciples do not belong to the group either of *paides* or of *neaniskoi*. We have not been able to determine why the authors came to this judgment.

master (Lk 3:23) would have been similar to that generally found in a circle of disciples throughout Judaism, particularly in the case of teenagers with the means to accompany a charismatic teacher. Jesus' role as a teacher is highlighted in all of the Gospels,[60] and to ignore this aspect is to overlook a major part of the Gospel record. The apostles and other disciples of Jesus are presented as having been educated by him directly. They attended, in a way, a formal Jewish school, namely that of the house of Jesus. The subject matter of their learning was constant: the Law and the Prophets; the coming Kingdom of God; and the role of their teacher in that coming Kingdom. This kind of education was a formal Jewish education in the first century. It did risk attracting the wrath of established schools, such as those based in or stemming from other Jewish groups, either from the Temple or from among the Pharisees.[61] In structure, Jesus' curriculum was not different from theirs, although his answers may not have been accepted by those schools. Given Jesus' lack of the traditional training of the *ḥakam,* Jesus' authority to teach is presented in the Gospels as having been challenged by those labeled as his "opponents." To be sure, there are elements of Jesus' interpretation of Torah that would have resonated with certain groups. His claim that he was the Messiah would have overshadowed any common ground in matters of Jewish legal interpretation.

Paul's Education

The Apostle Paul is a unique case in the New Testament, since according to the portrayal offered in Acts, he had received a rabbinic education

60. For studies of the portrayal of Jesus as teacher, see for example Samuel Byrskog, "Jesus as Messiah Teacher in the Gospel according to Matthew: Tradition History and/or Narrative Christology," in *The New Testament as Reception,* eds. Morgens Müller and Henrik Tronier (London: Sheffield Academic Press, 2002), 83–100; Herman Harrell Horne and Angus M. Gunn, *Jesus the Teacher: Examining His Expertise in Education* (Grand Rapids, Mich.: Kregel Publications, 1998); Marie Noël Keller, "Jesus the Teacher," *Currents in Theology and Mission* 25 (1998), 450–60; Gregory J. Riley, "Words and Deeds: Jesus as Teacher and Jesus as Pattern of Life," *Harvard Theological Review* 90 (1997), 427–36; and Perry W. H. Shaw, "Jesus: Oriental Teacher Par Excellence," *Christian Education Journal* 1.1 (1997), 83–94.

61. One finds relatively wide acknowledgment that teachers of the Law and scribes were trained in schools associated with the Temple; this was the pattern in the ancient Near East as a whole. The innovation was that the Pharisees brought education away from the Temple or from Jerusalem as such to the people and the countryside. Hengel, *Judaism and Hellenism,* 78–83, argues that "from pre-exilic times, there were certainly scribal schools in the temple and probably elsewhere in the country which served primarily to instruct suitable priests and Levites" (78). See also Bickerman, *From Ezra to the Last of the Maccabees,* 67–71, on the transition from schools "for future office-holders" (scribes and priests) to "the formation of a Jewish intelligentsia, different from the clergy and not dependent on the sanctuary" (67).

with Gamaliel (Acts 22:3), a teacher of the very house in which both Greek and Hebrew learning took place.[62] Whether Paul was raised primarily in Jerusalem or in Tarsus is of little concern for his primary education, as he could have received a Greek education through tutors or otherwise in Jerusalem.[63] He himself and the author of Acts stressed that his Jewish education was Pharisaic and that it took place in Jerusalem (Phil 3:5; Acts 23:6; 26:4–5). Paul was not shy about the quality of his education, stating that he had "advanced in Judaism beyond many among [his] people of the same age" (Gal 1:14). Such a comment indicates both Paul's ability and the wealth of his family, for to advance in education meant that the family was able to allow him the time and opportunity to study.

Paul's own writings show knowledge of Greek rhetorical techniques and some knowledge of Greco-Roman philosophical teachings,[64] both of which

---

62. There have been challenges to the historicity of Paul's education with Gamaliel, such as John Knox, *Chapters in a Life of Paul* (Nashville: Abingdon Press, 1950), ch. 2, but Knox makes the mistake of opposing "Hellenistic" to "Jewish" education. Paul certainly was well educated in Judaism, as his own words attest (Phil 3:5–6; Gal 1:14) and there is no reason to doubt that he received an education from Gamaliel. See also Calvin Roetzel, *The Letters of Paul: Conversations in Context* (Louisville, Ky.: Westminster John Knox Press, 1998), 36–44, who surveys his education, not his learning with Gamaliel as such.

63. W. C. van Unnik, "Tarsus or Jerusalem: The City of Paul's Youth," in *Sparsa Collecta*, vol. 1 (Leiden: E. J. Brill, 1973), 259–320; van Unnik, "Once Again: Tarsus or Jerusalem?" in *Sparsa Collecta*, vol. 1, 321–27; and Andreas B. Du Toit, "A Tale of Two Cities: 'Tarsus or Jerusalem' Revisited," *New Testament Studies* 46.3 (2000), 375–402.

64. For studies of different aspects of Paul's engagement with ancient rhetoric and philosophy, see Fredrick J. Long, *Ancient Rhetoric and Paul's Apology: The Compositional Unity of 2 Corinthians* (Cambridge: Cambridge University Press, 2004); Mark Douglas Given, *Paul's True Rhetoric: Ambiguity, Cunning, and Deception in Greece and Rome* (Harrisburg, Pa.: Trinity Press International, 2001); Troels Engberg-Pederson, *Paul and the Stoics* (Louisville, Ky.: Westminster John Knox Press, 2000); Dieter Kremendahl, *Die Botschaft der Form: Zum Verhältnis von antiker Epistolographie und Rhetorik im Galaterbrief* (Freiburg: Universitätsverlag, 2000); N. Clayton Croy, "Hellenistic Philosophies and the Preaching of the Resurrection (Acts 17:18, 32)," *Novum Testamentum* 39 (1997), 21–39; L. L. Welborn, *Politics and Rhetoric in the Corinthian Epistles* (Macon, Ga.: Mercer University Press, 1997); Bruce W. Winter, *Philo and Paul among the Sophists: Alexandrian and Corinthian Responses to a Julio-Claudian Movement* (Cambridge: Cambridge University Press, 1997; 2nd ed., Grand Rapids, Mich.: Eerdmans, 2002); R. Dean Anderson, *Ancient Rhetorical Theory and Paul* (Kampen, Netherlands: Kok Pharos, 1996); Mark D. Given, "The Unknown Paul: Philosophers and Sophists in Acts 17," *Society of Biblical Literature Seminar Papers* 35 (1996), 343–51; Marty L. Reid, *Augustinian and Pauline Rhetoric in Romans Five: A Study of Early Christian Rhetoric* (Lewiston, N.Y.: Mellen Biblical Press, 1996); Troels Engberg-Pederson, ed., *Paul in His Hellenistic Context* (Minneapolis: Fortress Press, 1995); Bruce W. Winter, "Is Paul among the Sophists," *Reformed Theological Review* 53 (1994), 28–38; Litfin A. Duane, *St. Paul's Theology of Proclamation: 1 Corinthians 1–4 and Greco-Roman Rhetoric* (Cambridge: Cambridge University Press, 1994); Abraham J. Malherbe, *Paul and the Popular*

suggest a Greco-Roman education at the secondary level. His vast knowledge of the Torah and oral Law relays his Pharisaic training. Of course, Paul also learned of the traditions of the Christians, but by that time he was an adult and we can no longer consider it the teaching of children. Whether the earliest teaching of the Church made explicit provisions for the teaching of children is difficult to determine, as no data support, for instance, the teaching of children in Antioch in the first century (Acts 13:1) or in Ephesus (Acts 19:9–10) where Paul was noted as a teacher.

Education in the Early Church

Since the focus of the New Testament texts is on adult members of the faith, little is known about how children were educated. In a given congregation, at least some would have been able to read and write, but during the early decades of the Church's history many children would have gained this education prior to becoming Christians.

Ephesians 6:1–4 instructs parents to bring their children (*tekna*) up in the instruction (*paideia* and *nouthesia*) of the Lord. This *paideia* implies some sort of formal education. We cannot expect that at this early stage it necessarily implied all of what *paideia* meant in a Greco-Roman or Jewish setting, that is, a full education in the liberal arts. In numerous passages Philo of Alexandria outlined all of what *paideia* could involve. His description takes us from an elementary stage of learning all the way to adolescence.[65] Philo accepted that such learning consisted of writing and reading initially (*Som.* 1.205), moving through knowledge of poets and history, and eventually moving on to grammatical and rhetorical knowledge (*Cong.* 148). Included in such study, ideally, were rhetoric, dialectic, geometry, arithmetic, music, and astronomy.[66] What holds with respect to Jewish education in Palestine, however, also is found in the Diaspora, even in a city as noted for learning as Alexandria. Such an education was available only to a "small proportion of the Jewish population" and Philo had in mind "only men of the Jewish upper classes," as Alan Mendelson argued.[67] Not

---

Philosophers (Minneapolis: Fortress Press, 1989); Christopher Forbes, "Comparison, Self-Praise and Irony: Paul's Boasting and the Conventions of Hellenistic Rhetoric," *New Testament Studies* 32.1 (1986), 1–30; Stanley K. Stowers, "Social Status, Public Speaking and Private Teaching: The Circumstances of Paul's Preaching Activity," *Novum Testamentum* 26 (1984), 59–82; Abraham J. Malherbe, "Exhortation in First Thessalonians," *Novum Testamentum* 25 (1983), 238–56; and Jan Nicolaas Sevenster, *Paul and Seneca* (Leiden: E. J. Brill, 1961).

65. Mendelson, *Secular Education in Philo of Alexandria*, 1–16.

66. Ibid., 6–16.   67. Ibid., 26–27.

only could the poorer Jews not afford such an education, they often did not approve of the *gymnasium* due to its connections to Greek and Roman gods.[68] Philo and those of his class nevertheless participated in the *gymnasium* (*Provid.* 58; *Prob.* 26, 141).

Yet this was not all of the *paideia* that was available to a faithful Jew like Philo. Rather, "Philo's knowledge of Scripture, Jewish custom and law speaks eloquently for the existence of an effective system of religious learning."[69] As in Palestine, it seems that a basic religious education was offered through synagogues (*Spec.* 2.62; *Mos.* 2.216; *Opif.* 128) and that many could participate in this education (*Spec.* 2.62; *Hypoth.* 7.11–13). Paul himself seems to indicate the teaching function of the synagogues, and perhaps of Jewish schools in general, when he sarcastically speaks of their role as "teacher of infants" *(didaskalon nēpiōn)* (Rom 2:20). As in Palestine, the teaching of children was one of the roles of the Diaspora synagogue as well. Education in the synagogue schools was education in Scripture. The "Christian instruction" envisioned by Ephesians probably was of the same kind. This letter in the Pauline tradition indicates that parents were given the primary task of educating their children, but the churches probably had started to provide this instruction as well. In fact, the burden placed on the parents to provide an education may only have meant that they brought their children to receive an education, not that they supplied it.

The context sketched out thus far may give us some sense of the situation in 2 Timothy. Timothy was raised with "Sacred Scriptures" "from infancy" *(apo brephous)* (2 Tm 3:14–15). Philo had stated that education in Judaism was acquired "from the cradle" (*Legat.* 115 and *Spec. Leg.* 4.149–150), and Paul suggested that a similar phenomenon was facilitated in the synagogues (Rom 2:20).[70] Timothy was to "remain" steadfast in what he

---

68. Ibid., 31.   69. Ibid., 26.

70. For consideration of this passage in the literature, see Arthur F. Katt, "From a child thou hast known the Holy Scriptures (2 Tim 3:15)," *Concordia Theological Monthly* 25 (1954), 766–73; Robert L. Wilken, "Christian Formation in the Early Church," in *Educating People of Faith: Exploring the History of Christian and Jewish Communities* (Grand Rapids, Mich.: Eerdmans, 2004), 48–62; Pio G. Alves de Sousa, "La familia cristiana en los escritos de los padres apostólicos," in *Cuestiones fundamentales sobre matrimonio y familia* (Pamplona, Spain: Ediciones Universidad de Navarra, 1980), 557–66; and Blake Leyerle, "Appealing to Children," *Journal of Early Christian Studies* 5 (1997), 243–70. The order of the texts of Scripture to be read by children shows close parallels to Jewish practices. See Michael Gärtner, *Die Familienerziehung in der Alten Kirche. Eine Untersuchung über die ersten vier Jahrhunderte des Christentums mit einer Übersetzung und einem Kommentar zu der Schrift des Johannes Chrysostomus über die Geltungssucht und Kindererziehung* (Cologne: Böhlau Verlag, 1985), 118.

had learned, as the Scriptures were able to "instruct" him to salvation in Jesus Christ. According to the letter's author, Scripture was for "teaching" (*didaskalia*) and "education" (*paideia*) (2 Tm 3:16). This very likely comprised education acquired both at home and at church, as Timothy is encouraged to move forward in the teaching and education of others. Paul himself placed the office of teacher right behind that of apostle and prophet (1 Cor 12:28). Throughout the Pastoral Epistles, teaching is seen as a key element of the minister's task, for Paul (1 Tm 2:7; 2 Tm 1:11), Timothy (2 Tm 2:24), and every bishop (1 Tm 3:2).

This teaching included adults and children. When parents could not accomplish it, the task of educating children in the Scriptures rested with synagogues, and the equivalent would have been the case for Christian parents coming from Jewish backgrounds as well. For most children, it may have been the only formal education they received. It probably consisted of basic literacy, but certainly of the memorization and recitation of passages from Scripture.[71] The previous chapter has already considered the passage from 1 John that spoke of the education of children (*teknia* and *paidia*) and young men (*neaniskoi*) (1 John 2:12–14). With respect to children, this education in the faith seems to have been one of the major tasks of the early Church.

The importance of teaching is noted in Titus 1:11. The Pastoral Epistles in general associate the orderliness of children with their Christian faith. Titus 1:10–11 states that "whole households" were upset by improper teaching on the part of some from the "circumcision," a reference either to members of the Jewish community or to those Jewish Christian authorities who insisted that observance of key elements of Torah were essential for all Christians. How exactly these teachers were related to the Church or to the families is not clear.[72] The claim, however, that their teaching was undertaken for "base gain" (*aischros*) would indicate teaching for financial gain.[73] It is unlikely that this referred to teaching on an elementary level,

71. Gerhardsson, *Memory and Manuscript,* 59–66, 288–323, and 326–35.

72. In the previous chapter we noted that those who engaged in this teaching were described in Titus 1:10 as *anypotaktoi,* or "unsubmissive." This seems to link them somehow to the Christian Church, for those outside of the Church could not well be described as "submissive" or "unsubmissive" to the authority of the Church. We considered above that these teachers may be the "unsubmissive" children of these households. Yet the "unsubmissive" teachers could also be the origin of "unsubmissive" children.

73. Bruce W. Winter, *Philo and Paul among the Sophists: Alexandrian and Corinthian Responses to a Julio-Claudian Movement* (Cambridge: Cambridge University Press, 1997; 2nd ed., Grand Rapids, Mich.: Eerdmans, 2002), 164–69 and 228–29.

that of basic literacy and the memorizing of passages of the Bible (or of the oral Gospel tradition). Rather, it probably involved teaching that engaged in the interpretation of Scripture or philosophy at a level that put the students at odds with the Church and their families. At the least it was teaching teenagers, those old enough to benefit from a higher level of teaching and bold enough to "upset" their parents' and the Church's teaching and understanding. Such was the risk of education, as the early Christian faithful also could have learned from the model offered of Jesus' warning his followers that his teaching would lead to divisions in families (Mt 10:34–36; Lk 12:51–53). By this time, however, it seems that it was teaching that was opposed to that of the Church that threatened relationships in Christian families.

Raising and Educating Children as Parental Obligation

Education was a function of the family, both having its locus in the family dwelling and insofar as parents brought their children to the gatherings of the Christian community. Education in the Scriptures was at the heart of such an approach, as it was in Judaism. The Pastoral Epistles envision a love for children as one of the qualities of Christian women, young mothers in particular. According to Titus 2:4, older women in the community were to instruct the young women in how to become "friends of children" or "lovers of children" *(philoteknous)* themselves. At least in the eyes of some early Christians, several passages in the Pastoral Epistles closely connected the task of bearing, raising, and educating children with the lives of women. In 1 Timothy 5:14, young widows were encouraged not only to remarry and lead a household, but also to bear children *(teknogonein)*. A case that was understood as illustrating both childbearing and child-raising is 1 Timothy 2:15.

In the course of giving instructions to women, the household codes in 1 Timothy 2:15 state that "[a woman] will be saved [*sōthēsetai*] through the bearing of children [*dia tēs teknogonias*], if they remain [*meinōsin*] in faith, love and holiness with self-discipline." One of the difficulties in interpreting this verse is the shift in person in the two verbs from singular to plural. While the subject of *sōthēsetai* can be established more easily as "woman," spoken of earlier on in the passage in verses 11 and 12,[74] the referent of

74. Within the narrative scope of 1 Timothy 2:11–15, the most likely candidate for the position of subject of *sōthēsetai* in 2:15 is *gynē* from 2:11, appearing again, yet in the position of

the plural *meinōsin* is not quite as obvious. Although modern exegetes either assume that one ought to understand "parents" or more often "women" as subject of *meinōsin*,[75] Jerome and John Chrysostom readily supplied "children," thus assuming that the children were the ones who were called upon to remain and live their lives in faith, love, and holiness. At least one other modern exegete is willing to join these two ancient authors in their interpretation.[76]

When hearing that women were to be saved through bearing children, an early Christian audience may have recalled another instance in the Pentateuch where a connection was established between women and childbirth. Genesis 3:16 (LXX) would ring familiar, but there the woman *(tēi gynaiki)* was told that, because she had to leave paradise, giving birth would be accompanied by groans *(en lypais texēi tekna)*. To the extent that Genesis and 1 Timothy 2 share a reference to "children" and "giving birth," some readers of 1 Timothy 2 may have seen a reversal or reinterpretation of the condemnatory character of the pains of childbirth into a sign of blessing. Moreover, the plural *tekna* in Gen 3:16 (LXX) could have facilitated a process on the readers' part of assuming that the noun *teknogonia* in 1 Timothy 2:15 already contained the plural *tekna* as the subject of *meinōsin*.[77] Having Christian children whose lives embodied key Christian virtues could have been seen as the reversal of Adam and Eve's expulsion from paradise.[78]

Once children were born, they needed to be raised as Christians. A concern for the Christian education of children arose quite clearly in the household code of Ephesians 6, building upon the household code in Co-

---

object in the dative as *gynaiki* in verse 12. When Eve and *hē gynē* are used as mutually explanatory terms in verses 13 and 14, the author employs *hē gynē* to establish Eve as a representative example of *gynē* in verses 11 and 12, thus intending to further characterize *gynē*, not Eve.

75. See, for example, Stanley E. Porter, "What Does It Mean to Be 'Saved by Childbirth' (1 Timothy 2:15)," *Journal for the Study of the New Testament* 49 (1993), 87–102, here 98–99.

76. Jerome, *Letters* 107.6 (ed. Hilberg, *Sancti Eusebii Hieronymi Epistulae*, CSEL 55, 297); John Chrysostom, *On Vainglory* 19 (ed. and trans. Malingrey, *Jean Chrysostome. Sur la vaine gloire et l'éducation des enfants*, 102–3). See also ibid., 102, n. 3; and Anne-Marie Malingrey, "Note sur l'exegèse de 1 Tim 2,15," *Studia Patristica* 12 (1975), 334–39; and Jarl Henning Ulrichsen, "Noen bemerkninger til 1 Tim 2:15," *Norsk teologisk tidsskrift* 84 (1983), 19–25.

77. Whether or not the Greek *teknogonia* contains the singular *teknon* or the plural *tekna* cannot be determined on the basis of the singular of "child" as a compound in "childbirth." German, for example, renders the Greek noun by employing the expression "Kindergebären," a noun, the first compound of which, "Kinder," is in the plural.

78. For slightly later discussions that connect the sin of Adam and Eve and childbearing, see also David G. Hunter, "On the sin of Adam and Eve: A little known defence of marriage and childbearing in Ambrosiaster," *Harvard Theological Review* 82 (1989), 283–99.

lossians 3.[79] Having spoken of the obligations of wives and husbands in 3:18–19, in verse 20 the author of Colossians turned to the behavior expected of children *(ta tekna)* and exhorted them to "be obedient to [their] parents [*hypokouete tois goneusin*] in everything, since this is pleasing to the Lord." Immediately following, the author warned fathers not to provoke their children, so that they would not lose courage. Ephesians 6:1–4 resumes the basic, two-part structure of Colossians 3:20–21, while at the same time expanding it, in verses 2–3, through inclusion of the fourth commandment (Ex 20:12; par. Dt 5:16). This is the requirement of children to honor their father and their mother so that they may receive blessings in the land, which the author observed was "the first commandment [made] with a promise" (Eph 6:2). The author of Ephesians placed remarkable emphasis on the key virtue and guarantor of right relationships in the family and household: respect by dependents and those who were younger in age for those who were in authority and older.

A second significant change from the text of Colossians 3 occurs in Ephesians 6:4.[80] Here fathers were instructed not to provoke their children *(tekna)* to anger. Compared to Colossians, this seems to raise the bar for what fathers might have been able to get away with. The authority with which fathers are shown to have been invested receives additional support when they are told to bring up *(ektrephete)* their children "in the discipline and instruction of the Lord *(en paideiāi kai nouthesiāi kyriou)*." While *tekna* as a noun is not necessarily limited to designating only young children, and Colossians more clearly had in view children of all ages within a family, the choice of the verb *ektrephein* in Ephesians 6:4, which literally means "to nourish," makes it likely that the author had young children in view. Thus that verse gives advice on how to raise little ones. The statement in verse 4, which speaks of "the discipline and instruction of the Lord," is multidimensional in at least two senses. At the time of the composition of Ephesians, at the end of the first century, *paideia* was to be read in the same way in which it was used in the Septuagint, carrying the double meaning

---

79. For studies of aspects of the household codes in the New Testament see, for example, James D. G. Dunn, "The Household Rules in the New Testament," in *The Family in Theological Perspective* (Edinburgh: T&T Clark, 1996), 43–63, with the literature cited therein; and David L. Balch, *Let Wives Be Submissive: The Domestic Code in 1 Peter* (Chico, Calif.: Scholars Press, 1981). For considerations of later early Christian ideas, see also N. V. Harrison, "Raising them right: Early Christian approaches to child rearing," *Theology Today* 56 (2000), 481–94.

80. For a helpful and brief discussion of the relationship between the two letters, see Mac-Donald, *Colossians and Ephesians,* 4–6.

of shaping human nature through education of body, mind, and spirit, as well as of correcting and disciplining any faults in this process. This idea is complemented in Ephesians 6:4 by the noun *nouthesia,* describing the activity of counseling a person with words in order to evoke change through the stimulation of the mind *(nous).*[81]

A second level of meaning in verse 4 can be discerned. It lays emphasis on the father's obligation to educate and instruct his children and at the same time, by introducing a reference to "the Lord [*kyriou*]," it provides a more comprehensive or more forceful authority as source and as grounding of a Christian education of children. Both father and children are made dependent upon "the Lord" and both have the obligation to be informed about and to be instructed in God's teachings.[82]

If one compares the overall tone of educational advice in the deutero-Pauline letters with other instructions for parents on how to educate their children that were circulating in the larger Hellenistic-Jewish world, the Pastoral Epistles are situated somewhere between a strict, disciplinarian attitude that emphasized physical punishment as the tool of choice in education, and a softer style of education that hoped to achieve its goal of raising proper children quite exclusively through words and kind gestures. The parents', especially the father's, authority was recognized, yet guidance was provided so that those responsible for the child's actions would themselves exercise restraint, not let their own anger take over, and not provoke the children in their care to anger either.[83]

Early Christianity gave rise to a pervasive understanding of education. The Christian idea of *paideia* envisioned the formation of the human person as a process that is directed toward the ultimate goal of human life, the state of being in a right relationship with God through Christ, a goal defined by the tension between the "fear of God" and the hope of *theopoiēsis*

---

81. On *nouthesia* consult Ceslas Spicq, *Theological Lexicon of the New Testament,* vol. 2 (Peabody, Mass.: Hendrickson Publishers, 1994), 548, who explains it as "a compound of *nous* and *tithēmi,* the verb *noutheteō* basically means 'put something in someone's mind,' hence 'instruct, lecture,' sometimes by way of refreshing the memory, sometimes by way of making observations or giving warnings. In the latter case, *nouthesia* often means 'reproach' or 'reprimand' (Wis. 16:6). This range of meanings is common to secular and biblical Greek, although the latter places greater emphasis on corporal punishment, punishment being above all an element of child-rearing."

82. This reading presupposes that *kyriou* refers to God and not to the father himself. For a discussion of references to parents as *kyrioi* or *despotai* of their children see Bohlen, *Die Ehrung der Eltern bei Ben Sira,* 212–14.

83. See also Gärtner, *Familienerziehung in der Alten Kirche,* 36.

or *theosis,* that is, divinization. Early Christian writers in the Greek language, from Origen to the Cappadocian Fathers, characterized this goal as the reestablishment of familiarity, kinship, or more literally, "household relationship" with God *(tēn pros theon oikeōsin).*[84] To reach that ultimate goal, early Christians, in unison with the Jewish tradition, emphasized the religious and moral formation and transformation of the human person.[85]

First- and second-century Christian authors did not focus much energy on how to educate children. The religion may simply have been too young for writers in the movement to consider an issue that had taken Greek and Jewish civilization hundreds of years to figure out. Another explanation for this relative lack is the expectation, during those formative stages of Christian development, of Christ's immediate return.[86] It seems that both the experience of martyrdom and the perception of the martyr as the ideal of the perfect Christian life explain why no Christian plan of how to raise and guide children for a life in this world emerged in the course of the second and third centuries either. Nevertheless, a few sources can be found that address aspects of how Christian children were to be reared and educated.

For the second-century apologist Theophilus of Antioch, it was quite obvious that a child would go through different stages of development as he or she was growing up. Some aspects of this developmental process pertained to physical growth and the increasing capabilities of the child's body. In his treatise *To Autolycus,* Theophilus observed, for example, that "when a child is born it cannot eat bread at once, but first it is fed with milk, and then, with increasing age, it comes to solid food."[87] Childhood development

84. Gregory Nazianzen, *Letters* 165.8 (ed. Paul Gallay, *Briefe. Gregor von Nazianz* [Berlin: Akademie Verlag, 1969], 120; trans. Michael Wittig, *Briefe. Gregor von Nazianz* [Stuttgart: Anton Hiersemann, 1981], 179). See also Origen, *Contra Celsum* 4.6 (ed. and trans. Borret, *Origène. Contre Celse. Tome 2 (Livres 3 & 4),* 200, l. 4); Clement of Alexandria, *Quis dives salvetur?* 7 (ed. Otto Stählin, Ludwig Früchtel, and Ursula Treu, *Clemens Alexandrinus. Dritter Band. Stromata Buch VII und VIII. Excerpta ex Theodoto—Eclogae Propheticae—Quis Dives Salvetur—Fragmente* [Berlin: Akademie Verlag, 1970], 159–91, here 164); Basil of Caesarea, *Against Eunomius* 2.24 (ed. and trans. Bernard Sesboüé, Georges-Matthieu de Durand, and Louis Doutreleau, *Contre Eunome: suivie par Eunome apologie. Basile de Césarée* [Paris: Les Éditions du Cerf, 1983], 98–105, see especially 100). For this collection of attestations, see also Robert C. Gregg, *Consolation Philosophy: Greek and Christian Paideia in Basil and the Two Gregories* (Cambridge, Mass.: Philadelphia Patristic Foundation, 1975), 175, n. 3.

85. Blomenkamp, "Erziehung," 521.

86. Ibid. See also K. Coyle, "Empire and eschaton: The early Church and the question of domestic relations," *Église et théologie* 12 (1981), 35–94.

87. Theophilus of Antioch, *To Autolycus* 2.25 (ed. and trans. Grant, *Theophilus of Antioch. Ad Autolycum,* 66–67).

was also noted in the initial limitations young children have with regard to acquiring knowledge. Employing the example of Adam as infant in paradise, Theophilus argued that "in his actual age, Adam was as old as an infant; therefore he was not yet able to acquire knowledge properly."[88] From the continuation of his argument it becomes clear that Theophilus based his point not on attempts at conducting intellectual conversations with children, but on the observation that a newborn child was unable to eat bread and had to be fed with milk. Such an image may have been drawn from real-life observation or from the image in Paul's letter to the Corinthians (1 Cor 3:2; cf. Heb 5:12–13; 1 Pt 2:2). Only over time does the child advance "to solid food." Moreover, Theophilus observed that "one grows in age in an orderly fashion." Consequently, the human being increased in wisdom over time and in accord with his or her growth in stature. For Theophilus, "it is shameful for infant children to have thoughts beyond their years." When cast in this light, the task of education now can be understood as an effort to facilitate this process of becoming wise or of "growing in [one's] ability to think."[89] Some early Christian sources have quite a bit to say about the need to educate children, what goals such a process should pursue, how it was to proceed, and what methods or tools were to be employed.

Toward an Educational Philosophy: Goals for Educating Children

Early Christian writers became increasingly concerned about the moral life of their flock, including children. Tertullian complained that in theaters, "every age and every rank" saw "the buffoon in woman's clothes" and the pantomimes and also "the very harlots, too, victims of the public lust," who were "brought upon the stage … [and were] paraded publicly," while "their abode, their gains, their praises are set forth." He was concerned that children, who were included among those of "every age and every rank," were exposed to such influences. These things, he knew, happened "even in the hearing of those who should not hear such things."[90] Christian parents were encouraged, in raising their children, to rely on models other than the

---

88. Ibid. For a discussion of early Christian ideas concerning Adam and Eve as infants in paradise, see M. C. Steenberg, "Children in Paradise: Adam and Eve as 'Infants' in Irenaeus of Lyons," *Journal of Early Christian Studies* 12 (2004), 1–22.

89. All material cited here comes from Theophilus of Antioch, *To Autolycus* 2.25 (ed. and trans. Grant, *Theophilus of Antioch. Ad Autolycum*, 66–67).

90. Tertullian, *De spectaculis* 17 (ed. and trans. Marie Turcan, *Les Spectacles. Tertullien* [Paris: Les Éditions du Cerf, 1986], 238–48).

ones provided by public entertainment. While early Christians did not formulate a structured, systematic approach to education, the goals of their educational efforts can be grasped from comments in texts beginning in the first century A.D.

One of the earliest values of Christian education was that children ought to be obedient to their parents.[91] Some aspects of this obedience were considered in the previous chapter, since obedience also was essential to early Christian views of the role of children in family life. The obedience of one's children was seen as a criterion for ordination. A bishop had to demonstrate that he managed "his own household well, keeping his children submissive [*tekna echonta en hypotagēi*] and respectful in every way [*meta pasēs semnotētos*]" (1 Tm 3:4). Children's obedience implied proper household management, and was seen as a guarantee that the respective parent would be able to "take care of God's church" (1 Tm 3:5). Also "elders" *(presbyterous)* were expected to have obedient children (Ti 1:5–6).

Raising obedient children indicated the ability to eliminate factions within the community and to refute possibly heretical opinions. Children of potential Christian leaders were to be believers *(tekna ... pista)* and they were not permitted to be among those "accused of wastefulness [*asōtias*] and disobedience [*anypotakta*]" (Ti 1:6). When the author of the Letter to Titus emphasized the need for obedience in children by placing this quality at the end of the list, he had in mind the need not only to select an appropriate candidate for office, but also to find a candidate who was "able both to preach with sound doctrine and to refute those who contradict it" (Ti 1:9), and thus one who was able to silence teachings that might arise from among "many disobedient [*polloi anypotaktoi*] vain talkers and deceivers" who were in the community, "especially [among] those of the circumcision" (Ti 1:10). It was essential to have Christian teachers who could effectively teach the youth in the Christian congregations. The latter reason may also have motivated the requirement that candidates for office have "believing children."[92]

---

91. Roman parents highly praised obedience in a child. See, for example, the tombstone inscription for the eight-year-old Torquatianus *(semper parentibus obsequens)* and his brother Laetianus. See Jane F. Gardner and Thomas Wiedemann, *The Roman Household: A Sourcebook* (London: Routledge, 1991), 64. Obedience as a virtue in children was also treasured in the Jewish community. See the discussion in Yarbrough, "Parents and Children in the Jewish Family of Antiquity," 51–53; and Adele Reinhartz, "Parents and Children: A Philonic Perspective," in *The Jewish Family in Antiquity*, ed. Shaye J. D. Cohen (Atlanta: Scholars Press, 1993), 61–88, here 79.

92. We may catch a glimpse here of early Christian households in which parents and

The third quality expected of children of future leaders in the Church was that of restraint, displayed by a lack of wastefulness or debauchery *(asōtias)*. This ideal of restraint reemerges as *enkrateia,* formulated as a personal requirement of the candidate for the office of bishop *(enkratē)* in Titus 1:8. This quality expected of children could be seen as an early indication of the Christian ideal of *askēsis,* which found its fuller development in the course of the second and third centuries.[93]

The emerging early Christian philosophy of education was also characterized by the goal of instilling in the child a proper sense of the fear of God. This feature is evidenced more strongly in texts coming from outside the canonical writings. The early-second-century *Epistle of Barnabas* and the *Didache* (both of which were considered canonical in some New Testament collections dating before the fifth century) provided instructions for Christian parents regarding the proper care and education of their offspring. Thus Barnabas's letter commanded, "You shall not withdraw your hand from your son, or from your daughter, but from their infancy you shall teach them in the fear of God [*phobon theou*]." *Didache* 4.9 repeated this basic instruction. In his *Letter to the Philippians,* written in the middle of the second century, Polycarp of Smyrna saw it as the task of a husband's wife "to train up their children in the knowledge and fear of God."[94] In his *Letter to the Philadelphians,* in its longer recension, Pseudo-Ignatius instructed the children to reverence their parents and the parents to educate their children "in the nurture and admonition of the Lord [*en paideiāi kai nouthesiāi kyriou*]."[95]

The same concern for children's instruction in the fear of the Lord can

---

children adhered to different religions or to different factions within Christianity. The question of mixed marriages, in which mainly wives had become Christians and the husbands had not, has received some scholarly attention. See MacDonald, "Early Christian Women Married to Unbelievers"; and our discussion of 1 Corinthians 7:12–16, in chapter 3, above. Fuller investigation of how differences in religious affiliation affected parent-child relationships remains a *desideratum.*

93. See the discussion below, and chapter 8.

94. *Epistle of Barnabas* 19 (ed. and trans. Ehrman, *Apostolic Fathers,* vol. 2, 76–77); *Didache* 4.9 (ed. and trans. Ehrman, *Apostolic Fathers,* vol. 1, 424–25); Polycarp, *Letter to the Philippians* 4 (ed. and trans. Ehrman, *Apostolic Fathers,* vol. 1, 338–39).

95. Pseudo-Ignatius, *Letter to the Philadelphians* 4.3 and 4.6 (ed. and trans. Franciscus Xavierus Funk, *Patres Apostolici,* 2 vols. [Tübingen: Libraria Henrici Laupp, 1901], vol. 2, 124–43, here 128–31). Likewise a *Letter to the Antiochians* exhorts parents to "impart a holy training to [their] children," while the children are told, "Honor your parents, that it may be well with you." See Pseudo-Ignatius, *Letter to the Antiochians* 9.2 (ed. and trans. Funk, *Patres Apostolici,* vol. 2, 163–73, here 168–69). Here instructions from Old Testament literature, the Ten Commandments, form the basis for the behavior expected of children. Although the *Letter to the*

be detected in the Church orders. The fourth-century *Didascalia Apostol-orum* resumed the theme of requiring candidates for Church office to be exemplary leaders of their own households as a guarantee of the success of their ecclesiastical leadership. Thus one reads in the fifth-century Syri-ac *Didascalia Apostolorum* 22 the instructions provided to parents on how to raise and educate their children: "And teach your children handicrafts, those which are fitting and suitable to the fear of God, lest through idle-ness they may serve wantonness. Indeed, if they are not chastened by their parents, they will do evil things, like the heathen."[96] The same text was not shy in encouraging parents to use the rod for disciplining their children, when it continued,

On this account spare it not [i.e., the rod] to rebuke and chastise and teach them. Indeed, you certainly will not kill them by chastising them, but rather save them alive, as our Lord also teaches us in the [Book of] Wisdom, saying thus: "Chasten your son, that there may be hope for him"; "indeed, you shall strike him with a rod, and deliver his soul from Sheol."[97]

The author did not intend the constant references to the rod to be un-derstood only in a literal sense. This becomes clear when he explains that "our rod, however, is the word of God, Jesus Christ."[98] The attempt to in-still in children the proper fear of God was redirected into warning parents that "every man ... who spares to speak a word of rebuke to his son, hates his son" and into encouraging them to "teach [their] sons the word of the Lord, and chastise them with stripes, and subdue them from their youth by [their] word of the fear of God." Reinforcing the warning for parents, the author told them that if their children went astray, the parents them-selves would be "guilty before God for the judgment of their souls."[99]

The proper ordering of Christian society required that young people

---

Antiochians and the longer recension of the *Letter to the Philippians* are not part of the authentic Ignatian corpus, but part of the spurious writings ascribed to Ignatius, these texts are evidenced since the fourth century and thus still witness to the philosophy of raising children current in the formative period of Christianity.

96. Syriac *Didascalia Apostolorum* 22 (ed. and trans. Vööbus, *The Didascalia apostolorum in Syriac*, vol. 407, 219 [Syriac], and vol. 408, 202 [English]).

97. Ibid. (vol. 408, 202–3 [English] modified). See also Proverbs 29:17.

98. See Jeremiah 1:11–12, with the NRSV rendering the wood as that of an "almond tree." Syriac *Didascalia Apostolorum* 22 (ed. and trans. Vööbus, *The Didascalia apostolorum in Syriac*, vol. 407, 219 [Syriac], and vol. 408, 203 [English]).

99. Both citations from Syriac *Didascalia Apostolorum* 22 (Vööbus, vol. 407, 219–20 [Syri-ac], and vol. 408, 203 [English; with modifications]).

show respect to their elders. This is one aspect of the educational philosophy that permeated the writings of early Christian authors. In *First Clement*, by tradition ascribed to Clement of Rome, Peter's presumed second successor, the author exhorted the recipients of the letter, "Let us honor the aged among us; let us train up the young men in the fear of God."[100] The immediate concern of the letter was with order in the community. Some younger folks had challenged the authority of the elders (*presbyteroi*) in the local church. Yet the juxtaposition of the two parallel demands, one requesting honor to be shown to the elders or aged in the community and the second encouraging the education of the youth in the fear of God, also reveals two educational goals of the Christian community. The use of the first-person plural pronoun "us" in the first statement allows one to see children as being included in the group of those who will learn to show respect for elders, whether elders in age or with regard to spiritual authority. Out of such a respect for age grows the respect, or "fear," which one owes to God. The letter promotes the insight that respect for elders and fear of God are connected. Both needed to be acquired in the course of one's education and both had to be practiced constantly.

That the training of children was on the mind of the author of *First Clement* in this paragraph is confirmed by a comment following directives for wives to display proper conduct. The author supplemented his instructions on women's behavior by saying, "Let your children be partakers of true Christian training; let them learn of how great avail humility is with God—how much the spirit of pure affection can prevail with Him—how excellent and great His fear is, and how it saves all those who walk in it with a pure mind."[101] Thus, humility was added as a further purpose of educating children. A child's inclination to act with a "spirit of pure affection" is referred to as a means that could aid in gaining favor with God. When the letter's author emphasized the need for a close collaboration between fulfilling the goals of training the young to practice humility, honor the elders, and fear God, he was preparing his readers for the main point of his letter, that young members of the community were not to rebel against the authority of the elders and usurp offices that did not belong to them.[102]

100. *First Letter of Clement to the Corinthians* 21 (ed. and trans. Ehrman, *Apostolic Fathers*, vol. 1, 74–75). See also Polycarp, *Letter to the Philippians* 4 (ed. and trans. Ehrman, *Apostolic Fathers*, vol. 1, 338–39).

101. *First Letter of Clement to the Corinthians* 21 (ed. and trans. Ehrman, *Apostolic Fathers*, vol. 1, 76–77).

102. Ibid. 44 (Ehrman, vol. 1, 112–15).

Some of the "instruction" relayed by Clement of Alexandria[103] and others consisted simply of discipline, corporal or otherwise. Some aspects of this instruction also were coextensive with education in the Christian faith. The use of verbs such as *didaskō*, "to teach," and *paideuō*, "to instruct," among early Christian writers was more than casual advice: education and teaching were at the heart of the Christian mission. In his treatise *Oratio ad Graecos*, Tatian spoke of "free instruction" given to old women and children, stressing that "every age" was welcome to receive this teaching.[104] Indeed, in the following chapter Tatian responded to criticism by those who claimed that the Christians taught only nonsense to women and boys, girls and old women.[105] He denied that what they taught was nonsense, but not that they taught to all who wanted to learn. The perception of this openness to universal outreach as a characteristic of Christian education is supported by Pliny's concern expressed in *Ep.* 10.96, that Christians were coming from all age groups and social backgrounds.[106] We do know that catechetical schools, such as the famous school in Alexandria, began to form in the second century, perhaps earlier, but we also suspect that they grew from catechetical teaching at home and in church settings.[107] Where children were present, education was going to take root.

A Fully Developed Plan: John Chrysostom on Education in the Family

H. I. Marrou saw in the young Roman male

the young aristocrat [who] was brought up to respect not only the national tradition, which all Romans shared in, but his own family traditions, too. We know how proud the great houses were of the magistrates they had given to

---

103. Clement of Alexandria, *Stromateis* 4.17.108, 4 (ed. Stählin and Früchtel, *Clemens Alexandrinus. Zweiter Band. Stromata. Buch I–VI*, 296).

104. See Tatian, *Oratio ad Graecos* 32 (ed. and trans. Molly Whittaker, *Tatian. "Oratio ad Graecos" and Fragments*, Oxford Early Christian Texts [Oxford: Clarendon Press, 1982], 58–59).

105. Ibid. 33 (Whittaker, 60–61).

106. Pliny the Younger, *Letters* 10.96 (ed. and trans. William Melmoth, rev. ed. W. M. L. Hutchinson, *Letters. Pliny the Younger*, 2 vols. [Cambridge, Mass.: Harvard University Press, 1961], vol. 2, 400–405, here 400–401).

107. For recent discussion of the early Christian catechetical school of Alexandria see, for example, Annick Martin, "Aux origines de l'Alexandrie chrétienne: topographie, liturgie, institutions," in *Origeniana octava: Origen and the Alexandrian tradition = Origene e la tradizione Alessandrina (Papers of the 8th International Origen Congress, Pisa, 27–31 August 2001)* (Louvain: Louvain University Press, 2003), 105–20; and Bernard Pouderon, "Réflexion sur la formation d'une

the curia under the Republic, and how they displayed this to all and sundry in their great funerals, in which effigies of their forefathers were carried in procession, and their fame was celebrated along with that of the dead person in the funeral oration. One can easily see what a great influence this would have on any child, when each day his eyes could not fail to light upon the glorified *imagines* set up in the family "atrium," nor his ears to hear the endless stories about them; unconsciously at first, but very consciously later on, he was induced to model his outlook and behaviour on a certain ideal which was, so to speak, the hallmark of his family.[108]

While the glory early Christians aimed for was located in the heavens, not in earthly processions or shrines, for them the family came to be the source of the child's understanding of his or her place in this world and in the world to come.

Early Christian texts witness to specific, consciously employed practices of which parents and other educators availed themselves in raising their children. John Chrysostom's treatise *On Vainglory and the Right Way for Parents to Bring up Their Children* is one of the main sources available to the modern reader who wishes to rediscover these practices. Although this text does not add up to a detailed, structured method or philosophy of education, its author provided an ordered program to be followed in educating children. In addition, Chrysostom supplied concrete examples of good educational practices.[109]

Unlike the earliest centuries, in which texts reflected upon a Christian education only occasionally and in the context of other discussions, Chrysostom offered his readers a fully developed plan, from birth to marriage, for how to raise a Christian child. From the earliest age on, the stage was set for her or his education. Chrysostom urged that parents should not follow the Greek custom of lighting candles at the birth of a child and giving a name according to the name assigned to the candle that burnt longest (ch. 48). Rather, children were to be named after the saints, not after their ancestors (chs. 49–50). The education he envisioned for bringing up an "athlete for Christ"[110] witnessed to how children were integrated into the life of the Church. His focus on prayers, Bible readings, fasting, and vig-

élite intellectuelle chrétienne au IIe siècle: les 'écoles' d'Athènes, de Rome et d'Alexandrie," in *Apologistes chrétiens et la culture grecque* (Paris: Beauchesne, 1998), 237–69.

108. Marrou, *History of Education*, 235.

109. See also Gärtner, *Familienerziehung in der Alten Kirche*.

110. John Chrysostom, *On Vainglory* 19 (ed. Malingrey, *Jean Chrysostome. Sur la vaine gloire et l'éducation des enfants*, 104).

ils oriented the reader to the child's full life in the Christian faith. Still, the presentation of this life of faith, as outlined by Chrysostom, has limitations for the historian who aims at reconstructing ancient childhood.

Chrysostom focused on the education of boys, commenting on girls only occasionally. In general, he assumed that the child would have an education in the liberal arts, the Greek *paideia,* and this assumption governed the kind of advice he offered. He also presumed that the child came from a well-to-do family (e.g., cf. chs. 16, 31, 37, 53, 67, 68, 70, and 71) and his casual dismissal throughout the treatise of the morality and education of slaves remains perhaps its most troubling feature (cf. chs. 62, 66, 69, 71, 73, and 79). His focus, therefore, was on a Christian education for a wealthy, educated, free boy whose family owned slaves.

John Chrysostom's treatise is organized around two images: the soul of the son is likened to a city, the gates of which must admit only the best influences (chs. 23–24); and the citizens of this city must have the best laws ordained for them (ch. 64). The one who builds and guards the gates and who trains the citizens with laws is the king, the father of the boy (ch. 23). In the first fifteen chapters the author laments the world's focus on honor, luxury, and prestige, even among Christians. The first impulse of a Christian father was not to train his son in virtue, but to dress him in fine clothing, something Chrysostom saw as problematic for the moral development of the boy because of the luxury it bespoke and the "effeminacy" it created in the boy (ch. 16). He likewise challenged the mother who raised a daughter in her quarters with luxury to focus instead on teaching the child virtue (ch. 17).

Chrysostom claimed that no one "discourses to them about virginity and sobriety or about contempt of wealth and fame, or of the precepts laid down in Scripture" (ch. 17). To live a life without instruction in virtue was to live a life without teachers. Chrysostom saw that children did not lack teachers in *paideia,* for he bemoaned the fact that a father would "train his boy in the arts and literature and speech," that is, the whole of the Greco-Roman curriculum, yet would not "exercise this child's soul in virtue" (ch. 18).

It is no surprise that Chrysostom returned to that first key of Christian education: discipline. He had given up optimism that in raising athletes for Christ, parents might send their children to the desert to forsake marriage and live a monastic life, although he tried to cling to a forlorn hope: "I wish for this and used to pray that all might embrace it" (ch. 19). In an earlier treatise he had attempted to convince both pagan and Christian parents that allowing their sons to become ascetics was the best they could do for their children and for themselves as well.[111] Over time, however, this idealistic goal had faded away. Still, his hope was strong that parents might mold their children while they were young, impressing good precepts on their soul while it was still soft, like a seal being pressed into soft wax (ch. 20). He likened mothers and fathers to artists creating "statues for God" (ch. 22). Parents were to watch out for licentious speech, be sober and vigilant, and teach their son to "shorten sleep for the sake of prayer" (ch. 22). Here we can find one of the few teachings in early Christian texts that directly relates to a religious practice of children.[112]

Becoming more detailed in his discussion, Chrysostom employed the image of the child's soul as a city with gates that had to be guarded (chapters 23 to 63). The king, that is, the father, had to wage war on wrongdoers as he began to secure his city. An early age was best suited to begin to enact and enforce laws, since those who grow up with bad laws can only be reformed with difficulty, whereas those who are young and inexperienced submit readily and accept laws a father may have established (ch. 25), as long as these laws are enforced (ch. 26). The gates by which one can protect the child from bad influences are the five senses (ch. 27), with speaking, hearing, and seeing being the most significant ones.

The tongue was the busiest gate and had to be made "golden," for the "King of the Universe" intended "to dwell in this city" (ch. 26). This gate was to be built from "the words of God," which always ought to be on the child's lips, praising God, singing hymns, and speaking about God and "heavenly philosophy" (ch. 28). The positive means by which Chrysostom desired to mold the boy's speech were the study of the Bible and especially the constant presence of godly speech on his tongue. Chrysostom did not see this as problematic as long as the boy was young, since the father could limit the influences of other young children on his own child (ch. 29).

If the boy began to speak ill of others, the father was to punish him with stern looks, words of reproach, gentleness and promises, and corporal punishment, but the last only rarely. A child should fear being struck, rather than receive such punishment (ch. 30). The boy also was not to mistreat "even a slave" (ch. 31), for if he could treat a slave with respect, how

111. John Chrysostom, *Against the Opponents of the Monastic Life* (trans. Hunter, *A Comparison between a King and a Monk / Against the Opponents of the Monastic Life. Two Treatises by John Chrysostom*, 77–176). See also the discussion below, and John Chrysostom's treatise *A Comparison between a King and a Monk* (ed. PG 47.387–392; trans. Hunter, 69–76).

112. For a discussion of the place of prayer in the life of early Christian children, see below, chapter 7.

much more would he be able to treat a free person from his own class with respect. Chrysostom also challenged fathers to make certain that their children did not behave toward slaves with disdain—"do not overlook it, but punish him who is free" (ch. 31). Lurking behind this discussion is the reality that slaves were treated as inferior or even as less than human and that from childhood on the education of a slave was primarily to create a servile character, one that took the abuse of free children without resistance, as a training for their future status as adult slaves of these same freeborn peers.[113]

Chrysostom argued that the mother, the tutor (*paedagogus*, usually a slave), and other slaves had to be engaged in stopping the child from "speaking evil" (chs. 31–32). Military fathers, he said, began training their sons from the earliest in the military arts. Thus it was only wise that Christians begin to train their sons in this "royal discipline" from the earliest age (ch. 34). Chrysostom relied on hymns to God to order the child's speech, forgoing "shameful songs and ill-timed tales" (ch. 34). Once the proper citizens of the city, the virtues, had entered and been made secure, other citizens, that is, unwelcome behavioral traits, should be put to death.

The next gate was that of hearing. Chrysostom was most worried about this gate since children were "tender shoots" and ought to hear "nothing harmful from servants or tutor[s] or nurses" (37). He was concerned with the influence of slaves and the tales they told the child. If parents could not find anyone among the slaves who was trustworthy, they were to "hire someone who is free, a virtuous man" (ch. 38). Whether this concern characterized a view of slaves and their character in general, or a belief that most slaves were not Christians and hence not morally trustworthy, it does indicate that slaves, whether Christian or not, did not have the same moral education that to him seemed appropriate for the freeborn child. Education in the moral life, like that in the liberal arts, was not generally available for slaves.

The child was to hear stories from the Bible, with his mother nearby.

---

113. For systematic studies of Chrysostom's view of slavery, see, e.g., Georg Kontoulis, *Zum Problem der Sklaverei (ΔΟΥΛΕΙΑ) bei den kappadokischen Kirchenvätern und Johannes Chrysostomus* (Bonn: Dr. Rudolf Habelt GmbH, 1993), 315–78; W. Jaeger, "Die Sklaverei bei Johannes Chrysostomus" (theology diss., University of Kiel, 1974); and J. A. Möhler, "Bruchstücke aus der Geschichte der Aufhebung der Sklaverei," in *Gesammelte Schriften und Aufsätze*, ed. J. J. I. Döllinger (Regensburg: Manz, 1939–40), vol. 2, 54–140, especially 89–97. See also the helpful comments in passing in Joy A. Schroeder, "John Chrysostom's Critique of Spousal Violence," *Journal of Early Christian Studies* 12.4 (2004), 413–42.

These stories were chosen with concern for their particular didactic value.[114] For instance, Chrysostom detailed the moral value of the Cain and Abel story (Gn 4) with precision. Although he was murdered, Abel went to heaven, but Cain lived in fear for his deed, just like the child when standing before the teacher was wondering if he would receive a whipping (ch. 39). The moral was clear—one cannot hide one's sin from God (ch. 40), let alone from one's schoolmaster, and the righteous one receives a just reward (ch. 42). Chrysostom spent even more time on the manner in which the lessons of these stories were learned. The parents should take turns telling and repeating the story, and the child was to retell it to them as well (ch. 40), so that when the story was heard at church, the child would pay heed (ch. 41). After the story of Cain and Abel, that of Jacob and Esau (Gn 25:29–34; 27:1–28:9; 32:3–33:17) should be told next as an instruction to show reverence to the fathers and disdain of the belly (ch. 43). Why Chrysostom thought that in a first round of recitation this story was to be told to a child without the names of the key characters is not clear (ch. 45). Perhaps what he meant was that the story of Jacob and Esau, which is interspersed in three parts in Genesis, should be simplified. Eventually, however, the meaning of the story could be explained in all its philosophical complexity (ch. 46).

When the child was slightly more advanced in age, parents were to begin to narrate more fearful stories from the Scriptures. Between eight and ten, children were ready to hear about the flood and the destruction of Sodom. Stories of hell, however, should wait until boys were fifteen (ch. 52). Chrysostom relegated the telling of "the deeds of the New Testament— deeds of grace and deeds of hell" (ch. 52) to an even later age. In general, the telling of stories was to proceed from the Old to the New Testament, but also within the Old Testament from the earliest stories of Genesis to later accounts. Whether Chrysostom expected that this should be continued from Genesis through the whole of the Old Testament until reaching

114. James L. Crenshaw, *Education in Ancient Israel: Across the Deadening Silence* (New York: Doubleday, 1998), 237, rejects as "unlikely that widespread copying of such books" as Job, Ecclesiastes, and Sirach "took place in educational establishments" in ancient Israel. His discussion of "a literary canon" of ancient Israelite society, which appears also to have included the Book of Proverbs corresponds remarkably well with evidence regarding a recommended canon and order of Scriptural readings for young children. For a canon of reading which parents set up for their children, see also Gregory of Nyssa, *Life of Macrina* 3 (ed. and trans. Pierre Maraval, *Grégoire de Nysse. Vie de Sainte Macrine* [Paris: Les Éditions du Cerf, 1971], 150–51; trans. Joan M. Petersen, *Handmaids of the Lord. Contemporary Descriptions of Feminine Asceticism in the First Six Christian Centuries* [Kalamazoo, Mich.: Cistercian Publications, 1996], 51–86, here 53–54).

the New Testament is not clearly stated. He gave this method considerable weight, as he intended it to counteract slaves' speaking lewdly and even the presence of girls ("from a young woman shield him as from fire") (ch. 53).

After a brief discussion of the gate of smell (ch. 54), Chrysostom moved on to consider the role of the eyes. In some ways it was not the boy's eyes, but the eyes of those on the street that he felt needed to be addressed. He first warned against ever letting the boy go to the theater,[115] yet his chief concern was with the eyes of men watching the child pass on the street. The attendants had to be especially watchful so that the boy never suffered "corruption" (ch. 56). Pederasty is clearly in view here, as Chrysostom believed that the means to guard against it was to cut the boy's hair, "the chief part of his physical charm" (ch. 57). Part of the technique for guarding the gate of the eyes was to tell the story of Gen 6:1–4, when the sons of God lapsed by falling into the arms of the daughters of men (ch. 58). In addition, the father was to show the boy fields, meadows, and good books (ch. 59). Nevertheless, Chrysostom acknowledged the problem inherent in keeping watch over this gate: natural desire.

This gate is difficult to guard, since there burns a fire within and, so to speak, a natural compulsion. Let him learn hymns. If he is not inwardly aroused, he will not wish to see outwardly. Let him not bathe in company with women—such familiarity is evil—and let him not be sent into a crowd of women (ch. 60).

Chrysostom saw limiting access to women as the key—although he did not suggest at what precise age this should take place, perhaps only after the "natural compulsion" arises, which elsewhere he dated to age fifteen (ch. 76).

Chrysostom advised the father to tell his boy stories of the patriarch Joseph (Gn 37 and 39–50) "continually" and to promise him the reward of the Kingdom of Heaven for his behavior (ch. 61). Without making the point explicit, Chrysostom could expect his readers to recognize in Joseph the model par excellence of youthful male beauty resisting and overcoming female wiles.

More practically, he asked the father to choose a girl for his son to marry, and to warn the boy that if he lacked virtue in himself, no virtuous girl would want him (ch. 61). Coupled with this the boy also had to develop a "resolute spirit against womankind" (ch. 62). He was to be taught a spirit

---

115. See Blake Leyerle, *Theatrical Shows and Ascetic Lives: John Chrysostom's Attack on Spiritual Marriage* (Berkeley: University of California Press, 2001), especially chapters 2 and 3.

which agreed that "to be despised by the slave woman is meet only for the slave" (ch. 62). It seems that the father was not to allow his son to have sexual relations with a slave girl or woman either, a situation that likely would lead to the slave woman's despising him. Instead, the boy should meet his betrothed as soon as possible, before he entered into his civic duties in politics or the military (ch. 81). The goal here was to produce a marriage between a virgin bride and a virgin groom.

Once the city gates were guarded, the father, as king of the city, was to introduce laws for the remaining citizens: the Spirit (located in the heart and breast), the Appetite (also called Desire, located in the soul), and Reason (also called Wisdom, located in the brain) (chs. 64–65). The Spirit could produce either sobriety and equability or rashness and ill-temper; Desire, or Appetite, could produce either sobriety or licentiousness; and Reason in its turn could produce either understanding or folly. In order to mold the Spirit, the boy was to receive training in patience from earliest childhood, even when he suffered wrongs, but he was to go forth with courage if he saw another person being wronged (ch. 66). Such behavior could be practiced among one's own slaves, simply by being patient when slighted or disobeyed. It is not discussed how the slave learned to order himself. A second means to challenge the boy to a right ordering of the passions was to teach him to fear hell and yearn for the promise of heaven (ch. 67). Yet Chrysostom was most concerned with the child's behavior among slaves and thus he returned to a discussion of this issue several times throughout this section. The boy was not to be indulgent or harsh with his slaves; when provoked either by his slaves or by his companions he was to learn equability; if he struck his slave, he had to be punished (chs. 68–69).

The Spirit was not to be driven out of the boy entirely, since some day he himself would become a father or a master of the slaves. Yet he could learn proper behavior through tales of men, like Moses and Paul, who defended others and not themselves (ch. 69). The boy was not to demand services that he could do himself, such as washing his feet or getting his own cloak, from slaves who attended to his needs. Yet some tasks, such as cooking, Chrysostom thought were not proper for a free boy (ch. 70). Indeed, there were differences between slaves and free persons and this fact had to be manifested in behavior that was superior to that of slaves. With a pungent comment to warn the child, Chrysostom remarked that some fathers had adopted slaves for sons and renounced their own sons (ch. 71). The father was to warn the boy continually to treat slaves like brothers and not to become angry, as children often do, for example, if a slave broke his writing implements (ch. 73). The boy was to learn equanimity, even if it meant letting a slave go unpunished or allowing a younger brother to take precedence (ch. 74).

Appetite, or Desire, was concerned primarily with the sexual drive, something which Chrysostom thought likely to strike around fifteen years of age (ch. 76). The boy was not to suffer "outrage" himself nor commit it against girls. He was not to frequent the theater (ch. 78). The fear of hell was the best argument Chrysostom knew to employ, but apart from techniques suggested earlier, such as prayer and the singing of hymns, he also proposed new ones. He understood that the theater had many attractions for older boys, but a freeborn boy should never enter it (ch. 76), since "the sight of naked women uttering shameful words . . . [was] for slaves" (ch. 78) only. The father had to introduce his son to other boys who did not go to the theater: this was the standard his own son had to attain. Chrysostom was a strong believer in the power of role models, ideally those who were of the same age as the child, to produce the desired effects in a boy or girl.[116] Other pleasures could be substituted, for example, showing the child saintly men, other recreations, and "many gifts" (ch. 78). Chrysostom suggested that the father keep his son from women at all costs, except for old female slaves, and if the family had slaves of good conduct, the father was to indicate to his child that it was not right that a slave be freer of passions than the free boy (ch. 79). The boy's conduct with and imitation of slaves clearly was the issue of concern here: the child was not to commit outrages against a male or female slave in the house; moreover, he was not to follow their behavior by attending the theater. Yet if the family had slaves who led good lives, the child was to be encouraged to imitate them, always being reminded that he needed to be superior to them. Such statements suggest that the boys of wealthy families did engage in sexual practices with their slaves and could be found at the theater as well, very likely more regularly than their Christian teachers and pastors would have wanted.

Chrysostom advised that the boy learn to fast on Wednesdays and Fridays, a recommendation already voiced in the *Didache*.[117] The child also should practice praying "with great contrition" (chs. 79–80). The boy was to meet the bishop and his father was to be more pleased with this encounter than with any other relationship (ch. 83).

116. For a helpful discussion of this aspect, see Gärtner, *Familienerziehung in der Alten Kirche*, 88–102; see also A. Lumpe, "Exemplum," in *RAC* 6 (1966), 1229–57.

117. *Didache* 8.1 (ed. and trans. Ehrmann, *Apostolic Fathers*, vol. 1, 416–43, here 428–29).

Finally, Chrysostom turned to the development of Reason or Wisdom in the child. This was the "master principle" by which all else was governed. Wisdom was the fear and knowledge of God and one was to form one's attitude toward worldly things on this basis (chs. 85–87). "The summit of wisdom is refusal to be excited at childish things" (ch. 87). These "childish" things, however, were not merely what children desired. They were the very things Chrysostom had warned against at the opening of his treatise: honor, prestige, and wealth. The goal of the Christian's education was to "think nothing" of wealth, reputation, power, death, or the present life (ch. 87). As such, as the boy prepared to leave the family home, he had to have learned not to need or want to have a big wedding celebration with flutes, harps, and dancing, but rather to appreciate a sober affair, with Christ invited to the party (ch. 88). If this was done, the child in turn would also raise his own children in this way. One ought not to think that a disdain for prestige, honor, power, or glory meant that Chrysostom proposed that these be given up altogether—except if the child chose the monastic life—only that the child attend to political affairs free from sin, that as a soldier he not seek after "base" gain, and that he defend the cause of those who had suffered wrong (ch. 89).

Chrysostom's advice was directed at that small minority of Christian boys whose families had sufficient wealth to educate them in the Greek *paideia* and who owned a substantial number of slaves. What kind of Christian education was imagined for those whose fathers were farmers on a small plot of land or for slaves who were Christians is not addressed. With respect to prayer, fasting, singing hymns, hearing Bible stories, and attending church, Chrysostom probably would have given similar advice to them as well. This was a Christian education. As to the moral development of slaves, such advice would have been less necessary as the temptations were not present to the same degree, either to use a slave sexually or to hurt one physically. Chrysostom's focus on the wealthy, which in many respects may seem offensive to the modern reader, suggested itself to him because of their need for instruction in the primary Christian virtues. They were at a greater risk of forgoing Christian teaching because of their ability to luxuriate in wealth. Certain passages at the beginning of the treatise suggest this (ch. 1–15). One also notes that only the better off in Chrysostom's diocese would have had the wealth and leisure to own or read manuals of Christian education like the one he produced.

Chrysostom presented a picture according to which many were at risk of seeking after vainglory, while only a few could revel in it. He directed his discourse "to the faithful among us who refuse to hand over a trifling sum to Christ" (ch. 12). He spoke of those who desired slaves, fine clothes, gold, silver, and a fine house, yet he stressed that one needed "none of these possessions; for, if they were needed, the greater part of the human race would have perished and been destroyed" (ch. 13). These were people Chrysostom had in sight not because he was impressed with their wealth, but because they were misusing their wealth, particularly in their poor education of their sons. "Place does not make a man's character" (ch. 14). Yet, for all of this, one still may be disappointed that he did not focus more on the education of those who were poor or slaves, that he did not stress the fact that the poor had access to these goods of the Christian life even without having access to money, or that slaves, although treated poorly and with disdain, nevertheless had access to all the virtues through Christ. One does not find such considerations here. The discussion of girls takes one no farther. In one short section he encouraged the mother "to train her daughter by these precepts" and to lead her away from a life of luxury and excitement (ch. 90; see also ch. 17).

That Chrysostom gave only scant attention to mothers and daughters in this treatise does not mean that mothers did not play a significant role in educating their daughters, and even their sons. It simply confirms that the sources focus less on their role. Gärtner offered a noteworthy suggestion regarding the role of women in the education of children in Christian families. He thought that "women were not exposed to pagan culture without protection, given that they often did not attend schools, but rather were instructed at home." Thus, "if they received any training at all," this could "perhaps have been the reason why in many families the mother was the carrier of the [Christian] faith."[118] In support of his point one may note that Augustine's mother, Monica, played precisely such a role in his life, encouraging him to cling to the Christian faith, but also not turning him from his pagan education. Also Macrina's mother was in charge of the plan of her daughter's education and its exercise, including her training in the Scriptures.[119]

---

118. Gärtner, *Familienerziehung in der Alten Kirche*, 137, n. 2: "Frauen, die oft die Schulen nicht besuchten, sondern, wenn überhaupt, zu Hause unterrichtet wurden, waren der heidnischen Bildung nicht so ungeschützt ausgeliefert. Vielleicht wurde deshalb der Glaube in vielen Familien besonders von der Mutter getragen."

119. See Augustine of Hippo, *Confessions* I xi (17) (ed. Verheijen, *Sancti Augustini. Confessionum Libri XIII*, 9–10; trans. Chadwick, *Saint Augustine: Confessions,* 13); and Gregory of Nyssa, *Life of Macrina* 3 (ed. and trans. Maraval, *Grégoire de Nysse. Vie de Sainte Macrine*, 150–51; trans. Petersen, *Handmaids of the Lord*, 53).

Members of the Larger Family and Friends as Educators

Grandparents

When considering the Christian family as the initial locus of the education of Christian children, one may not forget that aunts, uncles, and grandparents, insofar as they were Christians, could also play an important role. Grandparents did play a recognized role in the Christian education of very young children from biblical times on, as the case of Timothy's grandmother Lois (1 Tm 3:15) has already demonstrated. Also, Melania the Younger was entrusted to the model of her grandmother, Melania the Elder, by the very fact of receiving her name. That she followed her grandmother's ideals and lifestyle of pilgrimage and asceticism followed suit in its time.[120] In the fourth century, Basil of Caesarea saw it as a sign of the quality and reliability of his faith that he had received initial instruction in it from his grandmother Macrina the Elder. In *Letter* 204 he spoke of how she had raised her grandchildren while they were still little boys, formed them, and gave shape to their character through teachings that were appropriate to her piety.[121]

Friends of the Child

Another model of education was supplied from among a child's friends. Chrysostom was especially interested in the example set by peers. According to him, those who were of the same age as those to be educated were especially effective as examples. If one was able to show to a child other children of his or her own age who behaved in an exemplary manner, this would inspire special zeal in the child, who would strive to imitate those exemplary children.[122] Such a view of children as role models also speaks to

120. Melania the Elder played a significant role in early Christianity. For literature on her, see for example Hildegard Gosebrink, "Frauengestalten im palästinensischen Mönchtum," in *"… weil sie mehr liebte." Frauen im frühen Mönchtum*, ed. Jakobus Kaffanke (Beuron: Beuroner Kunstverlag, 2002), 55–73; Anne Jensen, "Frauen in der Asketengeschichte 'Das Paradies' von Palladios (Historia Lausiaca)," in *"… weil sie mehr liebte,"* 37–54; Elizabeth A. Clark, "Melania the Elder and the Origenist Controversy: the Status of the Body in a Late-Ancient Debate," in *Nova & Vetera: Patristic Studies in Honor of Thomas Patrick Halton*, ed. John Petruccione (Washington, D.C.: The Catholic University of America Press, 1998), 117–27; M. F. G. Parmentier, "Evagrius of Pontus' 'Letter to Melania,'" *Bijdragen* 46 (1985), 2–38; and Nicole Moine, "Melaniana," *Recherches augustiniennes* 15 (1980), 3–79.

121. Basil of Caesarea, *Letters* 204 (ed. and trans. Deferrari, *Saint Basil. The Letters*, vol. 3, 168–69; trans. Sister Agnes Clare Way, with notes by Roy I. Deferrari, *Saint Basil. Letters. Volume II (186–368)* [New York: Fathers of the Church, 1955], 70–78, here 76).

122. John Chrysostom, *On Vainglory* 77b, lines 925–30 (ed. and trans. Malingrey, *Jean Chrys-*

the educational value, if one may see it that way, of accounts of the martyrdom of young people for inspiring in the young a dedication and personal commitment to the Christian faith.[123] Those children who gave their lives for the faith modeled a desired behavior for other young children and teenagers. They clearly played a role in educating Christian children in the faith.

Children and Organized Structures of Catechesis

The place of children in the Church's developing catechetical system is not easy to determine. At times one finds individual Christian teachers comparing catechetical efforts to the world of education known from the school systems. Gregory of Nyssa, for example, revealed a significant pedagogical awareness and interest in catechesis of the young through his use of rhetoric.[124] His pedagogical intentions come to the fore in the proemium of his homily *De beneficentia*.[125] There he compared the Christian preacher with an elementary school teacher, who does not present to the students the most difficult subject matters for study at the very outset. Initially such a teacher merely teaches the students the letters of the alphabet. Afterwards follow lessons on syllables, and then the teacher moves on to having the students read and write complete words.[126] So also is the catechetical teacher to proceed from explaining the basics of the faith to more difficult subject matters. How many and how often children were recipients of such catechetical efforts cannot be established statistically.

On occasion, early Christian texts provide accounts of how systematic attempts were made to instruct children in the Christian faith, especially in cases of planned efforts to spread the faith in a whole region.[127] In his *History of the Armenians*, for example, the Armenian historian Agathangelos

---

ostome. Sur la vaine gloire et l'éducation des enfants, 178–81). See comments in Gärtner, *Familienerziehung in der Alten Kirche*, 102.

123. For a discussion of select examples of martyrdom accounts of children, see also below, chapter 6.

124. For the following, see also Ulrike Gantz, *Gregor von Nyssa: Oratio consolatoria in Pulcheriam* (Basel: Schwabe, 1999), 68–69 and n. 58.

125. Gregory of Nyssa, *De beneficentia* (ed. Jaeger, *Gregorii Nysseni Opera*, vol. 9, 93.3–16).

126. See also Christoph Klock, *Untersuchungen zu Stil und Rhythmus bei Gregor von Nyssa. Ein Beitrag zum Rhetorikverständnis der griechischen Väter* (Frankfurt am Main: Athenäum, 1987), 173–74.

127. For the comments in this and the following paragraphs, see also Cornelia B. Horn, "The Lives and Literary Roles of Children in Advancing Conversion to Christianity: Hagiography from the Caucasus in Late Antiquity and the Middle Ages," *Church History* 76.2 (2007), 262–97, here 294–96.

retells missionary efforts already recorded in the fifth-century Koriun's *Life of Mesrop Mashtots* [128] and speaks more directly of the formal, catechetical school system in the Christian east, specifically in Armenia:

Similarly he [i.e., Gregory the Illuminator] persuaded the king that from every province and region they should bring to various places numbers of children [*mankti,* gen. *manktwoy*] in order to instruct them. So these barbarous, savage and wild natives he took and cast into the furnace of instruction, and by the heat of his spiritual love burnt away the impurity and rust of the putrid demons and vain cults. [129]

Moreover, Agathangelos provided a description of the Armenian school system and the method of teaching:

And from every place within the borders of Armenia and from the lands and provinces of his realm king Trdat commanded many young children [*mankti,* gen. *manktwoy*] to be introduced to the art of writing and faithful teachers to be put in charge. Especially the families of the impure pagan priests and their children [*manouk,* pl. *mankoun*] were to be brought together in groups in suitable places, and an adequate stipend paid to them. These he divided into two groups, some being set to Syriac and others to Greek. Thus in the twinkling of an eye these savage and idle and oafish peasants suddenly became acquainted with the prophets and familiar with the apostles and heirs to the Gospel and fully informed about all the traditions of God. [130]

According to Agathangelos, Gregory the Illuminator had a particular interest in reeducating families of the religious leaders of pagan Armenia. Thus he also "took some of the pagan priests' sons [*ordik,* abl. pl. *yordwots‘*] and brought them up in his own sight and under his own care, giving them instruction and raising them with spiritual care and fear." [131] Subsequently, several of them were ordained as bishops for the newly established Christian Church.

Gregory the Illuminator is shown displaying a keen sense of how to transform a religious system from the inside. Although one needs to take note of his church-political strategy, it also is obvious that this catecheti-

128. R. W. Thomson, *Agathangelos. History of the Armenians* (Albany: State University of New York, 1976), 494–95, for identification of passages which Agathangelos took over directly from Koriun.

129. Agathangelos, *Patmout‘iwn Hayot‘s, History of the Armenians* §839 (trans. Thomson, *Agathangelos. History of the Armenians,* 372–73).

130. Ibid. §840 (Thomson, 374–75).

131. Ibid. §845 (Thomson, 378–79 [modified]).

cal system was the means by which children were introduced not only to Christianity, but also to education itself. At the heart of these excerpts are the Greek notion of the power of education to transform the soul and the Hebrew notion of education as the means to save the soul. Both of these combined to create a Christian model of catechesis.

Educating Orphans in the Christian Community

Christian authors did not show much, if any, interest in or concern with improving the educational level of children in slave families. Yet this is not to be understood as complete neglect on the part of Christians of all groups of children at the margins of society. The author of the *Didascalia Apostolorum*, for example, dedicated the whole of chapter 17 to the care the Christian community was called upon to provide for orphans, including their education. The treatment of this question is supplemented by additional comments in earlier chapters. For later texts, the instructions of the *Didascalia Apostolorum* on the care for orphans became an influential model in the Christian East.[132]

The care of orphans was to be shared by the bishop and the community. Yet the text highlights the responsibility that the leaders of the Church, both presbyters and bishop, had in this matter. When decisions were to be made about whom to elect as presbyter, one of the criteria for consideration was whether the candidate has been "as a father to the orphans."[133] One of the source texts of the *Didascalia Apostolorum*, the *Testament of Our Lord Jesus Christ (Testamentum Domini Nostri Iesu Christi)*, explicitly requested that a candidate who was to be appointed bishop be "a lover of toil, a lover of widows, a lover of orphans."[134] The bishop was to be seen as the necessary and controlling link of the charitable work of the community. At the same time, however, as much as the Israelites in the Old Testament were called upon to offer their tithe unto God as gifts for the altar in the Temple, so here a case was made that the Christian faithful were obligated to give offerings for the needs of orphans and widows. Caring

132. See also the discussion in Timothy S. Miller, *The Orphans of Byzantium: Child Welfare in the Christian Empire* (Washington, D.C.: The Catholic University of America Press, 2003), 113–14.

133. Syriac *Didascalia Apostolorum* 3.2 (ed. and trans. Vööbus, *The Didascalia apostolorum in Syriac*, vol. 401, 28 [Syriac], and vol. 402, 28 [English]).

134. *Testamentum Domini Nostri Iesu Christi* (ed. Arthur Vööbus, *The Synodicon in the West Syrian Tradition*, CSCO 367 and 368, Scriptores Syri 161 and 162 [Louvain: Secrétariat du CorpusSCO, 1975], 12 [Syriac] and 35 [English]).

for orphans was the concrete task of the Christian community, inextricably joined to Christ's invitation to table fellowship with him.

The bishop was responsible for bringing the needs of the poor to the attention of the community and to "let them work amongst themselves and give and in this way serve in righteousness."[135] Proper instruction of the people would lead to sufficient supplies for all needs and all who were in need. One aspect of such instruction and teaching to which the bishop was called was to advise one of the faithful "who has no children" to "take in" or "adopt" a child, in case "anyone of the children of Christians be an orphan."[136] Chapter 17 contains further points of consideration which a bishop might employ in his preaching when he was trying to mobilize resources from within his congregation to help alleviate the sufferings of orphans.

Special encouragement seems to have been necessary to motivate people to adopt girls or treat them as foster children in one's family.[137] Those who had no children were inclined to adopt a boy, in order to have an heir for the family property and in order to ensure that their name would not be cast into oblivion. As the Syriac *Didascalia Apostolorum* gave advice on how to arrange for the adoption of a Christian "orphan, whether boy or girl [*'ō ṭalyā 'ō ṭalītā*]," it recommended that someone who did not have *bᵉnayyā*—a word that can be rendered as "children" or as "sons"—ought to take into his house "the boy in the place of sons [*lᵉṭalyā bdūkat bᵉnayyā*]." The one, however, who already had a son *(bᵉrā)*, should take in the girl *(ṭalītā)*. As if to entice a potential adoptive parent further, the *Didascalia Apostolorum* followed up with another piece of advice, or one may also call it a promise of gain, for a parent adopting a girl. The text advises that "when her [i.e., the girl's] time is come," the bishop ought to have the adoptive father "give her [i.e., the girl] to him [i.e., his son] as a wife [*bᵉnēšē*],"[138] explaining that thus "his work may be completed in the service of God."[139] Thus the text implied that the adoptive father would not be losing the fruit of his efforts in raising and educating the girl in this way.

135. Syriac *Didascalia Apostolorum* 18 (ed. and trans. Vööbus, *The Didascalia apostolorum in Syriac,* vol. 407, 184 [Syriac], and vol. 408, 166 [English]).

136. Ibid. 17 (Vööbus, vol. 407, 176 [Syriac], and vol. 408, 160 [English]).

137. For the neglected field of the study of foster children, see John H. Corbert, "The Foster Child: A Neglected Theme in Early Christian Life and Thought," in *Traditions in Contact and Change: Selected Proceedings of the 14th Congress of the International Association for the History of Religions* (Waterloo, Canada: Wilfrid Laurier University Press, 1983), 307–21.

138. The Syriac uses the noun "wife" in the plural here.

139. Syriac *Didascalia Apostolorum* 17 (ed. and trans. Vööbus, *The Didascalia apostolorum in Syriac,* vol. 407, 176 [Syriac], and vol. 408, 160 [English]).

Other early Christian texts suggest that families from the lower social ranks in particular were accustomed to accepting foreign children into their families, and if they did not adopt them outright, they raised them as foster children. One learns, for example, from the hagiographical biography of the fifth-century ascetic Peter the Iberian that Peter's nurse Ota, who "gave him suck when he was a baby," had other foster children, the boys Qata and Murgaqis, who were of the same age as little Peter.[140] This snippet of information suggests that at times several children from different families appear to have been cared for and raised as foster children and nurslings in the same household. Not infrequently the children themselves seem to have developed affection for one another like that of brothers and sisters. Both the *Life of Peter the Iberian* and Basil of Caesarea's correspondence provide examples of this. Peter retained such affection for Qata and Murgaqis that once he had become a monk in Palestine, he included their names in an annual commemoration liturgy which he celebrated in honor of his family members and relatives who had been models of the faith for him.[141] In *Letter* 37, Basil of Caesarea prayerfully remembered his former milk-brother.[142] While these children were not technically orphans, as foster children in a foreign family their experience was not unlike that of orphans adopted into a new family.

The *Didascalia Apostolorum* also spoke of the humane efforts of the bishop to make certain that orphaned children were raised in Christian families and so educated in this manner as well. The practical implications of caring for and raising orphans were not simply their education in a schoolroom. Rather one also must note the emphasis placed on practical skills. As stated at the beginning of this chapter: education in Christianity may have been for all, and education in the family was to be available for all, including orphans, but education in the classroom was only for a few. The next chapter considers the types of practical education most children, boys and girls, would have received: an education in a particular craft or skill, or even a simple education in the necessity of work.

140. John Rufus, *Life of Peter the Iberian* 9 (ed. and trans. Cornelia B. Horn and Robert R. Phenix Jr., *John Rufus: The "Lives" of Peter the Iberian, Theodosius of Jerusalem, and the Monk Romanus,* Writings from the Greco-Roman World 24 [Atlanta: Society of Biblical Literature, 2008]), 10–11.

141. John Rufus, *Life of Peter the Iberian* 10 (ed. and trans. Horn and Phenix, *John Rufus: The "Lives,"* 10–11).

142. Basil of Caesarea, *Letters* 37 (ed. and trans. Yves Courtonne, *Saint Basile: Lettres,* vol. 1 [Paris: Société d'édition "Les Belles Lettres," 1957], 79–80, here 80).

five

Children and Daily Life

A Time to Work and a Time to Play

The previous chapter looked at the process of education. It suggested that a Christian education through the Church was available to all children, even if only on an informal and weekly basis. Yet a thorough Greco-Roman education, to which wealthy Christians as well as Greek and Roman pagans had access, was out of reach for most children.[1] Keith Bradley has shown that work was a key part of the lives of most children, with the exception of wealthy children, mostly boys, who were able to spend their childhood and young adulthood in formal education.[2]

Children at Work

The majority of children in the Roman Empire were involved in work at a young age.[3] Some of these children worked in their family's trade or busi-

1. As the Church became more settled in the Greco-Roman world, it seems less likely that advanced Jewish education continued to appeal to parents of Christian children. This is the case for former Gentiles, but the kind of education received in a *bet ha-midrash* would have clashed with Christian readings of Scripture and so was supplanted by Christian education in the Church.

2. See also above, chapter 1. For a fuller study of children at work in ancient Rome, see Christian Laes, *Kinderen bij de Romeinen. Zes eeuwen dagelijks leven* (Louvain: Uitgeverij Davidsfonds, 2006), 133–98; and Christian Laes, "Kinderarbeid in het Romeinse rijk. Een vergeten dossier?" *Kleio* 30 (2000), 2–20.

3. Bradley, "Child Labor," 103–10.

ness, or on their plot of land. The income they helped to generate was necessary for their family's livelihood. Most girls were engaged in the family home, where they worked alongside their mothers, preparing for similar tasks in their own homes some day. Some children, free and slave, would have gained apprenticeships to learn skilled crafts.[4] Bradley's work is sufficient to show that the vast majority of Greco-Roman children worked for a living. Some further details from ancient texts may help to fill out the picture.

Lucius Junius Moderatus Columella's writings *De re rustica* and *De arboribus* speak of agriculture in general, and indicate the age at which children worked, as well as the tasks that were open to them.[5] The works preserved under the name of Musonius Rufus also provide insight into the extent of child labor. They delineate the types of tasks for which upperclass girls were trained, and they argue for the same manner of education for both girls and boys.[6]

Columella on Children's Work

Columella was born in what is now Cádiz, Spain, in the early first century A.D., although precise dates for his life are not certain.[7] Information he provides on farming is significant for practices in the Roman Empire during the rise of Christianity. He addressed large estate owners, gentlemen and freeborn (*Rust.* Preface, 1.10), most of whom dwelt in cities and

4. Ibid., 110; see also Golden, "Childhood in Ancient Greece," 18, on children's work beginning at a very young age, especially for children laboring in agrarian settings; and Shapiro, "Fathers and Sons, Men and Boys," 111, n. 114. See Pearl, "Apprentice Contract," for a contract for a slave girl that provided her with a position that allowed her to learn how to weave. See Werner A. Krenkel, "Prostitution," in *Civilization of the Ancient Mediterranean: Greece and Rome,* vol. 2 (New York: Charles Scribner's Sons, 1988), 1291–97, here 1295–97, on slave boys forced to work in the prostitution business.

5. Columella's collected works can be found in three volumes of the LCL series: *De Re Rustica, I–IV Vol. I* (ed. H. B. Ash), *De Re Rustica, V–IX Vol. II* (eds. E. S. Forster and Edward Heffner), and *De Re Rustica, X–XII and De Arboribus Vol. III* (eds. E. S. Forster and Edward Heffner) (Cambridge, Mass.: Harvard University Press, 1948).

6. Musonius Rufus's most significant treatise for purposes of the present investigation is entitled "Should Daughters Receive the Same Education as Sons?" See Cora E. Lutz, "Musonius Rufus. 'The Roman Socrates,'" *Yale Classical Studies* 10 (1947), 3–147, here 42–49. Lutz supplies the Greek text also found in Stobaeus, *Anthologium* 2.31,123 (ed. Curtius Wachsmuth and Otto Hense, *Ioannis Stobaei Anthologium* [Berlin: Apud Weidmannos, 1884], vol. 2, 235–39). Other treatises that will be referenced can also be found in Lutz's work.

7. See the introductory comments to Columella's *De re rustica* in the LCL edition of his works, by H. B. Ash, trans., *De Re Rustica, Vol. I,* ix–xi. Ash places him in the days of Seneca (ca. 4 B.C.–A.D. 65) and Pliny the Elder (A.D. 23–79).

only on occasion visited their farms (*Rust.* Preface, 1.11–19; 1.1.18–20). These farms were run by slaves and tenant farmers (*Rust.* 1.1.18–20; 1.7.3; 1.8.1–19). Our concern is not farming as such, but rather details Columella supplied regarding children who worked on the farms. Mention of child labor in Columella's works is valuable precisely because he did not have ulterior motives for mentioning children in the first place.

When advising his readers on how to choose an overseer (*vilicus*) for their estate, Columella suggested that the owner select a slave who had been hardened by farm work "from his early childhood" (*ab infante*) and thus one who had been tested by his experience (*Rust.* 1.8.2). As with similar pronouncements about Timothy's learning the Scriptures "from early childhood," this phrase indicates a child who began to work on a farm from a fairly young age. This is clarified when Columella later tells the master to choose as overseer a slave who was hardened to work on a farm "from boyhood" (*a pueritia*) (*Rust.* 11.1.7).

Columella suggested that an overseer's illiteracy was not only of no concern, but actually desirable, since it meant that he would be less likely to falsify the accounting ledgers (*Rust.* 1.8.4). The overseer was responsible for the operation of the estate (*Rust.* 11.1.2–14; cf. 1.8.1–11). He had under his care all of the other workers, including all the slaves. These workers also included boys, just as the overseer himself had begun working on a farm from his boyhood. That boys were valued workers can be derived from the fact that the slave mother who had borne three boys for the estate was exempted from work. If she had more boys than that, she was manumitted (*Rust.* 1.8.19).

Slaves generally worked in the fields. Their work began at dawn (*Rust.* 11.1.14–17) and ended at twilight (*Rust.* 11.1.18). There was no distinction regarding age with respect to the work they performed or the time they engaged in it. The single exception pertained to the overseer, who was to be neither too old nor too young (*Rust.* 1.8.3; 11.1.3–6). Columella suggested that an overseer should not be a *iuvenis* (*Rust.* 1.8.3), but rather one of the *adolescentes* (*Rust.* 11.1.6). That the overseer was to assume the task of running the estate at such a young age indicates his intimate familiarity with the many tasks required of him already from boyhood on (*Rust.* 1.8.3), a point which accords with Isomachus's advice cited elsewhere in Columella that one should "train" one's own overseer (*Rust.* 11.1.4–5). That comment supports the conclusion that the young male slaves were in the fields working. An estate such as the one Columella imagined required numerous slaves. In his treatise on trees, *De arboribus,* Columella speaks of the necessity of sending fifty, sixty, or even eighty workers out to dig up the ground for a nursery (1.5–6). How many of these were children is impossible to determine, yet some boys would be among them.

Young female slaves most likely had to work in the home (*Rust*. 12; Preface, 2–6). Some may have been married, or had children to raise, as indicated by the example of the woman who was to be granted a discharge from work for having many boys (*Rust*. 1.8.19). The overseer himself was to have a wife (*contubernalis mulier*) (*Rust*. 1.8.5), known as the *vilica* (*Rust*. 12; Preface, 8). She should be young (*iuvenis*), but not a little girl (*puella*) (*Rust*. 12.1.1). Her numerous tasks focused on the home itself (*Rust*. 12.1.1–2.6). One of them was to ensure that slaves who worked in the fields actually went to the fields and that those who had tasks indoors indeed performed their work indoors (*Rust*. 12.1.5). Many young slaves also worked indoors, including boys, but the majority of these were girls. One of the main tasks for these young slaves was food service. Columella stated that one who functioned as a cook, a baker, or a cellar-person had to be chaste and continent (*Rust*. 12.4.2–3). Thus, food and drinking vessels should be handled only by children who had not reached puberty (*nisi aut ab impubi*) and who could still be defined as *pueri* or *virgines* (*Rust*. 12.4.3). These slave children would be under the age of twelve (girls) or fourteen (boys).

Not everyone who worked on the estate was a slave. Some may also have been tenant farmers (*Rust*. 1.7.1). Columella spoke of the most fortunate estate as one which had tenant farmers who were on the estate "from the cradle" and treated the land as if it were their own father's property (*Rust*. 1.7.3). Such land was rented out to families whose members grew up on the land and who worked the land together with their children. Country estates, therefore, seemed to have employed considerable numbers of child laborers, especially young slaves, who were performing duties alongside adult slaves both in the home and in the fields.

Work of Child Slaves in Urban Settings

In cities and towns, slave children performed any number of jobs. They were also employed in tasks of sexual gratification, including prostitution. We know that sexual relations with masters were imposed on the slaves, as Seneca stated that this was a necessity for slaves (*Controversiae* 4; Preface 10), whether boys or girls. Werner Krenkel observed:

Slave boys were sent out to attract customers, especially in harbor towns where they swarmed the dock areas like flies (Plautus, *The Little Carthaginian* [*Poenu-*

lus] 688–691): they roamed cities (Seneca the Younger, *Dialogues* 1.5.3) and infested baths (Pliny the Elder, *Natural History* 33.40).... To meet the demand for male prostitutes, beautiful boys were captured, imported by carriage and ship ... and prostituted.[8]

The situation was not any better for girls. Scholars have noted that a slave girl was "not in a position to refuse the sexual demands of her owner or anyone else to whom he granted the temporary use of her."[9] Kenneth James Dover recounted that slave girls "who took part in men's parties as dancers or musicians could also be mauled and importuned in a manner which might cost a man his life if he attempted it with a woman of citizen status."[10] The discussion in the following chapter of violence done to children revisits this topic, but it is important to note that a child slave's work was whatever a given master desired.

There is abundant evidence that points to the early engagement of children, slave and free, in work in the urban setting. In a discussion of food and the means by which it was distributed in Roman society and the family, Peter Garnsey noted that boys would fare well in their diet, as they made up "the bulk of the productive workforce."[11] Justinian's *Digest* stated that "if a slave is under five years of age or is infirm or is one who was unable to do any work for his owner, no estimation of the value of his services will be made."[12] In urban settings, the training of children for different tasks, as craftspeople, artisans, builders, and entertainers, started early. In the city, many children, free boys as well as slave girls and slave boys, were apprenticed to particular craftspeople in order to learn a trade. Bradley noted evidence in the form of contracts which indicated work for apprenticed children from sunrise to sunset.[13] Confirmation of such practice is to be found in the farm work that children were required to do from dawn to dusk, as mentioned in the writings of Columella (*Rust.* 11.1.14–18). Girls, slave and free, were also trained in the city for household tasks such as weaving and serving, even as they were on the country estates.[14] In fact, every girl was

8. Krenkel, "Prostitution," 1296.

9. Kenneth James Dover, "Classical Greek Attitudes to Sexual Behaviour," in *Sex and Difference in Ancient Greece and Rome* (Edinburgh: Edinburgh University Press, 2004), 114–30, here 118.

10. Ibid.

11. Garnsey, *Food and Society in Classical Antiquity*, 101.

12. Justinian, *Digest* 7.7.6.1 (ed. and trans. Mommsen, Krueger, and Watson, *The Digest of Justinian*, 242).

13. Bradley, "Child Labor," 110.

14. Pearl, "Apprentice Contract," 255–59, discusses a contract for a slave girl to learn weav-

to learn how to spin and weave,[15] a set of skills and tasks that characterized the life of practically every female in the ancient world.

Work and the Upper-Class Boy or Girl

From the writings of Musonius Rufus, a Stoic philosopher who lived from around A.D. 30 to 101,[16] and who was a member of an upper-class (equestrian) family, we gain insight into the work expectations of boys and young men and, especially, of girls and young women who came from this same class. Musonius argued for the education of girls in a manner similar to that of boys. His comments open up a window onto the common expectations for upper-class girls. When he asked whether a woman should study philosophy, he answered his own question in the affirmative, since he was convinced that such study prepared her to run the household (*oikonometē*) and the household slaves (*oiketoi*).[17] Philosophy, he claimed, will lead her to the philosophic virtues and teach her to be a blameless wife and a defender of her husband and children. He continued these themes in his treatise on daughters and sons, defending the position that girls should have access to *paideia* so that they might cultivate the same virtues (understanding, justice, self-control, and courage) as boys. Although Musonius pushed against the conventions of his time by suggesting that some girls might be best suited for outdoor work, whereas some boys might be more ready for indoor work, he did argue that most boys were suited for the *gymnasium* and outdoor work and most girls for spinning and indoor work.[18]

Musonius was concerned with the equal education of boys and girls because he desired an equality of virtue among men and women. Yet the skills that an upper-class girl needed to know remained those of lower-class and even slave girls: indoor work and weaving. Columella complained that in his day, in fact during the same era when Musonius was writing, the wives of estate owners no longer knew how to weave or do any household tasks, so taken were they with luxury (*Rust.* 12; Preface, 9–10). While these were clearly the tasks for which girls were to be prepared in the Greco-

---

ing, but these activities were common also for free girls. Weaving is a task that bound all women, free and slave, rich and poor, at least theoretically.

15. Bonner, *Education in Ancient Rome,* 7–8.

16. Cf. Lutz, "Musonius Rufus. 'The Roman Socrates,'" 14–18.

17. Musonius Rufus, "That Women Too Should Study Philosophy" (Lutz, 38–43; also edited in Stobaeus, *Anthologium* 2.31,126 [ed. Wachsmuth & Hense, *Ioannis Stobaei Anthologium,* II, 244–47]).

18. Musonius Rufus, "Should Daughters Receive the Same Education as Sons?" (Lutz, 44–47).

Roman world, the difference was that upper-class girls were also being trained to order the slaves to care for the home and perform the necessary tasks, although Musonius did not believe a woman should consider serving her husband a task suitable only for a slave and beneath her own dignity.[19]

For upper-class boys, especially those who were trained to lead a life devoted to philosophy, Musonius recommended farming. He acknowledged that this was little in favor in his day, as it was a task considered beneath the dignity of city dwellers and wealthy people.[20] He spoke of tenant farmers, those who worked the land owned by the state or private individuals, and of how they were able to feed their children and wives through their work. It should be taken for granted that the young sons of the tenant farmers also worked the land together with their fathers, while the young daughters worked indoors with their mothers. Musonius spoke highly of the "peasants" (*chōritai*) who engaged in this work and believed that his young students (*neoi*) would be able to benefit from the same kind of labor. However, the young men who could afford to study with him did not intend to begin farming. Such labor was for the tenant farmers and their children, and for the slaves and slave children who worked the land for estate owners.

Whether or not a child had to work for a living or received training to be able to do so depended on the child's social status. Examples of childhoods spent in luxury and the comforts of upper-class life are more readily documented in ancient literature. On the basis of the letters of Cicero and Pliny the Younger, for example, and from the cases treated therein of Cicero's son Marcus and of the young Minicia Marcella, who died in her early teens, Bradley deduced the basic paradigms of the lifestyles of privileged boys and girls.[21] These children did not work themselves. On the contrary, a diverse retinue of adult nurses, pedagogues, teachers, and doctors (many of whom were slaves) worked for them, as well as other slaves and servants who served in their parents' households.[22] One may easily imagine, for example, how the girl Minicia Marcella could have enlisted without much trouble the services of an *ornatrix*, a slave with special expertise in hair-

---

19. Musonius Rufus, "That Women Too Should Study Philosophy" (Lutz, 42–43).

20. Musonius Rufus, "What Means of Livelihood Is Appropriate for a Philosopher?" (Lutz, 80–85; also ed. in Stobaeus, *Florilegium* 56,18 (ed. August Meineke, *Ioannis Stobaei Florilegium* [Leipzig: B. G. Teubner, 1856], vol. II, 336–40).

21. Bradley, "Child Labor," 103–6.

22. See Pliny the Younger, *Letters* 5.16.3 (ed. and trans. Radice, *Pliny, Letters and Panegyricus*, vol. 1, 378–79); see also Bradley, "Child Labor," 106.

dressing, when she was preparing for her wedding to a young aristocratic lad. Such a scene may have occurred in a manner quite similar to that shown on a drawing after a painting from Herculaneum, which depicts a taller, female *ornatrix*, perhaps about twenty or twenty-five years of age, at work on the hairdo of a younger lady of shorter stature and seemingly in her early teens.[23] A table with the necessary wreaths, threads, and bands for ornamentation was placed conveniently next to the coiffeuse. Death cut short the same such preparations that would have taken place in Minicia Marcella's case. It forced the girl's parents, Pliny's friend C. Minicius Fundanus and his wife, Statoria Marcella, to spend "the money . . . intended for clothing, pearls and jewels" at their daughter's wedding "on incense, ointment and spices" at the girl's burial instead.[24]

Highly educated boys, who shared in this luxurious life, were trained for various vocations and careers, such as politics, the military, the legal professions, philosophy, architecture, medicine, the scholarly life, and the clergy.[25] Wealthy children had leisure in their training and education in order to take on the most prestigious of careers.

Work for Children in the Jewish World

The same basic characteristics of the work of children in Greco-Roman settings also seem to obtain in the Jewish world of late antiquity. We may recall comments made with regard to Alexandria, where "lower-class Jews neither received nor were in a position to receive encyclical education."[26] With respect to Jewish Palestine, Shaye Cohen contrasted the "aristocracy

23. See C. Daremberg and E. Saglio, eds., *Dictionnaire des antiquités grecques et romaines* (Paris: Hachette, 1877–1919), vol. 4.1, fig. 5429; reproduced in Antonio d'Ambrosio, *Women and Beauty in Pompeii*, trans. Graham Sells (Los Angeles: J. Paul Getty Museum, 2001), 16, lower picture. For the depiction of a young girl combing her hair, see the painting from Villa di Arianna, Stabiae (Museo Archeologico Nazionale, Naples, inv. 9088), shown in d'Ambrosio, *Women and Beauty*, 17, lower picture. It cannot be excluded that Propertius, *Elegies* II.18b (ed. and trans. G. P. Goold, *Propertius. Elegies* [Cambridge, Mass.: Harvard University Press, rev. ed. 1999], 154–55), asking a "crazy girl" whether she wants to "play at aping the painted Britons, tinting your hair with a foreign color," and instead telling her that "all looks are beautiful as nature has made them . . . even in the Underworld many ills befell that girl who foolishly changed her hair, lying" may witness to a certain popularity of the many different colors, including blond, red, blue, and purple, that were in use for dying hair, also among younger girls. See also d'Ambrosio, *Women and Beauty*, 17–18.

24. See Pliny the Younger, *Letters* 5.16.7 (ed. and trans. Radice, *Pliny, Letters and Panegyricus*, vol. 1, 380–81); see also Bradley, "Child Labor," 106.

25. Clarke, *Higher Education in the Ancient World*, 109–18.

26. Mendelson, *Secular Education*, 27.

and the learned elite" with the "silent majority," among whom most were poor.[27] With a particular but not an exclusive focus on Galilee, Jonathan Reed argued that "acrimonious rhetoric against the 'amei ha-aretz [i.e., the "people of the land"] by the rabbis was not directed at Galileans in general nor at a distinct Galilean religious character, but rather suggests differences due to social status." The majority of these Galileans were peasant farmers over whom social elites exerted control. In fact, Reed argued that in the first century many peasants lost their land in Galilee and became tenant farmers, day laborers, artisans, or worse.[28] This does not take into account slaves in Galilee, Palestine, or the Diaspora, but the situation for slaves was not much different among Jews than among Greeks and Romans.[29] Children in Palestine performed the same kinds of jobs and tasks at the same ages as other slave children did. When we consider the reality of slavery in the Greco-Roman world and the vast majority of the population who were also poor, we can say that most children were familiar with work, at an unskilled level, or training for a trade, at a skilled level, from early on in their lives.

Jews also apprenticed their children. Lieberman noted apprenticeship agreements, found in rabbinic literature (*PT Gittin* V.8, 47b), that contain discussions of forfeiture clauses set up to protect a father who sent his sons for training. According to Lieberman, such forfeiture clauses were also intended to protect the investment of the craftsperson, who had taken on the apprentice, not just the father. He points to first-century (*Pap. Ox.* II, 275, dated to A.D. 66) and second-century (*Pap. Ox.* IV, 725, dated to A.D. 183) papyri which include clauses specifying a sum of one hundred *drachmae* for the craftsperson if the father pulled his son out of the contractual obligation before a certain date: "If the master fails to instruct the boy fully he is liable to the same penalties."[30] These apprenticeship agreements give us a glimpse into a child's work, both in the Jewish and Greco-Roman worlds.

Wealthy Jewish boys were also trained for the professions. *Mishnah Aboth* 5:21 states that a boy at age twenty is ready for a vocation. This clearly indicates a certain type of boy, one whose father had the means to allow him leisure to study Scripture and the rabbinic texts prior to any considerations of employment. Significant discussion of a father's training of his son for a profession is to be found in *b. Kiddushin* 29a–31a, an extensive

---

27. Cohen, *From the Maccabees to the Mishnah*, 123 and 48.
28. Reed, *Archaeology and the Galilean Jesus*, 54, 66–68, and 85–87.
29. Martin, "Slavery and the Ancient Jewish Family," 113–29.
30. Lieberman, *Greek in Jewish Palestine*, 4.

conversation regarding the things a father needed to do for a son.[31] Yet, a father's obligation to teach his son a profession held true for any boy, not only those studying in a rabbinic school. R. Judah is cited as saying that if a father did not teach his son a craft, he taught him "brigandage" or thievery (*b. Kidd.* 29a and 30b).[32] Another rabbi responded (30b) by saying that failure to teach a son a craft is not teaching him thievery, but is "like" teaching the son thievery. According to the text, the rabbis differed over teaching the son a business. Apparently, R. Judah considered business so risky that only a craft would prepare the child for economic security. The preparation in a craft probably was a task fulfilled by the father himself, but the child could also have been hired out as an apprentice.

According to rabbinic literature, the kinds of jobs a boy could be prepared for were numerous. Samuel Krauss outlined a number of these professions, trades, or crafts in his classic study *Talmudische Archäologie.*[33] To be without work was considered "an evil."[34] It was necessary to have a practical profession as a balance to the theoretical study of the Torah. Yet not every craft or trade would do, since an agricultural worker was often out of work, due to the seasonal nature of his occupation.[35] Other jobs, such as weaving, haircutting, and making clothes, were seen as work fit only for a woman, a perspective also found in Greco-Roman sources. Nevertheless, despite such restrictions, many jobs remained open: Hillel was a woodcutter, Aqiba a shepherd, Judah a baker, and so on.[36] These jobs were learned at the feet of one's father.[37]

31. The relative lateness of the Babylonian Talmud certainly is one of the potential problems in attempting to use it to provide context for early Christianity. Yet three points may be noted here: a first point is that our concern is with children's work throughout the time of the whole of the early Church, a time frame into which the Babylonian Talmud fits; secondly, the training of children tended to be tradition-bound and so the dictates listed here probably preceded the time of redaction by many centuries; and thirdly, some of the rabbis listed are Tannaim whose practices indeed date to the time of the origin of the Church. On the question of using rabbis' names for dating, see Strack and Stemberger, *Introduction to Talmud and Midrash,* 63–66.

32. R. Judah is to be dated to the late second–early third century A.D. See Strack and Stemberger, *Introduction to Talmud and Midrash,* 89–90.

33. See Krauss, *Talmudische Archäologie II,* 248–49, who identified the range of professions, trades, and crafts more concisely with the German term "Gewerbe."

34. Ibid., 249, speaking of being without work as "Übel."

35. Ibid., 250, 252.

36. See Krauss, *Talmudische Archäologie II,* 254, for the complete list of professions the author could locate in the texts.

37. Ibid., 254–55, from whose perspective the father's profession or trade usually carried over and determined the field in which the son worked, or even for whom "die Beschäftigung des Vaters sich gewöhnlich auf den Sohn übertrug."

Children's Work in the Gospels

The New Testament and other early Christian documents witness to different kinds of work that children performed. We have already discussed major factors which relate to children and work—gender, ethnicity, class, and status in freedom—but other factors such as geography could also determine the type of work in which children engaged. While we may expect to find children in farming and domestic work on a regular basis, the types of jobs for which they were apprenticed varied depending on the region.[38] Given that already from the first century the early Christian world spanned such a wide geographical range, one would expect a wide range of jobs in which Christian children were employed.

Most apprenticeships took place under the watchful eye of a parent. In fact, the Gospels provide such a model. In Mark 1:16–20 (par. Mt 4:18–22; Lk 5:1–11) we see James and John working with their father in their boat. It is reasonable to assume that the father of James and John would have trained his sons in their profession from childhood.[39] The two were working alongside their father's "hired workers" (*misthōtoi*), who may have been adults or children.[40] The term may be equivalent to day laborers, but possibly also to apprentices.[41] The precise meaning would depend on the task in which the workers were engaged and on their contractual status. The origin

38. Suzanne Dixon, *The Roman Family* (Baltimore: Johns Hopkins University Press, 1992), 25 and 117.

39. In contrast, Destro and Pesce, "Fathers and Householders in the Jesus Movement," 211, 216–19, and 222, do not accept that these apostles were teenagers when they were called.

40. Biblical commentaries, dictionaries, and encyclopedias tend to omit discussions of "work" as such, and so relatively little research has been accomplished on the topic, let alone on the question of the work of children. Where the issue of work comes up, the discussion tends to focus on "economy" and not on the actual practice of work. See, for instance, the excellent contribution of Joel Marcus, *Mark 1–8*, The Anchor Bible Commentary, vol. 27 (New York: Doubleday, 2000), 180–81 and 184–85, who, unlike many commentators, actually discusses the apostles in Mark 1 as fishermen. Yet he does not speak about the craft as such, their potential age, or the question of who the hired hands may have been.

41. See Philo, *Spec. Leg.* 2.79–85 (ed. and trans. F. H. Colson, *Philo. Works*, vol. 7, LCL 320 [Cambridge, Mass.: Harvard University Press, 1954], 356–59), who discusses the differences between slaves and "hired workers." It is most likely, but not necessary, that these are hired laborers. See H. Preisker and E. Würthwein, "μισθός, μισθόω, μίσθιος, μισθωτός, μισθαποδότης, μισθαποδοσία, ἀντιμισθία," in *Theological Dictionary of the New Testament* (Grand Rapids, Mich.: Eerdmans, 1967), vol. 4, 695–728, here 695–701. *Misthos* is a reward for work on a daily, monthly, or yearly basis; *misthoō* describes the act of hiring someone or letting oneself be hired out for payment; *misthōtos* describes one who hires himself out for work or a day laborer; a *misthios* is a "hired hand." There is no reason to assume that these could not be children, especially when one keeps in mind the reality of child labor in the ancient world.

of the term, derived from the verb for "to hire" or "rent out," would link it to "day laborer" more conclusively, but apprentices were simply hired out on a longer-term basis. Even if we are dealing with day laborers, this does not exclude the possibility that they were children.[42] The synoptic parallels do not exactly clarify the situation, but Mark gives the most likely ancient scenario, with sons working alongside their father and hired workers. Matthew and Luke add little to this portrait.

Sons learning their trade and hired workers are not found only in this Markan passage in the Gospels. John 5:19 alerts us to the image of the father handing down practical knowledge in the workshop to his son. As noted earlier, Charles H. Dodd saw in the image "a picture from daily life," which John "spiritualized" to make a theological point.[43] For Dodd, John offered the image of a father handing down the tricks of the trade to his son in the family workshop. When Jesus is identified as the carpenter's son (Mt 13:55) or as the carpenter (Mk 6:3), a basic equivalence is indicated. To be the carpenter's son is to be the carpenter.[44] The trade Jesus learned was acquired starting from childhood and taught by his father.

In the parable of the Prodigal Son in Luke 15:11–32, the figure of the younger son points to two images of the hired worker. One is the son who hired himself out to a man after he had wasted his inheritance and thus was put to work feeding the pigs (Lk 15:14–16). Whether or not the son was still a child, the work he did was identical with the kind of work which children performed on large estates. The irony, of course, is that he came from such an estate himself, where as an upper-class son he never needed to engage in such humiliating work himself. His father, the owner of such an estate, also had *misthioi* ("hired workers") who had enough "bread," while his own son went hungry (Lk 15:17). These workers were not simply day laborers, since their description as being "of my father" and as "having enough bread" suggests an ongoing relationship with the father and the work of the estate.[45] Elsewhere in the parable one finds slaves (*doulos* in Lk 15:22, and *pais* in

---

42. For the time of Herod Antipas, Reed, *Archaeology and the Galilean Jesus*, 68, speaks of the removal of farmers off their own plots of land to tenancy farming and then into day labor. This placed stress on families (Reed, 98) and could have meant that children were required to look for work off of the family farm.

43. Dodd, *The Founder of Christianity*, 179, n. 4; see above, chapter 2.

44. Albright and Mann, *Matthew*, 172–73.

45. Against the definition of *misthios* in Preisker and Würthwein, "μισθός, μισθόω, μίσθιος, μισθωτός," 701, who see these workers as "day-laborers." While we accept that this is the general meaning of the term, the description of these workers in the parable suggests an ongoing relationship with the father. However, they would still be "hired" hands.

Lk 15:26), referred to in the plural. The picture in Luke's parable is quite similar to the type of estate Columella described, with day laborers, tenant farmers, and slaves engaged in farming crops or in raising animals.[46] Certainly, among these slave workers there were also children.

John 10:7–18 describes the same kind of agricultural worker. The account of the Good Shepherd in John 10 offers a theological image of Jesus' love for his people, but its relevance as a metaphor for Jesus' love derives from the ability to connect the image to everyday instances taken from life. Jesus is not a "hired worker" (*misthōtos*), but rather someone who cares for the sheep, who will lay down his life for the sheep (John 10:11–15). What, in contrast, will the hired worker do when the wolf comes? He (or she) will run. In verses 12 and 13 the term "hired worker" is used to describe someone who will dash off when the sheep are threatened. Here we have an image either of someone who works for the owner as a day laborer or of an apprentice. The worker leaves at the first sign of trouble, not being confident in his or her ability to fend off the wolf. What might be in the background is the image of a child for hire, as a day laborer or apprentice, someone who saves him- or herself when the wolf comes to threaten the flock. Admittedly, the assumption that the hired worker may be a child is somewhat speculative in this case. Yet children often filled these positions. The image of a child who cares for the sheep and then runs in fear cannot be discounted.[47]

Children's Work Elsewhere in the New Testament

The Apostle Paul received extensive education in Pharisaic schools (Phil 3:5; Gal 1:14; Acts 22:3), yet he may have been a tentmaker by trade (Acts 18:3). The picture we find in *b. Kiddushin* 29a–31a is brought to bear in this portrait of Paul.[48] While we do not know for sure where exactly his elementary education took place, we know that as a boy he would have started to study the Torah and the traditions of the fathers—later called

---

46. J. P. V. D. Baldson, *Life and Leisure in Ancient Rome* (New York: McGraw-Hill, 1969), 54, speaks of workers, free and slave, in agricultural settings working from dawn to dusk.

47. Raymond Brown, *The Gospel according to John (I–XII)*, The Anchor Bible Commentary, vol. 29 (New York: Doubleday, 1966), 388 and 395, sees these hired hands as synonymous with authorities, perhaps Pharisees, which is a likely reading of the one who cares for the sheep if not the Good Shepherd. We simply point to the actual agricultural image, which refers to situations in which children often served as shepherds and which gives the condemnation of these hired hands a powerful twist. On the image itself, Brown (387) helpfully draws attention to 4 Ezra 5:18.

48. Krauss, *Talmudische Archäologie II*, 254, lists Paul's occupation as a tentmaker among the trades of the rabbis.

"oral law"—and that he would have been trained in a trade. Given the dictates of later rabbinic teaching, it is reasonable to assume that Paul learned his trade as a boy while he was studying.

Numerous trades are listed in the Acts of the Apostles and elsewhere in the New Testament. Yet it is almost impossible to determine whether children are in view as practitioners. Not one of the specific practitioners mentioned in Acts seems to be a child. Still the crafts mentioned are of the kind for which apprenticeship, either in the home or in someone's workshop, was necessary. Some of these trades are those of the silversmith (Acts 19:24), the tanner (Acts 9:43 and 10:6), the coppersmith (2 Tm 4:14), or the seamstress (Acts 9:39). Acts 16:16–24 adds the story of a slave girl who made money for her masters by prophesying. Not infrequently, children were seen to possess this particular gift and were considered to have "a position intermediate between the human world and that of the gods."[49] This slave girl seems to fit exactly into such a category, one whose masters exploited her ominous and portentous sayings for financial gain. In Acts 19:13–20 we hear of seven Jewish exorcists, all sons of a high priest, Sceva. These sons were practicing exorcism in the name of Jesus until they were mastered by a demon and ran away defeated. We cannot discount as impossible an assumption that some of these brothers were still of a rather young age or that they may have begun their trade as children due to a special giftedness and concomitant training. Finally, we should also consider under this category Philip and his four daughters. The daughters are described as *parthenoi*, i.e., virgins, in Acts 21:9, who had the gift of prophecy. Reference to "virgins" alerts one to the possibility that they were still children, below or at the age of puberty. Children were considered suitable for the task of prophecy, functioning as intermediaries between the divine and human worlds in Greco-Roman society.[50] It is impossible to determine whether all of these children had actual spiritual gifts, were trained in this practice, were self-trained, or simply were exploited by masters and parents. In the end it may have been a combination of factors playing together in such instances.

49. Wiedemann, *Adults and Children in the Roman World*, 176; see also Horn, "The Depiction of Children and Young People."

50. See, for example, the discussion in Sarah Iles Johnston, "Charming Children: The Use of the Child in Ancient Divination," *Arethusa* 34.1 (2001), 97–118; and the comments and literature with brief discussion in Cornelia B. Horn, "Children as Pilgrims and the Cult of Holy Children in the Early Syriac Tradition: The Cases of Theodoret of Cyrrhus and the Child-Martyrs Behnām, Sarah, and Cyriacus," in Proceedings of the ARAM Twenty-First International Conference: "Pilgrimages and Shrines in the Syrian Orient" (University of Oxford), published in *ARAM Periodical* 18–19 (2006–7), 439–62, here 442–43.

Other tasks children performed required little or no training. The slave girl *(paidiskē)* who pointed out Peter's relationship to Jesus after Jesus' arrest was a slave of the high priest (Mk 14:66, 69), who engaged in the same domestic tasks as any household slave. The same can be said of Rhoda, a female slave whose name we know, and who worked in the home of Mary, mother of John Mark (Acts 12:13–14). Also her tasks would have been domestic, such as running errands and attending to the needs of the household. In fact, the reader of Acts meets her as she was answering the door at Peter's unexpected arrival.[51]

Children as Workers in Apocryphal Gospels and Acts

While children only occasionally make an appearance in canonical texts, apocryphal gospels and acts are rather well populated with children.[52] One of the liveliest sets of comments on children that also allows one to gain insight into children's lives and the type of work that was expected of them derives from the *Infancy Gospel of Thomas*. In this text, the boy Jesus is often shown as being engaged in tasks for his mother and father. When he is working with his father, the tasks are frequently related to livelihood or craft. At the age of six, Jesus is sent to get water for his mother (*IGTh* 11). While carrying the water, he breaks the jug, yet miraculously he is able to hold the water in his clothing. At planting time, Jesus sows seeds alongside his father and gains a miraculous harvest from only one grain of wheat (*IGTh* 12). Finally, in Joseph's workshop Jesus takes a beam that has been made too short and stretches it to its proper length (*IGTh* 13). All of Jesus' work involves miracles. Yet more important for the present purposes, it involves the mundane reality of a child's life in the second century, and likely also that of earlier centuries. Jesus the child carries out the basic and necessary chore of fetching water for his mother. A later chapter finds Joseph's son James gathering wood for the house (*IGTh* 16). An earlier chapter showed a friend in the workshop learning his craft (*IGTh* 10). What emerges is a rather authentic picture of a child's work in the service of an ordinary family in the ancient world.[53]

---

51. As a parallel case one may also include the slave girl *(paidiskē)* Juthine, who appears in the *Infancy Gospel of James* 2.2, 6 (ed. and trans. Hock, *The Infancy Gospels of James and Thomas*, 34–35), as the slave girl of Mary's mother, Anna. On the stock literary figure of the slave girl Rhoda, see J. Albert Harrill, *Slaves in the New Testament: Literary, Social, and Moral Dimensions* (Minneapolis: Fortress Press, 2006), 64–66.

52. See also Horn, "The Depiction of Children and Young People as Literary Device"; and Horn, "Suffering Children, Parental Authority, and the Quest for Liberation?" A fuller study of children in apocryphal literature is in preparation.

53. For stimulating discussion, also see forthcoming work by Reidar Aasgaard, including

On numerous occasions, apocryphal acts feature children running errands for their parents or other people. In the *Acts of Paul (and Thecla)*, Paul sent one of Onesiphorus's boys to buy food for the group.[54] In *Acts of John* and *Acts of Peter*, youths come and announce events to the respective apostles.[55] These situations do not qualify as work done for a wage or the acquisition of a skill, but such scenes do show young people or children working in the service of others. Running errands may generally be classified as unskilled labor. The *Acts of Peter* provides a further instance of unskilled labor that involved a certain doorkeeper *(hostiarius)* at the house of Marcellus.[56] Simon the Magician had instructed the young *(iuvenis)* doorkeeper to let Peter know that Simon was not at home, although he was hiding in the house. The evidence for this youthful doorkeeper is remarkable, since the tasks assigned to such doorkeepers call for people of a more mature age to fulfill these duties.[57]

The *Acts of Thomas* also provide the reader with an example of young female entertainers at the court of the king of Andrapolis. Thomas met a Hebrew flute-girl *(aulētria)* there, who played for the guests at the wedding of the king's young daughter.[58] Although the flute-girl's age is never specified, she is presented as an associate of the young. She seems to have been attracted by Thomas's youthful beauty and joined the young married couple when they assumed a life of asceticism, eventually going with them to India to meet Thomas. In the light of the evidence Bradley assembled on child entertainers in the ancient world, it is quite likely that this flute player still was a relatively young girl.

his "Christianity's First Nursery Tale? A Proposal for a New Interpretation of the Infancy Gospel of Thomas," paper presented at the annual meeting of the American Academy of Religion, Philadelphia, Pa., November 2005.

54. *Acts of Paul (and Thecla)* 23 (ed. Richard A. Lipsius and Maximilian Bonnet, *Acta Apostolorum Apocrypha* [Hildesheim: Georg Olms, repr. 1959], vol. 1, 235–72, here 251). The text does not specify which one of the two sons, Simmias or Zeno (see *Acts of Paul [and Thecla]* 2), was sent out. See also discussion below, chapter 7.

55. See *Acts of John* 86 (ed. and trans. Junod and Kaestli, *Acta Iohannis. Praefatio—Textus*, 293, §86, ll. 6–9 [Greek] & 292 [French]), and *Acts of Peter* 22 (eds. Richard A. Lipsius and Maximilian Bonnet, *Acta Apostolorum Apocrypha* [Hildesheim: Georg Olms, repr. 1959], vol. 1, 45–103, here 69).

56. *Acts of Peter* 9 (Lipsius and Bonnet, vol. 1, 56, ll. 27 [*hostiarius*] and 31 [*iuvenis*]).

57. See also Osiek and Balch, *Families in the New Testament World*, 25.

58. *Acts of Thomas* I.5, 8, 9, and 16 (ed. Bonnet, "Acta Philippi et Acta Thomae accedunt Acta Barnabae," in *Acta Apostolorum Apocrypha*, vol. 2.2, 108, 111–13, and 123).

The Nature of Children's Work

Social class, one's degree of freedom, and necessity determined whether or not children worked.[59] Children from better-off classes had no need to work themselves, but in their homes they witnessed slave children of their own age having to labor regularly. Free children either were apprenticed or learned crafts from their father or mother. The data we have been able to assemble from Christian texts is not as diverse as the types of employment Bradley outlined on the basis of data gathered more broadly from the Greco-Roman world. A fuller study of historiographical and hagiographical material may change that impression, given, for instance, the occasional example of a child working as a shepherd tending his parents' flocks that we have come across.[60]

The New Testament and other early Christian literature do not address at any noteworthy length the ethics of child labor. Children were not called to be free from work and without doubt the children of Christians did not stop working when their families converted. The slaves Christians continued to keep would have begun working as children. Christians may not have prostituted their slaves as readily as non-Christians, yet we do have evidence that Christian women sent their slave girls to appease the sexual desires of their husbands, because they themselves, as ascetically minded converts, were no longer willing to entertain such approaches.[61] Children worked at the professions and crafts of their fathers already at a young age, just as before the rise of Christianity, and daughters likewise learned to weave, just as before. An upper-class boy would have had the same leisurely upbringing independent of whether he was a Christian or a pagan boy. Although Chrysostom warned that wealthy freeborn sons could easily fall into a slothful existence, he accepted that cooking was not work a freeborn boy should have to do: a slave could cook for him.[62]

In general, the early Church did not develop a theology of work apart from those perspectives found in Judaism, as evidenced by Paul's desire to support himself (1 Cor 9), or in the Greco-Roman world, where most work

---

59. Bradley, "Child Labor," 109.

60. See, for example, the protagonist in the *Martyrdom of Abd al'Masih* (ed. and trans. Josephus Corluy, "Acta Sancti Mar Abdu'l Masich. Aramaice et Latine," *Analecta Bollandiana* 5 [1886], 5–52).

61. See, for example, the case of Eucleia in *Acts of Andrew* 22 (ed. and trans. Prieur, *Acta Andreae*, 468–69).

62. John Chrysostom, *On Vainglory* 70 (ed. and trans. Malingrey, *Jean Chrysostome. Sur la vaine gloire et l'éducation des enfants*, 170–71).

was apportioned as the task of slaves.[63] There does not seem to have been any explicit reflection on children and work in the ancient world. Some of this may have been due to the fact that children often needed to work, as their labor was essential for peasant families. Yet it also may have been due to the fact that Christianity conquered neither the division between enslaved and free people in the ancient world, nor that between the wealthy and the poor.[64]

Children at Play

Work did not define every minute of a child's existence. Play also was essential to the life of children in the ancient world.[65] Evidence in support of children's play comes not only from literary references, but also from examples of the material culture, which include toys, dolls, and visual representations of children playing games with balls and sticks as well as with their pets.[66] Christian children participated in games like any other children. Most of their games were traditional and ubiquitous, like those that children in the Jewish or Greco-Roman world had played in the past and continued to play. Play is essential to the formation and identity of the

63. See, for example, John Chrysostom, ibid.; and Augustine, *Confessions* I xix (30) (ed. Verheijen, *Sancti Augustini. Confessionum Libri XIII*, 16–17; trans. Chadwick, *St. Augustine. Confessions*, 21–22).

At times, the New Testament speaks of the need to work (1 Thes 4:11; 2 Thes 3:10–12). Indeed, Paul supported himself through labor (1 Cor 4:12; Acts 20:35). Yet the main focus for Christians was to do the work of God. Perhaps this perspective may account for the general lack of consideration of work, its nature, its meaning and purpose: the focus was on being engaged in the work of God in preparation for the eschaton. Jesus worked at his ministry and mission (Lk 3:23, 13:32; Jn 4:34, 6:29–30, and 17:4), while Paul spoke extensively of his and others' work for God (Rom 15:17, 16:3; 1 Cor 3:13–15; 2 Cor 6:1; Gal 4:11; Phil 2:22, 2:30, 4:3; and 1 Thes 1:3). This kind of work was not seen as an activity or manifestation of God (i.e., Gal 3:5; Eph 1:20; Col 1:10), but rather as work and effort expended for ministry: precisely this was the focus of the early Church.

64. Early Christians did show some concern for the plight of the poor. For recent work on poverty in early Christianity, see for example Susan Ashbrook Harvey, "The Holy and the Poor: Models from Early Syriac Christianity," in *Through the Eye of a Needle: Judeo-Christian Roots of Social Welfare* (Kirksville, Mo.: Thomas Jefferson University Press, 1994), 43–66; and Susan Holman, *The Hungry are Dying: Beggars and Bishops in Roman Cappadocia* (Oxford: Oxford University Press, 2001). See also the list of helpful further resources at www.povertystudies.org.

65. Golden, "Childhood in Ancient Greece," 22; Neils, "Children and Greek Religion," 146–50; and Foley, "Mothers and Daughters," 118.

66. For different types of games in which children engaged, see, for example, Rolf Hurschmann, "Kinderspiele," in *Der Neue Pauly*, vol. 6 (Stuttgart: J. B. Metzler, 1999), cols. 467–68; and Hurschmann, "Geschicklichkeitsspiele," in ibid., 4 (1998), cols. 1004–5.

child. It also prepares the child for his or her life in the adult community, usually without any consciousness of such a goal on the part of the child.[67] Lost in play, children participated in a slow process of transformation from childhood to the ideals and tasks of adulthood. Yet some Christian teachers and Church leaders such as Tertullian and John Chrysostom categorically rejected play *(ludus)* or the attendance at theater performances and other games.[68]

In the second part of this chapter we address both the play children engaged in and the way in which "play" was used as a form of children's social initiation into the life of the Christian community. As Horn has stated elsewhere regarding the understanding of the Christian as a "child" of God, the issue "also implicitly raises the question of how the idea of the Christian as a permanent child—enacted in eucharistic feedings as well as baptismal births—influenced and was influenced by the rituals of play that prepared children to participate as adults in the liturgical life of their communities."[69] Our discussion therefore considers ways in which children played, as children always and everywhere do, and also how this play related to their integration into the Christian community and to the preparation of children for life in it. We begin with a survey of games, play, and amusements in the ancient Greco-Roman world.

Rattles and Amulets

In the ancient world, as today, children had toys to amuse and distract them, appropriate to their age and abilities. Infants with limited motor skills were given basic toys to shake. These included rattles, *crepundia* and *crepitacula* (Greek: *platagē, platagōnion*), whose names are derived from the verbs meaning "to make noise," "to make noise by striking," and "to clap."[70] *Crepundia* were little ornaments, charms, or mini-toys, shaped in the form of swords, axes, tools, animals, flowers, or half moons, manufactured from clay, bronze, or, more rarely, gold or silver and pierced to allow for string-

---

67. Wiedemann, *Adults and Children in the Roman Empire*, 150.

68. See for instance Tertullian, *De spectaculis* (ed. and trans. Turcan, *Les Spectacles. Tertullien*); and Chrysostom, *On Vainglory*.

69. See Horn, "Children's Play as Social Ritual," 96. The present discussion resumes and expands upon the earlier work of that article, which was published in *Late Ancient Christianity: A People's History of Christianity*, vol. 2, ed. Virginia Burrus, Minneapolis: Fortress Press, 2005. This material is used here by permission of Augsburg Fortress Publishers.

70. See Rolf Hurschmann, "Crepundia," in *Der Neue Pauly*, vol. 3 (1997), col. 220; A. Mau, "Crepundia" and "Crepitaculum," in *Paulys Real-Encyclopädie der Christlichen Altertumswissenschaft*, vol. 4, cols. 1706–7 and 1705–6.

ing them together on a thread or a chain. *Crepundia* could be hung around a baby's neck and shoulder. The jingling and rattling noise produced by the child's movements kept the little one entertained, amused, and busy. The material artifacts bear witness to the multiple functions they performed: as toys; as indicators of the parents' wealth and status, when made from gold or another precious metal; and as a way to identify the child's family of origin. They often bore the name of the father and/or mother upon them, thus allowing a lost or even abducted child to be returned home safely.[71]

Crepitacula, on the other hand, were larger rattles which toddlers could shake or which could fit in an adult hand. They were made of clay, wood, bronze, sometimes even of the dried heads of poppy flowers and produced sound through the rattling or clattering of little pebbles or seeds placed inside. *Crepitacula* came in quite a range of shapes, including spheres, boxes, rolls, fruits such as pumpkins or pomegranates, as well as in the shape of animals, such as hedgehogs, owls, or pigs. One of the most striking rattles found is a rectangle shaped as a cradle with a baby shaking a rattle atop of it.[72]

Crepitacula were probably also used by mothers and nurses in order to calm a crying baby, attract its attention, or lull it to sleep. In ancient Greece, such rattles seem to have had apotropaic and cultic functions. Ancient Greek vases connected with funerary rites depict adults sitting opposite one another at a table or altar, holding rattles in their hands. When mothers and nurses used rattles to help the little ones fall asleep they may also have intended to ward off demonic influences.[73]

Ancient society developed customs and rites that accompanied and marked the passage of a newborn into childhood. One such custom found in ancient Rome was the placing of the *bulla* around the child's neck.[74]

---

71. Plautus, *Rudens*, IV.iv.1151–59 (ed. Edward Sonnenschein, *T. Macci Plauti. Rudens* [Oxford: Oxford University Press, 1891], 63), provides literary witness to such a usage. See also Jean-Pierre Néraudau, "Les jeux de l'enfance en Grèce et à Rome," in *Jouer dans l'Antiquité* (Marseille: Musées de Marseille, and Paris: Réunion des musées nationaux, 1992), 44–48, here 44; and Marie-Odille Kastner, "L'enfant et les jeux dans les documents d'époque romaine," *Bulletin de l'Association Guillaume Budé* (1995), 85–100, here 86.

72. The object was exhibited in the Museum of Cycladic Art, Athens, K. Politis Collection, no. 124, in January 2004. It is pictured in Plati, *Playing in Ancient Greece*, 26.

73. Pherekydes and Hellanikos (Schol. Apollonius Rhodos 2.1052–57a) identify the instruments used as *platagē*; Peisandros (*Paus.* 8.22.4) and Apollodorus (2.5.6) call them *krótala*; for the references see Karl R. Mühlbauer and Theresa Miller, "Spielzeug und Kult: Zur religiösen und kultischen Bedeutung von Kinderspielzeug in der griechischen Antike," *American Journal of Ancient History* 13.2 (1997), 154–69, here 155–56.

74. See also A. Mau, "Bulla, 2)," in *Paulys Real-Encyclopädie der Christlichen Altertumswissenschaft*, vol. 3, cols. 1048–51.

Boys and girls both wore the *bulla,* which was made of leather in the case of plebeian children, or, if the parents could afford it and came from patrician ranks, of two concave pieces of gold fastened together by a spring. Shortly after birth or on the *dies lustralis,* the day of purification,[75] the father placed the *bulla* around the little one's neck. It was worn on a cord, strap, or chain and it contained an amulet, which also pointed to the object's religious purpose as a protective charm against evil. By hanging the *bulla* around the newborn's neck, the father recognized him or her as part of the family and thus established his or her rank as child. It would have been difficult, how-ever, for a little baby boy or girl in the cradle to distinguish between the *bulla* and the *crepundia* that served him or her as entertainment. The child would have recognized both merely for their quality as toys.

Dolls and Balls

As children grew and developed their motor skills, parents gave them a wider range of toys to play with, including dolls *(pupae, korai),* tops *(stromboi, strobiloi, bembikes, kōnoi),* hoops *(trochus, trochoi, krikoi),* and balls *(sphairai).*[76] The variety among such items was vast. Latin-speaking chil-dren, for example, distinguished between five different types of balls: *paganica* (made of leather and feathers), *harpastum* (relatively hard and less elastic), *trigonalis* (small and very hard), *follis* (made of leather and inflated with air), and *folliculis* (a small balloon).[77]

Such toys were welcome gifts on feast days. On the Saturnalia, for ex-ample, a seven-day celebration encompassing the winter solstice, all mem-bers of Roman society could freely engage with one another, without re-strictions of status, rank, or rules otherwise in place between masters and slaves.[78] Gift-giving was one of the favorite activities during this feast, when schools closed and everyone practiced not-so-random acts of kindness.

75. Dixon, *Roman Family,* 101, see also 179, pl. 19, for a figure of a little boy with a bulla around his neck.

76. See also, for example, Rolf Hurschmann, "Puppen," in *Der Neue Pauly,* vol. 10 (2001), cols. 601–2; and U. Wagner, "Puppentheater," in ibid., cols. 602–4; Hurschmann, "Kreisel," in ibid., vol. 6 (1999), col. 824; Hurschmann, "Lauf- und Fangspiele," in ibid., cols. 1186–87.

77. For the classification of the different types of balls, see Kastner, "L'enfant et les jeux," 94. See also Hurschmann, "Ballspiele," in *Der Neue Pauly,* vol. 2 (1997), cols. 426–27; Hurschmann, "Harpaston," in ibid., vol. 5 (1998), cols. 163–64; and E. Wagner, "Kritische Bemerkungen zum Harpastum-Spiel," *Gymnasium* 70 (1963), 356–66.

78. See, for example, Karl-Wilhelm Weeber, "Geschenke II," in *Der Neue Pauly,* vol. 4 (1998), cols. 988–89, for the differentiation between *sigilla* (clay dolls dedicated to Saturn) and *sigillaria* (gifts exchanged at the occasion of the Saturnalia). For a fuller discussion of gift giving in the ancient world, see also Alfred Stuiber, "Geschenke," in *RAC* 10 (1978), 685–703. On the

Children partook of their fair share of cakes and sweetmeats, which were attached to boughs and exchanged between visitors and guests. Yet the *sigilla* and *sigillaria,* especially the doll-like clay figures children received as gifts, were their favorites. The rabbis bear witness to the attraction of these figures in *Tosefta Avodah Zarah* 2:6, when they outlaw participation in such gift-giving:

> One who goes to arenas or to the (Roman) camp and sees the sorcerers and charmers and clowns and buffoons and mimes and *sigillarion* and *sigillaria* behold, this is seating oneself with the scoffers. As it is written, "do not sit in the seat of the scoffers, but his delight is in the law of the Lord." You learn that these things cause a man to neglect the study of the Torah.[79]

Jewish children also seem to have found these toy statues appealing and their particular inclusion in this list of banned activities and objects is aimed at keeping Jewish children from participating in the gift-giving of Saturnalia.

Jewish concern would not have been limited to the *sigilla* and *sigillaria.* The ancient world recognized certain objects as part of cult celebrations, which today we see simply as toys or amusements. The swing, in particular, is such an item. Vase paintings show young women, often young girls, only infrequently little boys, seated on swings which satyrs or male adults keep in motion. These scenes have been interpreted as representing fertility rites or purification rituals at the Aiora-feast. This was a celebration connected in Greek mythology to the suicide of Athenian girls in revenge for the death of a male adult. Songs sung at that feast were known as *katabaukaleseis,* the same name given to songs sung by nurses to lull children into sleep.[80]

Spinning tops, sticks and hoops, and balls also had cult connections. The Greek gods had played with them, and like Hermes depicted on a vase as teaching Ganymede how to play with the top, had taught the divine offspring the necessary skills. In variations of the Bacchic mystery cult, the top was one of the identifiers of Dionysus' presence.[81] Whips, knucklebones, tops, and hoops are frequently found as votive offerings in ancient sanctuaries, pointing to their use as gifts given by boys and girls at the oc-

---

Saturnalia, see also, for example, Götz Distelrath, "Saturnalia," in *Der Neue Pauly,* vol. 11 (2001), cols. 113–15; and Dolansky, "Ritual, Gender, and Status in the Roman Family," 161–214.

79. Our translation. The distinction between *sigillarion* and *sigillaria* is not obvious, unless it is simply the replication of the singular and plural forms. The differences between the two are otherwise not clear, unless the rabbis have conflated the *sigilla* and *sigillaria* (see note 78 above). Nevertheless, the terms usually describe the small clay dolls associated with the festival.

80. Mühlbauer and Miller, "Spielzeug und Kult," 156–57.

81. Ibid., 158.

casion of initiatory rituals. The connection of more formal games to various cults must not be forgotten. Children participated in these games, and "sporting competitions were usually held as part of regular, recurring festivals in honor of gods and heroes."[82]

Dolls may also have had a particular cultic link, as they often were a part of offerings to gods and goddesses that marked the transition to adulthood. In the ancient world dolls were made from rags, clay, hard wood (e.g., ebony), bone, ivory, or wax. Some dolls had movable, jointed arms and legs. Although the literary references to dolls are relatively infrequent, the archaeological evidence is especially rewarding.[83]

There has been intense debate over whether dolls were primarily toys, or votive offerings to deities that only secondarily functioned also as toys for children. Depictions of children with dolls on tombstones, reliefs on other types of monuments, and paintings show the child holding the doll or looking at it; but there are no scenes of children actually playing with dolls.

Children seem to have shared toys with one another, and at times children of both sexes played with the same kinds of toys. Girls and boys played with nuts, pebbles, and knucklebones. Given that dolls were found in temples of Apollo, one of the two gods in the ancient world to whom boys dedicated their toys when entering adult life,[84] it is not unlikely that at least a few boys possessed and played with dolls. More often, however, dolls are found in tombs of girls and in temples and sanctuaries of female goddesses like Aphrodite, Venus, and Hera.

Many of the depictions of dolls, as well as physically preserved dolls, do not represent a baby's body but instead contain indicators of sexual differentiation. They represent a young marriageable girl or an already married adult woman. It seems likely that girls looked at dolls as role models. The Greek word *korē* is instructive: it is employed in a fourfold meaning to describe a doll, the figurines which priestesses offer to the gods or nymphs,

82. See Golden, *Sport in the Ancient World from A to Z*, 116–17, 121–22, and 147.

83. See especially Kate McKnight Elderkin, "Jointed Dolls in Antiquity," *American Journal of Archaeology* 34.2 (1930), 455–79; Michel Manson, "Les Poupées Antiques," in *Jeux et Jouets dans l'Antiquité et au Moyen Age, Dossiers de l'Archéologie* 168 (1992), 48–57; and Georges Lafaye, "Pupa," in *Dictionnaire des antiquités grecques et romaines*, vol. 4.1 (1905), 768–69.

84. The other one was Hermes. See *Anthologia Palatina* VI.309 (ed. and trans. W. R. Paton, *The Greek Anthology*, 5 vols. [Cambridge, Mass.: Harvard University Press, 1958–63], vol. 1, 466–67): "his favorite ball, and his noisy wooden rattle, and the knucklebones that he so wanted, and the top that he used to whip—all these Philokles offered to Hermes [when he grew up]." See also Beryl Rawson, "Adult-Child Relationships in Roman Society," in *Marriage, Divorce, and Children in Ancient Rome*, 7–30, here 19–20.

a young girl, or, later in the Christian era, the *Theotokos*, Mary, the Mother of God.[85] Dolls made from precious materials or beautifully dressed may have suggested to the little girl what her future life would look like and thus instilled in her the desire to grow up and be a chaste bride. When that goal was reached, on the eve of the wedding day, the doll, together with other toys, was offered as votive gift at the shrine of a female goddess. The example of Timarete is often referred to because she dedicated her tympana, a ball, a hair-band, her dolls, and her dolls' clothes to Artemis right before her wedding.[86] Girls made the transition to adulthood rapidly and giving up dolls for marriage represents only the sharpest of these transitions.[87]

At the age of seven boys had to give up some of their childhood toys too, as Wiedemann suggested.[88] To make the transition easier, new toys and games were developed in the service of learning how to read and write at school. In order to render the children's earliest attempts at acquiring the basics of the alphabet more effective and enjoyable, parents and instructors invented visual and tactile teaching tools, such as large, carved letter blocks. Quintilian spoke of such ivory letters made for schooling purposes.[89] Evidence of such letters carved from ivory also witnesses to the monetary resources parents needed to invest not only to make those reading lessons possible in the first place, but also to turn them into pleasurable, fun activities.

The Games Children Played

Few descriptions of the actual rules of children's games have come down to us. From the relatively little that survives, however, one gets the

---

85. Mühlbauer and Miller, "Spielzeug und Kult," 161. It is worth noting that in the Byzantine tradition, the *Theotokos* is also called *korē*, for example, in the *Canon to the Akathistos Hymn*, odes 8 and 9 (Greek text and English trans. N. Michael Vaporis and Evie Zachariades-Holmberg, *The Akathist Hymn and Small Compline* [Needham, Mass.: Themely Publications, 1992], 14–15). We are grateful to Robert R. Phenix for providing this reference.

86. *Anthologia Palatina* VI.280 (ed. and trans. Paton, *Greek Anthology*, vol. 1, 448–49).

87. In connection with the distancing of pre-teen children from their toys, it is of interest to note that recent research conducted by scientists at the University of Bath, England, has shown that girls more readily than boys tend to mutilate their Barbie® dolls when transitioning into their teenage years. See the announcements, for example, Alexandra Frean, "Barbarism Begins with Barbie, the Doll Children Love to Hate," *The Times* (U.K.), December 19, 2005; and Anastasia de Waal, "Barbie in the Microwave," *The Guardian*, December 22, 2005. We are grateful to Robert Phenix Jr. for alerting us to this phenomenon.

88. Wiedemann, *Adults and Children in the Roman Empire*, 153.

89. Quintilian, *De institutione oratoria* 1.1.26 (ed. and trans. Butler, *The Institutio oratoria of Quintilian*, vol. 1, 32–33).

impression that some of the games children played were quite similar to games still common in modern times. Such games included blind man's bluff, hide-and-seek, or forms of tug-of-war. Board games were also quite popular, but instead of the marbles or shaped pieces used nowadays, children in the ancient world played with pebbles or nuts. These could also be used for playing without a prescribed or drawn board. The sarcophagus of the boy Aemilius Daphnus shows a dozen little boys playing in small groups with nuts on the ground.[90]

Very popular, not only among children, was a game played with bones taken from the ankle joints of young calves, sheep, or goats. Those knucklebones *(astris, astrichos, astragaloi)* resembled dice and thus could be used in a similar manner, by assigning numeric value to the different sides.[91] Variations of the games played with these bones were among the best loved and most widespread forms of entertainment, judging from the many depictions of scenes of children engaged in them on vases, reliefs, and paintings and in sculptures, and from the plentiful archaeological evidence. In ancient times, knucklebones also served their users in petitioning an oracle or in making votive offerings in sanctuaries, and they were understood to be closely connected with Eros, the god of love, and Aphrodite, whose chosen toy they were. The throw of knucklebones that achieved the highest number of points was named after her.[92]

Boys and girls played at times by themselves, and at other times in groups, sometimes with members of their own sex, and at other times in mixed company. A young boy might enjoy rolling his hoop, as depicted and remembered by his family on a sarcophagus.[93] While it may be presumed that a little girl at times played with her doll or another toy by herself, depictions of such scenes are difficult to find. The late-second-century A.D. terracotta statue of a young girl playing knucklebones, preserved in the Staatliche Museen, Berlin, is among the very rare exceptions.[94] Most frequently children at play are seen as a part of a group. Minucius Felix preserves the rules for a game of throwing shells played by groups of boys:

90. Rawson, *Marriage, Divorce, and Children in Ancient Rome*, pl. 4b.

91. See also Hurschmann, "Astragal," in *Der Neue Pauly*, vol. 2 (1997), col. 120.

92. See François Poplin, "Les jeux d'osselets antiques," in *Jeux et Jouets dans l'Antiquité et au Moyen Age, Dossiers de l'Archéologie* 168 (1992), 46–47; and Mühlbauer and Miller, "Spielzeug und Kult," 159–60.

93. Paul Veyne, "The Roman Empire," in *A History of Private Life: I. From Pagan Rome to Byzantium* (Cambridge, Mass.: Harvard University Press, 1987), 5–234, here 16.

94. See the depiction in Poplin, "Les jeux d'osselets antiques," 46.

When we had reached the place where some boats, supported on oak plank-
ing, to save them from ground rot, were lying idle, we saw a party of boys com-
peting eagerly in their game of throwing sherds into the sea. The game is to
choose from the shore a flat sherd, one smoothed by the friction of the waves,
to catch hold of the sherd by the flat side, and then bending forward and
stooping, to send it spinning as far as one can on the top of the waves, so that
the missile either skims the surface of the sea and swims on its way, gliding
forward with a gentle impulse; or else shaves the tops of the waves, glancing
and jumping as it takes its successive leaps. The boy won, whose sherd went
furthest, and made [the] most hops.[95]

This is a game that continues to be played today at any seashore filled with
pebbles and children.

A second-century A.D. painting from an underground tomb shows
a group of boys hitting a ball to keep it up in the air and prevent it from
touching the ground.[96] Another marble relief shows teenage boys holding
what looks like field hockey sticks preparing to face off for possession.[97] A
relief on a second-century child's sarcophagus depicts separate groups of
boys and girls; three girls lined up behind one another, taking turns throwing a ball against the wall; and a group of four boys, two rolling a nut down
an inclined board, attempting to hit and demolish a tower of nuts by two
other boys.[98] Ovid specified the rules for this and related games with nuts
for future generations.[99] Other reliefs show groups of girls playing quoits
or knucklebones with one another. Less common are scenes that depict
groups of children of both sexes playing together.[100]

As one might expect, then as now, children could get rowdy and out
of control when playing with one another. In the midst of a game, a fight
could break out and a boy, for example, might start tearing the hair from

95. Minucius Felix, *Octavius* 3 (ed. and trans. Gerald H. Rendall, *Minucius Felix*, LCL [Lon-
don: William Heinemann, 1966], 314–437, here 318–19 [modified]).

96. For depiction, see Veyne, "The Roman Empire," 15.

97. Plati, *Playing in Ancient Greece*, 27. The marble relief is found in the Archaeological Museum, Athens.

98. See Veyne, "The Roman Empire," 16, for depiction.

99. Ovid, *Nux* 73–86 (ed. Fridericus Waltharius Lenz, *P. Ovidis Nasonis. Halievtica Fragmenta—Nux, Incerti: Consolatio ad Liviam* [Turin: G. B. Paravia, 1952], 139–41; trans. I. H. Mozley, *Ovid in Six Volumes*, vol. 2: *The Art of Love, and Other Poetry* [Cambridge, Mass.: Harvard
University Press, 1979], 298–301).

100. See also Kastner, "L'enfant et les jeux," 92. Depictions can be found in Veyne, "The
Roman Empire," 15–16 and 18; Poplin, "Les jeux d'osselets antiques," 47, showing two young
women playing knucklebones; and Wiedemann, *Adults and Children in the Roman Empire*,
pl. 20.

his playmate's head, as depicted on a sarcophagus, now in the Museo Chiaramonti.[101] Not necessarily causing "torrents of blood nor dead bodies," children's sport and pastime nonetheless reminded the observer of scenes of battle and war. To prevent children's play from becoming too destructive, forms of control were considered necessary. At official competitions, a *rhabdouchos* (pl. *rhabdouchoi*) was employed to keep order and punish rule breakers; such punishment could take the form of a strike with the rod *(rhabdos).*[102] People in the ancient world did not hesitate to exercise control over children via corporal punishment.

Children's Pets and Children as Pets

Children greatly enjoyed their pets. Sometimes boys caught mice and then harnessed them to a small toy cart or carriage. From the first Christian century onward, evidence for cats as children's pets emerges, at least in larger cities like Rome, but the evidence on the whole suggests that dogs were much more common. Children also played with other animals, like goats and rabbits, indicators of a childhood in the country. Aquatic creatures and birds were included in the range of animal companions for children as well. Pliny the Younger described how the children at Hippo in North Africa had once found a special friend in a tame dolphin alongside of which they used to swim. That spectacle, however, led to such a stream of curious tourists visiting town that the city's administrators ended up killing the dolphin in secret to restore order.[103]

The close bond that could develop between a child and its pet is also documented on tombstones. Presumably the parents of Avita, a little girl who died at the age of ten years and two months, memorialized their daughter by having her depicted as seated on a chair with an open book on her lap and a dog sitting right behind her to the left and looking up at her. A mid-first-century A.D. marble altar from Ostia depicts the five-year-old freeborn Egrilius firmly holding on to the left horn of a little goat to his right.[104]

A different aspect of the connection between children and pets emerg-

101. See Wiedemann, *Adults and Children in the Roman Empire*, pl. 20.

102. See Golden, *Sport in the Ancient World from A to Z*, 148. One also notes the use the Apostle Paul made of the term *rhabdos* in 1 Corinthians 4:21, when after describing himself as their spiritual father, he asked the Corinthians whether he should come with a spirit of gentleness or with a *rhabdos.*

103. Pliny the Younger, *Letters* 9.33 (ed. and trans. Radice, *Pliny, Letters and Panegyricus*, vol. 2, 146–49). See also Wiedemann, *Adults and Children in the Roman Empire*, 90.

104. For respective depictions of these two artifacts see Wiedemann, *Adults and Children in the Roman Empire*, pl. 22; and Rawson, *Marriage, Divorce, and Children in Ancient Rome*, pl. 3.

es when one considers how children at times became either the object or the expression of the playfulness of adults in the ancient world. As literary sources attest, some members of the imperial household, e.g., Livia, Domitian, and Commodus, thought of and treated little children, often very young slave girls or boys, as pets *(deliciae)*.[105] The nakedness of the child's body suggested fruitfulness, sensual pleasure, and playfulness in artistic depictions, as on a mid-second-century A.D. marble relief from Ostia that shows a couple with right hands joined in marital pose *(dextrarum iunctio)*, the wife leaning her left hand over her husband's right shoulder while holding a fruit or a ball in it. The two are framed by three naked young boys, the one in front at the bottom of the picture representing a real child, the couple's young son, the two to the upper right and left representing *putti*.[106] The naked body as such did not pose a moral problem for early Christians either, given that their central rite of initiation, baptism, required full immersion, and the chrismation of the body included the genitals. In the case of little children, such baptismal rituals continued well beyond the third-century turn to more body- and gender-conscious regulations, as Christians increasingly felt that practices of ascetic renunciation ought to include the renunciation of the naked body.

Preparation for Adulthood

Although many types of toys and games were common to children of both sexes, some of the toys children played with helped instill in them an idea of what their future roles and tasks in life might look like, similar to the role which fancifully dressed dolls played for girls. While some of the miniature furniture pieces and vessels that often accompany dolls found in sanctuaries and tombs may be interpreted as additional votive offerings or funer-

---

105. While commenting on Livia, Cassius Dio speaks of "one of the prattling boys, such as the women keep about them for their amusement, naked as a rule"; elsewhere he refers to "one of the naked 'whispering' boys" who filched away a two-leaved tablet of linden wood from under Domitian's pillow (*Roman History* 48.44, 67.15 [ed. and trans. Earnest Cary, *Dio's Roman History*, 9 vols. (Cambridge, Mass.: Harvard University Press, 1914), vol. 5, 312–15]). Herodian reports that "[Commodus] forgot about the little boy, who was one of those that fashionable Roman fops are pleased to keep in their households running around without any clothes on, decked out in gold and fine jewels. Commodus had such a favourite, whom he often used to sleep with. He used to call him Philocommodus, a name to show his fondness for the boy" (*History* 1.17.3 [ed. and trans. C. R. Whittaker, *Herodian. History of the Empire* (Cambridge, Mass.: Harvard University Press, 1969), vol. 1, 114–15]). See also Wiedemann, *Adults and Children in the Roman Empire*, 26 and 45, and the discussion in Laes, "Desperately Different?"

106. Rawson, *Marriage, Divorce, and Children in Ancient Rome*, plate preceding title page.

ary objects providing for the children's necessities in the afterlife, they also could have functioned as accessories to dolls with which the girls played, inspiring and modeling demands for proper household equipment for a future lady.[107] One does notice that children who raced in the ancient equivalent of a go-cart, i.e., a fit-to-size version of a chariot or carriage hitched to a small animal, often a goat or sturdy pony, are depicted as male.[108] In addition to the enjoyment the boys gained from the ride, they also may have imitated the latest winner of the horse races in the arena. At the same time, and with a view to their future life in public and on the road, they learned basic skills of how to handle such means of transportation.

Christian Children and Play

We have already seen how images of children at play can be gained from archaeological evidence of toys and other objects that may have functioned in the context of games and related activities, sometimes of a ritual or cultic nature. A significant amount of this type of archaeological data is drawn from reliefs on children's sarcophagi and from excavations of children's burial sites. Yet even with these scattered images, glimpses of children at play, the picture remains incomplete. Classicists and museum curators have started the process of piecing together the scattered literary and material data.[109] The following exploration attempts to begin the same process for images of Christian children at play to be found in literary sources.

New Testament Images of Play

The New Testament presents the reader with only a few images of children at play. The image in Matthew 11:17 (Lk 7:32) hearkens to the reality of

107. For depictions of miniature dishes see Agnès Durand, "Jeux et jouets de l'enfance en Grece et à Rome," in *Jeux et Jouets dans l'Antiquité et au Moyen Age, Dossiers de l'Archéologie* 168 (1992), 10–17, here 16; and Jean-Marie André, "Jeux et divertissements dans le monde greco-romain," in *Jeux et Jouets dans l'Antiquité et au Moyen Age, Dossiers de l'Archéologie* 168 (1992), 36–45, here 44.

108. Veyne, "The Roman Empire," 14, and probably also the picture of the section of the Tomb of the Haterii, depicted there on 24; see also Wiedemann, *Adults and Children in the Roman Empire*, pl. 18.

109. For example, in the studies of the classicists Wiedemann, *Adults and Children in the Roman Empire*; and Leslie Joan Shumka, "Children and Toys in the Roman World: A Contribution to the History of the Roman Family" (M.A. thesis, University of Victoria, Canada, 1993); as well as in the anonymously published exhibition catalogue *Jouer dans l'Antiquité*, Musée d'Archéologie Méditerranéenne, Centre de la Vieille Charité, Marseille, France (1992), and Plati, *Playing in Ancient Greece*.

children's lives, playing in the marketplaces *(agora)*, with parents nearby sell-ing their wares or with the children being alone, calling out to their friends. Matthew 7:11 (Lk 11:13) presents the idea of children *(tekna)* receiving "good" gifts from parents, much like the children celebrating the Saturnalia. Another image involving children's play is that of Paul putting aside "childish things" *(ta tou nēpiou*, "the things of childhood") when he became a man,[110] a com-ment which may bring to mind the formal and informal ways in which toys and games were offered up when a girl or boy reached the appropriate age.

Paul's writings also reflect awareness of the athletic contests in which both children and adults participated. It is not clear whether this knowl-edge is derived from his own experience in the *gymnasium*, from youth-ful participation in athletic contests, or simply from his observation of games, especially those at Corinth, the Isthmian Games.[111] In 1 Corinthi-ans 9:24–27, Paul used images from both boxing and running, sports in which both children and adults competed for prizes. As Robert Dutch has noted, "Boys, ephebes, and men trained, and competed, in the *gymnasium* as well as in games." He also commented that "in the Corinthian church the educated elite who were ephebes, or ex-ephebes, possibly *neoi*, had this intimate connection with the Isthmian games and may have competed in them and/or other contests."[112] Paul himself also employed athletic imag-ery in Philippians 3:14 and 1 Thessalonians 2:19, and such imagery can be found in 2 Timothy 2:5 as well. Whether Paul himself ever engaged in such games is beyond our ability to discern, yet his usage of athletic terminol-ogy and images constitutes evidence of his knowledge of youthful games and supposes that those in his congregations both knew the games and may even have competed in them, or trained for them in the *gymnasium*.

---

110. For studies of childhood matters in Paul's correspondence, see Reidar Aasgaard, "Paul as a Child: Children and Childhood in the Letters of the Apostle," *Journal of Biblical Literature* 126 (2007), 129–59; Christine Gerber, *Paulus und seine "Kinder": Studien zur Beziehungsmeta-phorik der paulinischen Briefe* (Berlin: de Gruyter, 2005); T. J. Burke, "Paul's Role as 'Father' to His Corinthian 'Children' in Socio-Historical Context (1 Corinthians 4:14–21)," in *Paul and the Corinthians: Studies on a Community in Conflict. Essays in Honour of Margaret Thrall*, ed. T. J. Burke and J. K. Elliott (Leiden: E. J. Brill, 2003), 95–113; and Yarbrough, "Parents and Children in the Letters of Paul."

111. For a general overview, see T. Wilson, *St. Paul and Paganism* (Edinburgh: T&T Clark, 1927); Victor C. Pfitzner, *Paul and the Agon Motif: Traditional Athletic Imagery in the Pauline Literature* (Leiden: E. J. Brill, 1967); Oscar Broneer, "Paul and the Pagan Cults at Isthmia," *Har-vard Theological Review* 64 (1971), 169–87, here 186–87; Robert S. Dutch, *The Educated Elite in 1 Corinthians: Education and Community Conflict in Graeco-Roman Context* (London: T&T Clark, 2005), 219–47.

112. Dutch, *The Educated Elite in 1 Corinthians*, 247.

This evidence also raises an issue that later Christians had to deal with more fully. The games of ancient Greece and Rome often had cultic associations, even those practiced in the *gymnasium*. Games such as the Isthmian Games, celebrated at Corinth, were sacred. It may be the case that the context for Paul's discussion of eating food offered to idols in 1 Corinthians 8–10 was that of youthful participants from the Corinthian church taking part in sacred meals.[113] The association of games and play with pagan rites was something which would trouble Church leaders for centuries.

Overall, the seriousness of the mission and task of Jesus and the earliest Christians seems to have overwhelmed any sense, and most images, of children at play. Even the images of children at play that occur in the New Testament material are used as counterpoints to a different spiritual reality, a reality of people who have not hearkened to God's voice, have not trusted God for spiritual gifts, or have not put aside an immature faith. These images are not employed to focus on the games and toys of children. In using the language and imagery of athletics Paul transformed this realm of children's participation in the life of the community into the spiritual contest.

Jesus at Play in the *Infancy Gospel of Thomas*

Other early Christian texts, those at the margins of canonical literature, presented their readers with a larger stock of images of children at play. Among these, the *Infancy Gospel of Thomas* describes the boy Jesus at play. In virtually no other text of early Christian provenance do we hear of Jesus playing. Between the ages of five and twelve, Jesus is presented as playing with many friends at a ford in the stream (*IGTh* 2.1) where he made twelve sparrows from clay and then gave them life (*IGTh* 2.3). Jesus also is shown playing in a house with playmates when one of them fell down and died (*IGTh* 9.1). Again, the focus of the *Infancy Gospel of Thomas* was upon Jesus' miraculous acts: birds from clay took on real life and Jesus raised a dead boy to life. One focus in reading this evidence may be on the mundane: Jesus played with playmates both indoors and outdoors in the water and mud, even though the games are not specified. This offers a rather common picture of children at play in a Jewish or Greco-Roman context. The games do not seem to have been organized, but children were together utilizing whatever was available for play.

---

113. Ibid., 244.

Christian Children and Religious Dimensions of Their Play

We do not know much about the toys or gifts given to infants in Judaism. Yet as noted above, Paul did speak about putting away the "things of childhood" (1 Cor 13:11). While these may be considered to be of only symbolic value—as references to childish speaking, thinking, or reasoning—we should not too quickly dismiss the thought that he also may be speaking of the experience of putting aside his toys, as many children did in the Greco-Roman world. Christian children were also given toys to play with. Even in infancy, the habit of wearing *bullae* or other amulets in a Greco-Roman context may have made it a natural transition for Christian children to wear cross pendants as signs of recognition as well. For Christian children, the transition from the Saturnalia to the later Christian celebration of Christmas, observed at the same time of year, would have been an easy task, given that they continued to receive the toys they so treasured.[114]

Christians were conscious of cultic connections associated with specific toys, but given the everyday nature of the objects involved, they may not have seen a need to despise their use as "un-Christian." Their teachers and catechists attempted to break such habits, however, just as we saw in a Jewish context with *Tosefta Avodah Zarah* 2:6. Clement of Alexandria's *Protreptikos*, a second-century prospectus for potential converts to Christianity, ridiculed the Dionysian mysteries and the central place which toys like tops and rattles held in it:

The mysteries of Dionysus are wholly inhuman; for while [Dionysus was] still a child, and the Curetes danced around [his cradle] clashing their weapons, and the Titans having come upon them by stealth, and having beguiled him with childish toys, these very Titans tore him limb from limb when but a child, as the bard of this mystery, the Thracian Orpheus, says:—"Cone, and spinning-top, and limb-moving rattles, And fair golden apples from the clear-toned Hesperides." And the useless symbols of this mystic rite it will not be useless to exhibit for condemnation. These are dice, ball, hoop, apples, top, looking-glass, tuft of wool.[115]

---

114. For gift giving in the service of advancing the early educational efforts of children, see also Jerome, *Letter* 128.1 (ed. Hilberg, *Sancti Eusebii Hieronymi Epistulae*, CSEL 56.1, 157, ll. 1–4): "In the meantime let her learn the alphabet, spelling, grammar, and syntax. To induce her to repeat her lessons with her little shrill voice, hold out to her as rewards cakes and mead and sweetmeat (*proponatur ei crustula mulsi praemia, et, quicquid gustu suaue est*)."

115. Clement of Alexandria, *Protreptikos* II.17.2–18.1 (ed. Marcovich, *Clementis Alexandrini*

Clement perceived it to be a danger that insufficiently educated new converts might continue to connect the toys and games of their childhood with the services and rites of gods they were called upon to leave behind when joining the Church, thus displaying the same concern which drove Paul's discussion of people participating in cultic meals in 1 Corinthians 8 and 10. Moreover, adults could pass these connections down to their children through the toys they bestowed on them as gifts.

That such fears were not completely unfounded even into the fifth century emerges from the description of a scene in Theodoret of Cyrrhus's *Ecclesiastical History*. Theodoret's main concern at this instance was to blackmail his opponent Lucius and the city's Arian faction. On that occasion, Theodoret also recorded that a group of boys subjected the ball with which they were playing to an ancient pre-Christian fire-based purification ritual for fear that it might have been polluted.

Some lads were playing ball in the market place and enjoying the game, when Lucius was passing by. It chanced that the ball was dropped and passed between the feet of the ass. The boys raised an outcry because they thought that their ball was polluted. On perceiving this Lucius told one of his suite to stop and learn what was going on. The boys lit a fire and tossed the ball through the flames with the idea that by so doing they purified it. I know indeed that this was but a boyish act, and a survival of the ancient ways; but it is none the less sufficient to prove in what hatred the town held the Arian faction.[116]

In a town torn apart by internal Christian bickering and strife, hatred against the Christian "other" appears to have taken up more space than working toward reconciliation. That the catechesis of children with an eye toward Christianizing aspects of their everyday activities may have fallen to the wayside, or at least been neglected, is not surprising.

Christian Girls Looking to Their Dolls as Role Models?

Christian references to girls and dolls suggest that little girls may have prized the doll more for its looks than for its potential as playing companion. In his advice on how to raise the little Pacatula, Jerome thought the

---

Protrepticus, 26–27; trans. William Wilson, *The Writings of Clement of Alexandria* [Edinburgh: T&T Clark, 1868], 29–30).

116. Theodoret of Cyrrhus, *Ecclesiastical History* 4.15.5–7 (ed. Leon Parmentier and Günther Christian Hansen, *Theodoret. Kirchengeschichte* [Berlin: Akademie Verlag, c1998], 236; trans. Blomfield Jackson, "The Ecclesiastical History of Theodoret," NPNF 2nd ser., vol. 3 [repr. Peabody, Mass.: Hendrickson Publishers, 1995], 33–159, here 117 [yet included in book 4, ch. 13]).

doll an appropriate reward for her. He was sure that she would "make haste to perform her tasks if she hopes afterwards to get some bright bunch of flowers, some glittering bauble, some enchanting doll."[117]

The evidence concerning the dedication of dolls from the classical and Hellenistic periods helps to augment and explain the limited Christian evidence for children dedicating their toys to God. Like other parents, Christian parents made decisions for their children's future. Such plans included the dedication of an infant to a religious life. In some instances parents who had made such decisions are presented in a way reflecting the votive offering of toys and dolls in particular. Jerome noted that "some mothers when they have vowed a daughter to virginity clothe her in somber garments, wrap her up in a dark cloak, and let her have neither linen nor gold ornaments. They wisely refuse to accustom her to what she will afterwards have to lay aside."[118] Such mothers manifested toward their daughters the same behavior they as girls would have shown toward dolls, dressing them in whatever outfit suited their fancy. In the Christian context, the chosen garments for the girls were appropriate to their destination for the ascetic life. Other Christian mothers adopted the opposite policy, realizing that "women are fond of finery and many whose chastity is beyond question dress not for men but for themselves." Thus the second group of mothers thought it better if they gave their daughters what they asked for so that they might "enjoy things to the full and so learn to despise them."[119]

The question of what kinds of dolls either group of mothers would have given their daughters to play with is intriguing. One might assume that the first group considered giving them dolls dressed in simple and dark-colored clothes in order to reinforce the desired vision of the future ascetic life. In the last chapter of his treatise *On Vainglory,* John Chrysostom seems to support such a proposition. While he does not speak of dolls specifically, he does reject daughters' being introduced to "extravagance and personal adornment" or "finery and excitement." His suggestion is simple: "let us repress all these tendencies."[120]

Yet neither archaeological nor most textual data support such assumptions of dolls in outfits appropriate for the ascetic lifestyle. Many of the

---

117. Jerome, *Letters* 128.1 (ed. Hilberg, *Sancti Eusebii Hieronymi Epistulae,* CSEL 56.1, 157, ll. 4–6).

118. Jerome, *Letters* 128.2 (ed. Hilberg, 157, ll. 11–14).

119. Jerome, *Letters* 128.2 (ed. Hilberg, 157, ll. 16–18).

120. John Chrysostom, *On Vainglory* 90 (ed. and trans. Malingrey, *Jean Chrysostome. Sur la vaine gloire et l'éducation des enfants,* 196–97).

dolls for which accessories or indications of clothing survive project the image of a well-groomed young lady. This observation holds true for dolls from non-Christian and Christian settings spanning a time frame of several hundred years. Among the better known examples are bone and ivory dolls of Vestal Virgins and child empresses. From the second century comes the example of an attractive jointed doll in bone, depicting a tall, elegant young woman, wearing a gold necklace as well as bracelets on wrist and ankle. The doll was found in the tomb of the Vestal Virgin Cossinia. Alongside the doll, excavators also found a small jewel casket made of red glass.[121] The second example consists of the second-century jointed ivory doll of Crepereia Try-phaena, which was found wearing two golden bracelets and a ring with an attached key. That doll displays an impressive, towering hairdo.[122] The third example is a clearly Christian one, consisting of two precious ivory dolls found in the coffin of the fifth-century empress Maria, baby bride of Hono-rius.[123] Yet dolls belonging to children of less elite status display no obvi-ous signs of having once been dressed in simple outfits either. It is plausible that the traditional usage of dolls elaborately adorned as brides continued because those dolls were understood as models of virginal chastity. Dolls presented girls with an image of the attractive wife,[124] a role for which they could become accustomed through play and for which they could prepare. Thus even a girl destined for the life of virginity, and perhaps especially such a girl, could, in the eyes of her parents and guardians, be encouraged to grow further toward internalizing and accepting the ideal of becoming the "bride of Christ" by playing with beautifully dressed and adorned dolls.

Serious Play

Some Christian children appear to have been soberly aware of the se-riousness of transitioning from one stage of childhood to another. A late

121. Manson, "Les Poupées Antiques," 56; Kastner, "L'enfant et les jeux," 90; Eugenia S. P. Ricotti, *Giochi e giocattoli* (Rome: Quasar, 1995), 57–58; M. R. Rinaldi, "Ricerche sui giocattoli nell'antichità a proposito di un'iscrizione di Brescello," *Epigraphica* 18 (1956), 104–29, here 118–19.

122. Elderkin, "Jointed Dolls," 471–72; Rinaldi, "Ricerche sui giocattoli nell'antichità," 116–17; A. Reith, "Die Puppe im Grab der Crepereia," *Atlantis* 33 (1961), 367–69; Jutta Väterlein, *Roma ludens: Kinder und Erwachsene beim Spiel im antiken Rom* (Amsterdam: B. R. Grüner, 1976), 29–30; Anna Mura Somella, *Crepereia Tryphaena; Le scoperte archeologiche nell'area del Palazzo di Giustizia* (Venice: Marsilo Editori, 1983); Ricotti, *Giochi e giocattoli,* 54–56; and Wie-demann, *Adults and Children in the Roman Empire,* 150.

123. See Elderkin, "Jointed Dolls," 475; Ricotti, *Giochi e giocattoli,* 58–59; and Wiedemann, *Adults and Children in the Roman Empire,* 149–50.

124. Wiedemann, *Adults and Children in the Roman Empire,* 149.

poem, a child's prayer, indicated this: "Today, dear God, I am seven years old, and must play no more. Here is my top, my hoop, and my ball: keep them all, my Lord."[125] From age seven on, playing and studying competed with one another for children's attention, even for children not willing to give up their toys quite yet. Jerome recommended the use of toy letters, such as those described by Quintilian for the education of girls, when he instructed Laeta that she should

have made for [little Paula] letters out of boxwood or ivory, and call each by its proper name. Let her play with these so that her play may also be instruction. And let her keep the letters in order in her mind, so that in her memory she may go over the names in a rhyme. However, often change the internal order and mix up the letters so that the last ones are in the middle and the middle ones at the beginning: thus she may know them not only by sound, but also by sight.[126]

Jerome was clear about the purpose of using such playful methods. It seemed he remembered being a child. During breaks, after school, and certainly during the holidays, children played wherever space allowed, even if it was "among the offices where the young slaves [worked]."[127] The learning process, as Jerome understood it, needed to "guard against [little Paula] hating her studies, lest a bitterness toward them learned early in childhood penetrate beyond her young years."[128] That such playful teaching could be placed at the immediate service of developing knowledge about the Christian faith was a welcome side effect for Jerome. The words and names little Paula was to spell with her toy letters were to be "those of the prophets and the apostles, or the list of the patriarchs descended from Adam, as in Matthew and Luke."[129]

Jerome knew that children enjoyed nursery tales.[130] Early Christian authors, who realized also that the mythological exploits and adventures of pagan gods could be put to the same use, disapproved of such storytelling. Clement of Alexandria, for example, documented the reluctance of early

---

125. Cited in Wiedemann, *Adults and Children in the Roman Empire*, 153.

126. Jerome, *Letters* 107.4 (ed. Hilberg, *Sancti Eusebii Hieronymi Epistulae*, CSEL 55, 294, ll. 4–9).

127. Jerome, *Apology against Rufinus* 1.30 (ed. and trans. Pierre Lardet, *Saint Jérôme. Apologie Contre Rufine* [Paris: Les Éditions du Cerf, 1983], 82, l. 34).

128. Jerome, *Letters* 107.4 (ed. Hilberg, *Sancti Eusebii Hieronymi Epistulae*, CSEL 55, 294, ll. 17–18).

129. Jerome, *Letters* 107.4 (Hilberg, 294, ll. 20–22).

130. Jerome, *Letters* 128.1 (Hilberg, CSEL 56.1, 156).

Christian parents, "who avoid[ed] the practice of soothing [their] crying children, as the saying goes, by telling them fabulous stories," "old wives' talk" "of fabulous and monstrous shapes" or the "terrifying apparition of strange demons," for fear "of fostering in [the children's] minds the impiety professed by those who, though wise in their own conceit, have no more knowledge of the truth than infants."[131] Chrysostom also had such a plan for storytelling. The stories narrated to children were to hold their attention and encourage their interest, but he was wary of the effect of nurses and tutors.[132] They told "harmful" stories, instead of those based upon the Bible.[133] Chrysostom gave extensive advice for what stories to tell and how to tell them, even those from the Bible, and he was most concerned about slaves' stories, which would steer the charge away from virtue.[134]

John Chrysostom rejected the theater and the things associated with it, hinting at the "corruption" associated with the theater, especially for boys with physical charms. He encouraged the father to introduce his son to flowers, meadows, and fair books and to mock the drunken patrons old and young alike as they spilled from the theater.[135] At times, for polemical purposes Christian authors effectively exploited potential cases of pedophilia or practices of displaying dancing and playing children for adult entertainment.[136] In his *Ecclesiastical History*, Theodoret of Cyrrhus, for example, accused the supporters of Lucius, his "Arian" competitor for the episcopal throne, of having set up on the altar at church

a boy who had forsworn his sex and would pass for a girl, with eyes, as it is written, smeared with antimony, and face reddened with rouge like their idols, in woman's dress ... to dance and wave his hands about and whirl round as though he had been at the front of some disreputable stage ... while the bystanders laughed aloud and rudely raised unseemly shouts.[137]

131. Clement of Alexandria, *Protreptikos* VI.1 (ed. Marcovich, *Clementis Alexandrini Protrepticus*, 102).

132. John Chrysostom, *On Vainglory* 37–38 (ed. and trans. Malingrey, *Jean Chrysostome. Sur la vaine gloire et l'éducation des enfants*, 128–31).

133. John Chrysostom, *On Vainglory* 34 and 37 (Malingrey, 124–26 and 128).

134. John Chrysostom, *On Vainglory* 43–45 and 52–53 (Malingrey, 140–44 and 150–52).

135. John Chrysostom, *On Vainglory* 56–57, 59, and 79 (Malingrey, 154–59 and 184–85).

136. As Dover, "Classical Greek Attitudes to Sexual Behaviour," 118, makes clear this polemic was with good reason.

137. Theodoret of Cyrrhus, *Ecclesiastical History* 4.22.7 (ed. Parmentier and Hansen, *Theodoret. Kirchengeschichte*, 251; trans. Jackson, "The Ecclesiastical History of Theodoret," 122 [yet marked as book 4, ch. 19]).

One can only imagine what Chrysostom's response to all this would have been, as he rejected the ornamentation and perfuming of boys as a terrible outrage.[138]

While knucklebones and games with dice were games of chance, early Christian authors do not appear to have advised their flock to avoid them. Rather, their texts witness to the still widespread use of such games. Intent on making Origen's vast knowledge accessible to a Latin-speaking audience, Rufinus witnessed to the popularity of playing with dice as a boy's pastime, asserting that the treatises he had in front of him were "Origen's recreation no less than dice are a boy's."[139] Yet the focus in so many Christian texts on prayer, the Bible, hymns, and avoiding the theater and potential pitfalls in the city streets warns the reader that Christians were critical of the structure of play in their culture.

Christian writers, for instance, warned parents against boys and girls playing together. John Chrysostom admonished the father to keep the boy away from baths with women, from slave girls, from any women or girls really, except his mother and older slave women.[140] Jerome, quite his usual self, was rather outspoken when in 413 he instructed Gaudentius, who had asked for advice on how to bring up his infant daughter Pacatula: "A girl should associate only with girls, she should know nothing of boys and should dread even playing with them."[141] Given the contrast between the visual depictions and such prescriptive statements, one may readily assume that quite the opposite was typical.

Children and Play Gone Wrong

Whereas cheerful tones very likely accompanied much of children's engagement in playful activities, not every opportunity for their participation in a game or in playing with companions ended in or was characterized by harmony and joy. At times, also, violent behavior manifested itself in chil-

---

138. John Chrysostom, *On Vainglory* 16 and 54 (ed. and trans. Malingrey, *Jean Chrysostome. Sur la vaine gloire et l'éducation des enfants*, 96–101 and 152–55).

139. Rufinus of Aquileia, *Apology against Jerome* 2.25 (ed. Manlio Simonetti, *Tyrannii Rufini Opera* [Turnhout: Brepols, 1961], 37–123, here 102, ll. 35–36; trans. William Henry Fremantle, "The Apology of Rufinus in Two Books," NPNF vol. 3, 2nd ser. [Peabody, Mass.: Hendrickson Publishers, 1995], 435–82, here 470 [here numbered bk. 2, ch. 22]), who cites Jerome in this passage.

140. John Chrysostom, *On Vainglory* 53, 59–60, and 62 (ed. and trans. Malingrey, *Jean Chrysostome. Sur la vaine gloire et l'éducation des enfants*, 152–53, 156–59, and 160–63).

141. Jerome, *Letters* 128.4 (ed. Hilberg, *Sancti Eusebii Hieronymi Epistulae*, CSEL 56.1, 160, ll. 3–5); see also ibid., 107.4 (Hilberg, CSEL 55, 294, ll. 2–4).

dren's games and play. John Chrysostom employed the image of war when he was describing the struggles of the soul against vices, leaving it open whether or not children he watched intentionally "played war."[142] War as one of the possible contexts for children's games was known already for centuries. Among the Spartans, a military training game took place within the framework of a ritual celebration that was intended to eradicate in the boys who played it any emotions or feelings of mercy for the opponent. The game, known as *platanistas,* named after the grove of plane trees on the island that served as the battleground, required the sacrifice of a puppy to Ares, the god of war, on the evening preceding the battle. Each team drew lots, and in their fight for possession of the island the boys "were allowed to kick, bite, and even to gouge their opponents' eyes."[143] That early Christians were keenly aware of the tight connections between war, military service, and pagan rituals and cults is demonstrated in numerous texts from patristic authors and hagiographic accounts.[144]

Children were also capable of carelessly using violence against other human beings, and they tended to do so especially when they were in a group. This is graphically illustrated in martyrdom accounts, even if one discounts the hagiographic exaggerations of such literature. In his *Ecclesiastical History,* Sozomen gives us a glimpse of the sometimes wild and brutal ballgames of young boys on city streets. When as part of the crowds a group of schoolboys witnessed how Bishop Mark of Arethusa's ears had been severed by ropes, they took the old man for their ball and "made game of him by tossing him aloft and rolling him over and over, sending him forward, catching him up, and unsparingly piercing him with their styles."[145] The boys' systematically violent moves blurred the boundaries between game and battle.

Chrysostom indicated the level of spite a child could display when

142. John Chrysostom, *On the Priesthood* 6.13 (trans. W. A. Jurgens, *The Priesthood. A Translation of the Peri hierosynes of St. John Chrysostom* [New York: Macmillan, 1955], 109); cf. also John Chrysostom, *On Vainglory* 23–24 and 27 (ed. Malingrey, *Jean Chrysostome. Sur la vaine gloire et l'éducation des enfants,* 108–10 and 112).

143. Walter S. Hett, "The Games of the Greek Boy," *Greece and Rome* 1 (1931), 24–29, here 26.

144. Very accessible is the collection in Louis J. Swift, *The Early Fathers on War and Military Service* (Wilmington, Del.: M. Glazier, c1983). See also the discussion of the connection between children's experience and war, below, chapter 6.

145. Sozomen, *Ecclesiastical History* 5.10.11 (ed. Joseph Bidez and Günther Christian Hansen, *Sozomenus. Kirchengeschichte,* GCS NF vol. 4 [Berlin: Akademie Verlag, 2nd, rev. ed., 1995], 208; trans. Chester D. Hartranft, "The Ecclesiastical History of Sozomen," NPNF 2nd ser., vol. 2 [Peabody, Mass.: Hendrickson Publishers, 1995], 179–427, here 333).

something happened of which he or she did not approve.[146] In the case he had in mind, a boy had had some of his things broken by his slave, likely his pencils or pens. Chrysostom knew that children could get angry when such things happened and thus explained that "children are made fractious by the loss of such articles and incline rather to lose their soul than to let the culprit go unpunished." Thus he encouraged the father to make the boy control his anger and not to replace the lost items immediately. The boy should control his passions when his friends or the slaves provoked him. If, however, a friend was being wronged, he should intercede for that friend.[147]

Augustine displayed quite a hot temper at the ballgames he played as a boy. Apart from his excitement about games,[148] he loved to win at them and preferred his games to studying; when he lost in a ball game, he felt jealousy and envy, admitting that he "loved the pride of winning."[149] The boys with whom he battled, however, were good friends of his, regardless of whether he wanted to beat them in games, because he remembered fondly an unnamed friend from boyhood.[150] Indeed, the joy Augustine felt on the night of the famed pear incident, apart from his later meditations on the nature of evil, come from his friendships and his experiences with the boys seeking games to play with him.[151] Later, as a teenager, he would go to the theater,[152] an activity which earlier in the *Confessions* he had called the games of adults.[153]

Children's Music

In order to direct children's energies in more creative ways, parents and educators promoted children's singing and playing music. It is rather difficult to reconstruct these songs, not least because material evidence that

---

146. John Chrysostom, *On Vainglory* 31, 66–69, and 73 (ed. and trans. Malingrey, *Jean Chrysostome. Sur la vaine gloire et l'éducation des enfants*, 122–25, 164–71, and 174–77). See also Ann Ellis Hanson, "'Your mother nursed you with bile': anger in babies and small children," in *Ancient Anger. Perspectives from Homer to Galen*, Yale Classical Studies, vol. 32, ed. Susanna Braund and Glenn W. Most (Cambridge: Cambridge University Press, 2003), 185–207.

147. John Chrysostom, *On Vainglory* 66, 68, and 73 (ed. Malingrey, *Jean Chrysostome. Sur la vaine gloire et l'éducation des enfants*, 164–69 and 174, l. 895 to 176, l. 898).

148. Augustine, *Confessions* I ix (15–16), xix (30) (ed. Verheijen, *Sancti Augustini. Confessionum Libri XIII*, 8–9 and 16–17; trans. Chadwick, *St. Augustine Confessions*, 12–13, 22).

149. Ibid. x (16) (Verheijen, 9, ll. 6–7; Chadwick, 12).

150. Ibid. IV iv (7) (Verheijen, 43; Chadwick, 56–57).

151. Ibid. II iv (9), ix (17) (Verheijen, 21–22, 26; Chadwick, 28–29, 34).

152. Ibid. III i (1)–ii (4) (Verheijen, 27–29; Chadwick, 35–37).

153. Ibid. I ix (15)–x (16) (Verheijen, 8–9; Chadwick, 12–13).

could point to that part of their life is scarce. Where we do find evidence of children singing songs, it often is in praise of a victor of athletic competitions. These songs were commissioned by the victors and written by notable poets, but they were sung by choirs of boys.[154] One suspects that these songs were not sung for the purpose of calming down an excited populace, children included.

If the theater was always problematic for Christians as a form of entertainment, music as such was not rejected out of hand. Chrysostom thought that music might aid in calming a rambunctious child. Parents were to teach their child "hymns to God, not shameful songs and ill-timed tales."[155] A few traces of children's musical engagement are preserved in the literary record, sometimes directly in the sacred texts. As portrayed in the Gospel of Luke, for example, Jesus availed himself of the image of "children sitting in the marketplace and calling to one another, 'We played the flute for you, and you did not dance; we wailed, and you did not weep,'" when chiding his audience for accepting neither John the Baptist nor the Son of Man (Lk 7:32–34). While children did not readily play all available instruments, some musical instruments elicited admiration and wonder from children, as Eusebius of Caesarea noted when he spoke disapprovingly of children who would "admire the seven-stringed lyre," but disregard the instrument's builder or the musician who knew how to play it.[156]

The energies needed for practice when children sang in choruses is not to be underestimated. The members of the virgin choirs who performed the *madrōshē*, or hymns, which Ephraem the Syrian composed for the liturgy and for religious instruction, needed not only good voices, but also linguistic skill, a good memory, and physical stamina. The hymns, for which Ephraem availed himself of more than fifty different syllable patterns,[157] fill more than a dozen volumes in Dom Edmund Beck's modern editions. While the virgins certainly included "daughters of the covenant" who had

154. See Golden, *Sport in the Ancient World from A to Z*, 61.

155. John Chrysostom, *On Vainglory* 34 (ed. and trans. Malingrey, *Jean Chrysostome. Sur la vaine gloire et l'éducation des enfants*, 126–27).

156. Eusebius of Caesarea, *Oration in Praise of Constantine* 11.9 (ed. Ivar A. Heikel, *Eusebius Werke. Erster Band. Über das Leben Constantins, Constantins Rede an die heilige Versammlung, Tricennatsrede an Constantin*, GCS [Leipzig: J. C. Hinrichs'sche Buchhandlung, 1902], 195–259, here 226, ll. 9–12; trans. Ernest Cushing Richardson, "The Oration of Eusebius Pamphilius in Praise of the Emperor Constantine," NPNF 2nd ser., vol. 1 [Peabody, Mass.: Hendrickson Publishers, 1995], 581–610, here 596).

157. Joseph Amar and Edward Mathews, *St. Ephrem the Syrian: Selected Prose Works* (Washington, D.C.: The Catholic University of America Press, 1994), 41.

committed themselves to a life of asceticism and whose circle consisted of women of all ages,[158] girls probably joined at an early age, thus being introduced in an entertaining way to the service of the Church. One hymn, now only extant as part of Ephraem's Armenian corpus, was composed for the day of dedication of a young girl as a "daughter of the covenant."[159] In a similar vein, Jerome referred to the examples of Miriam singing to the virgin choir (cf. Ex 15:21) and of Paula's daughter Eustochium who taught "her [young virgin] companions to be music girls for Christ, to be luteplayers for the Saviour."[160]

The content of the music was of great importance. When advising little Paula's mother, Laeta, on how to raise her daughter, Jerome was convinced that the girl who was to be shaped into a temple of God could dispense with the "knowledge of the world's songs." Rather her "tongue [had to] be steeped while still tender in the sweetness of the psalms."[161] He advised Gaudentius to "reward [his infant daughter] for singing psalms" so that she will "love what she has to learn."[162] There could not be enough of the proper, religious singing with sweet children's voices for Jerome, who foresaw that little Paula, when visiting with her grandfather, would "leap upon his breast, put her arms round his neck, and, whether he likes it or not, sing Alleluia [in his ears]."[163] As far as he knew, she had already started in the cradle singing "Alleluia."[164]

Not only were children instructed and encouraged to sing select passages from the Scriptures, most prominently the Psalms, but the whole Christian congregation would also regularly be reminded of the centrality of children's witness to the faith. Rufinus, for example, documented in his *Apology* that "the Hymn of the Three Children . . . is regularly sung on festivals in the Church of God" and even "martyrs or confessors . . . have

158. For a discussion of the daughters of the covenant and their role as singers, see Susan Ashbrook Harvey, "Revisiting the Daughters of the Covenant: Women's Choirs and Sacred Song in Ancient Syriac Christianity," *Hugoye: Journal of Syriac Studies* 8.2 (2005), http://syrcom.cua.edu/Hugoye/Vol8No2/HV8N2Harvey.html.

159. Ephraem the Syrian, *Armenian Hymns* 16 (ed. and trans. L. Mariès and Ch. Mercier, *Hymnes de Saint Ephrem conservées en version arménienne* [Paris: Firmin-Didot, 1961], 105–9). An English translation with commenting notes was published in Robert Murray, "'A Marriage for all eternity': The Consecration of a Syrian bride of Christ," *Sobornost* 11 (1989), 65–68.

160. Jerome, *Letters* 54.13 (ed. Hilberg, *Sancti Eusebii Hieronymi Epistulae*, CSEL 54, 480, ll. 22–23).

161. Ibid., 107.4 (Hilberg, CSEL 55, 294, l. 2).

162. Ibid., 128.1 (Hilberg, CSEL 56.1, 157, l. 9).

163. Ibid., 107.4 (Hilberg, CSEL 55, 295, ll. 19–20).

164. Ibid., 108.26 (Hilberg, CSEL 55, 345, ll. 12–13).

sung the Hymn of the Three Children."[165] The reference in Susanna 1:45 to Daniel as a "young lad" supported the identification of Shadrach, Meshach, and Abednego (Dn 3:1–18) as young children, as an alternative to their representation as young men as displayed on reliefs on sarcophagi.[166] If the music from the Scriptures was hailed, Chrysostom spoke against music for secular celebrations, urging that even flutes, harps, and dancing be kept from a Christian wedding celebration.[167]

Role-Playing

Ancient texts provide relatively ample evidence for the importance and frequency of different forms of role-playing in a child's play. Tales, gender-typical toys, and the imitation of "real life" roles played an important part in this process. By being encouraged to imitate aspects of adults' behavior, children's social imagination was cultivated, and early on they learned central features of future roles they might play in the world. Children's imitation of adult behavior was strongly encouraged and playfully introduced into child behavior in the ancient world. Across all strands of society, both among the elite and among the lower classes, the preferred roles for imitation were those of leadership and public office. Children played "kings" or "judges."[168] Any office that was visually distinguished by special garb was by that very virtue highly attractive for children's imitation. In the case of Gaius Caesar Caligula, whose surname meant "little boots," his early acquaintance with the training and dress of the soldier was retained in his very name.[169] Parents promoted the early display of oratorical skills in

165. Rufinus of Aquileia, *Apology against Jerome* 2.37 and 39 (ed. Simonetti, *Tyrannii Rufini Opera*, 111–12 and 114; trans. Fremantle, "The Apology of Rufinus," 475–76 [here numbered bk. 2, chs. 33 and 35]). This Hymn of the Three Children continues to be sung regularly to this day at such occasions in the Armenian Church. We are grateful to Robert R. Phenix Jr. for alerting us to this fact.

166. For paintings of the scene in the Roman catacombs, see Josef Wilpert, *Die Malereien der Katakomben Roms* (Freiburg i. Br.: Herdersche Verlagshandlung, 1903), pl. 13, 78.1, and 172.2. For a relief on a Christian sarcophagus, see S. R. F. Price, *Rituals and Power: The Roman Imperial Cult in Asia Minor* (Cambridge: Cambridge University Press, 1984), pl. 1c. See also Price, *Rituals and Power*, p. 199 and n. 156, for references to similar depictions on reliefs on Christian sarcophagi in Giuseppe (Josef) Wilpert, *I Sarcofagi Cristiani Antichi* (Rome: Pontificio istituto di archeologica christiana, 1932), vol. 2, 259–63; and Friedrich Wilhelm Deichmann, ed., *Repertorium der christlich-antiken Sarkophage* (Wiesbaden: F. Steiner, 1967), vol. 1, nos. 324, 338, 339, 351, 596, and 718.

167. John Chrysostom, *On Vainglory* 88 (ed. and trans. Malingrey, *Jean Chrysostome. Sur la vaine gloire et l'éducation des enfants*, 194–95).

168. Wiedemann, *Adults and Children in the Roman Empire*, 150–51.

169. Suetonius, *The Life of the Caesars: Gaius Caligula* 9 (text and trans. I. C. Rolfe, *Sue-*

order to advance the child's chances at serving in public office. At family gatherings, on feast days, or at burial ceremonies for family members, a boy may well have given a speech in honor of the occasion or the deceased relative. Among the best preserved and most impressive statues of children in the Roman world is one now kept in the Louvre, which depicts Nero in the pose of a young orator, identifiable as a child by the *bulla* he is still wearing around his neck.[170]

Participation in the music of the Church also encouraged Christian children in observing their role models. They did not necessarily have kings and judges to imitate, but bishops and priests.[171] One of the better-known examples is the behavior of little Athanasius, later the bishop of Alexandria. In their respective *Ecclesiastical Histories*, Socrates Scholasticus and Sozomen recounted a version of an incident that took place during the episcopacy of Alexander and on the feast of the commemoration of the martyr-bishop Peter.[172] According to Socrates, Alexander witnessed how a group of children, including the boy Athanasius, was engaged in a sacred game at the seashore, imitating the tasks "of the priesthood and the order of consecrated persons." The children had allotted Athanasius the bishop's throne, while each of the rest of the lads impersonated "either a presbyter or a deacon." Thus, according to Sozomen, the children were "imitating ... the ceremonies of the Church." For a while, Sozomen continued, Alexander thought of the mimicry as merely an innocent children's game and enjoyed watching what was going on. He behaved not much different from a Roman father who, having bought his son a new soldier's uniform, now took delight in how his son practiced the role of military commander among his playmates. Yet when Alexander realized that the children not only conducted the readings and prayers of the first part of the liturgy, but also performed in their play "the unutterable," as Sozomen called it, i.e., the offering of the gifts and the consecration, a part not known to catechumens, he either became concerned, as Sozomen portrayed him, or suspected a portent, as Socrates would have it. Alexander had the children summoned

---

tonius [Cambridge, Mass.: Harvard University Press, 1965], 414–17; trans. Catherine Edwards, *Suetonius. Lives of the Caesars* [Oxford: Oxford University Press, 2000], 139–40).

170. Wiedemann, *Adults and Children in the Roman Empire*, pl. 21.

171. For a favorite play of "kings and soldiers" in the ancient world, see also Rene Bloch, "Basilinda," in *Der Neue Pauly*, vol. 2 (1997), col. 482.

172. Socrates Scholasticus, *Ecclesiastical History* 1.15 (ed. and trans. Pierre Périchon and Pierre Maraval, *Socrate de Constantinople. Histoire Ecclésiastique* [Paris: Les Éditions du Cerf, 2004], 170–73); and Sozomen, *Ecclesiastical History* 2.17 (ed. Günther Christian Hansen, *Sozomenos. Historia Ecclesiastica. Kirchengeschichte* [Turnhout: Brepols, 2004], vol. 1, 256–63).

and carefully questioned about the roles each one had played, and what exactly they had done and said. Sure enough, the children confessed that Athanasius had not only fulfilled the role of being "their bishop and leader," but also had baptized many of them who thus far had not yet officially become initiated members of the Church. Thus Alexander first convinced himself that in their game the children had used and "accurately observed" "the exact routine of the Church." Then he concluded in agreement with the counsel of his fellow clergy that the young Athanasius's baptism of his playmates was indeed valid. No rebaptism "of those who, in their simplicity, had been judged worthy of the Divine grace" was necessary. Bishop Alexander did celebrate for them the mysteries, though, an indirect witness to children's full participation at the Eucharistic liturgy. While Socrates reported that Bishop Alexander had given "directions that [all] the children should be taken to the church, and instructed in learning," Sozomen included a comment that incorporated the request for collaboration on the part of the children's relatives to "[bring them] up for the Church and for leadership in what they had imitated," suggesting that all of them were destined to become office holders in the Church. Socrates stated specifically only for Athanasius that Alexander "ordained him deacon on his becoming of adult age."

While the church historians' nuanced presentation of Athanasius's revelation as bishop is a literary construct, and while one encounters other examples of children acting out the roles of bishops in works of Christian hagiography,[173] known for its embellishments, it is conceivable that early Christian children role-played parts that reflected some of their experiences at church.[174] Even Sozomen, who dramatized the events surrounding little Athanasius most elaborately, did not think it worthy of special note that some of the children, including Athanasius, had been baptized and had at least some general idea of "the ceremonies of the Church." What he found remarkable was that they knew "the exact routine of the Church

---

173. For example, *Acta Sanctorum*, May 4, 453–54.

174. Ambrose's brief description of the young girl seeking refuge at the altar from an enforced marriage by grabbing onto the altar cloth and using it as a veil, thus expressing her desire for the status of a veiled virgin, may be taken as another case in point. See Ambrose of Milan, *On Virgins (De virginibus ad Marcellinam sororem)* bk. 1, ch. 12, sect. 66 (ed. and Italian trans. M. Salvati, *Sant'Ambrogio. Verginità* [Turin: Societa Editrice Internazionale, 1955], 5–163, here 70–73; trans. H. de Romestin, E. de Romestin, and H. T. F. Duckworth, "Three Books of St. Ambrose, Bishop of Milan, concerning Virgins, to Marcellina, his Sister," NPNF 10, 2nd ser. [repr. Peabody, Mass.: Hendrickson Publishers, 1995], 363–87, here 373 [numbered as bk. 1, ch. 12, sect. 65–66]).

... accurately." At the least, therefore, the description of the event by the church historians witnesses to a general familiarity of some Christian children with the basics of the liturgy. It also speaks to the fact that the ancient Christian audience was familiar with the liturgy, and thus accepted the plausibility of children reenacting it when they played with one another. One may add that a further side effect of such playful liturgical imitation consisted in an increased, more active familiarity of the children with the liturgical routines. Indeed, Chrysostom presented the advice that the child, more specifically perhaps the boy, be introduced to the bishop "often" in order to encourage him to model himself after the bishop and to counteract the impact of other entertainments such as the theater. Earlier on in his treatise Chrysostom had stressed that the boy should be taken to church often and pay special heed when stories he knew were read from the lectern.[175]

Conclusions

For many children, particularly those of the less affluent classes, work was a central part of daily life. Also, many children worked from a relatively young age on. As much as working for a living would be part of their later lives as adults, so already during their early childhood years they practiced those very activities. How much time they actually had left in their days to spend playing is not obvious. Yet no matter the intensity with which even very young children were incorporated into the workforce, some aspects of play touched all children's lives.

On the whole, the sources are ambivalent about the value of toys and games for the development of Christian children. On the one hand, toys and games were often associated with the worship of Greek and Roman deities. On the other hand, it was important that children be positively enticed and rewarded with toys: the educational value of play was appreciated by Christian and non-Christian writers alike. We noted with interest the importance of the Christian child's learning of Old and New Testament writings, particularly of those texts that were important for the performance of the liturgy, i.e., the Psalms. Here playful contexts appeared to have enhanced learning. Since the experience of the Christian liturgy as well as the acquisition of the faith was a lifelong matter, it was seen as im-

---

175. John Chrysostom, *On Vainglory* 41 and 83 (ed. Malingrey, *Jean Chrysostome. Sur la vaine gloire et l'éducation des enfants*, 138–39 and 190, ll. 1010–12).

portant that children be able to associate amusement with learning already in their earliest years.

Christian children played games and enjoyed toys just as non-Christian children did. However, aspects of the Christian liturgy lent themselves readily to reenactment by younger children. This too had parallels in children playing with items that were significant for certain cults, such as that of Dionysus. Faint traces of such ancient customs seem to be preserved into modern times, both in the East and in the West, in the roles of young altar servants, who sometimes function alongside lectors and deacons, but at other times also replace them.

six

🖊

Exposing Children to Violence

At various points, earlier chapters have noted practices regarding the treatment of children that were common to Jews, Greeks, and Romans alike. Such similarities can be discovered in the areas of education, discipline, work, and the age at which girls married. Differences of a fundamental nature appear when one turns to the relatively broad category of violence to which children were subjected. Here violence is understood as the deliberate taking of a child's life; abandoning a child to the surroundings and elements, human and otherwise;[1] the sexual exploitation and prostitution of

1. On the broader category of the abuse of children from a modern perspective, see, for example, Scott Coltrane and Randall Collins, *Sociology of Marriage & the Family: Gender, Love, and Property,* 5th ed. (Australia: Wadsworth, Thomson Learning, 2001), 481–94. The literature on infanticide, exposure, and abandonment of children in the ancient world is of significant size. See for example Kleijwegt, "Kind," 875–80; Mireille Corbier, "Child Exposure and Abandonment," in *Childhood, Class and Kin in the Roman World,* ed. Suzanne Dixon (London: Routledge, 2001), 52–73; William V. Harris, "Child-Exposure in the Roman Empire," *Journal of Roman Studies* 84 (1994), 1–22; Lawrence E. Stager, "Eroticism and Infanticide at Ashkelon," *Biblical Archaeology Review* 17 (1991), 34–53; Juha Pentikäinen, "Child Abandonment as an Indicator of Christianization in the Nordic Countries," in *Old Norse and Finnish Religions and Cultic Place-Names,* ed. Tore Ahlbäck (Åbo, Finland: Donner Institute for Research in Religion and Cultural History, 1990), 72–91; A. Huys, "*Ekthesis* and *Apothesis:* The Terminology of Infant Exposure in Greek Antiquity," *L'Antiquité Classique* 58 (1989), 190–97; Friedolf Kudlien, "Kindesaussetzung im antiken Rom," in *Groningen Colloquia on the Novel 2,* ed. Heinz Hofmann (Groningen: Egbert Forsten, 1989), 25–44; Ryoji Motomura, "The Practice of Exposing Infants and Its Effects on the Development of Slavery in the Ancient World," in *Forms of Control and Subordination in Antiquity,* eds. Turo Yuge and Masaoki Doi (Tokyo: Society for Studies on Resistance Movements in Antiquity, 1988), 410–15; John Boswell, *The Kindness of Strangers:*

children; the enslavement of children; and the many forms of abuse and torture which often accompanied slavery. In most of these categories, Jews and Christians following them walked a path different from that trodden by many others in the Mediterranean world.

Jewish Criticism of Abortion, Infanticide, and Exposure

Prior to the rise of Christianity, Jews had already criticized the practices of Greeks and Romans in the areas of abortion, infanticide, and exposure. The reality of those practices in the Hellenistic world is not in doubt, neither from Greek or Roman nor from Jewish sources. Also not in doubt is the continuation of such violence committed against children during the time of early Christianity.[2] Daniel Schwartz has dealt with this issue most thoroughly and recently and the present examination of the Jewish response to the practices is indebted to his discussion.[3] He addressed relatively recent claims that Jews, too, might have engaged in such practices. Such views were advanced in work by Tal Ilan, Catherine Hezser, and Maren R. Niehoff, which proposed that Jews engaged in exposure and starva-

---

The Abandonment of Children in Western Europe from Late Antiquity to the Renaissance (Chicago: University of Chicago Press, 1988); Sarah B. Pomeroy, "Copronyms and the Exposure of Infants in Egypt," in *Studies in Roman Law in Memory of A. Arthur Schiller,* ed. A. Arthur Schiller and others (Leiden: E. J. Brill, 1986), 147–62; Donald Engels, "The Use of Historical Demography in Ancient History," *Classical Quarterly* 34 (1984), 386–93; John Boswell, "*Expositio* and *Oblatio:* The Abandonment of Children and the Ancient and Medieval Family," *American Historical Review* 89 (1984), 10–33, reprinted in Carol Neel, ed., *Medieval Families: Perspectives on Marriage, Household, and Children* (Toronto: University of Toronto Press, 2004), 234–72; William V. Harris, "The Theoretical Possibility of Extensive Infanticide in the Graeco-Roman World," *Classical Quarterly* 32 (1982), 114–16; Mark Golden, "Demography and the Exposure of Girls at Athens," *Phoenix* 35 (1981), 316–31; Emiel Eyben, "Family Planning in Graeco-Roman Antiquity," *Ancient Society* 11–12 (1980–81), 5–82; Donald Engels, "The Problem of Female Infanticide in the Greco-Roman World," *Classical Philology* 75 (1980), 112–20; William L. Langer, "Infanticide: A Historical Survey," *History of Childhood Quarterly* 1 (1974), 353–65; Franz Joseph Dölger, "Das Lebensrecht des ungeborenen Kindes und die Fruchtabtreibung in der Bewertung der heidnischen und christlichen Antike," *Antike und Christentum* 4 (1933), 1–61; H. Bennet, "The Exposure of Infants in Ancient Rome," *Classical Journal* 18 (1922–23), 341–51; and Leopoldo Armaroli, *Ricerche storiche sulla esposizione degli infanti presso gli antichi popoli e specialmente presso i Romani* (Venice: Antonelli, 1838).

2. On the early practice of infant exposure and infanticide in the ancient world see, for example, Plato, *Rep.* 460c (ed. and trans. Paul Shorey, *The Republic. Plato,* 2 vols. [Cambridge, Mass.: Harvard University Press, 1943], vol. 1, 462–63); and Aristotle, *Pol.* 1335b (text and trans. H. Rackham, *Aristotle in Twenty-Three Volumes,* vol. 21: *Politics* [Cambridge, Mass.: Harvard University Press, 1977], 622–23).

3. Schwartz, "Did the Jews Practice Infanticide in Antiquity?" 61–95.

tion of infants and at times even in child sacrifice (Niehoff).[4] Each of these authors cited the work of Adele Reinhartz, who had suggested the possibility of greater Jewish participation in the practices than previously considered.[5] Reinhartz, however, was restrained in her conclusions, formulating that one "may surmise that in family life, as in many other matters, Jews were not always different from, or better than, their neighbors"—a conclusion with which Schwartz concurred.[6] He clarified that the question was not whether or not there "were . . . Jews who exposed or murdered babies in antiquity." The answer to that was "obvious": "there were Jews who did such things. Could it possibly be otherwise?!" Rather the issue was "whether such practice and approval were common among ancient Jews." On this score his answer also is convincing, namely, that Jews did not commonly practice exposure or infanticide or abortion, or approve of such practices.[7]

Mishnah Avodah Zarah 2.1 allowed for a Gentile midwife to aid a Jewish woman giving birth, but the equivalent passage in *t. Avodah Zarah* 3.3 put strictures on such aid due to the suspicion that the non-Jewish midwife might commit infanticide. Rabbi Meir, who is cited in the *Tosefta*, would not allow a Gentile midwife to help deliver a Jewish child because she was "suspect" with regard to the life of the child; the rabbinic sages allowed for her help in delivering a Jewish woman only if someone else stood beside the Gentile midwife. Rabbi Meir's prohibition and the conditional acceptance by the rabbis show a concern for certain acts undertaken by the Gentile midwife which could put the child's life at risk. This kind of prejudice had its origin in actual practices among the neighbors of the Jews.[8] Musonius Rufus criticized those who were poor for carrying out the practice of infanticide or exposure, as well as abortion. He also accused those of the

---

4. Tal Ilan, *Integrating Women into Second Temple History* (Tübingen: Mohr-Siebeck, 1999); Catherine Hezser, "The Exposure and Sale of Infants in Rabbinic and Roman Law," in *Jewish Studies between the Disciplines / Judaistik zwischen den Disziplinen: Papers in Honor of Peter Schäfer on the Occasion of his 60th Birthday* (Leiden: E. J. Brill, 2003), 3–28; and Maren R. Niehoff, *Philo on Jewish Identity and Culture* (Tübingen: Mohr-Siebeck, 2001).

5. Adele Reinhartz, "Philo on Infanticide," *Studia Philonica Annual* 4 (1992), 42–58.

6. See ibid., 58; for Schwartz's citation of Reinhartz and his conclusion, see Schwartz, "Did the Jews Practice Infanticide in Antiquity?" 62.

7. Schwartz, "Did the Jews Practice Infanticide in Antiquity?" 63–65.

8. Musonius Rufus devotes a short treatise to the question: "Should Every Child That Is Born Be Raised?" (ed. and trans. Lutz, "Musonius Rufus. 'The Roman Socrates,'" 96–101; see also the prior edition in fragments in: a.) Stobaeus, *Florilegium* 75, 15 [ed. Meineke, *Ioannis Stobaei Florilegium*, III, 74–75]; b.) J. Enoch Powell, ed., *The Rendel Harris Papyri of Woodbrooke College, Birmingham* [Cambridge: Cambridge University Press, 1936; repr. Milano, 1974], vol. 1, 32–50; and c.) Stobaeus, *Florilegium* 84, 21 [ed. Meineke, *Ioannis Stobaei Florilegium*, III, 129]).

wealthy classes of killing children to avoid having to divide their property among several offspring.[9]

Some Jews, as Schwartz acknowledged, were involved in such practices.[10] Two passages in the Mishnah imply this, although one such text acknowledges that infant exposure was more common among Gentiles. *Mishnah Kiddushin* 4:1–3 speaks of the ten classes of people who came "up" from Babylon. Included in these groups were those who had been "gathered" *(asufi)*, that is, those who had been found abandoned as children. Most likely, they were children abandoned by other Jews. *Mishnah Maksherin* 2:7 discusses abandoned children and supposes that on occasion also Jewish children were exposed. The text suggests that if an abandoned child was found in a city which was predominantly Gentile, one might assume that the child was a Gentile. If, however, one found a child abandoned in a city which was predominantly Jewish, one should assume that the abandoned infant was Jewish. If the population of the city was evenly split, the rabbis state that one should assume Jewish birth. They give this advice not because of the likelihood that Jews abandoned children more often. In assuming that the child was Jewish, the rabbis desired not to exclude any possibly Jewish child from his or her birthright and preferred to err on the side of caution. It should also be noted that, if the child was a boy, such abandonment would probably have occurred during the first eight days of the child's life and so the infant could not be identified by circumcision. Perhaps one is to understand this passage with the assumption that girls were abandoned more often than boys.[11]

When reading accounts of such situations, one also has to keep in mind that the rabbinic texts are considering legal issues, that is, responses to situations with respect to the application of Torah, and do not imply approval of the practices as such. Abortion is condemned by Josephus (*Against Apion* 2.202)—who equates it with infanticide *(teknoktonos)*—by Pseudo-Phocylides, and by the *Sibylline Oracles*.[12] Exposure, which is the casting out

9. Musonius Rufus, "Should Every Child That Is Born Be Raised?" (ed. and trans. Lutz, "Musonius Rufus. 'The Roman Socrates,'" 98–101); on this question, see also Wiedemann, *Adults and Children in the Roman Empire*, 35–39; Scott, "Unpicking a Myth: The Infanticide of Female and Disabled Infants in Antiquity," 143–51; Scott, *The Archaeology of Infancy and Infant Death*; and Scott, "Killing the Female? Archaeological Narratives of Infanticide."

10. See also Hezser, "Exposure and Sale of Infants," 13–19.

11. Ibid., 5–6. See also the image of the bloody infant with umbilical cord still intact in Ezekiel 16:4; see Malul, "Adoption of Foundlings in the Bible and Mesopotamian Documents."

12. Pseudo-Phocylides, *Sentences* 184 (ed. and trans. Van der Horst, *The Sentences of Pseudo-Phocylides*, 100–101); and *Sibylline Oracles* 2.280–82 (ed. Geffcken, *Oracula Sibyllina*, 41–42).

of a child and does not necessarily lead to death, is condemned by Hecataeus of Abdera (Diodorus Siculus 40.3.8),[13] Philo (*Spec.* 3.110–119; *Virt.* 131–133; *Mos.* 1.10), and again the *Sibylline Oracles* 2.280–282. Infanticide as the deliberate killing of an infant is condemned by Josephus (*Against Apion* 2.202), Ps.-Phocylides (*Sentences,* 184), the *Sibylline Oracles* 3.765–766,[14] and Philo (*Spec.* 3.110–119), who gave a particularly gruesome description of infanticide. Tacitus did not condemn the practice, but reported on the Jewish rejection of infanticide.[15] These voices make it clear that the Jewish rejection of such violence against children was a mainstream opinion in Jewish circles, even if individual Jews practiced abortion.[16]

Jewish Criticism of Sexual Violence against Children

While we can hear some voices that condemn violence done to free children, it is more difficult to find comments of people who criticized the violence committed against children in general and slave children in particular. The kind of violence slave children suffered may be linked to exposure, since pimps or slave traders sometimes found children who were exposed and raised them as prostitutes, both boys and girls. Demosthenes offered the chilling account of one such pimp:

> Now, Nicarete—the freedwoman of Charisius of Elis and the wife of his cook—owned these seven girls from when they were small children. She was an expert in recognizing beauty in small children and understood how to rear and train them from long experience: this was her trade and she earned her living from them. . . . When she had reaped the profit of their prime, she sold their bodies, each and every one of the seven.[17]

Slaves in general were subject to physical and sexual abuse and this also was the case for slave children.[18] Moreover, children, including free chil-

---

13. Hecataeus of Abdera (Diodorus Siculus 40.3.8) (text and trans. Francis R. Walton and C. H. Oldfather, *Diodorus of Sicily in Twelve Volumes. Vol. XII: Fragments of Books XXXIII–XL* [Cambridge, Mass.: Harvard University Press, 1967], 284–85).

14. *Sibylline Oracles* 3.765–66 (ed. Geffcken, *Oracula Sibyllina,* 87).

15. Tacitus, *Histories* 5.5.3 (ed. Heraeus, *Historiarum libri qui supersunt,* vol. 2, 182–85).

16. Kleijwegt, "Kind," 902–3.

17. Demosthenes, *Speeches* 59.18–19 (*Contra Neaeram* 18–19) (ed. and trans. A. T. Murray, *Demosthenes. Private Orations. In Four Volumes. Vol. 3: Orations L–LIX,* LCL 318 [London: William Heinemann, 1936], 364–65); see also the citation in Golden, "Childhood in Ancient Greece," 19.

18. Glancy, *Slavery in Early Christianity,* 46.

dren, were more likely to be used sexually in Greco-Roman than in Jewish society.[19] Individual Jews might also engage in such behavior toward children, yet again the issue is "whether such practice and approval were common among ancient Jews."[20]

Jewish criticism of sexual practices in the Greco-Roman world often focused on the use of boys by pederasts *(hoi paiderastoi)*, those men who were attracted sexually to boys or ephebes.[21] In *Spec.* 2.50, Philo criticized pederasts among Greeks and barbarians in a general discussion of those who were "wicked," but in *Spec.* 3.37–42 he was concerned specifically with pederasty. In this extended criticism he dealt with both the pederasts and those young men *(neoi)* who were kept in a state of youthfulness by the use of make-up, perfume, and hair braiding. Philo's most extensive criticism of pederasty, however, came in *De vita contemplativa* 48–62. There he spoke of the banqueting common among both Greeks and barbarians (48), in which the focus was placed on beautiful slaves who poured the drinks (50). As Columella recommended (*Rust.* 12.4.3), the slaves were children. Yet unlike in Columella, the sexual nature of their serving is pronounced in Philo's discussion.[22] Boys *(pais)* poured the wine, while "older boys" or "bigger boys" *(boupais)*,[23] who were freshly made up with cosmetics, were to pour the water (50). In the background were the "teenagers" *(meirakion)* who, according to Philo (52), recently had been the "pets" of the pederasts. These comments should orient one to the age of the slave boys: they were about seven or eight to thirteen or fourteen.[24] Philo's comment on those who were *meirakia* as being past prime and standing in the background suggests that attention was on the younger boys. In a later passage Philo spoke of the damage done to the boyhoods of those so chosen. Yet he also

19. Golden, "Childhood in Ancient Greece," 22; see also J. N. Bremmer, "Adolescents, *Symposion,* and Pederasty," in *Sympotica: A Symposium on the Symposium* (Oxford: Oxford University Press, 1990), 135–48

20. Schwartz, "Did the Jews Practice Infanticide in Antiquity?" 64.

21. The literature on this score is extensive and several contributions have been mentioned already above. Here it suffices to refer to Dover, "Classical Greek Attitudes to Sexual Behaviour," 121–23; Marrou, *History of Education,* 25–37; and Krenkel, "Prostitution," 1295–97.

22. Bremmer, "Adolescents, *Symposion,* and Pederasty," 135–48.

23. *Boupais* is derived from *pais,* "child," and *bous,* "ox" or "cow," designating the offspring of an ox or cow as well as, secondarily, an older boy who is not yet an adolescent. See Henricus Stephanus, *Thesaurus Graecae Linguae* (Graz: Akademische Druck- und Verlagsanstalt, 1954), vol. 3, cols. 370–71.

24. Shapiro, "Fathers and Sons, Men and Boys," 111, n. 114, states that not all the boys who served wine were slaves, but they certainly are boys here in Philo's portrait. It seems most likely that they were fulfilling duties or activities that were part of what they usually did.

expressed awareness of the damage suffered by the pederast, who thought only of "the beloved boy" (Greek: *paidika*; a term equivalent to the Latin: *delicia*) (61). Given that young boys, who had smooth, hairless skin, were most desirable to ancient connoisseurs and that the slave boys were tossed aside as an object of sexual pleasure when they became too old, Philo may be pointing at this very constellation of factors in his differentiation of three sets of boys, with the youngest closest to the adults while the oldest wait in the background.[25]

It is of interest that later Christian texts continued to reveal an awareness of the preferred place that young boys played in a master's household, where they served at the tables. Within the orbit of traditions belonging to the apocryphal *Acts of Paul (and Thecla)*, the *Martyrdom of Paul*, for example, tells of Patroclus, Nero's cup-bearer, who is identified as *pais* in the Greek and *puer* in the Latin text, terms which designate both his servile status and his young age.[26] Nero is described as having become greatly saddened when he heard of the death of his slave boy. One might even include the little Patroclus in the category of *delicia*. Whether or not Nero is to be understood as having had sexual relations with him is open to conjecture. Yet he is portrayed as having been displeased by the fact that little Patroclus, once returned from the dead through Paul's prayers, had become a Christian. Thus he expelled the young boy from his palace and threw him into prison.

In his comments, Philo addressed the fate of slave boys specifically. They may have been most at risk to fall subject to their owner's desires. Yet other authors speak of the dangers faced by boys in general.[27] The *Sibylline Oracles* make reference to such practices in the Hellenistic world in at least four instances.[28] In each of these cases the text refers to the use of boys by grown men for sex, but does not designate the boys as slaves. Freeborn boys could be at risk, even from their own fathers, as Musonius Rufus indicates when he refers to a father who took his own son, noted for his "ripe beauty," and sold him into sexual slavery.[29]

25. On the smooth skin, see also Catullus, *Carmina* 61, adduced as evidence in Glancy, *Slavery in Early Christianity*, 23.

26. *Martyrdom of Paul* 1 (ed. R. A. Lipsius, "Passionis Pauli Fragmentum," in *Acta Apostolorum Apocrypha* 1 [Hildesheim: Georg Olms, repr. 1959], 104–17, here 106–7).

27. Glancy, *Slavery in Early Christianity*, 12. Freeborn boys may have been at less risk. Yet they still were exposed to that of being accosted by adult males out on the streets.

28. *Sibylline Oracles* 3.185–87, 3.596–600, 5.166–67, 5.387–89, and 5.430 (ed. Geffcken, *Oracula Sibyllina*, 57–58, 79, 112, 123, and 125).

29. Musonius Rufus, "Must One Obey One's Parents under All Circumstances?" (ed. and

Musonius also spoke of the sexual use of female slaves by masters, which was a common practice. He stated that men often had sexual relations with courtesans, unmarried freewomen, or their own slaves (*therapainē* or *doulē* at various points in the discussion).[30] Musonius rejected all of these relationships and said that entertaining intimate contact with a slave girl revealed the master as a "swine rejoicing in his own vileness." He acknowledged that many people considered sex with a female slave "blameless," "since every master is held to have it in his power to use his slave as he wishes." Musonius disagreed, suggesting rather that if a master believed his own behavior acceptable, he also ought not to mind if his wife had sexual relations with a male slave.[31] An aspect of this condemnation that is important for the present investigation is the acknowledgment that masters used their female slaves sexually, especially those who were not married, which in turn indicates that the slaves with whom masters slept often were girls.[32]

One of the purposes of sleeping with slave girls was to impregnate them so that they might bear more children for the master, a purpose also identified in Columella (*Rust.* 1.8.19). It might be either her own master or another slave who fulfilled the task of impregnating the slave.[33] The only rule in Roman law governing the sexual use of slave girls appears to have been that they be twelve years of age.[34] Regardless of the question of paternity, children born of such liaisons were slaves of the master and could be kept or sold as the master wished. He could also sell the mother if he so desired. Thus, slaves could not maintain family connections by any desire of their own or by any act of the will. Their relationships depended upon the wishes and whims of the master, since a slave marriage could not exist in law.[35] Accordingly, most considered sex with a slave a morally neutral act. It was not anything a slave could avoid, whether a girl or a boy.

---

trans. Lutz, "Musonius Rufus. 'The Roman Socrates,'" 100–107, here 102–3; also ed. Stobaeus, *Florilegium* 79, 51 [ed. Meineke, *Ioannis Stobaei Florilegium*, III, 90–94]).

30. Musonius Rufus, "On Sexual Indulgence" (ed. and trans. Lutz, "Musonius Rufus. 'The Roman Socrates,'" 84–89; also ed. in Stobaeus, *Anthologium* 3.6,23 [ed. Wachsmuth and Hense, *Ioannis Stobaei Anthologium*, III, 286–89]).

31. See also the *Martyrdom of Saints Ptolemaeus and Lucius* 6 and 15–17 (ed. and trans. Musurillo, *Acts of the Christian Martyrs*, 38–41, here 38–39), which does recount the story of a woman who prior to her conversion to Christianity used to sleep with her slaves and servants.

32. Glancy, *Slavery in Early Christianity*, 9. See also there, 21 and 23.

33. C. Wayne Tucker, "Women in the Manumission Inscriptions at Delphi," *Transactions of the American Philological Association* 112 (1982), 225–36, here 230–32.

34. Justinian, *Digest* 27.7.1, 4 (ed. and trans. Mommsen, Krueger, and Watson, *The Digest of Justinian*, vol. 2, 805).

35. Glancy, *Slavery in Early Christianity*, 26–27. The slave father was not a father in law nor

Closely related to the sexual exploitation of slaves, as well as of free-born boys, was raising up exposed children to a life of prostitution. Not every exposed child died, and many were taken in by pimps *(leno)* who brought them up to live a life of prostitution.[36] The fact that under Roman law many slaves were sold with a *ne serva prostituator* covenant suggested to Glancy that both in theory and in practice prostitution and slavery were closely aligned.[37] The most common method of procuring such slaves, however, was to go to the local dumping spot and pick up exposed infants.

Physical Abuse in the Ancient World

In the face of customary practices of abandonment, exposure, and sexual use of children, one should not overlook that most ubiquitous form of child abuse in the ancient world, namely, harsh physical punishment.[38] Children were beaten regularly, whether slave or free, but we cannot pretend that slaves were treated as well as freeborn children. As Garnsey argued, what distinguished the slave from the freeborn child was the level of physical punishment the slave had to bear.[39] Considered merely as "bodies," neither human nor object, slaves were subject to abuse at many levels. Their masters could punish them for deeds they had done, or were thought to have done. They could be made to take the punishment due their master by allowing their body to serve in place of his. In fact, by law "all testimony by slaves [was] to be given under torture" and this did not depend upon the age of the child, as we shall soon see.[40]

---

could he protect his wife or daughter from any unwanted sexual advances. The Greco-Roman world saw him as a man without honor and without a family. Yet see Tucker, "Women in the Manumission Inscriptions at Delphi," 228, who argues that family relationships were acknowledged by the enslaved and that slaves or former slaves may also have tried to put the family "together," at times by buying the release of still captive slaves by those who were manumitted.

36. Glancy, *Slavery in Early Christianity*, 54–55.

37. Ibid., 54. The *ne serva prostituator* covenant "forbade the buyer (including subsequent buyers) from forcing the slave into prostitution."

38. For discussion of aspects of corporal punishment in the ancient world, see DeBruyn, "Flogging a Son"; Fitzgerald, "Proverbs 3:11–12, Hebrews 12:5–6, and the Tradition of Corporal Punishment"; Cribiore, *Gymnastics of the Mind*, 65–73; Laes, *Kinderen bij de Romeinen*, 123–31; and Meir Bar-Ilan, "The Battered Jewish Child in Antiquity," http://faculty.biu.ac.il/~barilm/battered.html, 2003 (1996) (seen December 3, 2007).

39. Garnsey, "Sons, Slaves—and Christians," 101–21, especially 120.

40. Glancy, *Slavery in Early Christianity*, 51.

The Christian Response to Abortion, Exposure, and Infanticide

Under the influence both of Jewish moralists and biblical teachings, early Christians condemned exposure, infanticide, and abortion.[41] Created in the image of God, every child conceived and born was thought to have value. The New Testament does not speak of abortion, exposure, or infanticide. The only evidence of such practices that one may derive from the text is circumstantial.[42] It seems unlikely that this has to do with the lack of knowledge of such practices. Rather, it should be linked to the rarity of such practices among the Jews, given that the New Testament offers examples of disabled adults whose lives were preserved from infancy in spite of their disabilities (cf. John 9:1–2).[43]

It is only when Christians became engaged fully in Greco-Roman culture that their opposition to abortion, exposure, and infanticide was stated outright. The fact that such practices are mentioned in a rather uniform manner in documents from the late first and early second centuries may be connected to the increasing presence of the Church in Gentile regions and thus to the presence of Christians who were aware of such practices and might even have engaged in such behavior before their own conversions. The form in which one finds such criticisms suggests that it was a *topos* in early Christian catechesis and even in apologetic literature.[44] *Didache* 2.2 condemns both abortion and infanticide. So does *Barnabas* 19.5, using a Greek phrase that is almost identical to the formulation of the *Didache*.[45] Both texts issued their condemnations in a list of revised "com-

41. Kleijwegt, "Kind," 924.

42. By this, we mean, for instance, Jesus referring to eunuchs who have been made eunuchs by men (Mt 19:12), a comment which may indicate knowledge of slave boys being "castrated." Whether such a custom is advocated or not is not to be decided here. The passage merely may reflect some knowledge of the actual practice, which would give the saying some of its force. On this passage, see also Jerome Kodell, "The Celibacy Logion in Matthew 19:12," *Biblical Theology Bulletin* 8 (1978), 19–23; and Quentin Quesnell, "'Made Themselves Eunuchs for the Sake of the Kingdom of Heaven' (MT 19,12)," *CBQ* 30 (1968), 335–58.

43. Studies on children and disabilities in the ancient world have not made much progress. See Anne Allély, "Les enfants malformés et handicaps à Rome sous le Principat," *Revue des études anciennes* 106.1 (2004), 73–101; and a forthcoming study by N. Kelley.

44. This *topos* and others, for instance pederasty, seem to get their start in Christian thought from the description of the "Two Ways," a document type that may have emerged from a Jewish setting. For discussion of the origin and history of the "Two Ways" document, see Kurt Niederwimmer, *The Didache. Hermeneia*, trans. Linda M. Maloney (Minneapolis: Fortress Press, 1998), 30–54; and Marcello Del Verme, *Didache and Judaism: Jewish Roots of an Ancient Christian-Jewish Work* (New York: T&T Clark, 2004).

45. See *Didache* 2.2 (ed. and trans. Ehrman, *Apostolic Fathers*, vol. 1, 418–19); and *Epistle*

mandments." In the midst of "you shall not kill" and "you shall not commit adultery" come commandments enjoining one not to perform magic, not to perform abortions, not to murder children, and not to engage in pederasty. Our discussion first turns to what was in view of the commandments against abortion and infanticide.

The language describing acts of abortion and infanticide in *Didache* 2.2 and *Barnabas* 19.5 is identical: *ou phoneuseis teknon en phthora,* "you shall not kill a child by miscarriage." Immediately following this passage, both texts add the commandment not to commit infanticide: *oude gennēthen apokteneis,* "neither shall you kill a child."[46] It is entirely possible that one of these texts borrowed the passages from the other. Yet it may also be the case that a revised list of "commandments" for new converts and catechists was in circulation, and took into account common practices of the Greco-Roman world. The listing of these prohibitions, especially in a form strongly reminiscent of the Ten Commandments, suggests that these may have circulated or been recited orally in the early Church, or even that they may have had a Jewish prehistory.[47] They condemn both abortion and infanticide in clear terms and without discussion. In the second half of the second century, while defending Christians from charges of cannibalism, Athenagoras asked how Christians could be guilty of such acts when they condemn the murder of the child in the womb by the use of drugs.[48] In so doing, he compared abortion to murder, stating that the one guilty of it had to give account for this act to God. By commenting that drugs were used to achieve such abortions, Athenagoras's remark may alert one to the possibility that another prohibition in the *Didache* also may have been related to the ban on abortion. Just prior to the statement on abortion one finds a ban on the use of "poisons" or "medicines": *ou pharmakeuseis.* Because the prohibition appears between the one banning abortion and the one

---

of *Barnabas* 19.5 (ed. and trans. Ehrman, *Apostolic Fathers,* vol. 2, 76–77). On the relationship between the *Didache* and the *Epistle of Barnabas* and their use of "revised" lists of commandments, see Richard A. Freund, "The Decalogue in Early Judaism and Christianity," in *The Function of Scripture in Early Jewish and Christian Tradition,* eds. Craig A. Evans and James A. Sanders (Sheffield: Sheffield Academic Press, 1998), 124–41, here 133–35; and Willy Rordorf, "Does the Didache Contain Jesus Tradition Independently of the Synoptic Gospels," in *Jesus and the Oral Gospel Tradition,* ed. Henry Wansborough, JSNT Supplement Series 64 (Sheffield: Sheffield Academic Press, 1991), 394–423, here 396.

46. See Niederwimmer, *The Didache,* 89–90. The only difference between these two phrases is the appearance of *palin* in *Barnabas* 19.5 (ed. Ehrman, *Apostolic Fathers,* vol. 2, 76, l. 18).

47. See the literature listed and referenced in notes 44 and 45.

48. Athenagoras, *A Plea for the Christians* 35 (ed. Marcovich. *Athenagoras. Legatio Pro Christianis,* 108–10).

banning the use of magic, it is difficult to determine its precise meaning. It seems that it cannot be directed against the use of medicines to cure sickness. Thus, either it was intended against the use of medicines or poisons in sorcery or against medicines or poisons that promoted a miscarriage.[49]

The exposure of children likewise was condemned by a number of Christian authors. Clement of Alexandria spoke of it in *Paedagogus* 3.4, stating that pagans exposed children born to them, while at the same time caring for birds. He had condemned the exposure of infants for other reasons in *Paedagogus* 3.3, where he considered the possibility that the children a man had exposed might be brought up for a life of prostitution and subsequently a boy or girl with whom such a man had intercourse might in fact be his own child.[50] Justin Martyr claimed that most exposed children, both boys and girls, were taken into people's households for a life of prostitution.[51] Like Clement, he argued that the one who exposed a child could end up having sex with a prostitute who was his own offspring. Justin compared bringing up abandoned children for a life of prostitution to raising herds of animals. In fact, numerous children were raised for the very purpose of prostitution. Justin also criticized the government for taking taxes and duty from sexual slave traders, thereby approving of and promoting such actions.[52] Further accusations include the charges that some of the boys were castrated for the purposes of prostitution and other men hired out their own wives and children as prostitutes, a practice which Musonius Rufus also condemned. Christians' concern for exposed children arose not only from the possibility of their death, which would be tantamount to murder, but also from the fact that certain places were known as sites to pick up abandoned children for the purpose of prostituting them. Justin and Clement may seem to be offering odd reasons to oppose exposure, but that misses the point these authors were making. Many people who left a child in a particular location might have known that it would not die, but would be claimed and brought up as a prostitute. In their condemnations, Justin and Clement were responding to this reality. The Christian opposi-

---

49. Niederwimmer, *The Didache*, 89–90.

50. Clement of Alexandria, *Paedagogus* 3.3 (ed. Marcovich and van Winden, *Clementis Alexandrini "Paedagogus,"* 161). On the practice of raising up exposed children as slaves, see also I. Biezunska-Malowist, "Die Expositio von Kindern als Quelle der Sklavenbeschaffung im griechisch-römischen Ägypten," *Jahrbuch für Wirtschaftsgeschichte* 2 (1971), 129–33.

51. Justin Martyr, *First Apology* 27 (ed. Marcovich, *Iustini Martyris Apologiae Pro Christianis,* 67).

52. Whether this also was one of the thoughts on the mind of the author of 1 Timothy 1:10 when he criticized "slave-traders" (*andrapodistai*) can be neither proven nor excluded.

tion to the exposure of children was directed not only at the possible death of infants, but also at the life of prostitution that likely was to become their lot.[53] Justin dealt with this point directly in *Apol.* 1.29, where he said that those children who did not get picked up would die and that as a result those who exposed their children became murderers.[54] The reality was that exposure did not always lead to death, but in the eyes of Christian authors the life of slavery and sexual exploitation into which children were placed also was to be condemned.

Some have seen a lack of concern for children as a whole in the practice of abortion, infanticide, and exposure. Mark Golden took issue with this in *Children and Childhood in Classical Athens.* He argued that such practices did not imply that parents did not love the children they chose to keep.[55] While this reflection may be correct on some level, the practices do imply a willingness to distinguish between the relative worth of one human over another, and to deny the humanity of some for arbitrary or fleeting reasons. This is at the heart of Greco-Roman society and it is why prior to the rise of Christianity the use of some children for sexual purposes or of some as slaves caused barely a moral ripple, apart from Jewish writers and the odd Greco-Roman moralist like Musonius Rufus. If fate decreed such a future for certain people, so be it. Christian arguments were not based on accidents of birth, but on the inherent worth of each child as a child of God.[56]

The Christian Response to Sexual Exploitation

Many boys and girls survived exposure, and some of those, perhaps most, became prostitutes. The boys who survived were often castrated or had their testicles crushed. When it came to the sexual use of children, Chris-

53. See Krenkel, "Prostitution," 1295–97.

54. Justin Martyr, *First Apology* 29 (ed. Marcovich, *Iustini Martyris Apologiae Pro Christianis,* 75). Glancy, *Slavery in Early Christianity,* 76, suggests that early Christian sources are condemning not exposure, but infanticide. She is right to differentiate between the two. Infanticide, the killing of a child, was clearly condemned as a sort of murder, but how should exposure be condemned if the child did not die? Justin and Clement condemned it because it led to children's being raised up to a life of slavery and prostitution.

55. Golden, "Did the Ancients Care When Their Children Died?" 152–60.

56. Abortion and infanticide were discussed at the councils of Elvira (306) (canons 63 and 68) and of Ancyra (314) (canon 21). At the council gathered in Elvira, a city in modern-day Spain, canon 63 regulated that "if a woman, while her husband is away, conceives by adultery and after that crime commits abortion, she shall not be given communion even at the end, since she has doubled her crime." Having spoken in canon 63 of the case of a baptized Christian

tian authors seem to have coined a new phrase to express their dismay at such behavior, or at least they brought a particular phrase to more common usage.[57] The word they chose to use does not occur in any extant pagan source. It is found only once before the rise of the common era in a Jewish text, the *Testament of Levi,* which is generally dated to the second century B.C. The verb under discussion is *paidophthoreō,* which at times has been translated as "engaging in sodomy," a rather unacceptable rendering, and at other times as "committing pederasty," which misses the core meaning of the word. In the *Testament of Levi* a noun derived from this verb appears as a plural masculine noun, *paidophthoroi,* describing wicked priests at the end of time.[58] The verb itself is constructed from "child"

woman, the council ruled somewhat more leniently in the case of a catechumen. In canon 68 it formulated that "a catechumen, if she has conceived a child in adultery and then suffocated it, shall be baptized at the end [of her life]." In these two canons clearly both abortion and infanticide are addressed. A few years later, at the opposite end of the Mediterranean, the council of Ancyra, modern-day Ankara, Turkey, possibly referred to and modified the earlier council at Elvira when it regulated that "women who commit fornication, and destroy that which they have conceived, or who are employed in making drugs for abortion, a former decree excluded them until the hour of death, and to this some have assented. Nevertheless, being desirous to use somewhat greater leniency, we have ordained that they fulfill ten years [of penance], according to the prescribed degrees." With these two cases, we encounter church leaders developing a penal system that tries to handle such actions in an expanding Christian environment, not simply offer criticism of the world around them. Even if limited, the problem was now "in house." For the translation of canons 63 and 68 of the Council of Elvira, see Samuel Laeuchli, *Power and Sexuality: The Emergence of Canon Law at the Synod of Elvira* (Philadelphia: Temple University Press, 1972), 133–34. For a discussion of the documents of Elvira, see Maurice Meigne, "Concile ou collection d'Elvire," *Revue d'histoire ecclésiastique* 70 (1975), 361–87. For canon 21 of the Council of Ancrya, see R. B. Rackham, "The Text of the Canons of Ancyra: The Greek, Latin, Syriac and Armenian Versions," in *Studia Biblica et ecclesiastica,* ed. Samuel Roles Driver and others (Oxford: Clarendon Press, 1891), vol. 3, 139–216, here 153 [Greek text] and 208 [Latin trans. of Syriac, which is not printed]; reprinted as a separate booklet by Gorgias Press (Piscataway, N.J., 2006).

57. Will Deming, "Mark 9.42–10.12, Matthew 5.27–32, and B. Nid. 13b: A First Century Discussion of Male Sexuality," *New Testament Studies* 36 (1990), 130–41; and Raymond F. Collins, *Sexual Ethics and the New Testament: Behavior and Belief* (New York: Crossroad, 2000), 62–72, make the challenging observation that the "scandal" against which Jesus warns his disciples in Mark 9:42, in particular, is that of sexually abusing children. Our discussion again returns to these articles below, but it is to be noted here that it is entirely possible that these scholars are correct. While there is no question of implying that sexual abuse was unknown to the Jews, or that certain Jews did not engage in such a practice, it seems that it was not culturally approved or accepted. As such and in contrast to Jesus' condemnation of such a practice, later Christian condemnation was based on a more widespread observation and broader cultural acceptance of such activities in the regions where Christianity spread. See Niederwimmer, *The Didache,* 89, n. 7, on the use of the word *paidophthoreō* and its likely construction by Jewish/Christian moralists.

58. *Testament of Levi* 3.17.11.3 (ed. M. De Jonge, *The Testaments of the Twelve Patriarchs. A Critical Edition of the Greek Text* [Leiden: E. J. Brill, 1978], 45).

(*pais*) and *phthoreō*, which as a verb is not well attested outside of Christian literature. As a noun and adjective, the root *phthor-* carries the meaning of "destruction," "ruin" or "seduction," "seducer" or "corruptor," or, more generally, "committing injury," "causing destruction."[59] This is the case for the pre-Christian and Christian usage. When it is employed to speak of a seducer it can refer to one who seduces women. As a result, if context does not demand otherwise, the translation of the verb *paidophthoreō* should assume that the seduction or corruption of children, both girls and boys, is referenced, and prohibited.

Didache 2.2 places the teaching *ou paidophthorēseis*, "do not seduce/corrupt children," right in the middle of the same revised list of commandments in which the prohibitions on abortion and infanticide are formulated.[60] Following the commandments that forbid murder and adultery is a prohibition against the sexual corruption of children. The same constellation is to be found in the *Epistle of Barnabas* 19.4, where, following commandments prohibiting fornication and adultery, the author states, "Do not seduce/corrupt children" (*ou paidophthorēseis*).[61] Clement of Alexandria's *Exhortation to the Greeks* (*Protrepticus*) recites the same phrase, in the same immediate context as found in the *Didache*. As in the *Didache* and *Barnabas*, Clement states *ou paidophthorēseis*.[62] The exact phrase is found again in Clement's *Paedagogus* 2.10.89, following prohibitions of fornication and adultery, in *Paedagogus* 3.12.89, and in *Stromateis* 3.4.36.[63] In Clement and the *Didache*, the context is identical; in the *Epistle of Barnabas* the context is similar. In each case, the phrase is identical and makes use of a verb form not found prior to its appearance in these texts. It is possible that one of the authors in question simply "created" the verb and the others adopt-

---

59. See Liddell and Scott, *Greek-English Lexicon*, 1930, for the entry for *"phthora."* G. W. H. Lampe, *A Patristic Greek Lexicon* (Oxford: Clarendon Press, 1961), 997, translates the verb *paidophthoreō* as "to corrupt boys" and the feminine noun as "corruption of boys"; the masculine noun is translated as "corrupting boys."

60. *Didache* 2.2 (ed. Ehrman, *Apostolic Fathers*, vol. 1, 418, l. 2).

61. *Epistle of Barnabas* 19.4 (ed. Ehrman, *Apostolic Fathers*, vol. 2, 76, l. 10).

62. Clement of Alexandria, *Protreptikos* X.108.5 (ed. Marcovich, *Clementis Alexandrini "Protrepticus,"* 158, l. 16).

63. Clement of Alexandria, *Paedagogus* 2.10.89 (ed. Marcovich and van Winden, *Clementis Alexandrini "Paedagogus,"* 123, ll. 6–7); ibid., 3.12.89 (ed. Marcovich and van Winden, 197, l. 28); and Clement of Alexandria, *Stromateis* 3.4.36 (ed. Stählin and Früchtel, *Clemens Alexandrinus. Zweiter Band. Stromata. Buch I–VI*, 212, l. 23). Pseudo-Athanasius, *Syntagma doctrinae ad monachos* 1.5.2 (ed. Henri Hyvernat, "Le Syntagma Doctrinae dit de Saint Athanase," in *Studia Patristica. Études d'ancienne littérature chrétienne*, fasc. 2 [Paris: Henri Leroux, 1890], 119–60, here 122), also uses the identical phrase.

ed it, but it is also possible that the verb gave expression to an early Christian *topos* which had existed already prior to its literary use in Christian catechesis and apologetics and which was adopted by each of these authors independently of one another.

The word, as a verb or as a noun, is found in numerous other early Christian authors, always to decry the use of children in this manner. The noun, *paidophthoros,* occurs in the *Epistle of Barnabas* 10.6. In this allegorical interpretation of the dietary laws in the Pentateuch, the prohibition against eating rabbit, in Deuteronomy 14:7 (it chews the cud but does not have split hooves), is explained as a metaphor indicating the prohibition of the seduction of children.[64] Tatian also used the noun to describe Greek gods, calling them seducers of children and adulterers.[65] While Pseudo-Justin in his *Oration against the Greeks* leveled the same accusation against the Greek gods in the third century, Justin Martyr himself, in his *Dialogue with Trypho* the Jew, accused the "nations" of engaging in the practice of seducing children (*Dial.* 95.1). Theophilus described Zeus himself as guilty of incest, adultery, and the corruption of children. Clement used the noun also in *Paedagogus* 2.10.88 to decry the practice of corrupting children.[66] On four occasions, Origen listed the corruption of children as a sin, usually in conjunction with adultery, but also with other sins such as the use of medicines or potions, as observed above in the *Didache*.[67] In those cases describing the impious behavior of the Greek gods, the Christians were function-

---

64. *Epistle of Barnabas* 10.6 (ed. Ehrman, *Apostolic Fathers,* vol. 2, 48, l. 12). The noun is also found in feminine form in Origen (see first three references to Origen in note 67 below) and Clement of Alexandria, *Paedagogus* 2.10.88 (ed. Marcovich and van Winden, *Clementis Alexandrini "Paedagogus,"* 123, l. 3). Theophilus of Antioch, *To Autolycus* 3.27 (ed. Grant, *Theophilus of Antioch. Ad Autolycum,* 140), employs a composite of noun and verb (παῖδας διέφθειρεν).

65. Tatian, *Oratio ad Graecos* 8.1 (ed. and trans. Whittaker, *Tatian. "Oratio ad Graecos" and Fragments,* 14, l. 14).

66. Pseudo-Justin Martyr, *Oratio ad Graecos* 2 (trans. M. Dods, "[Justin Martyr] The Discourse to the Greeks," in ANF 1 [New York: Charles Scribner's Sons, 1913], 271–72, here 271). See also Quasten, *Patrology,* vol. 1, 205–6; and Campbell Bonner, "The Sibyl and the Bottle Imps," in *Quantulacumque. Studies Presented to Kirsopp Lake by Pupils, Colleagues, and Friends,* ed. Robert P. Casey, Silva Lake, and Agnes K. Lake (London: Christophers, c1937), 1–8. Justin Martyr, *Dialogue with Trypho* 95.1 (ed. Miroslav Marcovich, *Iustini Martyris Dialogus cum Tryphone* [Berlin: de Gruyter, 1997], 234, l. 8); Theophilus of Antioch, *To Autolycus* 1.9 (ed. and trans. Grant, *Theophilus of Antioch. Ad Autolycum,* 12–13); and Clement of Alexandria, *Paedagogus* 2.10.88 (ed. Marcovich and van Winden, *Clementis Alexandrini "Paedagogus,"* 123).

67. Origen of Alexandria, *Commentary on Matthew* 18:15 (ed. PG 13.3, cols. 825–1600, here col. 1173); Origen of Alexandria, *Fragments on Ephesians* 24.4 (ed. J. A. F. Gregg, "The Commentary of Origen upon the Epistle to the Ephesians," *JThS* 3 [1902], 233–44, 398–420, and 554–76, here 559); Origen of Alexandria, *Commentary on John* 20.22.178.2 (ed. Erwin Preuschen,

ing as apologists, defending themselves from false claims about their own religious practices and using Greek myths about the gods to attack paganism. In most of the other cases, the Christians of the first to third centuries A.D. were engaging in polemic regarding a common practice among their neighbors.[68] Without question, their criticism had become part of a stereotyped list, but it is also clear that such sexual abuse of children was a part of common Greco-Roman practice and as Christianity began to engage its culture both apologetically and critically it challenged that practice, in part by coining a new word for what they observed and knew took place among the Greeks and Romans. Christians did not refer to the person who had sex with children as the "(sexual) lover of children" *(paiderastēs)*, but as the "destroyer and seducer of children" *(paidophthoros)*.

That the surrounding Greco-Roman culture was slow to change its ways, even as the lands of the Roman Empire became more Christianized, is clear from further usage of this term and from criticism of the practice itself by later Christian theologians and authors. One also has to reckon with the possibility that it may have become part of a stock arsenal of accusations to be used in debates with pagans, but this does not mean that the practices did not continue.

Epiphanius denounced the practice, as did Gregory Nazianzus, Athanasius of Alexandria, and Pseudo-Basil of Seleucia.[69] In several places Pseudo-Basil and Athanasius, the latter especially in the *Life of Antony*, seem to be dependent upon the earliest Christian denunciations, since they reproduced the form of the lists of revised commandments found in those sources.[70] Christian traditions in Greek, ascribed to the pen of the fourth-

---

Origenes. Vierter Band, GCS [Leipzig: J. C. Hinrichs, 1903], 354); and Origen, *Selecta in Exodum* 12.284.54 (ed. PG 12.281–98, here 284).

68. See also Horn, "The *Pseudo-Clementines* and the Challenges of the Conversion of Families."

69. See Epiphanius, *Ancoratus* 105 (ed. PG 43.17–256, here 208); Gregory Nazianzus, *Orations* 27 (*Adversus Eunomium*) 6.6 (ed. and trans. Paul Gallay and Maurice Jourjon, *Grégoire de Nazianze. Discours 27–31* [Paris: Les Éditions du Cerf, 1978], 84); Athanasius of Alexandria, *Contra gentes* 12.38, 15.18, and 26.16 (ed. and trans. Robert W. Thomson, *Contra gentes; and, De Incarnatione. Athanasius* [Oxford: Clarendon Press, 1971], 36, 42, and 70); Athanasius of Alexandria, *Life of Antony* 74.3 (ed. and trans. G. J. M. Bartelink, *Athanase d'Alexandrie: Vie d'Antoine* [Paris: Les Éditions du Cerf, 1994], 324–25; trans. Robert C. Gregg, *Athanasius: The Life of Antony and the Letter to Marcellinus* [Mahwah, N.J.: Paulist Press, 1980], 29–99, here 84–85); and Pseudo-Basil of Seleucia, *De Vita et Miraculis sanctae Theclae* bk. 1 (ed. PG 85.477–617, here 497).

70. The same holds true for the traditions found in Pseudo-Athanasius, *Syntagma doctrinae ad monachos* 1.5.2 (ed. Hyvernat, "Le Syntagma Doctrinae," 122); and Pseudo-Athanasius, *Didascalia cccxviii patrum Nicaenorum* (ed. PG 28.1637–1644, here col. 1639, l. 40).

century poet-theologian Ephraem the Syrian, but in fact being the product of later, now anonymous Greek ascetic writers, refer to those who sexually use children in a number of lists, in which the texts renounce the practice among numerous others, such as adultery, stealing, drunkenness, sorcery, and destruction of the soul and body.[71] The lists bear some resemblance to those in Clement, the *Epistle of Barnabas,* and the *Didache,* but they do not seem to be based directly upon them.[72]

In the fragments of the work of Pseudo-Polemon (ca. 88–145) one finds the denunciation of seducers and corruptors of children amongst those of patricides and matricides. Chrysostom counted seducers of children with those who were lustful and gluttonous. The *Apostolic Constitutions* seems to include the behavior in the more general category of homosexual acts when it states *oude paidophthorēseis* and then describes "the evil of Sodom" as "contrary to nature." It remains possible, of course, that "the evil of Sodom" in the author's mind is the corruption of children specifically.[73]

Apart from the use of the verb *paidophthoreō,* the related noun, and the *topos* as a whole, Christian authors often condemned the use of children sexually. Here it suffices only to refer to a sampling of such passages. Tatian criticized the Romans for approving of pederasty while barbarians condemned it, and for gathering "herds of boys" for this purpose. In his *To Autolycus,* Theophilus disparaged those who engaged in pederasty and sold their children. Athenagoras described those who condemned Christians as "adulterers and pederasts," who maintained "resorts for the young

71. Ephraem Graecus, "Sermo in secundum adventum domini nostri Iesu Christi [Λόγος εἰς τὴν δευτέραν παρουσίαν τοῦ κυρίου ἡμῶν Ἰησοῦ Χριστοῦ]" (ed. Konstantin G. Phrantzolas, Ὁσίου Ἐφραῖμ τοῦ Σύρου. Ἔργα, vol. 4 [Thessaloniki: Ἐκδόσεις τό Περιβόλί τῆς Παναγίας, 1992], 9–46, here 17, l. 11, and 26, l. 3); Ephraem Graecus, "Interrogationes et responsiones [Ἐρωτήσεις καὶ ἀποκρίσεις]" (ed. Phrantzolas, Ὁσίου Ἐφραῖμ τοῦ Σύρου. Ἔργα, vol. 4, 76–110, here 80, l. 8, and 89, l. 7; and Ephraem Graecus, "De virtutibus et passionibus [Περὶ ἀρετῶν καὶ παθῶν [ψυχικῶν]]" (ed. Konstantin G. Phrantzolas, Ὁσίου Ἐφραῖμ τοῦ Σύρου. Ἔργα, vol. 5 [Thessaloniki: Ἐκδόσεις τό Περιβόλί τῆς Παναγίας, 1994], 392–410, here 396, ll. 3–4).

72. For the extent of the *Corpus Ephraemi Graeci,* see the list in M. Geerard, *Clavis Patrum Graecorum,* vol. 2 (Turnhout: Brepols, 1974), 366–468. Perhaps most conveniently accessible and still of great help is also Democratie Hemmerdinger-Illiadou, "Ephrém Grec" and "Ephrém Latin," in *Dictionnaire de Spiritualité* 4 (1960–61), cols. 800–819.

73. Pseudo-Polemon, *Physiognomonica* 17.11 (ed. R. Foerster, *Scriptores physiognomonici Graeci et Latini* [Leipzig: Teubner, 1893], vol. 1, 327). For a more easily accessible edition, see Simon Swain and George Boys-Stones, ed. and trans., *Seeing the Face, Seeing the Soul: Polemon's Physi[o]gnomy from Classical Antiquity to Medieval Islam* (Oxford: Oxford University Press, 2007). John Chrysostom, *De paenitentia,* sermon 2 (ed. PG 60.699–706, here col. 699, l. 28). *Apostolic Constitutions* 7.2.10 (ed. and trans. Marcel Metzger, *Les Constitutions Apostoliques, Tome III, Livres VII et VIII* [Paris: Les Éditions du Cerf, 1987], 30–31).

for every kind of vile pleasure."[74] In his *Paedagogus,* Clement of Alexandria warned against having too many servants, especially "herds of beautiful boys, like cattle, from whom they milk away their beauty." He also was able to see that these children were not engaging in these acts of their own accord. Thus he pitied "the boys possessed by slave dealers" for "they are not treated with ignominy by themselves, but by command the wretches are adorned for base gain." Elsewhere, Clement issued strong prohibitions against using children sexually, especially boys, whom he said one should consider as "sons" and not as sexual objects. While he spoke up for the distance to be kept from boys, he did not become an equally strong defender of girls. He only thought that it was never correct to touch boys in a sexual way "as though they were girls."[75]

The protection of children from sexual advances, at least in the case of boys, may be the one area of morality in which early Christianity was truly countercultural. Some of the passages that deal with the issue are directed at Christian audiences and sometimes they come in apologetic works that at least pretend to envision non-Christian Greeks or Romans as hearers. Yet whether the authors are speaking to Christians or pagans, it is clear that the critique of the sexual use of children was a significant theme of Christian morality that engaged the possibility of altering children's lives for the better.[76] In the present discussion one has to keep in mind, as Osiek and Balch also point out, that marriage itself was often between a much older man and a girl between twelve and fifteen.[77] A modern perspective may be inclined to classify this as the corruption of children as well. With respect to arranged

74. Tatian, *Oratio ad Graecos* 28 (ed. and trans. Whittaker, *Tatian. "Oratio ad Graecos" and Fragments,* 52–53); Theophilus, *To Autolycus* 1.2 (ed. and trans. Grant, *Theophilus of Antioch. Ad Autolycum,* 4–5); Athenagoras, *A Plea for the Christians* 34.1 (ed. Marcovich, *Athenagoras. Legatio Pro Christianis,* 106).

75. Clement of Alexandria, *Paedagogus* 2.10 and 3.3–4 (ed. Marcovich and van Winden, *Clementis Alexandrini "Paedagogus,"* 120–24, 160, and 164, ll. 6–7).

76. Bakke, *When Children Became People,* 142–49, discusses the reality of relations between children and men and notes that the Council of Elvira (306), canon 71 ("Men who sexually abuse boys shall not be given communion even at the end." Laeuchli, *Power and Sexuality,* 134), stipulates excommunication for those who have sex with boys (141). One may concur with his proposition that the fact that only one council saw fit to deal with the question suggests that such practices, although they were real, did not occur frequently (149). A few decades later and at the other end of the Mediterranean world, Gregory of Nyssa, *Epistula Canonica* 4 (ed. PG 45:221–236, here 229), for example, argued that excommunication should not be for life, but for nine years. One is left to wonder whether the different cultural context of Greek society was a factor contributing to the practical necessity of introducing more lenient laws in order not to deplete local congregations too severely.

77. Osiek and Balch, *Families in the New Testament World,* 118.

marriages for girls, therefore, and as far as one can tell, Christianity did not challenge the prevailing cultural norms, unless one is willing to classify the option of celibacy as such a challenge. This challenge, however, was not based on revulsion at the young age of girls at marriage, but on the perception of the superiority of the celibate life. On the other hand, the culturally accepted norm of marriage, no matter how much one may reject its ancient form, was considered an opportunity for girls to embark upon an honorable life; the same could not be said of the prostitution and enslavement of children to serve the sexual needs of adults throughout the Greco-Roman world. In this respect, Christians challenged what they perceived were the corrupt norms of the prevailing morality in clear and pronounced terms.

The Christian Response to Slavery

The slavery of children is a topic that is difficult to discuss, since in non-Christian and Christian sources alike there is hardly any distinction between adult slaves and child slaves. Child slaves predominantly came from two sources: exposed children who were picked up and enslaved, and children who were born to an enslaved mother.[78] According to Greco-Roman law, slaves could not contract a legal marriage, although they could cohabitate and have children. The children born in these relationships took on the status of the mother at the time of birth and were the property of the slave owner. These slave children were bought and sold freely, and could be used sexually by their masters, whether boys or girls. In order to answer the question of how Christianity altered the plight of these children, one first needs to trace some of the ways in which Christianity could have had any impact on their lives. Three types of slave children need to be distinguished: those who belonged to Christian families and were themselves Christians; those who belonged to Christian families and were not Christians; and those who were Christians, but whose masters were not. The impact of Christianity on the vast majority of slave children who neither were Christians nor had masters who were Christians would have been minimal in its first centuries. Christian influence increased gradually as Christianity moved toward rejecting slavery in late antiquity and began to have a greater impact on the culture at large.

There were child slaves of Christian masters. When such masters were

---

78. The number of children whom parents sold into slavery, such as reported by Musonius Rufus, was probably small and statistically insignificant. Not many child slaves were taken in war at this time either.

told to "stop threatening" their slaves (Eph 6:9) and treat them "justly and fairly" (Col 4:1), it is not clear if their slaves were Christians or not.[79] What we know with certainty is that many slaves of all ages were Christians. Pliny the Younger stated that Christianity spread to "many of all ages and every rank." He referred to "young slave girls" and called them deaconesses, but we do not know whether they came from Christian or pagan families.[80] Christian masters probably had among their slaves some who were Christians and some who were pagans.

Christian masters were not necessarily better than their pagan counterparts. While one hopes that the moral teachings of Christianity led Christian masters to stop abusing their child slaves in every way, and that the presence of churches in homes led to a more humane manner of dealing with slave children, one also hopes that cases like the beating to death of a slave girl at the hands of her Christian master recounted in the early-third-century *Acts of Andrew* illustrates the exception and not the norm.[81] Certainty on the matter is impossible in light of the present state of research on the question.[82]

When one considers the Christian slaves of pagan masters, the New Testament is ambivalent, depending on the perspective of the author. Paul wrote that "in Christ" there is equality, "neither slave nor free" (Gal 3:28; 1 Cor 12:13; cf. Col 3:11).[83] Paul's letter to Philemon stops short of a condemnation of slavery and does not demand that Philemon manumit Onesimus. The Pauline tradition varies on the question. In Ephesians, slaves were to

79. The royal official's household, the members of which came to believe in Jesus, included slaves (Jn 4:46–54). So, too, did the centurion's household in Luke 7:1–10 (cf. Mt 8:5–13), in which the faith of the centurion led Jesus to heal his slave. Cornelius, another centurion, and his household, all of whom were baptized, included among themselves slaves (Acts 10:7). Other households and their members, all of whom believed and were baptized, such as those of Lydia (Acts 16:14–15), the Philippian jailer (Acts 16:27–34), and Crispus (Acts 18:8), probably also included slaves. The same might be said for the household of Stephanas, the members of which Paul baptized in Corinth (1 Cor 1:16). With some probability, we can also include among the slaves who were Christians those from the household of Aristobulus and Narcissus (Rom 16:10–11) and perhaps those whom Paul converted in the household of Caesar (Phil 4:22). See also Glancy, *Slavery in Early Christianity*, 46–49.

80. Pliny the Younger, *Epistle* 10.96.8–9 (ed. and trans. Radice, *Pliny, Letters and Panegyricus*, vol. 2, 288–91). On these slave girls, see also J. Albert Harrill, "Servile Functionaries or Priestly Leaders? Roman Domestic Religion, Narrative Intertextuality, and Pliny's Reference to Christian Slave *Ministrae* (Ep. 10,96 8)," *Zeitschrift für die Neutestamentliche Wissenschaft* 97 (2006), 111–30.

81. *Acts of Andrew* 22 (ed. and trans. Prieur, *Acta Andreae*, 468–69).

82. With interest one awaits further results from the Feminist Sexual Ethics Project, directed by Bernadette Brooten at Brandeis University, particularly with regard to the intersection of women, slavery, and sexual violence. See also http://www.brandeis.edu/projects/fse.

83. What this "equality" looked like socially is pretty clear: it did not exist. See John H. Elliott, "The Jesus Movement Was Not Egalitarian," *Biblical Interpretation* 11.2 (2003), 187–98.

serve their earthly masters with "fear and trembling," giving service whether or not they were immediately subject to the watchful eye of the master (Eph 6:5–8). In Colossians, there is an inconsistency: slaves were to obey their earthly masters "in everything," as if serving the Lord (Col 3:22–25), a teaching which comes only verses after the proclamation of their spiritual equality (Col 3:11). First Peter asked that slaves accept the authority of their masters "with all deference," even those who were "harsh" (1 Pt 2:18–21). The Letter to Titus proposed that slaves be "submissive" to their masters "in all things" (Ti 2:9–10).[84] One needs to be conscious of and clear about the implications of obeying "harsh" pagan masters "in everything," "with all deference."

Although Christian slaves may have imbibed the teachings of the Church regarding sexual morality, they themselves often could not practice it; not if their master chose to use them. Jennifer Glancy asked whether slaves in such a situation could even find a place in a Pauline Church in which they were to avoid *porneia*, given that their bodies were not their own.[85] Whether or not they loved their parents, effectively it did not matter, not if their master chose to sell them. Whether or not the promise of equality in the Church or in the kingdom to come gave them hope, one simply has to reckon with the reality that if a master did not allow them to attend church, they could not have participated in liturgical services, especially the communal commemoration of the death and resurrection of Jesus. The baptism of Christian slaves who had non-Christian masters remains difficult to explain.

In cases where children were slaves of pagans, it is probable that nothing changed for them, neither in terms of options for marriage nor with regard to how they lived their lives in general. They would have been left to the whims of their masters, a situation which Christian texts continued to stress as a necessary means of control and order. These children would have had difficulty living a Christian life of their own accord. Slaves of Christians may have been treated better at times, and Christian masters, pressured by Christian moral instruction, may have felt a greater need to treat their slaves according to a moral standard significantly different from that of the non-Christian owner. Whether they treated these children as equal in Christ is another question. We also do not know whether it ever

---

84. It is still unclear if in 1 Corinthians 7:21–24 Paul is asking for slaves to gain freedom if possible or to stay in their station. Numerous commentators, modern and ancient, including John Chrysostom, have found it difficult to unravel this text. See Will Deming, "A Diatribe in 1 Cor 7:21–22: A New Perspective on Paul's Directions to Slaves," *Novum Testamentum* 37 (1995), 130–37.

85. Glancy, *Slavery in Early Christianity*, 49–70.

stopped them from selling children. In fact, it is difficult to say with certainty that much changed for slave children of Christian masters because of the one clear reality: Christians continued to keep slaves for centuries, a fact which suggests that either Christians continued to buy slaves or that the children born to their adult slaves continued to be raised as slaves. It is also possible, of course, that some became "Christian" slaves in later centuries due to the conversion of their masters.

Outside of the New Testament, comments regarding slaves in the late first to early second century indicate that not much had changed in the status of Christian slaves. Selected examples from two to three centuries later also do not show much improvement. While masters were ordered not to command their male or female slaves in "bitterness" *(pikria),* so that the slaves would not cease to trust in the same God who rules over slave and master (*Didache* 4:10), slaves were also told to obey their master as a "type" *(typos)* of God.[86] When grouped with general injunctions for slaves, such comments lent an additional theological impetus directed to slaves to practice obedience: they were told that their master was like God for them. *Barnabas* 19:7 contains the same injunctions as the text from the *Didache* in an arrangement that imitates the rhetoric of the commandments in the Pentateuch, "you shall obey your masters as a 'type' of God [*hōs typō theou*]." The author of *Barnabas* stated that slaves were to be "submissive" *(hypotassō)* and may have had in mind child slaves, since the master was told not to command his or her slave or slave girl *(paidiskē)* in "a bitter temper," especially since the slaves also were Christians.[87] In his letter to Polycarp, Ignatius of Antioch instructed his addressee not to be "haughty" to his female and male slaves. Yet slaves were instructed not to become "arrogant" or "puffed up" either.[88] Slaves were to endure slavery for the glory of God, and a better, spiritual freedom; as a result they were not to seek freedom at the Church's expense. This "haughtiness" of which Ignatius wrote may then refer to a desire for manumission on the part of slaves, a social reality to which Christians only responded in later centuries. This teaching was not related to Polycarp alone, of course, but to the Church and its social situation as a whole. Yet one should not think that Bishop Polycarp was not personally intended as well, since we know that he him-

---

86. *Didache* 4.10–11 (ed. Ehrman, *Apostolic Fathers,* vol. 1, 424–25); see also Niederwimmer, *The Didache,* 109–11.

87. *Epistle of Barnabas* 19.7 (ed. Ehrman, *Apostolic Fathers,* vol. 2, 78).

88. Ignatius of Antioch, *Letter to Polycarp* 4.3 (ed. and trans. Ehrman, *Apostolic Fathers,* vol. 1, 310–21, here 314–15).

self kept child slaves who ultimately suffered on his behalf when the Roman authorities were seeking him.[89]

Given that Christians were part of the slave population of Roman society at least until the fourth century, the question arises whether or not any aspects of the reality of slavery proved to be an impediment or detriment to the child slaves' spiritual life in the Church. If slaves were truly treated as equal partners in Christ, such an understanding may have gone a long way to ameliorating their situation in general. Commentators point to the fact that certain bishops may have been slaves as children. There has been a longstanding tradition that Pius, the mid-second-century bishop of Rome, was a slave, since it is observed that the extant fragment of the *Muratorian Canon* notes him as a brother of the author of the *Shepherd of Hermas*.[90] At the beginning of the *Shepherd,* Hermas related a scene in which he was sold to a certain Rhoda.[91] Thus it seems that Hermas was a slave child by birth or at least was sold into slavery. Yet what factual reality supports such an assumption and whether or not this may indicate that his brother also was a slave is a question that is not easy to resolve. The text of the *Shepherd of Hermas* seems to offer conflicting evidence, since later on Hermas is introduced to the woman who purchased him in slavery. One may also ask how a slave sold in infancy would know his brother if he too was a slave, or even if Pius had not been sold into slavery.[92] One seems to be on more solid ground with the claim that Callistus, bishop of Rome in the third century, was raised as a slave. The information for this identification comes from Hippolytus, who in a lengthy denunciation of Callistus and his theology speaks of him as a domestic slave of a certain Carpophorus.[93] This Carpo-

89. *Martyrdom of Polycarp* 6.1–2 (ed. and trans. Ehrman, *Apostolic Fathers,* vol. 1, 366–401, here 374–75).

90. See *Muratorian Canon* 75–77 (trans. Wilhelm Schneemelcher, "Haupteinleitung: a) Kanonverzeichnisse 1. Der Canon Muratori," in *Neutestamentliche Apokryphen in deutscher Übersetzung,* vol. 1: *Evangelien,* 5th ed. [Tübingen: Mohr-Siebeck, 1987], 27–29, here 29); see also Kirsopp Lake, trans., "The Shepherd," in *Apostolic Fathers II,* LCL 25 (Cambridge, Mass.: Harvard University Press, 1913), 3.

91. *Shepherd of Hermas,* visio 1.1 (ed. and trans. Ehrman, *Apostolic Fathers,* vol. 2, 174–473, here 174–75).

92. Carolyn Osiek, *Shepherd of Hermas. Hermeneia* (Minneapolis: Fortress Press, 1999), 42, accepts that the child Hermas, raised up as a foundling *(threptos),* could indeed have been found by Rhoda and later sold by her. Indeed, why would this not be the case, given that child slaves were bought and sold as other goods were? Technically it could also be the case that such a foundling was known by his birth family many years later, and a family that exposed a child could later claim it; see also Beryl Rawson, "Children in the Roman *Familia,*" in *The Family in Ancient Rome: New Perspectives* (Ithaca, N.Y.: Cornell University Press, 1986), 170–200, here 172–73.

93. Hippolytus, *Adv. Haer.* 9.7 (trans. J. H. MacMahon, "[Hippolytus] The Refutation of

phorus was a wealthy Christian and Callistus was placed in charge of some of his banking business. There is no reason to doubt this basic information, regardless of Hippolytus's negative assessment of Callistus.

One major change in the lives of Christian slaves that would affect young slaves in particular was the church blessing, or a growing sense of a sacramental character, of their marriages. Roman law did not admit slave marriages as legal institutions or the relationships of father, mother, son, or daughter to be sanctioned among slaves.[94] Roman law did not conceptualize a phenomenon like adultery with a slave woman, although a slave's owner could sue for injury to his or her property.[95] Christian teaching on the marriage of slaves allowed slave children a semblance of normal family life, but it is not certain that this meant that child slaves were never sold or that parents were never separated from their children by sale or work in some other holding of their own or another master.[96]

That these realities continued to vex the lives of young and old slaves into the third and fourth centuries is apparent even from Christian witnesses. It is also clear that Christian authors considered slaves to be promiscuous, just as Greco-Roman paganism did. Basil of Caesarea knew of slave girls who were joined in "secret" marriages and who, as he thought, by this brought impurity

---

All Heresies," ANF 5: *Fathers of the Third Century: Hippolytus, Cyprian, Caius, Novatian, Appendix* [repr. Peabody, Mass.: Hendrickson Publishers, 1995], 9–153, here 129).

94. See Justinian, *Digest* 38.10.10, 5 (ed. and trans. Mommsen, Krueger, and Watson, *The Digest of Justinian*, vol. 3, 353). Rawson, "Children in the Roman *Familia*," 171, however, states, "in the humbler classes, even amongst slaves, conditions for an enduring and stable family life could exist. At least members of a family group not infrequently combined to commemorate one of their number who had died . . . but the conditions of slavery and other economic or social factors must have disrupted or destroyed family life for many others."

95. Justinian, *Digest* 48.5.6, 1 (ed. and trans. Mommsen, Krueger, and Watson, *The Digest of Justinian*, vol. 4, 805); and Justinian, *Codex* 9.9, 23 (ed. Krueger, *Codex Iustinianus. Corpus Iuris Civilis*, vol. 2, 375).

96. *Apostolic Constitutions* 8.32 (ed. and trans. Metzger, *Les Constitutions Apostoliques, Tome III*, 234–41) (see also Hippolytus, *Apostolic Tradition* 15 [ed. and trans. Wilhelm Geerlings, "Traditio Apostolica. Apostolische Überlieferung," in *Didache. Zwölf-Apostel-Lehre. Traditio Apostolica. Apostolische Überlieferung*, 2nd ed. (Freiburg: Herder, 1992), 212–313, here 244–45]) gives us some insight into the practical changes said to have been worked by the Church and the limitations of such teachings. If the slave was married, he (or she) had to learn to be content with his (or her) spouse. If he (or she) was not married, the slave had to be content to enter into lawful marriage or remain chaste. This does indicate the Christian desire that a slave live in a chaste marriage, in much the same way as the free person, but it does not seem to acknowledge the fact that a Christian slave who belonged to a pagan owner may not have been able to maintain chastity of his or her own accord. Such a lack of chastity, due to sexual activity not desired by the slave, would render him or her unfit to fulfill the moral requirements of the life of a Christian.

on their owner's house.[97] Why they married in secret cannot be determined from his offhand comment. One reason may have been that they could not obtain a proper Christian wedding. Perhaps they simply wished to live a normal life that was denied them when their masters ignored their desires and needs. If the secret marriage of slaves was designed so that they would not live in promiscuity, it would be difficult to see why Basil considered such relationships between slaves as a threat to the purity of their owner's house. Yet he was aware that masters could force their slave girls into unwanted sexual relations—and he did not hold such girls morally culpable.[98]

The reality seems to have been that slaves remained slaves, even as the Church attempted to rectify their situation in some significant ways. John Chrysostom gives us a window onto the reality of slaves' lives in many of his treatises and homilies. What emerges from his writings is the stark differences between the life of a slave child and that of a free child in the family that owned slaves, even when all were Christians. Chrysostom's *On Vainglory* assumes throughout that slaves have loose morals, are drawn to bawdy entertainment, and are not worthy to be left alone with freeborn children because they will sexually corrupt them.[99] He perceived a clear distinction between the slave and free child in morality. It is also obvious that slaves, children and adults, were open to physical abuse even from children of the house, as he warned fathers to make certain that their sons did not strike the slaves but control their temper.[100] The servants were to be like brothers to the child, even though slave morality was seen as being different from that of free men.[101] Yet it is quite unlikely that the slave child, even in a Christian master's home, ever had much of a chance of being raised like the free child. Still, Chrysostom also knew that the morality of slave owners was not always different from that of slaves, for he criticized masters who went to the same woman as their slaves did for sexual intercourse.[102] While such a woman could have been a prostitute, one suspects that what Chrysostom had in

---

97. Basil of Caesarea, *Letters* 199.18 (ed. and trans. Deferrari, *Saint Basil. The Letters,* vol. 3, 106–7). For a discussion of Basil's view of slavery, see the study by Richard Klein, *Die Haltung der Kappadokischen Bischöfe Basilius von Caesarea, Gregor von Nazianz und Gregor von Nyssa zur Sklaverei* (Stuttgart: Franz Steiner Verlag, 2000).

98. Basil of Caesarea, *Letters* 199.49 (ed. and trans. Deferrari, *Saint Basil. The Letters,* vol. 3, 134–35).

99. John Chrysostom, *On Vainglory* 37–38, 53, 78–79 (ed. and trans. Malingrey, *Jean Chrysostome. Sur la vaine gloire et l'éducation des enfants,* 128–31, 152–53, and 180–85).

100. Ibid., 31, 68–73 (Malingrey, 122–25 and 166–77).

101. Ibid., 71–72 (Malingrey, 172–75).

102. John Chrysostom, *Homilies on 1 Thessalonians* 5.4 (ed. PG 62.391–468, here 427).

mind was more likely a slave owned by the master. On a different matter of morality, Chrysostom criticized slave owners for not bringing their slaves to church, but always taking them along to the bath or the theater.[103] Like so much else, the morality of slaves depended on the master's will. This is not to say that Christianity did not ultimately bring some real improvements in the conditions of slaves in the Roman Empire. However, to make the matter more concrete, one may imagine two children in a home, one born a slave and one who was born free.[104] One was born to the master's wife, the other to the slave girl he owned. Even if the master was a Christian, when we ask what child was more at risk of physical punishment, of sexual abuse, of separation from his or her mother, we know that a Christian slave was still a slave, and a child raised as a slave was still subject to the violence of others, those to whom he or she belonged.[105]

The Martyrdom of Children

Children were not spared from sporadic or more systematic violence directed against Christians in the Roman Empire, especially from the second to the fourth centuries A.D.[106] The *Martyrdom of Potamiaena and Basilides* presents a young girl, Potamiaena, struggling to defend her virginity (*parthe-*

---

103. John Chrysostom, *Homilies on Ephesians* 22 (ed. PG 62.9–176, here col. 158; rev. trans. Gross Alexander, in *Chrysostom: Homilies on Galatians, Ephesians, Philippians, Colossians, Thessalonians, Timothy, Titus and Philemon*, NPNF 13, first series [Peabody, Mass.: Hendrickson Publishers, repr. 1994], 49–172, here 159).

104. For the question of how slaves lived in the homes of their masters, and where they lived, consult George, "Domestic Architecture and Household Relations," 11, 13–14, and 21. The question of where they slept and how child slaves lived with the master's children is difficult to determine. Especially for child slaves, perhaps playmates of the free child, the distinctions in their life would become clearer bit by bit and day by day, as they realized that the life they would lead as a slave would be fundamentally different from that of their friend or playmate who was free. Chrysostom's comments, cited above, make these distinctions obvious. What is lacking is any sense of the psychological consequences, which likely attended and affected such slave children.

105. For extended studies on Christian views of slavery, see for example J. Albert Harrill, *Slaves in the New Testament: Literary, Social, and Moral Dimensions* (Minneapolis: Fortress Press, 2006); J. Albert Harrill, "The Domestic Enemy: A Moral Polarity of Household Slaves in Early Christian Apologies and Martyrdom," in *Early Christian Families in Context: An Interdisciplinary Dialogue*, eds. David L. Balch and Carolyn Osiek (Grand Rapids, Mich.: Eerdmans, 2003), 231–54; Glancy, *Slavery in Early Christianity*; Richard Klein, *Die Haltung der Kappadokischen Bischöfe Basilius von Caesarea, Gregor von Nazianz und Gregor von Nyssa zur Sklaverei* (Stuttgart: Franz Steiner Verlag, 2000); J. Albert Harrill, *The Manumission of Slaves in Early Christianity* (Tübingen: Mohr Siebeck, 1995); and Richard Klein, *Die Sklaverei in der Sicht der Bischöfe Ambrosius und Augustinus* (Stuttgart: Franz Steiner Verlag Wiesbaden GmbH, 1988).

106. Many of the texts on martyrdom in this section, unless otherwise noted, are taken

nia), her body and soul being in "full flower" *(akmaion)*.[107] This young girl *(korē)*, who was threatened with sexual violence, ultimately was martyred, but threats of sexual violence were a significant part of the terror martyrs experienced.[108] In the *Martyrdom of Saints Agapē, Irenē, and Chionē* at Thessalonika Irenē, one of the three young women on whom the account is centered (2.2–3), is described as of youthful age *(to neon tēs hēlikias)* (4.4). Eventually all three were martyred, together with four female companions who likewise are identified as of the same youthful age as Irenē (4.4). First, however, young Irenē was sentenced to be placed naked in a brothel, where according to the account God protected her from any sexual activity (5.8–6.2).[109] This threat to the girl's sexual purity also explains the call of Cyprian in the *Acts of Saint Cyprian*, when he ordered *"custodiri puellas"* ("guard the young girls") as he was arrested (2.5, 26).[110]

The *Martyrdom of Saints Marian and James* describes not only the martyrdom of two girls *(puella)* named Tertulla and Antonia (11.1), but also the martyrdom of two boys *(puer)* who had been killed together with their mother a few days prior to the events featured in the text (11.5).[111] At a later point in time, Marian rejoiced over her son's martyrdom, although it is not clear if her son was a child by virtue of age (13.1–3). In the *Martyrdom of Saints Montanus and Lucius* 8.1–7, a mother, Quartillosa, had lost her husband and son to martyrdom and subsequently was given a vision of her son in heaven.[112] Many of these martyrdom accounts reflect the in-

---

from Musurillo, *Acts of the Christian Martyrs*. See there, xi–liii, for a discussion of the dating of the texts and their historicity.

107. *Martyrdom of Potamiaena and Basilides* 1.1–6 (ed. and trans. Musurillo, *Acts of the Christian Martyrs*, 132–35, here 132).

108. For studies of martyrdom in early Christianity, see, for example, Elizabeth A. Castelli, *Martyrdom and Memory: Early Christian Culture Making* (New York: Columbia University Press, 2004); Joyce E. Salisbury, *The Blood of Martyrs: Unintended Consequences of Ancient Violence* (New York: Routledge, 2004); Daniel Boyarin, *Dying for God: Martyrdom and the Making of Christianity and Judaism* (Stanford, Calif.: Stanford University Press, 1999); Gus George Christo, *Martyrdom according to John Chrysostom: "To Live Is Christ, To Die Is Gain"* (Lewiston, N.Y.: Edwin Mellen Press, 1997); Glen Warren Bowersock, *Martyrdom and Rome* (Cambridge: Cambridge University Press, 1995); and Theofried Baumeister, *Genese und Entfaltung der altkirchlichen Theologie des Martyriums* (Bern: Peter Lang, 1991).

109. *Martyrdom of Saints Agapê, Irenê, and Chionê at Saloniki* (ed. and trans. Musurillo, *Acts of the Christian Martyrs*, 280–93).

110. *Acts of Saint Cyprian* (ed. and trans. Musurillo, *Acts of the Christian Martyrs*, 168–75).

111. *Martyrdom of Saints Marian and James* (ed. and trans. Musurillo, *Acts of the Christian Martyrs*, 194–213).

112. *Martyrdom of Saints Montanus and Lucius* (ed. and trans. Musurillo, *Acts of the Christian Martyrs*, 214–39).

fluence of 2 Maccabees 7, with its retelling of the martyrdom of the seven Jewish sons and their mother, as the text just mentioned does,[113] or in cases where there is no direct reference to a parent, such martyrdom accounts work with allusions to the story of the three young men of Daniel 3.[114]

Early Christian literature featured quite a few cases of children who suffered martyrdom and whose martyrdom was in fact the focus of a given *passio,* not merely an accompanying side story. In some instances, hagiographical layers are so thick that it is difficult to determine which details are credible and which are topical exaggerations. Cases of the martyrdom of two- or three-year-old children who talked back at their persecutors and endured beatings, burnings, and boiling in hot-water vessels without dying until God determined the time of their deaths probably had been composed more to make theological points than to accurately recount historical events. The cases of the martyrdom of the little Cyriacus and his mother Julitta or the martyrdom of Mar Ṭalya, both best known in the Syriac tradition, are excellent examples of such hagiographical traditions.[115] Of some interest for earlier considerations advanced in chapter 2 is a connection established in the *Martyrdom of Mar Ṭalya* between the young martyr and the symbol of the lamb. Given the clear parallel between Christ and the martyr Ṭalya that permeates this account of a child's long suffering and death, it is hardly remarkable that at the time of Ṭalya's birth the "voice of a lamb" was heard.[116] Although the parallel between Ṭalya and the lamb does not function on the philological level, this detail provides support at least on the level of motif to Jeremias's consideration of a connection between the ideas of "child" and "lamb" in the Gospel of John. When hearing the word *ṭalya,* speakers of Aramaic may indeed have been reminded both of a young child and of a lamb. In the immediate context of the martyrdom account of Ṭalya, the reference to the lamb enhanced the impact of a child as a young, relatively weak and helpless being, facing the persecutor as the embodiment of evil, without doubt a contrast that gave power of attraction and conviction to many an account of a child's martyrdom.

Of special note with regard to children's martyrdom accounts in early

---

113. Ibid., 13.1 (Musurillo, 224–27).

114. See, for example, ibid., 3.4 (Musurillo, 216–17).

115. For fuller discussion, see Cornelia Horn, "Children and Violence in Syriac Sources: The *Martyrdom of Mar Ṭalyā' of Cyrrhus* in the Light of Literary and Theological Implications," proceedings of the International Symposium Syriacum (Beirut, Lebanon 2004), published in *Parole de l'Orient* 31 (2006), 309–26.

116. *Martyrdom of Mar Ṭalya* (MS BM 12,174 fol. 426v, col. A). An edition of this text is in preparation.

Christian literature are the reactions of the children's parents to such situations. At times, one finds cases in which the parents were still pagans while their young children wanted to convert to Christianity. In such instances, the parents themselves could become the children's persecutors. Perhaps the most remarkable early case that Christian hagiography from the East provides for this constellation of factors is documented in the Georgian *Martyrdom of the Children of Kola*. Local Georgian tradition preserves the memory of the probably late-fourth-century martyrdom of a group of nine children from a village of the Kola valley, in the area of modern-day Göle, in northeastern Turkey.[117] Using a tenth-century manuscript, today kept on Mount Athos, Nicolai Marr published the brief account of their martyrdom in 1903.[118]

The nine pagan boys used to play with Christian children from the village, but they realized that they could not join the Christians when these went to church for prayer. Affection for their fellow playmates motivated the pagan boys, ages seven to nine, to ask to become Christians themselves. They received instruction and were baptized at night. With baptism also came a change in the boys' family allegiance, since from then on they stayed with the families of their Christian friends.

When their parents learned what had happened, they "forcibly dragged the children from the Christians' houses" and "beat them black and blue." The parents tried to force their sons to eat food sacrificed to idols and tried to bribe them to do so by promising them bright-colored clothes, without success. At their wits' end, the parents went to the local governor, who declared that since the children were their sons, the parents "had the right to do what [they] like with them." Thus on "the day of the supreme sacrifice of the holy martyrs," as the hagiographer recounted, the parents threw their young children into a deep hole and, without "pity for their own offspring," "smote the [children's] heads and broke open their skulls," while many of the people joined them in stoning the children. Here persecution originated in the family and affected members of the family at the same time.[119]

---

117. For a study of the valley with useful maps, see Robert W. Edwards, "The Vale of Kola: A Final Preliminary Report on the Marshlands of Northeast Turkey," *Dumbarton Oaks Papers* 42 (1988), 119–41.

118. The Georgian text can be found in N. Y. Marr, "Mučeničestvo otrokov' Kolaïcev'," in *Teksty i Razyskanija po Armjano-Gruzinskoï Filologii*, vol. 5 (St. Petersburg, 1903), 55–61. An English translation is available in David Marshall Lang, *Lives and Legends of the Georgian Saints, Selected and Translated from the Original Texts* (London: Macmillan, 1956), 40–43.

119. Lang, *Lives and Legends*, 42–43. For a fuller discussion of the *Martyrdom of the Children of Kola* in the context of early Georgian literature on children, see also Horn, "The Lives and Literary Roles of Children in Advancing Conversion to Christianity."

In the case of Christian parents, one can distinguish between two prominent attitudes presented in the sources. Parents either tried to hide their children from potential exposure to martyrdom, or they strongly encouraged them to suffer martyrdom, sometimes assuming that the children would be killed, together with the parents themselves. We turn first to the examination of one particular case of parents who encouraged their children to die.

One notices that in cases where Christian parents encouraged their children to martyrdom, the mother of the Maccabean brothers served as example *par excellence* for the literary representation of this type of parent, especially for the Christian mother supporting her sons or daughters and strengthening and encouraging them not to give in to the enticements of their persecutors but instead to hold out until the end and die. A convincing example of this kind of behavior is found in the martyrdom of Sophia and her children. It is true that the story is characterized by strongly legendary features, starting with the very names of Sophia's daughters, namely Pistis, Elpis, and Agapē, or Faith, Hope, and Love.[120] Yet as much as a modern-day parent may call his or her daughter "Esperanza" or "Grace," so also the girls' names as such are insufficient to dismiss the story as unhistorical. Even if one assumes that the account belongs to the realm of fiction, it nevertheless witnesses to what an early Christian audience accepted as an uplifting, inspiring, and believable example.

Turning to the narrative, one notices that as soon as the three girls were ready to confront their persecutors, their mother, Sophia, instructed them "not to 'look ... at the childishness of your years, nor at the superb beauty of your faces,' but rather to put on 'heavenly armour,' 'the breastplate of the Spirit,' and to 'place a crown upon your mother by your endurance.'"[121] Thus Sophia prepared her daughters to fight like spiritual soldiers. She further appealed to her daughters to be strong as she herself was strong when enduring the pains of giving birth to them, since now she was

---

120. For edition and translation of the Syriac text of the *Martyrdom of Sophia and Her Three Daughters*, see Agnes Smith Lewis, *Select Narratives of Holy Women from the Syro-Antiochene or Sinai Palimpsest, Studia Sinaitica* vols. 9 [Syriac text] and 10 [English translation] (London: C. J. Clay and Sons, 1900), 218–44 [Syriac] and 168–84 [English]. The edition of the Greek recension appeared in F. Halkin, *Légendes grecques de "martyres romaines"* (Brussels: Société des Bollandistes, 1973), 179–228. We rely here on the material as presented in the Syriac narrative.

121. Cornelia B. Horn, "'Fathers and Mothers Shall Rise Up Against Their Children and Kill Them': Martyrdom and Children in the Early Church," paper presented at the annual meeting of the American Academy of Religion/Society of Biblical Literature, Toronto, Canada, November 25, 2002, direct quote. For the citations included, see *Martyrdom of Sophia and Her Three Daughters* (trans. Smith, *Select Narratives*, vol. 10, 170).

ready to "offer to God the perfect sacrifice of [their] victory."[122] Even as So-phia saw "how Pistis's breasts were cut off and how she [was] roasted in a frying-pan,"[123] the mother continued to encourage her daughter, saying, "Be strong . . . in witnessing for our Redeemer."[124] Her other two daugh-ters, Elpis and Agapē, even joined their mother in cheering on their sister to endure the martyrdom until the end.[125] When the other two daughters themselves were exposed to suffering and persecution, their mother en-couraged each one of them not to give up, even emphasizing that the top of the crown of their martyrdom was formed by the addition of the crown of their childhood.[126] Like the mother of the Maccabean brothers, here So-phia encouraged her daughters not to withdraw from the persecutors and renounce their faith, but quite to the contrary, to accept martyrdom. Like the mother of the Maccabean brothers, Sophia watched her children die.

Martyrdom and Slavery

One of the most unfortunate consequences Christianity brought upon chil-dren was unintended by early Christians themselves. Slave children were tortured as a consequence of the persecution Christians suffered.[127] The *Martyrdom of Polycarp* reports that when a persecution broke out in Smyr-na, Polycarp was spirited away to a hiding place in the country against his own wishes. Since the pursuers could not find him, they took from his house two of his slave boys (*paidaria*, "little children")[128] and tortured them.

122. *Martyrdom of Sophia and Her Three Daughters* (trans. Smith, *Select Narratives*, vol. 10, 171–72, see also 176).

123. Horn, "'Fathers and Mothers Shall Rise Up Against Their Children and Kill Them.'" *The Martyrdom of Sophia and Her Three Daughters* provides a more elaborate account of the martyrdom. In that same paper, Horn also discussed in immediate proximity to the *Martyr-dom of Sophia and Her Three Daughters* the case of the martyrdom of the little baby boy in Pru-dentius, *Peristephanon* 10.827–38. Since a more in-depth work on children and martyrdom is in preparation, that material is not included in the present study.

124. *Martyrdom of Sophia and Her Three Daughters* (trans. Smith, *Select Narratives*, vol. 10, 175).

125. Ibid. (Smith, vol. 10, 176).

126. Smith, *Select Narratives*, vol. 10, 180: "Behold I see two crowns prepared for thy sisters, and on the head of them both the crown of thy childhood appears, and I am hoping to go on the road of thy victory."

127. Golden, "*Pais*, 'Child' and 'Slave,'" 99–102, esp. 102, n. 38, where Plutarch, *Moralia* 461b–463b, is cited explaining the differences between slaves and free persons: slave girls are tortured, but wives are scolded.

128. According to Golden, "*Pais*, 'Child' and 'Slave,'" 91, n. 3, *paidarion* means either "young boy" or "young slave."

One of the slave boys confessed and so the officials made that boy *(paidari-on)* lead them to Polycarp's hiding place.[129] It is not clear if these boys were Christians like Polycarp, although Pliny considered torturing slave girls who were Christians to extract some information from them.[130] Torture was the common method Romans employed to gain information from all slaves.[131] As noted earlier, a slave's testimony could not be accepted in Roman courts unless it was given under torture.

Justin Martyr recounted the tactics of Roman officials who took Christian slaves, either children or old women, and tortured them in order to have them "confess" the Christian wrongdoing they had witnessed.[132] A fragment of the works of Irenaeus states that the same procedure was used with the slaves of Christian catechumens to have them offer up "evidence" regarding trumped-up charges of Christian cannibalism.[133] Eusebius reports the use of the same tactic, in which slaves who were not Christians were either tortured or threatened with torture in order to have them tell of terrible Christian practices, which they supposedly had observed or heard of.[134] The age of the slaves in the last two examples is not given, but in the light of Justin's example one might consider that children were among them. It may also be emphasized that the text clearly designates these slaves as pagans and not as Christians. While Christians probably did not intend torture for the children, these children's lives were made even worse due to the Romans' attempts to suppress Christianity and root out what they perceived to be an illegitimate and stubborn group.

The extant sources also allow one to discern cases of slaves who were Christians and who themselves suffered martyrdom because of their faith. In their martyrdom account, Paeon, Hierax, and Evelpistus are all characterized as having been dragged away from parents and as having been or

---

129. *Martyrdom of Polycarp* 6.1–2 and 7.1–2 (ed. and trans. Ehrman, *Apostolic Fathers*, vol. 1, 374–77).

130. Pliny the Younger, *Epistle* 10.96.8 (ed. and trans. Radice, *Pliny, Letters and Panegyricus*, vol. 2, 288–89).

131. Glancy, *Slavery in Early Christianity*, 51.

132. Justin Martyr, *Second Apology* 12.4 (ed. Miroslav Marcovich, *Iustini Martyris Apologiae Pro Christianis* [Berlin: de Gruyter, 1994], 135–59, here 155).

133. See also the discussion in Franz Joseph Dölger, "'Sacramentum infanticidii.' Die Schlachtung eines Kindes und der Genuß seines Fleisches und Blutes als vermeintlicher Einweihungsakt im ältesten Christentum," *Antike und Christentum* 4 (1933), 188–228, here 199–204.

134. Eusebius of Caesarea, *Church History* 5.1.14 (*The Martyrs of Lyons* [*and Viennes*]) (ed. Schwartz, Mommsen, and Winkelmann, *Eusebius Werke, Zweiter Teil, Erster Band, Die Kirchengeschichte*, GCS N. F. 6.1, 406).

become slaves.[135] These three are not presented as having been married or as having children of their own. They are young, although it is not clear whether they were children. In the story of the *Martyrs of Lyons,* Blandina was shown to have been a slave girl, and she was tortured for her faith,[136] as were other young people *(nearoi).*[137]

In the *Martyrdom of Pionius the Presbyter and his Companions,* the reader encounters a Christian slave girl who was exiled by her "immoral" mistress Politta for being a Christian, but who was instructed by another Christian, Pionius, not to give out her actual name, Sabina, for fear of coming again under the influence of her wicked mistress. In this case, her impending martyrdom was preferable to being under the control of a master who attempted to change her faith. That Sabina was of a relatively young age is indicated by a comment about her being "terrified . . . that she may be weaned *(apotitthios genētai),*" which came from among those in the crowd who awaited her punishment at the jail.[138] The final child slave who died as a martyr to be considered here is Eunoikos. His story is told in the *Testament of the Forty Holy and Glorious Martyrs of Christ Who Died at Sebaste.* Eunoikos is presented as a *pais* who was instructed to care for the martyrs' tombs if he survived the ordeal of persecution. Otherwise, if he should die in the course of the persecutions, he was to be allowed to share in the same tomb with the other (freeborn) Christians.[139]

The Impact of Martyrdom on Children

Apart from child martyrs, persecution and the suffering of martyrdom created another class of child victims, namely, the children of martyrs. Ber-

135. *Martyrdom of Saints Justin, Chariton, Charito, Evelpistus, Hierax, Paeon, Liberian, and their Community* (ed. and trans. Musurillo, *Acts of the Christian Martyrs,* 42–61; the text is extant in four recensions [A–D]). See ibid. A, 6,23; B, 4.6, 15–17 (for Paeon); B, 4.8, 23–24 (for Hierax); and B, 4.3, 9–10; C, 3.4, 24–26 (for Evelpistus).

136. *The Martyrs of Lyons (and Vienne)* 18 (ed. and trans. Musurillo, *Acts of the Christian Martyrs,* 62–85, here 66, ll. 21–31); see also Eusebius of Caesarea, *Church History* 5.1.17–18 (ed. Schwartz, Mommsen, and Winkelmann, *Eusebius Werke, Zweiter Band, Erster Teil, Die Kirchengeschichte,* GCS, N. F. 6.1, 408).

137. *The Martyrs of Lyons (and Vienne)* 27 (ed. and trans. Musurillo, *Acts of the Christian Martyrs,* 70, ll. 17–19); see also Eusebius of Caesarea, *Church History* 5.1.28 (ed. Schwartz, Mommsen, and Winkelmann, *Eusebius Werke, Zweiter Band, Erster Teil, Die Kirchengeschichte,* GCS, N. F. 6.1, 412, l. 22).

138. *Martyrdom of Pionius the Presbyter and his Companions* 9.3–5 and 10.3 (ed. Musurillo, *Acts of the Christian Martyrs,* 136–67, here 146–49).

139. *Testament of the Forty Holy and Glorious Martyrs of Christ Who Died at Sebaste* 1.5 (ed. and trans. Musurillo, *Acts of the Christian Martyrs,* 354–61, here 356–57).

yl Rawson has asked how public spectacles of violence, especially those of the amphitheater, affected children in the Roman Empire, and this question deserves further research in its own right.[140] Children experienced the rending of their relationship with their parents and the certain knowledge that their parents were soon to die a gruesome death. The *Martyrdom of Perpetua and Felicitas* provides evidence that both Perpetua and Felicitas had to find a way to have their children raised by others when they themselves would be dead.[141] Perpetua's father attempted to talk her out of her martyrdom—as did Hilarianus the governor—for the sake of her child, but she refused to turn her back on her faith. The last we hear of her child, he was with her father.[142] Felicitas left her daughter in the care of one of the (Christian) sisters and we hear nothing more of the child.[143] The impact of their parents' death on children probably was great, although it may not have been any more intense than what a slave child suffered when its mother (or father) was sold away or the child itself was sold and had to leave his or her parents behind.

The young *(adolescens)* martyr Irenaeus was bewailed both by his children and by women (or his wife)[144] who cried because of his youth. Indeed, when questioned by the prefect Probus, and when asked directly who the people weeping were, Irenaeus denied that he had a family, since Jesus had directed him to love God more than an earthly family (cf. Mt 10:37; Lk 14:25). When Probus asked him to act on behalf of his children and offer sacrifice to the gods, Irenaeus simply stated that God would save his children.[145] The *Acts of Phileas* present the prefect Culcianus asking Phileas to think of his wife and children (Papyrus Bodmer, column IX, ll. 8–10), but although the text is preserved only in fragmentary form, Phileas, like Irenaeus, placed God over family.[146] The same scene is found in the B recension (Latin) in 3.3 and there the preeminence of God over family is clearer. Later Phileas's whole family pleaded with him to consider his wife and children, but he refused, claiming the apostles and martyrs as his true

140. Rawson, "'The Roman Family' in Recent Research," 133–34; see also the comments on children witnessing the attempted burning of Thecla in Horn, "Suffering Children," 126–27.

141. See *Martyrdom of Perpetua and Felicitas* 3.8–9, 5.3, 6.2, 6.8 (ed. and trans. Musurillo, *Acts of the Christian Martyrs,* 106–31, here 108–15) for Perpetua; and ibid., 15.7 (Musurillo, 124–25) for Felicitas.

142. Ibid., 6.8 (Musurillo, 114–15).   143. Ibid., 15.7 (Musurillo, 124–25).

144. Musurillo, *Acts of the Christian Martyrs,* 297, n. 4.

145. *Martyrdom of Saint Irenaeus, Bishop of Sirmium* 3.1–2, 4.5–6, and 4.8–9 (ed. and trans. Musurillo, *Acts of the Christian Martyrs,* 294–301, here 296–99).

146. *Acts of Phileas* (Papyrus Bodmer) column IX (ed. and trans. Musurillo, *Acts of the Christian Martyrs,* 328–45, here 338–39).

relatives.[147] Finally, Aetius, one of the martyrs in the *Testament of the Forty Holy and Glorious Martyrs of Christ Who Died at Sebaste,* said farewell to his family, including his little child *(paidion)*.[148]

The best-known example of such a child and one that shows another attitude regarding the martyrdom of Christian parents is the case of Origen of Alexandria. Through Eusebius of Caesarea's account in his *Church History,* one has access to a literary representation of Origen's experience as a young boy when his father suffered martyrdom. Certainly, Eusebius had reason to enhance Origen's profile of dedication to the Christian cause. While Origen's father, Leonides, was in prison and was suffering persecution for his Christian faith, Eusebius portrayed the young Origen as filled with an ardent longing for martyrdom, so much so that his mother's appeals to reason, as well as her entreaties to him to have mercy on her motherly feelings, were without success. Only when she hid all his clothing, obviously hoping that he would not dare to leave the house naked, could she force him to remain at home. Nevertheless, according to Eusebius, the young boy Origen "sent his father a letter [into prison] pressing him strongly on the subject of martyrdom, and advising him" to remain steadfast and not to change his mind, i.e., to suffer martyrdom.[149] Similar to some other Christian mothers, Origen's mother did not disapprove of martyrdom as such, at least in Eusebius's version of events. Nevertheless, she did not want her own child to be exposed to such an experience. She may very well have felt that she had already sacrificed and suffered enough by having other members of her family, particularly her husband, Leonides, thrown into prison.[150]

One can speculate as to how many children were affected by such martyrdoms and the burden they carried as a result, as much as one can witness the impact of such trauma in the present day and its impact on children in war zones and in places where persecution currently occurs. There is no reason to doubt the traumatic impact of such events on children in the ancient Church. Yet it should be remembered also that for a long time

147. *Acts of Phileas (recensio Latina)* 3.3 and 6.4 (ed. and trans. Musurillo, *Acts of the Christian Martyrs,* 345–53, here 346–47 and 350–51).

148. *Testament of the Forty Martyrs of Sebaste* 3.2 (ed. Musurillo, *Acts of the Christian Martyrs,* 360).

149. Eusebius of Caesarea, *Church History* 6.2.4–6 (ed. Schwartz, Mommsen, and Winkelmann, *Eusebius Werke, Zweiter Band, Zweiter Teil, Die Kirchengeschichte,* GCS, N. F. 6.2, 520; trans. Williamson, *Eusebius: The History of the Church from Christ to Constantine,* 180).

150. For this discussion of the episode concerning Origen of Alexandria, see also Horn, "'Fathers and Mothers Shall Rise Up Against Their Children and Kill Them.'"

persecution of Christians in the Roman Empire was sporadic, and even during the reign of Diocletian persecution was a means to frighten Christians rather than exterminate them. Certainly Christian children were affected by the loss of a parent, relation, or friend, but it is more likely that Christian children would have experienced fear, and the sense of being in a marginalized position in Roman society. Christians were in some way different, yet in most respects they participated in Greco-Roman life as their polytheistic neighbors did.

Children at War

In chapter 4, we noted that John Chrysostom and his audience were aware and made use of imagery that related children and their education to military experience. In his treatise *On Vainglory* (ch. 89), Chrysostom argued that fathers who were in the military or who were fond of the military began from the children's earliest days to train their sons in the military arts. In some accounts of early Christian martyrdom the identification of the Christian with the image of the soldier also affected children's imagination. When Nero's young cup-bearer Patroclus, for example, confessed to the emperor his newfound faith as a Christian, the little boy readily accepted Nero's designation of him as "soldier of that king" who was to come to overthrow all kingdoms, including Nero's. Together with Barsabas Justus, Urion the Cappadocian, and Festus the Galatian, all of whom are identified in the apocryphal *Martyrdom of Paul* as "Caesar's chief men" and all of whom identified themselves as "soldiers of the king of the ages," Patroclus first had to endure grievous tortures before being shut up in prison.[151] In such settings, the imagery of the military and the soldier's life did not apply to actual war situations, but it was coextensive with children's suffering, not much different from what children endured in real situations of war.

Next to such metaphorical and idealistic applications of the ever-present reality of the military and soldiery, which in the teachings of Christian authors most immediately served spiritual purposes, one cannot escape the reality of the tortures and sufferings caused by real war in children's lives.[152] To

---

151. *Martyrdom of Paul* 2 (ed. Lipsius, "Passionis Pauli Fragmentum," 106–11). See also *Passio Sancti Pauli Apostoli* 4–5 (ed. Lipsius, "Passio Sancti Pauli Apostoli," in *Acta Apostolorum Apocrypha*, vol. 1, 23–44, here 27–29).

152. John K. Evans, *War, Women and Children in Ancient Rome* (London: Routledge, 1991), includes a chapter on children at the end of his study, but does not discuss more concretely the role or place of children in situations of war. The topic of children in situations of war in the

the extent that war was almost an unavoidable reality of people's lives, especially at the border regions of the Roman Empire, families and children were exposed to and affected by war in much the same way in which the atrocities of war today affect and often ruin children's lives. Examples can be adduced both from the western and the eastern realms of the Mediterranean world, and beyond. Victor of Vita, for example, provided an account of the bloody attacks of the Vandals in North Africa. As they were killing many of the clergy among the Catholics, many child lectors (*plurimi lectores infantuli*) also suffered.[153] A moving example from the East is provided in the words of Cyrillona, a late-fourth-century poet writing in Syriac who may be identical to Absamya, nephew of Ephraem the Syrian.[154] In this instance, one even hears about the fate of children as war captives from their father's own voice. In Hymn 4, which deals with the invasion of the Huns in Syria in A.D. 395, Cyrillona described not only that he saw Syria's villages and its people chastised and devastated, but also that his own family was stricken with the plights of war. As a father in despair, Cyrillona implored God to remember that the Huns had ransacked his village and taken at least some of his children captive within the last year.[155] Afraid that at the Huns' second attack on his village his sons would be killed, Cyrillona prayed to God "not to surrender the lambs to the leopards, nor the sheep to the impure wolves."[156] For those used to the dangers of life in the Syrian countryside, war affecting their families and children clearly was worse.

---

ancient world, both in the Christian and non-Christian world, is one that lends itself to further investigation.

153. Victor of Vita, *Historia persecutionis* 3.34 (ed. Michael Petschenig, *Victoris Episcopi Vitensis Historia Persecutionis Africanae Provinciae* [Vindobonae: Apud C. Geroldi Filium Bibliopolam Academiae, 1881], 89, ll. 3–7; trans. Serge Lancel, *Victor de Vita: Histoire de la persécution Vandale en Afrique suivie de La passion des sept martyrs, Registre des provinces et des cités d'Afrique* [Paris: Les Belles Lettres, 2002], 94–212, here 193); similarly also Augustine of Hippo, *De consensu Evangelistarum* 1, 10, 15 (ed. PL 34.1041–1230, here col. 1019; trans. S. D. F. Salmond, "[Augustine's] The Harmony of the Gospels," NPNF 6 [repr. Peabody, Mass.: Hendrickson Publishers, 1995], 77–236, here 83). See also Kleijwegt, "Kind," 923.

154. Dominique Cerbelaud, *Cyrillonas. L'Agneau Véritable. Hymnes Cantiques et Homélies,* Collection "L'Esprit et le Feu" (Paris: Chevetogne, 1984), 8.

155. Cyrillona, *Hymns* 4.7 (ed. G. Bickell, "Die Gedichte des Cyrillonas nebst einigen anderen syrischen Ineditis," *Zeitschrift der Deutschen Morgenländischen Gesellschaft* 27 [1873], 566–99, here 587; trans. Cerbelaud, *Cyrillonas,* 78). Later corrections which G. Bickell, "Berichtigungen zu Cyrillonas," *Zeitschrift der Morgenländischen Gesellschaft* 35 (1881), 531–32, published, do not affect the Syriac text of the relevant passage.

156. Cyrillona, *Hymns* 4.7 (ed. Bickell, "Gedichte des Cyrillonas," 587; trans. Cerbelaud, *Cyrillonas,* 79).

Conclusions

The impact of Christianity on the lives of children in the ancient world was mixed. At the turn of the third century, one finds a greater sense of participation in the dominant culture. This involvement took the form of denouncing certain behaviors affecting children. Christian writers and homilists criticized the practices of sexual use of children, exposure of children, and abortion. One may assume that this had an impact on Christians themselves, who would have given children the chance to live and to do so free from sexual use by adults. For slave children, it seems possible that many belonging to Christian masters were Christians. One may hope that their lot was better than that of those who were owned by pagans, although Christian masters still needed to be warned about the treatment of slaves and one hears of no restriction on the sale of slave children. As a group, Christians were exhorted not to use their slave children sexually, but there is no way to test this conclusion other than accepting the Christian prohibitions of corrupting children as applicable to slave children as well. Of some concern also is the matter of slave children set upon by Roman officials to extract confessions regarding the whereabouts of their Christian masters or regarding the practices of Christians. Apart from this, children themselves suffered martyrdom and witnessed the death of their own parents. Thus while the reality of martyrdom for the most part was not the fault of Christians, it did affect both Christian children and slaves who may or may not have been Christians. This kind of violence against children must be balanced, however, by the strong Christian criticism of practices which for centuries were the fate of children throughout the Greco-Roman world. Over time, Christian criticism of practices of abuse, infanticide, abortion, and exposure led to improved lives for numerous children, in significant part because the Roman state embraced the Christian moral code in the course of the fourth and fifth centuries.

seven

🖋

Children and Worship in the
Early Christian Church

Noteworthy distinctions were made between children and adults in the ancient world. Yet Christianity had a relatively easy time accepting children as members of the Church. Early Christians did not place many restrictions on children's participation in Christian worship. Quite likely, this is related both to Jesus' teachings regarding children and to the example of children's participation in Judaism and Greco-Roman religion.[1] Children belonged to the religion of their parents or guardians. Christian writers saw no reason to exclude them from Christianity's liturgical services or from entry into the community, for as Irenaeus argued, Jesus had sanctified every stage of life, from infancy to old age.[2]

The first reception of children into the Christian community is attributed to Jesus, who in a number of sayings found in the synoptic Gospels welcomed children into the group of his followers or held them up as examples for all his disciples and as models of the kingdom of God. It is highly probable that the sayings are authentic teachings of Jesus because of their dissimilarity to attitudes of the Jewish and Greco-Roman world. Children were generally not held up as models of spiritual enlightenment in Judaism

---

1. For recent work, see for example I. C. Mantle, "The Roles of Children in Roman Religion," *Greece & Rome* 49.1 (2002), 85–106.

2. Irenaeus of Lyons, *Against Heresies* 2.22.4 (ed. and trans. Adelin Rousseau and Louis Doutreleau, *Irénée de Lyon. Contre les Hérésies*, Book 2, SCh 293–94 [Paris: Les Éditions du Cerf, 1982], here SCh 294, p. 220).

and only rarely in early Christianity. That is, Jesus' reception of children, precisely because they were children and not spiritual prodigies, did not proceed from any existing model in Judaism, nor did early Christians, who initially concentrated their ministry and missions mostly on adults, readily adopt Jesus' ministry to children or accept children as models of spiritual perfection or as model disciples.[3]

The sayings on children in the synoptic Gospels may be grouped into distinct forms, one, which may be called "welcoming a child in Jesus' name" (Mk 9:33–42, Mt 10:40–42, 18:1–10, and Lk 9:46–48, 17:1–2), and the second, to which one may give the title "bringing children to Jesus" (Mk 10:13–16, Mt 19:13–15, and Lk 18:15–17). Apart from their theological value, these sayings point to the social reality in Jesus' ministry that children were present, whether as children of bystanders or of apostles and disciples. The integration of the two blocks of sayings relating to children orients the reader to the perceived significance of children for Jesus. The task that presents itself is to determine how and why children were of such significance.[4]

3. For instance, the model of childhood presented in the Gospel of Luke, but especially in the non-canonical *Infancy Gospel of Thomas* and the *Infancy Gospel of James,* is that of Jesus and Mary as prodigies. We have seen in chapter 4, however, that early Christians also developed a sense of the need to connect education and catechesis of children, for example, in the material selected from Agathangelos's *History of the Armenians.* On the communal dimensions of the catechesis of children, from the beginning of ancient Jewish history onward, see also Karin Finsterbusch, "Die kollektive Identität und die Kinder. Bemerkungen zu einem Programm im Buch Deuteronomium," *Jahrbuch für Biblische Theologie* 17 (2002), 99–120, who shows how in the Book of Deuteronomy parents are instructed to teach their children regularly and systematically. Children are to learn to fear God and through being integrated into the worship of the community will become part of and continue into the future the people of God. The author strengthens the case for a long tradition of children's catechesis as well as for an ancient tradition of allowing, even requiring, children to be part of the religious celebrations of Israel.

4. Studies we have consulted include Francis J. Moloney, *The Gospel of Mark. A Commentary* (Peabody, Mass.: Hendrickson Publishers, 2002); John R. Donahue and Daniel J. Harrington, *The Gospel of Mark,* Sacra Pagina Series, vol. 2 (Collegeville, Minn.: Liturgical Press, 2002); Rudolf Schnackenburg, *The Gospel of Matthew,* trans. Robert Barr (Grand Rapids, Mich.: Eerdmans, 2002); Ben Witherington III, *The Gospel of Mark: A Socio-Rhetorical Commentary* (Grand Rapids, Mich.: Eerdmans, 2001); Raymond F. Collins, *Sexual Ethics and the New Testament: Behavior and Belief* (New York: Crossroad, 2000), esp. 62–72; Petri Luomanen, *Entering the Kingdom of Heaven* (Tübingen: Mohr Siebeck, 1998); Donald Senior, *Matthew,* Abingdon New Testament Commentaries (Nashville: Abingdon Press, 1998); Joel B. Green, *The Gospel of Luke* (Grand Rapids, Mich.: Eerdmans, 1997); Robert H. Gundry, *Mark: A Commentary on His Apology for the Cross* (Grand Rapids, Mich.: Eerdmans, 1993); E. P. Sanders, *The Historical Figure of Jesus* (London: Penguin Press, 1993); Daniel J. Harrington, *The Gospel of Matthew,* Sacra Pagina Series, vol. 1 (Collegeville, Minn.: Liturgical Press, 1991); Craig A. Evans, *Luke,* New

Welcoming a Child in Jesus' Name

One first has to determine the original form of the saying. Accepting that Mark preserves its earliest form in most respects, one finds two elements of the saying in Mark, which in Matthew and Luke have been separated. In Mark 9:33–37, Jesus speaks of welcoming the child, and in verses 41–42 he addresses the woe befalling the one who does not welcome, but rather harms, a child. An insertion that comments on someone casting out demons in Jesus' name (vv. 38–40) separates the two parts. This may be evidence that already by the time of the Gospel's redaction, early Christians had become somewhat distanced from Jesus' blunt teaching on the value and treatment of children.[5] In Matthew (18:1–10 and 10:40–42) and in Luke (9:46–48 and 17:1–2), these two aspects of the teaching have been separated not by verses but by chapters and context. The teaching concerning the "little ones" *(ta mikra)* now was applied to all of Jesus' disciples (Mt 10:40–42; Lk 17:1–2).[6]

In the basic teaching on welcoming children (Mk 9:33–37 and par.), Jesus speaks of how one must receive the kingdom.[7] The disciples were ask-

---

International Bible Commentary (Peabody, Mass.: Hendrickson Publishers, 1990); Will Deming, "Mark 9.42–10.12, Matthew 5.27–32, and B. Nid. 13b: A First Century Discussion of Male Sexuality," *New Testament Studies* 36 (1990), 130–41; Michael D. Goulder, *Luke. A New Paradigm,* vol. 2 (Sheffield: JSOT Press, 1989); Lamar Williamson Jr., *Mark. Interpretation. A Bible Commentary for Teaching and Preaching* (Atlanta: John Knox Press, 1983); E. Earle Ellis, *The Gospel of Luke,* The New Century Bible Commentary (Grand Rapids, Mich.: Eerdmans, 1981); Francis Wright Beare, *The Gospel according to Matthew* (San Francisco: Harper & Row, 1981); Joachim Jeremias, *Neutestamentliche Theologie. Erster Teil: Die Verkündigung Jesu* (Gütersloh: Gerd Mohn, 1971); Rudolf Bultmann, *The History of the Synoptic Tradition,* trans. John Marsh (New York: Harper & Row, 1968); and T. W. Manson, *The Sayings of Jesus* (London: SCM Press, 1949).

5. Rudolf Bultmann, *The History of the Synoptic Tradition* (New York: Harper & Row, 1968), 142, calls this an "alien insertion."

6. Many scholars comment on this, but see Bultmann, *History of the Synoptic Tradition,* 142 and 145, who speaks of the application and extension from children to all disciples as "christianizing" the term; cf. also John R. Donahue and Daniel J. Harrington, *The Gospel of Mark* (Collegeville, Minn.: Liturgical Press, 2002), 290; Deming, "Mark 9.42–10.12, Matthew 5.27–32, and B. Nid. 13b," 131–32; and Collins, *Sexual Ethics and the New Testament: Behavior and Belief,* 70.

7. Matthew Black, *An Aramaic Approach to the Gospels and Acts* (Peabody, Mass.: Hendrickson Publishers, 1998), 218–23, argues that the pericope is not clear, particularly the relationship of v. 37 ("child") to v. 35 ("servant"). Black asks if it could simply be faulty editing that places 9:37 here and not in the context of 10:15; he wonders, in fact, if the Markan editor had trouble with all of the material dealing with children (220). His solution takes us back to our discussion of "child of God" in chapter 2. Black suggests that the Greek *paidion* is actually a (mis)translation of the Aramaic *talya* or servant. One could assume this, since in v. 35, the Greek has *diakonos* (servant). In Greek, of course, there is no connection etymologically between "servant" and

ing him about greatness in the kingdom of God and he took or called a child from their midst, which indicates the presence of children among Jesus' followers and in his ministry.[8] The teaching is concrete: welcome this little child (Mk 9:36, Lk 9:47, and Mt 18:2: *paidion*) in my name and you are welcoming me. The one who welcomes Jesus is welcoming the one who sent him. One ought not move away from the concreteness of this example too quickly. Richard Horsley's notes to the NRSV translation of the Gospel of Mark, for instance, state that "a child was the lowest-status person in the household."[9] While one may see slaves as certainly inferior to freeborn children, the status of a child would imply that it does not have any authority or power. Marion Lloyd Soards's comment on Luke, on the other hand, states that "the reception of the little child requires generosity without expectation of gain."[10] Neither of these remarks gets to the heart of the issue of the reception of the child as a child. In Mark and Luke the disciples are not told to "become like children," but instead are instructed to "welcome this child."[11] The reception of a child did not grant the disciples status or gain of any kind. Yet, the import of the teaching is not thereby exhausted: one is left with the clear command to receive the child in Jesus' name. Mark presents the child, and thereby all children, as a welcome arrival in the kingdom, not simply as a metaphor for an adult who has broken through to a new stage of spiritual growth. The child also offers the opportunity for encountering Jesus and in this respect becomes his representative. There is something definitive and specific about the child as a means to encounter the presence of Jesus, which is not reducible to one or more attributes of childhood, such as vulnerability, innocence, or insignificance, even if all of these can be part of the reality of the life of the child.

The movement to understand this teaching as a metaphor for how one receives the kingdom comes with Matthew's interpretation of the passage.

"child," but in Aramaic there is: *ṭalya* stands for both (220–21). Black's suggestion is interesting, but the reality is that the child taken and placed in the midst of the disciples is still the measure of servanthood. One may also refer back to Jeremias who did translate *ṭalya* as child.

8. Robert H. Gundry, *Matthew: A Commentary on His Literary and Theological Art* (Grand Rapids, Mich.: Eerdmans, 1982), 383–84, believes that the children represent the "youth of the Church," and so a part of the community (with respect to Mt 19:13–15).

9. Richard A. Horsley, "The Gospel According to Mark," in *The New Oxford Annotated Bible: New Revised Standard Version with the Apocrypha*, 3rd ed. (Oxford: Oxford University Press, 2001), NT 56–92, here NT 75.

10. Mary Lloyd Soards, "The Gospel According to Luke," in *The New Oxford Annotated Bible*, NT 93–145, here NT 116.

11. Gundry-Volf, "The Least and the Greatest," 38–40.

Matthew 18:5 retains the teaching as found in Mark and Luke, and has Jesus state that "whoever welcomes one such child in my name welcomes me." In Matthew 18:3, Jesus demanded that the disciples "change and become like children" and in verse 4 that they become "humble like this child."[12] The focus of the teaching had changed. Now the movement was from the child's reception by Jesus to the disciples' reception of the kingdom. This nuancing offered through Matthew's interpretation has become the dominant understanding of these passages in general. While Jesus spoke on behalf of the actual reception of children, Matthew argued that the disciples should also adopt the humility of a child. Matthew 18:3 also belongs in the context of Matthew 19:13–15 (and par.). Matthew's movement of the phrase to this context may indeed be an attempt to "spiritualize" the saying for all disciples of Jesus instead of focusing on actual children.[13]

In revising Mark, Matthew introduces the child as a symbol of a spiritual state. In 18:3, he exhorted his audience to "change and become like children."[14] Matthew does not explain this statement, and the reader is left to wonder whether humility may be the virtue through which one attains spiritual perfection.[15] When understood as lowliness and vulnerability, humility certainly ranked high among the characteristics of the child, since the passages which follow in Matthew 18 warn the disciples not to "put a stumbling block" (skandalizō) before one of the "little ones" (hena tōn mikrōn) (v. 6) and not to "despise" (kataphroneō) one of the "little ones" (henos tōn mikrōn) (v. 10).[16] While these "little ones" may refer, as has been argued frequently, to all of the "little ones" who make up Jesus' disciples, those whose status and prestige render them small and insignificant by the standards of

---

12. Senior, *Matthew*, 205; Schnackenburg, *The Gospel of Matthew*, 172; Beare, *The Gospel according to Matthew*, 375–76; Harrington, *The Gospel of Matthew*, 265–66; and Gundry-Volf, "The Least and the Greatest," 40–42. Gundry, *Matthew*, 360, argues that "the child stands for a disciple" and that this is why the comment about Jesus hugging a child is dropped from the Markan account by Matthew, because a child already represents a disciple. If the child cannot be a child here, however, the whole force of this saying is gone.

13. Schnackenburg, *The Gospel of Matthew*, 186; and Beare, *The Gospel according to Matthew*, 392.

14. This saying is out of place: it belongs in the context of Mark 10:13–16; Luke 18:15–17; and Matthew 19:13–15. Gundry, *Matthew*, 384, says that 18:3 was dropped from 19:13–15 because it had been used already by Matthew.

15. Ulrich Luz, *Matthew 8–20. Hermeneia* (Minneapolis: Fortress Press, 2001), 427–28, offers an excellent discussion on the question of "what is a child?" As he notes, the text does not say what it is, and commentators have been influenced throughout the ages by whatever characteristic feature of children was most valued by their culture and age.

16. Luz, *Matthew*, 428–29; and Gundry-Volf, "The Least and the Greatest," 40–42.

the world,[17] it is at least as probable that following immediately upon the teaching of the reception of children, Jesus' initial thrust was to emphasize that one was not to hinder children in their discipleship or lead them astray. In this regard it is noteworthy that in 1 Timothy 4:12, Timothy was told that he should not let anyone "despise" or "look down on" him *(kataphroneitō)* because of his youthfulness, an instance in which the author employs the same verb which appears in Matthew 18:10.[18] Thus one may argue for the inclusion of Matthew 18:10 in the original teaching as well.

To return to Mark, the statement about children in 9:36–37 is given because Jesus' disciples "were arguing among themselves over who was greatest" (9:34). At the center of the *inclusio* formed by the two sayings on children is the question of the casting out of demons (9:38–41). John, representing the disciples, reports to Jesus that others are casting out demons in his name, without his authority. With Jesus' answer, Mark implies that the power of the name of Jesus is greater than the human authority that seeks to control access to that power. One may read this passage as implying that John seeks a limit on the increase of the disciples, but Jesus rejects any limitation. In effect, one does not have to be one of "the" disciples to be a disciple. A lesser disciple who is not among the elite of Jesus' entourage may be in fact their equal. Their authority comes from the name of Jesus, and not from any human source. This *inclusio* may have been added here in order to interpret independent sayings of Jesus about children as referring to the ideal disciples. Children have no authority over who belongs to the household; they must accept any other children whom their parents or guardians wish to include.

One may also understand this passage in Mark to imply that children were both welcomed and not to be harmed spiritually by exclusion from the kingdom.[19] Although Matthew offered a spiritualized interpretation of

---

17. See note 6 above. See also Bultmann, *History of the Synoptic Tradition*, 142 and 145; Gundry, *Mark*, 509–10; and Harrington, *The Gospel of Matthew*, 265. See also Conrad, "קָטֹן *qāṭōn;* קָטָן *qāṭān;* קֹטֶן *qōṭen*," 6, who defines *qāṭān* as referring to younger persons, children, but suggests that the term already in the Old Testament could refer comparatively and pejoratively to those who were weaker and inferior. It is possible, therefore, that Jesus had in mind both children and those who are "little ones" by virtue of lack of power, status, and prestige, especially as *qāṭān* must be the ground for the Greek translation *mikra.*

18. Schnackenburg, *The Gospel of Matthew*, 175.

19. Bultmann, *History of the Synoptic Tradition*, 142, certainly sees this as originally applying to children, as does Deming, "Mark 9.42–10.12, Matthew 5.27–32, and B. Nid. 13b," 132–35, especially related to little boys and a warning against pederasty; he argues that this is the meaning of the saying of not to "put a stumbling block *(skandalizō)*." While this is possible, it could

the children, which is to be seen as secondary or out of place, his edition of Mark preserves the link between welcoming children and not causing them to stumble.[20] Mark 9:41, however, preserved a saying of Jesus which originally was part of the teaching regarding children: "Whoever gives you [pl.] a cup of water in my name to drink, Amen, I say to you, this one will not lose his reward."[21] Yet Matthew 10:42 seems to have the more original saying: "Whoever gives to one of these little ones a cup of cold water to drink only because of the name of disciple, Amen, I say to you, this one will not lose his reward." "Little ones"—literally, "children"—and not a generalized "you," the disciples, are the ones whom Jesus addressed here. As a result, one may argue that Jesus' original teaching concerned the reception of children into the group of Jesus' followers in this manner:[22]

A) If you welcome a child in my name, you welcome me (Mk 9:37; Mt 18:5; Lk 9:47);

B) Whoever causes one of these little ones to sin, it would be better to be thrown into the sea with a millstone (Mk 9:42; Mt 18:5; cf. Lk 17:2);

C) See that you do not despise one of these little ones, for their angels always behold the face of my Father (Mt 18:10);

D) Whoever gives a cup of water to one of these little ones will not lose his reward (Mt 10:42; cf. Mk 9:41).

---

mean more than simply pederasty, particularly because it was fairly uncommon in Palestine; as our discussion in chapter 6 has shown. Collins, *Sexual Ethics and the New Testament: Behavior and Belief*, 66, also connects the offense to sexual abuse of children and, clearly, sees "little ones" as referring to children. Certainly it is not to be doubted that the harming of children spiritually could include their sexual abuse, and this indeed is a valuable and necessary insight. Yet it also remains to be noted that harming them could comprise activities of a broader category, including other forms of physical abuse.

20. Gundry, *Matthew*, 202–3, states that Matthew has changed Mark's "you" in 9:41 to "one of these little ones." As this is obviously the case, one needs to ask what the basis for this change is. Perhaps Matthew had access to a collection of Jesus' sayings, an oral one perhaps, in which the unity of the teachings on children was maintained. It is likely that Matthew is not creating this change of his own accord; in this case the "change" of Matthew seems to be primary in the tradition.

21. For children's prominent place as servants at the table, especially with regard to serving drinks, see chapter 6 above. See also in that chapter our reference to Nero's cup-bearer in the *Martyrdom of Paul*.

22. Joachim Jeremias, *Neutestamentliche Theologie. Erster Teil: Die Verkündigung Jesu* (Gütersloh: Gerd Mohn, 1971), 242, accepts Mark 9:37 as a "Jesuslogion," but does not discuss the whole pericope as a teaching of Jesus, generally because he reads "little ones" as all disciples; Bultmann, *History of the Synoptic Tradition*, 142 and 145, speaks of the "complicated" history of the saying—he does not attribute it to Jesus—but does believe the Markan parts originally belonged together, referring to children.

The teaching has a parallelism which is based on a larger structure that can be identified as consisting of the components: "welcome the child"; "if you do not welcome the child, you will be punished" // "do not despise the child"; "if you do not despise the child, you will get a reward." Jesus' original teaching regarding the reception of children, as far as we can reconstruct it from the sources, concerned the concrete reception of children into the Christian community as children. They were welcome as they were and they were to be protected from all who would prey on them.

This is not to say that Matthew's claim that all who desire to enter the kingdom should "become like children" or become "humble like this child" (Mt 18:3–4) is an improper extension of Jesus' teaching. Perhaps it simply is a teaching out of place. Rather, our observation argues that if the formulation in Matthew draws us away from Jesus' initial statement that children as children are welcome as preeminent representatives of Jesus, the implication of children's acceptance in the Church is weakened and even lost. There is something about children and their place in the kingdom that is simply not reducible to innocence, vulnerability, humility, lowliness, lack of prestige, simplicity, purity, nearness to God, openness to Christ, or any other attribute one may suggest. It is all of this and more, for their place in the kingdom is by virtue of their being simply children of God.

Bringing Children to Jesus

The following discussion turns to the pericope found in Mark 10:13–16, Matthew 19:13–15, 18:3, and Luke 18:15–17. Matthew 19 provides further context for situating Jesus' understanding of what it means to become "like a child" (Mt 18:3). After presenting his teaching on divorce (Mt 19:3–12), Matthew showed Jesus being challenged by his own disciples, who argued that given the strictures of his teachings on divorce, marriage was not worth undertaking (Mt 19:10).[23] Indeed, Matthew had Jesus make the case for celibacy (19:11–12). Yet he followed it by describing Jesus as receiving children who were brought to him (Mt 19:13–15); in Mark, the reception of the children follows the teaching on divorce directly (Mk 10:13–16), and in Luke, the teaching concerning receiving the kingdom of God like "a little child" is part of a short narration (Lk 18:15–17) which is set in a sequence of parables and sayings (Lk 14:7–18:34). The question arises whether Matthew understood the reception of the kingdom "like a child" as related to Jesus'

---

23. See Luz, *Matthew*, 496–503, on the history of interpretation of this passage.

teaching on celibacy. His spiritualizing of the concrete reception of children by Jesus in Matthew 18:3–4 and his placement of Jesus' teaching on celibacy in Matthew 19:10–13 indicate that this may indeed be the case.[24] For Matthew, to be like a child was to return to a prepubescent state prior to the onset of sexual desire.

This teaching, with all its possible connotations, is both concrete and symbolic (Mk 10:13–16; Mt 19:13–15; and Lk 18:15–17). In the case of both Mark and Matthew, people are bringing children (*paidia*) to Jesus in order that he might "touch" them (Mark) or "lay his hands" on them (Matthew). Luke has people bringing "even" infants (*brephē*) to Jesus in order that he "touch" them. The disciples "rebuke" the parents for their seemingly intrusive behavior, but Jesus becomes "indignant" (in Mark's account at v. 14) at his disciples and orders them to allow *paidia* to be brought to him, for to "such as them" is the kingdom of God.[25] This is the concrete reception of children and it locates their place in the kingdom. The next verse speaks of the reception of the kingdom by adults, in symbolic terms, as children. It is here where Matthew 18:3 has its appropriate place: Jesus challenges his disciples to receive the kingdom "like a child" (*hōs paidion*) or not to receive it at all.[26] In Matthew 18:15, Jesus lays his hands on the children; and in Mark 10:16, Jesus takes the children in his arms and blesses them by laying his hands on them. It is difficult to determine what the reception of the kingdom by the disciples "like children" precisely means. The positive characteristics that are typical of a child seem obvious. Yet whether the saying intends to address humility, simplicity, vulnerability, weakness, innocence, openness, or celibacy remains an open debate.

The Q tradition in Matthew 11:25–27 and Luke 10:21–22, "you have hidden these things from the wise and intelligent and revealed them to children (*nēpios*)," generally has been understood to refer to all of Jesus' disciples. This also is how the tradition reflected by Q, clearly shared by the

---

24. Harrington, *The Gospel of Matthew*, 274–76.

25. Whether this is a "formal" blessing is not significant, nor does it need to reflect infant baptism: see Luz, *Matthew*, 504–7. It is, however, Jesus' actual reception of children. Even if we accept that it does not indicate later sacramental practices, it remains to be explored what exactly it represents. The passage will have to be considered with regard to its potential impact on how Christians accept children in the Church. It does not rule out later sacramental acceptance of children and it should lead to serious thought about how children ought to be "received."

26. Johnson, *The Gospel of Luke*, 276, suggests that what is meant here is not that the disciples must receive the kingdom in the same manner in which a child receives it, but that they must accept the kingdom in the same manner in which they accept a child.

redactors of the Gospels, understood this saying.[27] It seems that in Jesus' initial teaching children, as children, became the model for other disciples. Adults had to imitate not simply their humility, vulnerability, or weakness. Rather, children themselves, as actual members of the community, were the models for how the community had to receive God and the kingdom. One cannot limit the expected understanding only to one or another aspect of childhood.

In his receiving children and welcoming them into the community, Jesus set the standard to be followed. That his teachings soon became spiritualized indicates the difficulty that early Christianity had accepting the teachings as concerning actual children. That early Christians maintained and passed on the traditions points to their authenticity and authority. The extension of these passages as a metaphor implying that all Christians are children of Christ may have received its impetus from Jesus' preaching about the relationship of all people to God the father, and perhaps even of a priority for those who were marginalized and outcasts. Yet this does not have to distract the reader from Jesus' reception of children into the community and his emphasis on these children as the model for other disciples.

In light of the preceding discussion, we reconstruct this passage according to its form in Mark:

A) They were bringing children to Jesus, but the disciples rebuked them (Mk 10:13; Mt 19:13; Lk 18:15);
B) Jesus said, "Let the children come to me, do not stop them; for the kingdom of God belongs to such as these" (Mk 10:14; Mt 19:14; Lk 18:16);
C) Whoever does not receive the kingdom of God like a child will not enter it (Mk 10:15; Lk 18:17; cf. Mt 18:3);
D) Jesus laid his hands on the children and blessed them (Mk 10:16; Mt 19:15).

The key to understanding this passage is that the children themselves were received and blessed. Adults in the community were to accept the kingdom of God "like a child." They had to receive the kingdom in the manner

27. See notes 6 and 12 above. See also Ben F. Meyer, *Five Speeches that Changed the World* (Collegeville, Minn.: Liturgical Press, 1994), 94–95, who connects the "little ones" with "the poor" and other disadvantaged persons; Beare, *The Gospel according to Matthew*, 376; and T. W. Manson, *The Sayings of Jesus* (London: SCM Press, 1949), 138, who also speaks of the transferring of sayings regarding "children" to disciples in general.

in which children responded to Jesus, with all the implications of what being a child meant, for example, showing greater faith in who Jesus is and greater knowledge as to the nature of following him in faith. Also, the way in which children themselves were received in the community was the measure and manner of the kingdom of God in the midst of the Christians. What remains and demands acceptance in either case is that children were seen as the measure of discipleship.

While interpreters of these passages both ancient and modern struggled to understand how precisely one must receive the kingdom of God "as a little child," on two occasions, in two sets of passages, Jesus points to children as model disciples. It is hard to find another group of people to whom Jesus points as models for imitation, with so little content offered on how to model oneself. On the other hand, children are ubiquitous, then and now. Jesus called on his followers to bring them to him, to welcome them, to preserve them from harm, and to learn from them. He asked them to accept him and to accept the children just as they are. Like Jesus and the kingdom, they are simply a gift to us from whom we are called to learn and whom we are encouraged to imitate.

Children in the Accounts of Jesus' Ministry of Healing

The two sayings concerning welcoming a child in Jesus' name and bringing children to Jesus do not exhaust the Gospels' presentation of Jesus' interaction with children. There are several passages in the synoptic Gospels that feature Jesus healing a child.[28] Mark's Gospel offers four such healings, those of the paralytic child (Mk 2:1–10; Mt 9:1–8; Lk 5:17–26); Jai-

---

28. For a selection of studies on healing or therapeutic miracles, which we have consulted for this section, see Harold Remus, *Jesus as Healer* (Cambridge: Cambridge University Press, 1997); René Latourelle, *The Miracles of Jesus and the Theology of Miracles*, trans. Matthew J. O'Connell (New York: Paulist Press, 1988); Birger Gerhardsson, *The Mighty Acts of Jesus according to Matthew* (Lund: CWK Gleerup, 1979); W. Nicol, *The Semeia in the Fourth Gospel: Tradition and Redaction* (Leiden: E. J. Brill, 1972); Rudolf Pesch, *Jesu ureigene Taten? Ein Beitrag zur Wunderfrage* (Freiburg: Herder, 1970); Alan Richardson, *The Miracle-Stories of the Gospels* (London: SCM Press, 1969); and H. Van der Loos, *The Miracles of Jesus* (Leiden: E. J. Brill, 1965). There are voluminous studies on the miracles, of course, but most do not consider the question of children, except to note that children appear, if they do that. As a result, the studies add little to our discussion. For some time now the focus with regard to miracle stories in the Gospels has been on the historicity of the accounts, on whether miracles are believable, on parallel sorts of miracle accounts in other cultures and literature, including the Old Testament, for instance the Elijah/Elisha cycles, and on the very genre of miracle stories. These kinds of emphases make good sense. Yet acknowledging that we are not arguing for historicity or

rus's daughter (Mk 5:21–43; Mt 9:18–26; Lk 8:40–56); the Syro-Phoenician woman's daughter (Mk 7:24–30; Mt 15:21–28); and the epileptic child (Mk 9:14–29; Mt 17:14–21; Lk 9:37–42).[29] We noted already that in all cases a parent or one or several friends sought out Jesus on the child's behalf, acted on behalf of it, and with much persistence showed great concern for the child's well-being. These stories include both boys and girls as the recipients of miraculous healing.[30] One may observe that in each case the child itself was silent, while the parent or friend pleaded his or her case.[31] The healing that followed indicates faith on the part of others, but also the children's openness to being healed.[32] Although the children are presented as silent in each of these cases, their silence should not be read as indicating indifference. Their silent acceptance of healing is a lesson to the adult readers and hearers. To accept Jesus is to accept divine intervention as it might occur. This may be the model of receiving the kingdom like a child: the child's silence acknowledges the true nature of Jesus and demonstrates faith that he will heal the one who needs healing.

Whether or not a parent ought to bring a child to Jesus is a further question that arises from the evidence. The specific healing miracles featuring children may point to an assumption of a general need to bring children to Jesus, even if the children have not expressed the desire or need. In the cases featured in the Gospels, a parent's or friend's faith seemed sufficient for healing. The children's illnesses, and in one case a child's death, also prompt the question of the link between sinfulness and illness.[33] It was a common assumption in ancient societies that illness was the result of an individual's loss of divine favor or of a protective spirit due to some transgression (which is rejected in John 9:3, but that did not put an end to the idea in early Christianity). To the extent that such an understanding lurked in the background of these stories, parents or a child's proxies were thought to be able to heal the children through their faith by bringing them to Jesus.

John 4:46–54 preserves a parallel to the healing accounts of a centu-

---

denying it, our concern is with what these particular accounts can tell us about attitudes to children, including what the early Church thought was believable about Jesus' attitude to children.

29. See also above, chapter 3.

30. Gerhardsson, *The Mighty Acts of Jesus according to Matthew*, 47.

31. Gundry-Volf, "The Least and the Greatest," 46–48, discusses Matthew 21:14–16 and argues that children have the greatest insight into the nature of who Jesus is, "they know Jesus' true identity" (47). Although they are mute, perhaps their healings indicate their knowledge and acceptance of who Jesus is in these miracle accounts.

32. Richardson, *The Miracle Stories of the Gospels*, 63.

33. Ibid., 60–61.

rion's slave in Matthew 8:5–13 and Luke 7:1–10.[34] In John's account the slave is a child, which raises the consideration of the age of the slave in the synoptic accounts, or even the question of whether it was initially a slave or a child in those instances. In all three cases, the healing took place in Capernaum. It involved a centurion in the synoptic accounts and a royal official *(basilikos)* in John's Gospel. In the latter, however, the one who was lying ill was the official's son, his *paidion* (Jn 4:47 and 4:51 = *pais*). In all three accounts the ill person was healed thanks to the faith of the master or father, which is similar to the four other healing stories involving children. All these accounts feature clear connections, yet it is difficult to determine what was at the heart of the original synoptic account: the healing may have concerned a child, not a slave. Perhaps the slave was a child, and that detail was lost in the synoptic authors, except for the use of *pais* (Mt 8:6, 8; Lk 7:7). John's account does portray Jesus healing a child. As with the synoptic accounts of children's healing, the faith of the adults was decisive and definitive for the restoration of the child's health.

At times, children have a presence in other miracles recounted in the Gospels. In the "first" miraculous feeding (the "twelve baskets account") that is found in all four Gospels, Matthew 14:21 mentions that women and children *(paidia)* were present at the scene, but John 6:9 alone tells of a "little boy" *(paidarion)* who actually supplied the food, a little child sharing his lunch of bread and fish. The presence and involvement of children in the ministry of Jesus are assumed.

One may consider the parable in Matthew 25:1–13 regarding the virgins *(parthenoi)* as a parable in which children play a central role.[35] The meaning of this parable remains ambiguous, at least with respect to the virgins. That it is an eschatological parable is clear, given its position among the other eschatological material in Matthew 24 and 25, and the metaphor of single-minded vigilance for the return of the Messiah.[36] Yet its possible social impact for the early Christian community can be detected. Except for the work of Bettina Eltrop, modern interpretations of this parable do not sufficiently stress that *parthenoi* usually were children, that is, girls prior to

34. See also the discussion in Nicol, *The Semeia in the Fourth Gospel*, 41–42 (especially 41, no. 1 on the question of the relationship of *pais* to *doulos*), and 55.

35. On this passage see also the discussion in Bettina Eltrop, "Problem Girls: A Transgressive Reading of the Parable of the Ten Virgins (Matthew 25:1–13)," in *Transgressors: Towards a Feminist Biblical Theology* (Collegeville, Minn.: Liturgical Press, 2002), 163–71.

36. Joachim Jeremias, *The Parables of Jesus* (London: SCM Press, 1963), 51–55; and Luomanen, *Entering the Kingdom of Heaven*, 187.

marriage.[37] The import of the parable may derive from an early Christian tendency toward preservation of virginity in the expectation of the imminent return of Jesus. Paul, who was convinced that the parousia was going to happen in his lifetime, did not provide clear rules governing chastity, certainly not any ascribed to Jesus (1 Cor 7:25). However, in light of his teaching regarding *parthenoi* in 1 Corinthians 7:25–31 and 36–38, this parable may reflect an increasing intensity in the early Christian formulation of the goal to keep unmarried girls focused on the life of virginity and the Christian community.[38] To the extent that this parable offers a window on the developing Christian understanding of the unmarried life for girls, it also portrays aspects of children's place and role in the Church and their rejection of the married life or their acquiescence to a celibacy imposed on them by their Christian parents or guardians.

Other material in the New Testament points to the presence of children in the world of the believers and Jesus' interest in children, but not their specific role in the community as such. This may have to do with the informal structure of the initial mission and the accompanying lack of a settled liturgical life. How many of Jesus' disciples fit the category of being children, even older ones or teenagers, is impossible to know. Some of them probably did, since one finds that several of Jesus' own disciples were unmarried and were traveling with their mothers. Given the strong focus on marriage in Judaism, with a few exceptions to be considered in the following final chapter, it is not likely that all of Jesus' disciples were adult males in an unmarried state when he first called them to follow him.[39] We hear of Mary, who traveled with her sons James the younger and Joses (Mk 15:40; Mt 27:56; Lk 24:10).[40] The mother of the sons of Zebedee appears in Matthew 27:56 and 20:20–23, pleading the case for her sons' role in Jesus' glory. We should consider that youths, without a wife or children, were precisely the age group who followed teachers like Jesus.[41] We have

---

37. For instance, neither Schnackenburg, *The Gospel of Matthew*, 250–51; nor Harrington, *The Gospel of Matthew*, 348–51; nor Senior, *Matthew*, 274–77, as a sample, mention the possible age of "virgins."

38. See the more extensive discussion of this passage below in chapter 8.

39. E. P. Sanders, *The Historical Figure of Jesus* (London: Penguin Press, 1993), 107, claims that, regarding Jesus' disciples, "some or all of them had homes and families." Without denying this, it is not clear whether this means that all of them were married and had children, or whether it means that a widowed mother may have followed her young son on the road in his itinerant ministry. This, too, would be a "family."

40. Sanders, *The Historical Figure of Jesus*, 124.

41. We refer, again, to the work of Destro and Pesce, "Fathers and Householders in the

already considered, in chapter 3, what the young age of some of Jesus' followers reveals about early Christian family structures. There we also saw a few examples from the apocryphal *Acts of Andrew* and the *Acts of Thomas* in which a tradition continued in early Christianity of separating children from their families in order to allow them to become followers of the Christian movement. The Gospel material stresses the priority of following Jesus and discourages familial life in the light of the eschaton.[42] Jesus permits children among his followers, even if it means turning families and family relationships upside down. Included in the call to follow were those very children about whom Jesus had said to his disciples, "Whoever welcomes one such child in my name, welcomes me" (Mk 9:37; Mt 18:5; cf. Lk 9:48). Children clearly were present and active in Jesus' ministry. Clearly, the discouragement of family connections applied also to children who followed Jesus, not just to adults who turned from their families. Chapter 8 below addresses the implications of this acceptance of children for the development of Christian asceticism and its role with regard to the ascetic and his or her biological family.

Children in Paul's Churches as Presented in Acts

Earlier on we highlighted elements of children's integration into house churches and the process of their early acquaintance with the Scriptures, an important feature of their preparation for participating in community worship. We shall discuss 1 Corinthians 7:36–38 in the final chapter, but we ought to keep in mind that the discussion of virgins there also acknowledges the presence of girls in the life of the community. The lives of these girls are determined in light of Christian teaching and faith.[43] In addition, the Acts of the Apostles provides some evidence for the presence of young

---

Jesus Movement," 211, 216–19, and 222. They note the absence of fathers (211, 216), but do not place any of the apostles as children or teenagers.

42. Balla, *The Child-Parent Relationship in the New Testament*, 131–33 and 138–42, acknowledges the tensions caused by children leaving their families, but draws back from the implications of the data, suggesting finally that Jesus did not have an "anti-family" ethos (155). Yet a focus on the priority of Christ and the Kingdom is not "anti-family" so much as it is a reorientation of who is family in light of the eschaton.

43. On the possible tension in Pauline house churches, see Balch, "Rich Pompeiian Houses," 27 and 37–40. While children are not discussed directly, we may imagine them as a part of the home. Some of the tension could be due to children's involvement against the wishes of their parents. For some discussion of the place of children in house churches, see also Osiek, MacDonald, and Tulloch, *A Woman's Place*, 50–67 (on newborn and infants and their care), and 68–94 (on children growing up).

people at a Christian service. Yet the presentation of children in the material in canonical Acts, particularly with respect to Paul, must be approached with some circumspection. The reliability of the account of Paul's activity in several instances is contradictory to what Paul himself provides in his authentic letters. The tendencies of the presentation of the church in Acts are well known, especially the aspect of communal unanimity in all matters of church organization and mission. Nevertheless, the passages that place children in the early Christian communities may reflect the author's concern with children (along with widows and other socially marginal groups) that characterizes Luke-Acts.

Acts 20:7–12 narrates Paul's last evening in Troas, in which a young man, Eutychus, falls asleep and then falls out of a third-story window in the room where Paul continued his discourse until midnight. Eutychus is described as both a *neanias* (v. 9) and a *pais* (v. 12). It is clear that these two terms are used as synonyms without implying two different and therefore conflicting accounts of Eutychus's age. One can surmise from the use of these two words that he was in his mid-teens. Two other aspects of this story may be mentioned. First, it is taken for granted that Eutychus was present without his parents, which suggests that children would or could attend services on their own. Secondly, one also notices that the boy was present at what seemed to have been a formal service, given that it took place on the first day of the week (Sunday), when the community met to break bread and listen to Paul's preaching.[44]

Elsewhere, Acts places both freeborn and slave children in narratives concerning Pauline churches (cf. 21:5). The author of Luke-Acts assumes that in Paul's churches children had some role to play, although their precise formal function is difficult to determine; in any event, they were integral to Luke's concept of the Christian community. While children may have had leadership roles in conjunction with a mentor such as Paul, they also seem to have had roles in Christian worship, in Luke's presentation of the Christian Church, evidenced, for example, by Philip's four daughters who prophesied.[45] Given that household churches were the norm at this

44. Ernst Haenchen, *The Acts of the Apostles* (Philadelphia: Westminster Press, 1971), 585, understands Eutychus to be a "youth"; Hans Conzelmann, *A Commentary on the Acts of the Apostles* (Philadelphia: Fortress Press, 1987), 169, remarks only that we cannot specify the limits of the formal nature of the service. Both see the raising of Eutychus from the dead as a miracle account.

45. Johnson, *The Acts of the Apostles,* 369–70, does not refer to the general age of the daughters as *parthenoi,* but he does note that virgin prophetesses are associated with a number of pagan cults, such as at Delphi.

point, children's attendance at these services seems to have been a typical phenomenon.[46]

Acts' picture of early Christians holding all things in common and eating together (Acts 2:44–46) constitutes another relevant datum. The children were present among the believers, whether at home or in the Temple; the structure of the community at this time suggests that children simply were a part of the daily Christian life. As such, it would also be their life in the same way that it was their parents' life. The following paragraphs examine more fully what one may be able to say about the inclusion of children more specifically in the sacramental life of the Church, including the issue of the baptism of infants and children.

Children's Socialization into the Church

Of all the questions pertaining to the life of Christian children during the earliest years of the Church, the question of infant and youth baptism is among the most vehemently debated. The discussion centers on a scholarly dispute between Joachim Jeremias and Kurt Aland, which played out in several publications appearing in the middle of the twentieth century. The debate received significantly more attention in Protestant than in Catholic circles. Based on arguments of parallelism between early Christian baptism and early Jewish proselyte baptisms, epigraphical data derived from burial and commemorative sites of children, and exegetical work on biblical and patristic texts, Jeremias assumed a more or less continuous practice of baptizing children in the Christian community from New Testament times to the late second and early third centuries.[47] Explicit attestation for such a practice, however, is available only in the form of a treatise on baptism by the North African theologian Tertullian of Carthage, a text written around

---

46. Unless there were simply no children among the early Christians, they also were a part of the worship of the earliest community. Granted that the description of the community is idealized in Acts 2:42–46 and 4:32–37 (as Johnson, *The Acts of the Apostles*, 61–64, and Haenchen, *The Acts of the Apostles*, 190–96 and 230–35, confirm), still if the community is gathering together and eating together, the children also need to be seen as being present and as participating.

47. See Joachim Jeremias, *Hat die Urkirche die Kindertaufe geübt?* (Göttingen: Vandenhoeck & Ruprecht, 1938; 2nd, rev. edition, 1949); Joachim Jeremias, *Die Kindertaufe in den ersten vier Jahrhunderten* (Göttingen: Vandenhoeck & Ruprecht, 1958; trans. David Cairns, *Infant Baptism in the First Four Centuries* [London: SCM Press, 1960; repr. London: Westminster Press, c.1962]); Joachim Jeremias, *Nochmals: Die Anfänge der Kindertaufe. Eine Replik auf Kurt Alands Schrift: Die Säuglingstaufe im Neuen Testament und in der Alten Kirche* (München: C. Kaiser, 1962; trans. Dorothea M. Barton, *The Origins of Infant Baptism: A Further Study in Reply to Kurt Aland* [London: SCM Press, 1963]).

A.D. 200.[48] Taking his cue from the lack of explicit evidence before Tertullian, Aland refuted Jeremias's discussion as an overinterpretation of the evidence. Aland made a distinction between infant baptism and the baptism of children and argued that the practice of baptizing infants cannot be documented before the third century.[49] He also questioned whether the practice of delaying baptism that one seems to observe in fourth-century sources really was a "crisis," as Jeremias had argued, or rather the continuation of a practice of baptism later in life, as had been the case also throughout the previous centuries, now merely better documented in the sources. The debate between Jeremias and Aland had precursors in Dietrich Bonhoeffer's reflections on baptism and Karl Barth's rejection of infant baptism in 1943.[50] Inspired by and responding to the positions formulated by Jeremias and Aland, several other scholars participated in the debate and followed up with studies of their own.[51] Helpful collections of relevant ancient sources have also become available.[52]

48. For discussion of this evidence, see below.

49. Kurt Aland, *Die Säuglingstaufe im Neuen Testament und in der alten Kirche. Eine Antwort auf Joachim Jeremias* (Munich: C. Kaiser, 1961; trans. G. R. Beasley-Murray, *Did the Early Church Baptize Infants?* [London: SCM Press, 1963]); Kurt Aland, *Die Stellung der Kinder in den frühen christlichen Gemeinden—und ihre Taufe* (Munich: C. Kaiser, 1967); and Kurt Aland, *Taufe und Kindertaufe. 40 Sätze zur Aussage des Neuen Testaments und dem historischen Befund, zur modernen Debatte darüber und den Folgerungen daraus für die kirchliche Praxis—zugleich eine Auseinandersetzung mit Karl Barths Lehre von der Taufe* (Gütersloh: Gerd Mohn, 1971).

50. See Dietrich Bonhoeffer, "Zur Tauffrage. Ein Gutachten," in *Dietrich Bonhoeffer, Gesammelte Schriften* (Munich: Gerd Mohn, 1960), vol. 3, 431–54; Karl Barth, *Die kirchliche Lehre von der Taufe* (Zürich: Evangelischer Verlag, 1943; trans. Ernest A. Payne, *The Teaching of the Church Regarding Baptism* [London: SCM Press, 1948]). For Barth's later position on infant baptism, see Karl Barth, *Kirchliche Dogmatik*, 4 vols. (Zollikon-Zürich: Evangelischer Verlag, 1948–70), vol. 4.4. See also the discussion in Aland, *Taufe und Kindertaufe. 40 Sätze*, 40–41 and 48–68.

51. For a summary of the controversy between Joachim Jeremias and Kurt Aland up to the year 1962, see also A. Strobel, "Säuglings- und Kindertaufe in der ältesten Kirche," in *Begründung und Gebrauch der heiligen Taufe. Aus der Arbeit einer Studientagung* (Berlin: Lutherisches Verlagshaus, 1963), 7–69. See also the work by Willi Marxsen, "Erwägungen zur neutestamentlichen Begründung der Taufe," in *Apophoreta. Festschrift für Ernst Haenchen zu seinem 70. Geburtstag am 10. Dezember 1964* (Berlin: Töpelmann, 1964), 169–77; Beasley-Murray, "Church and Child in the New Testament"; Hans Hubert, *Der Streit um die Kindertaufe. Eine Darstellung der von Karl Barth 1943 ausgelösten Diskussion um die Kindertaufe und ihre Bedeutung für die heutige Tauffrage* (Bern: Peter Lang, 1972); E. Ferguson, "Inscriptions and the Origin of Infant Baptism," *JThS* n.s. 30 (1979), 37–46; and G. R. Beasley-Murray, "The Theology of the Child," *American Baptist Quarterly* 1 (1982), 197–202.

52. For convenient collections of early Christian literary sources on the baptism of young children, see J. C. Didier, *Le baptême des enfants dans la tradition de l'Église* (Paris: Desclée, 1959); and Heinrich Kraft, *Texte zur Geschichte der Taufe, besonders der Kindertaufe in der alten Kirche. Unter Mitwirkung von Holger Hammerich*, 2nd ed. (Berlin: de Gruyter, 1969). A transla-

More recent contributions on the issue of children and their reception of baptism in the early centuries of Christianity have shifted attention away from the specific question of whether in the first and second centuries infants were baptized, toward practical consequences of baptism for the life of children, theological answers to why children ought to be baptized, and investigations of the larger process of the initiation or socialization of children into the Christian Church. Michael Gärtner, for example, has investigated the impact of children's baptism or lack thereof on the way children were raised in families and in the Christian Church.[53] Eduard Nagel and David Wright deepened the historical and theological analysis of how and why the practice of postponing baptism until adulthood noticeably changed by the fifth century, especially in the West under Augustine's influence.[54] More recently, David Wright has focused on ceremonies of infant dedications that appear to have functioned as substitutes for baptism,[55] while Cornelia Horn has raised the more fundamental question of what it took for children to be considered and to become full Christians. Within that horizon, various forms of children's play and their imitation of adult practices have to be considered indicators and promoters of children's socialization as Christians.[56]

As the primary sacrament of initiation, baptism certainly has a role to play in the process of becoming a member of the Christian community. In the course of the fifth century, moreover, debates between theologians, primarily in the West, decisively reinterpreted baptism as an indispensable sign of a child's Christian identification. Without baptism, children could not be counted as full Christians.

---

tion and commentary on Didier's collection is available in J. C. Didier and A. M. Roguet, *Faut-il baptiser les enfants? La réponse de la tradition* (Paris: Éditions du Cerf, 1967).

53. Gärtner, *Familienerziehung in der Alten Kirche*, 64–86.

54. Eduard Nagel, *Kindertaufe und Taufaufschub. Die Praxis vom 3.–5. Jahrhundert in Nordafrika und ihre theologische Einordnung bei Tertullian, Cyprian und Augustinus* (Frankfurt am Main: Peter Lang, 1980); and David F. Wright, "How Controversial Was the Development of Infant Baptism in the Early Church," in *Church, Word, and Spirit: Historical and Theological Essays in Honor of Geoffrey W. Bromiley* (Grand Rapids, Mich.: Eerdmans, c1987), 45–63. See also David F. Wright, "Out, In, Out: Jesus' Blessing of the Children and Infant Baptism," in *Dimensions of Baptism: Biblical and Theological Studies* (Sheffield: Sheffield Academic Press, 2002), 188–206.

55. David F. Wright, "Infant Dedication in the Early Church," in *Baptism, the New Testament and the Church: Historical and Contemporary Studies in Honour of R. E. O. White* (Sheffield: Sheffield Academic Press, 1999), 352–78.

56. Cornelia B. Horn, "How Children Became Christians: Three Models from Early Christian Practice," paper delivered at the regional meeting of the American Academy of Religion/Society of Biblical Literature, St. Paul, Minn., April 2004; see also Horn, "Play as Social Ritual."

Our discussion takes a broad perspective on the question of what options and possibilities governed the admission and participation of early Christian children in the life of the Church. One question to be addressed is how children's experience intersected with baptism and baptismal practices. Also to be investigated is the question of how children participated in the Christian liturgy of the Eucharist and the Church's worship life more broadly. Beyond that, ancient documents preserve rare insights into how children were guided into a life of prayer, both communal and private. The practice of private and public prayer is not to be underestimated as a means of establishing a bond of personal and communal relationship with God. The process of socializing children into the Christian Church was closely related to the quality and extent of the religious education and formation children received.

When we consider children becoming Christians in this context, we speak not only of the educational efforts of catechists, but also of the partially intangible sense of belonging to a group, of an individual's identification with a social unit. Since Christians were not clearly identifiable as "Jew" or "Greek," the manner in which they became a part of the Church was dependent upon their sense of belonging to something other or someone else. Some of this weight was carried by the Church's moral strictures, which often set Christians apart from their Greek and Roman neighbors. It also emerged from their theology, which differentiated them from Jews. Yet, children are not first motivated to belong either by theology or even by morality, but by the reality of the shape of their life. One might ask therefore how they knew that they were Christians and not Jews or followers of a Roman or Greek religion.

Some answers to these questions may have to be defined negatively. Children may have realized that they were not circumcised, did not celebrate certain festivals, did not go to the synagogue, did not worship before statues of the deities, did not have a *lararium* in their homes, or did not go to the same temples as the rest of their family, their aunts and uncles, cousins, or other children in the neighborhood. Such self-definitions have a limited appeal and Christian children had to be brought into the community by positive means. These means included their presence at and participation in the Christian liturgy, which amounted to a participation in ritual acts of which children would not even always be aware. These structured and directed services aided in the socialization process, just as catechesis did, but the effort had to go beyond this. Efforts at socialization, group formation, and the formation of personal character and identity are greatly enhanced by positive, receptive behavior on the part of the person who is to be socialized. Such positive responses are naturally motivated by systems of reward and recognition. From an early point on, this also included baptism, but one has to be certain not to overlook the many other ways in which children became Christians.

Children Becoming Christians: Initiation and Acceptance

From occasional remarks in second-century texts, as well as in later texts that refer to events taking place during the second century, one may conclude that some individual believers were Christians for most of their lives, including much if not all of their childhood. Justin Martyr, for example, commented on "men and women, who have been Christ's disciples from childhood." Indeed, there were "many" of them who remained "pure at the age of sixty or seventy years,"[57] a remark which in the immediate context of the passage probably identified them as not having committed adultery during their lives. The mid-second-century *Martyrdom of Polycarp* had Bishop Polycarp declare that for eighty-six years he had served Christ and saw no reason why he should turn against Christ, given that Christ had never done him any injury.[58] Eusebius of Caesarea recorded a comment in which Polycrates identified himself as one who had lived "sixty-five years in the Lord."[59] The references to the long duration of their lives as Christians make it likely that they had been initiated while still relatively young.

Irenaeus of Lyons provided a clear theological rationale for the incorporation of children into the Christian community. In his treatise *Against Heresies* he explained that Christ "came to save all through means of Himself—all, I say, who through Him are born again to God—infants, and children, and boys, and youths, and old men."[60] The salvation worked by Christ was clearly for all. The reference to being "born again to God," however, does bespeak some kind of special, post-natal process or ritual through which those of all ages mentioned appear to have passed. Ire-

57. Justin Martyr, *First Apology* 15.6 (ed. Marcovich, *Iustini Martyris Apologiae Pro Christianis*, 54; A. Cleveland Coxe, ed., "The First Apology of Justin," in ANF 1 [New York: Charles Scribner's Sons, 1913], 163–87, here 167).

58. *Martyrdom of Polycarp* 9.3 (ed. and trans. Ehrman, *Apostolic Fathers*, vol. 1, 380–81).

59. Eusebius of Caesarea, *Church History* 5.24.7 (ed. Schwartz, Mommsen, and Winkelmann, *Eusebius Werke, Zweiter Band, Erster Teil, Die Kirchengeschichte*, GCS, N. F. 6.1, 492, ll. 7–8).

60. Irenaeus of Lyons, *Against Heresies* 2.22.4 (ed. Rousseau and Doutreleau, *Irénée de Lyon. Contre les Hérésies*. Book 2, SCh 294, 220, ll. 103–5).

naeus's comment is among the earliest and most explicit remarks that combine imagery distinctive of the baptismal ritual and theology with express references to infants and children. From these observations questions arise as to how widespread such a practice of baptizing younger children was and what kind of theology may have supported or rationalized it.

Children and Baptism

No necessary restrictions seem to have been in place in early Christian times that would have made it impossible for children to receive baptism. The normal requirements for baptism appear to have been a desire on the part of the recipient and some evidence of the person's knowledge and acceptance of basic tenets of the community's Christian faith.[61] A minimum age does not emerge as a criterion, which should be considered when positive evidence for children's baptism from the earliest times is lacking. Indisputable, positive evidence for the actual baptism of children does exist from the early third century on. However, early Christian authors thought that when they baptized children, they continued a tradition that reached back to apostolic times. A witness for this conviction is Origen of Alexandria's statement in his *Commentary on Romans,* that the Church received from the apostles the tradition of baptizing little children.[62] The casual character of Origen's remark in the context of instruction on the forgiveness of sins, and not on baptism, argues against Origen's misrepresenting the history of the practice.[63]

Earlier evidence for children's baptism comes from the west of North Africa. In chapter 18 of his treatise *On Baptism,* Tertullian advised his audience not to administer baptism too quickly, given that according to Matthew 7:6 Jesus instructed his disciples not to cast pearls before swine.[64]

---

61. For the expectation that faith ought to be present in the one to be baptized, see Tertullian's comments, when he talks about the eunuch receiving baptism at the hands of the apostle Philip on the way from Jerusalem to Gaza (Acts 8:26–40), that faith was not lacking (*fides non moratur*). See Tertullian, *De baptismo* 18.1 (ed. and trans. R. P. Refoulé and M. Drouzy, *Tertullien. Traité du Baptême* [Paris: Les Éditions du Cerf, 2002], 91).

62. Origen of Alexandria, *Commentary on Romans* bk. 5.9 (ed. Caroline P. Hammond Bammel, *Der Römerbriefkommentar des Origenes. Kritische Ausgabe der Übersetzung Rufins,* 3 vols. [Freiburg.: Herder, 1990], vol. 2, 440, ll. 168–69): *et eclesia ab apostolis traditionem suscepit etiam parvulis baptismum dare.*

63. See also Horn, "How Children Became Christians."

64. Tertullian, *De baptismo* 18.1 (ed. and trans. Refoulé and Drouzy, *Tertullien. Traité du Baptême,* 91, l. 14).

"Easy" or "speedy" baptisms evidenced in the earliest Christian texts required significant preparatory work on God's part, Tertullian argued. In the case of Philip's baptism of the eunuch on the road from Jerusalem to Gaza (Acts 8:26–40), an appropriate time of prayer and study of Scripture on the eunuch's part had preceded baptismal initiation.[65] Speedy action, as in the case of Paul's baptism by Simon in Damascus, was only justified by the clear, approving signs God sent ahead of time. Thus, Tertullian's point with regard to baptism was that one ought to take into account a given person's individual condition and disposition, including his or her age, before admitting him or her to baptism. At times, he argued, "the delay of baptism is more useful, especially however in the case of small children."[66] While one might have expected Tertullian to develop this thought with a focus on children, he turned to a discussion of how the hasty baptism of children posed a danger for the children's baptismal sponsors (*sponsores*), who might have died before they were able to ensure that the children grew up to become morally responsible and conscious adults. Tertullian told his readers that at baptism the sponsors had to make promises that because of their own mortality they might not be able to fulfill. He did not specify the exact content or wording of such promises. His subsequent remarks concerning a sponsor's disappointment at children who developed evil dispositions as they grew up leads one to conclude that proper character formation of the child probably was part of what sponsors had to guarantee.[67] In light of the burden of responsibility placed on the sponsors' shoulders, Tertullian responded to those who insisted on early baptism and who referred to Jesus' command not to hinder children from coming to him (Mk 10:14; Mt 19:4; Lk 18:16), by stating that these children should "come, then, as they are growing up, they should come learning, while they are learning to where they should come."[68] He stressed that they should "become Christians, when they have become able to know Christ."[69] Older children or youths who had developed skills and understanding were better prepared. One may assume also that baptism was more useful for older children, because baptism, as Tertullian finally remarked, was understood as

65. Ibid., 18.2 (Refoulé and Drouzy, 91–92).

66. Ibid., 18.4 (Refoulé and Drouzy, 92, ll. 12–15; also ed. Didier, *Le baptême des enfants*, 17, ll. 4–5): *Itaque pro cuiusque personae condicione ac dispositione, etiam aetate, cunctatio baptismi utilior est, praecipue tamen circa parvulos.*

67. Tertullian, *De baptismo* 18.4 (ed. and trans. Refoulé and Drouzy, *Tertullien. Traité du Baptême*, 92).

68. Ibid., 18.5 (Refoulé and Drouzy, 92, l. 19–93, l. 1).

69. Ibid., 18.5 (Refoulé and Drouzy, 93, l. 2): *fiant Christiani cum Christum nosse potuerint.*

granting forgiveness of sins. For this very reason, innocent little children had no need to hasten such forgiveness of sin.[70] For Tertullian, baptism was a weighty matter *(pondus)*, and its reception needed to be approached with due fear and respect. Understanding its consequences ought to be treated as a *sine qua non* for its reception.

At the beginning of the third century in North Africa, one can observe serious efforts not to keep children from baptism, but to raise among adults an awareness of their responsibility for the proper instruction and supervision of their children's growth into full Christian maturity. Children not only had a right to become baptized Christians, but, more importantly, they had a right to understand what was happening to them when and while they were becoming Christians. When cautioning his audience regarding hasty acts of child baptism, Tertullian did not qualify children's baptism as a recent innovation. One may infer from this that in North Africa children probably had been baptized for quite some time, at least for the period of the later half of the second century.

The practice of children's baptism in the second century is also corroborated by evidence contained in the earliest church order, the *Apostolic Tradition*, which probably goes back to the end of the second century.[71] Customarily and with reasonable likelihood ascribed to Hippolytus of Rome, the *Apostolic Tradition* includes regulations of the order in which candidates for baptism are to be inducted at the Easter celebration. Its instructions stipulate that after the baptismal candidates take off their garments, one should begin first with the baptism of children *(parvulos)*. This group was composed of children of differing age and ability, since the text distinguishes people with regard to their ability to respond to the questions asked during baptism: "All those who can speak for themselves, shall do so." Younger children constituted at least a part of the group of those "who cannot speak for themselves." When these younger children were to come up for baptism, "their parents shall speak for them, or someone else from among their family relatives."[72] At least some of this second group of chil-

70. Ibid. (Refoulé and Drouzy, 93, ll. 2–3): *Quid festinat innocens aetas ad remissionem peccatorum?*

71. For questions of authorship, date, and related matters with regard to the *Traditio Apostolica*, see the discussion in Bruno Steimer, *Vertex Traditionis: Die Gattung der altchristlichen Kirchenordnungen* (Berlin: de Gruyter, 1992), 60–71. See also Bruno Steimer, "Traditio Apostolica," in *Dictionary of Early Christian Literature* (2000), 580–83; and Bruno Steimer, "Kirchenordnungen," in *Der Neue Pauly* 6 (1999), cols. 483–85.

72. Hippolytus, *Apostolic Tradition* 21 (ed. Bernard Botte, *Hippolyte de Rome. La Tradition apostolique d'après les anciennes versions*, 2nd ed. [Paris: Les Éditions du Cerf, 1968], 80–81; see

dren may have been very young children carried up to the baptismal pool in their parents' or relatives' arms, since a group of children who cannot yet speak may include at least some children too young to walk on their own. Only after all children had received baptism could adults—first men, then women—be baptized. This order of baptizing children first and adults afterwards is attested in later church orders as well, for example in the fifth-century *Testamentum Domini Nostri Iesu Christi.*[73]

Given that the *Apostolic Tradition* regulated baptismal order by including cases of infants who could not yet speak, it is likely that not everyone heeded Tertullian's caution. About a decade later Tertullian composed another treatise, *On the Soul (De anima)*, that also addressed questions involving children.[74] From his discussion of ritual practices surrounding childbirth one may conclude that he probably had changed his mind. Instead of highlighting children's innocence, he now emphasized that the evil spirit clings to every human being, "ready to entrap their souls from the very portal of their birth." Tertullian seems to have assumed that evil was welcomed into every child, because the evil spirit was "invited to be present in all those superstitious processes which accompany childbearing." Such practices included the use of certain fillets that were "wreathed before the idols" and pregnant mothers wore around their wombs. These strips of cloth seem to have functioned as a kind of good-luck charm during pregnancy. During the baby's delivery, midwives would lament and call out the names of "Lucina and Diana," given that Juno, under the name of Lucina, Diana Lucina, and Diana Lucifera, was venerated as a goddess of birth in ancient Rome. For the whole of the first week after birth, "a table is spread in honor of Juno," and "on the last day the fates of the horoscope are invoked." When the infant made its first step on the ground, this was dedicated as "sacred to the goddess Statina." There was no end to such rituals, according to Tertullian, for no one "fails to devote to idolatrous service the entire head of his son, or to take out a hair, or to shave off the whole with a razor, or to bind it up for an offering, or to seal it for sacred use—on behalf

---

also Geerlings, "Traditio Apostolica. Apostolische Überlieferung," 256, ll. 10–13): *Ponent autem vestes, et baptizate primum parvulos. Omnes autem qui possunt loqui pro se, loquantur. Qui autem non possunt loqui pro se, parentes eorum loquantur pro eis, vel aliquis ex eorum genere* γένος.

73. *Testamentum Domini Nostri Iesu Christi* (ed. and trans. Vööbus, *Synodicon in the West Syrian Tradition,* 36 [Syriac] and 54 [English]). See also Gärtner, *Familienerziehung in der Alten Kirche,* 66.

74. The following citations are all found in Tertullian, *De anima* 39 (ed. J. H. Waszink, "Q. S. Fl. Tertulliani *De anima*," in *Quinti Septimi Florentis Tertulliani Opera,* vol. 2: *Opera Montanistica* [Turnhout: Brepols, 1954], 779–869, here 842–43).

of the clan, of the ancestry, or for public devotion."[75] The additional practice of assigning to everyone a personal *genius* only meant to Tertullian that every child received his or her own personal evil spirit.[76]

Tertullian seems to have assumed that pagan childbearing customs also affected Christian children and thus rendered every birth impure.[77] Those at whose birth pagan midwives assisted had no escape from exposure to and thus defilement by such practices. One notices with interest the same critical distance from pagan midwives recommended here by Christian authors that we observed earlier in Jewish authors.[78] Children coming from mixed marriages, who may have taken recourse to 1 Corinthians 7:14 as their defense,[79] could hear Tertullian explain that, when Paul stated that if "either of the parents was sanctified, the children were holy," the Apostle made such a claim because sanctification of the child in such an instance depended on "the prerogative of the [Christian parent's] seed" as much as on "the discipline of the institution."[80] While Tertullian has been understood to be speaking of the institution of baptism in this instance, it is more likely that he had marriage in mind, especially since he referred to marriage again only a few lines later.[81] When Paul added the comment that "otherwise, [the children] would be impure," a comment which Tertullian expanded with "by birth,"[82] Tertullian did not allow for the full force of Paul's point to carry the day. He argued that the child was not in an actual state of purity at birth, but rather that it was designated for a state of holi-

---

75. For the rabbis' consideration of such hair offerings as idolatry, cf. *m. Avodah Zarah* 1.3.

76. Tertullian, *De anima* 39.3 (ed. Waszink, "Q. S. Fl. Tertulliani *De anima*," 842, ll. 17–18). Also Socrates, "while yet a boy, was found by the spirit of the demon," as Tertullian, *De anima* 39.3, states in this same context.

77. Tertullian, *De anima* 39.3 (Waszink, 842, ll. 18–19): *adeo nulla ferme nativitas munda est.*

78. See above, chapter 6, regarding discussion of midwives in *m.* and *t. Avodah Zarah* 2.1 and 3.3 and the *Infancy Gospels of James* 5.6–8 and 18–20 (ed. and trans. Hock, *Infancy Gospels of James and Thomas,* 40–41 and 64–69). See also Matthews and Benjamin, *Social World in Ancient Israel, 1250–587 B.C.E.,* 67–81, for the role of midwives in the ancient world.

79. For consideration of the patristic interpretation of 1 Corinthians 7:14, see also Beasley-Murray, "The Theology of the Child," who applies it to the Baptist tradition; for Tertullian's interpretation of 1 Corinthians 7 more broadly, see René Braun, "Tertullien et l'exégèse de 1 Cor 7," in *Épektasis; mélanges patristiques offerts au Cardinal Jean Daniélou* (Paris: Beauchesne, 1972), 21–28.

80. Tertullian, *De anima* 39.4 (ed. Waszink, "Q. S. Fl. Tertulliani *De anima*," 842–43, ll. 21–22).

81. Ibid. (Waszink, 843, ll. 24–25).

82. Ibid. (Waszink, 843, l. 22): *ceterum, inquit, immundi nascerentur.* Paul, in fact, does not speak of "birth" as a circumstance of the child's state of impurity. Yet given Tertullian's present context of talking about childbirth and the reference to John 3:5, a verse which he was about to quote only a few lines later, it seems likely that Tertullian understood him in that way.

ness and salvation by virtue of having a Christian parent and by virtue of benefiting from the institution of marriage in which the child's parents participated. In mixed marriages children still were not preserved from impurity, but were more easily set on the path toward purity.

Moreover, given that Tertullian had already highlighted the context of birth as the crucial point with his addition of the phrase "by birth" (*nascerentur*) to 1 Corinthians 7:14, he sealed his point by citing John 3:5, which states that no one will enter the kingdom of God, for Tertullian a phrase bespeaking holiness, unless "born of water and spirit," that is, baptized.[83] Every child, therefore, completely independent of its Christian parents, still had to reach the state of holiness. Tertullian says: "Every soul, then, is counted as belonging to Adam until it is reenrolled with Christ; it is impure, until it is reenrolled; it is sinful, because it is impure, not withdrawing the shame from its association with the flesh."[84] What applies to every soul, applies to every child. Baptism as remission of sin, which Tertullian had rejected for children a decade earlier, had become essential for a child's holiness and salvation.

Toward the middle of the third century, evidence for the practice of children's baptism can be found in the writings of Origen and Cyprian of Carthage. The theme of baptism as remission of sins with regard to children reemerged, somewhat in line with Tertullian's later views on the question. Origen, who understood baptism to be a continuous tradition from apostolic times, explained in his *Homilies on Luke* how he saw the purgative effect of baptism as necessary also in the case of children. Arguing from Job 14:4–5 (LXX) that "no one is free from defilement [*mundus a sorde*], even if his life were (only) one day," Origen took the opportunity to address a question often discussed among the faithful (*frequenter inter fratres quaeritur*).[85] He stated that "little children are baptized for the remission of sins,"[86] but he did not say what sins children might have committed or when they might have sinned. Rather, he reverted to the witness of Job

---

83. Ibid. (Waszink, 843, ll. 23–28): *quasi designatos tamen sanctitatis ac per hoc etiam salutis intelligi volens fidelium filios, ... Alioquin meminerat dominicae definitionis: nisi quis nascetur ex aqua et spiritu, non inibit in regnum Dei, it est non erit sanctus.*

84. *Ibid.*, 40.1 (Waszink, 843, ll. 1–4): *Ita omnis anima eo usque in Adam censetur, donec in Christo recenseatur, tamdiu immunda, quamdiu recenseatur; peccatrix autem, quia immunda, quamdiu recenseatur ex carnis societate.*

85. Origen, *Homiliae in Lucam* 14 (ed. and trans. Henri Crouzel, François Fournier, and Pierre Périchon, *Origène. Homélies sur S. Luc: text latin et fragments grecs* [Paris: Les Éditions du Cerf, 1962], 222).

86. Ibid. (Crouzel, Fournier, and Périchon, 222–23; also ed. Didier, *Le baptême des enfants*, 19–20): *Parvuli baptizantur in remissionem peccatorum.* See also Acts 2:38.

14:4–5 and reasoned that there could not exist any other reason for children to be baptized except that all humans are sinful.[87] Because the defilement of birth *(sordes nativitatis)* was laid aside through the sacrament of baptism *(per baptismi sacramentum)*, little children were being baptized *(propterea baptizantur et parvuli)*.[88] Like Tertullian, Origen concluded his point with a reference to John 3:5. In his *Homilies on Leviticus*, he corroborated his argument for the baptism of children for the sake of the remission of sins by adding to Job 14:4 the voice of David, who said in Psalms 51:5 that he was conceived in iniquities and that his mother had brought him forth in sin.[89] Thus, "since the baptism of the church is given for the remission of sins, in congruence with the observance of the church, baptism is also given to little children." That they needed it was clear for him, since "if there were nothing [sinful] in little children that required remission . . . the grace of baptism would seem superfluous."[90]

The third-century North African theologian Cyprian of Carthage's letters are a significant source for our knowledge of children's participation in, as well as their initial introduction into, the Christian community. *Letter 64*, addressed to his episcopal colleague Fidus,[91] was cited numerous times by Augustine against the Pelagians in defense of his position on the necessity of the baptism of little children. Jerome also relied on the letter's authority in his anti-Pelagian undertakings.[92]

87. James K. Zink, "Uncleanness and sin: a study of Job XIV 4 and Ps LI 7," *Vetus Testamentum* 17.3 (1967), 354–61, who considers the patristic interpretation of Psalm 51:7 (355), but does not take into account early Christian readings of Job 14:4 (356–57).

88. Origen, *Homiliae in Lucam* 14 (ed. and trans. Crouzel, Fournier, and Périchon, *Origène. Homélies sur S. Luc,* 222–23). See also Origen, *Commentary on Romans,* bk. 5:9 (ed. Hammond Bammel, *Der Römerbriefkommentar des Origenes,* vol. 2, 440, ll. 168–72): *Pro hoc et ecclesia ab apostolis traditionem suscepit etiam parvulis baptismum dare; sciebant enim illi quibus mysteriorum secreta commissa sunt divinorum, quia essent in omnibus genuinae sordes peccati quae per aquam et spiritum ablui deberent.*

89. Origen, *Homiliae in Leviticum* 8.3 (ed. Marcel Borret, *Origène. Homélies sur le Lévitique,* 2 vols. [Paris: Les Éditions du Cerf, 1981], vol. 2, 14–23, here 21; trans. Gary Wayne Barkley, *Origen. Homilies on Leviticus: 1–16* [Washington, D.C.: The Catholic University of America Press, c1990], 158).

90. Ibid. (Borret, vol. 2, 21; Barkley, 158): *Addi his etiam illud potest, ut requiratur quid causae sit, cum baptisma ecclesiae pro remissione peccatorum detur, secundum ecclesiae observantiam etiam parvulis baptismum dari; cum utique si nihil esset in parvulis quod ad remissionem deberet et indulgentiam pertinere, gratia baptismi superflua videretur.*

91. Cyprian of Carthage, *Letters* 64 (ed. G. F. Diercks, *Sancti Cypriani Episcopi Epistularium* [Turnhout: Brepols, 1996], 418–25).

92. For references to eight citations in Augustine and one in Jerome, see Didier, *Le baptême des enfants* 22, note a.

Cyprian's *Letter* 64 gained such weight not only because of its content, but also because it represented what purported to be the universal consensus of a council of sixty-six North African bishops. It carried the weight of regional church legislation when it spoke on the proper timeframe during which children ought to be baptized. The council had met and discussed questions about the readmission to the Church of those Christians who during persecution had renounced their faith and who, as lapsed Christians, were excluded from the Church.[93] Fidus also expressed his opinion that infants "ought not to be baptized within the second or third day after their birth." Rather, he thought "that the law of ancient circumcision should be regarded," which meant that a just-born baby ought "not to be baptized and sanctified within eight days" after birth. The council of bishops gathered around Cyprian unanimously seems to have disagreed with Fidus. In his letter, Cyprian told Fidus that "the mercy and grace of God is not to be refused" to any human being. Since infants are also the work of God, they reflect the Creator's majesty and cannot be wanting in anything. Cyprian argued not for the physical, but for "the divine and spiritual equality" of all, "whether infants or older people." In baptism, neither grace nor the Holy Spirit was given any differently to younger and to older people. For God did not consider either rank or age (*personam non accipit, sic nec aetatem*), but instead "shows Himself as Father to all."[94]

Based on such a theological argument and with the support of Titus 1:15, "to the pure all things are pure," Cyprian then argued that whatever one may think of the purity of a newborn baby, since God had deigned the baby worthy to be created, no hindrance to heavenly grace was to be deduced from the newborn's status. When Cyprian observed that "any one of us would still shudder at kissing" the freshly born infant,[95] his comment reveals acquaintance with the circumstances accompanying the delivery of a baby. The remark appears to reflect his impression of the messy sight of

---

93. Cyprian dealt more extensively with the question of how to treat lapsed Christians in his treatise *De lapsis*. For a discussion of the question of rebaptism that emerged in the North African Church in the context of having to decide how to handle the reconciliation of Christians who had left the flock during the times of the persecution and who afterwards wished to rejoin the Church, see, for example, Patout J. Burns, "On Rebaptism: Social Organization in the Third Century Church," *Journal of Early Christian Studies* 1 (1993), 367–403. See also John Hammond Taylor, "St. Cyprian and the Reconciliation of Apostates," *Theological Studies* 3.1 (1942), 27–46.

94. Cyprian of Carthage, *Letters* 64 ii.1–2 and 64 iii.1–2 (ed. Diercks, *Sancti Cypriani Episcopi Epistularium*, 419–22).

95. Ibid., 64 iv.1–2 (Diercks, 422, especially l. 59).

a newborn child, still covered in blood and afterbirth. The comment may also reflect the view that at their birth babies were still under the influence of spirits over which one had no control. As part of the early Christian baptismal ceremony, the ritual kiss aided in expressing the establishment of a relationship with the neophyte as a member of the Christian community.[96] In addition, Cyprian was willing to interpret such a kiss of a newborn as an act of kissing "the still recent hands of God themselves." When embracing "the human being lately formed and freshly born," one is "embracing that which God has made," and that on which the imprint of God's hand is still visible and touchable.[97]

With respect to Fidus's concern that one ought to wait on baptism until the eighth day, Cyprian argued on the basis of the supersession of the Old Law by the New Law "that spiritual circumcision ought not to be hindered by carnal circumcision." Given that God let Peter know that he "should call no man common or unclean" (Acts 10:28), Cyprian concluded that "absolutely every human being is to be admitted to the grace of Christ." If sinners guilty of the most heinous crimes were able to obtain remission of sins through baptism, Cyprian could not see any reason not to baptize "an infant, who, being lately born, has not sinned, except in that, being born after the flesh according to Adam, it has contracted the contagion of the ancient death at its earliest birth." When this infant is baptized it receives the forgiveness of sins, "not his own sins, but the sins of another." At the close of the letter, which, as Cyprian repeated, represented "our judgment in council [*in concilio nostra sententia*]," he enlisted the voices of the newborn infants in support of his conviction that they should receive baptism. For when "infants and newly born persons," who "deserve more from our help and from the divine mercy," are "lamenting and weeping from the first moment of their coming forth in birth," they are doing nothing else but asking to receive that grace of baptism.[98]

Cyprian's *Letter to Fidus* provided Augustine with a welcome precedent when Augustine was making the case for infant baptism in the early fourth

---

96. On the ritual of the kiss as baptismal practice, see F. J. Dölger, "Der Kuß im Tauf- und Firmungsritual nach Cyprian von Carthago und Hippolyt von Rom," *Antike und Christentum* (1929), 186–96. For the role of kissing in establishing family identity in the early Christian church, see the discussion by Michael L. Penn, "Performing Family: Ritual Kissing and the Construction of Early Christian Kinship," *Journal of Early Christian Studies* 10.2 (2002), 151–74.

97. Cyprian of Carthage, *Letters* 64 iv.2 (ed. Diercks, *Sancti Cypriani Episcopi Epistularium*, 422, ll. 61 and 63).

98. Ibid., 64 v.1–2 and 64 vi.2 (Diercks, 423–25).

century. In *Letter* 166, Augustine explicitly relied on "the blessed Cyprian," who wished "to correct those who thought that an infant should not be baptized before the eighth day." Augustine emphasized Cyprian's point of saving souls by declaring the practice of baptizing children before the eighth day not to be an incident of "inventing any new doctrine, but preserving the firmly established faith of the Church." Augustine thought "that a child may be properly baptized immediately after its birth."[99]

Whereas Cyprian's *Letter to Fidus* argued that Christians ought not take the practices surrounding circumcision as their model, around A.D. 400 Augustine was inclined to develop parallels between circumcision and baptism in his arguments. If people were to dismiss the authority of the Church and the apostolic authority of the councils, but still "seek for divine authority in this matter [of infant baptism]," as he argued against the Donatists, "the parallel of circumcision" could still allow one to "form a true conjecture" with regard to "the value of the sacrament of baptism in the case of infants." As one of "God's earlier people" Abraham "was justified" before he was circumcised, a scene which foreshadowed "Cornelius ... [who] was enriched with the gift of the Holy Spirit before he was baptized."[100] Augustine implied that arguments for the early baptism of infants based on comparisons with circumcision have to be regarded as valid.

In the controversies over Pelagius's teachings, the question of infant baptism continued to play an important role. In his treatise *On the Forgiveness of Sin and the Baptism of Children*, Augustine argued against the Pelagians that from their shared admission of the necessity of baptizing infants the Pelagians ought to be able to see that further doctrinal consequences, particularly the admission of original sin, had to be derived. Given that children were "being washed by the sacrament" and were "reconciled to God" to "live in Him, and be saved, and delivered, and redeemed, and enlightened," and given that they were thus set free "from death, and the vices, and guilt, and thralldom, and darkness of sin," given moreover that they did "not commit any sin in the tender age of infancy by their actual trans-

---

99. Augustine, *Letters* 166.23 (ed. A. Goldbacher, *S. Aureli Augustini Hipponensis Episcopi Epistulae, Pars III. Ep. CXXIV–CCXXXIV A* [Vindobonae: F. Tempsky, 1904], 579; trans. Sister Wilfrid Parsons, *Saint Augustine. Letters. Vol. IV (165–203)* [New York: Fathers of the Church, 1955], 27).

100. Augustine, *On Baptism against the Donatists* 4.24.31 (ed. M. Petschenig, *Sancti Aureli Augustini Scripta Contra Donatistas* [Vindobonae: F. Tempsky, 1908], 145–375, here 259; trans. J. R. King, "The Seven Books of Augustine, Bishop of Hippo, on Baptism, against the Donatists," in *Augustin: The Writings against the Manichaens and against the Donatists*, NPNF, 1st ser., vol. 4 [Peabody, Mass.: Hendrickson Publishers, repr. 1995], 411–514, here 461).

gression," original sin was the only explanation for why they were baptized in the first place.[101] Likewise in the context of the Pelagian controversies, Jerome availed himself of arguments related to the baptism of infants. To the question, "why little children are baptized," he responded without hesitation in A.D. 415 "that their sins may be forgiven."[102]

In earlier years, and in a context that required not polemics but rather pastoral, pedagogical, and diplomatic skills, Jerome could write to the parents of young children with the intention of demonstrating not only that they had the responsibility of bringing their child to baptism, but also that they themselves would derive benefit from doing so. In his *Letter* 107 to Laeta from A.D. 403, Jerome made it clear that until a child was able to discern good and evil, the child's parents were responsible for his or her actions. Jerome hypothesized that some parents might imagine "that, if they are not baptized, the children of Christians are liable for their own sins; and that no guilt attaches to parents who withhold from baptism those who by reason of their tender age can offer no objection to it." Yet Jerome attempted to dissuade parents from such a line of reasoning. He told them that since "baptism ensures the salvation of the child, this in turn brings advantage to the parents." In the end, however, he merely stated *that* there was an advantage for parents in having their children baptized; *what* exact-

---

101. Augustine, *De peccatorum meritis et remissione et de baptismo parvulorum ad Marcellinum libri tres* bk. 1, ch. 39 (ed. Carolus F. Urba and Ioseph Zycha, *Sancti Aureli Augustini De peccatorum meritis et remissione et de baptismo parvulorum ad Marcellinum libri tres, De spiritu et littera liber unus, de natura et gratia liber unus, de natura et origine animae liber quattuor, contra duas epistulas Pelagianorum libri quattuor* [Vindobonae: F. Tempsky, 1913], 3–151, here 38; trans. Peter Holmes, Robert Ernest Wallis, and Benjamin B. Warfield, "A Treatise on the Merits of Forgiveness of Sins, and on the Baptism of Infants," in *Augustin: Anti-Pelagian Writings,* NPNF 1st ser., vol. 5 [Peabody, Mass.: Hendrickson Publishers, repr. 1995], 15–78, here 30). For considerations of the role of baptism, particularly infant baptism, in Augustine and Pelagius, see also Martha Ellen Stortz, "'Where or When Was Your Servant Innocent?' Augustine on Childhood," in *The Child in Christian Thought* (Grand Rapids, Mich.: Eerdmans, 2001), 78–102 and 467–77; Alfred Vanneste, "La nouvelle théologie du péché originel," *Ephemerides theologicae Lovanienses* 67.4 (1991), 249–77; Gerald Bonner, "Baptismus parvulorum," in *Augustinus-Lexikon* vol. 1, fasc. 4 (Basel: Schwabe, 1990), 592–602; John Ferguson, "In Defence of Pelagius," *Theology* 83 (1980), 114–19; and John H. S. Burleigh, "St. Augustine on Baptism," *Reformed Theological Review* 15 (1956), 65–80. For later, Western perspectives on the baptism of infants, see also Peter Cramer, *Baptism and Change in the Early Middle Ages, c. 200–c. 1150* (Cambridge: Cambridge University Press, 1993), 131–36.

102. Jerome, *Against the Pelagians* 3.18 (ed. C. Moreschini, *S. Hieronymi Presbyteri Opera. Pars III. Opera Polemica 2. Dialogus adversus Pelagianos* [Turnhout: Brepols, 1990], 122; trans. John N. Hritzu, "The Dialogue against the Pelagians," in *Saint Jerome. Dogmatic and Polemical Works* [Washington, D.C.: The Catholic University of America Press, c1965], 221–378, here 375–76).

ly that advantage was he left to the parents' imagination. Jerome's emphasis, however, returned to the theme of parents' responsibility for the proper moral upbringing of their children. Once they had made the choice to baptize their child, parents imperiled themselves by neglecting the child's Christian development.[103]

Later councils in North Africa also came out more forcefully than Cyprian and his episcopal colleagues in their regulations concerning the question of infant baptism. Canon 2 of the Council of Carthage in 418, for example, decreed "that whoever says that infants fresh from their mothers' wombs ought not to be baptized, let him [or her] be anathema."[104] Such statements reflect the influence of Augustine, who three years earlier, in his *Letter* 166, had commented that "anyone [who] shall say that even infants who depart life without sharing in this sacrament [of baptism] shall be made alive in Christ ... certainly goes counter to the teaching of the Apostle and condemns the whole Church." Immediately following, Augustine argued that it was the Church's practice to "haste to baptize infants because of the unquestioned belief that otherwise they cannot possibly be made alive in Christ."[105]

Although the North African Church established official regulations pertaining to the early baptism of children and pressed for immediate baptism after birth, the example of Augustine of Hippo himself, having been born to a Christian mother but not receiving baptism until age thirty-three, is a clear indication that such regulations were not followed by all Christian parents. In North Africa at least, we may assume that into the fourth century there was no unified practice regarding the baptism of children who came from Christian families. While the practice of baptizing infants appears to have been widespread enough that debates were conducted as to whether one should baptize on the eighth day, or the second, or the third, in other cases infants in the households of Christian parents remained without baptism.[106] Moreover, the concerns in support of pressing for a very early baptismal date for children were not widely shared outside of North Africa.

103. Jerome, *Letters* 107.6 (ed. Hilberg, *Sancti Eusebii Hieronymi Epistulae,* CSEL 55, 297–98; trans. W. H. Fremantle, G. Lewis, and W. G. Martley, "Letters," in *Jerome: Letters and Select Works,* NPNF 2nd ser., vol. 6 [Peabody, Mass.: Hendrickson Publishers, repr. 1995], 1–295, here 192).

104. Council of Carthage, *Canons* 2 (ed. Didier, *Le baptême des enfants,* 121).

105. Augustine, *Letters* 166.21 (ed. Goldbacher, *S. Aureli Augustini Hipponensis Episcopi Epistulae, Pars III,* 576; trans. Parsons, *Saint Augustine. Letters. Vol. IV,* 25).

106. See also Gärtner, *Familienerziehung in der Alten Kirche,* 65–68.

Sources from the Christian West and East witness that infant baptism was not the only, nor even the dominant, practice. Examples from Cappadocia and from Italy illustrate both the delay of baptism until early adulthood and the possibility that at times the gender of the newborn child may have been a factor when deciding for or against baptism in infancy. Jerome, who saw himself as "a Christian born of Christian parents and bearing the banner of the cross on [his] brow,"[107] had been "nourished on catholic milk" "from the cradle,"[108] but received baptism only as an adult.[109] Ambrose was chosen to become bishop of Milan while still a catechumen.[110] Both Basil of Caesarea and his friend Gregory Nazianzen were dedicated to God before their birth,[111] but they did not receive baptism until their later twenties.

Whether or not such hesitation to baptize children also extended to cases of female infants is a more difficult question. It has been suggested that the same reluctance to baptize infant girls born to Christian families cannot be detected. Both Pierre-Thomas Camelot and, following him, Michael Gärtner believe we know with certainty that both Marcella, the sister of Ambrose of Milan, and Macrina, the sister of Basil the Great and Gregory of Nyssa, were baptized at an earlier age than their brothers, implying that these girls were baptized as children.[112] One could easily imagine that in the case of girls, parental supervision of youthful chastity may have been regarded as an easier task to accomplish than in the case of boys. Yet Gregory of Nyssa's *Life of Macrina*, the main source of our knowledge of

107. Jerome, *Preface to the Commentary on the Book of Job* (ed. PL 28.1079–1084, here col. 1082).

108. Jerome, *Letters* 82.2 (ed. Hilberg, *Sancti Eusebii Hieronymi Epistulae*, CSEL 55, 109, ll. 9–10).

109. See Wright, "Infant Dedication," 355–56.

110. For discussion of this part of his life, see Neil Brendan McLynn, *Ambrose of Milan: Church and Court in a Christian Capital* (Berkeley: University of California Press, c1994), 51.

111. Gregory Nazianzen, *Orations* 18.11 (*Funebris in Patrem*) (ed. PG 35.395–1252 and PG 36.11–664 [*Orations* 18: PG 35.985–1044], here PG 35.997; trans. McCauley and others, *Funeral Orations by Saint Gregory Nazianzen*, 119–56, here 127) (praise for his mother Nonna who promised him to God and dedicated him immediately after birth); Gregory Nazianzen, *Orations* 43.73 (*Funebris in laudem Basilii Magni*) (ed. J. Bernardi, *Grégoire de Nazianze. Discours 42–43* [Paris: Les Éditions du Cerf, 1992], 116–307, here 288; trans. McCauley and others, *Funeral Orations by Saint Gregory Nazianzen*, 27–99, here 92) (on Basil as consecrated to God from infancy and from the very womb of his mother). See also Wright, "Infant Dedication," 356.

112. See Pierre-Thomas Camelot, "Le baptême des petits enfants dans l'église des premiers siècles," *La Maison-Dieu* 88 (1966), 23–42, here 29; and Gärtner, *Familienerziehung in der Alten Kirche*, 67, n. 2. Neither one, however, provides references to texts that would support such a view.

her life, does not speak of her baptism. Gregory did say that while the girl's mother was still pregnant with her, she saw in a dream how "she was carrying in her arms the child who was still within her womb." Macrina's mother also saw "that a being of greater magnificence in form and appearance than a mortal man addressed the child whom she was carrying as Thecla," and he did so three times. The name "Thecla" then, the name of the young virgin who figured prominently in the apocryphal *Acts of Paul (and Thecla)* and the name of the young woman "whose fame is great among the virgins," as Gregory himself explained, was understood to be Macrina's "secret name."[113] The discussion of name-giving, a reference to Thecla that is reminiscent of her functioning as a patron saint for the little girl, and the comment that the person in the dream called the child three times, all could be understood as indicators of some kind of dedication ceremony for the little girl, even before her birth. Yet there is no explicit reference to baptism by water or to baptism by "fire and spirit." While one is free to assume that little Macrina was baptized, we have not been able to provide textual evidence for such an assumption. The case is similar to that of Ambrose's sister Marcella.

Marcella features prominently in Ambrose's three books *On Virgins*, which are directly addressed to her. The only reference to baptism occurs in book 3, in a passage that equates the martyrdom of young virgins with baptism. Both baptism and martyrdom have the same effect of forgiving sins and allowing one to reach the heavenly kingdom.[114] Yet neither Marcella's baptism nor the baptism by water of young girls is featured. Until further evidence can be adduced, one will have to assume that gender may not have been such a decisive criterion for distinguishing who was to be baptized at an early age and who in early adulthood.

One of the prominent illustrations of the baptismal theology of the Cappadocian fathers is Gregory Nazianzen's *Oration* 40.[115] In this sermon delivered in A.D. 381, Gregory commented on the question of children's

113. Gregory of Nyssa, *Life of Macrina* 2 (ed. Maraval, *Grégoire de Nysse. Vie de Sainte Macrine*, 144, l. 22–146, l. 30; trans. Petersen, *Handmaids of the Lord*, 52–53).

114. Ambrose of Milan, *On Virgins (De virginibus ad Marcellinam sororem)* bk. 3, ch. 7, par. 34 (ed. and Italian trans. Salvati, *Sant'Ambrogio. Verginità*, 158–59; trans. de Romestin, and others, "Three Books of St. Ambrose, Bishop of Milan, concerning Virgins," 387).

115. Gregory Nazianzen, *Orations* 40 (ed. and trans. Claudio Moreschini and Paul Gallay, *Grégoire de Nazianze. Discours 38–41* [Paris: Les Éditions du Cerf, 1990], 198–311); for Gregory Nazianzen's baptismal theology, primarily in his *Orations* 39 and 40, see Brian Matz, "The Purifying Work of Baptism and the Christian Post-Baptismal Life according to Gregory Nazianzen" (Ph.D. thesis, Saint Louis University, Missouri, 2006).

baptism. He eagerly attempted to help parents overcome their hesitation at having their children baptized. To the parents of infant children he recommended that they not "let sin get any opportunity." Rather, parents were to let their child "be sanctified from his childhood, from his most tender age," to be "consecrated by the Spirit."[116] A few paragraphs later, Gregory fine-tuned his recommendation and specified more exactly the circumstances when baptism of children at their most tender age should occur. To those who asked whether children ought to be baptized, Gregory responded that "if any danger presses," baptism should be administered immediately. He was convinced that it was "better that they should be unconsciously sanctified than that they should depart unsealed and uninitiated." The best time for baptism, however, was after a child had completed his or her third year of life.[117] Gregory's explanation indicates that baptism was not performed primarily to wash children clean of any sins. One may also note the position of John Chrysostom, who, just a few years after Gregory's sermon, confirmed a practice of baptizing infants in his Church. Yet he also explained that this was done despite the fact that "they are not guilty of any sins."[118] When the early Church in the East baptized children, the sacrament was primarily understood as an aid in protecting or sealing children off against the attacks of sin.

One of the few treatises from the Christian East that deals with children's death and its consequences on their age of baptism is Gregory of Nyssa's *On Infants' Early Deaths*.[119] Gregory considered what was to be thought of the case of

---

116. Gregory Nazianzen, *Orations* 40.17 (ed. and trans. Moreschini and Gallay, *Grégoire de Nazianze. Discours 38–41*, 232, ll. 15–16; trans. Charles Gordon Browne and James Edward Swallow, "Select Orations of Saint Gregory Nazianzen Sometime Archbishop of Constantinople," NPNF 2nd ser., vol. 7, 365).

117. Ibid., 40.28 (Moreschini and Gallay, 262, l. 4–11; Browne and Swallow, 370).

118. John Chrysostom, *Ad Neophytos*, Discours III, sect. 6 (ed. and trans. Antoine Wenger, *Jean Chrysostome. Huit Catéchèses baptismales inédites* [Paris: Les Éditions du Cerf, 1957], 150–67, here 154). See also J. P. Bouhot, "Version inédite du sermon 'Ad neophytos' de S. Jean Chrysostome, utilisée par S. Augustin," *Revue des études augustiniennes* 17 (1971), 27–41.

119. Gregory of Nyssa, *On Infants' Early Deaths* (ed. Hadwig Hörner, "De infantibus praemature abreptis," in *Gregorii Nysseni Opera Dogmatica Minora. Pars 2* [Leiden: E. J. Brill, 1987], lxxxv–cxlvi and 65–97; trans. William Moore and Henry Austin Wilson, "On Infants' Early Deaths," in *Select Writings and Letters of Gregory, Bishop of Nyssa*, NPNF 2nd ser., vol. 5, 372–81). See also the discussion by Jane Baune, "The Fate of Babies Dying before Baptism in Byzantium," in *The Church and Childhood*, 115–25. For detailed discussion of Gregory's treatise, see the papers collected in J. C. M. van Winden and A. van Heck, eds., "Colloquii Gregoriani III Leidensis. 18/23-IX-1974. Acta" (Leiden, 1976), typescript.

a human being [who] enters on the scene of life, draws in the air, beginning the process of living with a cry of pain, pays the tribute of a tear to Nature, just tastes life's sorrows, before any of its sweets have been his, before his feelings have gained any strength; still loose in all his joints, tender, pulpy, unset; in a word, before he is even human (if the gift of reason is man's peculiarity, and he has never had it in him), such a one, with no advantage over the embryo in the womb except that he has seen the air, so short-lived, dies and goes to pieces again; being either exposed or suffocated, or else of his own accord ceasing to live from weakness.[120]

Including both boys and girls without mentioning girls explicitly, Gregory wondered whether such a little one's soul would be judged, "stand with the rest before the tribunal," or "undergo its trial for deeds done in life." Yet he also was not sure whether a little child who died just as it had begun to live would "receive the just recompense by being purged, according to the Gospel utterances, in fire, or refreshed with the dew of blessing."[121] In the end, "recompense" or "retribution" *(antidosis)* was Gregory's key word. According to him, such a little child would not experience any retribution, neither in a negative nor in a positive sense. Thus Gregory explained,

We may speak, then, in this way also as regards this question of the infants: we may say that the enjoyment of that future life does indeed belong of right to the human being, but that, seeing [that] the plague of ignorance has seized almost all now living in the flesh, he who has purged himself of it by means of the necessary courses of treatment receives the due reward of his diligence, when he enters on the life that is truly natural; while he who refuses Virtue's purgatives and renders that plague of ignorance, through the pleasures he has been entrapped by, difficult in his case to cure, gets himself into an unnatural state, and so is estranged from the truly natural life, and has no share in the existence which of right belongs to us and is congenial to us. Whereas the innocent babe has no such plague before its soul's eyes obscuring its measure of light, and so it continues to exist in that natural life; it does not need the soundness, which comes from purgation, because it never admitted the plague into its soul at all.[122]

The reason that the baby who died would not receive any retribution or recompense was not so much that it had not received baptism. In fact, in the whole of Gregory's treatise the word baptism does not occur once. Rather,

---

120. Gregory of Nyssa, *On Infants' Early Deaths* (ed. Hörner, "De infantibus," 72–73; trans. Moore and Wilson, "On Infants' Early Deaths," 373–74 [modified]).

121. Ibid. (Hörner, 73; Moore and Wilson, 374).

122. Ibid. (Hörner, 82–83; Moore and Wilson, 376–77).

the baby had not developed beyond the natural stage of life, was still nourished only with milk and not with meat (cf. 1 Cor 3:2). Since the child had not been able to use reason to approach God, it had not had an opportunity to partake of God by knowing him. Thus it both did not have to and would not be able to approach God and become like God in the life thereafter in the same manner in which the person who led a virtuous life would be able to do. Yet what exactly happened to that child, no reasonable person would dare to say.[123] Christians in the East were significantly more concerned with a person's intellectual and spiritual development, at times parallel to or even independent of the person's integration into strict sacramental practices.

Returning to the West, one may notice that it is not necessary to claim that the phenomenon of withholding baptism for little children was a new practice introduced in the fourth century. At the turn from the second to the third century Tertullian argued that a delay in baptism was "more useful" and that baptism should be delayed until children could really understand what they believed.[124] Some have interpreted this as foreshadowing a "crisis" in the fourth century known as "baptismal delay," in which parents put off baptism for so long that children or young adults ran a greater risk of dying without initiation.[125] Yet in many places, it appears to have been a well-established practice, alongside infant baptism. Instead of baptizing one's child as an infant, one could enroll him or her in the ranks of the catechumens. Here again, Augustine's case serves as a good example.[126] His mother made sure he received the salt of the catechumens, but saw no need to have him baptized during his childhood years—except once when she felt he might die from a sickness, but then cancelled baptismal plans when the boy suddenly recovered.[127]

At least one other reason has to be considered as explanation why some parents did not have their young children baptized.[128] As the Church was forming, baptism of adults was the main and even, early on, the only means of obtaining remission of sins. With the growing intensity and refinement of developing penitential practices and systems, parents were hesitant to baptize their little children only to expose them to the necessity

---

123. Ibid. (Hörner, 84–85 and 87; Moore and Wilson, 378 and 379).

124. Tertullian, *De baptismo* 18 (ed. and trans. Refoulé and Drouzy, *Tertullien. Traité du Baptême*, 92–93).

125. See Jeremias, *Infant Baptism*, 87–97.

126. See the discussion and references in Wright, "Infant Dedication," 353–55.

127. Augustine of Hippo, *Confessions* I xi (17) (ed. Verheijen, *Sancti Augustini. Confessionum Libri XIII*, 9–10; trans. Chadwick, *Saint Augustine: Confessions*, 13–14).

128. Gärtner, *Familienerziehung in der Alten Kirche*, 86.

of undergoing rigorous and demanding penitential acts at a later point in their lives. If a young man, perhaps more often than a young woman, gave in to temptations and to the strong urges of desire, sexual and otherwise, during his teenage years and fell into sin, baptism postponed to one's early adult life was a more convenient way of taking care of the accumulated debts in the divine ledger.

Even when children were not baptized until later in their lives, it did not mean that they were not considered part of the Church or were not received in some formal way into the flock. For children in Christian families childhood clearly was not a time without participation in and exposure to the worship and prayer life of the community. In fact, sufficient evidence exists to suggest that even during the supposed time of the crisis of children's baptism, children of Christians were presented to the priest shortly after birth and were signed with the cross.[129] Different regions witness additional practices. Augustine, for example, reported in his *Confessions* that children in North Africa also received salt at that instance.[130] This ritual of the reception of the child into the Church, which is still conducted in Eastern Christian churches and is called either "churching" or "dedication,"[131] preferably was conducted on the fortieth day after birth, or at times also on the eighth day after birth, parallel to circumcision. It was not intended to replace baptism, yet it was not a merely private matter either. Rather, it was considered equivalent to the child's reception into the status of a catechumen.[132] After dedication but before baptism, the Christian child was

---

129. John Chrysostom, *Homilies on 1 Cor.* 12.7 (ed. PG 61.9–382, here 106); Jerome, *Preface to the Commentary on the Book of Job* (ed. PL 28, col. 1082); and Marc the Deacon, *Vita Porphyri* 45 (ed. and trans. Henri Grégoire and M.-A. Kugener, *Marc le Diacre. Vie de Porphyre, Évêque de Gaza* [Paris: Les Belles Lettres, 1930], 37–38). On the latter, see also Timothy D. Barnes, "The Baptism of Theodosius II," *Studia Patristica* 19 (1989), 8–12.

130. Augustine of Hippo, *Confessions* I xi (17) (ed. Verheijen, *Sancti Augustini. Confessionum Libri XIII*, 9, l. 4; trans. Chadwick, *Saint Augustine: Confessions*, 13); see also Wright, "Infant Dedication."

131. For discussions of this custom, see, for example, Charles Caspers, "Leviticus 12, Mary and Wax: Purification and Churching in Late Medieval Christianity," in *Purity and Holiness: The Heritage of Leviticus* (Boston: E. J. Brill, 2000), 295–309; Anne-Marie Korte, "Reclaiming Ritual: A Gendered Approach to (Im)Purity," in *Purity and Holiness: The Heritage of Leviticus*, ed. Marcel Poorthuis and Joshua Schwartz (Boston: E. J. Brill, 2000), 313–27; Walter von Arx, "The Churching of Women after Childbirth," in *Liturgy and Human Passage*, ed. David Power and Luis Maldonado (New York: Seabury Press, 1979), 63–72; and Günther Kehnscherper, "The 'Churching of Women': Leviticus 12 and Luke 2:21–24: The Law of Purity and the Benediction of Mothers," *Studia Patristica* 18.2 (1989), 380–84.

132. Augustine of Hippo, *Confessions*, V xiv (25) and VI xi (18) (ed. Verheijen, *Sancti Augus-*

looked at as an "unbaptized Christian" *(christianos abaptistos)*,[133] one who was already considered to be a "child of the Church," but who also needed and received special mention as a catechumen or otherwise during the prayers of intercession.[134] As catechumens, and certainly once they were baptized, children in Christian families were considered part of the Church and thus were allowed and expected to participate in the Christian liturgy.

Children's Participation in the Eucharistic Liturgy

Both the presence of children and the breaking of bread were features of the worship life of early Christians assembled in the *oikos* to praise God. Children were a part of the households that converted to the Christian faith. Acts 2:46 shows that from the very beginning early Christians in Jerusalem not only "spent much time together in the temple" but also "broke bread at home and ate their food with glad and generous hearts." The meal envisioned in Acts 2:42 can reasonably be argued to have been an *agapē* meal, which included a ritual commemoration of the death and resurrection of Jesus. To the extent that children were part of a given household in which such gatherings for the meal took place, nothing seems to preclude the assumption that they also participated in this meal. Evidence discussed in chapter 6 points to the preference in the Greco-Roman world for child slaves as servants at mealtime. This may be taken as an indication that children were not excluded from communal meals. We also have evidence from the Jewish world that indicates that children regularly participated in meals held at the occasion of special celebrations, such as the Passover.[135]

Given the clear connections between the Jewish Passover meal and the developing early Christian Eucharistic liturgy,[136] it is relevant to point to

---

tini. *Confessionum Libri XIII,* 71–72 and 85–86; trans. Chadwick, *Saint Augustine: Confessions,* 89 and 104); Kleijwegt, "Kind," 920.

133. See Heinzgerd Brakmann and M. Metzger, "Katechumenat," in *Reallexikon für Antike und Christentum* 20 (2003), 497–574, here 553.

134. *Apostolic Constitutions* 8.6.9 and 8.12.44 (ed. and trans. Metzger, *Les Constitutions Apostoliques, Tome III,* 154–55 and 202–3).

135. See Barclay, "The Family as the Bearer of Religion," 72, who cites Passover as particularly significant, listing Exodus 13:8; Philo, *Spec. leg.* 2.145–49; and *m. Pesahim* 10.4.

136. See, for example, the studies and comments by Clemens Leonhard, "Pessachhaggada und Osternacht. Gegenseitige Beeinflussung von jüdischer und christlicher Liturgie," *Kirche und Israel. Neukirchener Theologische Zeitschrift* 16 (2001), 45–47; Demetrius Dumm, "Passover and Eucharist," *Worship* 61 (1987), 199–208; and George S. Bebis, "Influence of Jewish Worship on Orthodox Christian Worship," *Greek Orthodox Theological Review* 22 (1977), 136–42.

the fact that children are pictured as participating rather naturally in meals that Christian families held at special occasions as well. The late-second-century *Acts of Paul (and Thecla),*[137] for example, tells of an instance when Onesiphorus, his wife, and his children accompanied the Apostle Paul on his flight. The group was in hiding "in an open sepulcher" on the way "from Iconium to Daphne." All had been fasting for a while, including the children. After a few days, the boys became hungry. Since there was no place nearby to buy any bread, and since Onesiphorus had left behind all his earthly possessions "and followed Paul with all his house," Paul gave his upper garment to one of the boys and told him to go and "buy several loaves and bring them." As the story goes, the boy also met Thecla on the way and brought her back with him to the group and to Paul. When all were reunited, "there was much love within the sepulcher, for Paul rejoiced, and Onesiphorus, and all of them. And they had five loaves, and herbs, and water (and salt), and they rejoiced for the holy works of Christ."[138] Quite obviously, the whole group including the children shared a meal together, which was a meal celebrated with "much love" and in rejoicing—or might one also understand thanksgiving?—"for the holy works of Christ." At the very least the reader witnesses how children participated in *agapē* meals of early Christians at the end of the second century.

Child communion in Cyprian's *De lapsis* is not spoken of as a novelty, but is introduced to the reader in the context of a discussion of lapsed Christians,[139] implying that children participated in the Eucharist. This is also the case in *Apostolic Constitutions* 8.12–14,[140] which describes the communion of children. In addition, early Christian documents provide specific instructions for how to handle children's reception of the Eucharist. Christian children who had been baptized were allowed to participate in the full liturgy without any restrictions. Those who were catechumens could participate only within the limits set for such catechumens.

With the development of the Eucharistic liturgy, the participation of children in the Eucharistic celebration and their partaking of the Eucharistic gifts continued and were seen as natural. What regulated children's

---

137. For the dating of the *Acts of Paul (and Thecla),* see Bremmer, "The Apocryphal Acts," 153.

138. *Acts of Paul (and Thecla)* 23 and 25 (ed. Lipsius and Bonnet, *Acta Apostolorum Apocrypha,* vol. 1, 251 and 253). For a discussion of the social context of children at family meals, see also Nielsen, "Roman Children at Mealtimes."

139. Cyprian of Carthage, *De lapsis* 9, 25, and 26 (ed. and trans. Maurice Bénevot, *Cyprian: "De Lapsis" and "De Ecclesiae Catholicae Unitate"* [Oxford: Clarendon Press, 1971], 2–55, here 14–15 and 36–39).

140. Ed. and trans. Metzger, *Les Constitutions Apostoliques, Tome III,* 176–211.

admission were the same penitential requirements that affected adults. In A.D. 459, in a letter to Rusticus, Leo the Great had to deal with a question pertaining to young Christians who, "after being baptized in infancy," were torn away from their parents' influence. Rusticus wanted to know whether such young Christians who had been captured by non-Christians, incorporated into their manner of life and religious system, but then repatriated "to Roman territory still being young people," were allowed to commune at the commemoration of the death of Jesus. Leo ruled that if such young people had "only lived with Gentiles and eaten sacrificial food," purification "by fasting and laying on of hands," with the assumption that in the future they would abstain "from things offered to idols," sufficed to admit them to Eucharistic fellowship. If they had actively "worshipped idols," killed someone, or committed acts of fornication, they could "be admitted to communion" only after having performed public penance.[141]

Within the church building, children formed a group of their own and were assigned to a special place, or were found with their mothers, especially the little ones on their mothers' arms.[142] While children were allowed to participate in processions taking place inside and outside of the church,[143] not all children seemed to have displayed the same exemplary behavior that Athanasius reported for little Antony.[144] The *Apostolic Constitutions* provides our fullest account of specific instructions regulating children's behavior during the Eucharistic prayers. At the time of the anaphora, a deacon kept guard over the children who stood at the bema, while the mothers received special instruction and admonition to keep their very small children with them. When the time came for the reception of the Eucharist, children followed immediately after the priests, deacons, and ascetics. Children clearly were given communion before the adult laity.[145] Inta

---

141. Leo the Great, *Letters* 167, question 19 (ed. PL 54.1197–1209, here col. 1209; trans. Charles Lett Feltoe, "Letters," NPNF 12, 2nd ser. [Peabody, Mass.: Hendrickson Publishers, 1995], 1–114, here 112).

142. *Didascalia Apostolorum* 2.57.8 (ed. F. X. Funk, *Didascalia et Constitutiones apostolorum* [repr. Turin: Bottega d'Erasmo, 1964], vol. 1, 164). See also Marc the Deacon, *Vita Porphyri* 66 (ed. and trans. Grégoire and Kugener, *Marc le Diacre. Vie de Porphyre, Évêque de Gaza,* 52).

143. Egeria, *Diary* 31.3 (ed. Aetio Franceschini and Robert Weber, "Itinerarium Egeriae," in *Itineraria et alia geographica* [Turnholt: Brepols, 1965], 37–90, here 77, l. 17; trans. John Wilkinson, *Egeria's Travel,* 3rd ed. [Warminster: Aries & Philips, 1999], 152).

144. Athanasius, *Life of Antony* 1.2 (ed. and trans. Bartelink, *Athanase d'Alexandrie: Vie d'Antoine,* 130, ll. 3–5; trans. Gregg, *Athanasius: The Life of Antony,* 30). See also the discussion in chapter 8.

145. *Apostolic Constitutions* 8.11.10, 8.12.2, and 8.13.14 (ed. and trans. Metzger, *Les Constitutions Apostoliques,* Tome III, 174–77 and 210–11). See also John Moschus, *Pratum Spirituale* 196

Ivanovska has convincingly argued that this ordering may reflect a conviction that due to their simplicity and perceived innocence before God children may have been seen as closer in worthiness to the ranks of the ordained and dedicated than the general adult laity.[146] A tradition of allowing children to receive communion prior to adults continued to be documented in later sources, such as the writings of the sixth-century Basileios Kilix.[147] There is no reason to assume that children received the Eucharist any less frequently, or more often, than adults did. Children who had been baptized seem to have received the Eucharist regularly from the earliest years of their life. As Cyprian witnessed, however, the very little ones received communion only under the species of wine, appropriate to their still limited capacities for eating and swallowing solid foods.[148] As they grew older, like everyone else children received the Eucharist under the species of both bread and wine. Consecrated gifts that were left over from the Eucharistic meal were given to little children to eat after the service, a practice documented in the *Church History* of Evagrius Scholasticus.[149]

Children and Prayer

Prayer surrounded the life of a Christian child. One of the first instances of a child's exposure to prayer was the occasion of its parents' prayer at its birth. The *Apology* of Aristides from the first half of the second century preserves precious evidence that at the birth of a child, the Christian parents "give thanks to God." In case of the death of the child, a common occurrence in pre-modern societies, prayer also accompanied the child's passing away. Aristides informed his reader that "if ... it [i.e., the child] happens to die in childhood," which is not limited to the time immediately following the birth, "they [i.e., the parents] give thanks to God the more, as for one who has passed through the world without sins."[150] While some

(ed. PG 87, 3, 2852–3112, here 3081B; trans. John Wortley, *The Spiritual Meadow of John Moschus* [Kalamazoo, Mich.: Cistercian Publications, 1992], 173).

146. See Inta Ivanovska, "Children in the Eucharistic Setting: A Study of the Christian Liturgical Practice from the Sub-Apostolic Period to Augustine," paper delivered to the Ph.D. seminar "God's Family," Saint Louis University, spring 2005.

147. See Kleijwegt, "Kind," 921.

148. Cyprian, *De lapsis* 25 (ed. and trans. Bénevot, *Cyprian: "De Lapsis" and "De Ecclesiae Catholicae Unitate,"* 38–39). For further references, see Kleijwegt, "Kind," 921.

149. Evagrius Scholasticus, *Church History* 4.36 (trans. Michael Whitby, *The Ecclesiastical History of Evagrius Scholasticus* [Liverpool: Liverpool University Press, 2000], 241). Kleijwegt, "Kind," 921, provides references to later texts from the hagiographical tradition as well.

150. Aristides, *Apology* 15.9 (ed. and trans. Bernard Pouderon, Marie-Joseph Pierre, with

scholars have seen the reference to thanksgiving as a reference to baptism, this is not a necessary explanation. One may quite as well understand the two occurrences of thanksgiving in Aristides's *Apology* as an illustration of parental prayer of thanksgiving for their child, one in gratitude for receiving the child from God's hands, and the other as a prayer of gratitude that the child returned directly into God's hand, given that no sin separated it from God.

Within the context of family life, children actively participated in family prayer. Clement of Alexandria spoke of their prayer together with their parents,[151] especially at the times of family meals.[152] Similar observations also are recorded in Cyprian.[153] Chrysostom wanted parents to wake up their children at night to join the parents in prayers.[154] Like other Christian teachers who recommended that children learn how to read by studying and reciting the Psalms,[155] Chrysostom desired that children learn the Psalms, which by the fifth century had developed into an essential component of the daily liturgy of the hours that monks prayed.[156] As crucial as the Psalms were for prayer, Chrysostom also insisted that children should acquire a more general acquaintance with the Holy Scriptures,[157] and that after the liturgy they should speak at home with their parents about what they had heard at church.[158] While one can also catch the occasional glimpse at a child's intimate and personal prayer to God, for example at the occasion of a girl's offering of her doll to the Lord and accompanying that act with a short prayer, Chrysostom saw a role for parents in guiding their

---

the collaboration of Bernard Outtier and Maria Guiorgadzé, *Aristide. Apologie* [Paris: Les Éditions du Cerf, 2003], 242 [Syriac] and 243 [French]).

151. Clement of Alexandria, *Stromateis* 3.9.68, 1 (ed. Stählin and Früchtel, *Clemens Alexandrinus. Zweiter Band. Stromata. Buch I–VI*, 226).

152. Clement of Alexandria, *Stromateis* 7.7.49.3–4 (ed. Otto Stählin, Ludwig Früchtel, and Ursula Treu, *Clemens Alexandrinus. Dritter Band. Stromata Buch VII–VIII. Excerpta ex Theodoto—Eclogae Propheticae—Quis Dives Salvetur—Fragmente* [Berlin: Akademie-Verlag, 1970], 37).

153. See also Cyprian, *Ad Donatum* 16 (ed. and trans. Jean Molager, *Cyprien de Carthage. A Donat et la vertue de patience* [Paris: Les Éditions du Cerf, 1982], 114–17).

154. John Chrysostom, *Homilies on Acts* 26.4 (ed. PG 60.97–204, here 203).

155. See Jerome, *Letters* 107.12 (ed. Hilberg, *Sancti Eusebii Hieronymi Epistulae*, CSEL 55, 302, l. 18), and *Letters* 128.4 (Hilberg, CSEL 56.1, 160, l. 11).

156. John Chrysostom, *On Vainglory* 34 and 60 (ed. and trans. Malingrey, *Jean Chrysostome. Sur la vaine gloire et l'éducation des enfants*, 126–27 and 158–59 [*tās theias epōdas*]); and John Chrysostom, *Homilies on Colossians* 9.2 (ed. PG 62.299–392, here 362).

157. John Chrysostom, *Homilies on Ephesians* 21.1 (ed. PG 62.9–176, here 150). See also chapter 4

158. John Chrysostom, *De ss. martyribus* 4 (ed. PG 50.645–54, here 652); and John Chrysostom, *De poenitentia* 6.1 (ed. PG 49.277–350, here 315).

children to the regular practice of prayer in the home and at church in a structured manner.[159]

Other witnesses that can be gathered from early Christian texts show how children's prayer life was enforced in different institutional settings, for example, in the monastery. While Basil of Caesarea recommended in his *Long Rules* that the living quarters of children who grew up in a monastery be separate from those of the brethren of more advanced age and stature, "the prayers assigned for recitation throughout the day should, however, be said in common by young and old."[160] This comment provides valuable evidence for children's participation in communal prayer, and more specifically for participation in the regular daily hours of the monastery. More formal roles for children at prayer times during the liturgy will be considered in the following discussion of children's official roles during the church's service.

Children and Church Offices

There is evidence that children played a visible and audible role in liturgical services in the early Church, fulfilling multiple official functions. They sang in choirs, served as lectors, and were assigned special roles during times of prayer. Our discussion of children's play has already considered aspects of children's singing, inside and outside of church. In the course of time children's church choirs developed into a permanent fixture of the liturgy.[161] Here the discussion will focus on children in the service of the spoken word, namely, children's roles as lectors in reading from the Scriptures and their special roles in the intercessory prayer of the Church.

159. For studies of Chrysostom's view of family life and children, see Leyerle, "Appealing to Children"; Vigen Guroian, "The ecclesial family: John Chrysostom on parenthood and children," in *The Child in Christian Thought*, ed. Marcia J. Bunge (Grand Rapids, Mich.: Eerdmans, 2001), 61–77 and 475–76; D. O'Roark, "Parenthood in Late Antiquity: The Evidence of Chrysostom," *Greek, Roman, and Byzantine Studies* 40 (1999), 53–81; and Vigen Guroian, "Family and Christian Virtue in a Post-Christendom World: Reflections on the Ecclesial Vision of John Chrysostom," *St. Vladimir's Theological Quarterly* 35.4 (1991), 327–50.

160. Basil of Caesarea, *Regulae fusius tractatae (Long Rules)*, quaestio 15.2 (ed. PG. 31.889–1052, here 953; trans. Sister M. Monica Wagner, *Basil of Caesarea. Ascetical Works* [New York: Fathers of the Church, 1950], 265).

161. Johannes Quasten has been able to gather and discuss a wealth of information on the topic in *Musik und Gesang in den Kulten der heidnischen Antike und christlichen Frühzeit*, 2nd enlarged ed. (Münster: Aschendorffsche Verlagsbuchhandlung, 1973), trans. Boniface Ramsey, *Music and Worship in Pagan and Christian Antiquity* (Washington, D.C.: National Association of Pastoral Musicians, 1983).

For the time from the fourth century on, epigraphical evidence is available that some Christian children served as lectors.[162] Lives of monks that contain information about the childhood of their protagonists at times provide information about special dedications or consecrations to liturgical services to which the ascetic was already commissioned as a little boy. Cyril of Scythopolis, for example, reported that Abba Euthymius's mother dedicated her infant son to the service of God. She gave her child over into the hands of Bishop Oltreios, who baptized Euthymius, tonsured him, and appointed him lector of his Church at the age of two. Moreover, Bishop Oltreios arranged that little Euthymius would become part of the bishop's household to be fed and raised there.[163] Cyril also knew of other monks in Palestine who as children were dedicated to a life in the service of the Church. Cyriacus, for example, who was the son of a presbyter and a relative of the bishop of Corinth, was ordained a lector as a little child.[164]

While not all lectors necessarily moved on to a clerical career, the evidence for those who did seems to be more plentiful than for those who did not. Epiphanius of Pavia, for example, was ordained a lector at age eight, but then had to wait until he was eighteen before he would be admitted to the next step in the ordination process and become a subdeacon.[165] Marc Kleijwegt noted that there exists a remarkable wealth of evidence for similar early ordinations throughout the Roman Empire. While Victor of Vita, as we saw in chapter 6, commented on the death of child lectors among the Catholic clergy in Carthage when they were attacked by the Vandals, decrees of the Roman bishops Siricius (A.D. 385), Innocence (404), and Zosimus (418) confirm that children could be ordained *"ab infantia"* to be-

---

162. *CIL* 8, 453 (ed. T. Mommsen, *Corpus Inscriptionum Latinarum*, vol. 8: *Inscriptiones Africae Latinae* [Berlin: G. Reiner, 1881], 64); *CIL* 11, 1709 (ed. E. Bormann, *Corpus Inscriptionum Latinarum*, vol. 9: *Inscriptiones Aemiliae, Etruriae, Umbriae Latinae* [Berlin: G. Reiner, 1888–1926], 391); see also G. W. Clark, "An illiterate lector?" *Zeitschrift für Papyrologie und Epigraphik* 57 (1984), 103–4, here 103; and E. Josi, "Lectores—scola cantorum—clerici," *Ephemerides Liturgica* 44 (1930), 282–90, here 283–84, who also provides further evidence for young lectors who had died while still young. See also Kleijwegt, "Kind," 922–24.

163. Cyril of Scythopolis, *Life of Euthymius* 2–3 (ed. Eduard Schwartz, *Kyrillos von Skythopolis* [Leipzig: J. C. Hinrichs Verlag, 1939], 6–85, here 9–11; trans. R. M. Price and John Binns, *Cyril of Scythopolis: The Lives of the Monks of Palestine* [Kalamazoo, Mich.: Cistercian Publications, 1991], 1–92, here 5–6).

164. Cyril of Scythopolis, *Life of Cyriacus* 1 (ed. Schwartz, *Kyrillos von Skythopolis*, 222–35, here 223, ll. 6–8; trans. Price and Binns, *Cyril: Lives of the Monks*, 245–61, here 245).

165. Felix Ennodius, *Life of Epiphanius of Pavia* 8 (ed. Wilhelm Hartel, *Magni Felicis Ennodii Opera Omnia* [Vindobonae: Apud C. Geroldi Filium Bibliopolam Academiae, 1882], 331–83, here 332–33, see especially 332, l. 25). See also Kleijwegt, "Kind," 923.

come lectors.[166] We agree with Kleijwegt, who sees that the main concerns that promoted such early ordinations were a general desire for children's early formation in the faith and control over young people's lifestyles, especially the sexual conduct of those in the clerical ranks. Assumptions about children's innocence, purity, and a special religious sensibility, as Johannes Quasten has suggested, may also have played a role in selecting young boys as lectors.[167] Girls do not seem to have been admitted to the ranks of lectors, but they took the veil at about the same time that they could have become married, which may indicate that less concern existed regarding their sexual corruption.

With the evidence for boys holding the ranks of lectors, we have seen some evidence for children's early participation in specific functions at the liturgy as well as children's early admission to certain ranks leading up the ladder of the ministerial hierarchy. Whether or not children had access to such services in the first place depended not only on their gender. It also appears to have been contingent on the quality of a given child's baptism, or more specifically on the quality and type of church affiliation of the person administering baptism to them. A canon of the so-called African Code, established in A.D. 419, required that further discussion was needed "concerning those infants ... who are baptized by Donatists." One was concerned that regulations be provided so that children should be converted to Christianity with a firm determination of their faith. Given that it had not been "of their own will" that they received baptism among the Donatists instead of among the Catholics, they should not have to feel the consequences of "the error of their parents," which might prevent them from approaching the Christian mysteries or exclude them from ordination.[168]

Next to gender-specific offices like that of the lector, children's choirs featured girls, especially in Syria, as we saw in chapter 5, where Ephraem the Syrian's hymns were composed explicitly for choirs of virgins. Yet a broader task, that of active participation in the prayers of the liturgy, was also open to both boys and girls. Especially appreciated was the children's

---

166. On the youthful age of lectors, see also E. Peterson, "Das jugendliche Alter der Lektoren," *Ephemerides Liturgica* 48 (1934), 437–42.

167. Quasten, *Musik und Gesang*, 133; see also Quasten, *Music and Worship*, 87–92.

168. *African Code (A.D. 419)*, Canon 47/51 (trans. Henry R. Percival, "The Canons of the CCXVII Blessed Fathers Who Assembled at Carthage. Commonly Called The Code of Canons of the African Church. A.D. 419," in *The Seven Ecumenical Councils of the Undivided Church. Their Canons and Decrees, together with the Canons of all the Local Synods which have Received Ecumenical Acceptance*, NPNF 2nd ser., vol. 14 [repr.: Peabody, Mass.: Hendrickson, 1995], 441–510, here 463).

prayer of intercession, for instance, for the catechumens.[169] During the litany of the faithful, participation in which was reserved for those who had
been baptized, children took over the prayers of intercession on behalf of
the concerns of the community of the faithful in Antioch. Chrysostom explained that because of their innocence and simplicity children were able to
function as mediators between God and the sinful adults in a special manner.[170] When the children were praying, they either recited the respective
prayer verse alone, or they stood while praying and adults knelt. At the occasion of her visit to the Church of Jerusalem, Egeria observed that at the
time of the evening prayer children (*pisinni*, literally "little ones") responded with *Kyrie eleison* to the reading of the individual names in the litany.[171]
The prayer of children seemed to be especially advantageous before God,
because their young age moved God to pity and "was most deserving of divine philanthropy," as Gregory Nazianzen explained.[172] Even during times
of famine, some parents, as Basil of Caesarea complained, sent only their
dependent and innocent children to the prayers of repentance at church.
Although the children may have found the service at church preferable to
school and teacher, Basil commented disapprovingly that the little children
did not really know how to pray.[173] Yet there are examples enshrined in the
memory of the early Church that children were more than willing to learn,
even in their own playful ways. As seen above, church historians provided
accounts of children imitating liturgical celebrations in their play, thus reinforcing and taking on as their own what they had seen at church.[174] An
example of a child who exceeded what Basil perhaps would have expected

169. *Apostolic Constitutions* 8.6.9 (ed. and trans. Metzger, *Les Constitutions Apostoliques,*
Tome III, 154–55).

170. John Chrysostom, *Homilies on Matthew* 71.4 (ed. PG 58.661–68, here 666). See also
Franz Joseph Dölger, *Sol salutis: Gebet und Gesang im christlichen Altertum, mit besonderer Rücksicht auf die Ostung in Gebet und Liturgie* (Münster: Aschendorff, 1972), vol. 1, 86–89.

171. Egeria, *Diary* 24.5 (ed. Franceschini and Weber, "Itinerarium Egeriae," 68, l. 39; trans.
Wilkinson, *Egeria's Travel*, 143).

172. Gregory Nazianzen, *Orations* 16.13 (ed. PG 35.952C). See also Pseudo-Clement of
Rome, *Recognitions* 5.30.5 (ed. Bernhard Rehm and Georg Strecker, *Die Pseudoklementinen II.
Rekognitionen in Rufins Übersetzung*, GCS [Berlin: Akademie Verlag, 1994], 183, l. 30; trans. André Schneider and Luigi Cirillo, *Les "Reconnaissances" du pseudo Clément. Roman chrétien des
premiers siècles* [Turnhout: Brepols, 1999], 333).

173. Basil of Caesarea, *Homilia dicta tempore famis et siccitatis* (ed. and trans. PG 31.303–328,
here 309 and 312).

174. See above, chapter 5. See also Rufinus of Aquileia, *Church History*, 10.15 (ed. Theodor
Mommsen, "Rufinus Vorrede, Einlage über Gregorius Thaumaturgus, Buch X und XI," in *Eusebius Werke. Zweiter Band. Zeiter Teil. Die Kirchengeschichte*, ed. Eduard Schwartz, Theodor Mommsen, and Friedhelm Winkelmann, GCS 6.2 [Berlin: Akademie Verlag, 1999], 951–1040, here

of children who knew how to pray is that of Simeon Stylites the Younger. He joined the monastery at the age of six all by himself, received his first pillar at the age of seven, and prayed fifty to eighty Psalms every day.[175]

Conclusions and Prospects

This chapter examined the manner in which children were incorporated into the Christian community. Beginning with the statements of the importance of children in the words attributed to Jesus in the canonical Gospels, children were essential to the concept of what it means to become a Christian. The evidence concerning the baptism of children is significant, suggesting a practice that, if not universal from the beginning of the second century, cannot be dismissed as nonexistent on the basis of contrary evidence. It is a safe assumption that children participated in some way in the liturgy and meal commemorating the death and resurrection of Jesus. Christianity's first churches were located in houses, and the fact that Christians assembled to partake of a communal meal in a domestic setting implies that children, at least those of the house where the celebration occurred, were present. From the third century on, the evidence for children as liturgical participants becomes much clearer.

The iconic value of children in Christian literature reflects the Greco-Roman belief that, by virtue of their innocence, their prepubescent "purity," and their honesty, children ought to be seen as being closer to the divine than adults. In this sense, children become signs of the myth of the First Humans, which is common to many foundation stories (Gn 2–3, the earliest Iranian religion, etc.). In this respect, the witness of apocryphal Christian material greatly enhances the background of the New Testament texts. The notion of seeking the "beginning" rather than the "end," found in *logia* in the *Gospel of Thomas* and other early traditions preserved in the apocrypha, can be seen as part of this First Human myth in which the idea of childhood in the Gospels is situated. A comprehensive discussion of this aspect of children remains a desideratum.

980–81); and John Moschus, *Pratum Spirituale* 196 and 197 (ed. PG 87, 3, 3080–3084 and 3084–3085; trans. Wortley, *The Spiritual Meadow*, 172–74 and 174–75).

175. *Vita Simeon Stylites Iunioris* 12, 15, 17 (ed. and trans. Paul van den Ven, *La vie ancienne de S. Syméon Stylite le jeune (521–592)* [Brussels: Société des Bollandistes, 1962], vol. 1, 11 and 13–14). For Theodoret of Cyrrhus's childhood experience of the performance of ascetics in Syria, including that of Simeon, see the discussion in Horn, "Children as Pilgrims and the Cult of Holy Children in the Early Syriac Tradition."

eight

𝒦

Children and Christian Asceticism

Early Christians generally displayed a positive attitude toward the child. Most Christians in antiquity continued to marry and many desired to have children. At times they struggled with then-current views that children could be seen as the guarantee of one's own resurrection.[1] Those who had children, as Clement of Alexandria acknowledged, loved their sons and daughters more than anything else. Christians offered their children parental affection and were acknowledged as "good fathers" and "good parents."[2] Although some important early Christian teachers demonstrated less than exuberant joy and interest in promoting marriage and procreation, and portrayed such lifestyle choices and participation in the world in depreciative terms, married life and the raising of children did have its defenders among Christian authors. Some of them encouraged boys and girls to choose the right kind of married life.

On the whole, however, voices other than those that praised, defended, and promoted marriage and childbearing were the stronger ones. A range of early Christian texts, including the New Testament, evince a tendency to highlight not so much the joys of having children as the burden of it all. Novatian saw virginity as the continuance of infancy, and since the virginal

1. See, for example, *Acts of Paul (and Thecla)* 14 (ed. Lipsius and Bonnet, *Acta Apostolorum Apocrypha*, vol. 1, 245, ll. 4–5).

2. Clement of Alexandria, *Paedagogus* 1.9 (ed. Marcovich and van Winden, *Clementis Alexandrini "Paedagogus,"* 46); and Clement of Alexandria, *Protreptikos* X.107.3 (ed. Marcovich, *Clementis Alexandrini "Protrepticus,"* 157).

state admitted no children and in fact had "contempt for offspring," it was free "from the calamity of the death of children."[3] Taking care of children also required much labor and energy on the part of the parents, and in the end was seen as diverting a person from pursuing the goal of the heavenly kingdom. Thus for some, children and family life did not seem to fit well with the life of the perfect Christian. As children grew up in this slowly emerging Christian tradition and absorbed the relatively new and greater emphasis on renunciation and abstention from married life, the option of living a life of virginity and withdrawal from worldly affairs in asceticism emerged as a real choice. This final chapter of our study explores some of the ways in which children encountered asceticism as both an increasingly established and a highly valued choice.[4]

Children and the Message of Renunciation in the New Testament

If understood as an undifferentiated whole, the New Testament is fraught with contradictions over the role of the family in the spiritual attainment of the individual. There are regulations for family life, and the ideal family is described, if only in an ad hoc manner. Yet the call of the gospels to abandon even one's family to follow Jesus seems squarely opposed to the ideals of family life. Matthew presents Jesus as acknowledging solitary Christians who are sexually continent (Mt 19:11–12). Identification of the "eunuchs for the kingdom of heaven" remains difficult.[5] The term strictly understood ex-

3. Novatian, *De bono pudicitiae* 7 (ed. Hartel, *S. Thasci Caecilli Cypriani Opera Omnia*, CSEL 3.3, 18; trans. Wallis, "Treatises Attributed to Cyprian: 'Of the Discipline and Advantage of Chastity,'" 589). See also chapter 3 above.

4. The literature on ancient asceticism is rather vast. Only a brief selection that aids in offering some orientation can be presented here. Raymond Van Dam, *Families and Friends in Late Roman Cappadocia* (Philadelphia: University of Pennsylvania Press, 2003), offers a study with an emphasis on family relationships within ascetic endeavors, and ascetic endeavors within family structures in Cappadocia. Vincent L. Wimbush and Richard Valantasis, eds., *Asceticism* (New York: Oxford University Press, 1995), includes helpful essays on methodological questions. Susanna Elm, *"Virgins of God": The Making of Asceticism in Late Antiquity* (Oxford: Oxford University Press, 1994), studies women's role in the ascetic enterprise within the geographically limited regions of Asia Minor and Egypt. Philip Rousseau, *Pachomius: The Making of a Community in Fourth-Century Egypt* (Berkeley: University of California Press, c1985), studies ascetical developments in Egypt. André Jean Festugière, *Antioche païenne et chrétienne; Libanius, Chrysostome et les moines de Syrie* (Paris: E. de Boccard, 1959), focuses on asceticism in the Syrian context.

5. For possible connections to Qumran, see Constantin Daniel, "Esséniens et eunuques, Matthieu 19:10–12," *Revue de Qumran* 6 (1968), 353–79. For selected early Christian voices on this verse, see, for example, Josef Blinzler, "Justinus Apol. I, 15,4 und Matthäus 19,11–12," in

cludes women from this category, and it implies an involuntary mutilation of the male genitalia so as to render him infertile, or even incapable of sexual intercourse, not the "voluntary celibacy" of the later Christian church.

Celibacy was a part of Second Temple Judaism and Matthew's *logion* may reflect a continuation of celibacy in the early rabbinic period. The two most prominent examples of Jewish celibacy were the Essenes, often identified (not without controversy) with the community at Qumran, and the Therapeutae, who are described by Philo of Alexandria.[6] Ancient evidence concerning the Essenes claimed that at least some of them lived a celibate life in their communities.[7] In *On the Contemplative Life,* Philo described the Therapeutae as a celibate group living on the outskirts of Alexandria. Their community showed striking parallels to later Christian monastic communities, with members who left their families behind, including children and wives (*Contempl.* 18), and who seemed to live not only in continence but also in chastity (*Contempl.* 65–68).[8] The members of the community spent most of their time alone, each in a "cell" called a *monastērion,* which is perhaps the earliest occurrence of this word in Greek literature (*Contempl.* 24, 30).[9]

As described by Philo, the ascetic life of the Therapeutae had many similarities to the life to which Jesus called his disciples, and to the life that children saw as the model of the Christian existence. Philo indicated that some members had been part of the community since childhood (*Contem-*

Mélanges bibliques. En homage au R. P. Béda Rigaux (Gembloux, Belgium: J. Duculot, 1970), 45–55; as well as Origen of Alexandria's experience, according to Eusebius of Caesarea, *Church History* 6.8.1–2 (ed. Schwartz, Mommsen, and Winkelmann, *Eusebius Werke. Zweiter Band. Zweiter Teil. Die Kirchengeschichte,* GCS, N. F. 6.2, 534).

6. While some have doubted the existence of this group, this is not the general consensus. For a recent discussion, consult Mary Ann Beavis, "Philo's *Therapeutai*: Philosopher's Dream or Utopian Construction," *Journal for the Study of the Pseudepigrapha* 14.1 (2004), 30–42, esp. 40–41, for her assessment that the Therapeutae were a historical community.

7. Pliny the Elder, *Natural History* 5.73 (ed. and trans. H. Rackham, *Pliny. Natural History. With an English Translation in Ten Volumes,* vol. II, *libri III–VII* [Cambridge, Mass.: Harvard University Press, 1942], vol. 2, 276–77); Josephus, *Jewish War* 2.120, 160–61 (ed. and trans. H. St. J. Thackeray, *Josephus. In Nine Volumes,* vol. 2: *The Jewish War. Books I–III* [London: William Heinemann, 1926], 368–69); and Philo, *Hypoth.* 11:14–17 (ed. and trans. Colson, *Philo,* vol. 9, 442–43), who cites his *Apologia pro Judaeis.* For a short discussion of the issue regarding the Essenes, the Qumran sectarians, and the Dead Sea Scrolls, see James C. VanderKam, *The Dead Sea Scrolls Today* (Grand Rapids, Mich.: Eerdmans 1994), 71–98, and especially 70–71 on the question of marriage.

8. Joan E. Taylor, "Virgin Mothers: Philo on the Women Therapeutae," *Journal for the Study of the Pseudepigrapha* 12.1 (2001), 37–63.

9. See F. H. Colson's note on *monastērion* in LCL, *Philo IX,* 519–20.

pl. 67). In support of the presence of children at other Jewish ascetic communities, one also notes with interest debates among scholars regarding archaeological evidence for the presence of children at Qumran.[10]

Celibacy is well attested at the Qumran community on the Dead Sea, which was dissolved in A.D. 68 during the First Jewish War with the Romans. In the Qumran context, celibacy was part of the training for the eschatological battle between the Sons of Light and the Sons of Darkness. Insofar as the kingdom of heaven in Matthew is an eschatological kingdom, Jesus' remark about the "eunuchs for the kingdom of heaven" may have reflected early Christian continuation of this idea, which was central to the Qumran community, at least in its earlier stages. This is supported by the fact that the Qumran community seems to have also admitted women and children in the first century A.D. A community in which there were clearly older celibate men and new recruits who had known family life may have been mirrored in Matthew's community. However, it is not clear whether the Qumran community required initiates who brought a family to remain celibate.

Similar to the challenges to family life that can be witnessed in the ascetic inclinations of the Essenes and Therapeutae, one can sense in Jesus' teaching the beginnings of a devaluation and revaluation of family ties for those who were part of the spiritual community. Jesus displays conflicting attitudes toward the care of family members. In Matthew 8:14–15, he is presented as visiting Peter's house, and upon seeing Peter's mother-in-law lying in bed sick with fever, he heals her through his touch, restoring her to family life. To the son who wished to delay following Jesus in order to bury his father, Matthew has Jesus say, "Follow me, and let the dead bury their own dead" (Mt 8:21–22). Taking care of funeral arrangements for one's parents was an acknowledged responsibility in the ancient world.[11] Jesus' call to radical discipleship challenged such established family customs and

---

10. Jodi Magness, "Women at Qumran?" in *What Athens Has to Do with Jerusalem: Essays on Classical, Jewish, and Early Christian Art and Archaeology in Honor of Gideon Foerster* (Louvain: Peeters, 2002), 89–123, here 90–93.

11. For studies of the Scripture passage's implications regarding ancient burial practices, see for example Herbert W. Basser, "Let the Dead Bury Their Dead: Rhetorical Features of Rabbinic and New Testament Literature," in *Historical, Literary, and Religious Studies*, eds. Herbert W. Basser and Simcha Fishbane, Approaches to Ancient Judaism, n.s., vol. 5 (Atlanta: Scholars Press, 1993), 79–95; and Byron R. McCane, "'Let the Dead Bury Their Own Dead': Secondary Burial and Matt 8:21–22," *Harvard Theological Review* 83 (1990), 31–43; Hans G. Klemm, "Das Wort von der Selbstbestattung der Toten: Beobachtungen zur Auslegungsgeschichte von Mt 8:22 Par.," *New Testament Studies* 16 (1969), 60–75, for rhetorical dimensions of the comment.

seemingly counteracted, disregarded, and frustrated the duties of children toward their parents.[12]

The narrative setting in which this Jesus-logion appears in the Gospel of Luke provides a context that explains more clearly why conflict between responsibilities toward family and the response to Jesus' call may have emerged. The author of Luke added an exhortation to Matthew 8:22, telling the son who wishes to bury his father to "go and proclaim the kingdom of God" (Lk 9:60). And in response to yet another person in this scene, who wished to follow Jesus but asked to be allowed to "first say farewell to those at [his] home" (Lk 9:61), Jesus again responded with a reference regarding the unfitness for the kingdom of God of the one who put a hand to the plow but then looked back (Lk 9:62). Unique in the New Testament Gospels, Luke 9:61–62 is an allusion to 1 Kings 19:20: "I will follow you, Lord, but let me first say goodbye to my family [lit. 'those in my house']." Jesus replies, "No one who puts a hand to the plow and looks back is fit for the kingdom of God." Luke, like Matthew, presents a saying concerning the eschatological nature of Christianity, one that may reflect the concept of the day of the Lord in the prophetic literature of the Hebrew Bible (cf. Zep 1:7ff.). Both parables are metaphors for vacillation between following Jesus and not following him. The literary mechanism that these two parables assume may be found in the Old and New Testaments. When the end time arrives, the eschatological parousia of Jesus, there will no longer be any time to decide whether one is for or against. This sudden aspect of the end time may in Luke's and Matthew's communities reflect their reception of Paul, such as 1 Thessalonians 5:2: "The day of the Lord will come like a thief in the night"; or it may allude to acts of persecution, when the individual must make a "yes or no" declaration of his or her allegiance to Jesus.

However, there are other social realities that these passages may suggest. Followers of Christ, especially those who committed themselves to preaching the Gospel and to striving for the kingdom of God, could not be tied down by emotional or customary family bonds. They had to be able to wander freely, without any strings attached, to wherever the work of spreading the Gospel would take them. When caught between obligations toward family and children on the one hand and the call to proclaim the message of salvation throughout the world on the other, bonds to fam-

---

12. See also the discussion in Horn, "Children at the Intersection of Classical and Early Christian Popular Literature."

ily and kin had to be severed.[13] Such a disruption of attachment to family, probably including children, may have been behind Peter's cry to Jesus in Matthew 19:27 that the apostles had left "everything" to follow Jesus.[14]

In the New Testament Gospels, breaking family bonds meant replacing the physical family with the spiritual one. Mark 10:29–30 presents Jesus' wry reply to Peter's statement that the disciples have left everything (10:28). Those who have left behind everything will gain all of it back "in this life" one hundredfold "with persecutions [*meta diōgmōn*]" and, yes, also eternal life in the world to come.[15] Here, Peter and the disciples, as elsewhere in Mark's Gospel, fundamentally misunderstand discipleship. In the previous passage, Jesus has told a rich man that he must give away all his possessions in order to gain "treasure in heaven" (Mk 10:17–22). The disciples are perplexed that Jesus then warns them that it is difficult for a rich man to enter the kingdom of heaven (Mk 10:23–27), which leads to Peter's statement that the disciples have given up "everything." It is the phrase "with persecution" that explains this entire sequence of passages. The rich man, like the disciples, misunderstands the physical sacrifice that the Christians of Mark's community perhaps grasped from firsthand experience, along with the fact that the reward for their witness to the Gospel would not be re-

---

13. For work on the perspectives of the Gospels regarding family division and the renunciation of the family, see for example Arland D. Jacobson, "Jesus against the Family: the Dissolution of Family Ties in the Gospel Tradition," in *From Quest to Q: Festschrift James M. Robinson*, eds. Jon M. Asgeirsson, Kristin de Toyer, and Marvin W. Meyer (Louvain: Louvain University Press, 2000), 189–218; Fred Strickert, "Jesus' True Family: The Synoptic Tradition and Thomas," in *For a Later Generation: The Transformation of Tradition in Israel, Early Judaism, and Early Christianity. Festschrift for George W. E. Nickelsburg*, eds. Randal A. Argall, Beverly A. Bow, and Rodney A. Werline (Harrisburg, Pa.: Trinity Press International, 2000), 246–57; Arland Dean Jacobson, "Divided Families and Christian Origins," in *The Gospel behind the Gospels: Current Studies on Q*, ed. Ronald A. Piper (Leiden: E. J. Brill, 1995), 361–80; Khiok-Khng Yeo, "The Mother and Brothers of Jesus (Lk 8:19–21, Mk 3:31–35, Mt 12:46–50)," *Asia Journal of Theology* 6 (1992), 311–17, which provides enlightening perspectives on the interpretation of the respective verses from Chinese conceptions of the family; Mahlon H. Smith, "Kinship Is Relative: Mark 3:31–35 and Parallels," *Forum* 6 (1990), 80–94; Marshall S. Scott, "Honor Thy Father and Mother: Scriptural Resources for Victims of Incest and Parental Abuse," *Journal of Pastoral Care* 42 (1988), 139–48, here 146–47 for a discussion of how such anti-familial or anti-parental perspectives can be used positively as sources of healing.

14. Luz, *Matthew*, 516–17; and Gundry, *Matthew*, 391–92.

15. See also the verses Matthew 19:29 and Luke 18:29, which do not expand in detail on the future reward by listing "houses, brothers and sisters, mothers and children" in the way Mark does. On these passages, see also David M. May, "Leaving and Receiving: A Social-Scientific Exegesis of Mark 10:29–31," *Perspectives in Religious Studies* 17 (1990), 141–51 and 154; Thomas E. Schmidt, "Mark 10:29–30, Matthew 19:29: 'Leave Houses . . . and Region'?" *New Testament Studies* 38 (1992), 617–20; and Robert H. Gundry, "Mark 10:29: Order in the List," *CBQ* 59 (1997), 465–75.

ceived until the next world. Having a larger family (perhaps a metaphor for the Christian community) also implies suffering. Whether one is rich or poor, or as a disciple has received more in this world than what one has suffered, Matthew and Luke define discipleship as persecution.

With this in mind, the expansion on the "hundredfold . . . in this age" does not include a mention of "father," and this omission may be taken as a clue to the new reality of the community of the followers of Christ gathered under the kingship of the one father in heaven. Mark brings one closer to the experiential reality of wandering preachers of the Jesus movement who left possessions and blood relationships behind, but who, through preaching the Gospel, gained new "brothers and sisters" in Christ. These, like Paul in 1 Corinthians 3:1–3, conceived of themselves as parents of new, spiritual children.[16] Wandering missionaries, whom Christians were invited to entertain and shelter at the most for three days, are also evidenced in the *Didache*.[17] Yet the question of what happened to such missionaries' offspring and spouses and how they dealt with the departure of their parent, husband, or wife did not play a role in the text.[18]

Subsequent early Christian texts emphasize the exchange of biological offspring for spiritual children. The model seems to have come from the earliest stages of Christianity. Paul renounced his right to travel with a believing wife (1 Cor 9:5–6, 12, 15) and willingly chose celibacy (1 Cor 7:8). He often mentions his spiritual children and his spiritual parentage. These spiritual children could be individuals, such as Onesimus (Phlm 10), Timothy (1 Cor 4:17), or the entire congregation of a given church (1 Cor 4:14; 2 Cor 6:13; Gal 4:19; 1 Thes 2:7, 11). One can see the model developed also in the apocryphal acts of apostles. In the *Acts of Thomas* I.12, Jesus promised a young couple on their wedding night "living children" if they would renounce sexual intercourse altogether.[19] In such instances, the

---

16. Amy-Jill Levine, "Gender, Judaism, and Literature: Unwelcome Guests in Household Configurations," *Biblical Interpretation* 11.2 (2003), 239–46, here 239, on the new family's being based on loyalty to Jesus.

17. *Didache* 12 (ed. and trans. Ehrman, *Apostolic Fathers*, vol. 1, 436–37).

18. For relevant literature on the impact of the spread of Christianity and the missionary impulse on the family, see for example S. Guijarro Oporto, *Fidelidades en conflicto: La ruptura con la familia por causa del discipulado y de la misión en la tradición sinóptica* (Salamanca: Publicaciones Universidad Pontificia, 1998); and David C. Sim, *The Gospel of Matthew and Christian Judaism: The History and Social Setting of the Matthean Community* (Edinburgh: T&T Clark, 1998). See also Halvor Moxnes, *Putting Jesus in His Place: A Radical Vision of Household and Kingdom* (London: Westminster John Knox Press, 2003).

19. *Acts of Thomas* I.12 (ed. Bonnet, *Acta Apostolorum Apocrypha*, vol. 2.2, 118, ll. 4–5).

renunciation of family for the sake of proclaiming the Gospel was replaced by sexual renunciation as a form of witness to Christ's message. Family ties and offspring had to be rejected while spiritual relatives and children in the Christian community were promised.

Neither of the synoptic parallels to Mark 10:29–30 in Matthew 19:29 and in Luke 18:29 expand the promise for this age to include a detailed list of relatives and offspring. Thus a significant portion of the synoptic tradition witnesses to the fact that Jesus did not announce any substitutes in this world for those who gave up family and children for the sake of the Gospel. The only reward was what one could expect in heaven. The traditions reflected in Matthew and Luke also show an even more radical dimension of the required rejection of family and offspring. Luke 14:25–26 has Jesus confront large crowds, saying, "Whoever comes to me and does not hate [*ou misei*] his [or her] father and mother [*ton patera heautou kai tēn mētera*], wife and children [*ta tekna*], brothers and sisters [*tous adelphous kai tas adelphas*], yes, and even life itself, cannot be my disciple."[20] In the Gospel of Matthew, the author phrased this *logion* less antagonistically by preferring a comparative mode of expression. There Jesus was made to say that "the one who loves son or daughter more than me [*philōn huion hē thygatera hyper eme*]" is "not worthy of me" (Mt 10:37).[21] Yet the basic message remains that a disciple of Jesus has to subordinate every relationship to the primacy of his or her relationship to Jesus. In both Matthew and Luke, the immediately following verse adds the requirement of carrying the cross as the necessary sign and condition of the disciple, thus emphasizing the radical nature of the decision that is required.

20. For discussion of some relevant aspects of Luke 14:26, see Robert H. Stein, "Luke 14:26 and the Question of Authenticity," *Forum* 5 (1989), 187–92, which elucidates the Old Testament background to divisions in the family, illustrated, for example, in Micah 7:5–6; Leif E. Vaage, "Q and the Historical Jesus: Some Peculiar Sayings (7:33–34, 9:57–58, 59–60, 14:26–27)," *Forum* 5 (1989), 159–76; and Ieuan Ellis, "Jesus and the Subversive Family," *Scottish Journal of Theology* 38.2 (1985), 173–88, which challenges the impression that may seem to be supported by Luke 14:26 that Jesus hated family life, or subscribed to an anti-family ideology more broadly.

21. George Howard, "The Textual Nature of an Old Hebrew Version of Matthew," *JBL* 105 (1986), 49–63, here 58, records as "interesting reading" the expansion "not worthy to be with me in the kingdom of heaven" for Matthew 10:37. For other studies, including those that consider Matthew 10:37 from the perspective of comparison with Luke 14:25–26, see J. Duncan M. Derrett, "Hating Father and Mother (Luke 14:26; Matthew 10:37)," *Downside Review* 117 (1999), 251–72; Harry Fleddermann, "The Cross and Discipleship in Q," *Society of Biblical Literature Seminar Papers* 27 (1988), 472–82; and Andrew S. Jacobs, "'Let Him Guard Pietas': Early Christian Exegesis and the Ascetic Family," *JECS* 11.3 (2003), 265–81, which lays open not so much expected anti-family, but rather pro-family attitudes in patristic exegesis of the verses.

One might also consider that this was a saying addressed to children concerning the rejection of family bonds. One notices that the possessive pronoun in Luke 14:26 only accompanies the mention of the father *(ton patera heautou)* in this long string of accusative objects, all of which follow their respective direct articles in the Greek. The author thus emphasized the *pater familias*. Whether or not one assumes that mother, wife, children, brothers, sisters, and "life itself" are all later additions, this emphasis on the father makes it possible to see the saying addressed primarily to those under the authority of the father, and therefore also to children.[22] In Matthew 10:37, the saying concerning preferential love falls into two halves, presented in parallel structure: first the mention of father and mother, and then a second group consisting of "son and daughter." It does not take much to see that the first half is addressed to children in relation to their parents, while the second half considers the perspective of parents. The character of the first half of the *logion* as one intended for children is even more obvious than in Luke 14:26. Matthew 10:37 and Luke 14:26 present evidence that the message of preferential love and attachment to Jesus, even to the point of rejection or "hate" for family bonds, is one strand of proclamation which early Christian children could absorb from their encounter with Scripture.

Children may also have seen Jesus as a model for renouncing family ties, or for distancing themselves from parents. In a scene recounted in all three synoptic Gospels, Jesus is informed that his mother and brothers wished to speak with him. He countered with a rhetorical question: "Who are my mother and my brothers?" (Mk 3:33; cf. Mt 12:48 and Lk 8:21). Then he followed up with a redefinition of family as those "who hear the word of God and do it" (Lk 8:21; cf. Mk 3:34), while identifying them with his disciples in Matthew 12:49.

Children's Asceticism in Paul's Letters: 1 Corinthians 7:36–38

Within the corpus of Paul's writings, 1 Corinthians 7:36–38 constitutes a key passage concerning the question of whether a "virgin" should choose the path of marriage or of virginity. In Paul's newly founded churches, cases seem to have arisen in which young people, some of whom were already promised and engaged to future spouses, began to reconsider whether mar-

---

22. Gärtner, *Familienerziehung in der Alten Kirche*, 149–50, considers the possibility of the verse being addressed originally to young people, whose primary personal ties are with their parents. He does not single out the father figure as such.

ried life was compatible with the Christian calling, or in which the parents of young people questioned whether married life was the proper choice for their children. Longstanding questions and debates have focused on how to translate this passage from the Greek. Critical readers have struggled in particular over whether Paul was responding to fathers who wanted their daughters to remain celibate or to a fiancé who wished to live in a celibate, or spiritual, marriage with his betrothed.[23] Regardless of its precise meaning, the questions this passage raised were fundamental for young persons considering marriage. They had to be concerned about whether marriage was still permissible for Christians or whether young couples who were engaged could resolve not to get married, but live in sexually inactive, celibate relationships. Parental or societal expectations or personal desires and passions for the opposite sex could create insurmountable pressures on the young people in such cases.

Older English translations of the Bible, such as the King James Version and the Jerusalem Bible, translated 1 Corinthians 7:36–38 as having to do with the question of whether or not fathers ought to let their daughters be married at all in light of Paul's teachings on the eschaton. At present, every major English translation (RSV, NRSV, NIV, NJB, NAB) rejects this reading and instead interprets these verses in light of the purported practice

---

23. See John Martens, "Fathers and Daughters in 1 Corinthians 7:36–38: The Social Implications for Children of Parents' Belief in Christ," paper presented at the Society of Biblical Literature meeting, Philadelphia, 2005, for a fuller discussion of the passage in light of Roman marriage law and practice. Gregory Lockwood, *1 Corinthians*, Concordia Commentary (St. Louis: Concordia Publishing House, 2000), 263–64, grounds the text in the life of a couple that is engaged to marry. Raymond F. Collins, *First Corinthians*, Sacra Pagina Series, vol. 7 (Collegeville, Minn.: Liturgical Press, 1999), 299, tends toward understanding Paul as writing about an engaged couple. For Richard Horsley, *1 Corinthians* (Nashville: Abingdon Press, 1998), 108, and Jerome Murphy-O'Connor, *1 Corinthians* (New York: Doubleday, 1998), 72, the passage focuses particularly on the sex drive of the male in the relationship. Hans-Josef Klauck, *1. Korintherbrief* (Würzburg: Echter Verlag, 1984), 57–58, shows that from the ancient Church to the nineteenth century, this passage was seen as referring to a father dealing with his virgin daughter. Yet he believes that "sexuelle Untertöne" in the passage make this unlikely. Thus he thinks that the passage more likely refers to engaged couples living together, which the Church fathers knew of also; he also thinks it could (possibly) refer to a relationship between a master and a slave girl. William F. Orr and James Arthur Walther, *1 Corinthians*, The Anchor Bible (New York: Doubleday, 1976), 223–24, sees the text as probably referring to a father and his daughter. See also the discussions in Robert Hurley, "To Marry or Not to Marry: The Interpretation of 1 Cor 7:36–38," *Estudios bíblicos* 58.1 (2000), 7–31; Giorgio R. Castellino, "1 Cor. VII, 36–38 nel diritto orientale e nella etnologia," in *Mélanges Eugène Tisserant. Vol. 1. Écriture Sainte—Ancien Orient*, vol. 1 of 7 (Vatican City: Biblioteca Apostolica Vaticana, 1964), vol. 1, 31–42; and Richard Kugelman, "1 Cor. 7:36–38," *CBQ* 10.1 (1948), 63–71.

in Corinth of spiritual marriage. Yet understanding the passage from such a perspective leads to numerous problems in dealing with the straightforward meaning of the Greek text. In addition, such interpretations do not pay close attention to the social context of the reception of Christianity in society or to the Greco-Roman understanding of marriage in the context of which daughters, often young ones, were given to their spouses by their fathers.[24] Young women did not, as the current translations of this passage suggest, make these bonds with fiancés of their own accord. Rather than providing a discussion of a decision-making process that was going on between the couple, it seems that 1 Corinthians 7 supplies the reader with a sense of the transformation which Christianity wrought in children's lives, as related to early Christian teachings on marriage and sexuality. Thus the passage should be read in light of the ideal of celibacy for girls reaching the age of marriage, and the concerns parents and the girls themselves had to face in the process.[25]

Whereas it is possible to read this passage in the manner pursued by most English translations today—that Paul was advising those who were engaged to get married if their passions were strong—the present discussion adopts a reading that takes the object of Paul's concerns to be the fathers of the young daughters of Corinth. At the heart of the passage is a young girl or virgin *(parthenos)*. Bettina Eltrop has made a case for understanding references to some young women identified as *parthenoi* in the New Testament as girls who were under the age of twelve and a half, still unmarried, dependent on their fathers for decisions regarding marriage, biologically virgins, and possibly facing plans to get married in the fu-

---

24. See Orr and Walther, *1 Corinthians,* 223–24; and Martens, "Fathers and Daughters in Corinth," for a thorough discussion of the Greek and the problematic nature of its translation. When deciding on the object of Paul's exhortation and teaching, most interpreters mention that any translation of this passage runs into difficulties that seem insurmountable. Yet the current translations do damage to the clear and accepted sense of a number of words in the passage. Based on a reading of the NRSV, one may list the following: *parthenos,* "girl," "virgin," or "maiden" is translated as "fiancée"; *hyperakmos,* "sexually well-developed," "in physical prime," to be in "full bloom" is translated as "strong passions"; *gamizō,* "to give in marriage," "to be given in marriage" is rendered as "to marry" (E. Stauffer, "γαμέω, γάμος," in *TDNT,* vol. 1, 648–57, here 648, states that this verb means "to give in marriage," but 1 Corinthians 7:36–38 is not discussed in the whole article); and *peri tou idiou,* "concerning all of one's possessions," or "concerning all that belongs to one," is translated as "his own desire" (with *thelēmatos*).

25. See Dale B. Martin, *The Corinthian Body* (New Haven, Conn.: Yale University Press, 1995), 219–28, for a return to some of the arguments we propose here. Martin, however, argues that the issue at stake is a girl's sexual passions, not whether her father should give her in marriage.

ture.[26] Paul was also speaking of such a young girl in 1 Corinthians 7:36–37. Whether he was addressing her fiancé or her father, either way the daughter or virgin would not have had much choice in the decision-making process.

First Corinthians 7 as a whole is a passage that offers Paul's response to the Corinthians who had asked whether or not "it is well for a man not to touch a woman" (1 Cor 7:1). Paul's response consists of a conditional affirmation of marriage. In verse 25 Paul confessed that he had no teaching from the Lord regarding the marriage of *parthenoi*, but that in light of the current "crisis" *(ananke)* it seemed best to him that one remain in one's current state.[27] If a *parthenos* did marry, she did not sin (7:28). Yet if she did not marry, she, like an unmarried woman *(gyne agamos)*, was able to concern herself with the matters pertaining to the Lord (7:34). For Paul, the matter was plain: the celibate life is the superior state. The remaining question is why Paul returned to a discussion of the *parthenos* in verses 36–38 and whether interpreters should understand the referent of *parthenos* in verses 25, 28, and 34 as somehow different from that of *parthenos* in 36–38. A related question also is whether the translation of *parthenos* should switch to "fiancée" in these later verses.

Earlier Paul had spoken more generally about the marriage of girls and had addressed the question of what was the good and what the better choice. Yet he remained interested in some further aspects of the issue of the *parthenoi*. What was at stake in the questions raised in verses 36–38 seemed to be the practical and social implications of whether or not one should "give" one's daughter in marriage. This is the direct meaning of the verb *gamizo*, which also in Matthew 22:30 and 24:38 carries this meaning and generally is translated as "to give" in marriage. It cannot refer either to a betrothed's desire to marry or to the girl's desire to marry.[28] Thus the verb must refer

26. Eltrop, "Problem Girls," 164–65, provides the description on 165. On 164, she sees *hyperakmos* as a reference to *parthenon* and regards this as a special case of an "overage virgin," who is older than twelve and a half and thus no longer under her father's control. While we accept her reading of *hyperakmos* as a girl who is "overage" and so ready for marriage, this does not indicate that she is "beyond" her father's control. There is no entry for *hyperakmos* in the *TDNT*, but Henry George Liddell and Robert Scott, *A Greek-English Lexicon*, revised by Henry Stuart Jones (Oxford: Clarendon Press, 1985), 1859, define it as "sexually well-developed" with reference to 1 Corinthians 7:36–38. The verb *hyperakmazo* is defined as "to surpass in vigour or bloom" (1859). The verb *akmazo* is defined as "to be in full bloom, at the prime" (51).

27. On *ananke*, see W. Grundmann, "ἀνάγκη," in *TDNT*, vol. 1, 344–47, who describes the word as "compulsion or necessity" (345) or as a "situation of need" (346). Again, 1 Corinthians 7:36–38 is not discussed.

28. See Stauffer, "γαμέω, γάμος," 650–51, who deals with Jesus' use of the verb as "to give" and "to be given."

to the father's "giving of" the girl in marriage. Aside from the theological considerations, which Paul addressed in verses 36–38, and which a Christian father may have been compelled to take into account, issues of honor associated with having an unmarried daughter in the family also played a role. A father or guardian had to consider the possibility of having to honor preexisting marriage contracts and the financial implications of caring for an unmarried daughter when terminating an engagement for religious reasons.

One of the stumbling blocks for translators has been the focus on "sexual tension" in the passage, a point which both Hans-Josef Klauck and Dale Martin perceived,[29] and one which finds its locus in the understanding of the word *hyperakmos*. With Eltrop, we see the term as referring to the virgins who are literally "past the peak" of eligibility.[30] Two other passages aid in providing the reader with a clearer sense of the word's proper meaning in this pericope. In a fragment contained in *Stobaeus*, Callicratidas talked about choosing a bride. He said it was best to be on the lookout for a *paidion* who had good ancestors, who was in "full bloom" *(akmazousan)* to be married *(gamiskē)*.[31] As far as it is discernible from the fragmentary nature of the text, the issue in this passage was not with sexual tension, but with a child who was reaching puberty; this is the force of the verb *akmazō* that is implied in *Stobaeus*. A second example, admittedly deriving from a different context, discussed a young Christian martyr who preserved her virginity before she died. In the *Martyrdom of Potamiaena and Basilides*, Potamiaena is described as a girl *(korē)* who struggled to defend her virginity *(parthenia)*, and also is described as being in "full flower" *(akmaion)*.[32] From the context of the passage, it is clear that "full flower" does not mean "in heat." The term is purely descriptive of her age, an application that also seems to hold true for the case of Callicratidas's statement above.[33]

In the light of the evidence derived from the two complementary passages and the preceding discussion, one may best translate 1 Corinthians 7:36–38 as follows (the parenthetical comments suggest how our translation takes careful account of Paul's discussion of virginity and first-century marriage law and practice):

29. Klauck, *1. Korintherbrief*, 57–58; and Martin, *The Corinthian Body*, 219–28.

30. Eltrop, "Problem Girls," 164.

31. Stobaeus, *Florilegium* 4.28.18 (ed. Meineke, *Ioannis Stobaei Florilegium*, vol. 4, 687).

32. *Martyrdom of Potamiaena and Basilides* 1 and 5 (ed. Musurillo, *Acts of the Christian Martyrs*, 133, ll. 6 and 25).

33. For a fuller discussion of the evidence of these two passages, see Martens, "Fathers and Daughters in Corinth."

36: But if anyone thinks that he is behaving dishonorably toward his "daughter" (*parthenos*), if she has reached a prime marriageable age (*hyperakmos*) and so he is obligated to (let marriage) take place, whoever wishes this, let it happen, it is no sin, let them marry.

37: But whoever stands steadfast in his heart, not having any necessity (*anankē*, translated in v. 25 with respect to Paul's teaching on virgins as "crisis"), but rather having the freedom of will concerning his own (family member, cf. Lk 18:28) (*peri tou idiou*) and he has judged in his own heart to keep his daughter (*parthenos*), he will do well.

38: So that if he gives his daughter (*parthenos*) in marriage (*gamizō*), he does well; but if he does not give her in marriage (*gamizō*), he will do better.

The social assumptions underlying Paul's option for virginity may be seen as that of a father who wished to keep his daughter as a virgin for the Lord, but who felt compelled to do otherwise by a previously existing marriage contract which was to take effect when his daughter was *akmaios*. At the time of Paul's letter, however, she was already *hyperakmos*. In such a case, the father would be obligated to allow the marriage to take place. According to the *Digest*, Roman law suggested that a previously established marriage contract was binding[34] and did not have to take place in the presence of the actual parties to the betrothal.[35] Thus it could be contracted by two sets of parents, or by the father of the bride and the husband-to-be. The girl could be engaged to be married under the age of twelve,[36] but not before the age of seven.[37] In this case, the situation in Corinth could have involved a marriage contracted prior to the family joining the Christian Church. Then Paul responded to a situation where a father, taking Paul's advice, began to reevaluate the agreement. It is true that a contract for mar-

---

34. Justinian, *Digest* 23.1.1 (ed. and trans. Mommsen, Krueger, and Watson, *The Digest of Justinian*, vol. 2, 656). The laws referred to in Justinian's *Digest*, the most significant part of the *Corpus Iuris Civilis*, were compiled under the guidance of the Emperor Justinian in the sixth century. The jurists referenced in the present section flourished for the most part in the early third century (Ulpian; Modestinus). Due caution, therefore, is necessary when claiming that these laws can be used to understand Paul's discussion in the middle of the first century. In general, it is fair to say that ancient law was not so much innovative as it was rather the compilation of the traditions and practices of a given people. It did not seek novelty, but continuity. This is especially the case with marriage law, which was bound by tradition, formality, and ancient practices. The respect with which precedent was treated can be seen by the very nature of Justinian's efforts to gather together the laws of the previous centuries.

35. Justinian, *Digest* 23.1.4 (ed. and trans. Mommsen, Krueger, and Watson, *The Digest of Justinian*, vol. 2, 656).

36. Ibid., 23.1.9 (Mommsen, Krueger, and Watson, vol. 2, 656).

37. Ibid., 23.1.14 (Mommsen, Krueger, and Watson, vol. 2, 657).

riage could be annulled by the father of the daughter in *potestas*,[38] but with conditions. The daughter could refuse the marriage only for limited reasons[39] and the father himself had limited ability to end the marriage without contracting for another. According to *Digest* 23.2.19, the father who refused to allow his daughter to marry could be forced to do so and could be forced to provide her with a dowry.[40] It is conceivable that this was the reason why Paul stated that it was no sin if they married.

If no marriage contract existed, a father would not face legal pressure to give his daughter in marriage. The preceding discussion understood *anankē* in verse 37 as "necessity" and interpreted this "necessity" as a legally binding marriage contract for the daughter.[41] Yet this does not have to be the case. It is possible to see *anankē* as any other kind of force, compulsion, constraint, or natural need. The compulsion could have been the daughter's desire for marriage, or the necessity may have resided in the inability to care for the daughter financially; but if no such need existed, whether contractually, socially, personally, or financially, the father could have felt free to care for her and not give her in marriage. Nevertheless, the second phrase of verse 37 implies a previously existing contractual obligation. If the father had *exousia* (freedom of choice, authority, the right to act, the right to dispose of one's property as one wishes), he could step out from the contract and keep his daughter. Given the theoretically unlimited control a father had in Roman law over the disposition of his property and his children, this compulsion had to have come from some external source. Within the family, the father could do whatever he chose to—although a Christian father would have had to acknowledge that the religion imposed certain moral constraints. We have translated the critical phrase concerning a situation where no compulsion existed as "he has freedom of will concerning his own (family member)." We also have translated *exousia* as "freedom of choice" and coupled it with *thelēmatos,* thus gaining the phrase "freedom of will." We have chosen to translate the phrase *peri tou idiou* as "concerning that which belongs to oneself," a phrase often used in the New Testament to refer to one's family (cf. Lk 18:28), and thus, by extension, "concerning his own family." Alternatively, it would also be possible to derive the same meaning by understanding *exousia* as "freedom of choice," as above, or "the authority to act," and by coupling this with *peri tou idiou*

38. Ibid., 23.1.10 (Mommsen, Krueger, and Watson, vol. 2, 656).
39. Ibid., 23.1.12 (Mommsen, Krueger, and Watson, vol. 2, 657).
40. Ibid., 23.2.19 (Mommsen, Krueger, and Watson, vol. 2, 660).
41. See also Orr and Walther, *1 Corinthians,* 224.

thelēmatos, thus reading the last phrase as "concerning his own action or decision." In that case, the final phrase of verse 37 would read: "he has the freedom of choice concerning his own action." Yet in either case, the father, free from compulsion, and with the power to act freely, could then with-hold his daughter from any marriage.

With his discussion in 1 Corinthians 7, Paul provided a presentation of and a response not just to his theological teaching regarding marriage and celibacy, but to altered social realities concerning the family and cultur-al dynamics. The impact on children and family was profound, especially with regard to the situation of young Christian girls who were struggling to find their place in this changing society. Independent of how exactly one translates the passage in question, celibacy was the preferred option rec-ommended to girls. Faced with such a message, a girl may have feared a life without the security of husband and children. Perhaps she may also have embraced celibacy as a new and welcome opportunity. Paul envisioned here a goal, and a good, higher and better than married life. He seems to have believed that a decision to preserve virginity was not only possible but advisable, and even better than the alternative of married existence. Whether this decision was based on a young man's ability to stand firm in the decision he had made in his heart, a reading of the passage we do not follow, or whether it was based on the father's ability to act without finan-cial concern or external pressure regarding the decision to be made for his daughter, in the end the reality created was the same: one would do better (*kreisson poiēsei*) to let the girl remain a virgin.

It is true that Paul took it for granted that the lives of young children, particularly girls, were affected by decisions that male persons made about their married or unmarried state of life. Subsequent early Christian tradi-tions show that both boys and, more frequently, young girls soon decided on their own not to marry but to live as virgins and become ascetics. Paul had made accessible a new form of life for them, an option that girls in par-ticular seem to have been eager to embrace.

Taking Hold of a Life of Virginity and Asceticism

Early Christian literature preserves examples of young boys and girls who struggled with the choices of married life and virginity. At times of their own accord, at other times motivated by ideals of the Christian faith, some boys and girls opted for a life of virginity. Of special interest are examples to be found in the apocryphal acts of apostles, texts that were composed in the second and third centuries. Like the canonical Acts, they reflect the influence of Greco-Roman popular literature. Written in a genre that somewhat resembled the canonical Acts of the Apostles, the apocryphal acts constitute a kind of expansion of the model set by the canonical Acts, showcasing the work of more of the apostles and allowing them to reach more remote regions.[42] Central also to the elaboration of the earliest history of Christianity in the apocryphal texts are the structures of family life and how these were affected by the message and ideals of the idealized portraits of Jesus' apostles. Once the radical novelty of Christianity began to wear off, already existing societal and cultural structures, like family life and biological developments in human existence, for example, the bearing and raising of children, were realities of life over and against which a more pronounced position had to be formulated within Christian teaching and experience. Measured against the canonical Acts of the Apostles, in the apocryphal acts children play a more prominent role.[43] A good number of examples of children choosing a life of virginity can be found in the apocryphal texts.

Acts of John 111 portrays the apostle praying aloud to God in the presence of young men *(neaniskoi)* whom John addressed as little children *(teknia)* and who had just finished digging a grave for him. In his prayer, John revealed that during his youth *(en neotēti)* he had wanted to get married, and needed three interventions by God before he realized that this was not to be. First, Jesus appeared and simply told John that he needed him. When John did not react, and marriage arrangements proceeded, God inflicted disease on him. And when the future apostle desired a third time to get married, Jesus made it clear to him that all his efforts would be in vain. If Jesus had not laid claim to him, he could be allowed to marry; yet that was not the case.[44] *Acts of John* attests to a choice for virginity made at

---

42. For a discussion of the distribution of missionary fields to individual apostles, see Jean-Daniel Kaestli, "Les scènes d'attribution des champs de mission et de départ de l'apôtre dans les Actes apocryphes," in *Les Actes apocryphes des apôtres. Christianisme et monde païen* (Geneva: Labor et Fides, 1981), 249–64.

43. For a more developed, comparative study of the role of children in canonical and apocryphal acts, see Horn, "The Depiction of Children and Young People as Literary Device." For other comparative work on the canonical and apocryphal acts, see Daniel Marguerat, "The Acts of Paul and the Canonical Acts: A Phenomenon of Rereading," trans. Ken McKinney, *Semeia* 80 (1997), 169–83; and François Bovon, "Canonical and Apocryphal Acts of Apostles," *Journal of Early Christian Studies* 11.2 (2003), 165–94.

44. *Acts of John* 111 and 113 (ed. Junod and Kaestli, *Acta Iohannis. Praefatio—Textus,* 306–7 and 311). All citations are from this edition.

a young age. John's proclamation of his decision functioned as an invitation to the young people surrounding him to do likewise. That John was about to die immediately following his prayer only heightened the urgency of his message to the young men digging his grave. It is important to note that childhood and youth clearly were emphasized as the important time in one's life to choose a life of virginity and asceticism and thus a life without establishing a natural family of one's own.

In the *Acts of Paul (and Thecla)*, the reader meets the young girl Thecla, who is portrayed as having listened to Paul when he was preaching in Iconium, modern-day Konya (Turkey).[45] Thecla was engaged to a young man, Thamyris, who eagerly waited for the time when they could get married. Given that Thecla's mother spoke of her daughter as *parthenos*,[46] and had a rigid expectation of marriage for her daughter, one may assume at least for the early part of the story that Thecla fit the category of a girl under the age of twelve and a half who was physiologically still a virgin.

Thecla's story illustrates the conflict of societal and cultural expectations of married life as the normal future of one's children with the preference given to virginity that is ascribed to Paul's preaching. Thecla's character shows that children themselves, here a young girl, may have decided on their own on a life of virginity. In manifest opposition to her mother's

45. For a fuller investigation of Thecla's character as a young girl and the model she set for children see Horn, "Suffering Children," 121–30. Both the figure of Thecla and the impact of her example on early Christian women's lives have been of interest to scholars. See the work accomplished on the reception history of Thecla in the eastern Mediterranean by Stephen J. Davis, *The Cult of Saint Thecla: A Tradition of Women's Piety in Late Antiquity* (New York: Oxford University Press, 2001). For other studies of traditions connected with Thecla, see Esther Yue L. Ng, "Acts of Paul and Thecla: Women's Stories and Precedent?" *Journal of Theological Studies* 55.1 (2004), 1–29; Catherine Burris and Lucas van Rompay, "Thecla in Syriac Christianity: Preliminary Observations," *Hugoye* 5.2 (2002) http://syrcom.cua.edu/Hugoye/Vol5No2/HV5N2BurrisVanRompay.html; Catherine Burris and Lucas van Rompay, "Some Further Notes on Thecla in Syriac Christianity," *Hugoye* 6.2 (2003) http://syrcom.cua.edu/Hugoye/Vol6No2/HV6N2BurrisVanRompay.html; Shelly Matthews, "Thinking of Thecla: Issues in Feminist Historiography," *Journal of Feminist Studies in Religion* 17.2 (2001), 39–55; Beate Wehn, "'Blessed are the bodies of those who are virgins': reflections on the image of Paul in the Acts of Thecla," trans. Brian McNeil, *Journal for the Study of the New Testament* 79 (2000), 149–64; Monika Pesthy, "Thecla among the Fathers of the Church," in *The Apocryphal Acts of Paul and Thecla*, ed. Jan N. Bremmer (Kampen: Kok Pharos, 1996), 164–78; Léonie Hayne, "Thecla and the Church Fathers," *Vigiliae Christianae* 48 (1994), 209–18; and Ruth Albrecht, *Das Leben der heiligen Makrina auf dem Hintergrund der Thekla-Traditionen. Studien zu den Ursprüngen des weiblichen Mönchtums im 4. Jahrhundert in Kleinasien* (Göttingen: Vandenhoeck & Ruprecht, 1986), 239–319, a work still to be considered a classic.

46. *Acts of Paul (and Thecla)* 8 and 9 (ed. Lipsius and Bonnet, *Acta Apostolorum Apocrypha*, vol. 1, 241, l. 15, and 242, l. 7).

wishes, Thecla refused to marry her fiancé, Thamyris. No appeals from the mouth of her fiancé or her mother could change her mind.[47] Not even attempts on her life moved her to change her mind, and she was willing to be burned as a martyr in the theater for her choice.[48] The beatification of "the bodies of the virgins" *(ta sōmata tōn parthenōn)*[49] became a spectacle for everyone to see, including the children who had brought the firewood for her execution to the theater.[50] Thecla's *exemplum* was radical, and it gained in weight and effectiveness not only through her gender but perhaps all the more through her youthful age.

Other apocryphal acts of apostles show that Thamyris was not the only one who thought he had reason to complain that a given apostle "did not allow young girls to marry."[51] In *Acts of Thomas* 11, King Misdeus came to regret that he had ever allowed his young daughter any contact with the apostle Judas Thomas, even if only for prayer. In this case, both of the young people, bride and bridegroom about to consummate their marriage, were dissuaded from doing so through the preaching of Jesus, who appeared to them in the guise of Judas Thomas.[52] The rejection of sexual intercourse and the bearing of children was significantly more graphic and negative than the positive portrayal of the blessing to be achieved by one's preservation of virginity, which had attracted the young Thecla.

Addressing the young bridal couple as "my children" *(tekna mou)*, Jesus promised that in exchange for their abstention from "this foul intercourse" they could "become holy temples." Instead of feeling the subjection to "impulses and pains," they would be pure and "acquire no cares of life or of children, whose end is destruction." Children in particular could tempt parents to commit great evils. If they were to have many children, parents might become greedy, "stripping orphans and overreaching widows," and ultimately be deserving of heinous punishments. Not only would having children lead parents to sin for their children's sake, children themselves would become idle, or be "oppressed by devils, some openly and some invisibly." If children did not become lunatics, crippled, or otherwise physi-

47. Ibid., 10 (Lipsius, vol. 1, 242–43).

48. Ibid., 20 and 22 (Lipsius, vol. 1, 249 and 250).

49. Ibid., 6 (Lipsius, vol. 1, 240, l. 2). For further discussion of this remarkable beatification, see also Magda Misset-van de Weg, "Blessed are the bodies of the virgins . . . ," in *Begin with the Body: Corporeality, Religion, and Gender* (Louvain: Peeters, 1998), 233–49.

50. *Acts of Paul (and Thecla)* 22 (ed. Lipsius, *Acta Apostolorum Apocrypha*, vol. 1, 250, ll. 5–6).

51. Ibid., 16 (Lipsius, vol. 1, 246, l. 3).

52. *Acts of Thomas* 11 (ed. Bonnet, *Acta Apostolorum Apocrypha*, vol. 2.2, 116).

cally deformed and impeded, no doubt they would become vain and engage in "useless or abominable acts" like "adultery or murder or theft or fornication."[53] This description of the woes, disadvantages, and outright horrors of having children met its match among other texts of apocryphal acts, but also more broadly among other early Christian writings of the same time period. That the young couple in the *Acts of Thomas* rejected the marital act in their bridal chamber is not much of a surprise.

At other times, early Christian authors enlisted more moderate arguments to convince children, or their parents, that marriage was not in the children's best interest. A scene from the *Acts of Andrew* serves well for purposes of illustrating how some authors attempted to counter a practice of marriage between blood relations, which was more widespread in certain areas of the early Christian world.[54]

In Gregory of Tours' Latin summary of a Latin version of the *Acts of Andrew*,[55] one reads of a case of a planned incestuous marriage at Philippi between two pairs of children or younger teenagers, two sons of one family and two daughters of a second family. The youths' fathers were brothers.[56] The text does not provide any information about the children's respective mothers, who do not appear at all in the decision-making process regarding their offspring's fate. Thus it is not clear whether the youths were full brothers and sisters, or only half-brothers and half-sisters. Like their mothers, the children also had no choice in influencing their fathers' agreement to marry them to their first cousins. This marriage was arranged to preserve and even enhance the social status of the two families.

Since the fathers, and by implication the children, possessed "great means" *(facultas magna),* in which the "great nobility" *(valde nobiles)* of their standing in society was grounded, the fathers agreed that given their "great riches" *(opes eximiae),* "there is no [family] in the community that is worthy to unite itself with [theirs]."[57] If sons and daughters were to marry, "all the more easily could [the families'] riches be joined [*coniungantur*]."[58]

---

53. Ibid., 12 (Bonnet, vol. 2.2, 116–18).

54. The custom seems to have been practiced more frequently in Egypt and Persia. See, for example, the discussion in W. Scheidel, "Brother-Sister and Parent-Child Marriage outside Royal Families in Ancient Egypt and Iran: A Challenge to the Sociobiological View of Incest Avoidance?" *Ethnology and Sociobiology* 17.5 (1996), 319–40.

55. See Prieur, *Acta Andreae,* 553.

56. Gregory of Tours, *Life of Andrew* 11, ll. 1 and 9 (ed. Prieur, *Acta Andreae,* 564–651, here 589 and 591, l. 9), identifies the father of the boys as *pater puerorum.*

57. Ibid., ll. 4–5 (Prieur, 589–91): *non est de civibus qui dignae copuletur generationi nostrae.*

58. Ibid., ll. 6–7 (Prieur, 591).

The Latin verb, taken from the same root from which the word for "spouse" *(coniunx)* is derived, turned the planned marriage of the children into a marriage of economic advantage. To the minds of these fathers, the union between their offspring was primarily a convenient means of uniting, and thus preserving, family property. That the combined possessions would make the new, single family *(una domus)* an even more powerful and more prestigious unit in the community is not spelled out, but is implied. On the part of the fathers, no signs of recognition or even the slightest awareness of potential problems in such an arrangement are hinted at. To the contrary, preparations for the wedding were made when, at the last moment, "on the wedding-day a word from God came to them," telling them to wait for instructions from God's servant Andrew.[59]

On the third day, when Andrew finally came, the message the parents heard was not praise of married life. Andrew addressed the parents as "my (little) children" and warned them "not to deceive these youths" into contracting a marriage. Moreover, the parents were required to do penance for having sinned against God.[60] The sin the parents had committed was their intention to unite blood relatives in marriage. The parents recognized their wrongdoing and implored the apostle to pray for them, pleading ignorance of the divine will in such matters. Gregory's summary does not say whether the youths preparing to marry subsequently rejected married life altogether. He simply stated that "the youths saw the apostle's face shining like the face of an angel," here using an image which in early Christian discourse often referred to ascetics who lived the angelic life.[61] The youths also acknowledged that Andrew's teaching was "great and without fault."[62] Admitting that they had not heard it before, the youths received it as if it were God's word.

The interpretation of this passage requires a further comment on the likely form of an earlier text of the *Acts of Andrew,* which may or may not have been identical with the one available to Gregory of Tours. The apocryphal *Epistle of Pseudo-Titus* draws attention to a passage that speaks of the apostle Andrew as having come to a wedding as a spoiler, separating the couple that was to be married and all the male and female guests who were present and exhorting them to lives of singleness like the saints for

---

59. Ibid., ll. 13 and 9–10 (Prieur, 591).   60. Ibid., ll. 22–23 (Prieur, 591).

61. Ibid., ll. 30–31 (Prieur, 593); see also Karl Suso Frank, *ΑΓΓΕΛΙΚΟΣ ΒΙΟΣ. Begriffsanalytische und begriffsgeschichtliche Untersuchung zum "engelgleichen Leben" im frühen Mönchtum* (Münster: Aschendorffsche Verlagsbuchhandlung, 1964).

62. Gregory of Tours, *Life of Andrew* 11, l. 32 (ed. Prieur, *Acta Andreae,* 593).

the glory of God.[63] The apostle's belated arrival, the multiple couples, and the last-minute cancellation of a marriage fit rather well with chapter 11 of Gregory of Tours' summary.[64] When Andrew therefore identified incest as the sin that was about to be committed in a marriage of the cousins, incest may not have been all that the apostle warned the parents and children about in this instance. The original *Acts of Andrew* may at that instance have contained further instruction against marriage.[65] Yet the latter summary of Gregory would have left out such passages, since the Western bishop had no interest in promoting extreme, encratite-like forms of rejecting family life, but rather wished to enlist apostolic support for ordered relationships in the Christian households of his own communities.

The subsequent identification of Andrew with an angel, and Andrew's concluding advice to the youths to preserve what they had heard without any defilement *(sine pollutione)* so that they would be able to receive eternal life, further supports the likelihood that an earlier version of the *Acts of Andrew* contained a clearer message not only rejecting incestuous marriage, but also urging the youth to refrain from married life altogether. In the end, the young cousins probably did not marry, thinking that with their ascetic choice they followed the better part of the Christian life.

As more varied, organized forms of asceticism developed and spread in the early Christian world, biographical and hagiographical literature began to preserve reminiscences not only of children who followed Paul's teaching regarding virginity as the better state of life, which in the second and third centuries was reinterpreted as a rejection of married life and sexual intercourse altogether. From the third century on, one also begins to see examples of children who opted to realize more fully what it might mean to renounce the world and thus to take up the cross. One finds examples of children who likewise integrated their pursuit of the virginal life with participation in developing forms of the eremitical and monastic life. A full study of children's experience of, contribution to, and participation

63. D. Domitien De Bruyn, "Epistula Titi, Discipuli Pauli, De dispositione Sanctimonii," *Revue Bénédictine* 37 (1925), 47–72, here 60, ll. 488–91: *Ut uenisset denique et andreas ad nupcias et ipse ad demonstrandam gloriam dei, destinatos sibi <<con>>iuges deiunxit, masculos et foeminas ab inuicem separauit et docuit eos singulari statu permanere sanctos;* see also D. De Bruyn, "Nouveaux Fragments des Actes de Pierre, de Paul, de Jean, d'André, et de l'Apocalypse d'Élie," *Revue Bénédictine* 25 (1908), 149–60, here 157; and Prieur, *Acta Andreae*, 21.

64. We agree with Prieur, *Acta Andreae*, 21, who also noted this resemblance. Whether or not the reference to incest is Gregory's invention does not have to be decided here.

65. Prieur, *Acta Andreae*, 590–91, n. 7, refers to the *Epistle of Pseudo-Titus* that makes such an assumption a likely one.

in asceticism remains an important future contribution scholarship could offer.[66]

The examples gleaned from apocryphal literature do not represent marginal trends in second- and third-century Christianity. Many Christian authors who are a part of mainstream Christian theology and thought fall squarely in the camp of those who asked Christian children to consider a life of celibacy. One certainly may also consider the earliest models of such asceticism, Jesus and Paul, as falling into that Christian mainstream. Other examples are abundant.

One significant area for exploration of the impact of asceticism on children's lives is the reconstruction of the childhood of male and female ascetics and members of monastic communities, about whose spiritual and physical pursuits and lives hagiographical texts attempt to inform the reader. In some of the earliest hagio-biographies of ascetic heroes that have come down to modern times, an important *topos* is that of developments and decisions these heroes made in childhood and early youth that later greatly influenced their spiritual progress. A few examples of male and female ascetics out of many that deserve study have to suffice as illustrations in the course of the following discussion.

Young Boys as Ascetics and the Role Models Available to Them

The fourth-century *Life of Antony* offers the earliest portrait of the education of a young ascetic. The young man was the offspring of prosperous Christian parents, who reared their son as a Christian.[67] That education, however, was not one of the intellect and the mind. Instead, somewhat in congruence with the idea of a child as a person who does not yet possess full rational and intellectual capacities and skills, the education toward the ideal life is presented as an effort to adapt one's lifestyle to that of the perfect Christian, who is removed from the desires and needs of this world, and who instead is in tune with the will of the heavenly parent. As author of the *Life*, Athanasius showed how the child Antony was not very receptive to knowledge that would have led to intellectual growth or even to the truth of the faith. Rather, according to Athanasius's description, every detail

66. See also Cornelia Horn, "Raising Martyrs and Monks: A Diachronic Comparison of the Use of Children's Role Models in Patristic Literature," paper delivered at the annual meeting of the North American Patristics Society, Chicago, May 2004.

67. Athanasius of Alexandria, *Life of Antony* 1.1 (ed. Bartelink, *Athanase d'Alexandrie: Vie d'Antoine*, 130, ll. 1–3; trans. Gregg, *Athanasius: The Life of Antony*, 30).

of Antony's life as a child manifested that he rejected secular learning and turned his entire being over to a Christocentric renunciation of the world.[68] "When he was a child [*paidion*], he lived with his parents, cognizant of little else besides them and his home." He was sheltered from the influences of the world, relating only to his parents, who are presented as initially having been the only examples of the Christian life for him. Little Antony "was obedient [*hypetasseto*] to his parents," displaying as a young child the virtue of monastic obedience. There was no doubt that "he accompanied his parents to the Lord's house."[69] He had already cultivated the asceticism of restraint: he knew only the way between his home and the local church. In effect, his Christian home and the Christian house of worship defined his identity, just as the ideal monk or virgin would remain within his or her enclosure, tending to the spiritual family, and worshipping with them.

The control Antony was able to exercise over his own body fittingly supported this ideal of contemplative asceticism. According to his hagiographer, Antony did not seek from his well-off parents the trappings of luxury, particularly with regard to food.[70] Antony was satisfied with what his parents provided for his nourishment, and wanted nothing more, thus displaying as a child a detachment from the cares of the world and the stomach, an important aspect of asceticism.[71] The picture that obtains is one in which Antony's parents were his first teachers in the faith and the ascetic life, even if Antony may have possessed a preternatural disposition to renunciation.[72] Within a few lines, Antony is presented as already following the path of obedience and poverty that was fundamental to asceticism in the East. Sexual chastity may have been perceived as not requiring any comment in reference to a young child. However, the author certainly presents Antony as sheltered from the world and its sources of sexual knowledge and experience. It is as though young Antony were a nonsexual being, whose appetites were never aroused through contact with corrupting influences.

68. Scholarly discussion continues to be divided about the authorship of the *Life*, but we assume the customary identification with Athanasius of Alexandria for the purposes of the present study. For more detailed perspectives see, for example, the work by Bernadette McNary-Zak, *Letters and Asceticism in Fourth-Century Egypt* (Lanham, Md.: University Press of America, 2000), 88–93.

69. Athanasius, *Life of Antony* 1.2–3 (ed. Bartelink, *Athanase: Vie d'Antoine*, 130, ll. 3–5 and ll. 10–13; trans. Gregg, *Athanasius: The Life of Antony*, 30 [modified]).

70. Ibid., 1.4 (Bartelink, 130, ll. 14–16; Gregg, 31).

71. Ibid. (Bartelink, 130, ll. 16–18; Gregg, 31).

72. Ibid., 1.1 and 1.4 (Bartelink, 130, ll. 1–2 and 15; Gregg, 30–31).

When Athanasius painted a picture of a "boy [*pais*] ... [who] could not bear to learn letters,"[73] he did not intend to portray a child who was intellectually incapable of studying and learning how to read and write. In fact, the collection of *Letters* written by Antony himself shows that the ascetic not only learned how to read and write, but that he had acquaintance with Platonic philosophy, at least in a more popular form, as well as with Alexandrian theological traditions.[74] Instead, Athanasius attempted to portray Antony as the antithesis of the intellectual and social butterfly, one who did not hop around from idea to idea or from one potential friend to another. Thus, according to Athanasius, little Antony wanted to "stand apart from friendship with other children." His "yearning ... was for living, an unaffected person [*hōs aplastos*], in his home." Distanced from the desires and longings of the world, and thus not affected by pain and emotions, the child Antony was portrayed as having been truly different from other children. Thus, Athanasius could say that "as a child [*hōs pais*] he was not frivolous, nor as a youth [*hōs tēi hēlikiāi prokoptōn*] did he grow contemptuous."[75]

In order to show that young Antony was well advanced in maturity of behavior and control over his thoughts and passions, Athanasius availed himself of the literary *topos* of the *puer senex* or *puer senilis*. The portrait of the young child who surpassed children of his or her age in abilities and skills, behaving and thinking like an adult of great distinction, was well known in classical, Jewish, and early Christian literature.[76] It became especially well known in the West through Gregory the Great's description of

73. Ibid., 1.2 (Bartelink, 130, ll. 6–7; Gregg, 30).

74. For ready access to these letters, see the English translation by Derwas J. Chitty, *The Letters of St. Antony the Great* (Oxford: S. L. G. Press, 1977); and more recently the Italian one in Matta El Meskin, *Secondo il Vangelo: le venti lettere di Antonio* (Magnano [Biella]: Qiqajon Comunità de Bose, c1999). See also the studies by Samuel Rubenson, *The Letters of St. Antony: Monasticism and the Making of a Saint* (Minneapolis: Fortress Press, 1995), 11, see also 95–99 and 109–15; and Janet Timbie, "Translating and Interpreting the Letters of Antony," in *A Multiform Heritage: Studies on Early Judaism and Christianity in Honor of Robert A. Kraft* (Atlanta: Scholars Press, 1999), 213–25.

75. Athanasius, *Life of Antony* 1.2–3 (ed. Bartelink, *Athanase: Vie d'Antoine*, 130, ll. 8–12; trans. Gregg, *Athanasius: The Life of Antony*, 30).

76. For the motif of the *puer senex*, see Ludwig Bieler, ΘΕΙΟΣ ΑΝΗΡ. *Das Bild des "göttlichen Menschen" in Spätantike und Frühchristentum* (Vienna: Oskar Höfels, 1935–36; repr. Darmstadt: Wissenschaftliche Buchgesellschaft, 1967), part 1, 34–36; Ernst Robert Curtius, *European Literature and the Latin Middle Ages* (New York: Pantheon, c1953; repr. Princeton, N.J.: Princeton University Press, 1990), 98–101, who also discusses the connection between the images of girl–old woman in early Christian literature (101–5); Elena Giannarelli, "L'infanzia nella biografia cristiana," *Studia Patristica* 18.2 (1989), 217–21, here 217–18; and Christian Gnilka, *Aetas spiritalis. Die Überwindung der natürlichen Altersstufen als Ideal frühchristlichen Lebens* (Bonn:

Benedict of Nursia, who was introduced at the beginning of his *Vita* as a man who "from his childhood had the understanding of an old man."[77]

Early Christian authors also used this *topos* when characterizing an ascetic who, although technically no longer a child, had reached at a relatively early age those heights of ascetic perfection and wisdom that normally were attained only at the end of a long life of struggle. The church historian Sozomen, for example, spoke of Macarius the Egyptian, who started the life of renunciation *(philosophein archomenos)* as a young man *(neos)*, but who excelled so quickly "that the monks called him 'child-elder' [*paidariogerōn*]"[78] before he was even forty. The monk Sabas seems to have been the only other revered ascetic who received that same title.[79] Another nuance of this connection between the notions of extreme youth and old age in one and the same person is to be found in the ascetic ideal of spiritualized childlikeness. The *Greek Life of Pachomius* noted that when the monks prepared to go to the weekly gathering of the community on Saturday or Sunday, they were required to take off the belt and goat skin that served as part of their habit during the week and instead "put on their heads soft cowls like children."[80] Inspiration for such a valuation of the monk as spiritually equivalent to the child was provided by various biblical texts that held up "becoming like a child" as the goal and ideal of the Christian life (Mt 18:3–4; Mk 10:14–15; and 1 Pt 2:1–3).[81] Ascetic texts in turn identified the simplicity attained by monks, desert dwellers, and hermits as fulfilling this commandment of being "like children."[82]

Peter Hanstein, 1972), at several places throughout; Kleijwegt, "Kind," 885–86 and 912–13. See also Martens, *One God, One Law: Philo of Alexandria on the Mosaic and Greco-Roman Law*, 92–95, and footnotes there for further literature on the ideal in Greco-Roman thought on kingship and in Philo. For the ideal in a Jewish context see Philo, *Mos.* 1.18–24.

77. Gregory the Great, *De vita et miraculis venerabilis Benedicti Abbatis* (ed. and trans. Adalbert de Vogüe and Paul Antin, *Grégoire le Grand. Dialogus. Tome II (Livres I–III)* [Paris: Les Éditions du Cerf, 1979], 126–249, here 126): *ab ipso suae pueritiae tempore cor gerens senile*. See also Curtius, *European Literature*, 100.

78. Sozomen, *Ecclesiastical History* 3.14.2 (ed. Bidez and Hansen, *Sozomenos. Kirchengeschichte*, GCS NF vol. 4, 118, ll. 15–16).

79. See Cyril of Scythopolis, *Life of Sabas* 11 (ed. Eduard Schwartz, *Kyrillos von Skythopolis* [Leipzig: J. C. Hinrichs Verlag, 1939], 85–200, here 94, l. 16).

80. In addition, a cross colored in red was to be affixed to these cowls. The variant recounted here depends on the version of the Greek life as found in MS Monac. graec 3 (trans. Hans Mertel, "Leben des Heiligen Pachomius aus dem Griechischen übersetzt," in *Des Heiligen Athanasius Schriften Gegen die Heiden, Über die Menschwerdung, Leben des Heiligen Antonius, mit einem Anhang Leben des Heiligen Pachomius* [Munich: Jos. Kösel & Fried. Pustet, n.d.], 781–900, here 787).

81. See also Curtius, *European Literature*, 100.

82. See, for example, Pseudo-Ephraem, *Homily on Hermits and Desert Dwellers and Mourn-*

Although the primary influence on the young Antony appears to have been the Christian household in which he grew up, Athanasius's text suggests two other figures who functioned as *exempla* for Antony during his childhood. Hearing Athanasius say that the little child "grew [*auxēsas*] and became a boy [*egeneto pais*], and was advancing [*proekopte tēi hēlikiāi*] in years,"[83] an ancient Christian might readily have recalled the very similar descriptions of the boy Jesus in Luke 2:40 and especially of the young John the Baptist, about whom one and the same verse (Lk 1:80) not only says that "the little child grew [*to de paidion ēuxanen*] and became strong [*ekrataiouto*] in spirit," but also that "he was in the wilderness [*en tais erēmois*] until the day he appeared publicly to Israel."[84] Although the connection between Athanasius's text and that of the Gospel of Luke is tentative, it is remarkable insofar as Christian tradition preserves a characterization of John the Baptist as a child ascetic.

In 1927 Alphonse Mingana edited and published a *Life of John the Baptist* that is extant in one recension in two manuscripts in Karshuni (i.e., Arabic, written in Syriac letters), one from 1527 (MS Mingana 22) and one from around 1750 (MS Mingana 183).[85] Mingana thought the earlier one was written for an Egyptian Christian audience, while the latter showed signs of Syriac Christians as the text's target audience. Mingana assumed that the Arabic was a translation from a Greek original into which one or more redactors incorporated other material.[86]

The narrator identified himself as Abba Serapion, an Egyptian bishop.[87] The present text is not a uniform composition. Rather it shows traces of having been put together from several written traditions.[88] Also, it starts

---

ers 413 (trans. Joseph Amar, "On Hermits and Desert Dwellers," in *Ascetic Behavior in Greco-Roman Antiquity: A Sourcebook* [Minneapolis: Fortress Press, 1990], 66–80, here 77).

83. Athanasius, *Life of Antony* 1.2 (ed. Bartelink, *Athanase: Vie d'Antoine*, 130, l. 6; trans. Gregg, *Athanasius: The Life of Antony*, 30).

84. For a comparison between Jesus and John in Luke's initial chapters, see Augustin George, "Le parallèle entre Jean-Baptiste et Jésus en Luc 1–2," in *Mélanges bibliques en homage au R. P. Béda Rigaux* (Gembloux, Belgium: J. Duculot, 1970), 147–71.

85. A. Mingana, "A New Life of John the Baptist," *Bulletin of the John Rylands Library* 11 (1927), 438–489; repr. in *Woodbrooke Studies. Christian Documents in Syriac, Arabic, and Garshūni*, vol. 1 (Cambridge: W. Heffer and Sons, 1927), 234–87.

86. Ibid., 234–36; 249, n. 2; but see also 243, nn. 1 and 4.

87. Ibid., 255.

88. These texts appear to have focused on the Baptist's nativity and youth on the one hand, and on his beheading and the subsequent cult of his relics on the other. Mingana, "A New Life," 247, seems to mark the dividing line between the two halves on the basis of inconsistencies regarding Herodias being portrayed as living together with Herod already and intriguing to be

out as a biography of John the Baptist, yet toward the end takes on the character of a homily or panegyric delivered at a feast commemorating the Baptist, perhaps in connection with the dedication of a church in his name in Alexandria. Internal evidence from the latter half of the text suggests that the panegyric was delivered toward the end of the fourth century, during the time when Theophilus held the see of Alexandria (385–412).[89] Yet that does not preclude the possibility that individual traditions recounted in this story may come from an earlier or later date. The extent to which the whole text reflects fifth-century popular Egyptian Christianity cannot be determined in detail here.

Of particular interest for our purposes is how this text develops the interpretative consequences of Luke 1:80, which can be understood as suggesting that as a young child, John the Baptist lived in the desert. The story tells that when "John grew up in a beautiful childhood and [had suckled] his mother two years," Herod "began to kill all the children of Bethlehem." John's mother, Elizabeth, fearing for his life, received advice from Zacharias, her husband, to go with her son "to the wilderness of 'Ain Karim" in order to save him. Before their departure, when Zacharias took his son "into the Temple and blessed him," the angel Gabriel brought down from heaven Elijah's raiment of camel's hair and Elisha's leather girdle, over which Zacharias prayed and which he then gave to his son. Shortly afterwards the text explains that Zacharias's blessing "made [the little two-year-old John] a priest." In an address to Elizabeth, the narrator next compared her to Hagar and said that she "did not care to provide food nor a little drinking water for the child." At a time when "there was neither a monastery in the desert nor a congregation of monks" with whom they could have stayed, little John emerges as a two-year-old ascetic in rough, desert garb, for which he would become famous later on. Often presented as having been the first ascetic in the desert, John is shown to have practiced the hardships of fasting from food and drink at a very early age. Although merely a child, John became the founder and initiator of ascetic life in the desert.[90]

---

taken into Herod's household (and bed) for the first time. That her daughter is called by two different names in this second half of the text may indicate that there were even more traditions from which the author or redactor drew for his composition. The extremely negative portrayal of Herodias and her daughter, which exempts Herod from almost any responsibility for the death of John the Baptist, may make a male author more likely than a female one.

89. Mingana, "A New Life," 235, 253, and 255–57. The mention of Emperor Theodosius the Great in the text at this instance allowed Mingana to narrow the time of composition further to A.D. 385 to 395.

90. Mingana, "A New Life," 238–41. For the parallel to Hagar, see Genesis 21.

One notes that the text suggests Elizabeth as the driving force behind turning little John into the initiator of desert asceticism. The narrator had her say that she "put on [her] son a raiment of camel's hair and a leathern girdle in order that the mountain of the holy wilderness may . . . be inhabited, and in order that monasteries and congregations of monks may increase in it and that sacrifice may be offered in it in the name of the Lord Jesus Christ." Also her husband, Zacharias, who in the meantime had been murdered in the Temple and become a martyr, witnessed to the fact that John's "mother took him into the desert."[91]

The Karshuni *Life of John the Baptist* adds another facet to the illustration of the especially supportive role of the mother in a child's experience of the ascetic life. The text describes how for about five years "the blessed John . . . wandered in the desert with his mother," while "God prepared for him locusts and wild honey as food."[92] While the reference to food eaten by the desert ascetic John is taken from Mark 1:6 (cf. Mt 3:4) and subsequently inspired significant discussion among early Christian teachers and ascetics,[93] the text suggests that John's mother had a role in selecting her son's diet. God is acknowledged as having prepared the foods, yet it was Elizabeth who "was told about him not to let any unclean food enter his mouth."[94] Inspired by concern for John's young age, the text later returns to the connection between the mother as provider of food and little John's life in the desert. In the Karshuni *Life of John the Baptist*, the Christ child is understood to have been two years younger than his kinsman John. Little Jesus had to console his own mother at the death of Elizabeth, as the Virgin Mary "wept immediately over the loneliness of John who was very young."[95] Instead of allowing her to take John, who now was "an orphan without anyone," away from the desert and into the Holy Family's own home, Jesus promised to "render the water of this spring of water [which was available in the wilderness of 'Ain Karim][96] as sweet and delicious to

---

91. Mingana, "A New Life," 241–42. See also James A. Kelhoffer, *The Diet of John the Baptist*, Wissenschaftliche Untersuchungen zum Neuen Testament 176 (Tübingen: Mohr Siebeck, 2005), 175, who notes "an explicit connection between how Elizabeth clothed John and monks who would later dress like John."

92. Mingana, "A New Life," 242.

93. See Kelhoffer, *The Diet of John the Baptist*.

94. Mingana, "A New Life," 242.

95. Ibid., 244.

96. For the purposes of the Karshuni *Life of John the Baptist*, the protagonist remained in the wilderness of 'Ain Karim all his life. There is no indication of a move to another wilderness area, for example, to the Judaean desert. 'Ain Karim is identical with "the wilderness in which

him as the milk he sucked from his mother."[97] Other interpreters of the Baptist's diet at times thought they followed the *Diatessaron* when they turned the locusts into milk.[98] Dionysius Bar Salibi (1166–71), a Syrian-Orthodox bishop and one of the important Syriac writers of the Middle Ages, even explained that "milk was proper to his youth."[99] Yet a reference to water that was to taste as "sweet and delicious" as the milk from Elizabeth's breasts is a rather unique invention of the Karshuni *Life of John the Baptist* and thus far has gone unnoticed. It appears that other writers merely assumed that John had water for drinking, given that they did not seem to have commented on his young age in the desert.[100] The influential role of a mother in leading her child into the ascetic life is remarkable, but not at all unique, as our later discussion will show.

Consideration of the ascetic character of the young Antony of Egypt has led us to explore examples of biblical children who were models of the ascetic life. Yet early Christian literature did not limit the pool of potential examples to those taken from the Christian Scriptures. Neither was the ascetic life restricted to young male practitioners. Young girls also adopted the ascetic life and had female role models available.

Girls as Ascetics and Their Role Models

Early Christian sources witness to girls who were introduced to the ascetic life by family members or acquaintances or who took up asceticism on their own initiative. When Antony of Egypt reached the end of his teens, his parents passed away and he was confronted with the task of having to take care of "one very young sister [*brachytatēs adelphēs*]." After responding to his obligation "both for the home and his sister" for about half a year, Antony felt called to "be perfect, go, sell what [he] possess[ed] and give it to the poor" in order to "have treasure in heaven" (Mt 19:21). As he promptly followed this call, he "entrusted his sister to the care of respect-

---

no soul lived" (Mingana, "A New Life," 241). Thus the titles provided for chs. 7 and 9 in Gerhard Schneider, *Evangelia Infantiae Apocrypha. Apocryphe Kindheitsevangelien* (Freiburg: Herder, 1995), 75, are misleading.

97. Mingana, "A New Life," 244.

98. See Kelhoffer, *The Diet of John the Baptist,* 141–48.

99. The fragment from Bar Salibi's work, as preserved in MS BM Add. 12,143, fol. 52 is cited in J. Rendel Harris, *Fragments of the Commentary of Ephrem Syrus upon the Diatessaron* (London: C. J. Clay and sons, 1895), 17; see also Kelhoffer, *The Diet of John the Baptist,* 143.

100. Kelhoffer, *The Diet of John the Baptist,* does not index references to "water." In a personal communication the author also remarked that John drinking water usually is not featured.

ed and trusted virgins [*gnōrimois kai pistais parthenois*] and gave her over to be raised in virginity [*eis parthenian*]."[101] Here the reader encounters a case in which a young lad committed his sister to a life of virginity. The "respected and trusted virgins" distinguished themselves by their lifestyle from other women in the village. Yet the text does not supply evidence of the existence of an organized monastic foundation of women at that time or in that location.[102] About midway through the *Life of Antony*, Athanasius again commented on Antony's sister, who by then had grown old in the virginal life and was directing the life of other virgins, possibly including young virgins too.[103] Thus, we have evidence that the girl was thought of as having continued all her life on the path of virginity, on which her brother, who had fulfilled for her the role of *pater familias*, had placed her and which the virgins who took care of her had modeled for her.

Evidence from the eastern regions of the early Christian world shows that families were encouraged to dedicate at least one of their children to the life of virginity. A collection of 107 canons, compiled in Egypt between A.D. 370 and 450 and known as *Pseudo-Athanasian Canons*, recommended that in every Christian house there ought to be a virgin, "for the salvation of this whole house is this one virgin."[104] The parents were instructed to encourage and educate all their children to live in virginity, but they were called upon to be attentive and examine carefully "which among [the] daughters is worthy of holiness."[105] The process of selection and examination had to cover all aspects of a girl's behavior, including whether she could control her gaze, was obedient even when scolded by her parents, and preferred fasting over eating and drinking. An anonymous, early-fourth-century Greek homily, probably written in Syria,[106] recommended that parents also ought to exam-

101. Athanasius, *Life of Antony* 2.1, 2.3, and 3.1 (ed. Bartelink, *Athanase: Vie d'Antoine*, 132 and 134–36; trans. Gregg, *Athanasius: The Life of Antony*, 31–32 [modified]).

102. See G. Garitte, "Un couvent de femmes au IIIe siècle? Note sur un passage de la vie grecque de S. Antoine," in *Scrinium Lovaniense: Mélanges historiques, historische opstellen Étienne van Cauwenbergh* (Louvain: J. Duculot Gembloux, 1961), 150–59; Bartelink, *Athanase: Vie d'Antoine*, 81–82 and 135, n. 4; and Elm, "*Virgins of God*," 227–28.

103. Athanasius, *Life of Antony* 54.8 (ed. Bartelink, *Athanase: Vie d'Antoine*, 280, ll. 28–30; trans. Gregg, *Athanasius: The Life of Antony*, 71–72).

104. *Pseudo-Athanasian Canons*, canon 98 (ed. and trans. Wilhelm Riedel and Walter Ewing Crum, *The Canons of Athanasius of Alexandria: The Arabic and Coptic Versions* [London: Williams and Norgate, 1904], ٥٢ – ٥٥ and 62–64); see also Elm, "*Virgins of God*," 231.

105. *Pseudo-Athanasian Canons*, canon 97 (ed. and trans. Riedel and Crum, *The Canons of Athanasius*, ٥٢ and 62); see also Elm, "*Virgins of God*," 231.

106. For Syria as the likely place of composition of this homily, see David Amand de Mendieta, "La virginité chez Eusèbe d'Emèse et l'ascétisme familial dans la première moitié du

ine their young daughter with regard to whether "her steps are honorable, her movements well ordered, her eye respectful ... what her intention is, of what type her desire is, whether human or heavenly, and of what intensity her fasts and all of her piety in Christ."[107] The selection process had to be completed at the latest when the daughter turned thirty, at which point she was no longer regarded as a potential candidate for the vow of virginity but had to be given into marriage.[108] It is to be assumed, however, that the selection process started in early childhood, given that those who did not display early signs of controlled behavior were never considered as possible candidates.

Early Christian literature in Latin also preserves examples of girls chosen by their parents from infancy for a life of consecrated virginity.[109] The corpus of Jerome's letters is an excellent source of information in this regard. In his letter to Laeta concerning her infant daughter, Paula (*Letter* 107), and in a letter to Gaudentius concerning his infant daughter, Pacatula (*Letter* 128), Jerome assumed the existence of the practice of consecrating girls to a life of virginity. The first, *Letter* 107, was written in 403 and the second in 413. The practice described was widespread and as such does not warrant much comment. One may notice, though, that each of the parents addressed in these letters was a person of means, and that consecrated virginity had become a trend in some educated and wealthy circles. One also notes that Jerome's advice to the parents on how to raise the girls is hardly applicable or practical without some measure of wealth on the parents' part.

Little Paula was consecrated to Christ before she was born, indeed before she had even been conceived, much like Hannah had dedicated Sam-

---

IVe siècle," *Revue d'histoire ecclésiastique* 50 (1955), 777–820, here 818; and Arthur Vööbus, "Die Syrische Herkunft der Pseudo-Basilianischen Homilie über die Jungfräulichkeit," *Oriens Christianus* 40 (1956), 69–77. See Frank, *ΑΓΓΕΛΙΚΟΣ ΒΙΟΣ*, 149–50, for some discussion of the example of ascetical life in the family illustrated in this homily.

107. See *Greek Homily on Virginity* II.18 (ed. David Amand de Mendieta and Matthieu-Charles Moons, "Une curieuse homélie grecque inédite sur la virginité addressée aux pères de famille," *Revue Bénédictine* 63 [1953], 18–69 and 211–38, here 39; trans. Teresa M. Shaw, "Homily: On Virginity," in *Ascetic Behavior in Greco-Roman Antiquity: A Sourcebook* [Minneapolis: Fortress Press, 1990], 29–44, here 32). For a discussion of this *Greek Homily on Virginity* with regard to the question of how parents ought to raise their children toward asceticism, see also Elm, *"Virgins of God,"* 34–39.

108. See Elm, *"Virgins of God,"* 231–32.

109. For some discussion of Jerome's letters as witness to girls' education, see also Joan M. Petersen, "The Education of Girls in Fourth-Century Rome," in *The Church and Childhood*, 29–37.

uel, and Elizabeth John the Baptist. Given such a dedication, Jerome delighted in directing Laeta in the correct way to bring up the little girl. Like Chrysostom, Jerome concentrated on the education of Paula's soul, which involved keeping the little one away from boys. He also directed practical advice to Laeta, such as how to teach her daughter how to write and how to reward her for her lessons, so that learning would not become burdensome to her. Again, as with Chrysostom in *On Vainglory,* Jerome was worried that little Paula's nurse or other women might direct silly talk her way or even teach her to pronounce words improperly; Jerome warned the parent that undoing these mistakes was much harder than getting it right the first time.[110]

Jerome made it clear that from an early age the girl should know that she was in Christ's "army" and that her grandmother (Paula) and her aunt (Eustochium) were already enrolled in the service of Christ at a monastery for female ascetics in Bethlehem. As a result, little Paula was not to become fond of fine clothes, make-up, or jewelry, since those who went back on their vows could bring upon themselves terrible punishment. Instead, the little girl had to become familiar with the interior life by regularly going to church. Also, she was to eat separately from her parents' table so that she would not long for tasty dishes. Yet Jerome was considerate enough to make sure that her Spartan diet of bread, herbs, apples, and a fish or two every now and then did not become a fast which extended for weeks on end; of this he could not approve for a little girl.[111]

Paula was to be an ascetic already as a young girl. Play did not seem to be in her future, music certainly was not, but study of the Bible was to be her sure daily portion. Apart from the Scriptures, Jerome directed her reading to certain Church fathers such as Cyprian, Athanasius, and Hilary. She was not to have any special slave girl to be her confidante, nor was she to pay attention to a boy's curly locks or return the attention of a boy's smile. Paula should learn how to spend her life in prayer, but also how to spin wool, as any girl preparing for marriage would do as well. Yet, since she was not preparing for marriage, she should be kept from the wedding celebrations of slaves, the household games, and the baths, while learning to mortify her flesh and drive out her sexual yearnings. Jerome acknowledged that raising her daughter in this manner might be too difficult a task

110. Jerome, *Letters* 107.3–4 (ed. Hilberg, *Sancti Eusebii Hieronymi Epistulae,* CSEL 55, 293–95).

111. Jerome, *Letters* 107.4–5 and 107.7–10 (Hilberg, CSEL 55, 296 and 298–301).

for Laeta and thus he suggested sending the girl to her grandmother and aunt, even while she was still a young girl, advice which Laeta subsequently followed.[112]

Jerome's letter to Gaudentius was similar in content, as he instructed Gaudentius on how to raise his little daughter Pacatula for the pursuit of the ascetic life. Pacatula was still an infant on the knee, a detail one can discern from Jerome's comment on how hard it was to write to a girl who could not understand the meaning of self-control. Nevertheless, he started from the beginning, instructing Gaudentius to teach the girl to read and write and to reward her for her lessons with cakes and other treats, such as a doll. This is advice similar to that given to Laeta for little Paula, but there Jerome did not identify the sorts of treats to be given. One also suspects that given the austere diet recommended for Paula, cakes would not be among the treats. Also Pacatula should learn how to spin as a very young girl, for even if the threads broke in her clumsy hands, someday she would learn how to do it properly. Jerome did acknowledge that when her lessons were over, little Pacatula might need a hug from her mother or kisses from her family.[113]

It seems that one encounters a kinder and gentler Jerome when he is writing to a father concerning matters of raising a mere infant. By the time he was sending advice to Gaudentius, Jerome seemed to have modified his advice on clothing as well. He told Laeta not to give little Paula any fine clothing, but here he left the decision in Gaudentius's hands, acknowledging that some parents liked to dress their daughters, even those beyond reproach, in nice clothing. He stated that girls liked pretty clothes and many women of chastity also enjoyed wearing beautiful garments.[114] Jerome was not intent on having those chosen for the life of virginity engage in indulgence, but he seemed to recognize that balance was needed, at least at times.

Jerome did return to other themes he had raised in the letter to Lae-

---

112. Ibid., 107.9–13 (Hilberg, CSEL 55, 300–305). On the central role of spinning and weaving in the life of women in the ancient world, see the article by Penelope Allison, "Artefact Distribution and Spatial Function in Pompeiian Houses," in *The Roman Family in Italy: Status, Sentiment, Space,* ed. Beryl Rawson and Paul Weaver (Oxford: Oxford University Press, 1999), 321–54, who discusses numerous artifacts related to weaving that were found throughout the ancient city. This sort of evidence is a nice addition to the literary evidence, which speaks constantly of weaving. Of course, there is no way to say that all the weaving artifacts found in Pompeii belonged to women, but on that score the literary evidence is unanimous.

113. Jerome, *Letters* 128.1 (Hilberg, CSEL 56.1, 156–57).

114. Ibid. 128.2 (Hilberg, CSEL 56.1, 157).

ta, not changing his advice on the girl's playmates or acquaintances: she should play only with girls, not with boys; as she got older, she should not turn her attention to handsome, curly-haired boys or the licentious songs of sweet girls. Again, one sees in Pacatula a girl of the wealthier classes, as she was to be kept from the coarseness of household speech and her nurses and tutors had to be sober and not given to rough speech. Jerome particularly warned Gaudentius not to let sweet-talking boys gain access to his daughter through her nurses and guardians; although he did not directly use this language, Jerome's description of the sparks that could lead to a flame suggest that the boys were understood to have had a very specific goal on their minds.[115]

Jerome may have had a particular issue on his mind as well when he was moderating his instructions on the education and the raising of little children to a life of virginity. *Letter* 128 has a long aside in which its author railed against those who had chosen a life of virginity—or had it chosen for them—but were not coping well. He addressed this section to both men and women. Jerome knew of men who were supposed to be living as virgins, but whose live-in helpers, Jerome suggested, were beautiful, voluptuous young girls.[116] He speaks of women, virgins or widows, who engaged in long conversations with men alone in their homes and perhaps engaged in even more, although the virgins claimed that these men were only there to help instruct them in the Scriptures.[117] Perhaps it was a fact of life that some Christians chosen for virginity from childhood did not have the calling, or that the things withheld from a person when he or she was still a child were desired all the more later on. In an offhanded way Jerome mentioned a little later in the text certain upper-class women who stated that

---

115. Ibid., 128.4 (Hilberg, CSEL 56.1, 160–61).

116. Ibid., 128.3 (Hilberg, CSEL 56.1, 158, l. 4, to 159, l. 17). On the practice of ascetics living together in "spiritual marriage" or as *syneisaktes,* see also John Chrysostom's many comments. The phenomenon has been studied extensively. See for example Greg Peters, "Spiritual Marriage in Early Christianity: 1 Cor 7:25–38 in Modern Exegesis and the Earliest Church," *Trinity Journal* 23.2 (2002), 211–24; Blake Leyerle, *Theatrical Shows and Ascetic Lives: John Chrysostom's Attack on Spiritual Marriage* (Berkeley: University of California Press, 2001); Blake Leyerle, "John Chrysostom on the Gaze," *Journal of Early Christian Studies* 1 (1993), 159–74; Rosemary Rader, "Christian Pre-Monastic Forms of Asceticism: Syneisaktism, or 'Spiritual Marriage,'" in *The Continuing Quest for God: Monastic Spirituality in Tradition & Transition,* ed. William Skudlarek (Collegeville, Minn.: Liturgical Press, 1982), 80–87; Elizabeth A. Clark, "John Chrysostom and the Subintroductae," *Church History* 46 (1977), 171–85; and Antoine Guillaumont, "Le nom des 'agapètes,'" *Vigiliae Christianae* 23.1 (1969), 30–37.

117. Jerome, *Letters* 128.3 (ed. Hilberg, *Sancti Eusebii Hieronymi Epistulae,* CSEL 56.1, 159, ll. 17–21).

they wanted a life of virginity, but who expressed such a desire only in order to cohabitate with a low-born man or even a slave. Some had even de-
serted their husbands on such a pretense to live with low-born men.[118] In
Letter 117, Jerome identified a widowed mother and her virgin daughter in
Gaul who instead of living together were living with men who were their
lovers.[119] Situations like these may have arisen when people saw the life of
virginity as a cover for other desires, or when women and men chosen for
the life did not feel called to it and so took for themselves a lover under the
cloak of secrecy. Yet if one does not give Jerome the benefit of the doubt,
his rigor in writing and advising parents on how to raise their little children
for the ascetic life may also reveal the harshness of a struggle going on in
his own soul regarding his choice of that way of life and the difficulties he
may have experienced as he tried to continue on the path.

With the rise of ascetic fervor from the fourth century on, many parents, or at least one of a child's parents, came to acquire such a longing
for the ascetic life that, although they were hindered from living it out
in their own lives, they designated their offspring for it. The *Life of Melania the Younger*, probably composed by the monk Gerontius of Jerusalem
in the first half of the fifth century,[120] reports that Melania was fourteen
when she was married to the seventeen-year-old Pinianus. "With much
piteous wailing," "she begged her husband" to live chastely with her, yet
Pinianus wished "to have two children" as heirs, before he was willing to
"renounce the world." As soon as "a daughter was born to them," however, "they promptly dedicated [her] to God for the virginal estate," while
"Melania's heart burned even more strongly with the divine fire," to which
she gave expression in ascetic practices. In the case of Melania's daughter,
both parents seem to have collaborated when committing the child to a life
of virginity. It is quite likely that the baby girl continued to dwell with her
parents and not in an organized ascetic community. What her parents, primarily her mother, desired for her future life may have been freedom from
the pressure of having to get married, an experience which for Melania had
been a great burden in her own life. Yet it never came to the point of conflict between society's expectations for a wealthy young lady and her par-

118. Ibid., 128.4 (Hilberg, CSEL 56.1, 161, ll. 2–5).

119. Ibid., 117 (Hilberg, CSEL 55, 422–34).

120. On the question of the authorship of the *Life of Melania the Younger*, see Denys Gorce,
Vie de Sainte Mélanie, Sources Chrétiennes 90 (Paris: Les Éditions du Cerf, 1962), 54–62; and
Elizabeth A. Clark, *The Life of Melania the Younger. Introduction, Translation, and Commentary*,
Studies in Women and Religion vol. 14 (Lewiston, N.Y.: Edwin Mellen Press, 1984), 24.

ents' or her own ascetic inclinations: the little girl passed away shortly after the death of her baby brother.[121] She never grew up either to resent or to willingly conform to her mother's choice for her life.

That the parents' desire to see their children take to the ascetic life became a problem in some areas is reflected in legal evidence. Canons were needed to curb parental efforts at pressuring their children toward asceticism. Church canons are preserved from fourth- and fifth-century Egypt that attempted to place some of the control over whether a young girl was to enter the ascetic life back into the girl's hands. Canon 36 of the *Pseudo-Basilian Canons,* for example, ruled that parents were not allowed to dress their daughters "in the garment of a virgin."[122] Thus, parents could not make the decision for their daughters. Instead, the girls had to examine their predispositions carefully on their own and make up their own minds about what station in life to choose.

Such decisions could be aided by supplying the young girls with proper models of young virgins, known from the Scriptures or early Christian popular literature, who had embarked on the path of the virginal ascetic life before them. The choice examples for girls were the five wise virgins, the Virgin Mary, and especially Thecla.

Christian authors advised parents who took care of a little virgin to "weave a pure crown with the words of chastity" gathered from the Scriptures. That crown, which was to contain "the words spoken to holy Mary by the angel: 'Hail, you who have received grace, the Lord is with you,'" was to be "set . . . before her, so that, longing for these things, she may enter eagerly into the undefiled nuptial chamber of Christ and gather there with the wise virgins." Boosting the girl's self-image by demonstrating to her the elect nature of her calling as virgin in imitation even of Christ's mother would, it was hoped, whet and sustain her appetite for the "crown of immortality."[123]

The preferred models to be presented to little female virgins undoubtedly were the five wise virgins and young Thecla. Reference to the "wise

---

121. Gerontius, *Vita Melaniae Iunioris* 1–2 and 6 (ed. Gorce, *Vie de Sainte Mélanie,* 132 and 136; trans. Clark, *The Life of Melania the Younger,* 28–30).

122. *Pseudo-Basilian Canons* 36, as cited in Elm, "*Virgins of God,*" 230.

123. See *Greek Homily on Virginity* II.43–44 (ed. de Mendieta and Moons, "Une curieuse homélie grecque," 45; trans. Shaw, "Homily: On Virginity," 34). Mary as a model for virgins is featured in many other places, yet the age of the respective virgins is not to be limited to children in most of these instances. See, for example, Syriac Pseudo-Athanasius, *On Virginity* 77–81 (ed. and trans. David Brakke, *Pseudo-Athanasius on Virginity,* CSCO 592 and 593, Scriptores Syri tt. 232 and 233 [Louvain: Peeters, 2002], 30–32 [Syriac] and 29–31 [English]). For a brief discussion of Mary as model of virgins, see also Elm, "*Virgins of God,*" 336–37.

virgins" allowed the little girls to imagine that in those five virgins they could find some sort of playmates with whom to spend their time in their elevated existence, removed from the world. Thinking of those wise virgins, the little girls could dream of having company when they "stretched out their bridal bed-curtain," "received the crown of the Kingdom of the Heavens," and "kept company with the immortal Bridegroom."[124]

The most glorious example of a virgin girl was Thecla, Paul's travel companion famous from the *Acts of Paul (and Thecla)*, who became a model and inspiration for women all across the eastern Christian world. The anonymous, fourth-century Greek homily already cited above provided suggestive evidence that Thecla was to be recommended as a model to little girls pursuing a life of virginity. The girls were to "follow in the footsteps of that famous one who has gone before you and of whom you have heard: Thecla." Whatever obstacles a little virgin girl might have had to face, a troubled mother, a lamenting or aggressive suitor, or the opposition of local law, Thecla's example could show how to overcome all such hurdles. When the homilist, who presumed a detailed acquaintance on the part of his audience with Thecla's story, commented that it was "profitable for young people [*neoi*] to be crucified [*anastaurousthai*] with Jesus Christ," he may have thought of a scene in the *Acts of Paul (and Thecla)* that featured Thecla as a young girl condemned to death by burning in the theater.[125] When "boys and girls" had "brought in wood and straw," Thecla "made the sign of the cross" (*ton typon tou staurou*) and climbed upon the wood.[126] As much as Thecla, who opposed her mother and fiancé in the *Acts of Paul (and Thecla)*, defended her choice of virginity, and in the theater became an example for "boys and girls," so did it seem appropriate to this homilist to continue to entertain her example for young virgin girls in his own congregation. Usage of the exemplary character of the virgin Thecla as marker and identifier of the virginal ideal for young girls is not limited to this one instance either. In a biography, rhetorically cast into the form of a letter, Gregory of Nyssa intended to commemorate the life of his sister Macrina. Emphasizing Macrina's eternal destination for the virginal and ascetical ideal, Gregory illustrated in an early chapter how even before

---

124. See *Greek Homily on Virginity* II.43–44 (ed. de Mendieta and Moons, "Une curieuse homélie grecque," 45; trans. Shaw, "Homily: On Virginity," 34).

125. See ibid., VIII.100–102 (de Mendieta and Moons, 61; Shaw, 40). For a fuller discussion of Thecla's characterization as a young girl in the earlier part of the *Acts of Paul (and Thecla)*, see Horn, "Suffering Children," 121–30.

126. *Acts of Paul (and Thecla)* 22 (ed. Lipsius, *Acta Apostolorum Apocrypha*, vol. 1, 250).

her birth little Macrina received Thecla as patron of her virginity and as spiritual role model.[127] For those girls who were selected to strive for the highest ideal of Christian perfection, specific examples were available for children, and Thecla was the choice model among them.

Parental Support and Opposition

While asceticism was in vogue with many of the Christian teachers and writers from the fourth century on, not everyone wholeheartedly believed that the life of renunciation was the one and only choice one had for living as a good Christian. The author of the *Didascalia Apostolorum,* for example, did not show much interest in promoting sexual asceticism. Yet that did not mean that he was not interested in establishing a properly ordered, Christian life in the communities. When commenting on the upbringing of children, he was concerned that Christian children, especially boys, should be married off as soon as possible.[128] In this way, the temptations of pre- and extramarital affairs could be avoided.[129] While church orders that considered the whole of the organization of Christian life did not display much if any interest in promoting asceticism among children, individual Christian parents and teachers could go very different routes.

Parents and caretakers are the earliest teachers of their children. Parental influence on children's development was clearly considered important in early Christian texts promoting asceticism. Yet not all parents and not all children were the same. The fourth-century Greek homily cited above saw a gender distinction between promoters of the ascetic life for boys and for girls. It recommended to "the father [to] persuade his son, and [to] the mother her daughter," while at the same time stating that "the children are common to both of them."[130] Both father and mother therefore received

127. Gregory of Nyssa, *Life of Macrina* 2 (ed. and trans. Maraval, *Grégoire de Nysse. Vie de Sainte Macrine,* 146–49; trans. Kevin Corrigan, *The Life of Saint Macrina by Gregory, Bishop of Nyssa* [Toronto: Peregrina, c.1987, repr. 1989], 27–28).

128. Syriac *Didascalia Apostolorum* 22 (ed. and trans. Vööbus, *The Didascalia apostolorum in Syriac,* vol. 407, 220 [Syriac], and vol. 408, 203 [English]); see also ibid., 17 (Vööbus, vol. 407, 176 [Syriac], and vol. 408, 160 [English]), recommending that the fathers of sons should adopt girl orphans as suitable future wives for their sons. See our discussion above, chapter 4

129. See Charlotte Methuen, "'For Pagans Laugh to Hear Women Teach': Gender Stereotypes in the *Didascalia Apostolorum,*" in *Gender and Christian Religion. Papers Read at the 1996 Summer Meeting and the 1997 Winter Meeting of the Ecclesiastical History Society* (Woodbridge, England: Boydell Press, 1998), 23–35, here 27.

130. See *Greek Homily on Virginity* II.10 (ed. de Mendieta and Moons, "Une curieuse homélie grecque," 37; trans. Shaw, "Homily: On Virginity," 31 [modified]).

advice on how to ease their children's path to the virginal and ascetic life. We also have seen Jerome writing letters to a mother in one case and to a father in another. While Christian teachers expended effort in convincing both mother and father to promote the ascetic future of their children, for boys and girls, it seems that for the most part they had a more difficult time handling a father's opposition. On the other hand one can see how women, at least those who received recognition from Christian writers, were more active in furthering and enhancing ascetic experiences for their children. Two examples, John Chrysostom's treatise *Against the Opponents of the Monastic Life* and Theodoret of Cyrrhus's account of his mother's efforts to expose him to holy men in the Syrian desert, serve well to illustrate this distinction.

Christian teachers wrote to promote the ascetic life of young virgins. The example taken from Jerome's work, who sent out letters from his location in Bethlehem in the East, could be amplified with material taken from the writings of Ambrose in the West. The Bishop of Milan, for instance, defended the ascetic choice of the young girl who, refusing to marry a promising suitor, walked up to the altar, placed her head under the altar cloth, and through this gesture demanded to be received among the ranks of the veiled virgins.[131] Yet instead of pursuing Ambrose's defense of the virginal life of Christian girls at greater length here, one may highlight a more systematic effort of Christian authors in the East, who in their treatises developed strategies for overcoming parental opposition to the choice of asceticism.[132] A young person may have shown a desire to become an ascetic, to the complete chagrin of the parent, and the need was felt to counter the parents' almost certain opposition.

One of the most prolific writers on the topic was John Chrysostom. Like other Eastern and Western patristic authors on educational matters who attempted to counter parents' opposition to the ascetic life, Chrysostom commented on the issue by consistently portraying Christian parents,

131. Ambrose of Milan, *On Virgins (De virginibus ad Marcellinam sororem)* bk. 1, ch. 12, sect. 66 (ed. and Italian trans. Salvati, *Sant'Ambrogio. Verginità,* 70–73; trans. de Romestin, and others, "Three Books of St. Ambrose, Bishop of Milan, concerning Virgins," 373 [numbered as bk. 1, ch. 12, sect. 65–66]).

132. For discussion concerning a more widespread opposition to the monastic life, see, for example, L. Gougaud, "Les critiques formulées contre les premiers moines d'occident," *Revue Mabillon* 24 (1934), 145–63; and Pierre de Labriolle, "Rutilius Claudius Namatianus et les moines," *Revue des Études Latines* 6 (1928), 30–41; for a discussion of how parental attitudes toward ascetic choices on the part of their children differed from the selection of martyrdom as an option, see Horn, "'Raising Martyrs and Monks.'"

especially from upper classes, as resisting their children's vocation. Those parents considered the monastic life a path that was shameful and unworthy of those of noble origins. In his consolation to the monk Stagirius,[133] Chrysostom recalled how Stagirius's father had said the monastic life made his son "shameful and unworthy of the brilliance of [his] ancestors." Through choosing such a path the son also was destroying his own father's glory. Had that particular father not been so strongly compelled by the bonds of nature, he would have "quickly disinherit[ed]" him.[134] In his youthful treatise *A Comparison between a King and a Monk,* Chrysostom argued with conviction for the benefits of asceticism as an ideal career for the young. Yet the most fully developed work on the subject matter was his treatise *Against the Opponents of the Monastic Life.* There the author challenged both pagan and Christian parents by asking them whether they really had their offspring's best interests at heart. In his response to pagan parents he showed that ascetics also possessed the goods that were valued by people of the world. Ascetics had control over money, health, glory, and power, yet they commanded them in a far superior way.[135] They did not need earthly treasures, physical well-being, or glory and power in this world, since they had control over the heavenly realities of such things, only imperfectly mirrored by what corresponded to them here on earth. Since ascetics lived the life of heaven on earth, theirs was the fulfillment of any longing a parent could ever have, when she or more often he was eager to find the best for her or his children. Thus Chrysostom advised parents to send their offspring to ascetics "for their higher education and moral training."[136]

Only a few texts are preserved in which Christian authors reflected on their own experiences as children. The best-known case, and often the only one cited, is Augustine of Hippo, writing about his childhood adventures in his *Confessions.* Thus far overlooked, however, are writers from the Christian East, particularly from Syria, among whom at least one shared his reflections on his own childhood. Writing in the fifth century, Theodoret of Cyrrhus provides an excellent example of the lasting impact of the

---

133. For a new effort at editing this text, see Daniel Ridings, "A New Edition of John Chrysostom's *Ad Stagirium a daemone vexatum,*" *Studia Patristica* 29 (1997), 508–14.

134. John Chrysostom, *Ad Stagirium a daemone vexatum* 2.3 (ed. PG 47.423–494, here col. 452; trans. Hunter, *Comparison / Against the Opponents,* 97, n. 11).

135. Ibid., 2.3–7 (ed. PG 47.451–460).

136. Johannes Quasten, *Patrology,* vol. 3: *The Golden Age of Greek Patristic Literature* (Westminster, Md.: Christian Classics, 1994), 463.

pilgrimage experience on a young child.[137] His mother exposed her young son regularly to holy men and a few holy women living in the rocky desert areas of the Syrian plateau. For the rest of his life, Theodoret could rely on his memories of these visits and he further developed the relationships established in this manner during the earliest years of his life.[138]

In Theodoret's *Religious History,* the reader can catch glimpses of how as a child he regularly went on pilgrimage visits to selected holy people. The most impressive memory he preserved was of visits with the ascetic Peter the Galatian. In his *Ecclesiastical History,* Theodoret spoke of Peter as an ascetic living on Mount Silpius, a little to the south of Antioch.[139] Throughout the stages of Peter's life, "victorious achievements of the child [*pais*], boy [*antipais*], adolescent [*meirakion*], adult [*andros*], middle-aged man, elderly man, and ancient man" could be observed.[140] As Theodoret admiringly reported, Peter had chosen to live as an ascetic from age seven. R. M. Price dated Peter's birth to around 304 and thus the beginning of the young boy's ascetic endeavors to about 311.[141] When exactly Peter went on pilgrimage to the Holy Land cannot be reconstructed. Although Price thought it was possible that Peter might have visited there prior to Constantine and Helena's building of Christian shrines, that assumption still does not allow one to derive a youthful age or even childhood as the age range for the pilgrim Peter. Eventually, Peter settled in the area south of Antioch, preferring as Theodoret knew to report, "not those of the same race and family but those of the same convictions."[142] In her early twenties,

137. For a discussion of children's place in the pilgrimage endeavors in the Syriac-speaking realm in early centuries, see also Horn, "Children as Pilgrims and the Cult of Holy Children in the Early Syriac Tradition." The present discussion summarizes some of the themes of that article.

138. On Theodoret of Cyrrhus and his relation to ascetics, see especially Pierre Canivet, *Le monachisme syrien selon Théodoret de Cyr* (Paris: Beauchesne, c1977). For a study of Theodoret's childhood, see also Alice Leroy-Molinghen, "Naissance et enfance de Théodoret," in *L'enfant dans les civilisations orientales / Het kind in de oosterse beschavingen,* ed. A. Théodoridès, P. Naster, and J. Ries (Louvain: Peeters, 1980), 153–58.

139. Theodoret of Cyrrhus, *Ecclesiastical History* 4.28.3 (ed. Parmentier and Hansen, *Theodoret. Kirchengeschichte,* 269).

140. Theodoret of Cyrrhus, *Religious History* 9.1 (Peter the Galatian) (ed. and trans. P. Canivet and A. Leroy-Molinghen, *Théodoret de Cyr: Histoire des moines de Syrie,* 2 vols. [Paris: Les Éditions du Cerf, 1977–79], vol. 1, 406–7; trans. R. M. Price, *Theodoret of Cyrrhus: A History of the Monks of Syria* [Kalamazoo, Mich.: Cistercian Publications, 1985], 81).

141. Price, *Theodoret of Cyrrhus: A History of the Monks of Syria,* 88.

142. Theodoret of Cyrrhus, *Religious History* 9.3 (Peter the Galatian) (ed. and trans. Canivet and Leroy-Molinghen, *Théodoret de Cyr: Histoire des moines de Syrie,* vol. 1, 410–11; trans. Price, *Theodoret of Cyrrhus: A History of the Monks of Syria,* 82).

Theodoret's mother had benefited from the instructions toward conversion to a simple life and from the healing powers of Peter. Throughout her life she preserved high respect and veneration for that holy man. Although she used to send her young son out to the ascetic "to reap his blessings once each week," Peter himself was reluctant to verify predictions that Theodoret would become a monk later in life. Nevertheless, as Theodoret remembered, Peter "often sat [him] on his knees and fed [him] with grapes and bread."[143] From his early acquaintance with the ascetic, Theodoret retained many stories of exorcisms and healings, which the saint worked on those in need. Theodoret never became an ascetic living in the desert himself. Yet impressed by his early and ongoing encounters with ascetics, he wrote about them later in life and thus became one of the strongest promoters of ascetic ideals and icons of the holy life among clergy and laity alike in the Eastern Christian world. The meeting between a young child and an ascetic that had been initiated, promoted, and sustained through motherly efforts bore fruit in a joint venture of episcopal and ascetic interests.

Children and the Institutional Structures of Asceticism

The discussion above has only begun to trace a few of the possible lines of research into the question of what the connections were between family life and asceticism more generally, and the role of children in the ascetic life more specifically. Much of what could be said about how children's lives were affected by the rise of asceticism has to remain unexplored here. For example, we have chosen not to consider in any depth the concrete place of children in institutions and structures of the ascetic life. This question deserves to be treated separately in a study dedicated explicitly to the topic of children and asceticism. Material for such inquiry abounds. We hear in the *Apophthegmata Patrum* of Abba Carion, who left his wife and two children in the world so that he might be able to take up life as a monk in Scetis, but at the time of famine had his young son join him there, quite to the dismay of several other ascetics in the settlement.[144] Why Abba Car-

---

143. Ibid., 9.4 (Canivet and Leroy-Molinghen, vol. 1, 414–15; Price, 83).

144. *Apophthegmata Patrum*, Sayings of Carion 2 (trans. Benedicta Ward, *The Sayings of the Desert Fathers. The Alphabetical Collection* [Kalamazoo, Mich.: Cistercian Publications, 1975], 100–101). See also Philip Rousseau, "Blood-Relationships among Early Eastern Ascetics," *Journal of Theological Studies* 23 (1972), 135–44. For further study of children and the young in the perspective of the Desert Fathers, see for example Louis Leloir, "Attitude des pères du désert vis-à-vis des jeunes," in *L'enfant dans les civilisations orientales / Het kind in de oosterse beschavingen*, 133–43.

ion's little daughter ran away when she saw her father as an ascetic and why she did not want to join and find shelter in the Scetis community is an open question with many possible answers. Opposition to the presence of children in ascetic settings also can be detected directly in Abba Carion's words, when he said that "a monk who lives with a boy, falls, if he is not stable; but even if he is stable and does not fall, he still does not make progress."[145] The danger of sexual temptation arising from the view of young bodies was seen as lurking in the background here. Other texts, like Basil of Caesarea's *Long Rules*,[146] provided instructions on how to raise and educate children who were part of the monastery. Basil deemed "every time of life, even the very earliest, suitable for receiving applicants" to the monastery.[147] Yet he also was aware of the fact that the tranquility necessary for ascetics' pursuit of their life of dedication to and labor for God may come into conflict with the necessary noise that accompanies the raising and training of children. Thus Basil instructed that "the children's quarters should be separate from those of the more advanced in perfection."[148] As we considered earlier, Cyril of Scythopolis witnessed to the fact that Abba Euthymius was introduced to asceticism by being tonsured at the age of two. As a little child he received his first training under the direction of his uncle, Bishop Otreius.[149] The *Rule of Benedict* provided advice regarding children, both of the rich and of the poor, who were left with the brethren of the monastery as oblates.[150] In the mountain villages of late antique Syria, children populated the monasteries of Symeon the Mountaineer after they had been forcefully taken from their families. Those families who refused to part with their children shortly afterwards had to mourn their children's deaths.[151] A future study of these and other witnesses to the

145. *Apophthegmata Patrum*, Sayings of Carion 3 (trans. Ward, *The Sayings of the Desert Fathers*, 101).

146. Basil of Caesarea, *Regulae fusius tractatae (Long Rules)*, quaestio 15 (ed. PG 31.952–957; trans. Wagner, *Saint Basil. Ascetical Works*, 264–68).

147. Ibid., quaestio 15.1 (PG 31.952; Wagner, 264).

148. Ibid., quaestio 15.2 (PG 31.953; Wagner, 265).

149. Cyril of Scythopolis, *Life of Euthymius* 3 (ed. Schwartz. *Kyrillos von Skythopolis*, 10–11; trans. Price and Binns, *Cyril: Lives of the Monks*, 6). See also chapter 7.

150. *Regula Benedicti* 59 [*De filiis nobiliium aut pauperum qui offeruntur*] (ed. and trans. Adalbert de Vogüe and Jean Neufville, *La Règle de Saint Benoît II (ch. VIII–LXXIII)* [Paris: Les Éditions du Cerf, 1972], 632–35). See also the discussion by Adalbert de Vogüe, *La Règle de Saint Benoît, tome VI, Commentaire Historique et Critique (Parties VII–IX et Index)* (Paris: Les Éditions du Cerf, 1971), 962–70 and 1355–68.

151. John of Ephesus, *Lives of the Eastern Saints* (ed. and trans. E. W. Brooks, *John of Ephesus. Lives of the Eastern Saints*, Patrologia Orientalis 17.1 [Paris: Firmin-Didot, Imprimeurs-

presence and conditions of life of children in ascetic structures may build upon and expand the preceding investigation of the numerous factors that played a role in preparing, exposing, and enticing children to take up asceticism as a possible option for their lives. Quite a few of them learned to see asceticism as the ideal way for the little ones to come to Jesus and to take possession of the kingdom of heaven, whose owners Jesus had proclaimed them already (Mt 19:14; Mk 10:14; and Lk 18:16).

Éditeurs, 1923], 245); see also Susan Ashbrook Harvey, *Asceticism and Society in Crisis. John of Ephesus and the "Lives of the Eastern Saints"* (Berkeley: University of California Press, 1990), 96; and Clark, "The Fathers and the Children," 1–2.

Conclusions

How well did the early Church live up to Jesus' command: "Let the little children come to me" (Mt 19:14)? To what extent did Jesus' followers welcome children as they welcomed the kingdom of God? Did early Christians themselves change and become "like little children"? These questions cannot be answered directly, which suggests that the early Church was not able to live up to Jesus' commands with respect to children. Early Christian treatment of children cannot always be viewed as a straightforward success. Yet it is also fair to judge the achievements of Christians in the early centuries in this regard not only in light of the ideal Jesus put forward, but in light of how well they succeeded in living up to other ideals set for his disciples. Did the Christians always love their neighbors as themselves? Were they able to forgive seven times, or seventy-seven times? Did they feed and clothe their enemies? Arguing in this manner is not an exercise in delineating the failures of early Christians. It is an exercise in checking reality and an acknowledgment of the transformed life to which Jesus' disciples were called. It is also an act of acknowledging human weakness, the reality of sin, which permeates all human life. This is not to say that early Christians did not evince successes in their rethinking of childhood and what it meant to be a child. They managed to transform practices and challenge whole cultures with respect to their treatment of children. It is easier to see the ways in which Christianity made life better for children, and ways in which they failed to do so, when we keep in mind the practices that flourished before the rise of Christianity and which continued alongside it.

These conclusions have to restate what we said at the beginning, namely, that Christianity did not discover children or childhood; it did not create childhood, nor did it invent the notion that children are people. Generalized comments about the low estate of children in the ancient world,

Jewish or Greco-Roman, must be tempered with a dose of equanimity. All throughout the Mediterranean basin men and women sought children and wanted to become fathers and mothers to perpetuate the family name, to bring honor to the family, to serve God, to work, and to have someone who would care for them, the parents, in their old age. Since childhood mortality, both in childbirth and subsequently, was remarkably high, a reality not to be conquered until the rise of modern medicine and still not conquered in every part of the world today, children were a precious commodity. As far as we are able to tell from literary and epigraphical evidence and from the remains of material culture, such as toys, jars, and sculpture, children were cared for, loved, and mourned in death. This is, of course, where we have to add qualifications. The care and love shown to some children was not applicable throughout the Greco-Roman world. Some children were cast out, unacceptable to the family; some were raised as sexual slaves; and many worked from an early age. Some boys were able to have the leisure of an education and a smooth path to a political or military career, while others worked beside their fathers in rented fields from childhood. Boys might be able to put off marriage for many years, studying and playing, while girls just reaching puberty were considered ready for marriage. Those who were educated, especially at high levels, had numerous advantages, but also the regular punishment, many blows, from teacher and *paedagogus* that accompanied an education. Such conditions illustrate well why it is so jarring to consider the place of children in ancient Greece or Rome: cruelty and brutality vied with love and care in the life of the child.

Christianity arose first from within Judaism. Children in the Jewish community were not regularly exposed or killed, nor were they regularly sexually abused, although it would be foolish to think such things never happened. In other respects, Judaism was exactly like its neighbors. Girls were married at a young age; students expected blows from their teachers; many children had to work from childhood; and a slave child working for a Jewish master could expect the life of a slave. Christianity emerged with many of these same attitudes, positive and negative, inherited from Judaism as it met the Greco-Roman world. It was armed with another tool: the radical teaching of Jesus with respect not only to children, but also to the world itself. When Christianity arose in the first century, life for children began to change, sometimes imperceptibly, sometimes quickly, and sometimes, it is true, not at all.

What began to change was the general attitude toward children: they were seen as valuable in themselves. Deriving from the understanding that all people are created in the image of God, that all people are children of God, that already the little child was such a "child of God," and that in the end everyone was called to become a "child of God," Christianity accepted children as persons, not on the basis of their reception into the family or their usefulness to the community, but on the basis of their very birth. It is true that Judaism had the same attitude toward children, and thus we cannot argue that the Christian attitude was without precedent. Yet Christianity did begin to influence Greco-Roman attitudes toward children more widely. This did not mean that children were no longer aborted, exposed, or killed, but it did mean that the cultures into which Christianity advanced were challenged as to their practices and attitudes concerning children. For those who were Christians, engaging in such practices meant that their own place in the Church was threatened, as were their very souls. Ultimately this lent itself to bringing about a change in practices. If such changes were not immediately apparent, eventually they did come.

If the child was accepted into the Church as a child, valuable as such, it is not true that Jesus' insights regarding the child as model for a disciple's acceptance of the kingdom and for the disciple's behavior gained much ground. We have some evidence that Jesus' teachings on the primacy of the child as a model disciple were already being changed and dispersed, extended to all disciples, as the Gospel material was being edited. As in Judaism and in a Greco-Roman setting, children were accepted as fully human in one sense, but only partly human in another sense. Lacking the fullness of reason, weak in the ability to control their emotions, children were in need of discipline and education before they could be a part of the human family. The measure of growth was the freeborn, educated male, which implied some recognizable level of wealth and social standing. The model was not a slave, not a woman, and certainly not a child. Jesus' own teachings confronted and defied those cultural expectations, in particular through his teachings concerning children, the weak, the outcast, and the marginalized and the way he acted upon this in his choice of apostles and disciples. Yet it was not long before the model Christian child was like every other model child in the ancient world: not someone to follow, but one who needed to be brought into line, educated, and made to take his or her place, whatever that would be for a slave child or a freeborn child, girl or boy. Perhaps this was inevitable—children, after all, *do* need to be raised, trained, and taught—but what went missing from Jesus' own teaching? And why was it cast aside so readily?

One reason is to be sought in the confrontation between the ideal and the necessities of everyday practical life. Children are dependent, they are vulnerable, they are weak, and, practically, they know very little. Christian families had to deal with this reality like all other families. They had to prepare their children for life, whatever that life and whatever their station in life might be. Here it seems that the pursuit of the ideal was most immediately lost. Jesus' focus on the kingdom, and the need to prepare for entry into the kingdom, was absolute. The family was to take second place to the preparation for the coming kingdom—fathers, mothers, brothers, and sisters were those who did the will of God—but quickly the family moved into its (regular and established) place of prominence in the emerging Christian culture. Children were what they always were: hope for the future, be that economically, in terms of their own progeny, or for reasons of the preservation and increase of honor. The ways in which honor was gained might have changed—children ought to be obedient to the Christian faith; wealth might no longer have been the true measure of power in the community—but children were expected to bear witness to their excellent upbringing. Although Christianity seems to have brought familial disruption in its wake, it is not clear that on the practical level a return to a more stable, settled life was not in the best interest of children in the long run.

From its earliest stages, Christianity brought with it changes in the manner in which some children were treated sexually. Sexual morality, far stricter among the Jews than among Greeks and Romans, retained a place of prominence among Christians. Yet among them its influence was even expanded, since so much of Christian identity rested upon sexual continence, the place of sex in marriage, and even celibacy. As a result of the teachings of Jesus and Paul and of many of those who followed after them, sexuality came to be a predominant issue for Christian morality. Positively, boys simply did not have to face the same likelihood of sexual abuse by an older male, so common in Greece and Rome, as a part of growing up. This did not mean that the sexual use of children did not exist in the cultures in which Christianity rested, or that there were no Christians who engaged in sexual contact with children, but such practices were not countenanced. From the perspective of Christian teachings, it was not acceptable that slave children, boys and girls, were raised to be prostitutes. Even though some Christian masters may and probably would have continued to use their slaves sexually, Christianity did not accept this behavior as normal, natural, or legal.

One practice that does not seem to have changed with the rise and early spread of Christianity was the age at which girls were married. Through-out the ancient Mediterranean world, the common age of marriage for fe-males was puberty. There simply is no evidence that this changed. What did change, however, was the availability of the option of leading a celibate life as an alternative to marriage. Although it seems that often the parents made the choice for their children, the evidence we have been able to in-vestigate suggests that this opportunity opened up new options for girls and boys and that many of them chose celibacy of their own accord and against the wishes of their parents. A life of celibacy offered boys and espe-cially girls the opportunity to focus on the spiritual life, free of the forces and expectations of marriage, which often was arranged and under the con-straints of ancient society. The ascetic life was not seen as a constraint, but as freedom: spiritual, to be sure, but also a form of freedom in the world to live a life consecrated to God. Children's involvement in religion was not a novelty that came about with the arrival of Christianity. Jews, Greeks, and Romans all had a place for children in their rites and practices. Children worshipped in numerous ways in all of these cultures, but the celibate life put children and their choices at the heart of the religious life and the life of the Christian community itself.

After all, education, play, and work for children seem not to have changed much for Christian children, although this comment requires some qualification. As one might suspect, Christian children brought Christian rites into their play; negatively, they could no longer attend cer-tain festivals and rites, the theater or games. Perhaps it comes as a surprise that education did not become formally Christian in its basic or advanced form for several centuries; the Christian education of antiquity was the pa-gan education of antiquity. For Christian children, catechesis was much like the study of Scripture among the Jews, and Christian children learned Scripture and Christian morality in the Church. Yet with the exception of components of physical education, the Greco-Roman education stayed the same. So, too, did work. Christian children had to work and partici-pate in the workforce, if their families depended on their assistance. The children of those Christian families that had sufficient wealth were educat-ed at leisure. Slave children worked as was necessary and as was required; Christianity does not seemed to have challenged the status quo in this regard, except for keeping slave children away from brothels and a life of prostitution.

At root, what Christianity brought that was new for children was a new way of looking at the world and a practical option grounded in a new spiritual reality: children were valuable as children; both boys and girls were brought into the Church in the same manner—baptism did not differentiate along the lines of gender; also slave children could become members of the Church, even though they remained bound to their masters; children might choose a life not of marriage, as was the common expectation in the ancient world, especially for girls, but of celibacy, of undivided devotion to God. The world around them accepted them as Christians, even as children. As the martyrdom accounts are eager to show, children were not immune from persecution or suffering. While freed from many of the violent effects of Greco-Roman culture, sexual and otherwise, for a number of centuries Christian children faced the same persecution and martyrdom that their adult brothers and sisters were confronted with. They were, indeed, Christians, even as children. Parallel to their equal participation in Christian witness through martyrdom, children's place in the Church also was prominent through baptism, the liturgy, and a life of devotion to the Church, monastically or in Church offices. Yet, in so many respects, although Christian children prepared for the world to come perhaps with greater intensity than their non-Christian peers, their lives were very similar to those of the children around them who were not Christian. They went to school, played, worked, and were brought up in families much like their neighbors. Jesus' teachings on the child as spiritual model seemed to recede, only to be located in the ascetic life. All members and subgroups of Christianity faced the same tension in the ancient world: how to be a part of the world while preparing for the world to come. Children were not sheltered from this struggle for balance. Would a given child make a decision for the married life or for the life of asceticism? Would the child opt to remain obedient to his or her family or to the family of God? The alternatives that posed themselves only increased.

We should not underestimate the advances in the lives of children which Christianity brought: the opportunity to share in life itself and the opportunity to be free of sexual violence. Nor can we omit the most significant spiritual reality: that children as children were seen to be valid partakers of the kingdom of heaven, even if they were not accepted by adult Christians as models of the kingdom Jesus had proposed. Children, too, had to get ready for the world to come. Such preparation did not remove them from the world around them—it placed them on the frontlines of Christian inculturation. Involved in the ordinary life of children, the life of the family, play, education, work, discipline, and training, Christian children were much like other children. As the privileged hearers of the words of Jesus, who said, "Let the little children come to me," they were brought into the Church and called to respond to the message, "unless you change and become like children, you will never enter the kingdom of heaven." Despite all the good the ancient Church was able to accomplish on behalf of them, early Christian children waited, as children today still wait, for the Church to catch up fully to the import of Jesus' teachings.

Bibliography

Primary Sources

Acts of Andrew. Ed. and trans. Jean-Marc Prieur. *Acta Andreae. Textus*. Corpus Christianorum Series Apocryphorum (hereafter CCSA) 6. Turnhout: Brepols, 1989.

Acts of John. Ed. and trans. Eric Junod and Jean-Daniel Kaestli. *Acta Iohannis. Praefatio—Textus*. CCSA 1. Turnhout: Brepols, 1983.

Acts of Paul (and Thecla). In *Acta Petri. Acta Pauli. Acta Petri et Pauli. Acta Pauli et Theclae. Acta Thaddaei*. Ed. Richard A. Lipsius. *Acta Apostolorum Apocrypha*. Vol. 1, 235–72. Ed. Richard A. Lipsius and Maximilian Bonnet. Leipzig: Hermann Mendelssohn, 1891; repr.: Hildesheim: Georg Olms, 1959.

Acts of Peter. In *Acta Petri. Acta Pauli. Acta Petri et Pauli. Acta Pauli et Theclae. Acta Thaddaei*. Ed. Richard A. Lipsius. *Acta Apostolorum Apocrypha*. Vol. 1, 45–103. Ed. Richard A. Lipsius and Maximilian Bonnet. Leipzig: Hermann Mendelssohn, 1891; repr: Hildesheim: Georg Olms, 1959.

Acts of Phileas (Papyrus Bodmer). Ed. and trans. Herbert Musurillo. *The Acts of the Christian Martyrs*, 328–45. Oxford: Clarendon Press, 1972.

Acts of Phileas (recensio Latina). Ed. and trans. Herbert Musurillo. *The Acts of the Christian Martyrs*, 345–53. Oxford: Clarendon Press, 1972.

Acts of Saint Cyprian. Ed. and trans. Herbert Musurillo. *The Acts of the Christian Martyrs*, 168–75. Oxford: Clarendon Press, 1972.

Acts of Thomas. In *Acta Philippi et Acta Thomae accedunt Acta Barnabae*. Ed. Maximilian Bonnet. *Acta Apostolorum Apocrypha*. Vol. 2.2, 99–291. Eds. Richard A. Lipsius and Maximilian Bonnet. Leipzig: Hermann Mendelssohn, 1903; repr.: Hildesheim: Georg Olms, 1959.

African Code (A.D. 419). Trans. Henry R. Percival. "The Canons of the CCXVII Blessed Fathers Who Assembled at Carthage. Commonly Called The Code of Canons of the African Church. A.D. 419." In *The Seven Ecumenical Councils of the Undivided Church. Their Canons and Decrees, together with the Canons of all the Local Synods which have Received Ecumenical Acceptance*. NPNF 2nd ser., vol. 14, 441–510. Repr.: Peabody, Mass.: Hendrickson Publishers, 1995.

Agathangelos. *Patmout'iwn Hayot's. History of the Armenians*. In *Agathangelos. History of the Armenians*. Trans. R. W. Thomson. Albany: State University of New York Press, 1976.

Alberigo, G., et al. *Conciliorum Oecumenicorum Decreta*. Bologna: Istituto per le Scienze Religiose, 1973.

Amar, Joseph, and Edward Mathews, trans. *St. Ephrem the Syrian: Selected Prose Works.* The Fathers of the Church 91. Washington, D.C.: The Catholic University of America Press, 1994.

Ambrose of Milan. *On Virgins* [*De virginibus ad Marcellinam sororem*]. Ed. M. Salvati. *Sant'Ambrogio. Verginità.* Corona Patrum Salesiana. Series Latina 6, 5–163. Turin: Societa Editrice Internazionale, 1955.

———. *On Virgins* [*De virginibus ad Marcellinam sororem*]. Trans. H. de Romestin, E. de Romestin, and H. T. F. Duckworth. "Three Books of St. Ambrose, Bishop of Milan, concerning Virgins, to Marcellina, his Sister." NPNF 2nd ser., vol. 10, 363–87. Repr.: Peabody, Mass.: Hendrickson Publishers, 1995.

Anthologia Palatina. Ed. W. R. Paton. *The Greek Anthology.* 5 vols. Loeb Classical Library (hereafter LCL) 67–68 and 84–86. Cambridge, Mass.: Harvard University Press, 1958–63.

Antony of Egypt. *Letters.* Trans. Derwas J. Chitty. *The Letters of St. Antony the Great.* Fairacres Publication 50. Oxford: S. L. G. Press, 1977.

———. *Letters.* Trans. Matta El Meskin. *Secondo il Vangelo: le venti lettere di Antonio.* Translated from Arabic into Italian by Maurizio Bagatin and Corrado Pettiti. Padri orientali. Magnano [Biella]: Qiqajon Comunità di Bose, c1999.

Apophthegmata Patrum. Trans. Benedicta Ward. *The Sayings of the Desert Fathers. The Alphabetical Collection.* Cistercian Studies Series 59. Kalamazoo, Mich.: Cistercian Publications, 1975.

Apostolic Constitutions. Ed. and trans. Marcel Metzger. *Les Constitutions Apostoliques.* 3 vols. Sources Chrétiennes (hereafter SCh) 320, 329, and 336. Paris: Les Éditions du Cerf, 1985–1987.

Apostolic Tradition. Ed. Bernard Botte. *Hippolyte de Rome. La Tradition apostolique d'après les anciennes versions.* SCh 11bis., 2nd ed. Paris: Les Éditions du Cerf, 1968.

———. Ed. and trans. Wilhelm Geerlings. *Traditio Apostolica. Apostolische Überlieferung,* 212–313. Fontes Christiani 1. Freiburg: Herder, c1991.

Aristides. *Apology.* Ed. and trans. Bernard Pouderon, Marie-Joseph Pierre, with the collaboration of Bernard Outtier and Maria Guiorgadzé. *Aristide. Apologie.* SCh 470. Paris: Les Éditions du Cerf, 2003.

Aristotle. *Politics.* Ed. W. D. Ross. *Aristotelis Politeia.* Oxford: Oxford University Press, 1973.

———. *Politics.* Text and trans. H. Rackham. *Aristotle in Twenty-Three Volumes.* Vol. 21. Cambridge, Mass.: Harvard University Press, 1977.

Athanasius. *Contra gentes.* Ed. Robert W. Thomson. *Contra gentes; and, De Incarnatione. Athanasius.* Oxford Early Christian Texts. Oxford: Clarendon Press, 1971.

———. *Life of Antony.* Trans. Robert C. Gregg. *Athanasius: The Life of Antony and the Letter to Marcellinus.* Classics of Western Spirituality, 29–99. Mahwah, N.J.: Paulist Press, 1980.

———. *Life of Antony.* Ed. and trans. G. J. M. Bartelink. *Athanase d'Alexandrie: Vie d'Antoine.* SCh 400. Paris: Les Éditions du Cerf, 1994.

Athenagoras. *A Plea for the Christians.* Ed. Miroslav Marcovich. *Athenagoras. Legatio Pro Christianis.* Berlin: de Gruyter, 1990.

Augustine of Hippo. *Confessions.* Ed. Lucas Verheijen. *Sancti Augustini Confessionum Libri XIII.* CCL 27. Turnhout: Brepols, 1981.

———. *Confessions.* Trans. Henry Chadwick. *St. Augustine Confessions.* Oxford World Classics. Oxford: Oxford University Press, c1991.

————. *De bono conjugale.* Trans. Charles T. Wilcox and others. *St. Augustine, Treatises on Marriage and Other Subjects.* Fathers of the Church 27, 9–51. New York: Fathers of the Church, 1955.

————. *De civitate Dei.* Ed. and trans. R. W. Dyson. *Augustine, The City of God against the Pagans.* Cambridge: Cambridge University Press, 1998.

————. *De consensu Evangelistarum.* Ed. PL 34.1041–1230.

————. *De consensu Evangelistarum.* Trans. S. D. F. Salmond. "[Augustine's] The Harmony of the Gospels." NPNF 1st ser., vol. 6, 77–236. Repr.: Peabody, Mass.: Hendrickson Publishers, 1995.

————. *De peccatorum meritis et remissione et de baptismo parvulorum ad Marcellinum libri tres.* Ed. Carolus F. Urba and Ioseph Zycha. *Sancti Aureli Augustini De peccatorum meritis et remissione et de baptismo parvulorum ad Marcellinum libri tres, De spiritu et littera liber unus, de natura et gratia liber unus, de natura et origine animae liber quattuor, contra duas epistulas Pelagianorum libri quattuor.* (= *Sancti Aureli Augustini Opera* [*sect. VIII, pars I*]). CSEL 60, 3–151. Vindobonae: F. Tempsky, 1913.

————. *De peccatorum meritis et remissione et de baptismo parvulorum ad Marcellinum libri tres.* Trans. Peter Holmes, Robert Ernest Wallis, and Benjamin B. Warfield. "A Treatise on the Merits of Forgiveness of Sins, and on the Baptism of Infants." In *Augustin: Anti-Pelagian Writings.* NPNF 1st ser., vol. 5, 15–78. Repr.: Peabody, Mass.: Hendrickson Publishers, 1995.

————. *Letters.* Ed. A. Goldbacher. *S. Aureli Augustini Hipponensis Episcopi Epistulae, Pars III. Ep. CXXIV–CCXXXIVa.* CSEL 44. Vindobonae: F. Tempsky, 1904.

————. *Letters.* Trans. Sister Wilfrid Parsons. *Saint Augustine. Letters. Vol. IV (165–203).* Fathers of the Church 30. New York: Fathers of the Church, 1955.

————. *On Baptism against the Donatists.* Ed. M. Petschenig. *Sancti Aureli Augustini Scripta Contra Donatistas,* 145–375. CSEL 51. Vindobonae: F. Tempsky, 1908.

————. *On Baptism against the Donatists.* Trans. J. R. King. "The Seven Books of Augustine, Bishop of Hippo, on Baptism, against the Donatists." In *Augustin: The Writings against the Manichaens and against the Donatists.* NPNF 1st ser., vol. 4, 411–514. Repr.: Peabody, Mass.: Hendrickson Publishers, 1995.

Basil of Caesarea. *Ad adolescentes.* Ed. N. G. Wilson. *Saint Basil on the Value of Greek Literature,* 19–36. London: Duckworth, c1975.

————. *Ad adolescentes.* In *Saint Basil. The Letters.* Greek text and English trans. Roy J. Deferrari. 4 vols. LCL. Vol. 4, 378–435. Cambridge, Mass.: Harvard University Press, 1934.

————. *Against Eunomius.* Ed. and trans. Bernard Sesboüé, Georges-Matthieu de Durand, and Louis Doutreleau. *Contre Eunome: suivie par Eunome apologie. Basile de Césarée.* SCh 305. Paris: Les Éditions du Cerf, 1983.

————. *Homilia dicta tempore famis et siccitatis.* Ed. and trans. PG 31.303–328.

————. *Letters.* Ed. and trans. Roy J. Deferrari. *Saint Basil. The Letters.* 4 vols. LCL. New York: G. P. Putnam's Sons, 1926–34.

————. *Letters.* Trans. Sister Agnes Clare Way. With notes by Roy I. Deferrari. *Saint Basil. Letters. Volume II (186–368).* Fathers of the Church 28. New York: Fathers of the Church, 1955.

————. *Letters.* Ed. and trans. Yves Courtonne. *Saint Basile: Lettres, Tome I.* Paris: Société d'édition "Les Belles Lettres," 1957.

————. *Long Rules.* Trans. Sister M. Monica Wagner. *Basil of Caesarea. Ascetical Works.* Fathers of the Church 9. New York: Fathers of the Church, 1950.

————. *Regulae fusius tractatae (Long Rules)*. Ed. PG. 31.889–1052.

Blackman, Philip. *Mishnayoth. Pointed Hebrew Text, English Translation, Introductions, Notes, Supplement, Appendix, Indexes, Addenda, Corrigenda.* 7 vols. 2nd rev. ed.: New York: The Judaica Press, 1990.

Bonnet, Maximilian, ed. *Acta Philippi et Acta Thomae accedunt Acta Barnabae. Acta Apostolorum Apocrypha* 2.2. Eds. Richard A. Lipsius and Maximilian Bonnet. Leipzig: Hermann Mendelssohn, 1903: repr.: Hildesheim: Georg Olms, 1959.

Brashler, James, and Douglas M. Parrott, eds. and trans. "The Act of Peter, BG, 4: 128,1–141,7." In *Nag Hammadi Codices V,2–5 and VI with Papyrus Berolinensis 8502,1 and 4*. Ed. Douglas M. Parrott. Nag Hammadi Studies 11, 473–93. Leiden: E. J. Brill, 1979.

Canon to the Akathistos Hymn. Greek text and English trans. N. Michael Vaporis and Evie Zachariades-Holmberg. *The Akathist Hymn and Small Compline.* Needham, Mass.: Themely Publications, 1992.

Cartlidge, David R., and David L. Dungan. *Documents for the Study of the Gospels.* London: Collins, 1980.

Cassius Dio. *Roman History.* Ed. and trans. Earnest Cary. *Dio's Roman History.* 9 vols. LCL 32, 37, 53, 66, 82–83, 175–77. Cambridge, Mass.: Harvard University Press, 1914–27.

Chitty, Derwas J. *The Letters of St. Antony the Great.* Fairacres Publication 50. Oxford: S. L. G. Press, 1977.

Cicero. *Letters to Atticus.* Ed. David Roy Shackleton Bailey. *M. Tullius Cicero. Epistulae ad Atticum.* 2 vols. Bibliotheca scriptorum Graecorum et Romanorum Teubneriana. Stuttgart: B. G. Teubner, 1987.

————. *Rosc. Am.* Ed. Karl Halm. *Ciceros Ausgewählte Reden.* Vol. 1: *Die Reden für Sex. Roscius aus Ameria and über das Imperium des Cn. Pompeius.* 12th ed. Berlin: Weidmannsche Buchhandlung, 1910.

————. *Tusculan Disputations.* Ed. Otto Heine. *Cicero. Tusculanarum Disputationum.* 2 vols. Leipzig: Teubner, 1957; repr.: Amsterdam: Verlag Adolf M. Hakkert, 1965.

Clement of Alexandria. *Paedagogus.* Ed. Miroslav Marcovich and J. C. M. van Winden. *Clementis Alexandrini. Paedagogus.* Supplements to Vigiliae Christianae 61. Leiden: E. J. Brill, 2002.

————. *Protreptikos.* Trans. William Wilson. *The Writings of Clement of Alexandria.* Ante-Nicene Christian Library 4. Edinburgh: T&T Clark, 1868.

————. *Protreptikos.* Ed. Miroslav Marcovich. *Clementis Alexandrini "Protrepticus."* Supplements to Vigiliae Christianae 34. Leiden: E. J. Brill, 1995.

————. *Quis Dives Salvetur.* Ed. Otto Stählin, Ludwig Früchtel, and Ursula Treu. *Clemens Alexandrinus. Dritter Band. Stromata Buch VII–VIII. Excerpta ex Theodoto—Eclogae Propheticae—Quis Dives Salvetur—Fragmente,* 159–91. GCS 3. Berlin: Akademie-Verlag, 1970.

————. *Stromateis.* Eds. Otto Stählin and Ludwig Früchtel. *Clemens Alexandrinus. Zweiter Band. Stromata. Buch I–VI.* GCS. Berlin: Akademie-Verlag, 1960.

————. *Stromateis.* Ed. Otto Stählin, Ludwig Früchtel, and Ursula Treu. *Clemens Alexandrinus. Dritter Band. Stromata Buch VII–VIII. Excerpta ex Theodoto—Eclogae Propheticae—Quis Dives Salvetur—Fragmente,* 3–102. GCS 3. Berlin: Akademie-Verlag, 1970.

Columella. *De re rustica.* Ed. and trans. Harrison Boyd Ash, *De Re Rustica, I–IV Vol. I*; eds. E. S. Forster and Edward Heffner, *De Re Rustica, V–IX Vol. II*; and eds.

E. S. Forster and Edward Heffner, *De Re Rustica, X–XII and De Arboribus Vol. III.* LCL 361, 407, and 408. Cambridge, Mass.: Harvard University Press, 1948.

Constantine (Emperor). "Oratio ad sanctorum coetum." In *Über das Leben Constantins; Constantins Rede an die heilige Versammlung; Tricennatsrede an Constantin.* Ed. Ivar August Heikel. GCS 7, 149–92.. Leipzig: J. C. Hinrichs, 1902.

Coogan, Michael D., ed., Mark Z. Brettler, Carol A. Newsom, and Pheme Perkins associate editors. *The New Oxford Annotated Bible: The New Revised Standard Version, with the Apocryphal/Deuterocanonical Books.* 3rd ed. Oxford: Oxford University Press, 2001.

Corpus Inscriptionum Latinarum. Ed. T. Mommsen. *Corpus Inscriptionum Latinarum,* vol. 8: *Inscriptiones Africae Latinae.* Berlin: G. Reiner, 1881.

———. Ed. E. Bormann. *Corpus Inscriptionum Latinarum,* vol. 11: *Inscriptiones Aemiliae, Etruriae, Umbriae Latinae.* Berlin: G. Reiner, 1888–1926.

Corrigan, Kevin. *The Life of Saint Macrina by Gregory, Bishop of Nyssa.* Toronto: Peregrina, c.1987, repr. 1989.

Cyprian of Carthage. *Ad Donatum.* Ed. and trans. Jean Molager. *Cyprien de Carthage. A Donat et la vertue de patience.* SCh 291. Paris: Les Éditions du Cerf, 1982.

———. *De lapsis.* Ed. and trans. Maurice Bénevot. *Cyprian. "De Lapsis" and "De Ecclesiae Catholicae Unitate,"* 2–55. Oxford: Clarendon Press, 1971.

———. *Letters.* Ed. G. F. Diercks. *Sancti Cypriani Episcopi Epistularium.* CCSL 3C: *Sancti Cypriani Episcopi Opera,* part 3.2. Turnhout: Brepols, 1996.

———. *On the Dress of Virgins.* Ed. G. Hartel. *S. Thasci Caecilli Cypriani Opera Omnia,* 185–205. CSEL 3.1. Vienna: Apud C. Geroldi filium, 1868.

———. *On the Dress of Virgins.* Trans. Roy J. Deferrari. *St. Cyprian. Treatises.* Fathers of the Church 36. New York: Fathers of the Church, 1958.

Cyril of Scythopolis. *Life of Cyriacus.* Ed. Eduard Schwartz. *Kyrillos von Skythopolis.* Texte und Untersuchungen zur Geschichte der altchristlichen Literatur 49.2, 222–35. Leipzig: J. C. Hinrichs Verlag, 1939.

———. *Life of Cyriacus.* Trans. R. M. Price and John Binns. *Cyril of Scythopolis: The Lives of the Monks of Palestine.* Cistercian Studies 114, 245–61. Kalamazoo, Mich.: Cistercian Publications, 1991.

———. *Life of Euthymius.* Ed. Eduard Schwartz. *Kyrillos von Skythopolis.* Texte und Untersuchungen zur Geschichte der altchristlichen Literatur 49.2, 6–85. Leipzig: J. C. Hinrichs Verlag, 1939.

———. *Life of Euthymius.* Trans. R. M. Price and John Binns. *Cyril of Scythopolis: The Lives of the Monks of Palestine.* Cistercian Studies 114, 1–92. Kalamazoo, Mich.: Cistercian Publications, 1991.

———. *Life of Sabas.* Ed. Eduard Schwartz. *Kyrillos von Skythopolis.* Texte und Untersuchungen zur Geschichte der altchristlichen Literatur 49.2, 85–200. Leipzig: J. C. Hinrichs Verlag, 1939.

Cyrillona. *Hymns.* Ed. G. Bickell. "Die Gedichte des Cyrillonas nebst einigen anderen syrischen Ineditis." *Zeitschrift der Deutschen Morgenländischen Gesellschaft* 27 (1873), 566–99.

———. *Hymns* (corrections). Ed. G. Bickell. "Berichtigungen zu Cyrillonas." *Zeitschrift der Deutschen Morgenländischen Gesellschaft* 35 (1881), 531–32.

———. *Hymns.* Trans. Dominique Cerbelaud. *Cyrillonas. L'Agneau Véritable. Hymnes Cantiques et Homélies.* Collection "L'Esprit et le Feu." Paris: Éditions de Chevetogne, 1984.

De Mendieta, David Amand, and Matthieu-Charles Moons. "Une curieuse homélie grecque inédite sur la virginité addressée aux pères de famille." *Revue Bénédictine* 63 (1953), 18–69 and 211–38.

Demosthenes. *Speeches*. Ed. and trans. Augustus Tabor Murray. *Demosthenes. Private Orations. In Four Volumes. Vol. 3: Orations L–LIX*. LCL 318. London: William Heinemann, 1936.

Didache. Eds. and trans. Willy Rordorf and André Tuilier. *La Doctrine des Douze Apôtres*. SCh 248. 2nd ed. Paris: Les Éditions du Cerf, 1998.

———. Ed. and trans. Bart D. Ehrman. *The Apostolic Fathers*. 2 vols. LCL 24 and 25. Vol. 1, 416–43. Cambridge, Mass.: Harvard University Press, 2003.

Didascalia Apostolorum. Ed. F. X. Funk. *Didascalia et Constitutiones apostolorum*. 2 vols. Repr.: Turin: Bottega d'Erasmo, 1964.

Didascalia Apostolorum (Syriac). In *The Didascalia apostolorum in Syriac*. Ed. and trans. Arthur Vööbus. CSCO 401–2 and 407–8, Scriptores Syri, tt. 175–76 and 179–80. Louvain: Secrétariat du CorpusSCO, 1979.

Didier, J. C. *Le baptême des enfants dans la tradition de l'Église*. Monumenta Christiana Selecta 7. Tournai: Desclée, 1959.

Didier, J. C., and A. M. Roguet. *Faut-il baptiser les enfants? La réponse de la tradition*. Paris: Éditions du Cerf, 1967.

Diodorus Siculus. Text and trans. Francis R. Walton and C. H. Oldfather. *Diodorus of Sicily in Twelve Volumes. Vol. 12: Fragments of Books XXXIII–XL*. Cambridge, Mass.: Harvard University Press, 1967.

Egeria. *Diary*. Ed. Aetio Franceschini and Robert Weber. "Itinerarium Egeriae." In *Itineraria et alia geographica*. CCSL 175, 37–90. Turnhout: Brepols, 1965.

———. *Diary*. Trans. John Wilkinson. *Egeria's Travel*. 3rd ed. Warminster: Aries & Philips, 1999.

Ehrman, Bart D. *The Apostolic Fathers*. 2 vols. LCL 24 and 25. Cambridge, Mass.: Harvard University Press, 2003.

El Meskin, Matta. *Secondo il Vangelo: le venti lettere di Antonio*. Translated from Arabic into Italian by Maurizio Bagatin and Corrado Pettiti. Padri orientali. Magnano (Biella): Qiqajon Comunità di Bose, c1999.

Ephraem Graecus. "Interrogationes et responsiones [Ἐρωτήσεις καὶ ἀποκρίσεις]." Ed. Konstantin G. Phrantzolas. Ὁσίου Ἐφραῖμ τοῦ Σύρου. Ἔργα. Vol. 4, 76–110. Thessaloniki: Ἐκδόσεις τὸ Περιβολὶ τῆς Παναγίας. Ἔργα Perivoli tes Panagias, 1992.

———. "Sermo in secundum adventum domini nostri Iesu Christi [Λόγος εἰς τὴν δευτέραν παρουσίαν τοῦ κυρίου ἡμῶν Ἰησοῦ Χριστοῦ]." Ed. Konstantin G. Phrantzolas. Ὁσίου Ἐφραῖμ τοῦ Σύρου. Ἔργα. Vol. 4, 9–46. Thessaloniki: Perivoli tes Panagias, 1992.

———. "De virtutibus et passionibus [Περὶ ἀρετῶν καὶ παθῶν [ψυχικῶν]]." Ed. Konstantin G. Phrantzolas. Ὁσίου Ἐφραῖμ τοῦ Σύρου. Ἔργα. Vol. 5, 392–410. Thessaloniki: Ἐκδόσεις τό Περιβολί τῆς Παναγίς Perivoli tes Panagias, 1994.

Ephraem the Syrian. *Armenian Hymns*. Ed. and trans. L. Mariès and Ch. Mercier. *Hymnes de Saint Ephrem conservées en version arménienne*. Patrologia Orientalis 30. Fascicle 1. Paris: Firmin-Didot, 1961.

Epiphanius. *Ancoratus*. Ed. PG 43.17–256.

Epistle of Barnabas. Ed. and trans. Bart D. Ehrman. *The Apostolic Fathers*. 2 vols. LCL 24 and 25. Vol. 2, 12–83. Cambridge, Mass.: Harvard University Press, 2003.

Eusebius of Caesarea. *Church History*. Ed. Kirsopp Lake. *Eusebius. The Ecclesiastical*

History. LCL 153. Cambridge, Mass.: Harvard University Press; and London: William Heinemann, 1926.

———. *Church History.* Trans. G. A. Williamson. *Eusebius: The History of the Church from Christ to Constantine.* Revised and edited with a new introduction by Andrew Louth. Penguin Classics. London: Penguin Books, c1969 and c1985.

———. *Church History.* Ed. Eduard Schwartz and Theodor Mommsen. 2nd ed. Friedrich Winkelmann. *Eusebius Werke: Die Kirchengeschichte.* 3 vols. GCS, N.F., vols. 6.1–3. Repr.: Berlin: Akademie Verlag, 1999.

———. *Oration in Praise of Constantine.* Ed. Ivar A. Heikel. *Eusebius Werke. Erster Band. Über das Leben Constantins, Constantins Rede an die heilige Versammlung, Tricennatsrede an Constantin,* 195–259. GCS. Leipzig: J. C. Hinrichs'sche Buchhandlung, 1902.

———. *Oration in Praise of Constantine.* Trans. Ernest Cushing Richardson. "The Oration of Eusebius Pamphilius in Praise of the Emperor Constantine." NPNF 2nd ser., vol. 1, 581–610. Repr: Peabody, Mass.: Hendrickson Publishers, 1995.

Evagrius Scholasticus. *Church History.* Trans. Michael Whitby. *The Ecclesiastical History of Evagrius Scholasticus.* Translated Texts for Historians 33. Liverpool: Liverpool University Press, 2000.

Felix Ennodius. *Life of Epiphanius of Pavia.* Ed. Wilhelm Hartel. *Magni Felicis Ennodii Opera Omnia.* CSEL 6, 331–83. Vindobonae: Apud C. Geroldi Filium Bibliopolam Academiae, 1882.

First Letter of Clement to the Corinthians. Ed. and trans. Bart D. Ehrman. *The Apostolic Fathers.* 2 vols. LCL 24 and 25. Vol. 1, 34–151. Cambridge, Mass.: Harvard University Press, 2003.

Greek Homily on Virginity. Trans. Teresa M. Shaw. "Homily: On Virginity." In *Ascetic Behavior in Greco-Roman Antiquity. A Sourcebook,* 29–44. Ed. Vincent L. Wimbush. Studies in Antiquity and Christianity. Minneapolis: Fortress Press, 1990.

Gregory Nazianzen. *Letters.* Ed. Paul Gallay. *Briefe. Gregor von Nazianz.* GCS 53. Berlin: Akademie Verlag, 1969.

———. *Letters.* Trans. Michael Wittig. *Briefe. Gregor von Nazianz.* Bibliothek der griechischen Literatur 13. Stuttgart: Anton Hiersemann, 1981.

———. *Orations.* Ed. PG 35.395–1252 and PG 36.11–664.

———. *Orations.* Trans. Leo P. McCauley, John J. Sullivan, Martin R. P. McGuire, and Roy J. Deferrari. *Funeral Orations by Saint Gregory Nazianzen and Saint Ambrose.* Fathers of the Church 22. New York: Fathers of the Church, 1953.

———. *Orations.* Ed. and trans. Paul Gallay and Maurice Jourjon. *Grégoire de Nazianze. Discours 27–31.* SCh 250. Paris: Les Éditions du Cerf, 1978.

———. *Orations.* Ed. and trans. Claudio Moreschini and Paul Gallay. *Grégoire de Nazianze. Discours 38–41.* SCh 358. Paris: Les Éditions du Cerf, 1990.

———. *Orations.* Ed. J. Bernardi. *Grégoire de Nazianze. Discours 42–43.* SCh 384. Paris: Les Éditions du Cerf, 1992.

———. *Orations.* Trans. Charles Gordon Browne and James Edward Swallow. "Select Orations of Saint Gregory Nazianzen Sometime Archbishop of Constantinople." In *Cyril of Jerusalem, Gregory Nazianzen.* Ed. Philip Schaff and Henry Wace. NPNF 2nd ser., vol. 7, 203–434. Repr.: Peabody, Mass.: Hendrickson Publishers, 1995.

Gregory of Nyssa. *De beneficentia.* Ed. Adrianus van Heck. In *Gregorii Nysseni Opera.* Ed. Werner Jaeger. Vol. 9, 91–108. Leiden: E. J. Brill, 1952–.

————. *Epistula Canonica*. Ed. PG 45:221–236.

————. *Life of Macrina*. Ed. and trans. Pierre Maraval. *Grégoire de Nysse. Vie de Sainte Macrine*. SCh 178. Paris: Les Éditions du Cerf, 1971.

————. *Life of Macrina*. Trans. Kevin Corrigan. *The Life of Saint Macrina by Gregory, Bishop of Nyssa*. Toronto: Peregrina, c.1987, repr. 1989.

————. *Life of Macrina*. Trans. Joan M. Petersen. *Handmaids of the Lord. Contemporary Descriptions of Feminine Asceticism in the First Six Christian Centuries*, 51–86. CSS 143. Kalamazoo, Mich.: Cistercian Publications, 1996.

————. *On Infants' Early Deaths*. Ed. Hadwig Hörner. "De infantibus praemature abreptis." In *Gregorii Nysseni Opera Dogmatica Minora. Pars 2*, lxxxv–cxlvi and 65–97. Ed. J. Kenneth Downing, Jacobus A. McDonough, and Hadwig Hörner. *Gregorii Nysseni Opera*, 3.2. Leiden: E. J. Brill, 1987.

————. *On Infants' Early Deaths*. Trans. William Moore and Henry Austin Wilson. "On Infants' Early Deaths." In *Select Writings and Letters of Gregory, Bishop of Nyssa*. Trans. William Moore and Henry Austin Wilson. NPNF 2nd ser., vol. 5, 372–81. Repr.: Peabody, Mass.: Hendrickson Publishers, 1995.

Gregory of Tours. *Life of Andrew*. Ed. Jean-Marc Prieur. *Acta Andreae. Textus*. CCSA 6, 553–651. Turnhout: Brepols, 1989.

Gregory the Great. *De vita et miraculis venerabilis Benedicti Abbatis*. Ed. and trans. Adalbert de Vogüe and Paul Antin. *Grégoire le Grand. Dialogus. Tome II (Livres I–III)*, 126–249. SCh 260. Paris: Les Éditions du Cerf, 1979.

Harris, J. Rendel. *Fragments of the Commentary of Ephrem Syrus upon the Diatessaron*. London: C. J. Clay and Sons, 1895.

Hennecke, Edgar, and Wilhelm Schneemelcher, eds. *Neutestamentliche Apokryphen in deutscher Übersetzung*. 2 vols. 5th ed. Tübingen: J. C. B. Mohr (Paul Siebeck), 1987–89.

Herodian. *History*. Ed. and trans. C. R. Whittaker. *Herodian. History of the Empire*. 2 vols. LCL 454 and 455. Cambridge, Mass.: Harvard University Press, 1969–70.

Hippolytus. *Adversus haereses*. Trans. J. H. MacMahon. "[Hippolytus] The Refutation of All Heresies." In *ANF* 5: *Fathers of the Third Century: Hippolytus, Cyprian, Caius, Novatian, Appendix*, 9–153. Repr.: Peabody, Mass.: Hendrickson Publishers, 1995.

————. *Apostolic Tradition*. Ed. and trans. Wilhelm Geerlings. "Traditio Apostolica. Apostolische Überlieferung." In *Didache. Zwölf-Apostel-Lehre. Traditio Apostolica. Apostolische Überlieferung*. Trans. Georg Schöllgen and Wilhelm Geerlings. Fontes Christiani 1, 212–313. 2nd ed. Freiburg: Herder, 1992.

History of Joseph the Carpenter. Ed. and trans. A. Battista and B. Bagatti. *Edizione critica del testo arabo della "Historia Iosephi Fabri Lignarii" e ricerche sulla sua origine*. Studium Biblicum Franciscanum. Collectio Minor 20. Jerusalem: Franciscan Printing Press, 1978.

————. Trans. with introduction by Anne Boud'hors. "Histoire de Joseph le Charpentier." In *Ecrits apocryphes chrétiens II*, 27–74. Eds. Pierre Geoltrain and Jean-Daniel Kaestli. Paris: Éditions Gallimard, 2005.

Hock, Ronald F., trans. *The Infancy Gospels of James and Thomas*. The Scholars Bible 2. Santa Rosa, Calif.: Polebridge Press, 1995.

Hunter, David G., trans. *A Comparison between a King and a Monk / Against the Opponents of the Monastic Life. Two Treatises by John Chrysostom*. Studies in the Bible and Early Christianity 13. Lewiston, N.Y.: Edwin Mellen Press, c1988.

Ignatius of Antioch. *Letters*. Ed. Bart D. Ehrman. *The Apostolic Fathers*. 2 vols. LCL

24 and 25. Vol. 1, 203–321. Cambridge, Mass.: Harvard University Press, 2003.

Infancy Gospel of Thomas. Ed. and trans. Ronald F. Hock. *The Infancy Gospels of James and Thomas,* 104–43. The Scholars Bible 2. Santa Rosa, Calif.: Polebridge Press, 1995.

Irenaeus of Lyons. *Against Heresies.* Ed. and trans. Adelin Rousseau and Louis Doutreleau. *Irénée de Lyon. Contre les Hérésies. Livre III.* SCh 210–11. Paris: Les Éditions du Cerf, 1974.

———. *Against Heresies.* Ed. and trans. Adelin Rousseau and Louis Doutreleau. *Irénée de Lyon. Contre les Hérésies. Livre II.* SCh 293–94. Paris: Les Éditions du Cerf, 1982.

Isidore of Seville. *Etymologiae.* Trans. Stephen A. Barney. *The Etymologies of Isidore of Seville.* New York: Cambridge University Press, 2005.

———. *Etymologiae.* In *Isidori Hispalensis Episcopi Etymologiarum sive originum libri XX.* Ed. W. M. Lindsay. New York: Oxford University Press, 1911, repr. 1985.

Jerome. *Against the Pelagians.* Trans. John N. Hritzu. "The Dialogue against the Pelagians." In *Saint Jerome. Dogmatic and Polemical Works.* Fathers of the Church 53, 221–378. Washington, D.C.: The Catholic University of America Press, c1965.

———. *Against the Pelagians.* Ed. C. Moreschini. *S. Hieronymi Presbyteri Opera. Pars III. Opera Polemica 2. Dialogus adversus Pelagianos.* CCSL 80. Turnhout: Brepols, 1990.

———. *Apology against Rufinus.* Ed. and trans. Pierre Lardet. *Saint Jérome. Apologie Contre Rufine.* SCh 303. Paris: Les Éditions du Cerf, 1983.

———. *Letters.* Trans. W. H. Fremantle, G. Lewis, and W. G. Martley. "Letters." In *Jerome: Letters and Select Works.* NPNF 2nd ser., vol. 6, 1–295. Repr.: Peabody, Mass.: Hendrickson Publishers, 1995.

———. *Letters.* Ed. Isidorus Hilberg. *Sancti Eusebii Hieronymi Epistulae.* 3 vols. CSEL 54–56. Vindobonae: F. Tempsky, 1910–18; repr. Vindobonae: Verlag der Österreichischen Akademie der Wissenschaften, 1996.

———. *Preface to the Commentary on the Book of Job.* Ed. PL 28.1079–1084.

John Chrysostom. *A Comparison between a King and a Monk.* Ed. PG 47.387–392.

———. *A Comparison between a King and a Monk.* Trans. David G. Hunter. *A Comparison between a King and a Monk / Against the Opponents of the Monastic Life. Two Treatises by John Chrysostom,* 69–76. Studies in the Bible and Early Christianity 13. Lewiston, N.Y.: Edwin Mellen Press, c1988.

———. *Ad Neophytos. Discours III.* Ed. and trans. Antoine Wenger. *Jean Chrysostome. Huit catéchèses baptismales inédites,* 150–67. SCh 50. Paris: Les Éditions du Cerf, 1957.

———. *Ad Stagirium a daemone vexatum.* Ed. PG 47.423–494.

———. *Against the Opponents of the Monastic Life.* Ed. PG 47.319–386.

———. *Against the Opponents of the Monastic Life.* Trans. David G. Hunter. *A Comparison between a King and a Monk / Against the Opponents of the Monastic Life. Two Treatises by John Chrysostom,* 77–176. Studies in the Bible and Early Christianity 13. Lewiston, N.Y.: Edwin Mellen Press, c1988.

———. *De inani gloria et de educandis liberis.* In *S. Joannis Chrysostomi De inani Gloria et de educandis liberis.* Ed. Franciscus Schulte. Progr. Gaesdonck. No. 627. Monasterii Guestfalorum: Ex Officina Societatis Typographiae Guestfalorum, 1914.

———. *De inani gloria et de educandis liberis.* In *Johannes Chrysostomos. Über Hoffart und Kindererziehung.* Ed. Basileios K. Exarchos. Munich: Max Hueber Verlag, 1952.

———. *De paenitentia.* Sermon 2. Ed. PG 60.699–706.

———. *De poenitentia.* Ed. PG 49.277–350.

———. *De ss. martyribus.* Ed. PG 50.645–654.

———. *Homilies on Acts.* Ed. PG 60.97–204.

———. *Homilies on Colossians* Ed. PG 62.299–392.

———. *Homilies on 1 Corinthians* Ed. PG 61.9–382.

———. *Homilies on Ephesians.* Ed. PG 62.9–176.

———. *Homilies on Ephesians.* Rev. trans. Gross Alexander. In *Chrysostom: Homilies on Galatians, Ephesians, Philippians, Colossians, Thessalonians, Timothy, Titus and Philemon.* NPNF 1st ser., vol 13, 49–172. Repr.: Peabody, Mass.: Hendrickson Publishers, 1994.

———. *Homilies on Matthew.* Homily 71. Ed. PG 58.661–668.

———. *Homilies on 1 Thessalonians.* Ed. PG 62.391–468.

———. *On the Priesthood.* Trans. W. A. Jurgens. *The Priesthood. A Translation of the "Peri hierosynes" of St. John Chrysostom.* New York: Macmillan, 1955.

———. *On Vainglory and the Right Way for Parents to Raise Their Children.* In *Christianity and Pagan Culture in the Later Roman Empire together with An English Translation of John Chrysostom's Address on Vainglory and the Right Way for Parents to Bring up Their Children,* 85–122. Trans. M. L. W. Laistner. Ithaca, N.Y.: Cornell University Press, c1951, repr. 1967.

———. *On Vainglory and the Right Way for Parents to Raise Their Children.* Ed. and trans. Anne-Marie Malingrey. *Jean Chrysostome. Sur la vaine gloire et l'éducation des enfants.* SCh 188. Paris: Les Éditions du Cerf, 1972.

John Moschus. *Pratum Spirituale.* Ed. PG 87, 3, 2852–3112.

———. *Pratum Spirituale.* Trans. John Wortley. *The Spiritual Meadow of John Moschus.* Cistercian Studies Series 139. Kalamazoo, Mich.: Cistercian Publications, 1992.

John of Ephesus. *Lives of the Eastern Saints.* Ed. and trans. E. W. Brooks. *John of Ephesus. Lives of the Eastern Saints.* Patrologia Orientalis 17.1 and 18.4. Paris: Firmin-Didot, 1923–24.

John Rufus. *Life of Peter the Iberian.* In *John Rufus: The "Lives" of Peter the Iberian, Theodosius of Jerusalem, and the Monk Romanus.* Ed. and trans. with an introduction and notes by Cornelia Horn and Robert R. Phenix Jr. Writings from the Greco-Roman World 24, 2–281. Atlanta: Society of Biblical Literature, 2008.

Josephus. *Against Apion.* Ed. and. trans. Henry St. John Thackeray. *Josephus.* LCL. 9 vols. Vol. 1: *The Life, Against Apion,* 161–411. Cambridge, Mass.: Harvard University Press, 1926.

———. *Jewish War.* Ed. and trans. Henry St. John Thackeray. *Josephus. In Nine Volumes.* Vol. 2: *The Jewish War. Books I–III.* LCL 203. London; William Heinemann, 1926.

Junod, Eric, and Jean-Daniel Kaestli, eds. *Acta Iohannis. Praefatio—Textus.* CCSA 1. Turnhout: Brepols, 1983.

Justin Martyr. *Dialogue with Trypho.* Ed. Miroslav Marcovich. *Iustini Martyris Dialogus cum Tryphone.* Patristische Texte und Studien 47. Berlin: de Gruyter, 1997.

———. *First Apology.* Translation edited by A. Cleveland Coxe. "The First Apology of Justin." In ANF 1, 163–87. New York: Charles Scribner's Sons, 1913.

———. *First Apology.* Ed. Miroslav Marcovich. *Iustini Martyris. Apologiae Pro Christianis,* 31–133. Patristische Texte und Studien 38. Berlin: de Gruyter, 1994.

———. *Second Apology.* Ed. Miroslav Marcovich. *Iustini Martyris. Apologiae Pro Christianis,* 135–59. Patristische Texte und Studien 38. Berlin: de Gruyter, 1994.

Justinian. *Codex.* Ed. P. Krueger. *Codex Iustinianus. Corpus Iuris Civilis.* 3 vols. Vol. 2: *Codex Iustinianus.* Berlin: Apud Weidmannos, repr. 1929.

———. *Digest.* Ed. Theodor Mommsen with the aid of Paul Krueger. Trans. Alan Watson. *The Digest of Justinian.* 4 vols. Philadelphia: University of Pennsylvania Press, 1985.

Kraft, Heinrich. *Texte zur Geschichte der Taufe, besonders der Kindertaufe in der alten Kirche. Unter Mitwirkung von Holger Hammerich.* Kleine Texte für Vorlesungen und Übungen 174. 2nd ed. Berlin: de Gruyter, 1969.

Laistner, M. L. W., trans. *Christianity and Pagan Culture in the Later Roman Empire together with An English Translation of John Chrysostom's Address on Vainglory and the Right Way for Parents to Bring up Their Children.* Ithaca, N.Y.: Cornell University Press, c1951, repr. 1967.

Lake, Kirsopp, trans. *The Apostolic Fathers.* 2 vols. LCL 24 and 25. Cambridge, Mass.: Harvard University Press, 1913.

Lang, David Marshall. *Lives and Legends of the Georgian Saints, Selected and Translated from the Original Texts.* New York: Macmillan, 1956.

Leo the Great. *Letter 167.* Ed. PL 54.1197–1209.

———. *Letters.* Trans. Charles Lett Feltoe. "Letters." NPNF 2nd ser., vol. 12, 1–114. Repr.: Peabody, Mass.: Hendrickson Publishers, 1995.

Life of Melania the Younger. Ed. and trans. Denys Gorce. *Vie de Sainte Mélanie.* SCh 90. Paris: Les Éditions du Cerf, 1962.

———. Trans. Elizabeth A. Clark. *The Life of Melania the Younger. Introduction, Translation, and Commentary.* Studies in Women and Religion 14. Lewiston, N.Y.: Edwin Mellen Press, 1984.

Lutz, Cora E. "Musonius Rufus. 'The Roman Socrates.'" *Yale Classical Studies* 10 (1947), 3–147.

Marc the Deacon. *Vita Porphyri.* Ed. and trans. Henri Grégoire and M.-A. Kugener. *Marc le Diacre. Vie de Porphyre, Évêque de Gaza.* Collection Byzantine. Paris: Société d'Édition "Les Belles Lettres," 1930.

Martyrdom of Abd al'Masih. Ed. and trans. Josephus Corluy. "Acta Sancti Mar Abdu'l Masich. Aramaice et Latine." *Analecta Bollandiana* 5 (1886), 5–52.

Martyrdom of Mar Talya. MS British Museum Add. 12,174. Fols. 426r–430r.

Martyrdom of Paul. In *Acta Petri, Acta Pauli, Acta Petri et Pauli, Acta Pauli et Theclae, Acta Thaddaei.* Ed. Richard A. Lipsius. *Acta Apostolorum Apocrypha* 1, 104–17. Ed. Richard A. Lipsius and Maximilian Bonnet. Leipzig: Hermann Mendelssohn, 1891; repr.: Hildesheim: Georg Olms, 1959.

Martyrdom of Pionius the Presbyter and his Companions. Ed. and trans. Herbert Musurillo. *The Acts of the Christian Martyrs,* 136–67. Oxford: Clarendon Press, 1972.

Martyrdom of Polycarp. Ed. and trans. Herbert Musurillo. *The Acts of the Christian Martyrs,* 2–21. Oxford: Clarendon Press, 1972.

———. Ed. and trans. Bart D. Ehrman. *The Apostolic Fathers.* LCL 24 and 25. Vol. 1, 366–401. Cambridge, Mass.: Harvard University Press, 2003.

Martyrdom of Potamiaena and Basilides. Ed. and trans. Herbert Musurillo. *The Acts of the Christian Martyrs,* 132–35. Oxford: Clarendon Press, 1972.

Martyrdom of Saint Irenaeus, Bishop of Sirmium. Ed. and trans. Herbert Musurillo. *The Acts of the Christian Martyrs*, 294–301. Oxford: Clarendon Press, 1972.

Martyrdom of Saints Agapē, Irenē, and Chionē at Saloniki. Ed. and trans. Herbert Musurillo. *The Acts of the Christian Martyrs*, 280–93. Oxford: Clarendon Press, 1972.

Martyrdom of Saints Justin, Chariton, Charito, Evelpistus, Hierax, Paeon, Liberian, and their Community. Ed. and trans. Herbert Musurillo. *The Acts of the Christian Martyrs*, 42–61. Oxford: Clarendon Press, 1972.

Martyrdom of Saints Marian and James. Ed. and trans. Herbert Musurillo. *The Acts of the Christian Martyrs*, 194–213. Oxford: Clarendon Press, 1972.

Martyrdom of Saints Montanus and Lucius. Ed. and trans. Herbert Musurillo. *The Acts of the Christian Martyrs*, 214–39. Oxford: Clarendon Press, 1972.

Martyrdom of Saints Perpetua and Felicitas. Ed. and trans. Herbert Musurillo. *The Acts of the Christian Martyrs*, 106–31. Oxford: Clarendon Press, 1972.

Martyrdom of Saints Ptolemaeus and Lucius. Ed. and trans. Herbert Musurillo. *The Acts of the Christian Martyrs*, 38–41. Oxford: Clarendon Press, 1972.

Martyrdom of Sophia and Her Three Daughters (Greek). Ed. F. Halkin. *Légendes grecques de "martyres romaines,"* 179–228. Subsidia hagiographica 55. Brussels: Société des Bollandistes, 1973.

Martyrdom of Sophia and Her Three Daughters (Syriac). Ed. and trans. Agnes Smith Lewis. *Select Narratives of Holy Women from the Syro-Antiochene or Sinai Palimpsest.* Studia Sinaitica. Vol. 9, 218–44 (Syriac text). Vol. 10, 168–84 (English translation). London: C. J. Clay and Sons, 1900.

Martyrdom of the Children of Kola. Ed. N. Y. Marr. "Mučeničestvo otrokov' Kolaïcev." In *Teksty i Razyskanija po Armjano-Gruzinskoï Filologii.* Vol. 5, 55–61. St. Petersburg, 1903.

———. Trans. David Marshall Lang. *Lives and Legends of the Georgian Saints, Selected and Translated from the Original Texts*, 40–43. New York: Macmillan, 1956.

Martyrs of Lyons (and Vienne). Ed. and trans. Herbert Musurillo. *The Acts of the Christian Martyrs*, 62–85. Oxford: Clarendon Press, 1972.

Mary of Cassobola. *Epistle of Mary the Proselyte (Mary of Cassobola) to Ignatius. Mariae Proselytae Chassaobolorum ad Ignatium Episcopum Antiochiae Epistula.* Ed. Franciscus Xavierus Funk. *Patres Apostolici.* 2 vols. Vol. 2, 46–53. Tübingen: Libraria Henrici Laupp, 1901.

Mertel, Hans, trans. "Leben des Heiligen Pachomius aus dem Griechischen übersetzt." In *Des Heiligen Athanasius Schriften Gegen die Heiden, Über die Menschwerdung, Leben des Heiligen Antonius, mit einem Anhang Leben des Heiligen Pachomius*, 781–900. Bibliothek der Kirchenväter 31. Munich: Jos. Kösel & Friedr. Pustet, n.d.

Mingana, A. "A New Life of John the Baptist." *Bulletin of the John Rylands Library* 11 (1927), 438–89. Repr. in *Woodbrooke Studies. Christian Documents in Syriac, Arabic, and Garshūni.* Edited and translated with a critical apparatus by A. Mingana, with introductions by Rendel Harris. Vol. 1, 234–87. Cambridge: W. Heffer & Sons, 1927.

Minucius Felix. *Octavius.* Ed. and trans. Gerald H. Rendall. *Minucius Felix*, 314–437. LCL. Cambridge, Mass.: Harvard University Press, 1966.

Muratorian Canon. Trans. Wilhelm Schneemelcher. "Haupteinleitung: a) Kanonverzeichnisse 1. Der Canon Muratori." In *Neutestamentliche Apokryphen in deutscher Übersetzung.* Vol. 1: *Evangelien*, 27–29. Ed. Wilhelm Schneemelcher. 5th ed. Tübingen: J. C. B. Mohr (Paul Siebeck), 1987.

Murray, Robert. "'A Marriage for all eternity': The Consecration of a Syrian bride of Christ." *Sobornost* 11 (1989), 65–68.

Musonius Rufus. "Must One Obey One's Parents under All Circumstances?" Ed. August Meineke. *Ioannis Stobaei Florilegium*. Vol. 3, 90–94. Leipzig: B. G. Teubner, 1856.

————. "Must One Obey One's Parents under All Circumstances?" Ed. and trans. Cora E. Lutz. "Musonius Rufus. 'The Roman Socrates.'" *Yale Classical Studies* 10 (1947), 3–147.

————. "On Sexual Indulgence." Ed. Curtius Wachsmuth and Otto Hense. *Ioannis Stobaei Anthologium*. Vol. 3, 286–89. Berlin: Apud Weidmannos, 1884.

————. "On Sexual Indulgence." Ed. and trans. Cora E. Lutz. "Musonius Rufus. 'The Roman Socrates.'" *Yale Classical Studies* 10 (1947), 3–147.

————. "Should Daughters Receive the Same Education as Sons?" Ed. Curtius Wachsmuth and Otto Hense. *Ioannis Stobaei Anthologium*. Vol. 2, 235–39. Berlin: Apud Weidmannos, 1884.

————. "Should Daughters Receive the Same Education as Sons?" Ed. and trans. Cora E. Lutz. "Musonius Rufus. 'The Roman Socrates.'" *Yale Classical Studies* 10 (1947), 3–147.

————. "Should Every Child That is Born Be Raised?" Ed. and trans. Cora E. Lutz. "Musonius Rufus. 'The Roman Socrates.'" *Yale Classical Studies* 10 (1947), 3–147.

————. "That Women Too Should Study Philosophy." Ed. Curtius Wachsmuth and Otto Hense. *Ioannis Stobaei Anthologium*. Vol. 2, 244–47. Berlin: Apud Weidmannos, 1884.

————. "That Women Too Should Study Philosophy." Ed. and trans. Cora E. Lutz. "Musonius Rufus. 'The Roman Socrates.'" *Yale Classical Studies* 10 (1947), 3–147.

————. "What Means of Livelihood Is Appropriate for a Philosopher?" Ed. August Meineke. *Ioannis Stobaei Florilegium*. Vol. 2, 336–40. Leipzig: B. G. Teubner, 1856.

————. "What Means of Livelihood Is Appropriate for a Philosopher?" Ed. and trans. Cora E. Lutz. "Musonius Rufus. 'The Roman Socrates.'" *Yale Classical Studies* 10 (1947), 3–147.

Musurillo, Herbert, ed. and trans. *The Acts of the Christian Martyrs*. Oxford: Clarendon Press, 1972.

Novatian. *De bono pudicitiae*. Ed. G. Hartel. *S. Thasci Caecilli Cypriani Opera Omnia*. CSEL 3.3, 13–25. Vienna: Apud C. Geroldi Filium, 1871.

————. *De bono pudicitiae*. Trans. Ernest Wallis. "Treatises Attributed to Cyprian: 'Of the Discipline and Advantage of Chastity.'" In *Hippolytus, Cyprian, Caius, Novatian, Appendix*. ANF 5, 587–92. Repr.: Peabody, Mass.: Hendrickson Publishers, 2004.

Odes of Solomon. In *The Odes of Solomon. The Syriac Text*. Ed. and trans. James H. Charlesworth. Society of Biblical Literature Texts and Translations 13. Pseudepigrapha Series 7. Missoula, Mont.: Scholars Press, c1977, 1978.

Origen. *Commentary on John*. Ed. Erwin Preuschen. *Origenes. Vierter Band*. GCS. Leipzig: J. C. Hinrichs, 1903.

————. *Commentary on Matthew*. Ed. PG 13.825–1600.

————. *Commentary on Romans*. Ed. Caroline P. Hammond Bammel. *Der Römerbriefkommentar des Origenes. Kritische Ausgabe der Übersetzung Rufins*. 3 vols. Aus der Geschichte der lateinischen Bibel 16, 33, and 34. Freiburg im Breisgau: Herder, 1990.

————. *Contra Celsum.* Ed. Marcel Borret. *Origène. Contre Celse. Tome 2 (Livres 3 & 4).* SCh 136. Paris: Les Éditions du Cerf, 1968.

————. *Contra Celsum.* Trans. R. Joseph Hoffmann. *Celsus. On The True Doctrine. A Discourse Against the Christians.* New York: Oxford University Press, 1987.

————. *Fragments on Ephesians.* Ed. J. A. F. Gregg. "The Commentary of Origen upon the Epistle to the Ephesians." *Journal of Theological Studies* (hereafter *JThS*) 3 (1902), 233–44, 398–420, and 554–76.

————. *Homiliae in Leviticum.* Ed. Marcel Borret. *Origène. Homélies sur le Lévitique.* SCh 286–87. Paris: Les Éditions du Cerf, 1981.

————. *Homiliae in Leviticum.* Trans. Gary Wayne Barkley. *Origen. Homilies on Leviticus: 1–16.* Fathers of the Church 83. Washington, D.C.: The Catholic University of America Press, c1990.

————. *Homiliae in Lucam.* Ed. and trans. Henri Crouzel, François Fournier, and Pierre Périchon. *Origène. Homélies sur S. Luc: text latin et fragments grecs.* SCh 87. Paris: Les Éditions du Cerf, 1962.

————. *Selecta in Exodum.* Ed. PG 12.281–298.

Ovid. *Nux.* Ed. Fridericus Waltharius Lenz. *P. Ovidis Nasonis. Halievtica Fragmenta— Nux, Incerti: Consolatio ad Liviam.* Corpus Scriptorum Latinorum Paravianum. Turin: G. B. Paravia, 1952.

————. *Nux.* Trans. I. H. Mozley. *Ovid in Six Volumes.* Vol. 2: *The Art of Love, and Other Poetry.* LCL 232. Cambridge, Mass.: Harvard University Press, 1979.

Passio Sancti Pauli Apostoli. In *Acta Petri. Acta Pauli. Acta Petri et Pauli. Acta Pauli et Theclae. Acta Thaddaei.* Ed. Richard A. Lipsius. *Acta Apostolorum Apocrypha 1,* 23–44. Ed. Richard A. Lipsius and Maximilian Bonnet. Leipzig: Hermann Mendelssohn, 1891; repr.: Hildesheim: Georg Olms, 1959.

Philo. 12 vols. (vols. 1–5, trans. Francis Henry Colson and Rev. George Herbert Whitaker; vols. 6–10, trans. F. H. Colson; vol. 11–12, trans. Ralph Marcus). LCL 226–27, 247, 261, 275, 289, 320, 341, 363, 379–80, and 401. Cambridge, Mass.: Harvard University Press, 1929–62, repr. 1981.

Philostratus. *Life of Apollonius of Tyana.* Ed. and trans. Christopher P. Jones. *Philostratus. The Life of Apollonius of Tyana.* LCL 16 and 17. Cambridge, Mass.: Harvard University Press, 2005.

Philoxenus of Mabbugh. *Discourses.* In *The Discourses of Philoxenus Bishop of Mabbôgh, A.D. 485–519.* Ed. and trans. E. A. Wallis Budge. 2 vols. London: Asher, 1893–94.

Plato. *Republic.* Ed. and trans. Paul Shorey. *The Republic. Plato.* 2 vols. LCL 237 and 276. Cambridge, Mass.: Harvard University Press, 1943.

Plautus. *Rudens.* Ed. Edward Sonnenschein. *T. Macci Plauti. Rudens.* Oxford: Oxford University Press, 1891.

Pliny the Elder. *Natural History.* Ed. and trans. H. Rackham. *Pliny. Natural History. With an English Translation in Ten Volumes, vol. II, libri III–VII.* LCL 352. Cambridge, Mass.: Harvard University Press, 1942.

Pliny the Younger. *Letters.* Ed. and trans. William Melmoth. Revised by W. M. L. Hutchinson. *Letters. Pliny the Younger.* 2 vols. LCL 55 and 59. Cambridge, Mass.: Harvard University Press, 1961.

————. *Letters.* Ed. and trans. Betty Radice. *Pliny, Letters and Panegyricus In Two Volumes.* LCL 55 and 59. Cambridge, Mass.: Harvard University Press, 1972–75.

Polycarp. *Letter to the Philippians.* Ed. Bart D. Ehrman. *The Apostolic Fathers.* 2 vols. LCL 24 and 25. Vol. 1, 332–53. Cambridge, Mass.: Harvard University Press, 2003.

Powell, J. Enoch, ed. *The Rendel Harris Papyri of Woodbrooke College, Birmingham.* Vol. 1. Cambridge: Cambridge University Press, 1936; repr. Milan: Cisalpino-Goliardica, 1974.

Prieur, Jean-Marc, ed. *Acta Andreae. Textus.* CCSA 6. Turnhout: Brepols, 1989.

Propertius. *Elegies.* Ed. and trans. G. P. Goold. *Propertius. Elegies.* LCL 18. Rev. ed. Cambridge, Mass.: Harvard University Press, 1999.

Protoevangelium of James. Ed. and trans. Ronald F. Hock. *The Infancy Gospels of James and Thomas,* 32–77. The Scholars Bible 2. Santa Rosa, Calif.: Polebridge Press, 1995.

Pseudo-Athanasian Canons. Ed. and trans. Wilhelm Riedel and Walter Ewing Crum. *The Canons of Athanasius of Alexandria: The Arabic and Coptic Versions.* London: Williams and Norgate, 1904.

Pseudo-Athanasius. *Didascalia cccxviii patrum Nicaenorum.* Ed. PG 28.1637–1644.

———. *Syntagma doctrinae ad monachos.* Ed. Henri Hyvernat. "Le Syntagma Doctrinae dit de Saint Athanase." In *Studia Patristica. Études d'ancienne littérature chrétienne,* fasc. 2, 119–60. Paris: Ernest Leroux, 1890.

Pseudo-Basil of Seleucia. *De vita et miraculis sanctae Theclae.* PG 85.477–617.

Pseudo-Clement of Rome. *Recognitions.* Ed. Bernhard Rehm and Georg Strecker. *Die Pseudoklementinen II. Rekognitionen in Rufins Übersetzung.* GCS. Berlin: Akademie Verlag, 1994.

———. *Recognitions.* Trans. André Schneider and Luigi Cirillo. *Les "Reconnaissances" du pseudo Clément. Roman chrétien des premiers siècles.* Apocryphes 10. Turnhout: Brepols, 1999.

Pseudo-Ephraem. *Homily on Hermits and Desert Dwellers and Mourners.* Trans. Joseph Amar. "On Hermits and Desert Dwellers." In *Ascetic Behavior in Greco-Roman Antiquity. A Sourcebook,* 66–80. Ed. Vincent L. Wimbush. Studies in Antiquity & Christianity. Minneapolis: Fortress Press, 1990.

Pseudo-Ignatius. *Letter to the Antiochians.* Ed. and trans. Francis X. Funk. *Patres Apostolici.* 2 vols. Vol. 2, 163–73. Tübingen: Libraria Henrici Laupp, 1901.

———. *Letter to the Philippians.* Ed. and trans. Franciscus Xavierus Funk. *Patres Apostolici.* 2 vols. Vol. 2, 124–43. Tübingen: Libraria Henrici Laupp, 1901.

Pseudo-Justin Martyr. *Oratio ad Graecos.* Trans. M. Dods. "[Justin Martyr] The Discourse to the Greeks." ANF 1, 271–72. New York: Charles Scribner's Sons, 1913.

Pseudo-Phocylides. *Sentences.* In *The Sentences of Pseudo-Phocylides. With Introduction and Commentary.* Ed. P. W. Van der Horst. Studia in Veteris Testamenti Pseudepigrapha 4. Leiden: E. J. Brill, 1978.

Pseudo-Polemon. *Physiognomonica.* Ed. R. Foerster. *Scriptores physiognomonici Graeci et Latini.* Vol. 1. Leipzig: Teubner, 1893.

———. *Physiognomonica.* Ed. and trans. Simon Swain and George Boys-Stones. *Seeing the Face, Seeing the Soul: Polemon's Physi[o]gnomy from Classical Antiquity to Medieval Islam.* Oxford: Oxford University Press, 2007.

Quintilian. *De institutione oratoria.* Trans. H. E. Butler. *The Institutio oratoria of Quintilian.* 4 vols. LCL 124–27. Cambridge, Mass.: Harvard University Press, 1961–66.

Rackham, R. B. "The Text of the Canons of Ancyra: The Greek, Latin, Syriac and Armenian Versions." In *Studia Biblica et ecclesiastica.* Ed. Samuel Roles Driver and others. Vol. 3, 139–216. Oxford: Clarendon Press, 1891. Reprinted as a separate booklet: Piscataway, N.J.: Gorgias Press, 2006.

Regula Benedicti. Ed. and trans. Adalbert de Vogüe and Jean Neufville. *La Règle de Saint Benoît II (ch. VIII–LXXIII).* SCh 182. Série des Textes Monastiques d'Occident 35. Paris: Les Éditions du Cerf, 1972.

Richardson, Cyril C., trans. *Early Christian Fathers.* New York: Simon & Schuster, 1996.

Riedel, Wilhelm, and Walter Ewing Crum, ed. and trans. *The Canons of Athanasius of Alexandria: The Arabic and Coptic Versions.* London: Williams and Norgate, 1904.

Rufinus of Aquileia. *Apology against Jerome.* Ed. Manlio Simonetti. *Tyrannii Rufini Opera,* 37–123. Turnhout: Brepols, 1961.

———. *Apology against Jerome.* Trans. William Henry Fremantle. "The Apology of Rufinus in Two Books." NPNF 2nd ser., vol. 3, 435–82. Peabody, Mass.: Hendrickson Publishers, 1995.

———. *Church History.* Ed. Theodor Mommsen. "Rufinus Vorrede, Einlage über Gregorius Thaumaturgus, Buch X und XI." In *Eusebius Werke. Zweiter Band. Zeiter Teil. Die Kirchengeschichte.* Ed. Eduard Schwartz, Theodor Mommsen, and Friedhelm Winkelmann. GCS 6.2, 951–1040. Berlin: Akademie Verlag, 1999.

Schneider, Gerhard, trans. *Evangelia Infantiae Apocrypha. Apocryphe Kindheitsevangelien.* Fontes Christiani 18. Freiburg: Herder, 1995.

Schwartz, Eduard, Theodor Mommsen, and Friedrich Winkelmann. *Eusebius Werke: Die Kirchengeschichte.* GCS, n.s., vols. 6.1–3. Repr.: Berlin: Akademie Verlag, 1999.

Seneca. *Controversiae.* Ed. Lennart Håkanson. *L. Annaeus Seneca. Oratorum et Rhetorum Sententiae, Divisiones, Colores.* Bibliotheca scriptorum Graecorum et Romanorum Teubneriana. Leipzig: B. G. Teubner, 1989.

Shaw, Teresa M., trans. "Homily: On Virginity." In *Ascetic Behavior in Greco-Roman Antiquity. A Sourcebook,* 29–44. Ed. Vincent L. Wimbush. Studies in Antiquity and Christianity. Minneapolis: Fortress Press, 1990.

Shepherd of Hermas. Trans. Kirsopp Lake. "The Shepherd." In *Apostolic Fathers II.* LCL 24 and 25. Cambridge, Mass.: Harvard University Press, 1913.

———. Ed. and trans. Bart D. Ehrman. *The Apostolic Fathers.* 2 vols. LCL 24 and 25. Vol. 2, 174–473. Cambridge, Mass.: Harvard University Press, 2003.

Sibylline Oracles. Ed. Johannes Geffcken. *Die Oracula Sibyllina.* GCS 8. Leipzig: J. C. Hinrichs'sche Buchhandlung, 1902; repr. in series: Greek Texts and Commentaries. New York: Arno Press, 1979.

Socrates Scholasticus. *Ecclesiastical History.* Ed. Pierre Périchon and Pierre Maraval. *Socrate de Constantinople. Histoire Ecclésiastique.* SCh 477 and 493. Paris: Les Éditions du Cerf, 2004–.

Sozomen. *Ecclesiastical History.* Ed. Joseph Bidez and Günther Christian Hansen. *Sozomenus. Kirchengeschichte.* GCS. NF vol. 4. 2nd rev. ed. Berlin: Akademie Verlag, 1995.

———. *Ecclesiastical History.* Trans. Chester D. Hartranft. "The Ecclesiastical History of Sozomen." NPNF 2nd ser., vol. 2, 179–427. Peabody, Mass.: Hendrickson Publishers, 1995.

———. *Ecclesiastical History.* Ed. and trans. Günther Christian Hansen. *Sozomenos. Historia Ecclesiastica. Kirchengeschichte.* 4 vols. Fontes Christiani 73/1–4. Turnhout: Brepols, 2004.

Stobaeus. *Anthologium.* Ed. Curtius Wachsmuth and Otto Hense. *Ioannis Stobaei Anthologium.* 4 vols. Berlin: Apud Weidmannos, 1884–1912.

———. *Florilegium.* Ed. Augustus Meineke. *Ioannis Stobaei Florilegium.* 4 vols. Leipzig: Teubner, 1855–57.

Strabo. *Geography*. In *The Geography of Strabo with an English translation by Horace Leonard Jones; based in part upon the unfinished version of John Robert Sitlington Sterret*. 8 vols. LCL. Cambridge, Mass.: Harvard University Press, 1982.

Suetonius. *The Life of the Caesars*. Text and trans. I. C. Rolfe. *Suetonius. With an English Translation by J. C. Rolfe. In Two Volumes*. LCL. Cambridge: Harvard University Press, 1965.

———. *The Life of the Caesars*. Trans. Catherine Edwards. *Suetonius. Lives of the Caesars*. Oxford World Classics. Oxford: Oxford University Press, 2000.

Swift, Louis J. *The Early Fathers on War and Military Service*. Message of the Fathers of the Church 19. Wilmington, Del.: M. Glazier, c1983.

Syriac Pseudo-Athanasius. *On Virginity*. Ed. and trans. David Brakke. *Pseudo-Athanasius on Virginity*. CSCO 592 and 593. Scriptores Syri, tt. 232 and 233. Louvain: Peeters, 2002.

Tacitus. *Histories*. Ed. Karl and Wilhelm Heraeus. *Historiarum libri qui supersunt*. Griechische und lateinische Schriftsteller. 2 vols. Leipzig: B. G. Teubner, 1927–29; repr. Amsterdam: A. M. Hakkert, 1966.

Tanner, Norman P., S.J. *Decrees of the Ecumenical Councils*. Vol. 1: *Nicaea I to Lateran V*. Washington, D.C.: Georgetown University Press, 1990.

Tatian. *Oratio ad Graecos*. Ed. and trans. Molly Whittaker. *Tatian. "Oratio ad Graecos" and Fragments*. Oxford Early Christian Texts. Oxford: Clarendon Press, 1982.

Tertullian. *Apologia*. Ed. and trans. T. R. Glover. *Tertullian. Apology. De Spectaculis*, 2–227. LCL. Cambridge, Mass.: Harvard University Press, 1966.

———. *De anima*. Ed. J. H. Waszink. "Q. S. Fl. Tertulliani *De anima*." In *Quinti Septimi Florentis Tertulliani Opera*. Vol. 2: *Opera Montanistica*. CCSL 2, 779–869. Turnhout: Brepols, 1954.

———. *De baptismo*. Ed. and trans. R. P. Refoulé and M. Drouzy. *Tertullien. Traité du Baptême*. SCh 35. Paris: Les Éditions du Cerf, 2002.

———. *De spectaculis*. Ed. and trans. Marie Turcan. *Les Spectacles. Tertullien*. SCh 332. Paris: Les Éditions du Cerf, 1986.

———. *Exhortation to Chastity*. Trans. William P. Le Saint. *Tertullian. Treatises on Marriage and Remarriage*, 42–64. Ancient Christian Writers 13. Westminster, Md.: Newman Press, 1951.

———. *Exhortation to Chastity*. Ed. Aem. Kroymann. "Q. S. Fl. Tertulliani *De Exhortatione Castitatis*." In *Quinti Septimi Florentis Tertulliani Opera*. Vol. 2: *Opera Montanistica*, 1013–35. CCSL 2. Turnhout: Brepols, 1954.

———. *To His Wife*. Ed. Charles Munier. *Tertullien. A Son Épouse*. SCh 273. Paris: Les Éditions du Cerf, 1980.

Testament of Levi. Ed. M. De Jonge. *The Testaments of the Twelve Patriarchs. A Critical Edition of the Greek Text*. Pseudepigrapha Veteris Testamenti Graece 1, pt. 2, 24–50. Leiden: E. J. Brill, 1978.

Testament of the Forty Holy and Glorious Martyrs of Christ Who Died at Sebaste. Ed. and trans. Herbert Musurillo. *The Acts of the Christian Martyrs*, 354–61. Oxford: Clarendon Press, 1972.

Testamentum Domini Nostri Iesu Christi. Ed. and trans. Arthur Vööbus. *The Synodicon in the West Syrian Tradition*. CSCO 367 and 368. Scriptores Syri, tt. 161 and 162; CSCO 367, 1–39 (Syriac) and CSCO 368, 27–57 (English). Louvain: Secrétariat du CorpusSCO, 1975.

Theodoret of Cyrrhus. *Commentary on the Letters of Paul*. PG 82.35–878.

————. *Commentary on the Letters of Paul.* Trans. Robert Hill. *Theodoret of Cyrus. Commentary on the Letters of St. Paul.* 2 vols. Brookline, Mass.: Holy Cross Orthodox Press, 2001.

————. *Ecclesiastical History.* Trans. Blomfield Jackson. "The Ecclesiastical History of Theodoret." NPNF 2nd ser., vol. 3, 33–159. Repr.: Peabody, Mass.: Hendrickson Publishers, 1995.

————. *Ecclesiastical History.* Ed. Leon Parmentier and Günther Christian Hansen. *Theodoret. Kirchengeschichte.* GCS. NF 5. Berlin: Akademie Verlag, c1998.

————. *Religious History.* Ed. and trans. P. Canivet and A. Leroy-Molinghen. *Theodoret de Cyr: Histoire des moines de Syrie.* 2 vols. SCh 234 and 257. Paris: Les Éditions du Cerf, 1977–79.

————. *Religious History.* Trans. R. M. Price. *Theodoret of Cyrrhus: A History of the Monks of Syria.* Cistercian Studies Series 88. Kalamazoo, Mich.: Cistercian Publications, 1985.

Theophilus of Antioch. *To Autolycus.* Ed. and trans. Robert M. Grant. *Theophilus of Antioch. Ad Autolycum. Text and Translation.* Oxford: Clarendon Press, 1970.

Victor of Vita. *Historia persecutionis.* Ed. Michael Petschenig. *Victoris Episcopi Vitensis Historia Persecutionis Africanae Provinciae.* CSEL 7. Vindobonae: Apud C. Geroldi Filium Bibliopolam Academiae, 1881.

————. *Historia persecutionis.* Ed. and trans. Serge Lancel. *Victor de Vita: Histoire de la persécution Vandale en Afrique suivie de La passion des sept martyrs, Registre des provinces et des cités d'Afrique,* 94–212. Collection des Universités de France. Paris: Les Belles Lettres, 2002.

Virgil. *Eclogae.* In *Vergil: Eclogues.* Ed. Robert Coleman. Cambridge Greek and Latin Classics. Cambridge: Cambridge University Press, 1977.

Vita Simeon Stylites Iunioris. Ed. and trans. Paul van den Ven. *La vie ancienne de S. Syméon Stylite le jeune (521–592).* 2 vols. Subsidia Hagiographica 32. Brussels: Société des Bollandistes, 1962–70.

Vööbus, Arthur, ed. *The Synodicon of the West Syrian Tradition.* 2 vols. CSCO 367–70. Scriptores Syri, tt. 161–64. Louvain: Secrétariat du CorpusSCO, 1975–76.

Xenophon. *Cyropaideia.* Trans. Wayne Ambler. *Xenophon. The Education of Cyrus.* Ithaca, N.Y.: Cornell University Press, 2001.

Secondary Sources

Aasgaard, Reidar. "Brotherhood in Plutarch and Paul: Its Role and Character." In *Constructing Early Christian Families: Family as Social Reality and Metaphor,* ed. Halvor Moxnes, 166–82. London: Routledge, 1997.

————. "Christianity's First Nursery Tale? A Proposal for a New Interpretation of the Infancy Gospel of Thomas." Paper presented at the annual meeting of the American Academy of Religion, Philadelphia, November 2005.

————. "Children in Antiquity and Early Christianity: Research History and Central Issues." *Familia* 33 (2006), 23–46.

————. "Paul as a Child: Children and Childhood in the Letters of the Apostle." *Journal of Biblical Literature* 126 (2007), 129–59.

Agouridēs, Savvas. "'Little Ones' in Matthew." *Bible Translator* 35 (1984), 329–34.

Aland, Kurt. *Die Säuglingstaufe im Neuen Testament und in der alten Kirche. Eine Antwort auf Joachim Jeremias.* Munich: C. Kaiser, 1961. Trans. G. R. Beasley-Murray.

Did the Early Church Baptize Infants? The Library of History and Doctrine. Philadelphia: Westminster Press, 1963.

———. *Die Stellung der Kinder in den frühen christlichen Gemeinden—und ihre Taufe.* Munich: C. Kaiser, 1967.

———. *Taufe und Kindertaufe. 40 Sätze zur Aussage des Neuen Testaments und dem historischen Befund, zur modernen Debatte darüber und den Folgerungen daraus für die kirchliche Praxis—zugleich eine Auseinandersetzung mit Karl Barths Lehre von der Taufe.* Gütersloh: Gütersloher Verlagshaus Gerd Mohn, 1971.

Albrecht, Ruth. *Das Leben der heiligen Makrina auf dem Hintergrund der Thekla-Traditionen. Studien zu den Ursprüngen des weiblichen Mönchtums im 4. Jahrhundert in Kleinasien.* Forschungen zur Kirchen- und Dogmengeschichte 38. Göttingen: Vandenhoeck & Ruprecht, 1986.

Albright, W. F., and C. S. Mann. *Matthew.* Anchor Bible Commentary 26. New York: Doubleday, 1971.

Allély, Anne. "Les enfants malformés et handicaps à Rome sous le Principat." *Revue des études anciennes* 106.1 (2004), 73–101.

Allison, Penelope. "Artefact Distribution and Spatial Function in Pompeiian Houses." In *The Roman Family in Italy: Status, Sentiment, Space,* eds. Beryl Rawson and Paul Weaver, 321–54. Oxford: Oxford University Press, 1999.

Alves de Sousa, Pio G. "La familia cristiana en los escritos de los padres apostólicos." In *Cuestiones fundamentales sobre matrimonio y familia,* ed. Augusto Sarmiento, 557–66. Pamplona, Spain: Ediciones Universidad de Navarra, 1980.

Anderson, R. Dean. *Ancient Rhetorical Theory and Paul.* Kampen, Netherlands: Kok Pharos, 1996.

André, Jean-Marie. "Jeux et divertissements dans le monde greco-romain." *Jeux et Jouets dans l'Antiquité et au Moyen Age, Dossiers de l'Archéologie* 168 (1992), 36–45.

Anonymous. "Children." In *Encyclopaedia Judaica* 5, cols. 426–28. Jerusalem: Keter Publishing, 1971.

Ariès, Philip. *L'Enfant et la Vie familiale sous l'Ancien Régime.* Paris: Plon, 1960. Trans. Robert Baldick. *Centuries of Childhood: A Social History of Family Life.* New York: Vintage Books, 1962.

Arjava, Antti. "Paternal Power in Late Antiquity." *Journal of Roman Studies* 88 (1988), 147–65.

———. *Women and Law in Late Antiquity.* Oxford: Clarendon Press, 1996.

Armaroli, Leopoldo. *Ricerche storiche sulla esposizione degli infanti presso gli antichi popoli e specialmente presso i Romani.* Venice: Antonelli, 1838.

Arnold, K. "Kind." In *Lexikon des Mittelalters,* vol. 5, fasc. 6, cols. 1142–45. Munich: Artemis Verlag, c1991.

Arx, Walter von. "The Churching of Women after Childbirth." In *Liturgy and Human Passage,* 63–72. Ed. David Power and Luis Maldonado. Concilium 112. New York: Seabury Press, 1979.

Aubin, M. M. "More apparent than real? Questioning the difference in marital age between Christian and non-Christian women of Rome during the third and fourth century." *Ancient History Bulletin* 14 (2000), 1–13.

Bakke, Odd M. *When Children Became People: The Birth of Childhood in Early Christianity.* Minneapolis: Fortress Press, 2005.

Balch, David. *Let Wives Be Submissive: The Domestic Code in 1 Peter.* Monograph Series, Society of Biblical Literature 26. Chico, Calif.: Scholars Press, 1981.

————. "Rich Pompeiian Houses, Shops for Rent, and the Huge Apartment Building in Herculaneum as Typical Spaces for Pauline House Churches." *Journal for the Study of the New Testament* (hereafter *JSNT*) 27.1 (2004), 27–46.

Balch, David L., and Carolyn Osiek, eds. *Early Christian Families in Context: An Interdisciplinary Dialogue.* Religion, Marriage, and Family series. Grand Rapids, Mich.: Eerdmans, 2003.

Baldson, J. P. V. D. *Life and Leisure in Ancient Rome.* New York: McGraw-Hill, 1969.

Balla, Peter. *The Child-Parent Relationship in the New Testament and Its Environments.* Wissenschaftliche Untersuchungen zum Neuen Testament 155. Tübingen: Mohr Siebeck, 2003.

Barclay, John M. G. "The Family as the Bearer of Religion in Judaism and Early Christianity." In *Constructing Early Christian Families: Family as Social Reality and Metaphor,* ed. Halvor Moxnes, 66–80. London: Routledge, 1997.

Bar-Ilan, Meir. "The Battered Jewish Child in Antiquity." http://faculty.biu .ac.il/~barilm/battered.html, 2003 (1996). Seen March 12, 2007.

Barnes, Timothy D. "The Baptism of Theodosius II." *Studia Patristica* 19 (1989), 8–12.

Barrow, Robin. *Greek and Roman Education.* Inside the Ancient World series. London: Bristol Classical Press, c1976, repr. 1996.

Barth, Karl. *Die kirchliche Lehre von der Taufe.* Zürich: Evangelischer Verlag, 1943. Trans. Ernest A. Payne. *The Teaching of the Church Regarding Baptism.* London: SCM Press, 1948.

————. *Kirchliche Dogmatik.* 4 vols. Zollikon-Zürich: Evangelischer Verlag, 1948–70.

Barton, S. C. *Discipleship and Family Ties in Mark and Matthew.* Society for New Testament Studies Monograph Series 80. Cambridge: Cambridge University Press, 1994.

Baskin, Judith R. "Rabbinic Reflections on the Barren Wife." *Harvard Theological Review* 82 (January 1989), 101–14.

Basser, Herbert W. "Let the Dead Bury Their Dead: Rhetorical Features of Rabbinic and New Testament Literature." In *Approaches to Ancient Judaism, New Series, Vol. 5: Historical, Literary, and Religious Studies,* eds. Herbert W. Basser and Simcha Fishbane, 79–95. South Florida Studies in the History of Judaism 82. Atlanta: Scholars Press, 1993.

Bauckham, Richard. *Jude and the Relatives of Jesus in the Early Church.* Edinburgh: T&T Clark, c1990.

Baumeister, Theofried. *Genese und Entfaltung der altkirchlichen Theologie des Martyriums.* Traditio Christiana 8. Bern: Peter Lang, 1991.

Baune, Jane. "The Fate of Babies Dying before Baptism in Byzantium." In *The Church and Childhood. Papers Presented at the 1993 Summer Meeting and the 1994 Winter Meeting of the Ecclesiastical History Society,* ed. Diana Wood, 115–25. Studies in Church History 31. Oxford: Blackwell Publishers, 1994.

Beare, Francis Wright. *The Gospel according to Matthew.* San Francisco: Harper & Row, 1981.

Beasley-Murray, George Raymond. "Church and Child in the New Testament." *Baptist Quarterly* 21 (1965–66), 206–18.

————. "The Theology of the Child." *American Baptist Quarterly* 1 (1982), 197–202.

Beavis, Mary Ann. "'Pluck the Rose but Shun the Thorns': The Ancient School and Christian Origins." *Studies in Religion/Sciences Religieuses* 29.4 (2000), 411–23.

———. "Philo's *Therapeutai*: Philosopher's Dream or Utopian Construction." *Journal for the Study of the Pseudepigrapha* 14.1 (2004), 30–42.

Bebis, George S. "Influence of Jewish Worship on Orthodox Christian Worship." *Greek Orthodox Theological Review* 22 (1977), 136–42.

Becker, M. J. "Roman period amphora burials of young children dating to the third century C.E. at Metaponto (Basilicata), Italy." *Archaeological News* 21–22 (1996–97), 20–26.

Bennet, H. "The Exposure of Infants in Ancient Rome." *Classical Journal* 18 (1922–23), 341–51.

Bernhard, Ludger. "Das frühchristliche Verständnis der Formel ΙΗΣΟΥΣ ΠΑΙΣ ΘΕΟΥ aufgrund der alten Bibelübersetzungen." In *Lingua Restituta Orientalis: Festgabe für Julius Aßfalg*, eds. Regine Schulz, Julius Aßfalg, and Manfred Görg, 21–29. Ägypten und Altes Testament 20. Wiesbaden: Otto Harrassowitz, 1990.

Betz, Hans Dieter. *Galatians*. Hermeneia Series. Philadelphia: Fortress Press, 1979.

Bickerman, Elias. *From Ezra to the Last of the Maccabees*. New York: Schocken Books, 1970.

Bieler, Ludwig. *ΘΕΙΟΣ ΑΝΗΡ. Das Bild des "göttlichen Menschen" in Spätantike und Frühchristentum*. Vienna: Oskar Höfels, 1935–36; repr.: Darmstadt: Wissenschaftliche Buchgesellschaft, 1967.

Biezunska-Malowist, I. "Die Expositio von Kindern als Quelle der Sklavenbeschaffung im griechisch-römischen Ägypten." *Jahrbuch für Wirtschaftsgeschichte* 2 (1971), 129–33.

Bird, Anthony E. "The Authorship of the Pastoral Epistles—Quantifying Literary Style." *Reformed Theological Review* 56 (1997), 118–37.

Black, Matthew. *An Aramaic Approach to the Gospels and Acts*. 3rd ed. Peabody, Mass.: Hendrickson Publishers, 1998.

Blass, F., and A. Debrunner. *A Greek Grammar of the New Testament and Other Early Christian Literature*. Trans. and ed. Robert W. Funk. Chicago: University of Chicago Press, 1961.

Blenkinsopp, Joseph. "The Family in First Temple Judaism." In *Families in Ancient Israel*, eds. Leo. J. Perdue, Joseph Blenkinsopp, John J. Collins, and Carol Meyers, 48–103. Louisville, Ky.: Westminster John Knox Press, 1997.

Blinzler, Josef. "Justinus Apol. I, 15,4 und Matthäus 19,11–12." In *Mélanges bibliques. En homage au R. P. Béda Rigaux*, eds. Albert-Louis Descamps and André de Halleux, 45–55. Gembloux, Belgium: J. Duculot, 1970.

Bloch, Rene. "Basilinda." In *Der Neue Pauly. Enzyklopädie der Antike*, ed. Hubert Cancik and Helmuth Schneider, vol. 2, col. 482. Stuttgart: Verlag J. B. Metzler, 1997.

Blomenkamp, P. "Erziehung." In *Reallexikon für Antike und Christentum* (hereafter *RAC*) 6 (1966), 502–59.

Boatwright, Mary T. "Children and Parents on the Tombstones of Pannonia." In *The Roman Family in the Empire: Rome, Italy, and Beyond*, ed. Michele George, 287–318. Oxford: Oxford University Press, 2005.

Bohlen, Reinhold. *Die Ehrung der Eltern bei Ben Sira. Studien zur Motivation und Interpretation eines familienethischen Grundwertes in frühhellenistischer Zeit*. Trierer Theologische Studien 51. Trier: Paulinus-Verlag, 1991.

Bonhoeffer, Dietrich. "Zur Tauffrage. Ein Gutachten." In *Dietrich Bonhoeffer, Gesam-*

melte Schriften, ed. Eberhard Bethge, vol. 3, 431–54. Munich: C. Kaiser, 1960.

Bonner, Campbell. "The Sibyl and the Bottle Imps." In *Quantulacumque. Studies Presented to Kirsopp Lake by Pupils, Colleagues, and Friends*, ed. Robert P. Casey, Silva Lake, and Agnes K. Lake, 1–8. London: Christophers, c1937.

Bonner, Gerald. "Baptismus parvulorum." In *Augustinus-Lexikon*, ed. Cornelius Mayer, and others, vol. 1, fasc. 4, 592–602. Basel: Schwabe, 1990.

Bonner, Stanley F. *Education in Ancient Rome*. Berkeley: University of California Press, 1977.

Boswell, John. *The Kindness of Strangers: The Abandonment of Children in Western Europe from late Antiquity to the Renaissance*. Chicago: University of Chicago Press, 1988.

———. "*Expositio* and *Oblatio:* The Abandonment of Children and the Ancient and Medieval Family." *American Historical Review* 89 (1984), 10–33. Reprinted in Carol Neel, ed. *Medieval Families: Perspectives on Marriage, Household, and Children*, 234–72. Medieval Academy Reprints for Teaching 40. Toronto: University of Toronto Press, 2004.

Bouhot, J. P. "Version inédite du sermon 'Ad neophytos' de S. Jean Chrysostome, utilisée par S. Augustin." *Revue des études augustiniennes* 17 (1971), 27–41.

Bovon, François. "Canonical and Apocryphal Acts of Apostles." *Journal of Early Christian Studies* (hereafter *JECS*) 11.2 (2003), 165–94.

Bowen, James. *A History of Western Education*. Vol. 1: *The Ancient World: Orient and Mediterranean 2000 B.C.–A.D. 1054*. New York: St. Martin's Press, 1972.

Bowersock, Glen Warren. *Martyrdom and Rome*. Cambridge: Cambridge University Press, 1995.

Boyarin, Daniel. *Carnal Israel: Reading Sex in Talmudic Culture*. Berkeley: University of California Press, 1993.

———. *Dying for God: Martyrdom and the Making of Christianity and Judaism*. Stanford, Calif.: Stanford University Press, 1999.

Bradley, Keith R. *Discovering the Roman Family: Studies in Roman Social History*. New York: Oxford University Press, 1991.

———. "Child Labor in the Roman World." In *Discovering the Roman Family: Studies in Roman Social History*, 103–24. New York: Oxford University Press, 1991.

———. "The Roman child in sickness and health." In *The Roman Family in the Empire: Rome, Italy, and Beyond*, ed. Michele George, 67–92. Oxford: Oxford University Press, 2005.

Brakmann, Heinzgerd, and M. Metzger. "Katechumenat." In *RAC* 20 (2003), 497–574.

Braun, René. "Tertullien et l'exégèse de 1 Cor 7." In *Épektasis; mélanges patristiques offerts au Cardinal Jean Daniélou*, ed. Jacques Fontaine and Charles Kannengiesser, 21–28. Paris: Beauchesne, 1972.

Bremmer, Jan N. "Adolescents, *Symposion*, and Pederasty." In *Sympotica: A Symposium on the Symposium*, ed. O. Murray, 135–48. Oxford: Oxford University Press, 1990.

———. "The Apocryphal Acts: Authors, Place, Time and Readership." In *The Apocryphal Acts of Thomas*, ed. Jan N. Bremmer, 149–70. Louvain: Peeters, 2001.

Brock, Sebastian. "Diachronic Aspects of Syriac Word Formation: An Aid for Dating Anonymous Texts." In *V Symposium Syriacum 1988*, Katholieke Universiteit, Louvain, August 29–31, 1988, ed. René Lavenant, S.J., 321–30. Orientalia Christiana Analecta 236. Rome: Pont. Institutum Studiorum Orientalium, 1990.

Broneer, Oscar. "Paul and the Pagan Cults at Isthmia." *Harvard Theological Review* 64 (1971), 169–87.

Brooten, Bernadette J. "'Junia—outstanding among the apostles' (Romans 16:7)." In *Women Priests: A Catholic Commentary on the Vatican Declaration,* eds. Leonard and Arlene Swidler, 141–44. New York: Paulist Press, 1977. German translation: "'Junia—hervorragend unter den Aposteln' (Rom 16:7)." In *Frauenbefreiung: biblische und theologische Argumente,* ed. Elisabeth Moltmann-Wendel, 148–51. Gesellschaft und Theologie: Systematische Beiträge 12. Munich: Chr. Kaiser Verlag, 1978.

———. "Der lange Schatten der Sklaverei im Leben von Frauen und Mädchen." In *Dem Tod nicht glauben. Sozialgeschichte der Bibel. Festschrift für Luise Schottroff zum 70. Geburtstag,* ed. Frank Crüsemann, Marlene Crüsemann, Claudia Janssen, Rainer Kessler, and Beate Wehn, 488–503. Gütersloh: Gütersloher Verlagshaus, 2004.

———. *The Feminist Sexual Ethics Project.* http://www.brandeis.edu/projects/fse.

Brothers, J. T. "The Interpretation of παῖς θεοῦ in Justin Martyr's *Dialogue with Trypho.*" *Studia Patristica* 9 (1966), 127–38.

Broudéhoux, J. P. *Marriage et Famille chez Clément d'Alexandrie.* Théologie Historique 11. Paris: Beauchesne et ses fils, c1970.

Brown, Peter. "Late Antiquity." In *A History of Private Life: I. From Pagan Rome to Byzantium,* ed. Paul Veyne, 237–311. Cambridge, Mass.: Harvard University Press, 1987.

Brown, F., S. Driver, and C. Briggs. *The Brown-Driver-Briggs Hebrew and English Lexicon.* Boston: Houghton, Mifflin, 1906; repr. Peabody, Mass.: Hendrickson Publishers, 1999.

Brown, Raymond E. *The Gospel according to John (I–XII).* The Anchor Bible Commentary, 29. New York: Doubleday, 1966.

———. *The Birth of the Messiah.* New York: Random House, 1993.

———. *An Introduction to the New Testament.* New York: Doubleday, 1997.

Brown, Raymond E., et al., eds. *Mary in the New Testament.* New York: Paulist Press, 1978.

Bultmann, Rudolf. *The History of the Synoptic Tradition.* Trans. John Marsh. New York: Harper & Row, 1968.

Burke, Trevor J. "Paul's Role as 'Father' to His Corinthian 'Children' in Socio-Historical Context (1 Corinthians 4:14–21)." In *Paul and the Corinthians: Studies on a Community in Conflict. Essays in Honour of Margaret Thrall,* ed. Trevor J. Burke and J. Keith Elliott, 95–113. Supplements to Novum Testamentum 109. Leiden: E. J. Brill, 2003.

Burleigh, John H. S. "St. Augustine on Baptism." *Reformed Theological Review* 15 (1956), 65–80.

Burns, Patout J. "On Rebaptism: Social Organization in the Third Century Church." *JECS* 1 (1993), 367–403.

Burris, Catherine, and Lucas van Rompay. "Thecla in Syriac Christianity: Preliminary Observations." *Hugoye: Journal of Syriac Studies* 5.2 (2002) http://syrcom.cua.edu/Hugoye/Vol5No2/HV5N2BurrisVanRompay.html.

———. "Some Further Notes on Thecla in Syriac Christianity." *Hugoye: Journal of Syriac Studies* 6.2 (2003) http://syrcom.cua.edu/Hugoye/Vol6No2/HV6N2BurrisVanRompay.html.

Burton, Ernest De Witt. *The Epistle to the Galatians.* The International Critical Commentary. Edinburgh: T&T Clark, 1975.

Buscemi, Alfio Marcello. "Libertà e *huiothesia:* studio esegetico di Gal 4,1–7." *Liber Annuus* 30 (1980), 93–136.

Byrskog, Samuel. "Jesus as Messiah Teacher in the Gospel according to Matthew: Tradition History and/or Narrative Christology." In *The New Testament as Reception,* eds. Morgens Müller and Henrik Tronier, 83–100. *JSNT* Supplement Series 230. Copenhagen International Seminar 11. London: Sheffield Academic Press, 2002.

Camelot, Pierre-Thomas. "Le baptême des petits enfants dans l'église des premiers siècles." *La Maison-Dieu* 88 (1966), 23–42.

Canivet, Pierre. *Le monachisme syrien selon Théodoret de Cyr.* Théologie historique 42. Paris: Beauchesne, c1977.

Carroll, John T. "Children in the Bible." *Interpretation* 55 (2001), 121–34.

Casey, James. *The History of the Family.* New Perspectives on the Past series. Oxford: Basil Blackwell, 1989.

Caspers, Charles. "Leviticus 12, Mary and Wax: Purification and Churching in Late Medieval Christianity." In *Purity and Holiness: The Heritage of Leviticus,* ed. Marcel Poorthuis and Joshua Schwartz, 295–309. Jewish and Christian Perspectives Series 2. Boston: E. J. Brill, 2000.

Castelli, Elizabeth A. *Martyrdom and Memory: Early Christian Culture Making.* New York: Columbia University Press, 2004.

Castellino, Giorgio R. "1 Cor. VII, 36–38 nel diritto orientale e nella etnologia." In *Mélanges Eugène Tisserant.* Vol. 1: *Écriture Sainte—Ancien Orient,* 31–42. Studi et Testi 231. Vatican City: Biblioteca Apostolica Vaticana, 1964.

Cattanei, Giovanni. "Significato formativo dell'obbedienza." In *L'educazione morale,* eds. Enzo Giammancheri and Marcello Peretti, 247–77. Brescia, Italy: Editrice la Scuola, 1977.

Chartrand-Burke, Tony. "Authorship and Identity in the Infancy Gospel of Thomas." *Toronto Journal of Theology* 14.1 (1998), 27–43.

———. "The Infancy Gospel of Thomas: The Text, Its Origin, and Its Transmission." Ph.D. thesis. University of Toronto, 2001.

———. "The Greek Manuscript Tradition of the Infancy Gospel of Thomas." *Apocrypha* 14 (2004), 129–51.

Christes, Johannes, Richard Klein, and Christoph Lüth, eds. *Handbuch der Erziehung und Bildung in der Antike.* Darmstadt: Wissenschaftliche Buchgesellschaft, 2006.

Christo, Gus George. *Martyrdom according to John Chrysostom: "To Live Is Christ, To Die Is Gain."* Lewiston, N.Y.: Edwin Mellen Press, 1997.

Clark, Elizabeth A. "John Chrysostom and the Subintroductae." *Church History* 46 (1977), 171–85.

———. *The Life of Melania the Younger. Introduction, Translation, and Commentary.* Studies in Women and Religion, vol. 14. Lewiston, N.Y.: Edwin Mellen Press, 1984.

———. "Melania the Elder and the Origenist Controversy: The Status of the Body in a Late-Ancient Debate." In *Nova & Vetera: Patristic Studies in Honor of Thomas Patrick Halton,* ed. John Petruccione, 117–27. Washington, D.C.: The Catholic Unversity of America Press, 1998.

Clark, G. W. "An illiterate lector?" *Zeitschrift für Papyrologie und Epigraphik* 57 (1984), 103–4.

Clark, Gillian. *Women in Late Antiquity: Pagan and Christian Lifestyles.* Oxford: Clarendon Press, 1993.

——. "The Fathers and the Children." In *The Church and Childhood: Papers Read at the 1993 Summer Meeting and the 1994 Winter Meeting of the Ecclesiastical History Society,* ed. Diana Wood, 1–27. Oxford: Blackwell Publishers, 1994.

Clark, M. L. *Higher Education in the Ancient World.* Albuquerque: University of New Mexico Press, 1971.

Claussen, Carsten. *Versammlung, Gemeinde, Synagoge: das hellenistisch-jüdische Umfeld der frühchristlichen Gemeinden.* Studien zur Umwelt des Neuen Testaments 27. Göttingen: Vandenhoeck & Ruprecht, 2002.

Coenen, Lothar, and Klaus Haacker, eds. *Theologisches Begriffslexikon zum Neuen Testament,* rev. ed., 2 vols. Wuppertal: R. Brockhaus Verlag and Neukirchener Verlag, 1997.

Cohen, Shaye J. D. "The Significance of Yavneh." *Hebrew Union College Annual* 55 (1984), 27–53.

——. *From the Maccabees to the Mishnah.* Library of Early Christianity 7. Philadelphia: Westminster Press, 1987.

——, ed. *The Jewish Family in Antiquity.* Brown Judaic Studies 289. Atlanta: Scholars Press, 1993.

Collins, John J. "Marriage, Divorce, and Family in Second Temple Judaism." In *Families in Ancient Israel,* eds. Leo. J. Perdue, Joseph Blenkinsopp, John J. Collins, and Carol Meyers, 104–62. Louisville, Ky.: Westminster John Knox Press, 1997.

Collins, Raymond F. *First Corinthians.* Sacra Pagina Series, vol. 7. Collegeville, Minn.: Liturgical Press, 1999.

——. *Sexual Ethics and the New Testament: Behavior and Belief.* New York: Crossroad, 2000.

Colón, A. R., with P. A. Colón. *A History of Children. A Socio-Cultural Survey across Millennia.* Westport, Conn.: Greenwood Press, 2001.

Colson, J. "L'évêque dans la Didascalie des Apôtres." *La Vie Spirituelle. Supplément* 5 (1951), 271–90.

Coltrane, Scott, and Randall Collins. *Sociology of Marriage & the Family: Gender, Love, and Property.* 5th ed. Australia: Wadsworth, Thomson Learning, 2001.

Conrad, J. "קָטֹן‎ *qāṭōn;* קָטָן‎ *qāṭān;* קֹטֶן‎ *qōṭen.*" In *Theological Dictionary of the Old Testament,* ed. G. Johannes Botterweck, Helmer Ringgren, and Heinz-Josef Fabry, trans. David E Green, vol. 13, 3–9. Grand Rapids, Mich.: Eerdmans, c2004.

Conzelmann, Hans. *A Commentary on the Acts of the Apostles.* Trans. James Limburg, A. Thomas Kraebel, and Donald H. Ivel, ed. Eldon Jay Epp with Christopher R. Matthews. Hermeneia Series. Philadelphia: Fortress Press, 1987.

Corbert, John H. "The Foster Child: A Neglected Theme in Early Christian Life and Thought." In *Traditions in Contact and Change: Selected Proceedings of the 14th Congress of the International Association for the History of Religions,* eds. Peter Slater and Donald Wiebe, 307–21. Waterloo, Canada: Wilfrid Laurier University Press, 1983.

Corbier, Mireille. "Child Exposure and Abandonment." In *Childhood, Class and Kin in the Roman World,* ed. Suzanne Dixon, 52–73. London: Routledge, 2001.

Coyle, K. "Empire and eschaton: The early Church and the question of domestic relations." *Église et théologie* 12 (1981), 35–94.

Cramer, Peter. *Baptism and Change in the Early Middle Ages, c. 200–c. 1150.* Cambridge Studies in Medieval Life and Thought. Cambridge: Cambridge University Press, 1993.

Crenshaw, James L. *Education in Ancient Israel: Across the Deadening Silence.* The Anchor Bible Reference Library. New York: Doubleday, 1998.

Cribiore, Raffaella. *Gymnastics of the Mind: Greek Education in Hellenistic and Roman Egypt.* Princeton, N.J.: Princeton University Press, c2001.

Crook, John A. *"Patria Potestas." Classical Quarterly* 17 (1967), 113–22.

Croy, N. Clayton. "Hellenistic Philosophies and the Preaching of the Resurrection (Acts 17:18, 32)." *Novum Testamentum* 39 (1997), 21–39.

Cullmann, Oscar. "Infancy Gospels." In *New Testament Apocrypha.* Vol. 1: *Gospels and Related Writings,* ed. Edgar Hennecke and Wilhelm Schneemelcher, ed. and trans. R. McL. Wilson, 363–69. Philadelphia: Westminster Press, 1963.

———. "Kindheitsevangelien." In *Neutestamentliche Apokryphen in deutscher Übersetzung, Bd. 1: Evangelien,* eds. Edgar Hennecke and Wilhelm Schneemelcher, 330–72. 5th ed. Tübingen: J. C. B. Mohr (Paul Siebeck), 1987.

Curtius, Ernst Robert. *European Literature and the Latin Middle Ages.* Trans. Willard R. Trask. Bollingen Series 36. New York: Pantheon, c1953; repr. Princeton, N.J.: Princeton University Press, 1990.

Daleas, Brian C. "Children in the Roman World: Status and the Growth of Identity." Ph.D. thesis. Indiana University, 1998.

D'Ambrosio, Antonio. *Women and Beauty in Pompeii.* Trans. Graham Sells. Los Angeles: J. Paul Getty Museum, 2001.

Daniel, Constantin. "Esséniens et eunuques, Matthieu 19:10–12." *Revue de Qumran* 6 (1968), 353–79.

Daremberg, C., and E. Saglio, eds. *Dictionnaire des antiquités grecques et romaines.* Paris: Hachette, 1877–1919.

Dasen, Véronique, ed. *Regards croisés sur la naissance et la petite enfance: actes du cycle de conferences "Naitre en 2001" / Geburt und frühe Kindheit: interdisziplinäre Aspekte: Beiträge der Vortragsreihe "Geboren im Jahr 2001."* Defis et dialogues / Herausforderung und Besinnung 18. Fribourg: Éditions Universitaires, 2002.

———, ed. *Naissance et petite enfance dans l'Antiquité. Actes du colloque de Fribourg, 28 novembre–1er décembre 2001.* Orbis Biblicus et Orientalis 203. Fribourg: Academic Press Fribourg, 2004.

Daube, D. *Roman Law: Linguistic, Social and Philosophical Aspects.* Gray Lectures 1966. Edinburgh: Edinburgh University Press, 1969.

Davis, Stephen J. *The Cult of Saint Thecla: A Tradition of Women's Piety in Late Antiquity.* New York: Oxford University Press, 2001.

Day, Linda. "Rhetoric and Domestic Violence in Ezekiel 16." *Biblical Interpretation* 8 (2000), 205–30.

De Bruyn, D. Domitien. "Nouveaux Fragments des Actes de Pierre, de Paul, de Jean, d'André, et de l'Apocalypse d'Élie." *Revue Bénédictine* 25 (1908), 149–60.

———. "Epistula Titi, Discipuli Pauli, De dispositione Sanctimonii." *Revue Bénédictine* 37 (1925), 47–72.

DeBruyn, Theodore S. "Flogging a Son: The Emergence of the *pater flagellans* in Latin Christian Discourse." *JECS* 7.2 (1999), 249–90.

Deichmann, Friedrich Wilhelm, ed. *Repertorium der christlich-antiken Sarkophage.* Vol. 1. Wiesbaden: F. Steiner, 1967.

del Agua Pérez, Agustin. "Procedimientos derásicos del Sal 2:7b en el Nuevo Testamento: Tu eres mi hijo, yo te he engendrado hoy." *Estudios bíblicos* 42 (1984), 391–414.

Delling, Gerhard. "Gotteskindschaft." In *RAC* 11 (1981), 1159–85.

Del Verme, Marcello. *Didache and Judaism: Jewish Roots of an Ancient Christian-Jewish Work.* New York: T&T Clark, 2004.

De Mendieta, David Amand. "La virginité chez Eusèbe d'Emèse et l'ascétisme familial dans la première moitié du IVe siècle." *Revue d'histoire ecclésiastique* 50 (1955), 777–820.

Deming, Will. "A Diatribe in 1 Cor 7:21–22: A New Perspective on Paul's Directions to Slaves." *Novum Testamentum* 37 (1995), 130–37.

———. "Mark 9.42–10.12, Matthew 5.27–32, and B. Nid. 13b: A First Century Discussion of Male Sexuality." *New Testament Studies* 36 (1990), 130–41.

Derrett, J. Duncan M. "Ananias, Sapphira, and the Right of Property." *Downside Review* 89 (1971), 225–32.

———. "Midrash in the New Testament: The Origin of Luke 22:67–68." *Studia Theologica* 29 (1975), 147–56.

———. "Hating Father and Mother (Luke 14:26; Matthew 10:37)." *Downside Review* 117 (1999), 251–72.

Dessau, H. "Liberalia." In *Paulys Real-Encyclopädie der Classischen Altertumswissenschaft,* ed. Georg Wissowa, vol. 13, cols. 81–82. Stuttgart: J. B. Metzler, 1937.

De Ste. Croix, Geoffrey Ernest Maurice. *The Class Struggle in the Ancient Greek World: From the Archaic Age to the Arab Conquests.* Ithaca, N.Y.: Cornell University Press, 1981.

Destro, Adrian, and Mauro Pesce. "Fathers and Householders in the Jesus Movement: The Perspective of the Gospel of Luke." *Biblical Interpretation* 11.2 (2003), 211–38.

De Waal, Anastasia. "Barbie in the Microwave." *The Guardian,* December 22, 2005.

Distelrath, Götz. "Saturnalia." In *Der Neue Pauly. Enzyklopädie der Antike,* ed. Hubert Cancik and Helmuth Schneider, vol. 11, cols. 113–15. Stuttgart: Verlag J. B. Metzler, 2001.

Dixon, Suzanne. *The Roman Mother.* Norman: University of Oklahoma Press, c1988.

———. *The Roman Family.* Baltimore: Johns Hopkins University Press, 1992.

———, ed. *Childhood, Class, and Kin in the Roman World.* London: Routledge, 2001.

Dodd, Charles H. *The Founder of Christianity.* New York: Macmillan, 1970.

Dolansky, Fanny L. "Coming of Age in Rome: The History and Social Significance of Assuming the *toga virilis.*" M.A. thesis. University of Victoria, Canada, 1999.

———. "Ritual, Gender, and Status in the Roman Family." Ph.D. thesis. University of Chicago, 2006.

Dölger, Franz Joseph. "Der Kuß im Tauf- und Firmungsritual nach Cyprian von Carthago und Hippolyt von Rom." *Antike und Christentum* (1929), 186–96.

———. "Das Lebensrecht des ungeborenen Kindes und die Fruchtabtreibung in der Bewertung der heidnischen und christlichen Antike." *Antike und Christentum* 4 (1933), 1–61.

———. "'*Sacramentum infanticidii.*' Die Schlachtung eines Kindes und der Genuß seines Fleisches und Blutes als vermeintlicher Einweihungsakt im ältesten Christentum." *Antike und Christentum* 4 (1933), 188–228.

———. *Sol salutis: Gebet und Gesang im christlichen Altertum, mit besonderer Rücksicht auf die Ostung in Gebet und Liturgie.* Liturgiewissenschaftliche Quellen und Forschungen 16–17. 2 vols. Münster: Aschendorff, 1972.

Donahue, John R., and Daniel J. Harrington. *The Gospel of Mark.* Sacra Pagina Series, vol. 2. Collegeville, Minn.: Liturgical Press, 2002.

Dover, Kenneth James. "Classical Greek Attitudes to Sexual Behaviour." In *Sex and Difference in Ancient Greece and Rome,* eds. Mark Golden and Peter Toohey, 114–30. Edinburgh: Edinburgh University Press, 2004.

Dresner, Samuel H. "Barren Rachel." *Judaism* 40 (Fall 1991), 442–51.

Duane, Litfin A. *St. Paul's Theology of Proclamation: 1 Corinthians 1–4 and Greco-Roman Rhetoric.* Cambridge: Cambridge University Press, 1994.

Dumm, Demetrius. "Passover and Eucharist." *Worship* 61 (1987), 199–208.

Dunn, James D. G. "The Household Rules in the New Testament." In *The Family in Theological Perspective,* ed. Stephen C. Barton, 43–63. Edinburgh: T&T Clark, 1996.

Dupont, Florence. *Daily Life in Ancient Rome.* Oxford: Basil Blackwell, 1993.

Dupont, J. "Community of Goods in the Early Church." In *Salvation of the Gentiles,* ed. J. Keating, 85–102. New York: Paulist Press, 1979.

Durand, Agnès. "Jeux et jouets de l'enfance en Grece et à Rome." *Jeux et Jouets dans l'Antiquité et au Moyen Age, Dossiers de l'Archéologie* 168 (1992), 10–17.

Durry, Marcel. "Le Marriage des Filles Impubères à Rome." *Comptes Rendus de l'Académie des Inscriptions* (1955), 84–91.

Dutch, Robert S. *The Educated Elite in 1 Corinthians: Education and Community Conflict in Graeco-Roman Context.* JSNT Supplement Series 271. London: T&T Clark, 2005.

Du Toit, Andreas B. "A Tale of Two Cities: 'Tarsus or Jerusalem' Revisited." *New Testament Studies* 46.3 (2000), 375–402.

Ebner, Martin. "'Kinderevangelium' oder markinische Sozialkritik? Mk 10,13–16 im Kontext." *Jahrbuch für Biblische Theologie* 17 (2002), 315–36.

Edwards, Bela Bates. "The Genuineness of the Pastoral Epistles." *Bibliotheca Sacra* 150 (1993), 131–39. Repr. from 1851 edition.

Edwards, Robert W. "The Vale of Kola: A Final Preliminary Report on the Marchlands of Northeast Turkey." *Dumbarton Oaks Papers* 42 (1988), 119–41.

Elderkin, Kate McKnight. "Jointed Dolls in Antiquity." *American Journal of Archaeology* 34.2 (1930), 455–79.

Elliott, John H. "The Jesus Movement Was Not Egalitarian." *Biblical Interpretation* 11.2 (2003), 187–98.

Ellis, E. Earle. *The Gospel of Luke.* The New Century Bible Commentary. Grand Rapids, Mich.: Eerdmans, 1981.

Ellis, Ieuan. "Jesus and the Subversive Family." *Scottish Journal of Theology* 38.2 (1985), 173–88.

Elm, Susanna. *"Virgins of God": The Making of Asceticism in Late Antiquity.* Oxford Classical Monographs. Oxford: Clarendon Press, c1994.

Eltrop, Bettina. *Denn solchen gehört das Himmelreich. Kinder im Matthäusevangelium. Eine feministisch-sozialgeschichtliche Untersuchung.* Stuttgart: Ulrich E. Grauer, 1996.

———. "Kinder im Neuen Testament. Eine sozialgeschichtliche Nachfrage." *Jahrbuch für Biblische Theologie* 17 (2002), 83–96.

———. "Problem Girls: A Transgressive Reading of the Parable of the Ten Virgins (Matthew 25:1–13)." In *Transgressors: Towards a Feminist Biblical Theology,* eds. Claudia Janssen, Ute Ochtendung, and Beate Wehn, trans. Linda M. Maloney, 163–71. Collegeville, Minn.: Liturgical Press, 2002.

Engberg-Pederson, Troels, ed. *Paul in His Hellenistic Context*. Minneapolis: Fortress Press, 1995.

————. *Paul and the Stoics*. Louisville, Ky.: Westminster John Knox, 2000.

Engels, Donald. "The Problem of Female Infanticide in the Greco-Roman World." *Classical Philology* 75 (1980), 112–20.

————. "The Use of Historical Demography in Ancient History." *Classical Quarterly* 34 (1984), 386–93.

Epp, Eldon Jay. *Junia: The First Woman Apostle*. Minneapolis: Fortress Press, 2005.

Esler, Philip E. "Family Imagery and Christian Identity in Gal. 5:13 to 6:10." In *Constructing Early Christian Families: Family as Social Reality and Metaphor*, ed. Halvor Moxnes, 121–49. London: Routledge, 1997.

————. "'Keeping it in the family': Culture, Kinship and Identity in 1 Thessalonians and Galatians." In *Families and Family Relations as Represented in Early Judaisms and Early Christianities: Texts and Fictions*, eds. Jan W. van Henten and Athalya Brenner, 145–84. Studies in Theology and Religion 2. Leiden: DEO Publishing, 2000.

Evans, Craig A. *Luke*. New International Bible Commentary. Peabody, Mass.: Hendrickson Publishers, 1990.

Evans, John K. *War, Women and Children in Ancient Rome*. London: Routledge, 1991.

Eyben, Emiel. "Family Planning in Graeco-Roman Antiquity." *Ancient Society* 11–12 (1980–81), 5–82.

————. "Fathers and Sons." In *Marriage, Divorce, and Children in Ancient Rome*, ed. Beryl Rawson, 114–43. Oxford: Oxford University Press, 1991.

————. *Restless Youth in Ancient Rome*. Trans. Patrick Daly. London: Routledge, 1993.

————. "Jugend." In *RAC* 19 (2001), 388–442.

Faley, Roland J. "Leviticus." In *The New Jerome Biblical Commentary*, eds. Raymond E. Brown, Joseph A. Fitzmyer, and Roland E. Murphy, 61–79. Englewood Cliffs, N.J.: Prentice Hall, 1990.

Fensham, F. C. "Father and Son as Terminology for Treaty and Covenant." In *Near Eastern Studies in Honor of William Foxwell Albright*, ed. Hans Goedicke, 121–35. Baltimore: Johns Hopkins University Press, 1971.

Ferguson, Everett. "Inscriptions and the Origin of Infant Baptism." *JThS* n.s. 30 (1979), 37–46.

Ferguson, John. "In Defence of Pelagius." *Theology* 83 (1980), 114–19.

Festugière, André Jean. *Antioche païenne et chrétienne; Libanius, Chrysostome et les moines de Syrie*. Bibliothèque des écoles françaises d'Athènes et de Rome 194. Paris: E. de Boccard, 1959.

Fiedler, Peter. "'The Servant of the Lord': Israel (Isaiah 42:1–4) and Jesus (Matthew 12:18)." *Covenant Quarterly* 56 (1997), 119–29.

Finsterbusch, Karin. "Die kollektive Identität und die Kinder. Bemerkungen zu einem Programm im Buch Deuteronomium." *Jahrbuch für Biblische Theologie* 17 (2002), 99–120.

Fischer, Irmtraud. "'. . . und sie war unfruchtbar.' Zur Stellung kinderloser Frauen in der Literatur Alt-Israels." In *Kinder machen. Strategien der Kontrolle weiblicher Fruchtbarkeit*, eds. Gertrude Pauritsch, Beate Frakele, and Elisabeth List, 116–26. Frauenforschung 6. Vienna: Wiener Frauenverlag, 1988.

————. "Über Lust und Last, Kinder zu haben. Soziale, genealogische und theologische Aspekte in der Literatur Alt-Israels." *Jahrbuch für Biblische Theologie* 17 (2002), 55–82.

Fitzgerald, John T. "Proverbs 3:11–12, Hebrews 12:5–6, and the Tradition of Corporal Punishment." In *Scripture and Traditions: Essays on Early Judaism and Christianity*, ed. G. O'Day and P. Gray, 291–317. Leiden: E. J. Brill, 2008.

———. "Early Christian Missionary Practice and Pagan Reaction: 1 Peter and Domestic Violence against Slaves and Wives." In *Renewing Tradition: Studies in Texts and Contexts in Honor of James W. Thompson*, ed. M. W. Hamilton, T. H. Olbricht, and J. Peterson, 24–44. Princeton Theological Monograph Series. Eugene, Ore.: Pickwick Publications, 2007.

Fitzmyer, Joseph A. *Luke*. Anchor Bible, vol. 28a. New York: Doubleday, 1981–85.

Fleddermann, Harry. "The Cross and Discipleship in Q." *Society of Biblical Literature Seminar Papers* 27 (1988), 472–82.

Foley, Helene. "Mothers and Daughters." In *Coming of Age in Ancient Greece: Images of Childhood from the Classical Past*, eds. Jenifer Neils and John H. Oakley, 113–37. New Haven, Conn.: Yale University Press, c2003, 2004.

Fonrobert, Charlotte. "The *Didascalia apostolorum*: A mishnah for the disciples of Jesus." *JECS* 9.4 (2001), 483–509.

Forbes, Christopher. "Comparison, Self-Praise and Irony: Paul's Boasting and the Conventions of Hellenistic Rhetoric." *New Testament Studies* 32.1 (1986), 1–30.

Francis, James. "Children and Childhood in the New Testament." In *The Family in Theological Perspective*, ed. Stephen C. Barton, 65–85. Edinburgh: T&T Clark, 1996.

Frank, Karl Suso. *ΑΓΓΕΛΙΚΟΣ ΒΙΟΣ. Begriffsanalytische und begriffsgeschichtliche Untersuchung zum "engelgleichen Leben" im frühen Mönchtum*. Beiträge zur Geschichte des alten Mönchtums und des Benediktinerordens 26. Münster: Aschendorffsche Verlagsbuchhandlung, 1964.

Frean, Alexandra. "Barbarism Begins with Barbie, the Doll Children Love to Hate." *The Times* (U.K.), December 19, 2005.

French, Valerie. "Children in Antiquity." In *Children in Historical and Comparative Perspective: An International Handbook and Research Guide*, eds. Joseph M. Hawes and N. Ray Hiner, 13–29. Westport, Conn.: Greenwood Press, 1991.

Freund, Richard A. "The Decalogue in Early Judaism and Christianity." In *The Function of Scripture in Early Jewish and Christian Tradition*, eds. Craig A. Evans and James A. Sanders, 124–41. JSNT Supplement Series 154. Sheffield: Sheffield Academic Press, 1998.

Frier, Bruce W., and Thomas A. J. McGinn. *A Casebook on Roman Family Law*. Classical Resources Series 5. New York: Oxford University Press, 2004.

Gaechter, Paul. "The Chronology from Mary's Betrothal to the Birth of Christ." *Theological Studies* 2.2 and 2.3 (1941), 145–70 and 347–68.

Galinsky, Karl. "Augustus' legislation on morals and marriage." *Philologus* 125 (1981), 126–44.

Gantz, Ulrike. *Gregor von Nyssa: Oratio consolatoria in Pulcheriam*. ΧΡΗΣΙΣ / CHRÊSIS. Die Methode der Kirchenväter im Umgang mit der antiken Kultur 6. Basel: Schwabe Verlag, 1999.

Gardner, Jane F. *Family and "Familia" in Roman Law and Life*. Oxford: Clarendon Press; and New York: Oxford University Press, 1998.

Gardner, Jane F., and Thomas Wiedemann. *The Roman Household. A Sourcebook*. London: Routledge, 1991.

Garitte, G. "Un couvent de femmes au IIIe siècle? Note sur un passage de la vie grecque de S. Antoine." In *Scrinium Lovaniense: Mélanges historiques, historische opstellen Étienne van Cauwenbergh*. Recueil de travaux d'histoire et de philologie 4, fasc. 24, 150–59. Louvain: J. Duculot Gembloux, 1961.

Garnsey, Peter. "Child Rearing in Ancient Italy." In *The Family in Italy from Antiquity to the Present*, eds. D. I. Kertzer and R. P. Saller, 48–65. New Haven, Conn.: Yale University Press, 1991.

———. *Food and Society in Classical Antiquity*. Cambridge: Cambridge University Press, 1999.

———. "Sons, Slaves—and Christians." In *The Roman Family in Italy: Status, Sentiment, Space*, eds. Beryl Rawson and Paul Weaver, 101–21. Oxford: Oxford University Press, 1999.

Gärtner, Michael. *Die Familienerziehung in der Alten Kirche. Eine Untersuchung über die ersten vier Jahrhunderte des Christentums mit einer Übersetzung und einem Kommentar zu der Schrift des Johannes Chrysostomus über die Geltungssucht und Kindererziehung*. Cologne: Böhlau Verlag, 1985.

Geerard, M. *Clavis Patrum Graecorum*. Vol. 2. Turnhout: Brepols, 1974.

George, Augustin. "Le parallèle entre Jean-Baptiste et Jésus en Luc 1–2." In *Mélanges bibliques en homage au R. P. Béda Rigaux*, ed. Albert-Louis Descamps and André de Halleux, 147–71. Gembloux, Belgium: J. Duculot, 1970.

George, Michele. "Domestic Architecture and Household Relations: Pompeii and Roman Ephesos." *JSNT* 27.1 (2004), 7–25.

Gerber, Christine. *Paulus und seine "Kinder": Studien zur Beziehungsmetaphorik der paulinischen Briefe*. Beihefte zur Zeitschrift für die neutestamentliche Wissenschaft und die Kunde der älteren Kirche 136. Berlin: de Gruyter, 2005.

Gerhardsson, Birger. *Memory and Manuscript: Oral Tradition and Written Transmission in Rabbinic Judaism and Early Christianity*. Volume 22: Acta Seminarii Neotestamentici Upsaliensis, trans. Eric J. Sharpe. Lund: C. W. K. Gleerup, 1961. Repr.: Grand Rapids, Mich.: Eerdmans, 1998.

———. *The Mighty Acts of Jesus according to Matthew*. Lund: C. W. K. Gleerup, 1979.

Gerö, Stephen. "Infancy Gospel of Thomas: A Study of the Textual and Literary Problems." *Novum Testamentum* 13.1 (1971), 46–80.

Giannarelli, Elena. "Nota sui dodici anni—l'età della scelta—nella tradizione letteraria antica." *Maia* 29–30 (1977–78), 127–33.

———. "L'infanzia nella biografia cristiana." *Studia Patristica* 18.2 (1989), 217–21.

———. "Infanzia e santità: un problema della biografia cristiana antica." In *Bambini santi: rappresentazioni dell'infanzia e modelli agiografici*, eds. Anna Benvenuti Papi and Elena Giannarelli, 25–58. Turin: Rosenberg & Sellier, 1991.

Ginestet, Pierre. *Les organizations de la jeunesse dans l'Occident Romain*. Collection Latomus 213. Brussels: Revue d'Études Latines, 1991.

Given, Mark Douglas. "The Unknown Paul: Philosophers and Sophists in Acts 17." *Society of Biblical Literature Seminar Papers* 35 (1996), 343–51.

———. *Paul's True Rhetoric: Ambiguity, Cunning, and Deception in Greece and Rome*. Harrisburg, Pa.: Trinity Press International, 2001.

Glancy, Jennifer. *Slavery in Early Christianity*. New York: Oxford University Press, 2002.

Gnilka, Christian. *Aetas spiritalis. Die Überwindung der natürlichen Altersstufen als Ideal frühchristlichen Lebens*. Theophaneia 24. Bonn: Peter Hanstein Verlag GmbH, 1972.

Golden, Mark. "Demography and the Exposure of Girls at Athens." *Phoenix* 35.4 (1981), 316–31.

―――. "Slavery and Homosexuality at Athens." *Phoenix* 38 (1984), 308–24.

―――. "*Pais*, 'Child,' and 'Slave.'" *L'Antiquité Classique* 54 (1985), 91–104.

―――. "Did the Ancients Care When Their Children Died?" *Greece & Rome* 35.2 (1988), 152–63.

―――. *Children and Childhood in Classical Athens.* Baltimore: Johns Hopkins University Press, 1990.

―――. "Childhood in Ancient Greece." In *Coming of Age in Ancient Greece: Images of Childhood from the Classical Past,* eds. Jenifer Neils and John H. Oakley, 12–29. New Haven, Conn.: Yale University Press, c2003, 2004.

―――. *Sport in the Ancient World from A to Z.* London: Routledge, 2004.

Goodblatt, David. "The Beruriah Traditions." *Journal of Jewish Studies* 26 (1975), 68–85.

Gorman, Michael J. *Abortion and the Early Church: Christian, Jewish and Pagan Attitudes in the Greco-Roman World.* New York: Paulist Press, 1982.

Gosebrink, Hildegard. "Frauengestalten im palästinensischen Mönchtum." In "*. . . weil sie mehr liebte.*" Frauen im frühen Mönchtum, ed. Jakobus Kaffanke, 55–73. Wegschritte: Tagungsberichte der Beuroner Tage für Spiritualität und Mystik, Erzabtei St. Martin Beuron. Beuron: Beuroner Kunstverlag, 2002.

Gougaud, L. "Les critiques formulées contre les premiers moines d'occident." *Revue Mabillon* 24 (1934), 145–63.

Goulder, Michael D. *Luke. A New Paradigm. Vol. II. JSNT* Supplement Series 20. Sheffield: JSOT Press, 1989.

Gourgues, Michel. "Lecture christologique du Psaume CX et fête de la Pentecôte." *Revue biblique* 83 (1976), 5–24.

Grassi, Joseph A. "Abba, Father (Mark 14:36): Another Approach." *Journal of the American Academy of Religion* 50 (1982), 449–58.

Green, Joel B. *The Gospel of Luke.* Grand Rapids, Mich.: Eerdmans, 1997.

Gregg, J. A. F. "The Commentary of Origen upon the Epistle to the Ephesians." *JThS* 3 (1902), 233–44, 398–420, and 554–76.

Gregg, Robert C. *Consolation Philosophy. Greek and Christian Paideia in Basil and the Two Gregories.* Patristic Monograph Series 3. Cambridge, Mass.: Philadelphia Patristic Foundation, 1975.

Grindel, John A. "Matthew 12:18–21." *Catholic Biblical Quarterly* (hereafter *CBQ*) 29 (1967), 110–15.

Gross, Walter Hatto. "Toga." In *Der Kleine Pauly: Lexikon der Antike, based on Pauly's Realencyclopädie der classischen Altertumswissenschaft,* ed. and enlarged by Konrat Ziegler, Walther Sontheimer, and Hans Gärtner, vol. 5, cols. 879–80. Munich: Druckenmüller, 1964–75.

Grubbs, Judith Evans. *Law and Family in Late Antiquity: The Emperor Constantine's Marriage Legislation.* Oxford: Clarendon Press, 1995.

―――. *Women and the Law in the Roman Empire: A Sourcebook on Marriage, Divorce and Widowhood.* London: Routledge, 2002.

Grundmann, W. "ἀνάγκη." In *Theological Dictionary of the New Testament,* ed. G. Kittel and G. Friedrich, trans. G. W. Bromley, vol. 1, 344–47. Grand Rapids, Mich.: Eerdmans, c1964.

Guijarro, Santiago. "The Family in First-Century Galilee." In *Constructing Early Christian Families: Family as Social Reality and Metaphor,* ed. Halvor Moxnes, 42–65. London: Routledge, 1997.

Guijarro Oporto, Santiago. *Fidelidades en conflicto: La ruptura con la familia por causa del discipulado y de la misión en la tradición sinóptica.* Plenitudo Temporis 4. Salamanca: Publicaciones Universidad Pontificia, 1998.

———. "Domestic Space, Family Relationships, and the Social Location of the Q People." *JSNT* 27.1 (2004), 69–81.

Guillaumont, Antoine. "Le nom des 'agapètes.'" *Vigiliae Christianae* 23.1 (1969), 30–37.

Gundry, Robert H. *Matthew. A Commentary on His Literary and Theological Art.* Grand Rapids, Mich.: Eerdmans, 1982.

———. *Mark: A Commentary on his Apology for the Cross.* Grand Rapids, Mich.: Eerdmans, 1993.

———. "Mark 10:29: Order in the List." *CBQ* 59 (1997), 465–75.

Gundry-Volf, Judith M. "The Least and the Greatest: Children in the New Testament." In *The Child in Christian Thought,* ed. Marcia J. Bunge, 29–60. Grand Rapids, Mich.: Eerdmans, 2001.

Guroian, Vigen. "Family and Christian Virtue in a Post-Christendom World: Reflections on the Ecclesial Vision of John Chrysostom." *St. Vladimir's Theological Quarterly* 35.4 (1991), 327–50.

———. "The ecclesial family: John Chrysostom on parenthood and children." In *The Child in Christian Thought,* ed. Marcia J. Bunge, 61–77 and 475–76. Grand Rapids, Mich.: Eerdmans, 2001.

Gwynn, Aubrey. *Roman Education from Cicero to Quintilian.* New York: Teachers College Press, 1926.

Haage, Herbert. "Der Gottesknecht bei Deuterojesaja im Verständnis der alten Kirche." *Freiburger Zeitschrift für Philosophie und Theologie* 31 (1984), 343–77.

Haenchen, Ernst. *The Acts of the Apostles.* Philadelphia: Westminster Press, 1971.

Halivni, David Weiss. "The Reception Accorded to Rabbi Judah's Mishnah." In *Jewish and Christian Self-Definition.* Vol. 2: *Aspects of Judaism in the Graeco-Roman World,* ed. E. P. Sanders, 204–12. London: SCM Press, 1981.

Hallett, Judith P. *Fathers and Daughters in Roman Society: Women and the Elite Family.* Princeton, N.J.: Princeton University Press, 1984.

———. "Roman Attitudes Toward Sex." In *Civilization of the Ancient Mediterranean: Greece and Rome,* eds. Michael Grant and Rachel Kitzinger, 1265–78. New York: Charles Scribner's Sons, 1988.

Hanson, Anthony T. "The Domestication of Paul: A Study in the Development of Early Christian Theology." *Bulletin of the John Rylands University Library of Manchester* 63.2 (1981), 402–18.

Hanson, Ann Ellis. "'Your mother nursed you with bile': Anger in babies and small children." In *Ancient Anger: Perspectives from Homer to Galen,* ed. Susanna Braund and Glenn W. Most, 185–203. Yale Classical Studies, *vol.* 32: Cambridge: Cambridge University Press, 2003.

Harnack, Adolf. "Die Bezeichnung Jesus als 'Knecht Gottes' und ihre Geschichte in der alten Kirche." *Sitzungsberichte der preussischen Akademie der Wissenschaften* 28 (1926), 212–38.

Harrill, J. Albert. *The Manumission of Slaves in Early Christianity.* Hermeneutische Untersuchungen zur Theologie 32. Tübingen: Mohr Siebeck, 1995.

———. "The Domestic Enemy: A Moral Polarity of Household Slaves in Early Christian Apologies and Martyrdom." In *Early Christian Families in Context: An Interdisciplinary Dialogue,* eds. David L. Balch and Carolyn Osiek, 231–54. Religion, Marriage, and Family series. Grand Rapids, Mich.: Eerdmans, 2003.

———. "Servile Functionaries or Priestly Leaders? Roman Domestic Religion, Narrative Intertextuality, and Pliny's Reference to Christian Slave Ministrae (Ep. 10,96 8)." *Zeitschrift für die Neutestamentliche Wissenschaft* 97 (2006), 111–30.

———. *Slaves in the New Testament: Literary, Social, and Moral Dimensions.* Minneapolis: Fortress Press, 2006.

Harrington, Daniel J. *The Gospel of Matthew.* Sacra Pagina Series, vol. 1. Collegeville, Minn.: Liturgical Press, 1991.

Harris, William V. "The Theoretical Possibility of Extensive Infanticide in the Graeco-Roman World." *Classical Quarterly* 32 (1982), 114–16.

———. "The Roman Father's Power of Life and Death." In *Studies in Roman Law in Memory of A. Arthur Schiller,* ed. Roger S. Bagnall and William V. Harris, 81–95. Columbia Studies in the Classical Tradition 13. Leiden: E. J. Brill, 1986.

———. "Child-Exposure in the Roman Empire." *Journal of Roman Studies* 84 (1994), 1–22.

Harrison, N. V. "Raising them right: Early Christian approaches to child rearing." *Theology Today* 56 (2000), 481–94.

Harrison, Verna E. F. "The allegorization of gender: Plato and Philo on spiritual childbearing." In *Asceticism,* eds. Vincent L. Wimbush and Richard Valantasis, 520–34. New York: Oxford University Press, 1995.

Harvey, Susan Ashbrook. *Asceticism and Society in Crisis: John of Ephesus and the "Lives of the Eastern Saints."* The Transformation of the Classical Heritage 18. Berkeley: University of California Press, 1990.

———. "Feminine Imagery for the Divine: The Holy Spirit, the Odes of Solomon, and Early Syriac Tradition." *St. Vladimir's Theological Quarterly* 37.2 (1993), 111–39.

———. "The Holy and the Poor: Models from Early Syriac Christianity." In *Through the Eye of a Needle: Judeo-Christian Roots of Social Welfare,* eds. Emily Albu Hanawalt and Carter Lindberg, 43–66. Kirksville, Mo.: Thomas Jefferson University Press, 1994.

———. "Revisiting the Daughters of the Covenant: Women's Choirs and Sacred Song in Ancient Syriac Christianity." *Hugoye: Journal of Syriac Studies* 8.2 (2005), http://syrcom.cua.edu/Hugoye/Vol8No2/HV8N2Harvey.html.

Hatlie, Peter. "The Religious Lives of Children and Adolescents." In *Byzantine Christianity. A People's History of Christianity,* vol. 3, ed. Derek Krueger, 182–200. Minneapolis: Fortress Press, 2006.

Hawes, Joseph M., and N. Ray Hiner, eds. *Children in Historical and Comparative Perspective: An International Handbook and Research Guide.* Westport, Conn.: Greenwood Press, 1991.

Hayne, Léonie. "Thecla and the Church Fathers." *Vigiliae Christianae* 48 (1994), 209–18.

Heichelheim, Fritz. "Toga." In *Paulys Real-Encyclopädie der Classischen Altertumswissenschaft,* ed. August Friedrich von Pauly, revised and enlarged by Georg Wissowa, Wilhelm Kroll, and Karl Mittelhaus, vol. 6, cols. 1651–60. Stuttgart: J. B. Metzler, 1937.

Hemmerdinger-Illiadou, Democratie. "Ephrém Grec" and "Ephrém Latin." In *Dictionnaire de Spiritualité* 4 (1960–61), cols. 800–819.

Henderson, Jeffrey. "Greek Attitudes Toward Sex." In *Civilization of the Ancient Medi-*

terranean: Greece and Rome, eds. Michael Grant and Rachel Kitzinger, 1249–63. New York: Charles Scribner's Sons, 1988.

Hengel, Martin. *Judaism and Hellenism.* Minneapolis: Fortress Press, 1991.

———. "Apostolische Ehen und Familien." In *The Interpretation of the Bible. The International Symposium in Slovenia,* ed. Jože Krašovec, 257–74. Journal for the Study of the Old Testament Supplement Series 289. Sheffield: Sheffield Academic Press, c1998.

Hennecke, Edgar. "Apostolische Pseudepigraphen." In *Pseudepigraphie in der heidnischen und jüdisch-christlichen Antike,* ed. Norbert Brox, 82–89. Wege der Forschung 484. Darmstadt: Wissenschaftliche Buchgesellschaft, 1977.

Hett, Walter S. "The Games of the Greek Boy." *Greece and Rome* 1 (1931), 24–29.

Hezser, Catherine. "The Exposure and Sale of Infants in Rabbinic and Roman Law." In *Jewish Studies between the Disciplines / Judaistik zwischen den Disziplinen: Papers in Honor of Peter Schäfer on the Occasion of his 60th Birthday,* eds. Klaus Herrmann, Margarete Schlüter, and Giuseppe Veltri, 3–28. Leiden: E. J. Brill, 2003.

Hiner, N. Ray, and Joseph M. Hawes. "Standing on Common Ground: Reflections on the History of Children and Childhood." In *Children in Historical and Comparative Perspective: An International Handbook and Research Guide,* eds. Joseph M. Hawes and N. Ray Hiner, 1–9. Westport, Conn.: Greenwood Press, 1991.

Holman, Susan. *The Hungry are Dying: Beggars and Bishops in Roman Cappadocia.* Oxford Studies in Historical Theology. Oxford: Oxford University Press, 2001.

Hopkins, K. "Everyday Life for the Roman Schoolboy." *History Today* 43.10 (1993), 25–30.

Hopkins, M. K. "The Age of Roman Girls at Marriage." *Population Studies* 18 (1965), 309–27.

Horn, Cornelia. "'Fathers and Mothers Shall Rise Up Against Their Children and Kill Them': Martyrdom and Children in the Early Church." Paper presented at the annual meeting of the American Academy of Religion / Society of Biblical Literature, Toronto, November 2002.

———. "How Children Became Christians: Three Models from Early Christian Practice." Paper delivered at the regional meeting of the American Academy of Religion / Society of Biblical Literature. St. Paul, Minn., April 2004.

———. "Raising Martyrs and Monks: A Diachronic Comparison of the Use of Children's Role Models in Patristic Literature." Paper delivered at the annual meeting of the North American Patristics Society, Chicago, May 2004.

———. "Children's Play as Social Ritual." In *Late Ancient Christianity. A People's History of Christianity,* vol. 2, ed. Virginia Burrus, 95–116. Minneapolis: Fortress Press, 2005.

———. *Asceticism and Christological Controversy in Fifth-Century Palestine: The Career of Peter the Iberian.* Oxford: Oxford University Press, 2006.

———. "Children and Violence in Syriac Sources: The *Martyrdom of Mar Ṭalyā'* of *Cyrrhus* in the Light of Literary and Theological Implications." *Parole de l'Orient* 31 (2006), 309–26.

———. "Children as Pilgrims and the Cult of Holy Children in the Early Syriac Tradition: The Cases of Theodoret of Cyrrhus and the Child-Martyrs Behnām, Sarah, and Cyriacus." *ARAM Periodical* 18–19 (2006–7), 439–62.

———. "Suffering Children, Parental Authority and the Quest for Liberation?: A

Tale of Three Girls in the *Acts of Paul (and Thecla)*, the *Act(s) of Peter*, the *Acts of Nerseus and Achilleus*, and the *Epistle of Pseudo-Titus*." In *A Feminist Companion to the New Testament Apocrypha*, ed. Amy-Jill Levine with Maria Mayo Robbins, 118–45. Feminist Companion to the New Testament and Early Christian Writings, vol. 11. New York: Continuum, 2006.

———. "The Virgin and the Perfect Virgin: Traces of Early Eastern Christian Mariology in the *Odes of Solomon*." *Studia Patristica* 40 (2006), 413–28.

———. "Children at the Intersection of Classical and Early Christian Popular Literature." Paper delivered at the annual meeting of the American Academy of Religion / Society of Biblical Literature. San Diego, November 2007.

———. "The Lives and Literary Roles of Children in Advancing Conversion to Christianity: Hagiography from the Caucasus in Late Antiquity and the Middle Ages." *Church History* 76.2 (2007), 262–97.

———. "The *Pseudo-Clementines* and the Challenges of the Conversion of Families." *lectio difficilior. European Electronic Journal for Feminist Exegesis* 2 (2007), http://www.lectio.unibe.ch/07_2/horn.html.

———. "The Depiction of Children and Young People as Literary Device in Canonical and Apocryphal Acts." In *Bringing the Underground to the Foreground: New Perspectives on Jewish and Christian Apocryphal Texts and Traditions*, proceedings of the Apocrypha and Pseudepigrapha Section of the Society for Biblical Literature International Meeting, Groningen, the Netherlands, July 2004, ed. Pierluigi Piovanelli. Forthcoming.

———. "Challenges to Childhood in the Eastern Mediterranean World in Ancient Christianity." Unpublished manuscript.

Hornblower, Simon, and Antony Spawforth, eds. *The Oxford Classical Dictionary*. Oxford: Oxford University Press, 1996.

Horne, Herman Harrell, and Angus M. Gunn. *Jesus the Teacher: Examining His Expertise in Education*. Grand Rapids, Mich.: Kregel Publications, 1998.

Horrell, David. "From ἀδελφοί to οἶκος θεοῦ: Social Transformation in Pauline Christianity." *Journal of Biblical Literature* 120.2 (2001), 293–311.

Horsley, Richard A. *1 Corinthians*. Abingdon New Testament Commentaries. Nashville: Abingdon Press, 1998.

———. "The Gospel According to Mark." In *The New Oxford Annotated Bible: New Revised Standard Version with the Apocryphal/Deuterocanonical Books*, 3rd edition, ed. Michael D. Coogan, Mark Z. Brettler, Carol A. Newsom, and Pheme Perkins, NT 56–92. Oxford: Oxford University Press, 2001.

Howard, George. "The Textual Nature of an Old Hebrew Version of Matthew." *Journal of Biblical Literature* 105 (1986), 49–63.

Hubert, Hans. *Der Streit um die Kindertaufe. Eine Darstellung der von Karl Barth 1943 ausgelösten Diskussion um die Kindertaufe und ihre Bedeutung für die heutige Tauffrage*. Europäische Hochschulschriften. Reihe XXIII. Theologie. Vol. 10. Bern: Herbert Lang, 1972.

Hübner, Ulrich. *Spiele und Spielzeug im antiken Palästina*. Orbis Biblicus et Orientalis 121. Freiburg, Schweiz: Universitätsverlag, 1992.

Hunter, David G. "On the sin of Adam and Eve: A little known defence of marriage and childbearing in Ambrosiaster." *Harvard Theological Review* 82 (1989), 283–99.

———. "Marriage." In *Augustine through the Ages: An Encyclopedia*, ed. Allan D. Fitzgerald, 535–37. Grand Rapids, Mich.: Eerdmans, 1999.

Hurley, Robert. "To Marry or Not to Marry: The Interpretation of 1 Cor 7:36–38." *Estudios bíblicos* 58.1 (2000), 7–31.

Hurschmann, Rolf. "Astragal" (vol. 2, col. 120), "Ballspiele" (2, 426–27), "Crepundia" (3, 220), "Geschicklichkeitsspiele" (4, 1004–5), "Harpaston" (5, 163–64), "Kinderspiele" (6, 467–68), "Kreisel" (6, 824), "Lauf- und Fangspiele" (6, 1186–87), and "Puppen" (10, 601–2). In *Der Neue Pauly. Enzyklopädie der Antike.* Ed. Hubert Cancik and Helmuth Schneider. Stuttgart: Verlag J. B. Metzler, 1997–2001.

Huskinson, J. *Roman Children's Sarcophagi: Their Decoration and Its Social Significance.* Oxford Monographs on Classical Archaeology. Oxford: Clarendon Press, 1996.

———. "Disappearing Children? Children in Roman Funerary Art of the First to the Fourth Century A.D." In *Hoping for Continuity: Childhood, Education and Death in Antiquity and the Middle Ages,* ed. K. Mustakallio, J. Hanska, H.-L. Sainio, and Ville Vuolanto, 91–103. Acta Instituti Romani Finlandiae 33. Rome: Institutum Romanum Finlandiae, 2005.

Huys, A. "*Ekthesis* and *Apothesis:* the Terminology of Infant Exposure in Greek Antiquity." *L'Antiquité Classique* 58 (1989), 190–97.

Ilan, Tal. *Integrating Women into Second Temple History.* Texte und Studien zum antiken Judentum 76. Tübingen: Mohr Siebeck, 1999; repr. Peabody, Mass.: Hendrickson Publishers, 2001.

Ingalls, W. "*Paida Nean Malista:* When Did Athenian Girls Really Marry?" *Mouseion* 1 (2001), 17–29.

Ison, David J. "The Constantinian Oration to the Saints—Authorship and Background." Diss., University of London, 1985.

———. "ΠΑΙΣ ΘΕΟΥ in the Age of Constantine." *JThS* 38 (1987), 412–19.

Ivanovska, Inta. "Children in the Eucharistic Setting: A Study of the Christian Liturgical Practice from the Sub-Apostolic Period to Augustine." Ph.D. seminar paper, Saint Louis University, Spring 2005.

Jacobs, Andrew S. "'Let Him Guard Pietas': Early Christian Exegesis and the Ascetic Family." *JECS* 11.3 (2003), 265–81.

Jacobson, Arland D. "Divided Families and Christian Origins." In *The Gospel behind the Gospels: Current Studies on Q,* ed. Ronald A. Piper, 361–80. Supplements to Novum Testamentum 75. Leiden: E. J. Brill, 1995.

———. "Jesus against the Family: The Dissolution of Family Ties in the Gospel Tradition." In *From Quest to Q: Festschrift James M. Robinson,* eds. Jon M. Asgeirsson, Kristin de Toyer, and Marvin W. Meyer, 189–218. Bibliotheca Ephemeridum theologicarum Lovaniensium 146. Louvain: Louvain University Press, 2000.

Jaeger, W. "Die Sklaverei bei Johannes Chrysostomus." Theol. Diss. University of Kiel, 1974.

Jastrow, Marcus. *Dictionary of the Targumim, Talmud Babli, Yerushalmi, and Midrashic Literature.* New York: The Judaica Press, 1982.

Jensen, Anne. "Frauen in der Asketengeschichte 'Das Paradies' von Palladios (Historia Lausiaca)." In *"... weil sie mehr liebte." Frauen im frühen Mönchtum,* ed. Jakobus Kaffanke, 37–54. Wegschritte: Tagungsberichte der Beuroner Tage für Spiritualität und Mystik, Erzabtei St. Martin Beuron. Beuron: Beuroner Kunstverlag, 2002.

Jeremias, Joachim. *Hat die Urkirche die Kindertaufe geübt?* Göttingen: Vandenhoeck & Ruprecht, 1938; 2nd revised edition, 1949.

————. *Die Kindertaufe in den ersten vier Jahrhunderten.* Göttingen: Vandenhoeck & Ruprecht, 1958. Trans. David Cairns. *Infant Baptism in the First Four Centuries.* London: SCM Press, 1960; repr. London: Westminster Press, c1962.

————. *Nochmals: Die Anfänge der Kindertaufe. Eine Replik auf Kurt Alands Schrift: Die Säuglingstaufe im Neuen Testament und in der Alten Kirche.* Munich: C. Kaiser, 1962. Trans. Dorothea M. Barton. *The Origins of Infant Baptism: A Further Study in Reply to Kurt Aland.* London: SCM Press, 1963.

————. *The Parables of Jesus.* Rev. ed. London: SCM Press, 1963.

————. *Neutestamentliche Theologie. Erster Teil: Die Verkündigung Jesu.* Gütersloh: Gerd Mohn, 1971.

Johann, Horst-Theodor, ed. *Erziehung und Bildung in der heidnischen und christlichen Antike.* Wege der Forschung 377. Darmstadt: Wissenschaftliche Buchgesellschaft, 1976.

Johnson, Luke Timothy. *Sharing Possessions: Mandate and Symbol of Faith.* Overtures to Biblical Theology. Philadelphia: Fortress Press, 1981.

————. *The Acts of the Apostles.* Sacra Pagina Series, vol. 5. Collegeville, Minn.: Liturgical Press, 1991.

————. *The Gospel of Luke.* Sacra Pagina Series, vol. 3. Collegeville, Minn.: Liturgical Press, 1991.

Johnson, Marshall D. *The Purpose of the Biblical Genealogies.* 2nd ed. Cambridge: Cambridge University Press, 1988.

Johnston, Sarah Iles. "Charming Children: The Use of the Child in Ancient Divination." *Arethusa* 34.1 (2001), 97–118.

Joshel, S. "Nurturing the Master's Child: Slavery and the Roman Child Nurse." *Signs* 12 (1986), 3–22.

Josi, E. "Lectores—scola cantorum—clerici." *Ephemerides Liturgica* 44 (1930), 282–90.

Jouer dans l'Antiquité. Musée d'Archéologie Méditerranéenne. Centre de la Vieille Charité, catalogue of exhibition held from November 22, 1991 to February 16, 1992. Marseille, France: Musées de Marseille—Réunion des Musées Nationaux, 1992.

Jungbauer, Harry. *"Ehre Vater und Mutter": Der Weg des Elterngebots in der biblischen Tradition.* Wissenschaftliche Untersuchungen zum Neuen Testament. 2nd. ser. Vol. 146. Tübingen: Mohr-Siebeck, 2002.

Jüngling, Hans-Winfried. "'Was anders ist Gott für den Menschen, wenn nicht sein Vater und seine Mutter?' Zu einer Doppelmetapher der religiösen Sprache." In *Ein Gott allein? JHWH-Verehrung und biblischer Monotheismus im Kontext der israelitischen und altorientalischen Religionsgeschichte,* eds. Walter Dietrich and Martin A. Klopfenstein, 365–86. Orbis Biblicus et Orientalis 139. Göttingen: Vandenhoeck & Ruprecht, 1994.

Kaestli, Jean-Daniel. "Les scènes d'attribution des champs de mission et de départ de l'apôtre dans les Actes apocryphes." In *Les Actes apocryphes des apôtres. Christianisme et monde païen,* ed. François Bovon and others, 249–64. Publications de la Faculté de théologie de l'Université de Genève 4. Geneva: Labor et Fides, 1981.

————. "Luke-Acts and the Pastoral Epistles: The Thesis of a Common Authorship." In *Luke's Literary Achievement: Collected Essays,* ed. Christopher M. Tuckett, 110–26. *JSNT* Supplement Series 116. Sheffield: Sheffield Academic Press, 1995.

Kalmin, Richard. "Levirate Law." In *The Anchor Bible Dictionary* 4, ed. David Noel Freedman, 296–97. New York: Doubleday, 1992.

Kanarfogel, Ephraim. "Attitudes toward Childhood and Children in Medieval Jewish Society." In *Approaches to Judaism in Medieval Times*, vol. 2, ed. David R. Blumenthal, 1–34. Brown Judaic Studies 54. Chico, Calif.: Scholars Press, 1985.

Kastner, Marie-Odille. "L'enfant et les jeux dans les documents d'époque romaine." *Bulletin de l'Association Guillaume Budé* (1995), 85–100.

Katt, Arthur F. "From a child thou hast known the Holy Scriptures (2 Tim 3:15)." *Concordia Theological Monthly* 25 (1954), 766–73.

Kehnscherper, Günther. "The 'Churching of Women': Leviticus 12 and Luke 2:21–24: The Law of Purity and the Benediction of Mothers." *Studia Patristica* 18.2 (1989), 380–84.

Kelhoffer, James A. *The Diet of John the Baptist*. WUNT 176. Tübingen: Mohr Siebeck, 2005.

Keller, Marie Noël. "Jesus the Teacher." *Currents in Theology and Mission* 25 (1998), 450–60.

Kinder, Donald. "Clement of Alexandria: Conflicting Views on Women." *Second Century: A Journal of Early Christian Studies* 7.4 (1989–90), 213–20.

Kinney, Anne Behnke. *Representations of Childhood and Youth in Early China*. Stanford, Calif.: Stanford University Press, 2004.

Klassen, William. "'A Child of Peace' (Luke 10:6) in First Century Context." *New Testament Studies* 27 (1981), 488–506.

Klauck, Hans-Josef. *Hausgemeinde und Hauskirche im frühen Christentum*. Stuttgarter Bibelstudien 103. Stuttgart: Verlag Katholisches Bibelwerk, 1981.

———. *1. Korintherbrief*. Die Neue Echter Bibel. Würzburg: Echter Verlag, 1984.

———. "Die heilige Stadt: Jerusalem bei Philo und Lukas." *Kairos* 28.3–4 (1986), 129–51.

Kleijwegt, Marc. *Ancient Youth: The Ambiguity of Youth and the Absence of Adolescence in Greco-Roman Society*. Dutch Monographs on Ancient History and Archaeology 8. Amsterdam: J. C. Gieben, 1991.

———. "Kind." In *RAC* 11 (2004), 865–947.

Klein, Richard. *Die Sklaverei in der Sicht der Bischöfe Ambrosius und Augustinus*. Forschungen zur Antiken Sklaverei 20. Stuttgart: Franz Steiner Verlag, 1988.

———. *Die Haltung der Kappadokischen Bischöfe Basilius von Caesarea, Gregor von Nazianz und Gregor von Nyssa zur Sklaverei*. Forschungen zur Antiken Sklaverei 32. Stuttgart: Franz Steiner Verlag, 2000.

Klemm, Hans G. "Das Wort von der Selbstbestattung der Toten: Beobachtungen zur Auslegungsgeschichte von Mt 8:22 Par." *New Testament Studies* 16 (1969), 60–75.

Klock, Christoph. *Untersuchungen zu Stil und Rhythmus bei Gregor von Nyssa. Ein Beitrag zum Rhetorikverständnis der griechischen Väter*. Beiträge zur klassischen Philologie 173. Frankfurt a. M.: Athenäum, 1987.

Knox, John. *Chapters in a Life of Paul*. Nashville: Abingdon Press, 1950.

Koch, K. "Der König als Sohn Gottes in Ägypten und Israel." In *"Mein Sohn bist du" (Ps 2,7): Studien zu den Königspsalmen*, ed. Eckart Otto and Erich Zenger, 1–32. Stuttgarter Bibelstudien 192. Stuttgart: Verlag Katholisches Bibelwerk, 2002.

Kodell, Jerome. "The Celibacy Logion in Matthew 19:12." *Biblical Theology Bulletin* 8 (1978), 19–23.

Kontoulis, Georg. *Zum Problem der Sklaverei (ΔΟΥΛΕΙΑ) bei den kappadokischen Kirchenvätern und Johannes Chrysostomus.* Habelts Dissertationsdrucke Reihe Alte Geschichte 38. Bonn: Dr. Rudolf Habelt, 1993.

Korbin, Jill. "Prologue. A Perspective from Contemporary Childhood Studies." In *Coming of Age in Ancient Greece: Images of Childhood from the Classical Past,* eds. Jenifer Neils and John H. Oakley, 7–11. New Haven, Conn.: Yale University Press, c2003, 2004.

Korte, Anne-Marie. "Reclaiming Ritual: A Gendered Approach to (Im)Purity." In *Purity and Holiness: The Heritage of Leviticus,* ed. Marcel Poorthuis and Joshua Schwartz, 313–27. Jewish and Christian Perspectives Series 2. Boston: E. J. Brill, 2000.

Kraemer, David. "Images of Childhood and Adolescence in Talmudic Literature." In *Exploring Judaism: The Collected Essays of David Kraemer,* ed. David Kraemer, 37–50. South Florida Studies in the History of Judaism 210. Atlanta: Scholars Press, c1999.

Kraemer, Ross Shepard. *Her Share of the Blessings: Women's Religions among Pagans, Jews, and Christians in the Greco-Roman World.* New York: Oxford University Press, 1992.

Krauss, Samuel. *Talmudische Archäologie II.* Hildesheim: Georg Olms, 1966.

Kremendahl, Dieter. *Die Botschaft der Form: Zum Verhältnis von antiker Epistolographie und Rhetorik im Galaterbrief.* Freiburg: Universitätsverlag, 2000.

Krenkel, Werner A. "Prostitution." In *Civilization of the Ancient Mediterranean: Greece and Rome,* vol. 2, eds. Michael Grant and Rachel Kitzinger, 1291–97. New York: Charles Scribner's Sons, 1988.

Krinetzki, Leo. *Der Einfluß von Is 52:13–53:12 Par auf Phil 2:6–11.* Rome: Pontificium Athenaeum Anselmianum, 1959.

Krückemeier, Nils. "Der Zwölfjährige Jesus im Tempel (Lk 2:40–52) und die biografische Literatur der hellenistischen Antike." *New Testament Studies* 50.3 (2004), 307–19.

Kudlien, Friedolf. "Kindesaussetzung im antiken Rom." *Groningen Colloquia on the Novel* 2, ed. Heinz Hofmann, 25–44. Groningen: Egbert Forsten, 1989.

Kuefler, Mathew. *The Manly Eunuch: Masculinity, Gender Ambiguity, and Christian Ideology in Late Antiquity.* Chicago: University of Chicago Press, 2001.

Kugelman, Richard. "1 Cor. 7:36–38." *CBQ* 10.1 (1948), 63–71.

Kügler, Joachim. "Die Windeln Jesu als Zeichen: Religionsgeschichtliche Anmerkungen zu ΣΠΑΡΓΑΝΟΩ in Lk 2." *Biblische Notizen* 77 (1995), 20–28.

———. "Die Windeln Jesu (Lk 2)—Nachtrag. Zum Gebrauch von ΣΠΑΡΓΑΝΟΝ bei Philo von Alexandrien." *Biblische Notizen* 81 (1996), 8–14.

———. "Der Sohn als Abbild des Vaters: kulturgeschichtliche Notizen zu Sir 30,4–6." *Biblische Notizen* 107–8 (2001), 78–92.

Labriolle, Pierre de. "Rutilius Claudius Namatianus et les moines." *Revue des Études Latines* 6 (1928), 30–41.

Lacey, Walter Kirkpatrick. *The Family in Classical Greece.* Ithaca, N.Y.: Cornell University Press, 1984.

———. "Patria Potestas." In *The Family in Ancient Rome: New Perspectives,* ed. Beryl Rawson, 121–44. Ithaca, N.Y.: Cornell University Press, 1986.

Laes, Christian. "Kinderarbeid in het Romeinse rijk. Een vergeten dossier?" *Kleio* 30 (2000), 2–20.

———. "Desperately Different? *Delicia* Children in the Roman Household." In *Ear-*

ly Christian Families in Context: An Interdisciplinary Dialogue, eds. David L. Balch and Carolyn Osiek, 298–324. Religion, Marriage, and Family series. Grand Rapids, Mich.: Eerdmans, 2003.

———. "High Hopes, Bitter Grief: Children and Their Virtues in Latin Literary Inscriptions." In *Virtutis imago: Studies on the Conceptualisation and Transformation of an Ancient Ideal,* ed. Gert Partoens, Geert Roskam, and Toon Van Houdt, 43–75. Collection d'études classiques 19. Louvain: Peeters, 2004.

———. *Kinderen bij de Romeinen. Zes eeuwen dagelijks leven.* Louvain: Uitgeverij Davidsfonds, 2006.

Laeuchli, Samuel. *Power and Sexuality: The Emergence of Canon Law at the Synod of Elvira.* Philadelphia: Temple University Press, 1972.

Lafaye, Georges. "Pupa." In *Dictionnaire des antiquités grecques et romaines,* eds. C. Daremberg and E. Saglio, vol. 4.1, 768–69. Paris: Hachette, 1905.

Lampe, G. W. H. *A Patristic Greek Lexicon.* Oxford: Clarendon Press, 1961.

Langer, William L. "Infanticide: A Historical Survey." *History of Childhood Quarterly* 1 (1974), 353–65.

Latourelle, René. *The Miracles of Jesus and the Theology of Miracles.* Trans. Matthew J. O'Connell. New York: Paulist Press, 1988.

Lattke, Michael. *Oden Salomos: Text, Übersetzung, Kommentar.* NTOA 41.1–3. Freiburg: Universitätsverlag, 1999–2005.

Lebendiger, I. "The Minor in Jewish Law." *Jewish Quarterly Review* 6 (1915–16), 459–93, and 7 (1916–17), 89–111 and 145–74.

Légasse, Simon. *Jésus et l'enfant: "enfant," "petits" et "simples" dans la tradition synoptique.* Paris: Lecoffre, 1969.

Lelis, Arnold A., William A. Percy, and Beert C. Verstraete. *The Age of Marriage in Ancient Rome.* Studies in Classics 26. Lewiston, N.Y.: Edwin Mellen Press, 2003.

Leloir, Louis. "Attitude des pères du désert vis-à-vis des jeunes." In *L'enfant dans les civilisations orientales / Het kind in de oosterse beschavingen,* ed. A. Théodoridès, P. Naster, and J. Ries, 133–43. Acta Orientalia Belgica 2. Louvain: Peeters, 1980.

Leonhard, Clemens. "Pessachhaggada und Osternacht. Gegenseitige Beeinflussung von jüdischer und christlicher Liturgie." *Kirche und Israel. Neukirchener Theologische Zeitschrift* 16 (2001), 45–47.

Leroy-Molinghen, Alice. "Naissance et enfance de Théodoret." In *L'enfant dans les civilisations orientales / Het kind in de oosterse beschavingen,* ed. A. Théodoridès, P. Naster, and J. Ries, 153–58. Acta Orientalia Belgica 2. Louvain: Peeters, 1980.

Lesky, E., and J. H. Waszink. "Embryologie." In *RAC* 4 (1959), 1228–44.

Levenson, Jon D. *The Death and Resurrection of the Beloved Son: The Transformation of Child Sacrifice in Judaism and Christianity.* New Haven, Conn: Yale University Press, 1993.

Levine, Amy-Jill. "Gender, Judaism, and Literature: Unwelcome Guests in Household Configurations." *Biblical Interpretation* 11.2 (2003), 239–46.

Levine, Lee I. *The Ancient Synagogue: The First Thousand Years.* New Haven, Conn.: Yale University Press, 2000.

Lewis, Mary E. *The Bioarchaeology of Children: Perspectives from Biological and Forensic Anthropology.* Cambridge Studies in Biology and Evolutionary Anthropology 50. Cambridge: Cambridge University Press, 2007.

Lewis, Naphtali. "On Paternal Authority in Roman Egypt." *Revue internationale des droits de l'antiquité* 17 (1970), 251–58.

Leyerle, Blake. "John Chrysostom on the Gaze." *JECS* 1 (1993), 159–74.

———. "Appealing to Children." *JECS* 5 (1997), 243–70.

———. *Theatrical Shows and Ascetic Lives: John Chrysostom's Attack on Spiritual Marriage.* Berkeley: University of California Press, 2001.

Liddell, Henry George, and Robert Scott. *A Greek-English Lexicon: Abridged.* Oxford: Clarendon Press, 1958. Revised by Henry Stuart Jones. Oxford: Clarendon Press, 1985.

Lieberman, Saul. *Greek in Jewish Palestine.* New York: Philip Feldheim, 1965.

Lightfoot, J. B. *St. Paul's Epistle to the Galatians.* Repr. Lynn, Mass.: Hendrickson Publishers, 1982.

Limburg, James. "The Book of Psalms." In *The Anchor Bible Dictionary* 5, ed. David Noel Freedman, 522–36. New York: Doubleday, 1992.

Lindemann, Andreas. "'Do Not Let a Woman Destroy the Unborn Baby in Her Belly': Abortion in Ancient Judaism and Christianity." *Studia Theologica* 49 (1995), 253–71.

———. "The beginnings of Christian life in Jerusalem according to the summaries in the Acts of the Apostles (Acts 2:42–47; 4:32–37; 5:12–16)." In *Common Life in the Early Church: Essays Honoring Graydon F. Snyde,* ed. Julian V. Hills, 202–18. Harrisburg, Pa.: Trinity Press International, 1998.

Loader, William R. G. "Christ at the Right Hand: Ps 110:1 in the New Testament." *New Testament Studies* 24 (1978), 199–217.

Lockwood, Gregory. *1 Corinthians.* Concordia Commentary. St. Louis: Concordia Publishing House, 2000.

Lohfink, Gerhard. "Die Vermittlung des Paulinismus zu den Pastoralbriefen." *Biblische Zeitschrift* 32.2 (1988), 169–88.

Long, Fredrick J. *Ancient Rhetoric and Paul's Apology: The Compositional Unity of 2 Corinthians.* Cambridge: Cambridge University Press, 2004.

Longenecker, Richard N. *Galatians.* Word Biblical Commentary, vol. 41. Dallas, Tex.: Word Books, 1990.

Lumpe, A. "Exemplum." In *RAC* 6 (1966), 1229–57.

Luomanen, Petri. *Entering the Kingdom of Heaven.* WUNT 2nd. ser. Vol. 101. Tübingen: Mohr Siebeck, 1998.

Luz, Ulrich. *Matthew 8–20. Hermeneia.* Ed. Helmut Koester. Trans. James E. Crouch. Minneapolis: Fortress Press, 2001.

Lyall, Francis. "Legal Metaphors in the Epistles." *Tyndale Bulletin* 32 (1981), 79–95.

MacDonald, Margaret Y. *The Pauline Churches: A Socio-historical Study of Institutionalization in the Pauline and Deutero-Pauline Churches.* Society of New Testament Studies Monograph Series 60. Cambridge: Cambridge University Press, 1988.

———. "Early Christian Women Married to Unbelievers." *Studies in Religion/Sciences religieuses* 19 (1990), 221–34.

———. *Colossians and Ephesians.* Sacra Pagina series 17. Collegeville, Minn.: Liturgical Press, 2000.

MacMullen, Ramsey. *Changes in the Roman Empire.* Princeton, N.J.: Princeton University Press, 1990.

Magness, Jodi. "Women at Qumran?" In *What Athens Has To Do with Jerusalem: Essays on Classical, Jewish, and Early Christian Art and Archaeology in Honor of Gideon Foerster,* ed. Leonard Victor Rutgers, 89–123. Interdisciplinary Studies in Ancient Culture and Religion 1. Louvain: Peeters, 2002.

Maier, Harry O. *The Social Setting of the Ministry as Reflected in the Writings of Her-*

mas, Clement, and Ignatius. Études sur le christianisme et le judaïsme 11. Waterloo: Wilfrid Laurier University Press, 2002.

Malherbe, Abraham J. "Exhortation in First Thessalonians." *Novum Testamentum* 25 (1983), 238–56.

———. *Paul and the Popular Philosophers.* Minneapolis: Fortress Press, 1989.

———. "The Christianization of a *Topos* (Luke 12:13–34)." *Novum Testamentum* 38 (1996), 123–35.

Malina, Bruce J. "Patron and Client: The Analogy behind Synoptic Theology." In *The Social World of Jesus and the Gospels,* 143–75. London: Routledge, 1996.

Malingrey, Anne-Marie. "Note sur l'exegèse de 1 Tim 2,15." *Studia Patristica* 12 (1975), 334–39.

Malul, Meir. "Adoption of Foundlings in the Bible and Mesopotamian Documents: A Study of Some Legal Metaphors in Ezekiel 16.1–7." *Journal for the Study of the Old Testament* (hereafter *JSOT*) 46 (1990), 97–126.

Manson, M. "The emergence of the small child in Rome (third century BC–first century AD)." *History of Education* 12 (1983), 149–59.

Manson, Michel. "Les Poupées Antiques." *Jeux et Jouets dans l'Antiquité et au Moyen Age, Dossiers de l'Archéologie* 168 (1992), 48–57.

Manson, T. W. *The Sayings of Jesus.* London: SCM Press, 1949.

Mantle, I. C. "The Roles of Children in Roman Religion." *Greece & Rome* 49.1 (2002), 85–106.

Marcus, Joel. *Mark 1–8.* The Anchor Bible Commentary, vol. 27. New York: Doubleday, 2000.

Marguerat, Daniel. "The Acts of Paul and the Canonical Acts: A Phenomenon of Rereading." Trans. Ken McKinney. *Semeia* 80 (1997), 169–83.

Marrou, Henri Irénée. *Histoire de l'éducation dans l'antiquité.* Paris: Editions du Seuil, 1948. Trans. George Lamb. *A History of Education in Antiquity.* Sheed and Ward, Inc., c1956, repr. 1982. Reprinted on demand: Wisconsin Studies in Classics. Madison: University of Wisconsin Press, 2005.

Marshall, I. Howard. "Recent Study of the Pastoral Epistles." *Themelios* 23 (1997), 3–29.

Martens, John W. "What Difference Did Christianity Make?" Paper presented at the annual meeting of the American Academy of Religion / Society of Bibilical Literature, Toronto, November 2002.

———. *One God, One Law: Philo of Alexandria on the Mosaic and Greco-Roman Law.* Ancient Mediterranean and Medieval Texts and Contexts. Studies in Philo of Alexandria and Mediterranean Antiquity 2. Leiden: Brill Academic, 2003.

———. "Fathers and Daughters in 1 Corinthians 7:36–38: The Social Implications for Children of Parents' Belief in Christ." Paper presented at the annual meeting of the Society of Biblical Literature, Philadelphia, November 2005.

Martin, Annick. "Aux origines de l'Alexandrie chrétienne: topographie, liturgie, institutions." In *Origeniana octava: Origen and the Alexandrian tradition = Origene e la tradizione Alessandrina,* papers of the eighth International Origen Congress, Pisa, August 2001, ed. P. Bernardino, D. Marchini, and Lorenzo Perrone, 105–20. Bibliotheca Ephemeridum theologicarum Lovaniensium 164. Louvain: Louvain University Press, 2003.

Martin, Dale B. "Slavery and the Ancient Jewish Family." In *The Jewish Family in Antiquity,* ed. Shaye J. D. Cohen, 113–29. Brown Judaic Studies 289. Atlanta: Scholars Press, 1993.

————. *The Corinthian Body*. New Haven, Conn.: Yale University Press, 1995.

————. "Slave Families and Slaves in Families." In *Early Christian Families in Context: An Interdisciplinary Dialogue*, eds. David L. Balch and Carolyn Osiek, 207–30. Religion, Marriage, and Family series. Grand Rapids, Mich.: Eerdmans, 2003.

Martin, Troy W. "The Brother Body: Addressing and Describing the Galatians and the Agitators as Ἀδελφοί." *Biblical Research* 47 (2002), 5–18.

Martyn, J. Louis. *Galatians*. The Anchor Bible. New York: Doubleday, 1997.

Marxen, Willi. "Erwägungen zur neutestamentlichen Begründung der Taufe." In *Apophoreta. Festschrift für Ernst Haenchen zu seinem 70. Geburtstag am 10. Dezember 1964*, 169–77. Beihefte zur Zeitschrift für die neutestamentliche Wissenschaft und die Kunde der älteren Kirche 30. Berlin: Töpelmann, 1964.

Matringe, G. "La puissance paternelle et le mariage des fils et filles de famille en droit romain (sous l'Empire et en Occident)." In *Studi in onore di Edoardo Volterra*, vol. 5, 191–237. Pubblicazioni della Facoltà di giurisprudenza dell'Università di Roma 40–45. Milan: A. Giuffrè, 1971.

Matthews, Shelly. "Thinking of Thecla: Issues in Feminist Historiography." *Journal of Feminist Studies in Religion* 17.2 (2001), 39–55.

Matthews, Victor H., and Don C. Benjamin. *The Social World of Ancient Israel, 1250–587 B.C.E.* Peabody, Mass.: Hendrickson Publishers, 1993.

Matz, Brian. "The Purifying Work of Baptism and the Christian Post-Baptismal Life according to Gregory Nazianzen." Ph.D. thesis, Saint Louis University, Missouri, 2006.

Mau, A. "Bulla, 2)." In *Paulys Real-Encyclopädie der Christlichen Altertumswissenschaft*, ed. Georg Wissowa, vol. 3, cols. 1048–51. Stuttgart: J. B. Metzlersche Buchhandlung, 1899.

————. "Crepitaculum" and "Crepundia." In *Paulys Real-Encyclopädie der Christlichen Altertumswissenschaft*, ed. Georg Wissowa, vol. 4, cols. 1705–6 and 1706–7. Stuttgart: J. B. Metzlersche Buchhandlung, 1901.

May, David M. "Leaving and Receiving: A Social-Scientific Exegesis of Mark 10:29–31." *Perspectives in Religious Studies* 17 (1990), 141–51 and 154.

McCane, Byron R. "'Let the Dead Bury Their Own Dead': Secondary Burial and Matt 8:21–22." *Harvard Theological Review* 83 (1990), 31–43.

McDonnell, Kilian. *The Baptism of Jesus in the Jordan: The Trinitarian and Cosmic Order of Salvation*. Collegeville, Minn.: Liturgical Press, 1996.

McLynn, Neil Brendan. *Ambrose of Milan: Church and Court in a Christian Capital*. Transformation of the Classical Heritage 22. Berkeley: University of California Press, c1994.

McNary-Zak, Bernadette. *Letters and Asceticism in Fourth-Century Egypt*. Lanham, Md.: University Press of America, 2000.

McNeil, Brian. "Jesus and the Alphabet." *JThS* 27 (1976), 126–28.

Meeks, W. A. *The First Urban Christians*. New Haven, Conn.: Yale University Press, 1983.

Meigne, Maurice. "Concile ou collection d'Elvire." *Revue d'histoire ecclésiastique* 70 (1975), 361–87.

Melnyk, Janet L. R. "When Israel was a child: Ancient Near Eastern adoption formulas and the relationship between God and Israel." In *History and Interpretation: Essays in Honour of John H. Hayes*, eds. M. Patrick Graham, William P. Brown, and Jeffrey K. Kuan, 245–59. JSOT Supplement Series 173. Sheffield: JSOT Press, 1993.

Ménard, Jacques E. "*Pais Theou* as Messianic Title in the Book of Acts." *CBQ* 19 (1957), 83–92.

Mendelson, Alan. *Secular Education in Philo of Alexandria.* Monographs of the Hebrew Union College 7. Cincinnati: Hebrew Union College Press, 1982.

Menken, Martinus J. J. "The Quotation from Isaiah 42:1–4 in Matthew 12:18–21." *Bijdragen* 59 (1998), 251–66.

Menoud, Ph.-H. "La mort d'Ananias et de Sapphira (Actes 5.1–11)." In *Aux Sources de la Tradition Chrétienne: Mélanges offerts à M. Maurice Goguel à l'occasion de son soixante-dixième anniversaire,* 146–54. Bibliothèque Théologique. Neuchatel: Delachaux et Nièstle, 1950.

Methuen, Charlotte. "Widows, Bishops and the Struggle for Authority in the *Didascalia Apostolorum.*" *Journal of Ecclesiastical History* 46 (1995), 197–213.

———. "'For Pagans Laugh to Hear Women Teach': Gender Stereotypes in the *Didascalia Apostolorum.*" In *Gender and Christian Religion. Papers Read at the 1996 Summer Meeting and the 1997 Winter Meeting of the Ecclesiastical History Society,* ed. R. N. Swanson, 23–35. Studies in Church History 34. Woodbridge, England: The Boydell Press, 1998.

Mette-Dittmann, Angelika. *Die Ehegesetze des Augustus. Eine Untersuchung im Rahmen der Gesellschaftspolitik des Princeps.* Historia Einzelschrift 67. Stuttgart: F. Steiner, 1991.

Meyer, Ben F. *Five Speeches that Changed the World.* Collegeville, Minn.: Liturgical Press, 1994.

———. *Reality and Illusion in New Testament Scholarship.* Collegeville, Minn.: Liturgical Press, 1994.

Meyers, Carol. "The Family in Early Israel." In *Families in Ancient Israel,* eds. Leo J. Perdue, Joseph Blenkinsopp, John J. Collins, and Carol Meyers, 1–47. Louisville, Ky.: Westminster John Knox Press, c1997.

Millard, A. R. "Abraham." In *The Anchor Bible Dictionary* 1, ed. David Noel Freedman, 35–41. New York: Doubleday, 1992.

Millard, Alan. "Literacy in the time of Jesus: Could his words have been recorded in his lifetime?" *Biblical Archaeology Review* 29.4 (2003), 36–45.

Miller, Timothy S. *The Orphans of Byzantium. Child Welfare in the Christian Empire.* Washington, D.C.: The Catholic University of America Press, 2003.

Misset-van de Weg, Magda. "Blessed are the bodies of the virgins . . ." In *Begin with the Body: Corporeality, Religion, and Gender,* ed. Jonneke Bekkenkamp and Maaike de Haardt, 233–49. Louvain: Peeters, 1998.

Moehring, Horst. "Arithmology as an Exegetical Tool in the Writings of Philo of Alexandria." In *The School of Moses: Studies in Philo and Hellenistic Religion: In Memory of Horst R. Moehring,* ed. John Peter Kenney, 141–76. Brown Judaic Studies 304. Studia Philonica Monographs 1. Atlanta: Scholars Press, 1995.

Möhler, J. A. "Bruchstücke aus der Geschichte der Aufhebung der Sklaverei." In *Gesammelte Schriften und Aufsätze,* ed. J. J. I. Döllinger, vol. 2, 54–140. Regensburg: Manz, 1939–40.

Moine, Nicole. "Melaniana." *Recherches augustiniennes* 15 (1980), 3–79.

Moloney, Francis J. *The Gospel of Mark. A Commentary.* Peabody, Mass.: Hendrickson Publishers, 2002.

Moore, Jenny, and Eleanor Scott, eds. *Invisible People and Processes: Writing Gender and Childhood into European Archaeology.* London: Leicester University Press, 1997.

Morgan, Teresa. *Literate Education in the Hellenistic and Roman Worlds*. Cambridge Classical Studies. Cambridge: Cambridge University Press, 1998.

Motomura, Ryoji. "The Practice of Exposing Infants and Its Effects on the Development of Slavery in the Ancient World." In *Forms of Control and Subordination in Antiquity*, proceedings of the International Symposium for Studies on Ancient Worlds, Tokyo, January 1986, eds. Toru Yuge and Masaoki Doi, 410–15. Leiden: E. J. Brill, 1988.

Moxnes, Halvor. *Putting Jesus in His Place: A Radical Vision of Household and Kingdom*. London: Westminster John Knox Press, 2003.

Mühlbauer, Karl R., and Theresa Miller. "Spielzeug und Kult: Zur religiösen und kultischen Bedeutung von Kinderspielzeug in der griechischen Antike." *American Journal of Ancient History* 13.2 (1997), 154–69.

Müller, Peter. *In der Mitte der Gemeinde. Kinder im Neuen Testament*. Neukirchen-Vluyn: Neukirchener Verlag, 1992.

———. "Die Metapher vom 'Kind Gottes' und die neutestamentliche Theologie." In *". . . was ihr auf dem Weg verhandelt habt": Beiträge zur Exegese und Theologie des Neuen Testaments. Festschrift für Ferdinand Hahn zum 75. Geburtstag*, eds. Peter Müller, Christine Gerber, and Thomas Knöppler, 192–203. Neukirchen-Vluyn: Neukirchener Verlag, 2001.

———. "Gottes Kinder. Zur Metaphorik der Gotteskindschaft im Neuen Testament." *Jahrbuch für Biblische Theologie* 17 (2002), 141–61.

Murphy-O'Connor, Jerome. *1 Corinthians*. Doubleday Bible Commentary. New York: Doubleday, 1998.

Nagel, Eduard. *Kindertaufe und Taufaufschub. Die Praxis vom 3.–5. Jahrhundert in Nordafrika und ihre theologische Einordnung bei Tertullian, Cyprian und Augustinus*. Europäische Hochschulschriften, Reihe XXIII: Theologie, vol. 144. Frankfurt am Main: Peter D. Lang, 1980.

Nardi, Enzo. *Procurato aborto nel mondo Greco Romano*. Milan: Dott. A. Giuffrè Editore, 1971.

Neils, Jenifer. "Children and Greek Religion." In *Coming of Age in Ancient Greece: Images of Childhood from the Classical Past*, eds. Jenifer Neils and John H. Oakley, 139–61. New Haven, Conn.: Yale University Press, c2003, 2004.

Neils, Jenifer, and John H. Oakley, eds. *Coming of Age in Ancient Greece: Images of Childhood from the Classical Past*. With the Assistance of Katherine Hart. New Haven, Conn.: Yale University Press, c2003, 2004.

Néraudau, Jean-Pierre. "Les jeux de l'enfance en Grèce et à Rome." In *Jouer dans l'Antiquité*, 44–48. Marseille: Musées de Marseille, 1992.

Ng, Esther Yue L. "Acts of Paul and Thecla: Women's Stories and Precedent?" *JThS* 55.1 (2004), 1–29.

Nicol, W. *The Semeia in the Fourth Gospel: Tradition and Redaction*. Leiden: E. J. Brill, 1972.

Niederwimmer, Kurt. *The Didache. Hermeneia*. Trans. Linda M. Maloney. Minneapolis: Fortress Press, 1998.

Niehoff, Maren R. *Philo on Jewish Identity and Culture*. Texte und Studien zum antiken Judentum 86. Tübingen: Mohr Siebeck, 2001.

Nielsen, Hanne Sigismund. "Roman Children at Mealtimes." In *Meals in a Social Context: Aspects of the Communal Meal in the Hellenistic and Roman World*, ed. Inge Nielsen and Hanne Sigismund Nielsen, 56–66. Aarhus Studies in Mediterranean Antiquity 1. Aarhus: Aarhus University Press, c1998.

Norden, Eduard. *Die Geburt des Kindes: Geschichte einer religiösen Idee.* Studien der Bibliothek Warburg 3. Leipzig: B. G. Teubner, 1924, repr. 1958.

Norman, Naomi J. "Death and Burial of Roman Children: The Case of the Yasmina Cemetery at Carthage—Part II, The Archaeological Evidence." *Mortality* 8.1 (2003), 36–47.

Oakley, John H., and Rebecca H. Sinos. *The Wedding in Ancient Athens.* Madison: University of Wisconsin Press, 1993.

O'Roark, D. "Parenthood in Late Antiquity: The Evidence of Chrysostom." *Greek, Roman, and Byzantine Studies* 40 (1999), 53–81.

Orr, William F., and James Arthur Walther. *1 Corinthians.* The Anchor Bible. New York: Doubleday, 1976.

Orton, David E. "We felt like grasshoppers: The little ones in biblical interpretation." *Biblical Interpretation* 11 (2003), 488–502.

Osiek, Carolyn. *Shepherd of Hermas. Hermeneia.* Minneapolis: Fortress Press, 1999.

———. "Female Slaves, *Porneia*, and the Limits of Obedience." In *Early Christian Families in Context: An Interdisciplinary Dialogue,* eds. David L. Balch and Carolyn Osiek, 255–74. Religion, Marriage, and Family series. Grand Rapids, Mich.: Eerdmans, 2003.

Osiek, Carolyn, and David L. Balch. *Families in the New Testament World: Households and House Churches.* Louisville, Ky.: Westminster John Knox, 1997.

Osiek, Carolyn, Margaret Y. MacDonald, and Janet H. Tulloch. *A Woman's Place: House Churches in Earliest Christianity.* Minneapolis: Fortress Press, 2006.

O'Toole, Robert F. "How Does Luke Portray Jesus as Servant of YHWH." *Biblica* 81 (2000), 328–46.

Parmentier, M. F. G. "Evagrius of Pontus' 'Letter to Melania.'" *Bijdragen* 46 (1985), 2–38.

Pearl, Orsamus. "Apprentice Contract." *Bulletin of the American Society of Papyrologists* 22 (1985), 255–59.

Penn, Michael L. "'Bold and Having No Shame': Ambiguous Widows, Controlling Clergy, and Early Syrian Communities." *Hugoye: Journal of Syriac Studies* 4.2 (2001), http://syrcom.cua.edu/Hugoye/Vol4No2/HV4N2Penn.html.

———. "Performing Family: Ritual Kissing and the Construction of Early Christian Kinship." *JECS* 10.2 (2002), 151–74.

Pentikäinen, Juha. "Child Abandonment as an Indicator of Christianization in the Nordic Countries." In *Old Norse and Finnish Religions and Cultic Place-Names,* ed. Tore Ahlbäck, 72–91. Scripta Instituti Donneriani Aboensis 13. Åbo, Finland: Donner Institute for Research in Religion and Cultural History, 1990.

Perkins, Pheme. "The Gospel according to John." In *The New Jerome Biblical Commentary,* eds. Raymond E. Brown, Joseph A Fitzmyer, and Roland E. Murphy, 942–85. Englewood Cliffs, N.J.: Prentice Hall, 1990.

Pesch, Rudolf. *Jesu ureigene Taten? Ein Beitrag zur Wunderfrage.* Quaestiones disputatae 52. Freiburg: Herder, 1970.

Pesthy, Monika. "Thecla among the Fathers of the Church." In *The Apocryphal Acts of Paul and Thecla,* ed. Jan N. Bremmer, 164–78. Kampen: Kok Pharos, 1996.

Peters, Greg. "Spiritual Marriage in Early Christianity: 1 Cor 7:25–38 in Modern Exegesis and the Earliest Church." *Trinity Journal* 23.2 (2002), 211–24.

Petersen, Joan M. "The Education of Girls in Fourth-Century Rome." In *The Church and Childhood, Papers Read at the 1993 Summer Meeting and the 1994 Winter Meeting of the Ecclesiastical History Society,* ed. Diana Wood, 29–37. Studies in

Church History 31. Oxford: Blackwell Publishers, 1994; repr. in *Christianity and Society: The Social World of Early Christianity*, ed. Everett Ferguson, 77–85. New York: Garland Publishing, 1999.

Peterson, E. "Das jugendliche Alter der Lektoren." *Ephemerides Liturgica* 48 (1934), 437–42.

Pfitzner, Victor C. *Paul and the Agon Motif: Traditional Athletic Imagery in the Pauline Literature*. Leiden: E. J. Brill, 1967.

Pitre, Brant James. "Blessing the barren and warning the fecund: Jesus' message for women concerning pregnancy and childbirth." *JSNT* 81 (2001), 59–80.

Plati, Marina. *Playing in Ancient Greece . . . with Lysis and Timarete*. Athens: N. P. Goulandris Foundation-Museum of Cycladic Art, 1999.

Pöhlmann, Wolfgang. *Der Verlorene Sohn und das Haus. Studien zu Lukas 15,11–32 im Horizont der antiken Lehre von Haus, Erziehung und Ackerbau*. Wissenschaftliche Untersuchungen zum Neuen Testament 68. Tübingen: J. C. B. Mohr (Paul Siebeck), 1993.

Pomeroy, Sarah B. "Copronyms and the Exposure of Infants in Egypt." In *Studies in Roman Law in Memory of A. Arthur Schiller*, ed. A. Arthur Schiller and others, 147–62. Leiden: E. J. Brill, 1986.

———. *Families in Classical and Hellenistic Greece*. Oxford: Clarendon Press, 1997.

Poplin, François. "Les jeux d'osselets antiques." *Jeux et Jouets dans l'Antiquité et au Moyen Age, Dossiers de l'Archéologie* 168 (1992), 46–47.

Porter, Stanley E. "What Does It Mean to Be 'Saved by Childbirth' (1 Timothy 2:15)." *JSNT* 49 (1993), 87–102.

Pouderon, Bernard. "Réflexion sur la formation d'une élite intellectuelle chrétienne au IIe siècle: les 'écoles' d'Athènes, de Rome et d'Alexandrie." In *Apologistes chrétiens et la culture grecque*, ed. Bernard Pouderon and Joseph Doré, 237–69. Théologie Historique 105. Paris: Beauchesne, 1998.

Preisker, H., and E. Würthwein. "μισθός, μισθόω, μίσθιος, μισθωτός, μισθαποδότης, μισθαποδοσία, ἀντιμισθία." In *Theological Dictionary of the New Testament*, ed. G. Kittel and G. Friedrich, trans. G. W. Bromley, vol. 4, 695–728. Grand Rapids, Mich.: Eerdmans, c1967.

Price, S. R. F. *Rituals and Power: The Roman Imperial Cult in Asia Minor*. Cambridge: Cambridge University Press, 1984.

Prostmeier, F. R. "Ignatius of Antioch." In *Dictionary of Early Christian Literature*, eds. Siegmar Döpp and Wilhelm Geerlings, trans. Matthew O'Connell, 296–98. New York: Crossroad, 2000.

Quasten, Johannes. *Musik und Gesang in den Kulten der heidnischen Antike und christlichen Frühzeit*. Liturgiewissenschaftliche Quellen und Forschungen 25. Münster: Aschendorffsche Verlagsbuchhandlung, 2nd ed. 1973. Trans. Boniface Ramsey. *Music & Worship in Pagan and Christian Antiquity*. Washington, D.C.: National Association of Pastoral Musicians, 1983.

———. *Patrology*. Vol. 1: *The Beginnings of Patristic Literature*, vol. 2: *The Ante-Nicene Literature After Irenaeus*. Allen, Tex.: Christian Classics, 1950, repr. 1995. Vol. 3: *The Golden Age of Greek Patristic Literature*. Westminster, Md.: Christian Classics, repr. 1994.

Quesnell, Quentin. "'Made Themselves Eunuchs for the Sake of the Kingdom of Heaven' (MT 19,12)." *CBQ* 30 (1968), 335–58.

Rader, Rosemary. "Christian Pre-Monastic Forms of Asceticism: Syneisaktism, or

'Spiritual Marriage.'" In *The Continuing Quest for God: Monastic Spirituality in Tradition & Transition,* ed. William Skudlarek, 80–87. Collegeville, Minn.: Liturgical Press, 1982.

Raditsa, L. F. "Augustus' Legislation Concerning Marriage, Procreation, Love Affairs and Adultery." In *Aufstieg und Niedergang der Römischen Welt* II.13 (1980), 278–339.

Rawson, Beryl. "Children in the Roman *Familia.*" In *The Family in Ancient Rome: New Perspectives,* ed. Beryl Rawson, 170–200. Ithaca, N.Y.: Cornell University Press, 1986.

———, ed. *The Family in Ancient Rome: New Perspectives.* Ithaca, N.Y.: Cornell University Press, 1986.

———. "The Roman Family." In *The Family in Ancient Rome: New Perspectives,* ed. Beryl Rawson, 1–57. Ithaca, N.Y.: Cornell University Press, 1986.

———. "Adult-Child Relationships in Roman Society." In *Marriage, Divorce, and Children in Ancient Rome,* ed. Beryl Rawson, 7–30. Oxford: Clarendon Press, 1991.

———, ed. *Marriage, Divorce, and Children in Ancient Rome.* Oxford: Clarendon Press, 1991.

———. *Children and Childhood in Roman Italy.* Oxford: Oxford University Press, 2003.

———. "'The Roman Family' in Recent Research: State of the Question." *Biblical Interpretation* 11.2 (2003), 119–38.

Rawson, Beryl, and Paul Weaver, eds. *The Roman Family in Italy: Status, Sentiment, Space.* Oxford: Clarendon Press, 1997.

Reed, Jonathan. *Archaeology and the Galilean Jesus: A Re-examination of the Evidence.* Harrisburg, Pa.: Trinity Press International, 2001.

Rehm, Merlin D. "Levites and Priests." In *The Anchor Bible Dictionary* 4, ed. David Noel Freedman, 297–310. New York: Doubleday, 1992.

Reichert, Andreas. "Israel, the firstborn of God: A topic of early Deuteronomic theology." In *Proceedings of the Sixth World Congress of Jewish Studies,* Hebrew University of Jerusalem, 1973, ed. Avigador Shinan, vol. 1, 341–49. Jerusalem: World Union of Jewish Studies, 1977.

Reichmann, V. "Feige I (Ficus Carica)." In *RAC* 7 (1969), 640–82.

Reid, Marty L. *Augustinian and Pauline Rhetoric in Romans Five: A Study of Early Christian Rhetoric.* Lewiston, N.Y.: Mellen Biblical Press, 1996.

Reinhartz, Adele. "Philo on Infanticide." *Studia Philonica Annual* 4 (1992), 42–58.

———. "Parents and Children: A Philonic Perspective." In *The Jewish Family in Antiquity,* ed. Shaye J. D. Cohen, 61–88. Brown Judaic Studies 289. Atlanta, Ga.: Scholars Press, c1993.

Reith, A. "Die Puppe im Grab der Crepereia." *Atlantis* 33 (1961), 367–69.

Remus, Harold. *Jesus as Healer.* Cambridge: Cambridge University Press, 1997.

Richardson, Alan. *The Miracle-Stories of the Gospels.* London: SCM Press, 1969.

Richardson, Peter. "Towards a Typology of Levantine/Palestinian Houses." *JSNT* 27.1 (2004), 47–68.

Ricotti, Eugenia S. P. *Giochi e giocattoli.* Vita e costumi dei romani antichi 18. Rome: Quasar, 1995.

Ridings, Daniel. "A New Edition of John Chrysostom's *Ad Stagirium a daemone vexatum.*" *Studia Patristica* 29 (1997), 508–14.

Riesner, Rainer. *Jesus als Lehrer.* WUNT 2. Reihe. Vol. 7. Tübingen: Mohr Siebeck, 1988.

Riley, Gregory J. "Words and Deeds: Jesus as Teacher and Jesus as Pattern of Life." *Harvard Theological Review* 90 (1997), 427–36.

Rinaldi, M. R. "Ricerche sui giocattoli nell'antichità a proposito di un'iscrizione di Brescello." *Epigraphica* 18 (1956), 104–29.

Roetzel, Calvin. *The Letters of Paul: Conversations in Context.* Louisville, Ky.: Westminster John Knox Press, 1998.

Rogerson, John. "The Family and Structures of Grace in the Old Testament." In *The Family in Theological Perspective,* ed. Stephen C. Barton, 25–42. Edinburgh: T&T Clark, 1996.

Rohrbaugh, Richard L. "Ethnocentrism and Historical Questions about Jesus." In *The Social Setting of Jesus and the Gospels,* eds. Wolfgang Stegemann, Bruce J. Malina, and Gerd Theissen, 27–43. Minneapolis: Fortress Press, 2002.

Rordorf, Willy. "Does the Didache Contain Jesus Tradition Independently of the Synoptic Gospels." In *Jesus and the Oral Gospel Tradition,* ed. Henry Wansborough, 394–423. *JSNT* Supplement Series 64. Sheffield: Sheffield Academic Press, 1991.

Rousseau, Philip. "Blood-Relationships among Early Eastern Ascetics." *JThS* 23 (1972), 135–44.

———. *Pachomius: The Making of a Community in Fourth-Century Egypt.* Transformation of the Classical Heritage 6. Berkeley: University of California Press, c1985.

Royse, James R. "A Philonic use of ΠΑΝΔΟΧΕΙΟΝ (Luke X 34)." *Novum Testamentum* 23 (1981), 193–94.

Rubenson, Samuel. *The Letters of St. Antony: Monasticism and the Making of a Saint.* Studies in Antiquity and Christianity. Minneapolis: Fortress Press, 1995.

Runesson, Anders. "The Origins of the Synagogue in Past and Present Research—Some Comments on Definitions, Theories, and Sources." *Studia Theologica* 57 (2003), 60–76.

Runia, David. *Philo in Early Christian Literature. Compendia Rerum Iudaicarum ad Novum Testamentum,* section 3, vol. 3. Assen: Van Gorcum, 1993.

Rusam, D. *Die Gemeinschaft der Kinder Gottes: Das Motiv der Gotteskindschaft und die Gemeinden der johanneischen Briefe.* Beiträge zur Wissenschaft vom Alten und Neuen Testament, 7. Folge, Heft 13. Stuttgart: Verlag W. Kohlhammer, 1993.

Salisbury, Joyce E. *The Blood of Martyrs: Unintended Consequences of Ancient Violence.* New York: Routledge, 2004.

Saller, Richard P. "Men's Age at Marriage and its Consequences in the Roman Family." *Classical Philology* 82 (1987), 21–34.

———. "Corporal Punishment, Authority, Obedience in the Roman Household." In *Marriage, Divorce and Children in Ancient Rome,* ed. B. Rawson, 144–65. Oxford: Oxford University Press, 1991.

———. *Patriarchy, Property, and Death in the Roman Family.* Cambridge: Cambridge University Press, 1994.

Sanders, E. P. *The Historical Figure of Jesus.* London: The Penguin Press, 1993.

Sandnes, Karl Olav. "Equality within Patriarchal Structures." In *Constructing Early Christian Families: Family as Social Reality and Metaphor,* ed. Halvor Moxnes, 150–65. London: Routledge, 1997.

Satlow, Michael L. *Jewish Marriage in Antiquity.* Princeton, N.J.: Princeton University Press, 2001.

Sawyer, Deborah F. *Women and Religion in the First Christian Centuries*. London: Routledge, 1996, repr. 1998.

Schaberg, Jane. *The Illegitimacy of Jesus: A Feminist Theological Interpretation of the Infancy Narratives*. New York: Crossroad, c1987.

Scheidel, W. "Brother-Sister and Parent-Child Marriage outside Royal Families in Ancient Egypt and Iran: A Challenge to the Sociobiological View of Incest Avoidance?" *Ethnology and Sociobiology* 17.5 (1996), 319–40.

Schereschewsky, Ben Zion (Benno). "Child Marriage." In *Encyclopaedia Judaica* 5, cols. 423–26. Jerusalem: Keter Publishing, 1971.

Schiemann, Gottfried. *"Manus"* and *"Mater familias."* In *Der Neue Pauly. Enzyklopädie der Antike* 7, cols. 839–41 and 998. Stuttgart: Verlag J. B. Metzler, 1996.

Schlatter, Adolf. *Geschichte Israels von Alexander dem Großen bis Hadrian*. Stuttgart: Calwer, 1925.

Schmidt, Thomas E. "Mark 10:29–30, Matthew 19:29: 'Leave Houses . . . and Region'?" *New Testament Studies* 38 (1992), 617–20.

Schmitt, John J. "The Motherhood of God and Zion as Mother." *Revue biblique* 92 (1985), 557–69.

Schnackenburg, Rudolf. *The Gospel of Matthew*. Trans. Robert Barr. Grand Rapids, Mich.: Eerdmans, 2002.

Schöllgen, Georg. *Die Anfänge der Professionalisierung des Klerus und das kirchliche Amt in der Syrischen Didaskalie*. Jahrbuch für Antike und Christentum. Ergänzungsband 26. Münster: Aschendorffsche Verlagsbuchhandlung, c1998.

Schroeder, Hans-Hartmut. *Eltern und Kinder in der Verkündigung Jesu: Eine hermeneutische und exegetische Untersuchung*. Theologische Forschung Wissenschaftliche Beiträge zur kirchlich-evangelischen Lehre 53. Hamburg-Bergstedt: Herbert Reich, Evangelischer Verlag, 1972.

Schroeder, Joy A. "John Chrysostom's Critique of Spousal Violence." *JECS* 12.4 (2004), 413–42.

Schüssler Fiorenza, Elisabeth. *Jesus: Miriam's Child, Sophia's Prophet*. Critical Issues in Feminist Christology. New York: Continuum, 1994.

Schwartz, Daniel. "Did the Jews Practice Infant Exposure and Infanticide in Antiquity?" *Studia Philonica Annual* 16 (2004), 61–95.

Scott, Eleanor. *The Archaeology of Infancy and Infant Death*. British Archaeological Reports International Series 819. Oxford: Archaeopress, 1999.

———. "Killing the Female? Archaeological Narratives of Infanticide." In *Gender and the Archaeology of Death*, eds. Bettina Arnold and Nancy L. Wicker, 3–21. Gender and Archaeology Series. Walnut Creek, Calif.: AltaMira Press, 2001.

———. "Unpicking a Myth: The Infanticide of Female and Disabled Infants in Antiquity." In *TRAC 2000*, proceedings of the tenth annual Theoretical Roman Archaeology Conference, Institute of Archaeology, University College London, April 2000, ed. Gwyn Davies, Andrew Gardner, and Kris Lockyear, 143–51. Oxford: Oxbow Books, 2001.

Scott, Marshall S. "Honor Thy Father and Mother: Scriptural Resources for Victims of Incest and Parental Abuse." *Journal of Pastoral Care* 42 (1988), 139–48.

Seeliger, H. R. "Constantine I (the Great), Emperor." In *Dictionary of Early Christian Literature*, eds. Siegmar Döpp and Wilhelm Geerlings, trans. Matthew O'Connell, 141–42. New York: Crossroad, 2000.

Senior, Donald. *Matthew*. Abingdon New Testament Commentaries. Nashville: Abingdon Press, 1998.

Sevenster, Jan Nicolaas. *Paul and Seneca*. Leiden: E. J. Brill, 1961.

Shapiro, H. A. "Fathers and Sons, Men and Boys." In *Coming of Age in Ancient Greece: Images of Childhood from the Classical Past,* eds. Jenifer Neils and John H. Oakley, 85–111. New Haven, Conn.: Yale University Press, c2003, 2004.

Shaw, Brent D. "The Age of Roman Girls at Marriage: Some Reconsiderations." *Journal of Roman Studies* 77 (1987), 30–46.

———. "Raising and Killing Children: Two Roman Myths." *Mnemosyne* 54.1 (2001), 31–77.

Shaw, Perry W. H. "Jesus: Oriental Teacher Par Excellence." *Christian Education Journal* 1.1 (1997), 83–94.

Shumka, Leslie Joan. "Children and Toys in the Roman World: A Contribution to the History of the Roman Family." M.A. thesis. University of Victoria, Canada, 1993.

Sim, David C. *The Gospel of Matthew and Christian Judaism: The History and Social Setting of the Matthean Community*. Edinburgh: T&T Clark, 1998.

Skeat, I. C. "Appendix to A. H. M. Jones, Notes on the Genuineness of the Constantinian Documents in Eusebius's *Life of Constantine*." *Journal of Ecclesiastical History* 5 (1954), 196–200.

Skemp, Vincent. "ἈΔΕΛΦΟΣ and the Theme of Kinship in Tobit." *Ephemerides theologicae Lovanienses* 75.1 (1999), 92–103.

Sly, Dorothy. *Philo's Perception of Women*. Atlanta: Scholar's Press, 1990.

Smith, Duane Andre. "Kinship and Covenant in Hosea 11:1–4." *Horizons in Biblical Theology* 16 (1994), 41–53.

Smith, Mahlon H. "Kinship Is Relative: Mark 3:31–35 and Parallels." *Forum* 6 (1990), 80–94.

Smith, William A. *Ancient Education*. New York: Philosophical Library, 1955.

Snowman, Leonard V. "Circumcision." In *Encyclopaedia Judaica* 5, cols. 567–76. Jerusalem: Keter Publishing, 1978.

Soards, Mary Lloyd. "The Gospel According to Luke." In *The New Oxford Annotated Bible: New Revised Standard Version with the Apocryphal/Deuterocanonical Books, Third Edition,* ed. Michael D. Coogan, NT 93–145. Oxford: Oxford University Press, 2001.

Soliday, Gerald L., ed. *History of the Family and Kinship: A Select International Bibliography*. Millwood, N.Y.: Kraus International Publications, c1980.

Somella, Anna Mura. *Crepereia Tryphaena; Le scoperte archeologiche nell'area del Palazzo di Giustizia*. Venice: Marsilio Editori, 1983.

Spicq, Ceslas. *Theological Lexicon of the New Testament*. Vol. 2. Ed. and trans. James D. Ernest. Peabody, Mass.: Hendrickson Publishers, 1994.

Stager, Lawrence E. "Eroticism and Infanticide at Ashkelon." *Biblical Archaeology Review* 17 (1991), 34–53.

Stauffer, E. "γαμέω, γάμος." In *Theological Dictionary of the New Testament,* ed. G. Kittel and G. Friedrich, trans. G. W. Bromley, vol. 1, 648–57. Grand Rapids, Mich.: Eerdmans, c1964.

Stauffer, Ethelbert. "Zur Kindertaufe in der Urkirche." *Deutsches Pfarrblatt* 49 (1949), 152–54.

Steenberg, M. C. "Children in Paradise: Adam and Eve as 'Infants' in Irenaeus of Lyons." *JECS* 12 (2004), 1–22.

Steimer, Bruno. *Vertex Traditionis: Die Gattung der altchristlichen Kirchenordnungen*. Beihefte zur Zeitschrift für die neutestamentliche Wissenschaft und die Kunde der älteren Kirche 63. Berlin: de Gruyter, 1992.

———. "Kirchenordnungen." In *Der Neue Pauly. Enzyklopädie der Antike,* ed. Hubert Cancik and Helmuth Schneider, vol. 6, cols. 483–85. Stuttgart: Verlag J. B. Metzler, 1999.

———. "Traditio Apostolica." In *Dictionary of Early Christian Literature,* eds. Siegmar Döpp and Wilhelm Geerlings, trans. Matthew O'Connell, 580–83. New York: Crossroad, 2000.

Stein, Robert H. "Luke 14:26 and the Question of Authenticity." *Forum* 5 (1989), 187–92.

Stemberger, Günter. "Kinder lernen Tora. Rabbinische Perspektiven." *Jahrbuch für Biblische Theologie* 17 (2002), 121–37.

Stephanus, Henricus. *Thesaurus Graecae Linguae.* Graz: Akademische Druck- und Verlagsanstalt, 1954.

Stortz, Martha Ellen. "'Where or When Was Your Servant Innocent?' Augustine on Childhood." In *The Child in Christian Thought,* ed. Marcia Bunge, 78–102 and 467–77. Grand Rapids, Mich.: Eerdmans, 2001.

Stowers, Stanley K. "Social Status, Public Speaking and Private Teaching: The Circumstances of Paul's Preaching Activity." *Novum Testamentum* 26 (1984), 59–82.

Strack, H. L., and Günter Stemberger. *Introduction to the Talmud and Midrash.* Minneapolis: Fortress Press, 1992.

Strange, William A. *Children in the Early Church: Children in the Ancient World, the New Testament and the Early Church.* Carlisle, U.K.: Paternoster, 1996; reprinted on demand: Eugene, Ore.: Wipf & Stock, 2004.

Strickert, Fred. "Jesus' True Family: The Synoptic Tradition and Thomas." In *For a Later Generation: The Transformation of Tradition in Israel, Early Judaism, and Early Christianity. Festschrift for George W. E. Nickelsburg,* eds. Randal A. Argall, Beverly A. Bow, and Rodney A. Werline, 246–57. Harrisburg, Pa.: Trinity Press International, 2000.

Strobel, A. "Säuglings- und Kindertaufe in der ältesten Kirche." In *Begründung und Gebrauch der heiligen Taufe. Aus der Arbeit einer Studientagung,* ed. Otto Perels, 7–69. Berlin: Lutherisches Verlagshaus, 1963.

Stuiber, Alfred. "Geschenke." In *RAC* 10 (1978), 685–703.

Swidler, Leonard. *Women in Judaism: The Status of Women in Formative Judaism.* Metuchen, N.J.: Scarecrow Press, 1976.

Tassin, Claude. "Matthieu 'targumiste?': L'exemple de Mt 12,18 (= Is 42,1)." *Estudios bíblicos* 48 (1990), 199–214.

Taylor, Joan E. "Virgin Mothers: Philo on the Women Therapeutae." *Journal for the Study of the Pseudepigrapha* 12.1 (2001), 37–63.

Taylor, John Hammond. "St. Cyprian and the Reconciliation of Apostates." *Theological Studies* 3.1 (1942), 27–46.

Thrams, Peter, and Wolfram Drews. "Kinderlosigkeit." In *RAC* 20 (2004), 947–64.

Timbie, Janet. "Translating and Interpreting the Letters of Antony." In *A Multiform Heritage: Studies on Early Judaism and Christianity in Honor of Robert A. Kraft,* ed. Benjamin G. Wright III, 213–25. Scholars Press Homage Series 24. Atlanta: Scholars Press, 1999.

Torjesen, Karen Jo. "The episcopacy—sacerdotal or monarchical? The appeal to Old Testament Institutions by Cyprian and the *Didascalia.*" *Studia Patristica* 36 (2001), 387–406.

Treggiari, Susan. *Roman Marriage: iusti coniuges from the Time of Cicero to the Time of Ulpian.* New York: Oxford University Press, 1991.

Trible, Phyllis. "Ruth." In *The Anchor Bible Dictionary* 5, ed. David Noel Freedman, 842–47. New York: Doubleday, 1992.

Troost, Arie. "Elizabeth and Mary—Naomi and Ruth: Gender-Response Criticism in Luke 1–2." In *A Feminist Companion to the Hebrew Bible in the New Testament,* ed. Athalya Brenner, 159–96. The Feminist Companion to the Bible 10. Sheffield: Sheffield Academic Press, 1996.

Tucker, C. Wayne. "Women in the Manumission Inscriptions at Delphi." *Transactions of the American Philological Association* 112 (1982), 225–36.

Tuckett, Christopher. "Sources and Methods." In *The Cambridge Companion to Jesus,* ed. Markus Bockmuehl, 121–37. Cambridge: Cambridge University Press, 2001.

Ubieta, Carmen Bernabé. "'Neither *xenoi* nor *paroikoi, sympolitai* and *oikeioi tou theou*' (Eph 2:19): Pauline Christian Communities: Defining a New Territoriality." In *Social Scientific Models for Interpreting the Bible: Essays by the Context Group in Honor of Bruce J. Malina,* ed. John J. Pilch, 260–80. Biblical Interpretation Series 53. Leiden: E. J. Brill, 2001.

Ulrichsen, Jarl Henning. "Noen bemerkninger til 1 Tim 2:15." *Norsk teologisk tidsskrift* 84 (1983), 19–25.

Urbach, Ephraim Elimelech. *The Sages: Their Concepts and Beliefs.* 2 vols. Trans. Israel Abrahams. Jerusalem: Magnes Press and Hebrew University, 1975.

Vaage, Leif E. "Q and the Historical Jesus: Some Peculiar Sayings (7:33–34, 9:57–58, 59–60, 14:26–27)." *Forum* 5 (1989), 159–76.

Vakaloudi, Anastasia D. *Contraception and Abortion from Antiquity to Byzantium* [in Greek]. N.p.: Ant. Stamoulis Editions, 2003.

Van Dam, Raymond. *Families and Friends in Late Roman Cappadocia.* Philadelphia: University of Pennsylvania Press, 2003.

VanderKam, James C. *The Dead Sea Scrolls Today.* Grand Rapids, Mich.: Eerdmans, 1994.

Van der Kooij, Arie. "'The Servant of the Lord': A Particular Group of Jews in Egypt according to the Old Greek of Isaiah—Some Comments on LXX Isa 49,1–6 and Related Passages." In *Studies in the Book of Isaiah: Festschrift Willem A. M. Beuken,* eds. Jacques van Ruiten and Marc Vervenne, 383–96. Bibliotheca Ephemeridum theologicarum Lovaniensium 132. Louvain: Peeters, 1997.

Van der Loos, H. *The Miracles of Jesus.* Leiden: E. J. Brill, 1965.

Van Henten, Jan Willem, and Athalya Brenner, eds. *Families and Family Relations as Represented in Early Judaisms and Early Christianities: Texts and Fictions.* Studies in Theology and Religion 2. Leiden: DEO Publishing, 2000.

Vanneste, Alfred. "La nouvelle théologie du péché originel." *Ephemerides theologicae Lovanienses* 67.4 (1991), 249–77.

van Unnik, Willem Cornelis. "Once Again: Tarsus or Jerusalem?" In *Sparsa Collecta. The Collected Essays of W. C. van Unnik,* vol. 1, 259–320. Supplements to Novum Testamentum 29, 321–27. Leiden: E. J. Brill, 1973.

———. "Tarsus or Jerusalem: The City of Paul's Youth." In *Sparsa Collecta. The Collected Essays of W. C. van Unnik,* vol. 1, 259–320. Supplements to Novum Testamentum 29. Leiden: E. J. Brill, 1973.

Van Winden, J. C. M., and A. van Heck, eds. "Colloquii Gregoriani III Leidensis. 18/23-IX-1974. Acta." Leiden, 1976. Typescript.

Van Winkle, D. W. "The Relationship of the Nations to Yahweh and to Israel in Isaiah 40:55." *Vetus Testamentum* 35 (1985), 446–58.

Väterlein, Jutta. *Roma ludens: Kinder und Erwachsene beim Spiel im antiken Rom.* Amsterdam: B. R. Grüner, 1976.

Vegge, Tor. "The Literacy of Jesus the Carpenter's Son." *Studia Theologica* 59 (2005), 19–37.

Verpeaux, Jean. "Les *oikeioi*: notes d'histoire institutionnelle et sociale." *Revue des études byzantines* 23 (1965), 89–99.

Veyne, Paul. "The Roman Empire." In *A History of Private Life: I. From Pagan Rome to Byzantium,* ed. Paul Veyne, 5–234. Cambridge, Mass.: Harvard University Press, 1987.

Vigne, Daniel. *Christ au Jourdain: Le Baptême de Jésus dans la tradition judéo-chrétienne.* Paris: Librairie Lecoffre, 1992.

Viviano, Benedict T. "The Gospel According to Matthew." In *The New Jerome Biblical Commentary,* eds. Raymond E. Brown, Joseph A. Fitzmyer, and Roland E. Murphy, 630–74. Englewood Cliffs, N.J.: Prentice Hall, 1990.

Vogüe, Adalbert de. *La Règle de Saint Benoît, tome VI, Commentaire Historique et Critique (Parties VII–IX et Index).* SCh 186. Paris: Les Éditions du Cerf, 1971.

Volterra, D. "Quelques observations sur le mariage des *filiifamilias.*" *Revue internationale des droits de l'antiquité* 1 (1948), 213–42.

Vööbus, Arthur. "Die Syrische Herkunft der Pseudo-Basilianischen Homilie über die Jungfräulichkeit." *Oriens Christianus* 40 (1956), 69–77.

Wagner, E. "Kritische Bemerkungen zum Harpastum-Spiel." *Gymnasium* 70 (1963), 356–66.

Wagner, U. "Puppentheater." In *Der Neue Pauly. Enzyklopädie der Antike,* ed. Hubert Cancik and Helmuth Schneider, vol. 10, cols. 602–4. Stuttgart: Verlag J. B. Metzler, 2001.

Watson, Nigel M. "'And if children, then heirs' (Rom 8:17)—why not sons?" *Australian Biblical Review* 49 (2001), 53–56.

Weber, Hans-Ruedi. *Jesus and the Children: Biblical Resources for Study and Preaching.* Atlanta: John Knox, 1979.

Weeber, Karl-Wilhelm. "Geschenke II." In *Der Neue Pauly. Enzyklopädie der Antike,* ed. Hubert Cancik and Helmuth Schneider, vol. 4, cols. 988–89. Stuttgart: Verlag J. B. Metzler, 1998.

Wehn, Beate. "'Blessed are the bodies of those who are virgins': Reflections on the image of Paul in the Acts of Thecla." Trans. Brian McNeil. *JSNT* 79 (2000), 149–64.

———. "'Geschunden die einen, und die anderen leben . . .' Über Herrschaft, Gewalt und Tod in einem christlichen Schreckenstext (Andreas-Akten 17–22)." In *Dem Tod nicht glauben. Sozialgeschichte der Bibel. Festschrift für Luise Schottroff zum 70. Geburtstag,* ed. Frank Crüsemann, Marlene Crüsemann, Claudia Janssen, Rainer Kessler, and Beate Wehn, 465–87. Gütersloh: Gütersloher Verlagshaus, 2004.

Weigandt, Peter. "Zur sogenannten 'Oikosformel.'" *Novum Testamentum* 6 (1963), 49–74.

Welborn, L. L. *Politics and Rhetoric in the Corinthian Epistles.* Macon, Ga.: Mercer University Press, 1997.

Widdicombe, Peter. *The Fatherhood of God from Origen to Athanasius.* Oxford Theological Monographs. Oxford: Clarendon Press; rev. paperback. ed., New York: Oxford University Press, 2000.

Wiedemann, Thomas. *Adults and Children in the Roman Empire.* New Haven, Conn.: Routledge, 1989.

Wilken, Robert L. "Christian Formation in the Early Church." In *Educating People of Faith: Exploring the History of Christian and Jewish Communities,* ed. John van Engen, 48–62. Grand Rapids, Mich.: Eerdmans, 2004.

Williams, James G. "The Beautiful and the Barren: Conventions in Biblical Type-Scenes." *JSOT* 17 (1980), 107–19.

Williamson, Lamar, Jr. *Mark. Interpretation. A Bible Commentary for Teaching and Preaching.* Atlanta: John Knox Press, 1983.

Wilpert, Giuseppe (Josef). *I Sarcofagi Cristiani Antichi.* Vol. 2. Rome: Pontificio istituto di archeologia cristiana, 1932.

Wilpert, Josef. *Die Malereien der Katakomben Roms.* Freiburg i. Br.: Herdersche Verlagshandlung, 1903.

Wilson, T. *St. Paul and Paganism.* Edinburgh: T&T Clark, 1927.

Wimbush, Vincent L., and Richard Valantasis, eds. *Asceticism.* New York: Oxford University Press, 1995.

Winston, David. "Philo and the Rabbis on Sex and the Body." In *The Ancestral Philosophy: Hellenistic Philosophy in Second Temple Judaism. Essays of David Winston,* ed. Gregory E. Sterling, 199–219. Studia Philonica Monographs 4. Providence, R.I.: Brown Judaic Studies, 2001.

Winter, Bruce W. "Is Paul among the Sophists." *Reformed Theological Review* 53 (1994), 28–38.

———. *Philo and Paul among the Sophists: Alexandrian and Corinthian Responses to a Julio-Claudian Movement.* Society for New Testament Studies Monograph 96. Cambridge: Cambridge University Press, 1997; 2nd ed., Eerdmans, 2002.

Witherington, Ben, III. *The Gospel of Mark: A Socio-Rhetorical Commentary.* Grand Rapids, Mich.: Eerdmans, 2001.

Wolfson, Harry A. *Philo: Foundations of Religious Philosophy in Judaism, Christianity, and Islam.* Vol. 2. Cambridge, Mass.: Harvard University Press, 1947.

———. *The Philosophy of the Church Fathers: Faith, Trinity, Incarnation.* Cambridge, Mass.: Harvard University Press, 1956.

Wright, David. F. "How Controversial Was the Development of Infant Baptism in the Early Church." In *Church, Word, and Spirit: Historical and Theological Essays in Honor of Geoffrey W. Bromiley,* ed. James E. Bradley and Richard A. Muller, 45–63. Grand Rapids, Mich.: Eerdmans, c1987.

———. "Infant Dedication in the Early Church." In *Baptism, the New Testament and the Church: Historical and Contemporary Studies in Honour of R. E. O. White,* ed. Stanley E. Porter and Anthony R. Cross, 352–78. JSNT Supplement Series 171. Sheffield: Sheffield Academic Press, 1999.

———. "Out, In, Out: Jesus' Blessing of the Children and Infant Baptism." In *Dimensions of Baptism. Biblical and Theological Studies,* ed. Stanley E. Porter and Anthony R. Cross, 188–206. JSNT Supplement Series 234. Sheffield: Sheffield Academic Press, 2002.

Yarbrough, O. Larry. "Parents and Children in the Jewish Family of Antiquity." In *The Jewish Family in Antiquity,* ed. Shaye J. D. Cohen, 39–59. Brown Judaic Studies 289. Atlanta: Scholars Press, c1993.

———. "Parents and Children in the Letters of Paul." In *The Social World of the First Christians: Essays in Honor of Wayne A. Meeks,* ed. L. M. White and O. L. Yarbrough, 126–41. Minneapolis: Fortress, 1995.

Yeo, Khiok-Khng. "The Mother and Brothers of Jesus (Lk 8:19–21, Mk 3:31–35, Mt 12:46–50)." *Asia Journal of Theology* 6 (1992), 311–17.

Yun Lee Too. "Introduction: Writing the History of Ancient Education." In *Education in Greek and Roman Antiquity,* ed. Yun Lee Too, 1–21. Leiden: E. J. Brill, 2001.

Zimmerli, Walther, and Joachim Jeremias. "παῖς θεοῦ." In *Theological Dictionary of the New Testament,* ed. G. Kittel and G. Friedrich, trans. G. W. Bromley, vol. 5, 645–717. Grand Rapids, Mich.: Eerdmans, 1964–.

Zink, James K. "Uncleanness and sin: A study of Job XIV 4 and Ps LI 7." *Vetus Testamentum* 17:3 (1967), 354–61.

Ziolkowski, Eric. *Evil Children in Religion, Literature, and Art.* Cross-Currents in Religion and Culture series. New York: Palgrave, 2001.

Index of Biblical References

Old Testament

New Testament

Index of Ancient Authors

Graeco-Roman Sources

Jewish Sources

Christian Sources

Index of Subjects and Modern Authors